Baby Names

A Complete Book of Names For Babies , with Tens of Thousands of Names for Boys and Girls- Meaning, Origin, and Uniqueness

Table of contents

Introduction..5

Chapter 1 What's in a Name? 6

Girls... 12

Boys... 198

Chapter 2 Inspiring Baby Names from Hindu 404

Chapter 3 Traditional names that never fade............................... 409

Chapter 4 FAQs..410

Chapter 5 Famous Names 412

Chapter 6 Biblical Namesand Meanings 414

Chapter 7 Names Based on Locations 418

Introduction

Finding a name for your baby can be a long and frustrating process. There are so many things to think about and so little time. Why can't the name just fall out of the sky or be given by God as it is in some movies? If only there was a simple way of finding the perfect name for my baby.

If this thought has crossed your mind, worry no more! With the help of this book, we doubt that you will have any difficulty with regards to finding the perfect name. In this book, you will find thousands of names with meaning and origin. Some you will adore, and some you will not, but see this process of searching as a gold miner does. You have to cut through some stone in order to get to the gold.

At the end of the book, you will get a checklist so you can test to see if you have found the right one.

So, without further ado, shall we get started?

Chapter 1
What's in a Name?

Deciding what to name your child is one of the most difficult and most important decisions you may ever make. After all, it sets the tone for his or her life! This guide will take you to step by step through the process of choosing a baby name, from what to avoid to what's trending.

Choosing the Perfect Name

Unfortunately, there's no one-size-fits-all formula for choosing the perfect baby name. A lot of the process depends on your preferences, traditions, and expectations. If you go into the baby naming process knowing you want a two-syllable girl's name that starts with an "S", this process will likely go a lot faster than if you were waiting to be surprised with the gender and are going into the process with no parameters.

Lucky for you, regardless of where you're at in the process, we've got you covered. Even if you think you already know what you want to name your son or daughter, there's no harm in making sure you don't make a mistake you might not even realize is a mistake. If you're certain about a name, make sure it follows all the things you should keep in mind, avoids any pitfalls, and falls in line with the final checklist. This guide is here to help you narrow your focus and avoid making a name mistake that will stay with your child for the rest of his or her life. We're here to make sure you choose the perfect name!

What to Keep in Mind When Choosing Your Baby's Name

The Popularity Factor

It happens... we hear a name we like on a TV show, or at the playground, or in a restaurant. It's easy to get stuck on a name and decide that that's the name your child is going to have, but do your research first. If you heard the name, that means at least one other person in your area has the name. There's a chance it could be a unique name you just happened to overhear, or it could be one of the most popular baby names this year. Names like Ava and Emma are adorable, but your daughter is bound to have two neighbors named Ava and four friends at her daycare named Emma, so you might want to think twice before giving your child a popular name. Noah has topped the list of popular boys' names for the past four years. Unless you want your son to share his name with thousands of others his age, opt against Noah until the popularity fades a bit.

Studies have even been done that found that nearly half of the parents who regret the name they gave their child feel that way because the name got way too popular. Do some research and ask 5 a few close friends—especially those with young kids in daycare and school— their thoughts. If this is your first child, or you haven't had children in the past three or five years, you might be out of touch with the current trends. Names that were popular when you were a kid are likely old news now, and names that you might think are unique could be topping all the baby name lists.

How Has It Been Used?

While naming after pop culture characters and celebrities is very on-trend right now (more about that later), consider how ordinary names are used in pop culture before deciding on those names for your child. For example, you may love the name Miley for a girl, but know that she will undoubtedly be asked at least once a week for the rest of her life if she's named after Miley Cyrus. If you're crazy about the name Stephanie but are looking for a unique spelling and opt for Stefani, you will constantly be asked if you're a big Gwen Stefani fan.

Along the same lines, you certainly don't want to choose a name that is associated with negativity. Obvious examples include Adolf, Osama, Ted, or any "O" name with a middle name or prefix that would result in them being called "OJ". You might want to go so far as to not naming after any fictional villains, like Lord Voldemort from the Harry Potter series or Cruella deVil from 101 Dalmatians.

Potential Nicknames

You certainly don't want to choose a name that just has a bunch of awful puns or rhymes waiting around the corner. We've all been through middle school and high school and know how cruel kids can be. Consider any possible nicknames or rhymes that can develop from the name you like to ensure that other children don't have a nice laugh at the expense of your child's name.

For example, the name Chuck rhymes with some words that aren't so nice and you probably wouldn't want other kids using in reference to your child. There's also Fatty Patty, Harry who's Hairy, Icky Vicky, Smelleanor, Elliott... the list goes on! Go through the alphabet and make sure the name(s) you like don't have any unfortunate rhymes, and take to the internet to do a quick search on whether or not there are any not-so-great nicknames for your chosen name(s).

Pronunciation is Key

Let's not beat around the bush. To go along with refraining from giving your child a name that is completely unheard of or ridiculous, don't give your child a name that is difficult to pronounce. Sure, there are people everywhere that can mispronounce names as simple as Michael or Kristin, but don't make it any harder on your child than it has to be. If their name is pronounced as Kylie, there is no need to spell it Khileighe. If you want a unique spelling, maybe go for something that is different from the normal Kylie but still can be read without missing a beat, like Kiley or Kyleigh.

This is something that can impact your child from the time they're born until they're in their sixties and beyond. It's simple: have some people read the name as you want to spell it, and make sure that at least 90% of them read it correctly at first glance. If you're set on giving your child a unique name that no one else has, by no means, go for it! Please just make sure it's easily pronounceable.

We don't mean to scare you if the name you love is just a bit different, because what we're talking about are simply absurd spelling and made-up names. Let's take a look at some of the names we're talking about:

- Maaike
- Kyler
- Saoirse
- Chiwetel
- Ioan
- Anais
- Maureen
- Kaia

7

If you're set on a name like Siobhan, Schuyler, or Isla, you'll also have to accept the fact that you and your child will be subject to answering pronunciation questions at least once a day for the rest of your/their lives.

Remember That They Grow Up

This is a big one that not a lot of parents think about. Sure, a six-month-old girl named Charlie or Lily is cute, but what about a 40-year-old with the same name? When naming a child, most people don't think about how the name will impact them for years to come, but it's a name they're stuck with forever. Picture them in high school, college, and beyond. If you would be embarrassed to have a name at any of those ages, you probably shouldn't make your child endure it.

Nicknames are the best solution to this problem. Instead of naming your son Johnny, name him Jonathan and simply call him Johnny when he's young. As he gets older, he can decide what he wants to be called. You can always use nicknames that change with age, so consider going with Charlotte and calling her Charlie when she's young, then switching to Charlotte as she gets older. If you give your child a name like Ellie, Davey, or Izzy, they're stuck with the name as they get older, so consider that before opting for a name because it's "cute"!

Adventures in Baby Naming

The name is the first gift you will give to your bundle of joy, and picking the right name is almost certainly one of the most important decisions you can make before the big day arrives.

How to choose a name can be both a challenging and stressful task for parents. A name that you feel comfortable saying and a name that your child will be proud of throughout his/her life are just a few of the many considerations when choosing a name. With an overwhelming number of options to choose from, picking that perfect name for your child may seem difficult.

Whether you are looking for a unique name for your child or you want something meaningful, this book offers an excellent selection of baby names for boys and girls including their meanings.

The process of pregnancy, getting everything ready for the big day, and deciding what you are going to name your baby can sometimes feel like a chore to fit in your already jam-packed schedule. So to make the task of choosing a nameless stressful, the following are some ideas that you can try:

1. Jot down all the names you have in mind. You can also ask your family and friends to contribute a possible name for the baby.
2. Announce it. Tell all your friends and family members that you are looking for that perfect name for your baby and that their suggestions would be very much appreciated.
3. Narrow down your choices. Pick at least five names that sound good when you say them. Write each one on a card and read them out every day for a week. You will see that at the end of the week, one will probably become your favorite.
4. Along with this book, you can leaf through magazines and even phone books to see if there are names that sound good to you.
5. Practice saying different names loudly and several times in a row. Then ask family members which ones they like best.
6. Read through the following names of boys and girls in this book, and note down your favorites!

When beginning the baby-naming process, don't be overwhelmed. Try to have fun and don't be stressed. Plan a get-together with a group of friends over dinner or coffee to talk through ideas. Have a date night with your spouse, partner, or S.O. and begin an informal discussion about names you like. If you already know the sex of your baby, cut the task time in half, since you will only have to focus on either male or female names. Maybe you're even one of the lucky ones who've already had a few names picked out long before you got the news that you were expecting. You may have plenty of time to make this decision, so take it at a comfortable pace and enjoy the adventure.

Tips for Choosing a Good Name

When you come up with a preliminary list of names you like, ask yourself the following questions about each name:

- Does it have a positive association for you or remind you of someone you like and respect?
- Is it compatible with your last name?
- Does it feel fresh or timeless?
- If heritage matters, does it reflect your family's culture?
- Does it have a definition that feels suitable?
- Will others respond well to the name?
- Is it easy to spell, easy to pronounce, and easy to remember?
- Do you like the initials the full name creates?
- Will it lend itself to a cute and kind nickname?
- Will the name stand the test of time and sound as good to you in thirty years as it does today?

If you cannot narrow down your names to one favorite, consider turning one into a middle name. Or create a middle name from the mother's maiden name. As a final thought, once you narrow down your top few choices, take a few days to see if you are as enthusiastic about your choice tomorrow as you are today.

Baby Name "Don'ts"

On the other side of the spectrum, here are a few things NOT to do when deciding on your baby's name:

Don't choose a name that other kids are apt to pick on. Some kids can be cruel, and you want to protect your child from others' ignorance.

Don't get too trendy. Britney is cute today, but how will "Nana Britney" sound?

Don't pick a name that rhymes with anything bad or sounds too similar to a word that is negative, obscene, or too slangy.

Don't go to the extreme with alternative spellings. A unique spelling makes a common name more distinctive, but you're also guaranteed that you and your child will always have to spell it out to others.

Don't choose a name that when coupled with your last name forms the name of someone famous (like "George Clooney" or "Katy Perry"), because those comparisons will be made for a lifetime.

Don't pick a name that sounds like it would be better suited for a pet. Fifi, Smokey, and Misty are cute for dogs and cats ... not so cute for kids.

Don't let choosing a name to create a rift between you and your partner. The process should be unifying, not divisive.

Don't tell too many people about the name you selected until it's on the birth certificate. Everyone has an opinion, and you're sure to hear it. Yours is the only one that counts.

Puzzles

Some people just prefer to keep the names from the family, or give them a "rearrangement" to contain more names or the same letters. Depends on what the parents wish in this direction; some parents combine part or all of their first names to create a name for their child. Of course, not every set of names lends itself to this trick but when it works, it's quite amazing.

Spontaneity

This interesting and very used method of choosing a name finds its use especially when time is short and the parents just don't seem to reach a final agreement regarding the name. It can come to you at your workplace, when driving or listening to the radio, when talking to someone or during any activity. It has no rules, just appears like a Eureka moment and can impress you so much that it makes you adopt him forever. The story behind the name is also a funny thing to remember and tell your baby about when he will ask how did you think about his name.

Stealing names

We are not suggesting that you steal your sister's favorite baby name right out from under her pregnant nose but statistics say that a surprising number of people do steal baby names! Pay attention around you and leave your ears open to any suggestions, even from other future parents. There have been many complaints about names that have been "stolen" but the reality is that once a name gets to be liked especially by a pregnant mother like you, or a responsible father looking for a baby name, there is no way you can convince anyone to give up and look for another. And nobody wants to upset a pregnant woman or a euphoric father!

Family and heritage

Family might drive you crazy when it comes to the name of your baby. Depending on the type of family (rich, aristocratic, independent or authoritarian), they might want to include a name from the family's lineage in your baby's name. Your child's heritage has importance if you want to accept it, and the solution can be found in accepting two names instead of one or to be flexible and modify slightly the names when necessary. Some say that it is recommended to continue the line of a certain family tradition in order to have the child protected and receive its welldeserved place in the family. Either way, it's advisable to consult family members especially if they have an important role in your baby's life. What is Meaning?

No one is likely to treat your daughter or son differently because their name means "hero" or "warrior" but the derivation of your baby's name is something you may want to think about. Especially if you are one of those people who care about symbols and meanings to everything in general. Depending on your language and culture, every name has a significance given by the religion, history or the word itself. You can name your child after a known leader or king (Attila, Franklin, Diana, Ludovic) or whatever you feel like, a color (Purple), a precious stone (Esmeralda) or some innovative combination (Isamar), but most probably people, including your child someday, will want to know what it means. This meaning gives not only a rational (or irrational explanation), but also a certain weight to your baby's personality. Each name carries energy derived from the vibration of the sound and also from it's more believed history. Everyone thinks of a particular personality when hearing "Lola", "Agatha", "Benjamin" or "Carmen". Pick your name and search its meaning, it will reflect maybe your expectations towards your child's life and character.

Anticipating nicknames

A nickname is so usual nowadays that it is advisable to think of it before you decide a name. Especially kids can be cruel when it comes to inventing a reason to laugh or mock someone, so try to anticipate any potentially embarrassing ones. The chances that you won't think of all the possibilities are obvious, but remember that nicknames are a passing period and won't stick forever. They will be invented or associated with some particularity of the child even if it has nothing to do with the name. Your duty is just to check for weird or ugly nicknames that could derive from your chosen name.

Initials

Especially when your baby has two names, the recommendation is to check how they sound together. Of course, if you already picked a perfect name and the initials are not so perfect then stick with the names, nothing else is important. Initials are not so commonly used and the best thing for everyone including your child is to pronounce the name entirely, not pieces, nicknames, initials or inventions. You know, of course, that is not truly possible when you involve your feelings and use diminutives to spoil and show tenderness. So going from Miguel to Miguelito or from Christina to Christy it's almost as natural as your real baby name.

Girls

A

'**Aolani** (Hawaiian) heavenly cloud.

'**Aulani** (Hawaiian) royal messenger.

A'lexus (American) a form of Alexis.

Aaleyah (Hebrew) a form of Aliya.

Aaliah (Hebrew) a form of Aliya.

Aalisha (Greek) a form of Alisha.

Aaliya (Hebrew) a form of Aliya.

Aaliyah ☆ (Hebrew) a form of Aliya.

Aalyiah (Hebrew) a form of Aliya.

Aaron BG (Hebrew) enlightened.(Arabic) messenger. Bible: the brother of Moses and the first high priest. **Aarti** (Hebrew, Hindi) a form of Arti.

Aasta (Norse) love.

Aba (Fante, Twi) born on Thursday.

Abagael, Abagail, Abbagail (Hebrew) forms of Abigail.

Abauro (Greek) tint of the sky at sunrise.

Abbey GB (Hebrew) a familiar form of Abigail.

Abbi, Abbie, Abby (Hebrew) familiar forms of Abigail.

Abbigail, Abbigale, Abbigayle, Abigael, Abigayle (Hebrew) forms of Abigail.

Abbygail, Abygail (Hebrew) forms of Abigail.

Abeer (Hebrew) a short form of Abira.

Abegail (Hebrew) a form of Abigail.

Abelarda (Arabic) servant of Allah.

Abelina (American) a combination of Abbey + Lina.

Abeliñe (Basque) a form of Abelina.

Abena (Akan) born on Tuesday.

Aberfa (Welsh) one who comes from the mouth of the river.

Abertha (Welsh) to sacrifice.

Abia (Arabic) great.

Abiann, Abianne (American) combinations of Abbey + Ann.

Abida (Arabic) worshiper.

Abidán (Hebrew) my father is judge.

Abiel (Hebrew) God is my father.

Abigail ☆ (Hebrew) father's joy. Bible: one of the wives of King David. .

Abigaíl (Spanish) a form of Abigail.

Abinaya (American) a form of Abiann.

Abira (Hebrew) my strength.

Abiram (Hebrew) my father is great.

Abra (Hebrew) mother of many nations.

Abria (Hebrew) a form of Abra.

Abrial (French) open; secure, protected.

Abriana, Abrianna (Italian) forms of Abra.

Abrielle (French) a form of Abrial.

Abrienda (Spanish) opening.

Abril (French) a form of Abrial.

Abundia (Latin) abundance.

Acacia (Greek) thorny. Mythology: the acacia tree symbolizes immortality and resurrection. Acacitlu (Nahuatl) rabbit of the water.

Acalia (Latin) Mythology: another name for Acca Larentia, the adoptive mother of Romulus and Remus.

Achcauhtli (Nahuatl) leader.

Achilla (Greek) a form of Achilles (Acima (Illyrian) praised by God.

Acindina (Greek) safe.

Acquilina (Greek) a form of Aquilla.

Ada (German) a short form of Adelaide. (English) prosperous; happy. (Hebrew) a form of Adah.

Adabella (Spanish) a combination of Ada and Bella.

Adah (Hebrew) ornament. (German, English) a form of Ada.

Adair GB (Greek) a form of Adara.

Adalcira (Spanish) a combination of Ada and Alcira.

Adalene (Spanish) a form of Adalia.

Adalgisa (German) noble hostage.

Adalia (German, Spanish) noble.

Adalsinda (German) noble strength.

Adaluz (Spanish) a combination of Ada and Luz.

Adama (Phoenician, Hebrew) a form of Adam.

Adamma (Ibo) child of beauty.

Adán (Spanish) a form of Adam (Adana (Spanish) a form of Adama.

Adanna (Nigerian) her father's daughter.

Adar GB (Syrian) ruler. (Hebrew) noble; exalted.

Adara (Greek) beauty. (Arabic) virgin.

Adawna (Latin) beautiful sunrise.

Adaya (American) a form of Ada.

Addie (Greek, German) a familiar form of Adelaide, Adrienne.

Addilyn (English) noble.

Addison ★ BG (English) child of Adam.

Addolorata (Italian) a form of Dolores.

Addy GB (Greek, German) a familiar form of Adelaide, Adrienne.

Addyson, Adyson (English) forms of Addison.

Adela (English) a short form of Adelaide.

Adelaida (German) a form of Adelaide.

Adelaide (German) noble and serene. Adelais (French) a form of Adelaide.

Adelaisa (Italian) a form of Adelaida.

Adele, Adelle (English) short forms of Adelaide, Adeline.

Adelia (Spanish) a form of Adelaide.

Adelina (English) a form of Adeline.

Adelinda (Teutonic) noble; serpent.

Adeline (English) a form of Adelaide.

Adelma (Teutonic) protector of the needy.

Adelmira (Arabic) exalted.

Adelpha (Greek) sister.

Adeltruda (German) strong and noble.

Adelvina (German) ennobled by victory.

Adena (Hebrew) noble; adorned.

Adhara (Arabic) maiden. Astronomy: a star in the Canis Major constellation.

Adia (Swahili) gift.

Adiel (Hebrew) ornament of the Lord. (African) goat.

Adien (Welsh) beautiful.

Adila (Arabic) equal.

Adilene (English) a form of Adeline.

Adina (Hebrew) a form of Adena.

Adira (Hebrew) strong.

Adison BG (English) a form of Addison.

Aditi (Hindi) unbound. Religion: the mother of the Hindu sun gods.

Adleigh (Hebrew) my ornament.

Adolfa (Arabic) exalted.

Adoncia (Spanish) sweet.

Adonia (Spanish) beautiful.

Adora (Latin) beloved. Adoración (Latin) the action of venerating the magical gods.

Adra (Arabic) virgin.

Adreana, Adreanna (Latin) forms of Adrienne.

Adrenilda (German) mother of the warrior.

Adria (English) a short form of Adriana, Adrienne.

Adriadna (Greek) she who is very holy, who doesn't yield.

Adrian BG (English) a form of Adrienne.

Adrián (Hispanic) from the Adriatic Sea.

Adriana, Adrianna (Italian) forms of Adrienne.

Adriane, Adrianne, Adrien, Adriene (English) forms of Adrienne.

Adrielle (Hebrew) member of God's flock.

Adrien BG (Greek, Latin) a form of Adrienne.

Adrienna (Italian) a form of Adrienne. **Adrienne** (Greek) rich. (Latin) dark.

Adrina (English) a short form of Adriana.

Adriyanna (American) a form of Adrienne.

Adya (Hindi) Sunday.

Aelwyd (Welsh) one that comes from the chimney.

Aerial, Aeriel (Hebrew) forms of Ariel.

Aerin (Hebrew, Arabic) a form of Aaron, Arin.

Aerona (Welsh) berry.

Afi (African) born on Friday.

Afilia (Germanic) of noble lineage.

Afina (Hebrew) young doe.

Afra (Hebrew) young doe. (Arabic) earth color.

Africa (Latin, Greek) sunny; not cold. Geography: one of the seven continents.

África (Spanish) a form of Africa.

Afrika (Irish) a form of Africa.

Afrodite (Greek) a form of Aphrodite.

Afton GB (English) from Afton, England.

Agalia (Spanish) bright; joy.

Aganetha (Greek) a form of Agnes.

Ágape (Latin) love.

Agapita (Greek) she who is beloved and wanted.

Agar (Hebrew) she who fled.

Ágata (Greek) friendly with everyone.

Agate (English) a semiprecious stone.

Agatha (Greek) good, kind. Literature: Agatha Christie was a British writer of more than seventy detective novels.

Agathe (Greek) a form of Agatha.

Agdta (Spanish) a form of Ágata.

Aggie (Greek) a short form of Agatha, Agnes.

Agilberta (German) famous sword of combat.

Aglaia (Greek) beautiful.

Agnella (Greek) a form of Agnes.

Agnes (Greek) pure.

Agnieszka (Greek) a form of Agnes.

Agrippina (Latin) born feet first.

Aguas Vivas (Spanish) living waters.

Agüeda (Greek) having many virtues.

Águeda (Spanish) a form of Ágata.

Ahava (Hebrew) beloved.

Ahlam (Arabic) witty; or who has pleasant drea

Ahliya (Hebrew) a forɪ Aliya.

Ahuiliztli (Nahuatl) joy.

Ahulani (Hawaiian) heavenly shrine.

Ai (Japanese) love; indigo blue.

Aida (Latin) helpful. (English) a form of Ada.

Aída (Latin) a form of Aida.

Aidan 🅱🅶 (Latin) a form of Aida.

Aide (Latin, English) a short form of Aida.

Aidé (Greek) a form of Haidee.

Aiden 🅱🅶 (Latin) a form of Aida.

Aidia (Spanish) a form of Aida.

Aiesha (Swahili, Arabic) a form of Aisha.

Aiko (Japanese) beloved.

Ailani (Hawaiian) chief.

Aileen (Scottish) light bearer. (Irish) a form of Helen. Ailén (Mapuche) ember.

Aili (Scottish) a form of Alice. (Finnish) a form of Helen.

Ailín, Aillén (Mapuche) transparent, very clear.

Ailis (Irish) a form of Adelaide.

Ailsa (Scottish) island dweller. Geography: Ailsa Craig is an island in Scotland.

Ailya (Hebrew) a form of Aliya.

Aime, Aimie (Latin, French) forms of Aimee.

Aimee (Latin) a form of Amy.

Aina (Hebrew) a form of Anna.

Ainara (Basque) swallow.

Ainhoa (Basque) allusion to the Virgin Mary.

Ainoa (Basque) she who has fertile soil.

Ainona (Hebrew) a form of Aina.

Ainsley 🅶🅱 (Scottish) my own meadow.

Ainslie (Scottish) a form of Ainsley.

Aintzane (Spanish) glorious.

Airiana (English) a form of Ariana.

Airiél (Hebrew) a form of Ariel.

Airleas (Irish) promise.

Aisha (Swahili) life. (Arabic) woman.

Aishia (Swahili, Arabic) a form of Aisha.

Aisling (Irish) a form of Aislinn.

Aislinn, Aislynn (Irish) forms of Ashlyn.

Aisone (Basque) a form of Asunción.

Aixa (Latin, German) a form of Axelle.

Aiyana (Native American) forever flowering.

Aiyanna (Native American) a form of

Aiyana. (Hindi) a form of Ayanna.

Aja (Hindi) goat.

Ajah (Hindi) a form of Aja.

Ajanae (American) a combination of the letter A + Janae.

Ajee, Ajée (Punjabi, American) forms of Ajay Ajia (Hindi) a form of Aja.

Akasha (American) a form of Akeisha.

Akayla (American) a combination of the letter A + Kayla.

Akeisha (American) a combination of the letter A + Keisha.

Akela (Hawaiian) noble.

Akeria (American) a form of Akira.

Akeyla (Hawaiian) a form of Akela.

Aki (Japanese) born in autumn.

Akia (American) a combination of the letter A + Kia.

Akiko (Japanese) bright light.

Akila (Arabic) a form of Akilah.

Akilah (Arabic) intelligent.

Akili 🅱🅶 (Tanzanian) wisdom.

Akilina (Greek) a form of Aquilla.

Akina (Japanese) spring flower.

Akira GB (American) a combination of the letter A + Kira.

Alaa GB (Arabic) a form of Aladdin Alaia (Basque) happy, of good cheer.

Alaina (Irish) a form of Alana.

Alair (French) a form of Hilary.

Alamea (Hawaiian) ripe; precious.

Alameda (Spanish) poplar tree.

Alana (Irish) attractive; peaceful. (Hawaiian) offering.

Alanah (Irish, Hawaiian) a form of Alana.

Alandra (Spanish) a form of Alexandra, Alexandria.

Alandria (Spanish) a form of Alexandra, Alexandria.

Alani (Hawaiian) orange tree. (Irish) a form of Alana.

Alanis (Irish) beautiful; bright.

Alanna, Alannah (Irish) forms of Alana.

Alanza (Spanish) noble and eager.

Alarice (German) ruler of all.

Alastrina (Scottish) defender of humankind.

Alatea (Spanish, Greek) truth.

Alaura (American) a form of Alora.

Alaya (Hebrew) a form of Aliya.

Alayna (Irish) a form of Alana.

Alaysha, Alaysia (American) forms of Alicia.

Alazne (Spanish) miracle.

Alba (Latin) from Alba Longa, an ancient city near Rome, Italy.

Alberta (German, French) noble and bright. Alborada (Latin) brandy-colored dawn.

Albreanna (American) a combination of Alberta + Breanna (see Breana).

Alcina (Greek) strong-minded.

Alcira (German) adornment of nobility.

Alda (German) old; elder.

Aldana (Spanish) a combination of Alda + Ana.

Aldegunda (German) famous leader.

Alden BG (English) old; wise protector.

Aldetruda (German) strong leader.

Aldina, Aldine (Hebrew) forms of Alda.

Aldonsa, Aldonza (Spanish) nice.

Aldora (English) gift; superior.

Alea, Aleah (Arabic) high, exalted. (Persian) God's being.

Aleaha (Arabic, Persian) a form of Alea.

Aleasha (Greek) a form of Alisha.

Alecia (Greek) a form of Alicia.

Aleea (Arabic, Persian) a form of Alea. (Hebrew) a form of Aliya.

Aleecia (Greek) a form of Alicia.

Aleela (Swahili) she cries.

Aleena (Dutch) a form of Aleene.

Aleene (Dutch) alone.

Aleesa (Greek) a form of Alice, Alyssa. **Aleesha** (Greek) a form of Alisha.

Aleeya (Hebrew) a form of Aliya.

Aleeza (Hebrew) a form of AlizaAlegía, Alegría, Allegría (Spanish) forms of Allegra.

Alegria (Spanish) cheerful.

Aleia, Aleigha (Arabic, Persian) forms of Alea.

Aleisha (Greek) a form of Alicia, Alisha.

Aleja (Spanish) a form of Alejandra.

Alejandra (Spanish) a form of Alexandra.

Alejandrina (Spanish) a form of Alejandra.

Aleka (Hawaiian) a form of Alice.

Aleksa (Greek) a form of Alexa.

Aleksandra (Greek) a form of Alexandra.

Alena (Russian) a form of Helen.

Aleria (Latin) eagle.

Alesha (Greek) a form of Alicia, Alisha.

Aleshia (Greek) a form of Alicia, Alisha.

Alesia, Alessia (Greek) forms of Alice, Alicia, Alisha.

Alessa (Greek) a form of Alice.

Alessandra (Italian) a form of Alexandra.

Aleta (Greek) a form of Alida.

Aleth (Greek) a form of Alethea.

Aletha (Greek) a short form of Alethea.

Alethea (Greek) truth.

Alette (Latin) wing.

Alex BG (Greek) a short form of Alexander, Alexandra.

Alex Ann, Alex Anne, Alexane, Alexanne (American) combinations of Alex + Ann.

Alexa (Greek) a short form of Alexandra.

Alexander BG (Greek) defender of mankind. History: Alexander the Great was the conqueror of the Greek Empire.

Alexanderia (Greek) a form of Alexandria.

Alexandra (Greek) a form of Alexander. History: the last czarina of Russia. .

Alexandre BG (Greek) a form of Alexandra.

Alexandrea (Greek) a form of Alexandria.

Alexandria (Greek) a form of Alexandra.

Alexandrine (Greek) a form of AlexandraAlexas, Alexes, Alexiss, Alexsis, Alexus, Alexxis, Alexxus, Alexys, Allexis, Allexus (Greek) forms of Alexis.

Alexcia (Greek) a form of Alexia.

Alexe (Greek) a form of Alex.

Alexi GB (Greek) a short form of Alexandra.

Alexia (Greek) a short form of Alexandria. **Alexie** (Greek) a short form of Alexandra.

Alexis

GB (Greek) a short form of Alexandra.

Alexius (Greek) a form of Alexis.

Alexsa (Greek) a form of Alexa.

Alexsandra (Greek) a form of Alexandra.

Alexzandra (Greek) a form of Alexandra.

Alexzandria (Greek) a form of Alexandria.

Aleya, Aleyah (Hebrew) forms of Aliya.

Aleyda (Greek) she who is like Athena.

Alfie BG (English) a familiar form of Alfreda.

Alfilda (German) she who helps the elves.

Alfonsa (German) noble and eager.

Alfreda (English) elf counselor; wise counselor. Alhertina (Spanish) noble.

Ali BG (Greek) a familiar form of Alice, Alicia, Alisha, Alison.

Alia, Aliah, Allia, Alliah (Hebrew) forms of Aliya.

Alice (Greek) truthful. (German) noble.

Alicen, Alicyn, Alisyn, Allisyn (English) forms of Alison.

Alicia (English) a form of Alice. .

Alicja (English) a form of Alicia.

Alida (Latin) small and winged. (Spanish) noble. .

Álida (Hebrew) a form of Hélida.

Alie, Alley, Alli, Allie, Ally, Aly (Greek)

18

familiar forms of Alice, Alicia, Alisha, Alison.

Aliesha (Greek) a form of Alisha.

Alika (Hawaiian) truthful. (Swahili) most beautiful.

Alima (Arabic) sea maiden; musical.

Alina (Slavic) bright. (Scottish) fair. (English) a short form of Adeline.

Aline (Scottish) a form of Aileen, Alina.

Alisa, Allisa (Greek) forms of Alice, Alyssa. **Alise, Allise** (Greek) forms of Alice.

Alisha (Greek) truthful. (German) noble. (English) a form of Alicia. Alishia (English) a form of Alisha.

Alisia, Alissia (English) forms of Alisha.

Alison (English) a form of Alice. .

Alissa, Allissa (Greek) forms of Alice, Alyssa.

Alita (Spanish) a form of Alida.

Alivia (Latin) a form of Olivia.

Alix GB (Greek) a short form of Alexandra, Alice.

Alixandra (Greek) a form of Alexandra.

Alixandria (Greek) a form of Alexandria.

Aliya (Hebrew) ascender.

Aliyah, Alliyah (Hebrew) forms of Aliya.

Aliye (Arabic) noble.

Aliza (Hebrew) joyful.

Alizabeth (Hebrew) a form of Elizabeth.

Alize (Greek, German) a form of Alice. (Hebrew) a short form of Aliza.

Allana, Allanah (Irish) forms of Alana.

Allegra (Latin) cheerful.

Allena (Irish) a form of Alana.

Allene (Dutch) a form of Aleene. (Scottish) a form of Aline.

Allethea (Greek) a form of Alethea.

Allicia (English) a form of Alicia.

Allisha (Greek, German, English) a form of Alisha.

Allison ☆

GB (English) a form of Alison.

Allyn (Scottish) a form of Aileen, Alina.

Allyssa (Greek) forms of Alyssa.

Allysen, **Allyson, Alyson** (English) forms of Alison.

Allysha, Alycia, Alysha, Alysia (English) forms of Alicia.

Alma (Arabic) learned. (Latin) soul.

Almeda (Arabic) ambitious.

Almira (Arabic) aristocratic, princess; exalted. (Spanish) from Almeíra, Spain.

Almita (Latin) kind.

Almodis (German) very happy, animated lady.

Almudena (Spanish) the city.

Almunda (Spanish) refers to the Virgin Mary.

Almundena, Almundina (Spanish) forms of Almunda.

Alodía (Basque) free land.

Alodie (English) rich.

Aloha (Hawaiian) loving, kindhearted, charitable.

Aloisa (German) famous warrior.

Aloise (Spanish) a form of Aloisa.

Aloma (Latin) a short form of Paloma.

Alonda (Spanish) a form of Alexandra.

Alondra (Spanish) a form of Alexandra.

Alonna (Irish) a form of Alana.

Alonsa (English) a form of Alonza.

Alonza BG (English) noble and eager.

Alora (American) a combination of the letter A + Lora.

Alpha (Greek) first-born. Linguistics: the first letter of the Greek alphabet.

Alta (Latin) high; tall.

Altagracia (Spanish) refers to the high grace of the Virgin Mary.

Altair BG (Greek) star. (Arabic) flying eagle.

Altamira (Spanish) place with a beautiful view.

Althea (Greek) wholesome; healer. History: Althea Gibson was the first African American to win a major tennis title. Aluminé (Mapuche) she who shines.

Alva BG (Latin, Spanish) white; light skinned. Alvarita (Spanish) speaker of truth.

Alvera (Latin) honest.

Alvina (English) friend to all; noble friend; friend to elves.

Alyah (Hebrew) a form of Aliya.

Alyce, Alyse, Alysse (Greek) forms of Alice.

Alyiah (Hebrew) a form of Aliya.

Alyna (Dutch) a form of Aleene. (Slavic, Scottish, English) a form of Alina.

Alysa (Greek) a form of Alyssa.

Alyshia (English) a form of Alicia.

Alyssa ☆ (Greek) rational. Botany: alyssum is a flowering herb.

Alyssia (Greek) a form of Alyssa.

Alyx (Greek) a form of Alex.

Alyxandra (Greek) a form of Alexandra.

Alyxandria (Greek) a form of Alexandria.

Alyxis (Greek) a form of Alexis.

Alzena (Arabic) woman.

Am (Vietnamese) lunar; female.

Ama (African) born on Saturday.

Amabel (Latin) lovable.

Amada (Spanish) beloved.

Amadea (Latin) loves God.

Amadis (Latin) the great love, the most beloved.

Amairani, Amairany (Greek) forms of Amara.

Amal GB (Hebrew) worker. (Arabic) hopeful.

Amalberta (German) brilliant work.

Amalia (German) a form of Amelia.

Amalie (German) a form of Amelia.

Amaline (German) a form of Amelia.

Amalsinda (German) the one God points to.

Amalur, Amalure (Spanish) homeland.

Aman BG (Arabic) a short form of Amani.

Amanada (Latin) a form of Amanda.

Amancai, Amancái, Amancay (Quechua) yellow flower streaked with red.

Amancia (Latin) lover.

Amanda GB (Latin) lovable. .

Amandeep BG (Punjabi) peaceful light.

Amani GB (Arabic) a form of Imani.

Amania (Hebrew) artist of God.

Amanjot (Punjabi) a form of Amandeep.

Amanpreet BG (Punjabi) a form of Amandeep.

Amapola (Arabic) poppy.

Amara (Greek) eternally beautiful.

Amaranta (Spanish) a flower that never fades.

Amari BG (Greek) a form of Amara.

Amarilia, Amarilla, Amarinda (Greek) she who shines.

Amarina (Australian) rain.

Amaris (Hebrew) promised by God.

Amarú (Quechua) snake, boa.

Amaryllis (Greek) fresh; flower.

Amatista (Greek) full of wine.

Amaui (Hawaiian) thrush.

Amaya (Japanese) night rain.

Amazona (Greek) Mythology: the Amazons were a tribe of warrior women.

Ambar GB (French) a form of Amber.

Ámbar (Arabic) the aroma of an exotic perfume.

Amber ☀ (French) amber.

Amber-Lynn, Amberlyn, **Amberlynn** (American) combinations of Amber + Lynn.

Amberlee, Amberley, Amberly (American) familiar forms of Amber.

Ambra (American) a form of Amber.

Ambria (American) a form of Amber.

Ambrosia (Greek) immortal.

Ambyr (French) a form of Amber.

Amedia (Spanish) a form of Amy.

Amee, Ami, Amie, Amiee (French) forms of Amy.

Ameena (Arabic) a form of Amina.

Ameera (Hebrew, Arabic) a form of Amira.

Amelberga (German) protected work.

Amelia ☀ (German) hard working. (Latin) a form of Emily. History: Amelia Earhart, an American aviator, was the first woman to fly solo across the Atlantic Ocean. Amélia (Portuguese) a form of Amelia.

Amelie, Amely (French) forms of Amelia.

Amelinda (American) a combination of Amelia + Linda.

America (Teutonic) industrious.

América (Teutonic) a form of America.

Amethyst (Greek) wine; purple-violet gemstone. History: in the ancient world, the amethyst stone was believed to help prevent drunkenness.

Amia (Hebrew) a form of Amy.

Amiana (Latin) a form of Amina.

Amilia (Latin, German) a form of Amelia.

Amilie (Latin, German) a form of Amelia.

Amina (Arabic) trustworthy, faithful. History: the mother of the prophet Muhammad.

Aminah (Arabic) a form of Amina.

Amira (Hebrew) speech; utterance.

Amirah (Hebrew, Arabic) a form of Amira.

Amiram (Hebrew) my land is lifted up.

Amissa (Hebrew) truth.

Amita (Hebrew) truth.

Amity (Latin) friendship.

Amlika (Hindi) mother.

Amma (Hindi) mother.

Amor, Amora (Spanish) love.

Amorette (Latin) beloved; loving.

Amorie (German) industrious leader.

Amorina (Spanish) she who falls in love easily.

Amoxtli (Nahuatl) book.

Amparo (Spanish) protected.

Amrit BG (Sanskrit) nectar.

Amrita (Spanish) a form of Amorette.

Amser (Welsh) time.

Amuillan (Mapuche) useful, helpful.

Amunet (Egyptian) Mythology: Amaunet is a guardian goddess of the pharaohs.

Amy (Latin) beloved.

An BG (Chinese) peaceful.

Ana (Hawaiian, Spanish) a form of Hannah.

Anaba (Native American) she returns from battle.

Anabel, Anabelle, Annabell (English) forms of Annabel.

Anaclara (Spanish) a combination of Ana + Carla.

Anacleta (Greek) she who has been called on; the required one.

Anahi, Anahy (Persian) short forms of Anahita.

Anahí, Anahid (Guarani) alluding to the flower of the ceibo tree.

Anahit (Persian) a short form of Anahita.

Anahita (Persian) the immaculate one. Mythology: a water goddess.

Anai (Hawaiian, Spanish) a form of Ana.

Anais (Hebrew) gracious.

Anaís (Hebrew) God has mercy.

Anakaren (English) a combination of Ana + Karen.

Anala (Hindi) fine.

Analaura (English) a combination of Ana + Laura.

Analena (Spanish) a form of Ana.

Anali (Hindi, Indian) fire, fiery.

Analía (Spanish) a combination of Ana and Lía.

Analicia (English) a form of Analisa.

Analiria (Spanish) native of Almeria, Spain.

Analisa, Annalisa (English) combinations of Anna + Lisa.

Analise, Annalise (English) forms of Analisa.

Anamaria (English) a combination of Ana + Maria.

Anan, Anán, Anani (Hebrew) cloudy.

Ananda (Hindi) blissful.

Anarosa (English) a combination of Ana + Rosa.

Anastacia, Anastazia, Annastasia (Greek) forms of Anastasia.

Anastasia (Greek) resurrection. .

Anat (Egyptian) Mythology: a consort of Seth.

Anatola (Greek) from the east.

Ancarla (Spanish) a combination of Ana and Carla.

Ancelín (Latin) single woman.

Anci (Hungarian) a form of Hannah.

Andeana (Spanish) leaving.

Andee, Andi, Andie (American) short forms of Andrea, Fernanda.

Andere (Greek) a form of Andrea.

Andra GB (Greek, Latin) a short form of Andrea.

Andrea GB (Greek) strong; courageous. **Andréa** (French) a form of Andrea.

Andreana, Andreanna (Greek) forms of Andrea.

Andreane, Andreanne, Andree Ann, Andree Anne (Greek) combinations of Andrea + Ann.

Andree (Greek) a short form of Andrea.

Andreia (Greek) a form of Andrea.

Andréia (Portuguese) a form of Andrea.

Andreina (Greek) a form of Andrea.

Andreína (Spanish) a form of Andrea.

Andresa (Spanish) a form of Andrea.

Andreya (Greek) a form of Andrea.

Andria (Greek) a form of Andrea.

Andriana, Andrianna (Greek) forms of Andrea.

Andromaca, Andrómana, Andrónica,

Andrómaca (Greek) she who is victorious over men.

Andromeda (Greek) Mythology: the daughter of Cepheus and Cassiopeia.

Anechka (Russian) grace.

Aneesa (Greek) a form of Agnes.

Aneesha (Greek) a form of Agnes.

Aneko (Japanese) older sister.

Anel (Hawaiian) a short form of Anela.

Anela (Hawaiian) angel.

Anelida (Spanish) a combination of Ana + Elida.

Anelina (Spanish) a combination of Ana + Lina.

Anémona (Greek) she who is victorious over men.

Anesha (Greek) a form of Agnes.

Aneshia (Greek) a form of Agnes.

Anesia (Greek) a form of Agnes.

Anessa, Annessa (Greek) forms of Agnes.

Aneta (Spanish) a form of Anita. (French) a form of Annette.

Anetra (American) a form of Annette.

Anezka (Czech) a form of Hannah.

Anfitrita (Greek) wind, breeze.

Angel 🅱🅶 (Greek) a short form of Angela.

Angela (Greek) angel; messenger. Ángela (Spanish) a form of Angela.

Angele, Angell, Angelle (Greek) short forms of Angela.

Angelea, Angelie (Greek) forms of Angela.

Angelena (Russian) a form of Angela.

Angeles (Spanish) a form of Angela.

Ángeles (Catalan) a form of Angeles.

Angelia (Greek) a form of Angela.

Angelic (Russian) a short form of Angelica.

Angelica, Angelika, Angellica (Greek) forms of Angela. **Angélica** (Spanish) a form of Angelica.

Angelicia (Russian) a form of Angelica.

Angelina (Russian) a form of Angela.

Angeline, Angelyn (Russian) forms of Angela.

Angelique (French) a form of Angela.

Angelisa (American) a combination of Angela + Lisa.

Angelita (Spanish) a form of Angela.

Angella (Greek) a form of Angela.

Angeni (Native American) spirit.

Angie (Greek) a familiar form of Angela.

Angustias (Latin) she who suffers from grief or sorrow.

Anh 🅶🅱 (Vietnamese) peace; safety.

Ani (Hawaiian) beautiful.

Ania (Polish) a form of Hannah.

Anica, Anika (Czech) familiar forms of Anna.

Anice, Anise (English) forms of Agnes.

Aniceta (Spanish) she who is invincible because of her great strength.

Aniela (Polish) a form of Anna.

Anik (Czech) a short form of Anica.

Anila (Hindi) Religion: an attendant of the Hindu god Vishnu.

Anillang (Mapuche) stable altar; decisive and courageously noble.

Anippe (Egyptian) daughter of the Nile.

Aniqua (Czech) a form of Anica.

Anisa, Anisah (Arabic) friendly. Anisha, Annisha

(English) forms of Agnes, Ann.

Anisia (Greek) she who fulfills her obligations.

Anissa (English) a form of Agnes, Ann. (Arabic) a form of Anisa.

Anita (Spanish) a form of Ann, Anna. .

Anitchka (Russian) a form of Anna.

Anitra (Spanish) a form of Anita.

Aniya (Russian) a form of Anya.

Anja (Russian) a form of Anya.

Anjali (Hindi) offering with both hands. (Indian) offering with devotion.

Anjela (Greek) a form of Angela.

Anjelica (Greek) a form of Angela.

Anjélica (Spanish) a form of Angelica.

Anjelita (Spanish) a form of Angela.

Anka GB (Polish) a familiar form of Hannah.

Ann, Anne (English) gracious.

Ann Catherine, Anne Catherine (American) combinations of Ann + Catherine.

Ann Julie, Anne Julie (American) combinations of Ann + Julie.

Ann Marie, Ann-Marie, Anne Marie, Anne-Marie, Annemarie, Annmarie (English) combinations of Ann + Marie.

Ann Sophie, Anne Sophie, Anne-Sophie (American) combinations of Ann + Sophie.

Anna ⭐ (German, Italian, Czech, Swedish) gracious. Culture: Anna Pavlova was a famous Russian ballerina.

Anna Maria, Annamaria (English) combinations of Anna + Maria.

Anna Marie, Anna-Marie, Annamarie (English) combinations of Anna + Marie.

Annabel (English) a combination of Anna + Bel.

Annabella (English) a form of Annabel.

Annabelle ⭐ (English) a form of Annabel.

Annah (German, Italian, Czech, Swedish) a form of Anna.

Annalee (Finnish) a form of Annalie.

Annalie (Finnish) a form of Hannah.

Annaliese (English) a form of Analisa.

Anneka (Swedish) a form of Hannah.

Anneke (Czech) a form of Anik. (Swedish) a form of Anneka.

Anneliese, Annelise (English) forms of Annelisa.

Annelisa (English) a combination of Ann + Lisa.

Annette (French) a form of Ann Annick, Annik (Russian) short forms of Annika.

Annie, Anny (English) familiar forms of Ann.

Annie Claude (American) a combination of Annie + Claude.

Annie Kim (American) a combination of Annie + Kim.

Annie Pier (American) a combination of Annie + Pier.

Annika (Russian) a form of Ann. (Swedish) a form of Anneka.

Annina (Hebrew) graceful.

Annisa, Annissa (Arabic) forms of Anisa. (English) a form of Anissa.

Anniston (American) Movies: Jennifer Aniston is an American movie star.

Annjanette (American) a combination of Ann + Janette (see Janett).

Annmaria (American) a combination of Ann + Maria.

Annora (Latin) honor.

Anona (English) pineapple.

Anouhea (Hawaiian) cool, soft fragrance.

Anouk (Dutch) a familiar form of Anna.

Anselma (German) divine protector.

Ansleigh (Scottish) a form of Ainsley.

Ansley GB (Scottish) a form of Ainsley.

Antania (Greek, Latin) a form of Antonia.

Antea (Greek) a form of Anthea.

Anthea (Greek) flower.

Anthony BG (Latin) praiseworthy. (Greek) flourishing.

Antía (Galician) a form of Antonia.

Antífona (Greek) opposite of her race.

Antígona (Greek) distinguished by her brothers.

Antigua (Spanish) old.

Antionette (French) a form of Antonia.

Antoinette (French) a form of AntoniaAntolina (Spanish) a form of Antonia.

Antonella (French) a form of Antoinette.

Antonette (French) a form of Antoinette.

Antonia (Greek) flourishing. (Latin) praiseworthy. Antónia (Portuguese) a form of Antonia.

Antonice (Latin) a form of Antonia.

Antonina (Greek, Latin) a form of Antonia.

Antoniña (Latin) she who confronts or is the adversary.

Antonique (French) a form of Antoinette.

Antonisha (Latin) a form of Antonice.

Anuncia (Latin) announcer, messenger.

Anunciación (Spanish) annunciation.

Anunciada, Anunciata (Spanish) forms of Anunciación.

Anya (Russian) a form of Anna.

Anyssa (English) a form of Anissa.

Anzia (Italian) one-armed.

Aparecida (Latin) appearance.

Aparicia (Latin) ghost.

Aphra (Hebrew) young doe.

Aphrodite (Greek) Mythology: the goddess of love and beauty.

Apia (Latin) devout woman.

Apolinaria, Apolinia (Spanish) forms of Appollonia.

Apoline (Greek) a form of Appollonia.

Appollonia (Greek) a form of Apollo .

April (Latin) opening.

Apryl (Latin) a form of April.

Apuleya (Latin) impulsive woman.

Aquene (Native American) peaceful.

Aquila GB (Latin, Spanish) eagle.

Aquilina (Latin) a form of Aquilla.

Aquiline (Greek) a form of Aquilla.

Aquilinia (Spanish) a form of Aquilla.

Aquilla (Latin, Spanish) a form of Aquila.

Ara BG (Arabic) opinionated.

Arabella (Latin) beautiful altar. **Araceli, Aracely** (Latin) heavenly altar.

Aracelis (Spanish) a form of Araceli.

Arama (Spanish) reference to the Virgin Mary.

Arán (Catalan) she is a conflicted virgin.

Arantxa (Basque) a form of Arantzazu.

Arantzazu, Aránzazu (Basque) are you among the thorns?

Aranzuru (Spanish) a form of Arantzazu.

Araseli (Latin) a form of Araceli.

Araya (Arabic) a form of Ara.

Arbogasta (Greek) the rich woman.

Arcadia, Arcadía (Greek) from Arcadia, a region in Greece.

Arcángela (Greek) archangel.

Arcelia (Latin) a form of Araceli.

Archibalda (German) born free.

Arcilla (Latin) a form of Araceli.

Ardelle (Latin) warm; enthusiastic.

Arden GB (English) valley of the eagle. Literature: in Shakespeare, a romantic place of refuge.

Ardi (Hebrew) a short form of Arden, Ardice, Ardith.

Ardice (Hebrew) a form of Ardith.

Ardith (Hebrew) flowering field.

Arebela (Latin) a form of Arabella.

Areil (American) a form of Areli.

Areli, Arely (American) forms of Oralee.

Arella (Hebrew) angel; messenger.

Aretha (Greek) virtuous. Aretusa (Greek) Mythology: Artheusa was one of the Nereids.

Argel (Welsh) refuge.

Argelia (Latin) jewelry boxes full of treasures.

Argenea (Latin) she who has platinum-colored hair.

Argenis (Latin) a form of Argenea.

Argentina (Latin) she who shines like gold. Geography: a country in South America.

Argimon (German) defensive army.

Argraff (Welsh) impression.

Ari BG (Hebrew) a short form of Ariel.

Aria ☆ (Hebrew) a form of Ariel.

Ariadna (Greek) a form of Ariadne.

Ariadne (Greek) holy. Mythology: the daughter of King Minos of Crete.

Ariah (Hebrew) a form of Aria.

Arial (Hebrew) a form of Ariel.

Arian BG (French) a form of Ariana.

Ariana ☆ (Greek) holy.

Ariane (French) a form of Ariana.

Arianna ☆ (Greek) a form of Ariana.

Arianne (English) a form of Ariana.

Arica, Arika (Scandinavian) forms of Erica.

Aricela (Latin) a form of Araceli.

Arie BG (Hebrew) a short form of Ariel.

Arieanna (Greek) a form of Ariana.

Ariel GB (Hebrew) lioness of God.

Ariela, Ariella (Hebrew) forms of Ariel.

Ariele, Ariell, Arielle, Arriel (French) forms of Ariel.

Aries GB (Greek) Mythology: Ares was the Greek god of war. (Latin) ram.

Arietta (Italian) short aria, melody.

Arin BG (Hebrew, Arabic) a form of Aaron. Ariona, Arionna **(Greek) forms of Ariana.**

Arissa (Greek) a form of Arista.

Arista (Greek) best.

Arla (German) a form of Carla.

Arlais (Welsh) what comes from the temple.

Arleen (Irish) a form of Arlene.

Arleigh (English) a form of Harley.

Arlena (Irish) a form of Arlene.

Arlene (Irish) pledge. **Arlette** (English) a form of Arlene.

Arlynn (American) a combination of Arlene + Lynn.

Armada, Armida (Spanish) forms of Armide.

Armanda (Latin) noble.

Armandina (French) a form of Armide.

Armani BG (Persian) desire, goal.

Armentaria (Latin) pastor of older livestock.

Armide (Latin) armed warrior.

Arminda (German) a form of Armide.

Armine (Latin) noble. (German) soldier. (French) a form of Herman Armonía (Spanish) balance, harmony.

Arnalda (Spanish) strong as an eagle.

Arnelle (German) eagle.

Arnette BG (English) little eagle.

Arnina (Hebrew) enlightened. (Arabic) a form of Aaron.

Arnulfa (German) eagle wolf.

Aroa (German) good person.

Arriana (Greek) a form of Ariana.

Artaith (Welsh) storm.

Artemia (Greek) a form of Artemis.

Artemis (Greek) Mythology: the goddess of the hunt and the moon.

Artha (Hindi) wealthy, prosperous.

Arti (Hebrew) a form of Ardi. (Hindi) a familiar form of Artha.

Artis BG (Irish) noble; lofty hill. (Scottish) bear. (English) rock. (Icelandic) follower of Thor.

Artura (Celtic) noble.

Aryana, Aryanna (Italian) forms of Ariana.

Aryel, Aryelle (Hebrew) forms of Ariel.

Aryn GB (Hebrew) a form of Aaron.

Aryssa (Greek) a form of Arissa.

Asa BG (Japanese) born in the morning.

Ascención (Spanish) ascension.

Asela (Latin) small donkey.

Asenka (Russian) grace.

Asgre (Welsh) heart.

Asha (Arabic, Swahili) a form of Aisha, Ashia.

Ashante, Ashanté (Swahili) forms of Ashanti.

Ashanti GB (Swahili) from a tribe in West Africa.

Asheley, Ashely (English) forms of Ashley.

Ashia (Arabic) life.

Ashira (Hebrew) rich.

Ashlan, Ashlen, Ashlin (English) forms of Ashlyn.

Ashle, Ashlea, Ashlee, Ashlei, Ashleigh, Ashli, Ashlie, Ashliegh, Ashly (English) forms of Ashley.

Ashleen (Irish) a form of Ashlyn.

Ashley ✧ GB (English) ash-tree meadow. .

Ashlyn, Ashlynn, Ashlynne (English) ash-tree pool. (Irish) vision, dream.

Ashonti (Swahili) a form of Ashanti.

Ashten GB (English) a form of Ashton.

Ashtin GB (English) a form of Ashton.

Ashton BG (English) ash-tree settlement.

Ashtyn (English) a form of Ashton.

Ashya (Arabic) a form of Ashia.

Asia (Greek) resurrection. (English) eastern sunrise. (Swahili) a form of Aisha.

Asiah (Greek, English, Swahili) a form of Asia.

Asiya (Arabic) one who tends to the weak, one who heals.

Asja (American) a form of Asia.

Asma (Arabic) excellent; precious.

Aspacia, Aspasia (Greek) welcome.

Aspen GB (English) aspen tree.

Aspyn (English) a form of Aspen.

Assumpta (Catalan) a form of Asunción.

Assunção (Portuguese) a form of Asunción.

Astarte (Egyptian) Mythology: a consort of Seth.

Aster (English) a form of Astra.

Astra (Greek) star.

Astrid (Scandinavian) divine strength.

Astriz (German) a form of Astra.

Asunción (Spanish) assumption.

Asunta (Spanish) to ascend.

Asya (Greek, English, Swahili) a form of Asia.

Atala, Atalia (Greek) young.

Atalanta (Greek) mighty huntress. Mythology: an athletic young woman who refused to marry any man who could not outrun her in a footrace.

Atalía (Spanish) guard tower.

Atanasia (Spanish) one who will be reborn; immortal.

Atara (Hebrew) crown.

Atenea (Greek) a form of Athena.

Atgas (Welsh) hate.

Athalia (Hebrew) the Lord is mighty.

Athena (Greek) wise. Mythology: the goddess of wisdom.

Athina (Greek) a form of Athena.

Ática (Greek) the city of Athens.

Atilia (Latin) woman who has difficulty walking.

Atira (Hebrew) prayer.

Atiya (Arabic) gift.

Atl (Nahuatl) water.

Atlanta (Greek) a form of Atalanta.

Atocha (Arabic) esparto grass.

Auberte (French) a form of Alberta.

Aubree ☆ (French) a form of Aubrey.

Aubrey ☆ (German) noble; bearlike. (French) blond ruler; elf ruler.

Aubri, Aubrie, Aubry (French) forms of Aubrey.

Aubriana, Aubrianna (English) combinations of Aubrey + Anna.

Aubrielle (French) a form of Aubrey.

Auburn GB (Latin) reddish brown.

Aude, Audey (English) familiar forms of Audrey.

Audelina (German) a form of Audrey.

Audra (French) a form of Audrey.

Audrea (French) a form of Audrey.

Audreanne, Audrey Ann, Audrey Anne (English) combinations of Audrey + Ann.

Audree, Audrie, Audry (English) forms of Audrey.

Audrey ☆ (English) noble strength.

Audrey Maud, Audrey Maude (English) combinations of Audrey + Maud.

Audriana, Audrianna (English) combinations of Audrey + Anna.

Audrina (English) a form of Audriana.

Audris (German) fortunate, wealthy.

August BG (Latin) born in the eighth month. A short form of Augustine.

Augusta (Latin) a short form of Augustine.

Augustine BG (Latin) majestic. Religion: Saint Augustine was the first archbishop of Canterbury.

Aundrea (Greek) a form of Andrea.

Aura (Greek) soft breeze. (Latin) golden.

Aúrea (Latin) she who has blond hair.

Aurelia (Latin) golden. Aurelie (Latin) a form of Aurelia.

Auriel (Hebrew) a form of Ariel.

Auristela (Latin) golden star.

Aurora (Latin) dawn. Mythology: the goddess of dawn.

Aurquena, Aurquene (Spanish) present.

Auset (Egyptian) Mythology: Aset is another name for Isis.

Austen BG (Latin) a short form of Augustine.

Austin BG (Latin) a short form of Augustine.

Austyn BG (Latin) a short form of Augustine.

Autum (American) a form of Autumn.

Autumn ☀ (Latin) autumn.

Auxiliadora (Latin) she who protects and helps.

Ava ☀ (Greek) a form of Eva.

Avaline (English) a form of Evelyn.

Avalon (Latin) island.

Averi, Averie (English) forms of Aubrey.

Avery ☀ (English) a form of Aubrey.

Aviana (Latin) a form of Avis.

Avis (Latin) bird.

Aviva (Hebrew) springtime.

Avneet (Hebrew) a form of Avner.

Avril (French) a form of April.

Awel (Welsh) gentle breeze.

Axelle (Latin) axe. (German) small oak tree; source of life.

Aya (Hebrew) bird; fly swiftly.

Ayah (Hebrew) a form of Aya.

Ayalga (Asturian) treasure.

Ayan (Hindi) a short form of Ayanna.

Ayana (Native American) a form of Aiyana. (Hindi) a form of Ayanna.

Ayanna (Hindi) innocent.

Ayat (Islamic) sign, revelation.

Ayelen, Aylén (Mapuche) joy.

Ayelén (Araucanian) a form of Ayelen.

Ayesha (Persian) a form of Aisha.

Ayinhual (Mapuche) beloved, darling; generous.

Ayinleo (Mapuche) inextinguishable love.

Ayiqueo (Mapuche) soft-spoken; pleasant.

Ayita (Cherokee) first in the dance.

Ayla (Hebrew) oak tree.

Aymara (Spanish) people and language of the south Andes.

Ayme (Mapuche) significant.

Aynkan (Indigenous) older sister.

Aysha (Persian) a form of Aisha.

Aysia (English) a form of Asia. (Persian) a form of Aisha.

Aza (Arabic) comfort.

Azalea (Greek) dry. Botany: a shrub with showy, colorful flowers that grows in dry soil.

Azaria (Hebrew) a form of Azuriah.

Azia (Arabic) a form of Aza.

Aziza (Swahili) precious.

Azucena (Arabic) admirable mother.

Azul (Arabic) color of the sky without clouds.

Azura (Persian) blue semiprecious stone.

Azure (Persian) a form of Azura.

B

Baba (African) born on Thursday.

Babe (Latin) a familiar form of Barbara. (American) a form of Baby.

Babesne (Arabic) a form of Amparo.

Babette (French, German) a familiar form of Barbara.

Babs (American) a familiar form of Barbara.

Baby (American) baby.

Badia (Arabic) elegant.

Bahiti (Egyptian) fortune.

Bailee, Baileigh, Baili, Bailie, Baillie, Baily (English) forms of Bailey.

Bailey GB (English) bailiff.

Baka (Hindi) crane.

Bakana (Australian) guardian.

Bakari BG (Swahili) noble promise.

Bakarne (Basque) solitude.

Bakula (Hindi) flower.

Balbina (Latin) stammerer.

Baldomera (Spanish) bold; famous.

Balduina (German) brave friend.

Baleigh (English) a form of Bailey.

Bambi (Italian) child.

Ban (Arabic) has revealed oneself; has appeared.

Bandi BG (Punjabi) prisoner.

Banon (Welsh) queen.

Bao GB (Chinese) treasure.

Baptista (Latin) baptizer.

Bara, Barra (Hebrew) chosen.

Barb (Latin) a short form of Barbara.

Barbada (Arabic) blessing.

Barbara (Latin) stranger, foreigner. **Bárbara** (Greek) a form of Barbara.

Barbie (American) a familiar form of Barbara.

Barbra (American) a form of Barbara.

Bardon (Hispanic) full of hair.

Bari (Irish) a form of Barrie.

Barika (Swahili) success.

Barran (Irish) top of a small hill. (Russian) ram.

Barrett BG (German) strong as a bear.

Barrie (Irish) spear; markswoman.

Bartola, Bartolina (Aramaic) she who tills the soil.

Bartolomea (Spanish) child of Talmaí.

Basemat (Hebrew) balm.

Basia (Hebrew) daughter of God.

Basiana (Spanish) acute judgment.

Basillia (Greek, Latin) royal; queenly.

Bastet (Egyptian) Mythology: cat-headed goddess.

Bathany (Aramaic) a form of Bethany.

Bathilda (German) warrior.

Bathsheba (Hebrew) daughter of the oath; seventh daughter. Bible: a wife of King David.

Batilde (German) a form of Bathilda.

Batini (Swahili) inner thoughts.

Batoul (Arabic) virgin.

Baudilia (Teutonic) audacious and brave.

Baylea, Bayleigh, Bayli, Baylie (English) forms of Bailey.

Baylee GB (English) a form of Bailey.

Bayley GB (English) a form of Bailey.

Bayo **(Yoruba) joy is found.**

Bea (American) a short form of Beatrice.

Beata (Latin) a short form of Beatrice.

Beatrice (Latin) blessed; happy; bringer of joy.

Beatris, Beatriz (Latin) forms of Beatrice.

Bebe BG (Spanish) a form of Barbara, Beatrice.

Becca (Hebrew) a short form of Rebecca.

Becka (Hebrew) a form of Becca.

Becky (American) a familiar form of Rebecca.

Bedelia (Irish) a form of Bridget.

Bee BG (American) a short form of Beatrice.

Bega (Germanic) illustrious; brilliant.

Begoña (Basque) the place of the dominant hill.

Begonia (Spanish) begonia.

Bel (Hindi) sacred wood of apple trees. A short form of Amabel, Belinda, Isabel.

Bela BG (Czech) white. (Hungarian) bright.

Belarmina (Spanish) beautiful armor.

Belen GB (Greek) arrow. (Spanish) Bethlehem.

Belicia (Spanish) dedicated to God.

Belinda (Spanish) beautiful. Literature: a name coined by English poet Alexander Pope in *The Rape of the Lock*.

Belisa (Latin) the most slender.

Belisaria (Greek) right-handed archer; she who shoots arrows skillfully.

Bella ☆ (Latin) beautiful.

Belle (French) beautiful. A short form of Arabella, Belinda, Isabel.

Belva (Latin) beautiful view.

Bena (Native American) pheasant.

Benate (Basque) a form of Bernadette.

Benecia (Latin) a short form of Benedicta.

Benedicta (Latin) blessed.

Benedicte (Latin) a form of Benedicta.

Benedicto (Latin) a form of Benedicta.

Benedita (Portuguese) a form of Benedicta.

Benicio (Spanish) benevolent one.

Benigna (Spanish) kind.

Benilda (German) she who fights with bears.

Benilde (Spanish) a form of Benilda.

Benita (Spanish) a form of Benedicta.

Benjamina (Spanish) a form of Benjamin

Bennett BG (Latin) little blessed one.

Benni (Latin) a familiar form of Benedicta.

Bennu (Egyptian) eagle.

Bente (Latin) blessed.

Berdine (German) glorious; inner light.

Berengaria (German) strong as a bear.

Berenice, Berenise (Greek) forms of Bernice.

Berget (Irish) a form of Bridget.

Berit (German) glorious.

Berkley BG (Scottish, English) birch-tree meadow.

Berlynn (English) a combination of Bertha + Lynn.

Bernabela, Bernabella (Hebrew) child of prophecy.

Bernadette (French) a form of Bernadine.

Bernadine (English, German) brave as a bear.

Berneta (French) a short form of Bernadette.

Berni (English) a familiar form of Bernadine, Bernice.

Bernice (Greek) bringer of victory. .

Berry BG (English) berry. A short form of Bernice.

Berta (German) a form of Berit, Bertha.

Bertha (German) bright; illustrious; brilliant ruler. A short form of Alberta.

Berti (German, English) a familiar form of Gilberte, Bertina.

Bertila, Bertilia (German) forms of Bertilda.

Bertilda (German) she who fights; the distinguished one.

Bertille (French) a form of Bertha.

Bertina (English) bright, shining.

Bertoaria (German) brilliant city or army.

Bertolda (German) a form of Bertha.

Berwyn BG (Welsh) white head.

Beryl (Greek) sea green jewel.

Bess (Hebrew) a short form of Bessie.

Bessie (Hebrew) a familiar form of Elizabeth.

Betania (Hebrew) a form of Bethany.

Beth (Hebrew, Aramaic) house of God. A short form of Bethany, Elizabeth.

Bethani, Bethanie (Aramaic) forms of Bethany.

Bethann (English) a combination of Beth + Ann.

Bethany (Aramaic) house of figs. Bible: the site of Lazarus's resurrection.

Bethel (Hebrew) from God's house.

Betiñe (Basque) a form of Perpetua.

Betsabe, Betsabé (Hebrew) daughter of an oath or pact.

Betsy (American) a familiar form of Elizabeth.

Bette (French) a form of Betty.

Bettina (American) a combination of Beth + Tina.

Betty (Hebrew) consecrated to God. (English) a familiar form of Elizabeth.

Betula (Hebrew) girl, maiden.

Betulia (Hebrew) birch-tree garden.

Beulah (Hebrew) married. Bible: Beulah is a name for Israel.

Bev (English) a short form of Beverly.

Bevanne (Welsh) child of Evan.

Beverley (English) a form of Beverly.

Beverly GB (English) beaver field.

Beverlyann (American) a combination of Beverly + Ann.

Bian (Vietnamese) hidden; secretive.

Bianca (Italian) white.

Bianka (Italian) a form of Bianca.

Bibi (Latin) a short form of Bibiana. (Arabic) lady. (Spanish) a form of Bebe.

Bibiana (Latin) lively.

Bibiñe (Basque) a form of Viviana.

Biblis (Latin) swallow.

Biddy (Irish) a familiar form of Bedelia.

Bienvenida (Spanish) welcome.

Bilal (Basque) born during summertime.

Billi (English) a form of Billie.

Billie GB (English) strong willed. (German, French) a familiar form of Belle, Wilhelmina.

Billie-Jean (American) a combination of Billie + Jean.

Billie-Jo (American) a combination of Billie + Jo.

Billy BG (English) a form of Billie.

Bina (Hebrew) wise; understanding. (Swahili) dancer. (Latin) a short form of Sabina.

Binney (English) a familiar form of Benedicta, Bianca, Bina.

Bionca (Italian) a form of Bianca.

Birdie (English) bird. (German) a familiar form of Bertha.

Birgitte (Swedish) a form of Bridget.

Birkide (Basque) a form of Bridget.

Bitilda (German) a form of Bathilda.

Bjorg (Scandinavian) salvation.

Bladina (Latin) friendly.

Blaine BG (Irish) thin.

Blair BG (Scottish) plains dweller.

Blaire (Scottish) a form of Blair.

Blaise BG (French) one who stammers.

Blake BG (English) dark.

Blakely BG (English) dark meadow.

Blanca (Italian) a form of Bianca.

Blanche (French) a form of Bianca.

Blanda (Latin) delicate; soft.

Blandina (Latin) flattering.

Blasa (French) a form of Blaise.

Blasina, Blasona (Latin) forms of Blaise.

Blayne BG (Irish) a form of Blaine.

Blenda (German) white; brilliant.

Blesila (Celtic) firebrand.

Blinda (American) a short form of Belinda.

Bliss GB (English) blissful, joyful.

Blodwyn (Welsh) flower.

Blondelle (French) blond, fair haired.

Blondie (American) a familiar form of Blondelle.

Blossom (English) flower.

Blum (Yiddish) flower.

Blythe (English) happy, cheerful.

Bo BG (Chinese) precious.

Boacha (Hebrew) blessed.

Bobbette (American) a familiar form of Roberta.

Bobbi (American) a familiar form of Barbara, Roberta.

Bobbi-Ann, Bobbie-Ann (American) combinations of Bobbi + Ann.

Bobbi-Jo, Bobbie-Jo (American) combinations of Bobbi + Jo.

Bobbi-Lee (American) a combination of Bobbi + Lee.

Bobbie GB (American) a familiar form of Barbara, Roberta.

Bodana, Bohdana (Russian) gift from God.

Bodil BG (Norwegian) mighty ruler.

Bolivia (Spanish) Geography: Bolivia is a country in South America.

Bolona (German) friend.

Bolonia (Italian) Geography: a form of Bologna, an Italian city.

Bonajunta (Latin) good; united.

Bonfila, Bonfilia (Italian) good daughter.

Bonifacia (Italian) benefactor.

Bonita (Spanish) pretty.

Bonnie, Bonny (English, Scottish) beautiful, pretty. (Spanish) familiar forms of Bonita.

Bonnie-Bell (American) a combination of Bonnie + Belle.

Bonosa (Spanish) willingly; with kindness.

Bova (German) brave; illustrious.

Bracken (English) fern.

Bradley 🅱🅶 (English) broad meadow.

Brady 🅱🅶 (Irish) spirited.

Braeden 🅱🅶 (English) broad hill.

Braelyn (American) a combination of Braeden + Lynn.

Braith (Welsh) freckle.

Branca (Portuguese) white.

Branda (Hebrew) blessing.

Brande, Brandee, Brandi, Brandie (Dutch) forms of Brandy.

Branden 🅱🅶 (English) beacon valley.

Brandis (Dutch) a form of Brandy.

Brandon 🅱🅶 (English) a form of Branden.

Brandy (Dutch) an after-dinner drink made from distilled wine.

Brandy-Lynn (American) a combination of Brandy + Lynn.

Braulia (Teutonic) gleaming.

Braulio (German) ardent; one who burns.

Braxton 🅱🅶 (English) Brock's town.

Bre (Irish, English) a form of Bree.

Brea, Breah (Irish) short forms of Breana, Briana.

Breahna (Irish) a form of Breana, Briana.

Breana, Bréana, Breanna, Bréanna (Irish) forms of Briana.

Breann, Breanne (Irish) short forms of Briana.

Breasha (Russian) a familiar form of Breana.

Breauna, Breaunna, Breunna, Briauna, Briaunna (Irish) forms of Briana.

Breck 🅱🅶 (Irish) freckled.

Bree (English) broth. (Irish) a short form of Breann.

Breean (Irish) a short form of Briana.

Breeana, Breeanna (Irish) forms of Briana.

Breena (Irish) fairy palace. A form of Brina.

Breeze **(English) light wind; carefree.**

Bregus (Welsh) fragile.

Breiana, Breianna (Irish) forms of Briana.

Breigh (Irish) a form of Bree.

Brena, Brenna (Irish) forms of Brenda.

Brenda (Irish) little raven. (English) sword.

Brenda-Lee (American) a combination of Brenda + Lee.

Brennan 🅱🅶 (English) a form of Brendan

Breona, Bréona,

Breonna, Bréonna (Irish) forms of Briana.

Breonia (Irish) a form of Breona.

Bret 🅱🅶 (Irish) a short form of Britany.

Brett 🅱🅶 (Irish) a short form of Britany.

Brette (Irish) a short form of Britany.

Breyana, Breyann, Breyanna (Irish) forms of Briana.

Breyona, Breyonna (Irish) forms of Briana.

Bria, Briah (Irish) short forms of Briana.

Briahna (Irish) a form of Briana.

Briana (Irish) strong; virtuous, honorable.

Brianca (Irish) a form of Briana.

Brianda (Irish) a form of Briana.

Briann, Brianne (Irish) short forms of Briana.

Brianna ⭐ (Irish) a form of Briana.

Briannah (Irish) a form of Briana.

Briar 🅱🅶 (French) heather.

Brice 🅱🅶 (Welsh) a form of Bryce.

Bricia (Spanish) a form of Bridget.

34

Bridey (Irish) a familiar form of Bridget.

Bridget (Irish) strong.

Bridgett, Bridgette (Irish) forms of Bridget.

Brie (French) a type of cheese. Geography: a region in France known for its cheese.

Brieana, Brieanna (American) combinations of Brie + Anna.

Brieann, Brieanne (American) combinations of Brie + Ann.

Briel, Brielle (French) forms of Brie.

Brienna (Irish) a form of Briana.

Brienne (French) a short form of Briana.

Brieonna (Irish) a form of Briana.

Brigette (French) a form of Bridget.

Brighton BG (English) bright town.

Brigid (Irish) a form of Bridget.

Brígida, Brigidia (Celtic) forms of Bridget.

Brigit, Brigitte (French) forms of Bridget.

Briley (American) a combination of "B" + Riley.

Brillana (English) from the city of Brill, England.

Brina (Latin) a short form of Sabrina. (Irish) a familiar form of Briana.

Brinley (English) burnt meadow.

Briona, Brionna (Irish) forms of Briana.

Brisa (Spanish) beloved. Mythology: Briseis was the Greek name of Achilles's beloved.

Brisda (Celtic) a form of Bridget.

Briselda (Spanish) a form of Bridget.

Brisia, Briza (Greek) forms of Brisa.

Bristol (English) the site of the bridge; from Bristol, England.

Brita (Irish) a form of Bridget. (English) a short form of Britany.

Britaney, Britani, Britanie, Brittaney (English) forms of Britany.

Britany, Brittany (English) from Britain.

Britin, Brittin (English) from Britain.

British (English) from Britain.

Britnee, Britney, Britni, Britnie, Britny, Brittnay, Brittnee,

Brittney, Brittni, Brittnie, Brittny (English) forms of Britany.

Briton BG (English) a form of Britin.

Britt BG (Swedish, Latin) a short form of Britta.

Britta (Swedish) strong. (Latin) a short form of Britany.

Brittan BG (English) a form of Britin. A short form of Britany.

Brittanny (English) a form of Britany.

Britten BG (English) a form of Britin. A short form of Britany.

Britteny (English) a form of Britany.

Brittiany (English) a form of Britany.

Brittin (English) a form of Britin.

Brittini, Brittiny (English) forms of Britany.

Britton BG (English) a form of Britin.

Brittony (English) a form of Britany.

Briyana, Briyanna (Irish) forms of Briana.

Brodie BG (Irish) ditch; canal builder.

Brogan BG (Irish) a heavy work shoe.

Bronnie (Welsh) a familiar form of Bronwyn.

Bronte (Greek) thunder. (Gaelic) bestower. Literature: Charlotte, Emily, and Anne Brontë were sister writers from England.

Bronwen (Welsh) a form of Bronwyn.

Bronwyn (Welsh) white breasted. **Brook** (English) brook, stream.

Brooke (English) brook, stream.

Brooke-Lynn, Brookelyn, Brookelynn (American) forms of Brooklyn.

Brooklin (American) a form of Brooklyn.

Brooklyn, Brooklyne, Brooklynn, Brooklynne (American) combinations of Brook + Lynn.

Brooks BG (English) a form of Brook.

Bruna (German) a short form of Brunhilda.

Brunela (Italian) a form of Brunhilda.

Brunhilda (German) armored warrior.

Brunilda (German) a form of Brunhilda.

Bryana, Bryanna (Irish) forms of Briana.

Bryanne (Irish) a short form of Bryana.

Bryce BG (Welsh) alert; ambitious.

Bryga (Polish) a form of Bridget.

Brylee, Brylie (American) combinations of the letter B + Riley.

Bryn GB (Latin) from the boundary line. (Welsh) mound.

Bryna (Latin, Irish) a form of Brina.

Brynn (Latin) from the boundary line. (Welsh) mound.

Brynne (Latin, Welsh) a form of Bryn.

Bryona, Bryonna (Irish) forms of Briana.

Bryttani, Bryttany (English) forms of Britany.

Bryttni (English) a form of Britany.

Buena (Spanish) good.

Buenaventura (Castilian) good fortune.

Buffy (American) buffalo; from the plains.

Bunny (Greek) a familiar form of Bernice. (English) little rabbit.

Burgundy (French) Geography: a region of France known for its Burgundy wine.

Bushra (Arabic) good omen.

Byanna (Irish) a form of Briana.

C

Cabeza (Spanish) head.

Cache, Cachet (French) prestigious; desirous.

Cadence (Latin) rhythm.

Cadie, Cady (English) forms of Kady.

Cadwyn (Welsh) channel.

Cadyna (English) a form of Cadence.

Caecey (Irish) a form of Casey.

Caela (Hebrew) a form of Kayla.

Caeley (American) a form of Kaylee, Kelly.

Caelin, Caelyn (American) forms of Kaelyn.

Caethes (Welsh) slave.

Cafleen (Irish) a form of Cathleen.

Cai BG (Vietnamese) feminine.

Caicey (Irish) a form of Casey.

Caila (Hebrew) a form of Kayla.

Cailee, Caileigh, Cailey (American) forms of Kaylee, Kelly.

Cailida (Spanish) adoring.

Cailin, Cailyn (American) forms of Caitlin.

Caitlan, Caitlen, Caitlyn, Caitlynn, Caitlynne

(Irish) forms of Caitlin, Kaitlan.

Caitlin (Irish) pure.

Cala, Calla (Arabic) castle, fortress.

Calala (Spanish) a familiar form of Chandelaria.

Calamanda (Latin) Geography: a region in Mexico.

Calandra (Greek) lark.

Calantha (Greek) beautiful blossom.

Caledonia (Latin) from Scotland.

Calee, Caleigh, Calley (American) forms of Caeley.

Calefagia (Greek) pleasant.

Caley 🄶🄱 (American) a form of Caeley.

Calfuray (Mapuche) blue violet flower.

Cali, Calli (Greek) forms of Calie.

Calida (Spanish) warm; ardent.

Cálida (Spanish) a form of Calida.

Calie, Callie, Cally (Greek, Arabic) familiar forms of Cala, Calista.

Calinda (Hindi) a form of Kalinda.

Calínica (Greek) she who wins a great victory.

Calíope (Greek) a form of Calliope.

Calirroe (Greek) walks with beauty.

Calista, Callista (Greek) most beautiful.

Calistena, Calistenia (Greek) beautiful strength.

Calisto (Spanish, Portuguese) a form of Calista.

Calixta, Calixto (Greek) forms of Calista.

Callan 🄶🄱 (German) likes to talk, chatter.

Callidora (Greek) gift of beauty.

Calliope (Greek) beautiful voice. Mythology: Calliope was the Muse of epic poetry.

Callula (Latin) beauty; light.

Caltha (Latin) yellow flower.

Calumina (Irish) dove.

Calvina (Latin) bald.

Calyca (Greek) a form of Kalyca.

Calyn (Scottish) a form of Caelan American) a form of Caelin. (German) a form of Callan.

Calypso (Greek) concealer. Botany: a pink orchid

native to northern regions. Mythology: the sea nymph who held Odysseus captive for seven years.

Cam 🄱🄶 (Vietnamese) sweet citrus.
Kam

Camara (American) a form of Cameron.

Camarin (Scottish) a form of Cameron.

Camberly (American) a form of Kimberly.

Cambria (Latin) from Wales.

Camden 🄱🄶 (Scottish) winding valley.

Camelia, Camellia (Italian) Botany: a camellia is an evergreen tree or shrub with fragrant roselike flowers.

Cameo (Latin) gem or shell on which a portrait is carved.

Camera (American) a form of Cameron.

Cameron 🄱🄶 (Scottish) crooked nose. **Camesha** (American) a form of Camisha.

Cami, Camie, Cammie, Cammy (French) short forms of Camille.

Camila ☆ (Italian) a form of Camille. .

Camilla (Italian) a form of Camille.

Camille GB (French) young ceremonial attendant.

Camino, Camiño (Spanish) road.

Camisha (American) a combination of Cami + Aisha.

Campbell BG (Latin, French) beautiful field. (Scottish) crooked mouth.

Camri, Camrie, Camry (American) short forms of Camryn.

Camryn GB (American) a form of Cameron.

Camylle (French) a form of Camille.

Cancia (Spanish) native of Anzio, Italy.

Canciana, Cancianila (Spanish) forms of Cancia.

Canda (Greek) a form of Candace. (Spanish) a short form of Chandelaria.

Candace (Greek) glittering white; glowing. History: the title of the queens of ancient Ethiopia.

Candela, Candelas (Spanish) candle; fire.

Candelaria (Spanish) a form of Chandelaria.

Candi (American) a familiar form of Candace, Candice, Candida. (Spanish) a familiar form of Chandelaria.

Candice, Candis (Greek) forms of Candace.

Candida (Latin) bright white.

Cándida (Latin) a form of Candida.

Candie, Candy (American) familiar forms of Candace, Candice, Candida.

Candra (Latin) glowing.

Candyce (Greek) a form of Candace.

Canela (Latin) cinnamon.

Caniad (Welsh) a form of Carmen.

Canita (Hebrew, Latin) a form of Carmen.

Cantara (Arabic) small crossing.

Cantrelle (French) song.

Canuta (German) of good origin.

Capitolina (Latin) she who lives with the gods.

Capri (Italian) a short form of Caprice. Geography: an island off the west coast of Italy.

Caprice (Italian) fanciful.

Cara, Carah (Latin) dear. (Irish) friend.

Caralampia (Greek) illuminated by happiness.

Caralee (Irish) a form of Cara.

Caralyn (English) a form of Caroline.

Carelyn (English) a form of Caroline.

Carem (Spanish) a form of Karen.

Caren (Welsh) a form of Caron. (Italian) a form of Carina.

Carenza (Irish) a form of Karenza.

Caressa (French) a form of Carissa.

Carey BG (Welsh) a familiar form of Cara, Caroline, Karen, Katherine. **Cari, Carie** (Welsh) forms of Carey, Kari.

Caridad, Caridade (Latin) love; affection.

Carilyn (English) a form of Caroline.

Carina (Italian) dear little one. (Greek) a familiar form of Cora. (Swedish) a form of Karen.

Carine (Italian) a form of Carina.

Carisa, Carrisa, Carrissa (Greek) forms of Carissa.

Carisma (Greek) a form of Karisma.

Carissa (Greek) beloved.
Carita (Latin) charitable.

Caritina (Latin) grace.

Carla (German) farmer. (English) strong. (Latin) a form of Carol, Caroline.

Carlee, Carleigh, Carley, Carli, Carlie (English) forms of Carly.

Carleen, Carlene (English) forms of Caroline.

Carlena (English) a form of Caroline.

Carlin BG (Irish) little champion. (Latin) a short form of Caroline.

Carlina (Latin, Irish) a form of Carlin.

Carling (Latin, Irish) a form of Carlin.

Carlisa (American) a form of Carlissa.

Carlisha (American) a form of Carlissa.

Carlissa (American) a combination of Carla + Lissa.

Carlita (Italian) a form of Carlotta.

Carlotta (Italian) a form of Charlotte.

Carly (English) a familiar form of Caroline, Charlotte.

Carlyle BG (English) Carla's island.

Carlyn, Carlynn (Irish) forms of Carlin.

Carman (Latin) a form of Carmen.

Carme (Galician) a form of Carmela.

Carmel GB (Hebrew) a short form of Carmela.

Carmela, Carmella (Hebrew) garden; vineyard. Bible: Mount Carmel in Israel is often thought of as paradise.

Carmelit (Hebrew) a short form of Carmelita.

Carmelita (Hebrew) a form of Carmela.

Carmelo (Spanish) a form of Carmela.

Carmen GB (Latin) song. Religion: *Nuestra Señora del Carmen*—Our Lady of Mount Carmel—is one of the titles of the Virgin Mary.

Carmina (Latin) a form of Carmine.

Carmiña, Carminda (Spanish) forms of Carmen.

Carmine BG (Latin) song; red.

Carmo (Portuguese) a form of Carmela.

Carnelian (Latin) clear, reddish stone.

Carniela (Greek) a form of Karniela.

Carol (German) farmer. (French) song of joy. (English) strong,

Carol Ann, Carol Anne, Carolan, Carolane, Carolanne (American) combinations of Carol + Ann. Forms of Caroline.

Carole (English) a form of Carol.

Carolina (Italian) a form of Caroline.

Caroline ☆ (French) little and strong.

Carolyn, Carolyne, Carolynn (English) forms of Caroline. .

Caron (Welsh) loving, kindhearted, charitable.

Carona (Spanish) a form of Corona.

Carpófora (Greek) one who carries fruits.

Carra (Irish) a form of Cara.

Carrie (English) a familiar form of Carol, Caroline.

Carrigan (Irish) a form of Corrigan.

Carrington 🆎 (Welsh) rocky town.

Carrola (French) a form of Carol.

Carson 🆎 (English) child of Carr.

Carter 🆎 (English) cart driver.

Cary 🆎 (Welsh) a form of Carey.

Caryl (Latin) a form of Carol.

Caryn (Danish) a form of Karen.

Carys (Welsh) love.

Casandra (Greek) a form of Cassandra.

Casey 🆎 (Irish) brave. (Greek) a familiar form of Acacia.

Cashmere (Slavic) a form of Casimir.

Casi, Casie (Irish) forms of Casey.

Casiana (Latin) empty; vain.

Casidy, Cassidee, Cassidi, Cassidie (Irish) forms of Cassidy.

Casiel (Latin) mother of the earth.

Casilda (Arabic) virgin carrier of the lance.

Casimir (Polish) a form of Casimira.

Casimira (Slavic) peacemaker. .

Cass 🆎 (Greek) a short form of Cassandra.

Cassady (Irish) a form of Cassidy.

Cassandra (Greek) helper of men. Mythology: a prophetess of ancient Greece whose prophesies were not believed.

Cassandre (Greek) a form of Cassandra.

Cassaundra (Greek) a form of Cassandra.

Cassey, Cassi, Cassy (Greek) familiar forms of Cassandra, Catherine.

Cassia (Greek) a cinnamon-like spice.

Cassidy 🆖 (Irish) clever.

Cassie (Greek) a familiar form of Cassandra, Catherine.

Cassiopeia (Greek) clever. Mythology: the wife of the Ethiopian king Cepheus; the mother of Andromeda.

Cassondra (Greek) a form of Cassandra.

Casta (Greek) pure.

Castalia (Greek) fountain of purity.

Castel (Spanish) to the castle.

Castora (Spanish) brilliant.

Cástula (Greek) a form of Casta.

Cataleya (Spanish) a form of Cattleya. Botany: Cattleya is a genus of orchid that grows in Colombia.

Catalín (Spanish) a form of Caitlin.

Catalina (Spanish) a form of Catherine. .

Catalonia (Spanish) a region of Spain.

Catarina (German) a form of Catherine.

Catelin, Catelyn, Catelynn (Irish) forms of Caitlin.

Caterina (German) a form of Catherine.

Catharine (Greek) a form of Catherine.

Catherine (Greek) pure. (English) a form of Katherine.

Catheryn (Greek, English) a form of Catherine.

Cathi (Greek) a form of Cathy.

Cathleen (Irish) a form of Catherine.

Cathrine, Cathryn (Greek) forms of Catherine.

Cathy (Greek) a familiar form of Catherine, Cathleen. ,

Catia (Russian) a form of Katia.

Catie (English) a form of Katie.

Catina (English) a form of Katina.

Catlin GB (Irish) a form of Caitlin.

Catriel (Hebrew) a form of Katriel.

Catrina (Slavic) a form of Catherine, Katrina.

Catriona (Slavic) a form of Catherine, Katrina.

Cayce (Greek, Irish) a form of Casey.

Cayetana (Spanish) native of the city of Gaeta, Italy.

Cayfutray (Mapuche) celestial waterfall from heaven.

Cayla, Caylah (Hebrew) forms of Kayla.

Caylee, Cayleigh, Cayley, Cayli, Caylie (American) forms of Kaylee, Kelly.

Caylen, Caylin (American) forms of Caitlin.

Ceaira (Irish) a form of Ciara.

Ceanna (Italian) a form of Ciana.

Ceara, Cearra (Irish) forms of Ciara.

Cecelia (Latin) a form of Cecilia.

Cecile (Latin) a form of Cecilia.

Cecilia (Latin) blind.

Cecília (Portuguese) a form of Cecilia.

Cecily (Latin) a form of Cecilia.

Cedar BG (Latin) a kind of evergreen conifer.

Cedrica (English) battle chieftain.

Ceferina (German) caresses like a soft wind.

Ceil (Latin) a short form Cecilia.

Ceilidh (Irish) country dance.

Ceira, Ceirra (Irish) forms of Ciara.

Celandine (Latin) an herb with yellow flowers. (Greek) swallow.

Celedonia (German) a form of Celidonia.

Celena (Greek) a form of Selena.

Celene (Greek) a form of Celena.

Celerina (Spanish) quick.

Celesta (Latin) a form of Celeste.

Celeste (Latin) celestial, heavenly.

Celestina (Latin) a form of Celeste.

Celestine (Latin) a form of Celeste.

Celia (Latin) a short form of Cecilia.

Célia (Portuguese) a form of Celia.

Celidonia (Greek) celandine herb.

Celina (Greek) a form of Celena.

Celine (Greek) a form of Celena.

Celmira (Arabic) brilliant one.

Celosia (Greek) dry; burning.

Celsa (Latin) very spiritual.

Celsey (Scandinavian, Scottish, English) a form of Kelsey.

Cemelia (Punic) she has God present.

Cenobia (Greek) stranger.

Centehua (Nahuatl) only one.

Centola (Arabic) light of knowledge.

Cera (French) a short form of Cerise.

Cercira (Greek) Geography: native of Syrtis, an ancient name for the gulf of the Mediterranean Sea.

Cerella (Latin) springtime.

Ceres (Latin) Mythology: the Roman goddess of agriculture. Astronomy: the first asteroid discovered to have an orbit between Mars and Saturn.

Ceridwen (Welsh) poetic goddess.

Cerise (French) cherry; cherry red.

Cesara, Cesaria, Cesira, Cesírea (Latin) forms of Cesare.

Cesare (Latin) long-haired. History: Roman emperors were given the title *Caesar.*

Cesarina (Latin) a form of Cesare.

Cesilia (Latin) a form of Cecilia.

Chabela (Hebrew) a form of Isabel.

Chabeli (French) a form of Chablis.

Chablis (French) a dry white wine. Geography: a region in France where wine grapes are grown.

Chadee (French) from Chad, a country in north-central Africa. .

Chahna (Hindi, Indian) love; light, illumination.

Chai (Hebrew) life.

Chaka (Sanskrit) a form of Chakra.

Chakra (Sanskrit) circle of energy.

Chalchiuitl (Nahuatl) emerald.

Chalice (French) goblet.

Chalina (Spanish) a form of Rose.

Chalonna (American) a combination of the prefix Cha + Lona.

Chambray (French) a lightweight fabric.

Chamique (American) a form of Shamika.

Champagne (French) a province in eastern France; a wine made in this province.

Chan BG (Cambodian) sweet-smelling tree.

Chana (Hebrew) a form of Hannah.

Chance BG (English) a short form of Chancey.

Chancey BG (English) chancellor; church official.

Chanda (Sanskrit) short tempered. Religion: the demon defeated by the Hindu goddess Chamunda.

Chandani (Hindi) moonlight.

Chandelaria (Spanish) candle.

Chandelle (French) candle.

Chandi (Indian) moonlight. (Sanskrit) a form of Chanda.

Chandler BG (Hindi) moon. (Old English) candlemaker.

Chanel, Channel (English) channel.

Chanell, Chanelle, Channelle (English) forms of Chanel.

Chaney BG (French) oak.

Chanice, Chanise (American) forms of Shanice.

Channa (Hindi) chickpea.

Channing BG (English) wise. (French) canon; church official.

Chantal, Chantale, Chantalle (French) song.

Chantara (American) a form of Chantal.

Chante BG (French) a short form of Chantal.

Chanté (French) a short form of Chantal.

Chantel, Chantele, Chantell, Chantelle (French) forms of Chantal.

Chantia (French) a form of Chante.

Chantile (French) a form of Chantal.

Chantilly (French) fine lace.

Chantrea (Cambodian) moon; moonbeam.

Chantrice (French) singer.

Chardae, Charde (Punjabi) charitable. (French) short forms of Chardonnay.

Chardonnay (French) a dry white wine.

Charice (Greek) a form of Charis.

Charis (Greek) grace; kindness.

Charisma (Greek) the gift of leadership.

Charissa (Greek) a form of Charity.

Charisse (Greek) a form of Charity.

Charity (Latin) charity, kindness.

Charla (French, English) a short form of Charlene, Charlotte.

Charlaine (English) a form of Charlene.

Charlee, Charleigh, Charli (German, English) forms of Charlie.

Charleen, Charline (English) forms of Charlene.

Charlene (English) a form of Caroline.

Charley BG (German, English) a form of Charlie.

Charlie BG (German, English) strong.

Charlisa (French) a form of Charlotte.

Charlize (South African) a feminine form of Charles, Charlie. Movies: Charlize Theron is a movie star from South Africa.

Charlotte ⭐ (French) a form of Caroline. Literature: Charlotte Brontë was a British novelist and poet best known for her novel *Jane Eyre*.

Charly BG (German, English) a form of Charlie.

Charmaine (French) a form of Carmen.
  Charmane (French) a form of Charmaine.

Charnette (American) a combination of Charo + Annette.

Charnika (American) a combination of Charo + Nika.

Charo (Spanish) a familiar form of Rosa.

Charyanna (American) a combination of Charo + Anna.

Chase BG (French) hunter.

Chasidy, Chassidy (Latin) forms of Chastity.

Chasity (Latin) a form of Chastity.

Chastity (Latin) pure.

Chauntel (French) a form of Chantal.

Chava (Hebrew) life. (Yiddish) bird. Religion: the original name of Eve.

Chavella (Spanish) a form of Isabel.

Chavi (Gypsy) girl.

Chavon (Hebrew) a form of Jane.

Chavonne (Hebrew) a form of Chavon. (American) a combination of the prefix Cha + Yvonne.

Chaya (Hebrew) life; living.

Chayla (English) a form of Chaylea.

Chaylea (English) a combination of Chaya + Lea.

Chela, Chelo (Spanish) forms of Consuelo.

Chelby (English) a form of Shelby.

Chelci, Chelcie, Chelsec, Chelsey, Chelsi, Chelsie, Chelsy (English) forms of Chelsea.

Chelley (English) a form of Shelley.

Chelsa (English) a form of Chelsea.

Chelse (English) a form of Chelsea.

Chelsea (English) seaport.

Chelsia (English) a form of Chelsea.

Chemarin (Hebrew) girl in black.

Chenelle (English) a form of Chanel.

Chenetta (French) oak tree.

Chenoa (Native American) white dove.

Chepa (Hebrew) chaste.

Cher (French) beloved, dearest. (English) a short form of Cherilyn.

Cherelle, Cherrell,

Cherrelle (French) forms of Cheryl. .

Cherese (Greek) a form of Cherish.

Cheri, Cherie, Cherri (French) familiar forms of Cher.

Cherice, Cherise, Cherisse (French) forms of Cherish.

Cherilyn (English) a combination of Cheryl + Lynn. .

Cherish (English) dearly held, precious.

Cherita (Latin) a form of Charity.

Cherokee GB (Native American) a tribal name.

Cherry (Latin) a familiar form of Charity. (French) cherry; cherry red.

Cheryl (French) beloved.

Chesarey (American) a form of Desiree.

Chesna (Slavic) peaceful.

Chesney (Slavic) a form of Chesna.

Chessa (American) a short form of Chesarey.

Chevelle (Spanish) a form of Chavella.

Cheyann, Cheyanne (Cheyenne) forms of Cheyenne.

Cheyanna (Cheyenne) a form of Cheyenne.

Cheyene (Cheyenne) a form of Cheyenne.

Cheyenna (Cheyenne) a form of Cheyenne.

Cheyenne GB (Cheyenne) a tribal name.

Cheyla (American) a form of Sheila.

Cheyna (American) a short form of Cheyenne.

Chi BG (Cheyenne) a short form of Cheyenne.

Chiara (Italian) a form of Clara.

Chicahua (Nahuatl) strong.

Chika (Japanese) near and dear.

Chiku (Swahili) chatterer.

Chila (Greek) a form of Cecilia.

Chilali (Native American) snowbird.

China (Chinese) fine porcelain. Geography: a country in eastern Asia.

Chinira (Swahili) God receives.

Chinue (Ibo) God's own blessing.

Chione (Egyptian) daughter of the Nile.

Chipahua (Nahuatl) clean.

Chiquita (Spanish) little one. **Chiyo** (Japanese) eternal.

Chloe ☆ (Greek) blooming, verdant. Mythology: another name for Demeter, the goddess of agriculture.

Chloris (Greek) pale. Mythology: the only daughter of Niobe to escape the vengeful arrows of Apollo and Artemis.

Chlorissa (Greek) a form of Chloris.

Cho (Korean) beautiful.

Cholena (Native American) bird.

Chriki (Swahili) blessing.

Chris BG (Greek) a short form of Christopher, Christina.

Chrissa (Greek) a short form of Christina.

Chrissanth (Greek) gold flower. Botany: chrysanthemums are ornamental, showy flowers.

Chrissie, Chrissy (English) familiar forms of Christina.

Christa (German) a short form of Christina. History: Christa McAuliffe, an American school teacher, was the first civilian on a U.S. space flight.

Christabel (Latin, French) beautiful Christian.

Christain BG (Greek) a form of Christina.

Christal (Latin) a form of Crystal. (Scottish) a form of Christina.

Christan BG (Greek) a short form of Christina.

Christel, Christelle, Chrystel (French) forms of Christal.

Christen, Christin GB (Greek) short forms of Christina.

Christena (Greek) a form of Christina.

Christene (Greek) a form of Christina.

Christi, Christie (Greek) short forms of Christina, Christine.

Christian BG (Greek) a form of Christina.

Christiana, Christianna (Greek) forms of Christina.

Christiane, Christianne (Greek) forms of Christina.

Christina (Greek) Christian; anointed. ,

Christine (French, English) a form of Christina.

Christophe BG (Greek) a form of Christopher.

Christopher BG (Greek) Christ-bearer.

Christy (English) a short form of Christina, Christine.

Christyn (Greek) a short form of Christina.

Chrys (English) a form of Chris.

Chrysta (German) a short form of Christina.

Chrystal (Latin) a form of Christal.

Chrystel (French) a form of Christal.

Chu Hua (Chinese) chrysanthemum.

Chumani (Lakota) dewdrops.

Chun BG (Burmese) nature's renewal.

Chyann, Chyanne (Cheyenne) forms of Cheyenne.

Chyenne (Cheyenne) a form of Cheyenne.

Chyna, Chynna (Chinese) forms of China.

Cian BG (Irish) ancient.

Ciana, Cianna (Chinese) forms of China. (Italian) forms of Jane.

Ciara, Ciarra (Irish) black. Cyarrah

Cibeles (Greek) Mythology: another name for the goddess Cybele.

Cicely (English) a form of Cecilia.

Cidney (French) a form of Sydney.

Ciearra (Irish) a form of Ciara.

Cielo (Latin) she who is celestial.

Cienna (Italian) a form of Ciana.

Ciera, Cierra (Irish) forms of Ciara.

Cihuaton (Nahuatl) little woman.

Cim (English) a form of Kim.

Cimberleigh (English) a form of Kimberly.

Cinderella (French, English) little cinder girl. Literature: a fairy-tale heroine.

Cindi (Greek) a form of Cindy.

Cindy (Greek) moon. (Latin) a familiar form of Cynthia.

Cinnamon (Greek) aromatic, reddish-brown spice.

Cinnia (Latin) curly haired.

Cinta (Spanish) a short form of Jacinta.

Cinthia, Cinthya (Greek) forms of Cynthia.

Cintia (Greek) a form of Cynthia.

Cíntia (Portuguese) a form of Cynthia.

Cipriana (Italian) from the island of Cyprus.

Cipriano (Greek) born in Cyprus.

Ciprina (Spanish) blessed by the goddess of love.

Cira (Spanish) a form of Cyrilla.

Circe (Greek) Mythology: a goddess who fell in love with Odysseus in Homer's *Odyssey*.

Cirenia, Cirinea (Greek) native of Cyrene, Libya.

Ciri (Greek) ladylike.

Ciriaca, Ciríaca (Greek) belonging to God.

Ciro (Spanish) sun.

Cissy (American) a familiar form of Cecilia, Cicely.

Citlali (Nahuatl) star.

Citlalmina (Nahuatl) greatest of our heroes.

Clair (French) a form of Clara.

Claire ✦ (French) a form of Clair.

Clairissa (Greek) a form of Clarissa.

Clancy BG (Irish) redheaded fighter.

Clara (Latin) clear; bright. Music: Clara Schumann was a famous nineteenthcentury German composerbright and beautiful.

Clare GB (English) a form of Clara.

Clarenza (Latin) clear; victorious.

Claribel (Latin) a form of Clarabelle.

Clarice, Clarisse (Italian) forms of Clara.

Clarie (Latin) a familiar form of Clara.

Clarinda (Latin, Spanish) bright; beautiful.

Clarisa (Greek) a form of Clarissa.

Clarissa (Greek) brilliant. (Italian) a form of Clara.

Clarita (Spanish) a form of Clara,

Claude BG (Latin, French) lame.

Claudel (Latin) a form of Claude, Claudia.

Claudette (French) a form of Claudia.

Claudia (Latin) a form of Claude.

Claudía (Latin) a form of Claudia.

Claudie (Latin) a form of Claudia.

Claudine (French) a form of Claudia.

Clea (Greek) a form of Cleo, Clio.

Cleantha (English) glory.

Clelia (Latin) a form of Celia.

Clematis (Greek) creeping vine. Botany: a climbing plant with colorful flowers or decorative fruit clusters.

Clemence GB (Latin) a form of Clementine.

Clementina (German) a form of Clementine.

Clementine (Latin) merciful. Clemira **(Arabic) brilliant princess.**

Cleo BG (Greek) a short form of Cleopatra.

Cleodora (Greek) gift of God.

Cleofe (Greek) she who shows signs of glory.

Cleone (Greek) famous.

Cleopatra (Greek) her father's fame. History: a great Egyptian queen.

Cleta (Greek) illustrious.

Cleva (English) dwells at the cliffs.

Clidia, Clidía (Greek) agitated in the sea.

Clímaca (Nahuatl) star.

Climena, Climent (Greek) impassioned by glory.

Clio (Greek) proclaimer; glorifier. Mythology: the Muse of history.

Clío (Greek) a form of Clio.

Clitemestra (Greek) Mythology: Clytemnestra was the daughter of Tyndareus and Leda.

Clitia (Greek) she who likes to keep herself clean.

Clodomira (German) famous.

Clodovea, Clodoveo (Spanish) forms of Clovis.

Cloe (Greek) a form of Chloe.

Cloelia (Latin) a form of Celia.

Clorinda (Greek) fresh; vital.

Closinda (German) famous, notable.

Clotilda (German) heroine.

Clovis (Teutonic) famous warrior.

Coatlicue (Greek) one from the skirts of serpents.

Coaxoch (Nahuatl) serpent flower.

Cochiti (Spanish) forgotten.

Coco GB (Spanish) coconut.

Codi BG (English) cushion.

Codie, Cody BG (English) cushion.

Coia (Catalan) a form of Misericordia.

Cointa (Egyptian) fifth.

Colbi, Colbie (English) forms of Colby.

Colby BG (English) coal town. Geography: a region in England known for cheese-making.

Coleen (Irish) a form of Colleen.

Colette, Collette (Greek, French) familiar forms of Nicole.

Colleen (Irish) girl.

Collina (Irish) a form of Colleen.

Collins (Greek) son of Colin. (Irish) holly.

Collipal (Mapuche) colored star.

Colman, Colmana (Latin) forms of Colomba.

Coloma (Spanish) a form of Colomba.

Colomba (Latin) dove.

Colombia (Spanish) Geography: a country in South America.

Colombina (Latin) a form of Colomba.

Columba BG (Latin) dove.

Concelia (Spanish) a form of Concepción.

Concepcion (Spanish) a form of Concepción.

Concepción (Spanish) refers to the Immaculate Conception.

Concesa (Latin) award.

Conceta, Concheta (Spanish) forms of Concetta.

Concetta (Italian) pure.

Conchita (Spanish) a form of Concepción.

Concordia (Latin) harmonious. Mythology: the goddess governing the peace after war.

Concordía (Latin) a form of Concordia.

Conner 🅱🅶 (Scottish) wise. (Irish) praised; exalted.

Connie 🅶🅱 (Latin) a familiar form of Constance.

Connor 🅱🅶 (Scottish) wise. (Irish) praised; exalted.

Consejo (Hispanic) a form of Consuelo.

Consolación (Latin) consolation.

Consorcia (Latin) association.

Constance (Latin) constant; firm. History: Constance Motley was the first African American woman to be appointed as a U.S. federal judge.

Constanza (Spanish) a form of Constance.

Consuela (Spanish) a form of Consuelo.

Consuelo (Spanish) consolation. Religion: *Nuestra Señora del Consuelo*—Our Lady of Consolation—is a name for the Virgin Mary.

Contessa (Italian) an Italian countess.

Cooper 🅱🅶 (English) barrel maker.

Cora (Greek) maiden. Mythology: Kore is another name for Persephone, the goddess of the underworld.

Corabelle (American) a combination of Cora + Belle.

Coral (Latin) corala combination of Cora + Lee.

Coralie (American) a form of Coralee.

Corazana (Spanish) a form of Corazon.

Corazon (Spanish) heart.

Corazón (Spanish) a form of Corazon.

Corbin 🅱🅶 (Latin) raven.

Cordasha (American) a combination of Cora + Dasha.

Cordelia (Latin) warm-hearted. (Welsh) sea jewel.

Cordella (French) rope maker.

Cordi (Welsh) a short form of Cordelia.

Córdula (Latin) she who is out of time.

Coreen (Greek) a form of Corinne.

Coreena (Greek) a form of Corinne.

Coretta (Greek) a familiar form of Cora.

Corey 🅱🅶 (Irish) from the hollow. (Greek) a familiar form of Cora.

Cori 🅶🅱 (Irish) a form of Corey.

Coriann, Corianne (American) combinations of Cori + Ann.

Corie 🅶🅱 (Irish) a form of Corey.

Corin 🅱🅶 (Greek) a form of Corinne.

Corina, Corinna, Corrina (Greek) forms of Corinne.

Corine (Greek) a form of Corinne.

Corinne (Greek) maiden.

Corisande, Corisanda (Spanish) flower of the heart.

Corissa (Greek) a familiar form of Cora.

Corliss 🅱🅶 (English) cheerful; goodhearted.

Cornelia (Latin) horn colored. Coro **(Spanish) chorus.**

Corona (Latin) crown.

Corrie (Irish) a form of Corey.

Corrin 🅶🅱 (Greek) a form of Corinne.

Corrine, Corrinne (Greek) forms of Corinne.

Corsen (Welsh) red.

Cortina (American) a form of Kortina.

Cortnee, Cortni, Cortnie (English) forms of Courtney.

Cortney 🅶🅱 (English) a form of Courtney.

Cory 🅱🅖 (Irish) from the hollow. (Greek) a familiar form of Cora.

Coryn, Corynn (Greek) forms of Corinne.

Cosette (French) a familiar form of Nicole.

Cosima (Greek) orderly; harmonious; universe.

Coszcatl (Nahuatl) jewel.

Courtenay (English) form of Courtney.

Courtline, Courtlyn (English) forms of Courtney.

Courtnee, Courtnei, Courtnie (English) forms of Courtney.

Courtney 🅖🅑 (English) from the court.

Covadonga (Spanish) cavern of the lady. Religion: large cave that is the scene of a shrine to the Virgin Mary.

Cozamalotl (Nahuatl) rainbow.

Cragen (Welsh) shell.

Cree (Algonquin) a Native American tribe and language of central North America.

Crescencia (Latin) growth.

Crescenciana (Spanish) a form of Crescencia.

Crimilda (German) she fights wearing a helmet.

Crisana, Crisanta (Spanish) forms of Crisantema.

Crisantema (Greek) chrysanthemum, golden flower.

Crisbell (American) a combination of Crista + Belle.

Crispina (Latin) curly haired.

Críspula (Greek) a form of Crispina.

Crista (Italian) a form of Christa.
Cristah

Cristal (Latin) a form of Crystal.

Cristan, Cristen, Cristin **(Greek) forms of Christan.** Cristeta **(Greek) a form of Crista.**

Cristi, Cristy (English) familiar forms of Cristina. Forms of Christy.
Cristian 🅱🅖 (Greek) a form of Christian.

Cristina (Greek) a form of Christina. **Cristine** (Greek) a form of Christine.

Cruz (Spanish) cross.

Cruzita (Spanish) a form of Cruz.

Crysta (Italian) a form of Christa.

Crystal (Latin) clear, brilliant glass.
S**Crystalin** (Latin) crystal pool,

Crystel (Latin) a form of Crystal.

Crystina (Greek) a form of Christina.

Cualli (Nahuatl) good.

Cuartila (Hispanic) a form of Quartilla.

Cucufata (Spanish) caped lady.

Cuicatl (Nahuatl) song.

Cunegunda (German) brave and famous.

Cuniberga (German) guardedly famous.

Curipán (Mapuche) brave lioness; black mountain; valorous soul.

Curran 🅱🅖 (Irish) heroine.

Custodia, Custodía (Latin) guardian angel.

Cutburga (German) protector of the wise person.

Cuthberta (English) brilliant.

Cuyen (Mapuche) moon.

Cybele (Greek) a form of Sybil.

Cydnee, Cydney, Cydni (French) forms of Sydney.

Cyerra (Irish) a form of Ciara.

Cym (Welsh) a form of Kim.

Cymreiges (Welsh) woman of Wales.

Cynara (Greek) thistle.

Cyndee, Cyndi (Greek) forms of Cindy.

Cynthia (Greek) moon. Mythology: another name for Artemis, the moon goddess. See Cyntia **(Greek) a form of Cynthia.**

Cypress (Greek) a coniferous tree.

Cyrena (Greek) a form of Sirena.

Cyrilla (Greek) noble.

Cyteria (Greek) Mythology: Cytherea is another name for Aphrodite.

Czarina (German) a Russian empress.

D

D'andra (American) a form of Deandra.

D'andrea (American) a form of Deandra.

D'asia (American) a form of Dasia.

D'ericka (American) a form of Derika.

D'onna (American) a form of Donna.

Da'jah (American) a form of Daja.

Dabria (Latin) Religion: one of the angelic scribes.

Dacey GB (Irish) southerner. (Greek) a familiar form of Candace.

Dacia (Irish) a form of Dacey.

Dacil (Aboriginal) History: a Guanche princess from the Canary Islands.

Dae (English) day. Daeja (French) a form of Déja.

Daelynn (American) a combination of Dae + Lynn.

Daere, Dera (Welsh) oak tree.

Daesha (American) a form of Dasha.

Daeshandra (American) a combination of Dae + Shandra.

Daeshawna (American) a combination of Dae + Shawna.

Daeshonda (American) a combination of Dae + Shonda.

Dafny (American) a form of Daphne.

Dagmar (German) glorious.

Dagny (Scandinavian) day.

Dagoberta (German) radiant as the day.

Dahlia (Scandinavian) valley. Botany: a perennial flower.

Dai GB (Japanese) great. **Daija, Daijah** (French) forms of Déja.

Daina (English) a form of Dana.

Daisey (English) a form of Daisy.

Daisha (American) a form of Dasha.

Daisia (American) a form of Dasha.

Daisy (English) day's eye. Botany: a white and yellow flower.

Daiya (Polish) present.

Daja, Dajah (French) forms of Déja.

Dakayla (American) a combination of the prefix Da + Kayla.

Dakira (American) a combination of the prefix Da + Kira.

Dakoda BG (Dakota) a form of Dakota.

Dakota GB (Dakota) a tribal name.

Dakotah BG (Dakota) a form of Dakota.

Dale BG (English) valley.

Dalena (English) a form of Dale.

Dalia, Daliah (Hebrew) branch.

Dalila (Swahili) gentle.

Dalisha (American) a form of Dallas.

Dallas BG (Irish) wise.

Dallis BG (Irish) a form of Dallas.

Dalma (Spanish) a form of Dalmacia.

Dalmacia (Latin) Geography: native of Dalmatia, a region on the Adriatic Sea.

Dalmira (Teutonic) illustrious; respected for her noble ancestry.

Dalton 🅱🅶 (English) town in the valley.

Damara (Greek) a form of Damaris.

Damaris (Greek) gentle girl. .

Damasia (Spanish) a form of Dalmacia.

Damesha (Spanish) a form of Damita.

Damia (Greek) a short form of Damiana.

Damiana (Greek) tamer, soother.

Damica (French) friendly.

Damira (Hebrew) long live the world.

Damita (Spanish) small noblewoman.

Damonica (American) a combination of the prefix Da + Monica.

Damzel (French) lady, maiden.

Dana 🅶🅱 (English) from Denmark; bright as day.

Danae (Greek) Mythology: the mother of Perseus.

Dánae (Greek) a form of Danae.

Danah (English) a form of Dana.

Danalyn (American) a combination of Dana + Lynn.

Danas (Spanish) a form of Dana.

Danasia (American) a form of Danessa.

Daneil (Hebrew) a form of Danielle.

Daneisha (American) a form of Danessa.

Danella (American) a form of Danielle.

Danelle (Hebrew) a form of Danielle.

Danesha (American) a form of Danessa.

Daneshia (American) a form of Danessa.

Danessa (American) a combination of Danielle + Vanessa.

Danessia (American) a form of Danessa.

Danette (American) a form of Danielle.

Dani, Danni (Hebrew) familiar forms of Danielle.

Dania, Danya (Hebrew) short forms of Danielle.

Danica, Danika (Slavic) morning star. (Hebrew) forms of Danielle.

Danice (American) a combination of Danielle + Janice.

Daniel 🅱🅶 (Hebrew, French) a form of Danielle.

Daniela (Italian) a form of Danielle.

Danielan (Spanish) a form of Danielle.

Daniele (Hebrew, French) a form of Danielle.

Daniell, Dannielle (Hebrew, French) forms of Danielle.

Daniella (English) a form of Dana, Danielle.

Danielle ⭐ (Hebrew, French) God is my judge.

Daniesha (American) a form of Danessa.

Danille (American) a form of Danielle.

Daniqua (Hebrew, Slavic) a form of Danica.

Danisha (American) a form of Danessa.

Danit (Hebrew) a form of Danielle.

Danita (Hebrew) a form of Danielle.

Danna, Dannah (American) short forms of Danella. (Hebrew) forms of Dana.

Dannica (Hebrew, Slavic) a form of Danica.

Danyale, Danyell, Danyelle (American) forms of Danielle.

Danyel GB (American) a form of Danielle.

Danyka (American) a form of Danica.

Daphne (Greek) laurel tree.

Daphnee, Daphney (Greek) forms of Daphne.

Dara GB (Hebrew) compassionate.

Darah, Darrah (Hebrew) forms of Dara.

Daralis (English) beloved.

Darbi (Irish, Scandinavian) a form of Darby.

Darby GB (Irish) free. (Scandinavian) deer estate.

Darcelle (French) a form of Darcy.

Darci, Darcie (Irish, French) forms of Darcy.

Darcy GB (Irish) dark. (French) fortress.

Daria (Greek) wealthy.

Daría (Greek) a form of Daria.

Darian BG (Greek) a form of Daron.

Dariane, Darianne (Greek) forms of Daron.

Darianna (Greek) a form of Daron.

Darice (Persian) queen, ruler.

Dariel BG (French) a form of Daryl.

Darielle, Darrielle (French) forms of Daryl.

Darien BG (Greek) a form of Daron.

Darienne (Greek) a form of Daron.

Darilynn (American) a form of Darlene.

Darion BG (Irish) a form of Daron.

Darla (English) a short form of Darlene.

Darlene (French) little darling.

Darlin, Darlyn (French) forms of Darlene.

Darnee (Irish) a familiar form of Darnelle.

Darneisha (American) a form of Darnelle.

Darnelle BG (English) hidden place.

Darnesha (American) a form of Darnelle.

Darnisha (American) a form of Darnelle.

Daron BG (Irish) a form of Daryn.

Daronica (American) a form of Daron.

Darrian BG (Greek) a form of Daron.

Darrien BG (Greek) a form of Daron.

Darrion BG (Irish) a form of Daron.

Darselle (French) a form of Darcelle.

Daru (Hindi) pine tree.

Darya (Greek) a form of Daria.

Daryan (Greek, Irish) a form of Daryn.

Daryl BG (English) beloved. (French) a short form of Darlene.

Daryn BG (Greek) gifts. (Irish) great.

Dasha (Russian) a form of Dorothy.

Dashawn BG (American) a short form of Dashawna.

Dashawna (American) a combination of the prefix Da + Shawna.

Dashay (American) a familiar form of Dashawna.

Dashia (Russian) a form of Dorothy.

Dashiki (Swahili) loose-fitting shirt worn in Africa.

Dashonda (American) a combination of the prefix Da + Shonda.

Dasia (Russian) a form of Dasha.

Davalinda (American) a combination of Davida + Linda.

Davalynda (American) a form of Davalinda.

Davalynn (American) a combination of Davida + Lynn.

David 🅱🅶 (Hebrew) beloved. Bible: the second king of Israel.

Davida (Hebrew) a form of David.

Davina (Scottish) a form of Davida.

Davisha (American) a combination of the prefix Da + Aisha.

Davita (Scottish) a form of Davina.

Davon 🅱🅶 (Scottish, English) a short form of Davonna.

Davonna (Scottish, English) a form of Davina, Devonna.

Dawn (English) sunrise, dawn.

Dawna (English) a form of Dawn.

Dawnetta (American) a form of Dawn.

Dawnisha (American) a form of Dawn.

Dawnyelle (American) a combination of Dawn + Danielle.

Dayana, Dayanna (Latin) forms of Diana.

Dayanira, Deyanira (Greek) she stirs up great passions.

Dayla (English) a form of Dale.

Daylan 🅱🅶 (English) a form of Dale.

Dayle (English) a form of Dale.

Daylin 🅱🅶 (English) a form of Dale.

Dayna (Scandinavian) a form of Dana.

Daysha (American) a form of Dasha.

Daysi (English) a form of Daisy.

Dayton 🅱🅶 (English) day town; bright, sunny town.

Daytona 🅱🅶 (English) day town; bright, sunny town.

De'ja, Deja, Dejá, Dejah, Déjah (French) forms of Déja.

Deana (Latin) divine. (English) valley.

Deandra 🅶🅱 (American) a combination of Dee + Andrea.

Deandrea (American) a form of Deandra.

Deangela (Italian) a combination of the prefix De + Angela.

Deann, Deanne (Latin) forms of Diane.

Deanna, Déanna (Latin) forms of Deana, Diana.

Deasia, Déasia (American) forms of Dasia.

Deaundra (American) a form of Deandra.

Debbie, Debby (Hebrew) familiar forms of Deborah.

Debora (Hebrew) a form of Deborah.

Débora, Déborah, Dèbora (Hebrew) forms of Deborah.

Deborah (Hebrew) bee. Bible: a great Hebrew prophetess.

Debra (American) a form of Deborah.

December (Latin) born in the twelfth month.

Decia (Latin) tenth child.

Dedra (American) a form of Deirdre.

Dedriana (American) a combination of Dedra + Adriana.

Dee (Welsh) black, dark.

Deeanna (Latin) a form of Deana, Diana.

Deedra (American) a form of Deirdre.

Deena (American) a form of Deana, Dena, Dinah.

Deianeira (Greek) Mythology: Deianira was the wife of the Greek hero Heracles.

Deidamia (Greek) she who is patient in battle.

Deidra, Deidre (Irish) forms of Deirdre.

Deifila, Deifilia (Greek) from the face of Zeus; loved by God.

Deina (Spanish) religious holiday.

Deirdre (Irish) sorrowful; wanderer.

Deisy (English) a form of Daisy.

Deitra (Greek) a short form of Demetria.

Déja (French) before.

Dejanae (French) a form of Déja.

Dejanelle (French) a form of Déja.

Dejanira (Greek) destroyer of men.

Dejon BG (French) a form of Déja.

Deka (Somali) pleasing.
Dekah

Delacey, Delacy (American) combinations of the prefix De + Lacey.

Delaina (German) a form of Delana.

Delaine (Irish) a short form of Delainey.

Delainey (Irish) a form of Delaney.

Delana (German) noble protector.

Delaney GB (Irish) descendant of the challenger. (English) a form of Adeline.

Delanie (Irish) a form of Delaney.

Delayna (German) a form of Delana.

Deleena (French) dear; small.

Delfia (Spanish) dolphin. Religion: refers to the thirteenth-century French Saint Delphine.

Delfina (Spanish) dolphin. (Greek) a form of Delphine.

Delia (Greek) visible; from Delos, Greece. (German, Welsh) a short form of Adelaide, Cordelia. Mythology: a festival of Apollo held in ancient Greece.

Dèlia (Catalan) a form of Delia.

Delicia (English) delightful.

Delicias (Spanish) delights.

Delilah (Hebrew) brooder. Bible: the companion of Samson. **Delina** (French) a form of Deleena.

Delisa (English) a form of Delicia.

Delisha (English) a form of Delicia.

Della (English) a short form of Adelaide, Cordelia, Delaney.

Delmar BG (Latin) sea.

Delmira (Spanish) a form of Dalmira.

Delores, Deloris (Spanish) forms of Dolores.

Delphine (Greek) from Delphi, Greece familiar form of Delores.

Delta (Greek) door. Linguistics: the fourth letter in the Greek alphabet. Geography: a triangular land mass at the mouth of a river.

Delwyn (English) proud friend; friend from the valley.

Demetra (Greek) a short form of Demetria.

Demetria (Greek) cover of the earth. Mythology: Demeter was the Greek goddess of the harvest.

Demi (French) half. (Greek) a short form of Demetria.

Demitria (Greek) a form of Demetria.

Demofila (Greek) friend of the village.

Dena (English, Native American) valley. (Hebrew) a form of Dinah. ,

Denae (Hebrew) a form of Dena.

Deneisha (American) a form of Denisha.

Denesha (American) a form of Denisha.

Deni (French) a short form of Denise.

Denica, Denika (Slavic) forms of Danica.

Denice (French) a form of Denise.

Denis BG (French) a form of Denise.

Denisa (Spanish) a form of Denise.

Denise (French) Mythology: follower of Dionysus, the god of wine.

Denisha (American) a form of Denise.

Denisse (French) a form of Denise.

Denita (Hebrew) a form of Danita.

Denver BG (English) green valley. Geography: the capital of Colorado.

Deodata (Latin) delivered to God.

Deogracias (Latin) born by the grace of God.

Deon BG (English) a short form of Deona.

Deona, Deonna (English) forms of Dena.

Deondra GB (American, Greek, English) a form of Deandra, Deona, Diona.

Deonilde (German) she who fights.

Derfuta (Latin) she who flees.

Derian BG (Greek) a form of Daryn.

Derica, Derricka (German) forms of Derika.

Derifa (Arabic) graceful.

Derika (German) ruler of the people.

Derry BG (Irish) redhead.

Derwen (Welsh) oak tree.

Deryn (Welsh) bird.

Desarae, Desaray (French) forms of Desiree.

Desdemona, Desdémona (Greek) unfortunate; unhappy.

Deserae, Deseray, Deseree (French) forms of Desiree.

Desgracias (Latin) a form of Deogracias.

Deshawn BG (American) a short form of Deshawna.

Deshawna (American) a combination of the prefix De + Shawna.

Deshawnda (American) a combination of the prefix De + Shawnda.

Deshay (American) a familiar form of Deshawna.

Desi BG (French) a short form of Desiree.

Desideria (French) a form of Desirae.

Desirae, Desiray, Desirea, Desireé, Desirée, Desiree' (French) forms of Desiree.

Desire (French) a form of Desiree.

Desiree (French) desired, longed for.

Despina (Greek) a form of Despoina.

Despoina (Greek) mistress, lady.

Dessa (Greek) wanderer. (French) a form of Desiree.

Desta (Ethiopian) happy. (French) a short form of Destiny.

Destanee, Destaney, Destani, Destanie, Destany (French) forms of Destiny.

Desteny (French) a form of Destiny.

Destin BG (French) a short form of Destiny.

Destina (Spanish) a form of Destiny.

Destine, Destinee, Destinée, Destiney, Destini, Destinie (French) forms of Destiny.

Destiny (French) fate.

Destyne, Destynee, Destyni (French) forms of Destiny.

Deva (Hindi) divine.

Devan BG (Irish) a form of Devin.

Devera (Spanish) task.

Devi (Hindi) goddess. Religion: the Hindu goddess of power and destruction.

Devika (Sanskrit) little goddess.

Devin BG (Irish) poet.

Devina (Scottish, Irish, Latin) a form of Davina, Devin, Divina.

Devinne (Irish) a form of Devin.

Devon BG (English) a short form of Devonna. (Irish) a form of Devin.

Devona (English) a form of Devonna.

Devonna (English) from Devonshire.

Devora (Hebrew) a form of Deborah.

Devota (Latin) devoted to God.

Devyn BG (Irish) a form of Devin.

Devynn (Irish) a form of Devin.

Dextra (Latin) adroit, skillful.

Deysi (English) a form of Daisy.

Dezarae, Dezaray, Dezaree (French) forms of Desiree.

Dezirae, Deziray, Deziree (French) forms of Desiree.

Dhara (Indian) earth.

Di (Latin) a short form of Diana, Diane.

Dia (Latin) a short form of Diana, Diane.

Día (Spanish) day.

Díamantina (Latin) unconquerable.

Diamon (Latin) a short form of Diamond.

Diamond GB (Latin) precious gem.

Diamonique (American, Latin) a form of Damonica, Diamond.

Diana (Latin) divine. Mythology: the goddess of the hunt, the moon, and fertility. Díana **(Greek) a form of Diana.**

Diandra (American, Latin) a form of Deandra, Diana.

Diane, Dianne (Latin) short forms of Diana.

Dianna (Latin) a form of Diana.

Dianora, Díanora (Italian) forms of Diana.

Diantha (Greek) divine flower.

Dicra (Welsh) slowly.

Diedra (Irish) a form of Deirdre.

Diega (Spanish) supplanter.

Diella (Latin) she who adores God.

Difyr (Welsh) fun.

Digna (Latin) worthy.

Dil, Dill (Welsh) sincere.

Dillan BG (Irish) loyal, faithful.

Dillian BG (Latin) worshipped.

Dilly (Welsh) a form of Dil.

Dilys (Welsh) perfect; true.

.

Dimitra (Greek) a form of Demetria.

Dimna (Irish) convenient.

Dina (Hebrew) a form of Dinah.

Dinah (Hebrew) vindicated. Bible: a daughter of Jacob and Leah.

Dinesha (American) a form of Danessa.

Dinka (Swahili) people.

Dinora (Hebrew) avenged or vindicated.

Dinorah (Aramaic) she who personifies light.

Diomira (Spanish) a form of Teodomira.

Diona, Dionna (Greek) forms of Dionne.

Diondra (Greek) a form of Dionne.

Dionis, Dionisa, Dionisia (Spanish) from Dionysus, god of wine.

Dionne GB (Greek) divine queen. Mythology: Dione was the mother of Aphrodite, the goddess of love.

Dior (French) golden.

Dirce (Greek) fruit of the pine.

Dita (Spanish) a form of Edith.

Divinia (Latin) divine.

Divya (Latin) a form of Divinia.

Dixie (French) tenth. (English) wall; dike. Geography: a nickname for the American South.

Diya (Hindi) dazzling personality.

Diza (Hebrew) joyful.

Djanira (Portuguese) a form of Dayanira.

Doanne (English) low, rolling hills.

Docila (Latin) gentle; docile.

Dodie (Hebrew) beloved. (Greek) a familiar form of Dorothy.

Dolly (American) a short form of Dolores, Dorothy.

Dolores (Spanish) sorrowful. Religion: *Nuestra Señora de los Dolores*—Our Lady of Sorrows—is a name for the Virgin Mary.

Domana (Latin) domestic.

Domanique (French) a form of Dominica.

Domenica (Latin) a form of Dominica.

Doménica, Domínica (Latin) forms of Dominica.

Domenique (French) a form of Dominica.

Domicia (Greek) she who loves her house.

Domiciana (Spanish) a form of Domicia.

Domilia (Latin) related to the house.

Dominica, Dominika (Latin) belonging to the Lord. .

Dominique GB (French) a form of Dominica.

Domino (English) a short form of Dominica.

Dominque BG (French) a short form of Dominique.

Domitila (Latin) a form of Domicia.

Domnina (Latin) lord, master.

Domonique (French) a form of Dominique.

Dona (English) world leader; proud ruler. (Italian) a form of Donna.

Doña (Italian) a form of Donna.

Donata (Latin) gift.

Donatila (Latin) a form of Donata.

Doncia (Spanish) sweet.

Dondi (American) a familiar form of Donna.

Doneisha (American) a form of Danessa.

Donesha (American) a form of Danessa.

Doneshia (American) a form of Danessa.

Donetsi (Basque) a form of Benita.

Donia **(Italian) a form of Donna.**

Donielle (American) a form of Danielle.

Donina (Latin) a form of Dorothy.

Donisha, Donnisha (American) forms of Danessa.

Donna (Italian) lady.

Donniella (American) a form of Danielle.

Donosa (Latin) she who has grace and charm.

Donvina (Latin) vigorous.

Donya (Italian) a form of Donna.

Dora (Greek) gift. A short form of Adora, Eudora, Pandora, Theodora.

Dorabella (English) a combination of Dora + Bella.

Doralynn (English) a combination of Dora + Lynn.

Dorbeta (Spanish) reference to the Virgin Mary.

Dorcas (Greek) gazelle. Bible: New Testament translation of the name Tabitha.

Doreen (Irish) moody, sullen. (French) golden. (Greek) a form of Dora.

Dores (Portuguese, Galician) a form of Dolores.

Doretta (American) a form of Dora, Dorothy.

Dori, Dory (American) familiar forms of Dora, Doria, Doris, Dorothy.

Doria (Greek) a form of Dorian.

Dorian BG (Greek) from Doris, Greece.

Doriane, Dorianne (Greek) from Doris, Greece.

Dorila (Greek) a form of Teodora.

Dorinda (Spanish) a form of Dora.

Doris (Greek) sea. Mythology: wife of Nereus and mother of the Nereids or sea nymphs.

Doroteia (Spanish) a form of Dorothy.

Dorotéia (Portuguese) a form of Dorothy.

Dorothea (Greek) a form of Dorothy. Dorothee (Greek) a form of Dorothy.

Dorothy (Greek) gift of God. .

Dorrit (Greek) dwelling. (Hebrew) generation.

Dottie, Dotty (Greek) familiar forms of Dorothy.

Dreama (English) dreamer.

Drew BG (Greek) courageous; strong. (Latin) a short form of Drusilla.

Drina (Spanish) a form of Alexandrine.

Drucilla (Latin) a form of Drusilla.

Drue BG (Greek) a form of Drew.

Drusi (Latin) a short form of Drusilla.

Drusilla (Latin) descendant of Drusus, the strong one. .

Drysi (Russian) one who comes from Demeter.

Duena (Spanish) chaperon.

Dueña (Spanish) owner.

Dula (Greek) slave.

Dulce (Latin) sweet.

Dulcina, Dulcinia (Spanish) forms of Dulcinea.

Dulcinea (Spanish) sweet. Literature: Don Quixote's love interest.

Duna (German) hill.

Dunia (Hebrew, Arabic) life.

Duquine, Duquinea (Spanish) forms of Dulcinea.

Durene (Latin) enduring.

Duscha (Russian) soul; sweetheart; term of endearment.

Dusti (English) a familiar form of Dustin.

Dustin BG (German) valiant fighter. (English) brown rock quarry.

Dustine (German) a form of Dustin.

Dusty BG (English) a familiar form of Dustin.

Dyamond (Latin) a form of Diamond.

Dyana, Dyanna (Latin) forms of Diana.

Dyani (Native American) deer.

Dylan BG (Welsh) sea.

Dylana (Welsh) a form of Dylan.

Dyllis (Welsh) sincere.

Dymond (Latin) a form of Diamond.

Dympna (Irish) convenient.

Dynasty (Latin) powerful ruler.

Dyshawna (American) a combination of the prefix Dy + Shawna.

E

Eadda (English) wealthy; successful.

Eadmund (English) a form of Edmunda.

Eadwine (English) a form of Edwina.

Earlene (Irish) pledge. (English) noblewoman.

Earna (English) eagle.

Earnestyna (English) a form of Ernestina.

Eartha (English) earthy.

Earwyn, Earwyna (English) forms of Erwina.

58

Easter (English) Easter time. History: a name for a child born on Easter.

Eastre (Germanic) a form of Easter.

Eathelin, Eathelyn (English) noble waterfall.

Eavan (Irish) fair.

Ebe (Greek) youthful like a flower.

Eber (German) wild boar.

Ebone, Eboné, Ebonee, Eboney, Eboni, Ebonie (Greek) forms of Ebony.

Ebony (Greek) a hard, dark wood.

Ebrill (Welsh) born in April.

Echidna (Egyptian) wild boar.

Echo (Greek) repeated sound. Mythology: the nymph who pined for the love of Narcissus until only her voice remained.

Eda (Irish, English) a short form of Edana, Edith.

Edana (Irish) ardent; flame.

Edda (German) a form of Hedda.

Eddy 🆎 (American) a familiar form of Edwina.

Edelburga, Edilburga (English) noble protector.

Edelia, Edilia (Greek) remains young.

Edeline (English) noble; kind.

Edelira (Spanish) a form of Edelmira.

Edelma, Edilma (Greek) forms of Edelia.

Edelmira (Teutonic) known for her noble heritage.

Eden 🆖 (Babylonian) a plain. (Hebrew) delightful. Bible: the earthly paradise.

Edén (Hebrew) a form of Eden.

Edesia (Latin) feast.

Edeva (English) expensive present.

Edgarda (Teutonic) defends her homeland.

Edian (Hebrew) decoration for God.

Edie (English) a familiar form of Edith.

Edilberta (German) she who comes from a long heritage.

Ediltrudis (German) strong; noble.

Edina (English) prosperous fort.

Edisa (Castilian) a form of Esther.

Edith (English) rich gift.

Edlen (English) noble waterfall.

Edlyn (English) prosperous; noble.

Edmanda (English) a form of Edmunda.

Edmunda (English) prosperous protector.

Edna (Hebrew) rejuvenation. Religion: the wife of Enoch, according to the Book of Enoch.

Edrea (English) a short form of Edrice, Edrianna.

Edrianna (Greek) a form of Adrienne.

Edrice (English) prosperous ruler.

Eduarda, Eduardo (English) forms of Edwardina.

Edurne (Basque) snow.

Eduviges (Teutonic) fighting woman.

Eduvigis, Eduvijis (German) victorious fighter.

Eduvixes (German) battle.

Edvina (German) a form of Edwina.

Edwardina (English) prosperous guardian.

Edwina (English) prosperous friend.

Effia (Ghanaian) born on Friday.

Effie (Greek) spoken well of. (English) a short form of Alfreda, Euphemia.

Efigenia (Greek) a form of Eugenia.

Efigênia (Portuguese) a form of Eugenia.

Efrata (Hebrew) honored.

Efrona (Hebrew) songbird.

Egberta (English) bright sword.

Egbertina, Egbertine, Egbertyne (English) forms of Egberta.

Egda (Greek) shield bearer.

Egeria (Greek) she who gives encouragement.

Egida (Spanish) a form of Eladia.

Egidia (Greek) a form of Eladía.

Eglantina (French) wild rose.

Egle (Greek) she who possesses splendor and shine.

Eider (Basque) beautiful.

Eileen (Irish) a form of Helen. .

Eira (Welsh) snow.

Eirene (Greek) a form of Irene.

Eiru (Indigenous) bee.

Eirween (Welsh) white snow.

Ekaterina (Russian) a form of Katherine.

Ela (Polish) a form of Adelaide.

Eladia (Greek) native of Elade, Greece.

Eladía (Greek) warrior with a shield of goat skin.

Elaina (French) a form of Helen.

Elaine (French) a form of Helen.

Elana (Greek) a short form of Eleanor. **Elanora** (Australian) from the shore.

Elata (Latin) elevated.

Elayna (French) a form of Elaina.

Elberta (English) a form of Alberta.

Elbertyna (Greek) one who comes from Greece.

Elcira (Teutonic) noble adornment.

Elda (German) she who battles.

Eldora (Spanish) golden, gilded.

Eldrida (English) wise counselor.

Eleadora (Spanish) a form of Eleodora.

Eleanor ✰ (Greek) light. History: Anna Eleanor Roosevelt was a U.S. delegate to the United Nations, a writer, and the thirty-second First Lady of the United States.

Eleanora (Greek) a form of Eleanor.

Eleanore (Greek) a form of Eleanor.

Electa (Greek) a form of Electra.

Electra (Greek) shining; brilliant. Mythology: the daughter of Agamemnon, leader of the Greeks in the Trojan War.

Eleebana (Australian) beautiful.

Elena (Greek) a form of Eleanor. (Italian) a form of Helen.

Eleni (Greek) a familiar form of Eleanor.

Eleodora, Eliodora (Greek) she who came from the sun.

Eleora (Hebrew) the Lord is my light.

Elesha (Greek, Hebrew) a form of Elisha.

Elethea, Elethia (English) healer.

Eletta (English) elf; mischievous.

Eleuia (Nahuatl) wish.

Eleusipa (Greek) she who arrives on horseback.

Eleuteria (Greek) liberty.

Eleutería, Eleuterio (Spanish) forms of Eleuteria.

Elexis, Elexus (Greek) forms of Alexis.

Élfega (German) brightness in the heights.

Elfelda (Spanish) tall; powerful.

Elfida, Élfida (Greek) daughter of the wind.

Élfreda (Greek) she who the geniuses protect.

Elfrida (German) peaceful.

Elga (Norwegian) pious. (German) a form of Helga.

Eli 🔲 (Hebrew) uplifted.

Elia 🔲 (Hebrew) a short form of Eliana.

Eliana (Hebrew) my God has answered me. **Eliane, Elianne** (Hebrew) forms of Eliana.

Elicia (Hebrew) a form of Elisha. .

Elida (Latin) a form of Alida.

Élida (Greek) Geography: the Olympic city in ancient Greece.

Elide (Latin) a form of Elida.

Eligia (Italian, Spanish) chosen one.

Elijah 🔲 (Hebrew) the Lord is my God. Bible: a great Hebrew prophet.

Elili (Tamil) beautiful.

Elimena (Latin) stranger.

Elina (Greek, Italian) a form of Elena. (English) a form of Ellen.

Elinor (Greek) a form of Eleanor.

Elionor (Greek) a form of Helen.

Elisa, Ellisa (Spanish, Italian, English) short forms of Elizabeth.

Elisabet (Hebrew) a form of Elizabeth.

Elisabeth (Hebrew) a form of Elizabeth.

Elise (French, English) a short form of Elizabeth, Elysia.

Elisea (Hebrew) God is salvation; protect my health.

Elisenda (Hebrew) a form of Elisa.

Elisha 🔲 (Hebrew) consecrated to God. (Greek) a form of Alisha.

Elisheva (Hebrew) a form of Elisabeth.

Elisia (Hebrew) a form of Elisha.

Elissa (Greek, English) a form of Elizabeth. A short form of Melissa.

Elita (Latin, French) chosen.

Eliza (Hebrew) a short form of Elizabeth.

Elizabet (Hebrew) a form of Elizabeth.

Elizabeth ✴ (Hebrew) consecrated to God. Bible: the mother of John the Baptist.

Elizaveta (Polish, English) a form of Elizabeth.

Elizebeth (Hebrew) a form of Elizabeth.

Elka (Polish) a form of Elizabeth.

Elke (German) a form of Adelaide, Alice.

Ella ✴ (English) elfin; beautiful fairy-woman. (Greek) a short form of Eleanor.

Elle (Greek) a short form of Eleanor. (French) she.

Ellen (English) a form of Eleanor, Helen.

Ellena (Greek, Italian) a form of Elena. (English) a form of Ellen.

Ellery 🔲 (English) elder-tree island.

Ellfreda (German) a form of Alfreda.

Elli, Elly (English) short forms of Eleanor.

Ellie ✴ (English) a short form of Eleanor, Ella, Ellen. **Ellice** (English) a form of Elise.

Elliot 🔲 (English) forms of Eli, Elijah.

Ellis 🔲 (English) a form of Elias

Ellison 🔲 (English) child of Ellis.

Ellyn (English) a form of Ellen.

Elma (Turkish) sweet fruit.

Elmina (English) noble.

Elmira (Arabic, Spanish) a form of Almira.

Elnora (American) a combination of Ella + Nora.

Elodie (English) a form of Alodie.

Eloina (French) a form of Eloisa.

Eloína (Latin) predestined.

Eloisa (French) a form of Eloise.

Eloísa (Spanish) a form of Eloise.

Eloise (French) a form of Louise.

Elora (American) a short form of Elnora.

Eloxochitl (Nahuatl) magnolia.

Elpidia, Elpidía (Greek) waits with faith.

Elsa (German) noble. (Hebrew) a short form of Elizabeth.

Elsbeth (German) a form of Elizabeth.

Elsie (German) a familiar form of Elsa, Helsa.

Elspeth (Scottish) a form of Elizabeth.

Elva (English) elfin. , German) a form of Elvira.

Elvia (English) a form of Elva.

Elvie (English) a form of Elva.

Elvina (English) a form of Alvina.

Elvira (Latin) white; blond. (German) closed up. (Spanish) elfin. Geography: the town in Spain that hosted a Catholic synod in 300 a.d.

Elvisa (Teutonic) a form of Eloise.

Elvita (Spanish) truth.

Elycia (Hebrew) a form of Elisha.
Ellycia

Elysa (Spanish, Italian, English) a form of Elisa.

Elyse (French, English) a form of Elise. (Latin) a form of Elysia.

Elysha (Hebrew) a form of Elisha.

Elysia (Greek) sweet; blissful. Mythology: Elysium was the dwelling place of happy souls.

Elyssa (Greek, English) a form of Elissa. (Latin) a form of Elysia.

Ema (German) a form of Emma.

Emalee, Emaleigh, Emalie, Emaly (American) forms of Emily.

Eman BG (Arabic) a short form of Emani.

Emani (Arabic) a form of Iman.

Emanuelle (Hebrew) a form of Emmanuelle.

Emari (German) a form of Emery.

Ember (French) a form of Amber.

Emelia (Latin) a form of Amelia.

Emelie, Emely (Latin) forms of Emily.

Emelinda (Teutonic) a form of Emily.

Emeline (French) a form of Emily.

Emerald (French) bright green gemstone.

Emeralda (Spanish) a form of Emerald.

Emerenciana (Latin) she who will be rewarded.

Emerita (Latin) a form of Emerenciana.

Emérita (Latin) veteran; licensed.

Emerson GB (German) Emery's son. Philosophy: Ralph Waldo Emerson was a proponent of individualism.

Emery GB (German) industrious leader.

Emesta (Spanish) serious.

Emeteria (Greek) half lion.

Emie, Emmie (German) forms of Emmy.

Emile BG (English) a form of Emily.

Emilee, Emileigh, Emiley, Emili, Emilie,

62

Emilly, Emmily
(English) forms of Emily.

Emilia (Italian) a form of Amelia, Emily.

Emilse (German) a combination of Emily + Ilse.

Emily ⚝ (Latin) flatterer. (German) industrious.

Emilyann (American) a combination of Emily + Ann.

Emilyn (American) a **form of Emmalynn.**

Emma ⚝ (German) a short form of Emily. Emmalee, Emmalie (American) combinations of Emma + Lee. Forms of Emily.

Emmaline (French) a form of Emily.

Emmalynn (American) a combination of Emma + Lynn.

Emmanuelle (Hebrew) God is with us.

Emmeline (French) a form of Emmaline.

Emmy, Emy (German) familiar forms of Emma.

Emmylou (American) a combination of Emmy + Lou.

Emna (Teutonic) a form of Emma.

Emory GB (German) a form of Emery.

Emperatriz (Latin) empress.

Emylee (American) a form of Emily.

Ena, Enna (Irish) forms of Helen.

Enara (Basque) swallow.

Enat (Irish) little.

Encarna, Encarnita (Spanish) forms of Encarnación.

Encarnación (Latin) incarnation of Jesus in his mother, Mary.

Enchantra (English) enchanting.

Endora (Hebrew) fountain.

Enedina (Greek) warm; indulgent.

Engel (Greek) a form of Angel.

Engela (Greek) a form of Angela.

Engelica (Greek) a form of Angelica.

Engracia (Spanish) graceful.

Enid (Welsh) life; spirit.

Enimia (Greek) well dressed.

Ennata (Greek) ninth.

Enrica (Spanish) a form of Henrietta. .

Enricua (Spanish) ruler.

Enya (Scottish) jewel; blazing.

Enye (Hebrew) grace.

Epifana, Epifanía (Spanish) forms of Epiphany.

Epiphany (Greek) manifestation. Religion: a Christian feast on January 6 celebrating the manifestation of Jesus' divine nature to the Magi.

.

Eppie (English) a familiar form of Euphemia.

Erasma (Greek) lovable.
Erasmah

Ercilia, Ercilla (Greek) delicate; gentle.

Erda (Anglo-Saxon) Mythology: an earth goddess after which the planet Earth is named.

Erea (Galician) a form of Irene.

Erela (Hebrew) angel.

Erendira, Eréndira, Erendiria (Spanish) one with a smile.

Eres (Welsh) beautiful.

Erica (Scandinavian) ruler of all. (English) brave ruler. **Érica** (German) a form of Erica.

Ericka (Scandinavian) a form of Erica.

Erika, Erikka (Scandinavian) forms of Erica.

63

Erin ⭐ (Irish) peace.
History: another name for
Ireland.

Erinn, Errin (Irish) forms
of Erin.

Erma (Latin) a short form
of Ermine, Hermina.

Ermenburga (German)
strong city.

Ermengarda (German)
where strength dwells.

Ermengardis (German)
strong garden.

Ermenilda (German)
powerful warrior.

Ermerinda (Latin) a form
of Erma.

Ermine (Latin) a form of
Hermina.

Ermitana (Greek) sparsely
populated place.

Erna (English) a short form
of Ernestine.

Ernestina (English) a form
of Ernestine.

Ernestine (English)
earnest, sincere.

Ernesto (Germanic) a form
of Ernestine.

Erosina (Greek) erotic
lady.

Erundina (Latin) like a
swallow.

Erwina, Erwyna
(English) sea friend.

Eryn, Erynn (Irish) forms
of Erin.

Escama, Escame
(Spanish) forms of
Escarna.

**Escarna, Escarne,
Eskarne** (Spanish)
merciful.

Escolástica (Latin) she
who knows much and
teaches.

Eshe (Swahili) life.

Esmé (French) a familiar
form of Esmeralda. A
form of Amy.

Esmerada (Latin) shining;
standing out.

Esmeralda (Greek,
Spanish) a form of
Emerald.

Esperanza (Spanish)
hope.

Essence (Latin) life;
existence.

Essie (English) a short
form of Estelle, Esther.

Estaquia (Spanish)
possessor of a head of
wheat.

Estebana (Spanish) a form
of Stephanie.

Estee (English) a short
form of Estelle, Esther.

Estefani, Estefany
(Spanish) forms of
Stephanie.

**Estefaní, Estéfani,
Estéfany** (Spanish)
forms of Stephanie.

Estefania (Spanish) a form
of Stephanie.

Estefanía (Greek) a form
of Stephanie.

Estela, Estella (French)
forms of Estelle.

Estelinda (Teutonic) she
who is noble and protects
the village.

Estelle (French) a form of
Esther.

Estephanie, Estephany
(Spanish) forms of
Stephanie.

Ester (Persian) a form of
Esther.

Éster, Ésther (Spanish)
forms of Esther.

Esterina (Greek) strong
and vital.

Estervina (German) friend
from the east.

Esteva, Estevana (Greek)
forms of Stephanie.

Esther (Persian) star.
Bible: the Jewish captive
whom Ahasuerus made
his queen.

Estíbalitz (Basque) sweet
as honey.

Estíbaliz (Castilian) a form
of Estíbalitz.

Estila (Latin) column.

Estrada (Latin) road.

Estralita (Spanish) a form
of Estrella.

Estrella (French) star.

Etaina (Celtic) she who shines.

Etapalli (Nahuatl) wing.

Etel (Spanish) a short form of Etelvina.

Etelburga (English) a form of Edelburga.

Etelinda (German) noble one who protects her village.

Etelreda (German) noble advice.

Etelvina (German) loyal and noble friend.

Eteria (Greek) pure air.

Eternity (Latin) eternity.

Ethana (Hebrew) **strong; firm.**

Ethel (English) noble.

Etienne 🆂🅶 (French) a form of Stephan.

Etilka (Hebrew) noble.

Étoile (French) star.

Etta (German) little. (English) a short form of Henrietta.

Euda (German) childhood.

Eudocia, Eudosia, Eudoxia (Greek) famous; knowledgeable.

Eudora (Greek) honored gift.

Eufonia (Greek) she who has a beautiful voice.

Eufrasia (Greek) she who is full of joy.

Eufrosina (Greek) joyful thought.

Eugena (Greek) a form of Eugenia.

Eugenia (Greek) born to nobility.

Eugênia (Portuguese) a form of Eugenia.

Eugenie (Greek) a form of Eugenia.

Eulalia (Greek) well-spoken.

Eulália (Portuguese) a form of Eulalia.

Eulampia (Greek) brilliant.

Eulogia (Greek) a form of Eulalia.

Eumelia (Greek) she who sings well.

Eun (Korean) silver.

Eunice (Greek) happy; victorious. Bible: the mother of Saint Timothy.

Eunomia (Greek) good order.

Euphemia (Greek) spoken well of, in good repute. History: a fourth-century Christian martyr.

Euporia (Greek) she who has a beautiful voice.

Eurídice (Greek) a form of Eurydice.

Eurneid (Russian) child of Clydno.

Eurosia (Greek) eloquent.

Eurydice (Greek) wide, broad. Mythology: the wife of Orpheus.

Eusebia (Greek) respectful; pious.

Eustacia (Greek) productive. (Latin) stable; calm.

Eustaquia (Greek) well-built.

Eustolia (Greek) agile.

Eustoquia (Greek) good mother.

Eutalia (Greek) abundant.

Euterpe (Greek) walks with grace.

Eutimia (Spanish) benevolent.

Eutiquia (Greek) she who entertains.

Eutropia (Greek) good character.

Euxenia (Greek) from a good family name.

Eva ⭐ (Greek) a short form of Evangelina. (Hebrew) a form of Eve.

Evaline (French) a form of Evelyn.

Evan 🆂🅶 (Irish) young warrior. (English) a form of John

Evangelina (Greek) bearer of good news.

Evangeline (Greek) a form of Evangelina.

Evania (Greek, Irish) a form of Evan.

Evanthe (Greek) flower.

Evarista (Greek) excellent one.

Eve (Hebrew) life. Bible: the first woman created by God. (French) a short form of Evonne Eve Marie **(English)** a combination of Eve + Marie.

Evelia (Hebrew) a form of Eve.

Evelin, Eveline, Evelyne (English) forms of Evelyn.

Evelina (English) a form of Evelyn.

Everly (Old English) from the grazing meadow.

Evelyn ☆

GB (English) hazelnut.

Everett BG (German) courageous as a boar.

Everilda (German) a form of Everett.

Evette (French) a form of Yvette. A familiar form of Evonne.

Evie (Hungarian) a form of Eve.

Evita (Spanish) a form of Eve.

Evline (English) a form of Evelyn.

Evodia (Greek) she who wishes others a good trip.

Evonne (French) a form of Yvonne. .

Exal (Spanish) a short form of Exaltación.

Exaltación (Spanish) exalted, lifted up.

Expedita (Greek) ready to fight.

Expósita (Latin) exposed.

Exuperancia (Latin) abundant.

Exuperia (Latin) a form of Exuperancia.

Eyén (Aboriginal) break of day.

Eyota BG (Native American) great.

Ezmeralda (Spanish) a form of Esmeralda.

Ezrela (Hebrew) reaffirming faith.

Ezri (Hebrew) helper; **strong.**

Eztli (Nahuatl) blood.

F

Fabia (Latin) bean grower.

Fabiana (Latin) a form of Fabia.

Fabienne (Latin) a form of Fabia.

Fabiola (Latin) a form of Fabia.

Fabricia (Latin) a form of Fabrizia.

Fabrienne (French) little blacksmith; apprentice.

Fabrizia (Italian) craftswoman.

Facunda (Latin) eloquent speaker.

Fadila (Arabic) generous.

Faina (English) happy.

Fairlee (English) from a yellow meadow.

Faith ☆ (English) faithful; fidelity.

Faiza, Faizah (Arabic) victorious.

Falda (Icelandic) folded wings.

Falicia (Latin) a form of Felicia.

Faline (Latin) catlike.

Falisha (Latin) a form of Felicia.

Fallon (Irish) grandchild of the ruler.

Falon (Irish) a form of Fallon.

Falviana (Spanish) a form of Flavia.

Falyn (Irish) a form of Fallon.

Fanchone (French) freedom.

Fancy (French) betrothed. (English) whimsical; decorative.

Fannie, Fanny
(American) familiar
forms of Frances.
Fantasia (Greek)
imagination.
Fany (American) a form of
Fannie.

Faqueza (Spanish)
weakness.
Farah, Farrah (English)
beautiful; pleasant.
Faren, Farren (English)
wanderer.
Faría (Hebrew) pharaoh.
Farica (German) peaceful
ruler.
Farida (Arabic) unique.
Fariha (Muslim, Arabic)
happy, joyful, cheerful,
glad.
Fatema (Arabic) a form of
Fatima.
Fátim, Fátima (Arabic)
forms of Fatima.
Fatima (Arabic) daughter
of the prophet. History:
the daughter of
Muhammad.
Fatimah (Arabic) a form of
Fatima.
Fatma, Fatme (Arabic)
short forms of Fatima.
Faustine (Latin) lucky,
fortunate.
Favia (Latin) a form of
Fabia.
Faviola (Latin) a form of
Fabia.
Fawn (French) young deer.

Fawna (French) a form of
Fawn.
Faxon BG (German) long-
haired.
Fay (French, English) a
form of Faye.
Fayana (French) a form of
Faye.
Faye (French) fairy; elf.
(English) a form of Faith.
Fayette (French) a form of
Faye.
Fayola (Nigerian) lucky.
Fayre (English) fair; light
haired.
Fayruz (Arabic) Turkish
woman.
Faythe (English) a form of
Faith.
Fe (Latin) trust; belief.
Febe (Greek) a form of
Phoebe.
Febronia (Latin) sacrifice
of atonement.
Fedra (Greek) splendid
one.
Feena (Irish) small fawn.
Felberta (English)
brilliant.
Felecia (Latin) a form of
Felicia.
Felecidade (Portuguese) a
form of Felicity.
Felica (Spanish) a short
form of Felicia.
Felice (Latin) a short form
of Felicia.
Felicia (Latin) fortunate;
happy.

Feliciana (Italian,
Spanish) a form of Felicia.

Felicidade (Latin) a form
of Felicity.
Felicísima (Spanish) a
form of Felicity.
Felicitas (Italian) a form of
Felicia.
Felícitas (Spanish) a form
of Felicity.
Felicity (English) a form of
Felicia.
Felícula (Latin) kitty.
Felisa (Latin) a form of
Felicia.
Felisha (Latin) a form of
Felicia.
Femi (French) woman.
(Nigerian) love me.
Fenella (Irish) a form of
Fionnula.
Fenna (Irish) fair-haired.
Feodora (Greek) gift of
God.
Fermina (Spanish) strong.
Fern (English) fern.
(German) a short form of
Fernanda.
Fernanda (German)
daring, adventurous.

Fernley (English) from the
fern meadow.

Feronia (Latin)
Mythology: goddess of
freedom.
Fiala (Czech) violet flower.
Fidelia (Latin) a form of
Fidelity.

Fidelity (Latin) faithful, true.

Fidencia (Latin) a form of Fidelity.

Fifi (French) a familiar form of Josephine.

Filadelfia (Greek) a form of Filia.

Filandra (Greek) she who loves humankind.

Filemona (Greek) a form of Philomena.

Filia (Greek) friend.

Filiberta (Greek) brilliant.

Filippa (Italian) a form of Philippa.

Filis (Greek) adorned with leaves.

Filma (German) veiled.

Filomena (Italian) a form of Philomena.

Filotea (Greek) she who loves God.

Finley 𝗚𝗕 (Irish) blond-haired soldier.

Fiona (Irish) fair, white.

Fionnula (Irish) white shouldered. ,

Fiorel (Latin) a form of Flora.

Fiorela (Italian) a form of Flora.

Fiorella (Italian) little flower.

Fira (English) fiery.

Flair (English) style; verve.

Flaminia (Latin) one who belongs to a religious order.

Flanna (Irish) a short form of Flannery.

Flannery (Irish) redhead. Literature: Flannery O'Connor was a renowned American writer.

Flavia (Latin) blond, golden haired.

Flávia (Portuguese) a form of Flavia.

Flaviana (Italian) a form of Flavia.

Flavie (Latin) a form of Flavia.

Flérida (Greek) exuberant lady.

Fleta (English) swift, fast.

Fleur (French) flower.

Fleurette (French) a form of Fleur.

Fliora (Irish) a form of Flora.

Flo (American) a short form of Florence.

Flor (Latin) a short form of Florence.

Flora (Latin) flower. A short form of Florence.

Floralia (Greek) a form of Flora.

Floramaría (Spanish) flower of Mary.

Floreal (French) flowers. History: the eighth month in the old French calendar.

Florelle (Latin) a form of Flora.

Florence (Latin) blooming; flowery; prosperous. History: Florence Nightingale, a British nurse, is considered the founder of modern nursing.

Flores (Spanish) a form of Flora.

Floria (Basque) a form of Flora.

Florian 𝗕𝗚 (Latin) flowering, blooming.

Florida (Spanish) a form of Florence.

Florie (English) a familiar form of Florence.

Florimel (Greek) sweet nectar.

Florinia (Latin) a form of Florence.

Floris (English) a form of Florence.

Florisel (Spanish) a form of Flora.

Flossie (English) a familiar form of Florence.

Flyta (English) rapid.

Fola (Yoruba) honorable.

Foluke 𝗕𝗚 (Yoruba) given to God.

Fonda (Latin) foundation. (Spanish) inn.

Fontanna (French) fountain.

Forrest 🅱🅶 (French) forest; forester.

Fortuna (Latin) fortune; fortunate.

Fosette (French) dimpled.

Fotina (Greek) light.

Fran 🅶🅱 (Latin) a short form of Frances.

Frances (Latin) free; from France.

Francesca, Franceska (Italian) forms of Frances.

Franchesca, Francheska (Italian) forms of Francesca.

Franchette (French) a form of Frances.

Franci (Hungarian) a familiar form of Francine.

Francine (French) a form of Frances.

Francis 🅱🅶 (Latin) a form of Frances.

Francisca (Italian) a form of Frances.

Francoise, Françoise (French) forms of Frances.

Franki (American) a familiar form of Frances.

Frankie 🅱🅶 (American) a familiar form of Frances.

Frannie, Franny (English) familiar forms of Frances.

Franqueira (German) open space.

Franzea (Spanish) a form of Frances.

Freda (German) a short form of Alfreda, Elfrida, Frederica, Sigfreda.

Freddi (English) a familiar form of Frederica, Winifred.

Freddie 🅱🅶 (English) a familiar form of Frederica, Winifred.

Fredella (English) a form of Frederica.

Frederica (German) peaceful ruler.

Frederika (German) a form of Frederica.

Frederike (German) a form of Frederica.

Frederique 🅶🅱 (French) a form of Frederica.

Fredesvinda (German) strength of the country.

Fredricka (German) a short form of Frederika.

Freedom (English) freedom.

Freida (German) a form of Frida.

Freira (Spanish) sister.

Freja (Scandinavian) a form of Freya.

Frescura (Spanish) freshness.

Freya (Scandinavian) noblewoman. Mythology: the Norse goddess of love.

Freyra (Slavic) a form of Freya.

Frida (German) a short form of Alfreda, Elfrida, Frederica, Sigfreda.

Frine, Friné (Greek) female toad.

Fritzi (German) a familiar form of Frederica.

Frodina (German) wise friend.

Froilana (Greek) rapid.

Fronde (Latin) leafy branch.

Fronya (Latin) forehead.

Fructuosa (Spanish) fruitful.

Fuensanta (Spanish) holy fountain.

Fukayna (Egyptian) intelligent.

Fulgencia (Spanish) she who excels because of her great kindness.

Fulla (German) full.

Fusca (Latin) dark.

Futura (Latin) future.

Fynballa (Irish) fair.

G

Gabele (French) a short form of Gabrielle.

Gabina (Latin) she who is a native of Gabio, an ancient city near Rome.

Gabor (Hungarian) God is my strength.

Gabriel 🅱🅶 (French) a form of Gabrielle.

Gabriela (Italian) a form of Gabrielle.

Gabriele GB (French) a form of Gabrielle.

Gabriell GB (French) a form of Gabrielle.

Gabriella ☆ (Italian) a form of Gabriela.

Gabrielle GB (French) devoted to God.

Gaby (French) a familiar form of Gabrielle.

Gada (Hebrew) lucky.

Gaea (Greek) planet Earth. Mythology: the Greek goddess of Earth.

Gaetana (Italian) from Gaeta. Geography: Gaeta is a city in southern Italy.

Gagandeep BG (Sikh) sky's light.

Gage BG (French) promise.

Gail (English) merry, lively. (Hebrew) a short form of Abigail.

Gailine (English) a form of Gail.

Gala (Norwegian) singer.

Galatea (Greek) Mythology: Galatea was a statue of a beautiful woman carved by Pygmalion, who fell in love with her and persuaded the goddess Aphrodite to bring the statue to life.

Galaxy (Latin) universe; the Milky Way.

Galen BG (Greek) healer; calm. (Irish) little and lively.

Galena (Greek) healer; calm.

Galenia (Greek) a form of Galena.

Gali (Hebrew) hill; fountain; spring.

Galilah (Hebrew) important; exalted.

Galilea (Hebrew) from Galilee.

Galina (Russian) a form of Helen.

Gamela (Scandinavian) elder.

Gamila (Arabic) beautiful.

Ganesa (Hindi) fortunate. Religion: Ganesha was the Hindu god of wisdom.

Ganya BG (Hebrew) garden of the Lord. (Zulu) clever.

Garabina, Garabine, Garbina, Garbine (Spanish) purification.

Garaitz (Basque) victory.

García (Latin) she who demonstrates her charm and grace.

Gardenia (English) Botany: a sweet-smelling flower.

Garland BG (French) wreath of flowers.

Garnet BG (English) dark red gem.

Garoa (Basque) fern.

Garyn (English) spear carrier.

Gasha (Russian) a familiar form of Agatha.

Gaspara (Spanish) treasure.

Gasparina (Persian) treasure.

Gaudencia (Spanish) happy, content.

Gavriella (Hebrew) a form of Gabrielle.

Gay (French) merry.

Gayla (English) a form of Gail.

Gayle (English) a form of Gail.

Gaylia (English) a form of Gail.

Gayna (English) a familiar form of Guinevere.

Gea (Greek) a form of Gaea.

Geanna (Italian) a form of Giana.

Gechina (Basque) grace.

Geela (Hebrew) joyful.

Geena (American) a form of Gena.

Gelasia (Greek) smiling lady.

Gelya (Russian) angelic.

Gema, Gemma (Latin, Italian) jewel, precious stone.

Gemini (Greek) twin.

Geminiana (Latin) a form of Gemini.

Gen (Japanese) spring. A short form of names beginning with "Gen."

Gena (French) a form of Gina. A short form of Geneva, Genevieve, Iphigenia.

Geneen (Scottish) a form of Jeanine.

Genell (American) a form of Jenell.

Generosa (Spanish) generous.

Genesis ✨ GB (Latin) origin; birth.

Genessis (Latin) a form of Genesis.

Geneva (French) juniper tree. A short form of Genevieve. Geography: a city in Switzerland.

Genevieve (German, French) a form of Guinevere. .

Genevra (French, Welsh) a form of Guinevere.

Genice (American) a form of Janice.

Genie (French) a familiar form of Gena.

Genita (American) a form of Janita.

Genna (English) a form of Jenna.

Gennifer (American) a form of Jennifer.

Genovieve (French) a form of Genevieve.

Gentil (Latin) kind.

Gentry BG (English) a form of Gent Georgeann,

Georgeanne (English) combinations of Georgia + Ann.

Georgeanna (English) a combination of Georgia + Anna.

Georgene (English) a familiar form of Georgia.

Georgette (French) a form of Georgia.

Georgia (Greek) farmer. Art: Georgia O'Keeffe was an American painter known especially for her paintings of flowers. Geography: a southern American state; a country in Eastern Europe.

Georgiana, Georgianna (English) forms of Georgeanna.

Georgie (English) a familiar form of Georgeanne, Georgia, Georgiana.

Georgina (English) a form of Georgia.

Geovanna (Italian) a form of Giovanna.

Geralda (German) a short form of Geraldine.

Geraldine (German) mighty with a spear. .

Geralyn (American) a combination of Geraldine + Lynn.

Geranio (Greek) she is as beautiful as a geranium.

Gerarda (English) brave spearwoman.

Gerásima (Greek) prize.

Gerda (Norwegian) protector. (German) a familiar form of Gertrude.

Geri, Gerri (American) familiar forms of Geraldine.

Germaine BG (French) from Germany.

Gertie (German) a familiar form of Gertrude.

Gertrude (German) beloved warrior.

Gertrudes (Spanish) a form of Gertrude.

Gervaise BG (French) skilled with a spear.

Gervasi (Spanish) a form of Gervaise.

Gervasia (German) a form of Gervaise.

Gessica (Italian) a form of Jessica.

Geva (Hebrew) hill.

Gezana, Gezane (Spanish) reference to the incarnation of Jesus.

Ghada (Arabic) young; tender.

Ghita (Italian) pearly.

Gia GB (Italian) a short form of Giana.

Giacinta (Italian) a form of Hyacinth.

Giacobba (Hebrew) supplanter, substitute.

Giada (Italian) jade.

Giana (Italian) a short form of Giovanna. .

Gianira (Greek) nymph from the sea.

Gianna ☆ (Italian) a form of Giana.

Gibitruda (German) she who gives strength.

Gidget (English) giddy.

Gigi (French) a familiar form of Gilberte.

Gilana (Hebrew) joyful.

Gilberte (German) brilliant; pledge; trustworthy.

Gilda (English) covered with gold.

Gill (Latin, German) a short form of Gilberte, Gillian.

Gillian (Latin) a form of Jillian.

Gimena (Spanish) a form of Jimena.

Gin (Japanese) silver. A short form of names beginning with "Gin."

Gina (Italian) a short form of Angelina, Eugenia, Regina, Virginia.

Ginebra (Celtic) white as foam.

Gines (Greek) she who engenders life.

Ginesa (Spanish) white.

Ginette (English) a form of Genevieve.

Ginger (Latin) flower; spice. A familiar form of Virginia.

Ginia (Latin) a familiar form of Virginia.

Ginnifer (English) white; smooth; soft. (Welsh) a form of Jennifer.

Ginny (English) a familiar form of Ginger, Virginia.

Gioconda (Latin) she who engenders life.

Giordana (Italian) a form of Jordana.

Giorgianna (English) a form of Georgeanna.

Giorsala (Scottish) graceful.

Giovanna (Italian) a form of Jane.

Giovanni BG (Italian) a form of Giovanna.

Gisa (Hebrew) carved stone.

Gisal (Welsh) a form of Giselle.

Gisel, Gisell, Gissel, Gisselle (German) forms of Giselle.

Gisela (German) a form of Giselle.

Giselle (German) pledge; hostage.

Gita (Yiddish) good. (Polish) a short form of Margaret.

Gitana (Spanish) gypsy; wanderer.

Gitel (Hebrew) good.

Githa (Greek) good. (English) gift.

Gitta (Irish) a short form of Bridget.

Giulana (Italian) a form of Guilia.

Giulia (Italian) a form of Julia.

Giunia (Latin) she who was born in June.

Giuseppina (Italian) a form of Josephine.

Giustina (Italian) a form of Justine.

Gizela (Czech) a form of Giselle.

Gizelle (Czech) a form of Giselle.

Gladis (Irish) a form of Gladys.

Gladys (Latin) small sword. (Irish) princess. (Welsh) a form of Claudia.

Glafira (Greek) fine, elegant.

Glauca (Greek) green.

Glaucia (Portuguese) brave gift.

Gleda (English) happy.

Glenda (Welsh) a form of Glenna.

Glenna (Irish) valley, glen.
.

Glennesha (American) a form of Glenna.

Gliceria (Greek) sweet.

Gloria (Latin) glory.
History: Gloria Steinem, an American feminist, founded *Ms.* magazine.

Gloriann, Glorianne (American) combinations of Gloria + Ann.

Glory (Latin) a form of Gloria.

Glosinda (German) sweet glory.

Glynnis (Welsh) a form of Glenna.

Godalupe (Spanish) reference to the Virgin Mary.

Godgifu (English) a form of Godiva.

Godiva (English) God's present.

Godoberta (German) brightness of God.

Golda (English) gold.
History: Golda Meir was a Russian-born politician who served as prime minister of Israel.

Goldie (English) a familiar form of Golda.

Goldine (English) a form of Golda.

Goma (Swahili) joyful dance.

Gontilda (German) famous warrior.

Gorane (Spanish) holy cross.

Goratze (Basque) a form of Exaltación.

Gorawén (Welsh) happiness.

Gorgonia (Greek) Mythology: Gorgons were monsters who turned people to stone.

Gotzone (Spanish) angel.

Graça (Portuguese) a form of Grace.

Grace ⭐ (Latin) graceful.

Graceann, Graceanne (English) combinations of Grace + Ann.

Gracelyn, Gracelynn, Gracelynne (English) combinations of Grace + Lynn.

Gracen, Gracyn (English) short forms of Graceanne.

Gracia (Spanish) a form of Grace.

Gracie (English) a familiar form of Grace.

Graciela (Spanish) a form of Grace.

Gracilia (Latin) graceful; slender.

Grant BG (English) great; giving.

Gratiana (Hebrew) graceful.

Grayce (Latin) a form of Grace.

Grayson BG (English) bailiff's child.

Graziella (Italian) a form of Grace.

Grecia (Latin) a form of Grace.

Greekria (Spanish) a form of Greekrina.

Greekriana (Spanish) a form of Greekria.

Greekrina (Latin) vigilant watchperson.

Greer (Scottish) vigilant.

Greta, Gretta (German) short forms of Gretchen, Margaret.

Gretchen (German) a form of Margaret.

Gretel (German) a form of Margaret.

Gricelda (German) a form of Griselda.

Grimalda (Latin) happiness.

Grise (Welsh) a form of Griselda.

Grisel (German) a short form of Griselda.

Grisela (Spanish) a form of Griselda.

Griselda (German) gray woman warrior.

Guadalupe (Arabic) river of black stones.

Gualberta (German) brilliant power.

Gualteria (German) a form of Walter

Gudelia, Gúdula (Latin) God.

Gudrun (Scandinavian) battler.

Güendolina (English) a form of Gwendolyn.

Guía (Spanish) guide.

Guillelmina (Italian, Spanish) a form of Guillermina.

Guillerma (Spanish) a short form of Guillermina.

Guillermina (Spanish) a form of Wilhelmina.

Guinevere (French, Welsh) white wave; white phantom. Literature: the wife of King Arthur.

Guioma (Spanish) a form of Guiomar.

Guiomar (German) famous in combat.

Gunda (Norwegian) female warrior.

Gundelina (Teutonic) she who helps in battle.

Gundelinda (German) pious one in the battle.

Gundenes (German) famous.

Gundenia (German) fighter.

Gurit (Hebrew) innocent baby.

Gurleen (Sikh) follower of the guru.

Gurley (Australian) **willow.**

Gurpreet BG (Punjabi) religion.

Gusta (Latin) a short form of Augusta.

Gustava (Scandinavian) staff of the Goths.

Gustey (English) windy.

Gwen (Welsh) a short form of Guinevere, Gwendolyn.

Gwenda (Welsh) a familiar form of Gwendolyn.

Gwendolyn (Welsh) white wave; white browed; new moon. Literature: Gwendoloena was the wife of Merlin, the magician.

Gwyn GB (Welsh) a short form of Gwyneth.

Gwyneth (Welsh) a form of Gwendolyn.

Gypsy (English) wanderer.

H

Habiba (Arabic) beloved.

Hachi (Japanese) eight; good luck. (Native American) river.

Hada, Hadda (Hebrew) she who radiates joy.

Hadara (Hebrew) adorned with beauty.

Hadasa (Hebrew) a form of Hadassah.

Hadassah (Hebrew) myrtle tree.

Hadaza (Guanche) distracted; lost.

Hadeel (Arabic) a form of Hadil.

Hadil (Arabic) cooing of pigeons.

Hadiya (Swahili) gift.

Hadley ☆ GB (English) field of heather.

Hadriane (Greek, Latin) a form of Adrienne.

Hae (Korean) ocean.

Haeley (English) a form of Hayley.

Hafsa (Muslim) cub; young lioness.

Hafwen (Welsh) pleasant summer.

Hágale (Greek) beautiful.

Hagar GB (Hebrew) forsaken; stranger. Bible: Sarah's handmaiden, the mother of Ishmael.

Haidee (Greek) modest.

Haidée, Haydée (Greek) forms of Haidee.

Haiden BG (English) heather-covered hill.

Haile, Hailee, Haileigh, Haili, Hailie, Haily (English) forms of Hayley.

Hailey ☆ (English) a form of Haile.

Haizea (Basque) wind.

Hajar (Hebrew) a form of Hagar.

Hala (African) a form of Halla.

Haldana (Norwegian) half Danish.

Halee, Haleigh, Halie, Hallee, Halli, Hallie (Scandinavian) forms of Haley.

Haley GB (Scandinavian) heroine.

Hali GB (Scandinavian) a form of Haley.

Halia (Hawaiian) in loving memory.

Haliaka (Hawaiian) leader.

Halima (Arabic) a form of Halimah.

Halimah (Arabic) gentle; patient.

Halimeda (Greek) loves the sea.

Halina (Hawaiian) likeness. (Russian) a form of Helen.

Halla (African) unexpected gift.

Halle (African) a form of Halla. (Scandinavian) a form of Halcy.

Halley GB (Scandinavian) a form of Haley.

Halona (Native American) fortunate.

Halsey GB (English) Hall's island.

Hama (Japanese) shore.

Hana, Hanah (Japanese) flower. (Arabic) happiness. (Slavic) forms of Hannah.

Hanako (Japanese) flower child.

Hanan GB (Japanese, Arabic, Slavic) a form of Hana.

Haneen (Japanese, Arabic, Slavic) a form of Hana.

Hanele (Hebrew) compassionate.

Hania (Hebrew) resting place.

Hanifa (Arabic) true believer.

Hanna (Hebrew) a form of Hannah.

Hannah ☆ (Hebrew) gracious. Bible: the mother of Samuel**Honnah**

Hanni (Hebrew) a familiar form of Hannah.

Happy (English) happy.

Hara GB (Hindi) tawny. Religion: another name for the Hindu god Shiva, the destroyer.

Haralda (Scandinavian) army ruler.

Harjot BG (Sikh) God's light.

Harlee, Harleigh, Harli, Harlie (English) forms of Harley.

Harleen, Harlene (English) forms of Harley.

Harley GB (English) meadow of the hare.

Harleyann (English) a combination of Harley + Ann.

Harlow (Old English) protector of the people. Movies: Jean Harlow was a glamorous, blond movie star in the 1930s.

Harmony (Latin) harmonious.

Harper ☆ (English) harp player.

Harpreet GB (Punjabi) devoted to God.

Harriet (French) ruler of the household. (English) a form of Henrietta. Literature: Harriet Beecher Stowe was an American writer noted for her novel *Uncle Tom's Cabin.*

Haru (Japanese) spring.

Hasana (Swahili) she arrived first. Culture: a name used for the first-born female twin. **Hasia** (Hebrew) protected by God.

Hasina (Swahili) good.

Hateya (Moquelumnan) footprints.

Hathor (Egyptian) goddess of the sky.

Hattie (English) a familiar form of Harriet, Henrietta.

Haukea (Hawaiian) snow.

Hausu (Moquelumnan) like a bear yawning upon awakening.

Hava (Hebrew) a form of Chava.

Haven GB (English) a form of Heaven.

Haviva (Hebrew) beloved.

Haya (Arabic) humble, modest.

Hayat (Arabic) life.

Hayden BG (English) a form of Haiden.

Hayfa (Arabic) shapely.

Hayle, Haylea, Haylee, Hayleigh, Hayli, Haylie (English) forms of Hayley.

Hayley (English) hay meadow.

Hazel (English) hazelnut tree; commanding authority.

Heather (English) flowering heather.

Heaven (English) place of beauty and happiness. Bible: where God and angels are said to dwell.

Heavenly (English) a form of Heaven.

Heba (Greek) a form of Hebe.

Hebe (Greek) Mythology: the Greek goddess of youth and spring.

Hecuba (Greek) Mythology: wife of Priam, king of Troy.

Hedda (German) battler.

Hedwig BG (German) warrior.

Hedy (Greek) delightful; sweet. (German) a familiar form of Hedda.

Heidi, Heidy (German) short forms of Adelaide.

Helah (Hebrew) rust.

Helaina (Greek) a form of Helena.

Helaku BG (Native American) sunny day.

Helana (Greek) a form of Helena.

Helda (German) a form of Hedda.

Helen (Greek) light.

Helena (Greek) a form of Helen.

Helene (French) a form of Helen.

Helga (German) pious. (Scandinavian) a form of Olga.

Heli (Spanish) a short form of Heliana.

Helia, Heliena (Greek) sun.

Heliana (Greek) she who offers herself to God.

Helice (Greek) spiral.

Hélida (Hebrew) of God.

Heliodora (Greek) gift from the sun.

Helki BG (Native American) touched.

Hellen (Greek) a form of Helen.

Helma (German) a short form of Wilhelmina.

Heloísa (Spanish) a form of Heloise.

Heloise (French) a form of Louise.

Helsa (Danish) a form of Elizabeth.

Heltu (Moquelumnan) like a bear reaching out.

Helvecia (Latin) happy friend. History: Helvetians were ancient inhabitants of Switzerland.

Helvia (Latin) blond hair.

Henar (Spanish) hay field.

Hendrika (Dutch) a form of Henrietta.

Henedina (Greek) indulgent.

Henimia (Greek) well-dressed.

Henley (English) Geography: Henley-on-Thames is the site of the Henley Royal Regatta, a rowing race between Oxford and Cambridge.

Henna (English) a familiar form of Henrietta.

Henrietta (English) ruler of the household.

Henriette (French) a form of Henrietta.

Henriqua (Spanish) a form of Henrietta.

Hera (Greek) queen; jealous. Mythology: the queen of heaven and the wife of Zeus.

Heraclia (Greek) a form of Hera.

Herberta (German) glorious soldier.

Hercilia, Hersilia (Greek) she who is delicate and kind.

Herculana (Greek) a form of Hercules

Herena, Herenia (Greek) forms of Irene.

Heresvida (German) numerous troops.

Heriberta (German) a form of Herberta.

Heriberto (Spanish) ruler.

Herlinda (German) pleasant, sweet.

Hermelinda (German) shield of strength.

Hermenegilda (Spanish) she who offers sacrifices to God.

Hermenexilda (German) warrior.

Hermia (Greek) messenger.

Hermilda (German) battle of force.

Hermina (Latin) noble. (German) soldier.

Herminda (Greek) a form of Hermia.

Herminia (Latin, German) a form of Hermina.

Hermínia (Portuguese) a form of Hermione.

Hermione (Greek) earthy.

Hermisenda (Germanic) path of strength.

Hermosa (Spanish) beautiful.

Hernanda (Spanish) bold voyager.

Hertha (English) child of the earth.

Herundina (Latin) like a swallow.

Hester (Dutch) a form of Esther.

Hestia (Persian) star. Mythology: the Greek goddess of the hearth and home.

Heta (Native American) racer.

Hetta (German) a form of Hedda. (English) a familiar form of Henrietta.

Hettie (German) a familiar form of Henrietta, Hester.

Hialeah (Cherokee) lovely meadow.

Hiawatha BG (Iroquoian) creator of rivers. History: the Onondagan leader who organized the Iroquois confederacy.

Hiba (Arabic) a form of Hibah.

Hibah GB (Arabic) gift.

Hibernia (Latin) comes from Ireland.

Hibiscus (Latin) Botany: tropical trees or shrubs with large, showy, colorful flowers.

Hidalgo (Spanish) noble one.

Higinia (Greek) she who enjoys good health.

Hilary GB (Greek) cheerful, merry.

Hilda (German) a short form of Brunhilda, Hildegarde.

Hildebranda (German) battle sword.

Hildegarda (German) a form of Hildegarde.

Hildegarde (German) fortress.

Hildegunda (German) heroic fighter.

Hildelita, Hildeliva (Latin) warrior.

Hildemarca (German) noble warrior.

Hildemare (German) splendid.

Hillary (Greek) cheerful, merry.

Hilma (German) protected.

Hilmer (German) famous warrior.

Hiltruda, Hiltrudes, Hiltrudis (German) strong warrior.

Himana (Greek) membrane.

Hinda (Hebrew) hind; doe.

Hipatia (Greek) best.

Hipólita (Greek) horsewoman.

Hiriko (Japanese) generous.

Hisa **(Japanese) long lasting.**

Hiti (Eskimo) hyena.

Hoa (Vietnamese) flower; peace.

Hoda (Muslim, Arabic) a form of Huda.

Hogolina (Teutonic) great intelligence.

Hola (Hopi) seed-filled club.

Holain (Greek) a form of Helen.

Holda (Hebrew) hidden.

Holland GB (French) Geography: A popular name for the Netherlands.

Hollee, Holley, Holli, Hollie (English) forms of Holly.

Hollis BG (English) near the holly bushes.

Holly (English) holly tree.

Hollyann (English) a combination of Holly + Ann.

Hollyn (English) a short form of Hollyann.

Hombelina, Humbelina (German) boss, leader.

Homera (German) woman who cannot see.

Honbria (English) sweet.

Honesta (Latin) honest.

Honesty (Latin) honesty.

Honey (English) sweet. (Latin) a familiar form of Honora.

Hong (Vietnamese) pink.

Honora (Latin) honorable.

Honoratas (Spanish) a form of Honora.

Honovi BG (Native American) strong.

Hope (English) hope.

Hopi (Hopi) peaceful.

Horatia (Latin) keeper of the hours.

Hortense (Latin) gardener.

Hosanna (Latin) a shout of praise or adoration derived from the Hebrew phrase "Save now!"

Hoshi (Japanese) star.

Howi BG (Moquelumnan) turtledove.

Hua (Chinese) flower.

Huanquyi (Mapuche) announcer, she who shouted.

Huata (Moquelumnan) basket carrier.

Huberta (German) bright mind; bright spirit.

Huda (Muslim, Arabic) to lead upon the right path.

Huette (German) bright mind; bright spirit.

Huilen, Huillen, Hullen (Araucanian) spring.

Humildad (Latin) a form of Humilia.

Humilia (Polish) humble.

Humiliana (Italian) a form of Humilia.

Hunter BG (English) hunter.

Huong (Vietnamese) flower.

Huseina (Swahili) a form of Hasana.

Hyacinth (Greek) Botany: a plant with colorful, fragrant flowers.

Hydi, Hydeia (German) forms of Heidi.

Hye (Korean) graceful.

I

Ia (Greek) voice; shout.

Iafa (Hebrew) strong and beautiful.

Ian BG (Hebrew) God is gracious.

Ianina (Hebrew) a form of Juana.

Ianira (Greek) enchantress.

Ianthe (Greek) violet flower.

Iara (Tupi) lady.

Iberia (Latin) she who is a native of Iberia.

Ibi (Indigenous) earth.

Icess (Egyptian) a form of Isis.

Ichtaca (Nahuatl) secret.

Icía (Galician) a form of Cecilia.

Iciar (Basque) name of the Virgin Mary.

Icnoyotl (Nahuatl) friendship.

Ida (German) hard working. (English) prosperous.

Idabelle (English) a combination of Ida + Belle.

Idalia (Greek) sun.

Idalina (English) a combination of Ida + Lina.

Idalis (English) a form of Ida.

Idara (Latin) well-organized woman.

Ideashia (American) a combination of Ida + Iesha.

Idelgunda (German) combative.

Idelia (German) noble.

Idelina (German) a form of Idelia.

Idelle (Welsh) a form of Ida.

Idil (Welsh) a form of Ida.

Idla (English) battle.

Idoberga, Iduberga (German) woman; shelter.

Idoia (Spanish) reference to the Virgin Mary.

Idolina (Latin) idol.

Idoya (Spanish) pond. Religion: a place of worship of the Virgin Mary.

Idumea (Latin) red.

Idurre (Spanish) reference to the Virgin Mary.

Ieasha (American) a form of Iesha.

Iedidá (Hebrew) loved.

Ieisha (American) a form of Iesha.

Iesha (American) a form of Aisha.

Ieshia (American) a form of Iesha.

Ife (Egyptian) love.

Ifigenia (Greek) a form of Iphigenia.

Ifiginia (Spanish) a form of Iphigenia.

Ignacia (Latin) fiery, ardent.

Ignia (Latin) a short form of Ignacia.

Igone (Spanish) ascension.

Igraine (Irish) graceful.

Ihuicatl (Nahuatl) sky.

Ilragarte (Basque) a form of Anunciación.

Ikerne (Basque) a form of Visitación.

Ikia (Hebrew) God is my salvation. (Hawaiian) a form of Isaiah.

Ila (Hungarian) a form of Helen.

Ilaina (Hebrew) a form of Ilana.

Ilana (Hebrew) tree.

Ilchahueque (Mapuche) young virginal woman.

Ilda (German) heroine in battle.

Ilde (English) battle.

Ildefonsa (German) ready for battle.

Ildegunda (German) she who knows how to battle.

Ileana (Hebrew) a form of Iliana.

Ilena (Greek) a form of Helena.

Ilene (Irish) a form of Helen.

Ilhuitl (Nahuatl) day.

Iliana (Greek) from Troy.

Ilima (Hawaiian) flower of Oahu.

Ilisa (Scottish, English) a form of Alisa, Elisa.

Ilise (German) a form of Elise.

Ilisha (Hebrew) a form of Alisha, Elisha.

Ilka (Hungarian) a familiar form of Ilona.

Ilona (Hungarian) a form of Helen.

Ilsa (German) a form of Ilse.

Ilse (German) a form of Elizabeth.

Iluminada (Spanish) shining.

Ilyssa (Scottish, English) a form of Ilisa.

Ima (Japanese) presently. (German) a familiar form of Amelia.

Imaculada (Portuguese) a form of Inmaculada.

Imala (Native American) strong-minded.

Iman GB (Arabic) believer.

Imani GB (Arabic) a form of Iman.

Imber (Polish) ginger.

Imelda (German) warrior.

Imena (African) dream.

Immaculada (Spanish) a form of Inmaculada. Religion: refers to the Immaculate Conception.

Imogene (Latin) image, likeness.

Imoni (Arabic) a form of Iman.

Imperia, Imperio (Latin) imperial ruler.

Ina (Irish) a form of Agnes.

Inalén (Aboriginal) to be close by.

Inari (Finnish) lake.

Inca (Spanish) ruler. History: a Quechuan people from highland Peru who established an empire from northern Ecuador to central Chile before being conquered by the Spanish.

Indalecia (Latin) compassionate lady.

Indamira, Indemira (Arabic) the guest of the princess.

India (Sanskrit) river. Geography: a country of southern Asia.

Indiana BG (American) Geography: a state in the north-central United States.

Indíana (American) a form of Indiana.

Indigo (Latin) dark blue color.

Indira (Hindi) splendid. History: Indira Nehru Gandi was an Indian politician and prime minister.

Indya (Sanskrit) a form of India.

Ines, Inez (Spanish) forms of Agnes.

Inês (Portuguese) a form of Ines.

Inéz (Spanish) a form of Ines.

Infantita (Spanish) immaculate child.

Infiniti (Latin) a form of Infinity.

Infinity (Latin) infinity.

Inga (Scandinavian) a short form of Ingrid.

Ingrid (Scandinavian) hero's daughter; beautiful daughter.

Iniga (Latin) fiery, ardent.

Inmaculada (Latin) immaculate.

Inoa (Hawaiian) name.

Inocencia (Spanish) innocent.

Inoceneia, Inocenta (Spanish) forms of Inocencia.

Inti (Quechua) sunshine. Mythology: Inca sun god.

Invención (Latin) invention.

Ió, Ioes (Greek) forms of Iola.

Ioana (Romanian) a form of Joan.

Iola (Greek) dawn; violet colored. (Welsh) worthy of the Lord.

Iolana (Hawaiian) soaring like a hawk.

Iolanthe (English) a form of Yolanda.

Iona (Greek) violet flower.

Iosune (Basque) a form of Jesus.

Iphigenia (Greek) sacrifice. Mythology: the daughter of the Greek leader Agamemnon.

Ipi (Mapuche) harvester; careful.

Iquerne (Spanish) visitation.

Ira BG (Hebrew) watchful. (Russian) a short form of Irina.

Iracema (Tupi) from where the honey comes.

Iragarzte (Basque) annunciation.

Iraida, Iraides, Iraís (Greek) descendent of Hera.

Irakusne (Basque) a form of Estefania.

Irati (Navarro) Geography: a jungle of Navarra, Spain.

Iratze (Basque) reference to the Virgin Mary.

Ireland (Irish) Geography: an island in the North Atlantic to the west of Great Britain.

Irena (Russian) a form of Irene.

Irene (Greek) peaceful. Mythology: the goddess of peace.

Ireny (Greek) a familiar form of Irene.

Iria (English) lady.

Iridia (Latin) belonging to Iris.

Iriel (Hebrew) God is my light.

Irimia (Spanish) Geography: where the Miño River starts.

Irina (Russian) a form of Irene.

Iris (Greek) rainbow. Mythology: the goddess of the rainbow and messenger of the gods.

Irma (Latin) a form of Erma. (German) a short form of Irmgaard.

Irmã (Portuguese) a form of Irma.

Irma de la Paz (Spanish) peaceful Irma.

Irmgaard (German) noble.

Irmine (Latin) noble.

Irta (Russian) a form of Rita.

Irune (Basque) reference to the Holy Trinity.

Irupe, Irupé (Guarani) irupe flower.

Irvette (Irish) attractive. (Welsh) white river. (English) sea friend.

Isa BG (Spanish) a short form of Isabel.

Isabeau (French) a form of Isabel.

Isabel (Spanish) consecrated to God.

Isabela (Italian) a form of Isabel.

Isabelina (Hebrew) a form of Isabel.

Isabell, Isabelle ✨ (French) forms of Isabel.

Isabella ✨ (Italian) a form of Isabel.

Isadora (Latin) gift of Isis.

Isaldina, Isolina (German) powerful warrior.

Isamar (Hebrew) a form of Itamar.

Isaura (Greek) native of Isauria, an ancient region in Asia Minor.

Isberga (German) a form of Ismelda.

Isel (Scottish) a short form of Isela.

Isela (Scottish) a form of Isla.

Iselda (German) she who remains faithful.

Iseult (Welsh) Literature: also known as Isolde, a princess in the Arthurian legends; a heroine of medieval romance.

Isha **(American) a form of Aisha.**

Ishi (Japanese) rock.

Isi (Spanish) a short form of Isabel.

Isibeal (Irish) a form of Isabel.

Isis (Egyptian) supreme goddess. Mythology: the goddess of nature and fertility.

Isla (Scottish) Geography: the River Isla in Scotland.

Isleta (Spanish) small island.

Ismaela (Hebrew) God will hear.

Ismelda (German) she who battles with sword.

Ismena (Greek) wise.

Isobel (Spanish) a form of Isabel.

Isoka (Benin) gift from God.

Isolde (Welsh) fair lady. Literature: also known as Iseult, a princess in the Arthurian legends; a heroine of medieval romance.

Isona (Spanish) a form of Isabel.

Isra (Iranian) rainbow.

Issie (Spanish) a familiar form of Isabel.

Ita (Irish) thirsty.
Itah

Italia (Italian) from Italy.

Italina (Italian) a form of Italia.

Itamar (Hebrew) palm **island.**

Itatay (Guarani) hand bell.

Itati, Itatí (Guarani) white rock.

Itotia (Nahuatl) dance.

Itsaso (Basque) sea.

Itsel (Spanish) a form of Itzel.

Itxaro (Spanish) hope.

Itzal (Basque) shadow.

Itzayana (Spanish) a form of Itzel.

Itzel (Spanish) protected.

Itziar (Basque) high area covered by pines overlooking the ocean.

Iuitl (Nahuatl) feather.

Iulene (Basque) soft.

Iva (Slavic) a short form of Ivana.

Ivana (Slavic) God is gracious.

Ivanna (Slavic) a form of Ivana.

Iverem (Tiv) good fortune; blessing.

Iverna (Latin) from Ireland.

Iveta (French) a form of Yvette.

Ivette (French) a form of Yvette.

Ivey (English) a form of Ivy.

Ivon (French) a form of Ivonne.

Ivón (Spanish) a form of Ivonne.

Ivonne (French) a form of Yvonne.

Ivory GB (Latin) made of ivory.

Ivria (Hebrew) from the land of Abraham.

Ivy (English) ivy tree.

Ixcatzin (Nahuatl) like cotton.

Ixtli (Nahuatl) face.

Iyabo (Yoruba) mother has returned.

Iyana, Iyanna (Hebrew) forms of Ian.

Iyesha (American) a form of Iesha.

Izabella (Spanish) a form of Isabel.

Izar, Izarra, Izarre (Basque) star.

Izarbe (Aragonese) Virgin Mary of the Pyrenees Mountains.

Izaskum (Basque) above the valley.

Izazcun, Izazkun (Spanish) reference to the Virgin Mary.

Izel (Nahuatl) unique.

Iziar (Basque) name of the Virgin Mary.

Izusa (Native American) white stone.

J

Ja BG (Korean) attractive. (Hawaiian) fiery.

Ja'lisa (American) a form of Jalisa.

Ja'nae (American) a form of Janae.

Jaafar (Arabic) small stream.

Jaamini (Hindi) evening.

Jabel (Hebrew) flowing stream.

Jabrea, Jabria (American) combinations of the prefix Ja + Brea.

Jacalyn (American) a form of Jacqueline.

Jacarandá (Tupi) fragrant flower.

Jacee, Jaci, Jacie (Greek) forms of Jacey.

Jacelyn (American) a form of Jocelyn.

Jacey GB (American) a combination of the

initials J. + C. (Greek) a familiar form of Jacinda.

Jacinda (Greek) beautiful, attractive. (Spanish) a form of Hyacinth.

Jacinta (Greek) a form of Jacinda.

Jacinthe (Spanish) a form of Jacinda.

Jackalyn (American) a form of Jacqueline.

Jackeline, Jackelyn (American) forms of Jacqueline.

Jacki (American) a familiar form of Jacqueline.

Jackie BG (American) a familiar form of Jacqueline.

Jackilyn (American) a form of Jacqueline.

Jacklyn, Jacklynn (American) short forms of Jacqueline.

Jackolyn (American) a form of Jacqueline.

Jackquel (French) a short form of Jacqueline.

Jackquelyn (French) a form of Jacqueline.

Jackson BG (English) child of Jack.

Jaclyn, Jaclynn (American) short forms of Jacqueline.

Jacob BG (Hebrew) supplanter, substitute.

Bible: son of Isaac, brother of Esau.

Jacobella (Italian) a form of Jacobi.

Jacobi BG (Hebrew) a form of Jacob.

Jacolyn (American) a form of Jacqueline.

Jacqualine (French) a form of Jacqueline.

Jacqueena (French) a form of Jacqueline.

Jacquelin, Jacquelyn, Jacquelyne, Jacquelynn (French) forms of Jacqueline.

Jacqueline (French) supplanter, substitute; little Jacqui.

Jacquetta (French) a form of Jacqueline.

Jacqui (French) a short form of Jacqueline.

Jacquiline (French) a form of Jacqueline.

Jacqulin, Jacquline, Jacqulyn (American) forms of Jacqueline.

Jacy GB (American) a combination of the initials J. + C. (Greek) a familiar form of Jacinda.

Jacyline (French) a form of Jacqueline.

Jacynthe (Spanish) a form of Jacinda.

Jada (Hebrew) wise. (Spanish) a form of Jade.

Jade (Spanish) jade.

Jadelyn (American) a combination of Jade + Lynn.

Jaden BG (Spanish) a form of Jade.

Jadie (Spanish) a familiar form of Jade.
Jadi

Jadyn GB (Spanish) a form of Jade.

Jadzia (Spanish) a form of Jade.

Jae BG (Latin) jaybird. (French) a familiar form of Jacqueline.

Jaeda (Spanish) a form of Jada.

Jaedyn (Spanish) a form of Jade.

Jael GB (Hebrew) mountain goat; climber.

Jaela (Hebrew) a form of Jael.

Jaelyn, Jaelynn (American) combinations of Jae + Lynn.

Jaffa (Hebrew) a form of Yaffa.

Jaha (Swahili) dignified.

Jahaira (Swahili) a form of Jaha.

Jahna (American) a form of Johna.

Jai BG (Tai) heart. (Latin) a form of Jaye.

Jaid, Jaide (Spanish) forms of Jade.

83

Jaida (Hebrew, Spanish) a form of Jada.

Jaiden BG (Spanish) a form of Jade.

Jaidyn (Spanish) a form of Jade.

Jaila (Hebrew) a form of Jael.

Jailene (American) a form of Jaelyn.

Jailyn (American) a form of Jaelyn.

Jaime BG (French) I love.

Jaimee, Jaimi, Jaimie (French) forms of Jaime.

Jaimica (Spanish) a form of James.

Jaimilynn (English) a combination of Jaime + Lynn.

Jaina (Hebrew, American) a form of Janae.

Jaione (Spanish) reference to the nativity.

Jaira (Spanish) Jehovah teaches.

Jakalyn (American) a form of Jacqueline.

Jakeisha (American) a combination of Jakki + Aisha.

Jakelin (American) a form of Jacqueline.

Jakeria (American) a form of Jacki.

Jakia (American) a form of Jacki.

Jakinda (Spanish) a form of Jacinda.

Jakki (American) a form of Jacki.

Jakolyn (American) a form of Jacqueline.

Jakqueline (French) a form of Jacqueline.

Jakyra (American) a form of Jacki.

Jala (Iranian) brightness. (Arabic) clarity, elucidation.

Jalea, Jalia (American) combinations of Jae + Leah.

Jalecia (American) a form of Jalisa.

Jaleesa (American) a form of Jalisa.

Jalen BG (American) a short form of Jalena.

Jalena (American) a combination of Jane + Lena.

Jalene BG (American) a form of Jalena.

Jalesa, Jalessa (American) forms of Jalisa.

Jalicia, Jalisha (American) forms of Jalisa.

Jalila (Arabic) great.

Jalinda (American) a combination of Jae + Linda.

Jalini (Hindi) lives next to the ocean.

Jalisa, Jalissa (American) combinations of Jae + Lisa.

Jaliyah (American) a combination of Jae + Aaliyah.

Jalyn GB (American) a combination of Jae + Lynn.

Jalynn (American) a combination of Jae + Lynn.

Jalysa (American) a form of Jalisa.

Jama (Sanskrit) daughter.

Jamaica (Spanish) Geography: an island in the Caribbean.

Jamani (American) a form of Jami.

Jamara (American) a form of Jamaria.

Jamaria (American) a combination of Jae + Maria.

Jamecia (Spanish) a form of Jamaica.

Jamee (French) a form of Jaime.

Jameela (Arabic) a form of Jamila.

Jameika (Spanish) a form of Jamaica.

Jameisha (American) a form of Jami.

Jameka (Spanish) a form of Jamaica.

Jamekia (Spanish) a form of Jamaica.

Jamelia (Arabic) a form of Jamila.

James BG (Hebrew) supplanter, substitute. (English) a form of Jacob. Bible: James the Great and James the Less were two of the Twelve Apostles.

Jamese (American) a form of Jami.

Jamesha (American) a form of Jami.

Jameshia (American) a form of Jami.

Jamesia (American) a form of Jami.

Jamey GB (English) a form of Jami.

Jami (Hebrew, English) a form of James.

Jamia (English) a form of Jami.

Jamica, Jamika (Spanish) forms of Jamaica.

Jamie GB (Hebrew, English) a form of James.

Jamie-Lee (American) a form of Jamilee.

Jamie-Lynn (American) a form of Jamilynn.

Jamila (Arabic) beautiful.

Jamilah, Jamilla (Arabic) forms of Jamillah, Jamila.

Jamilee (English) a combination of Jami + Lee.

Jamilia (Arabic) a form of Jamila.

Jamilynn (English) a combination of Jami + Lynn.

Jamira (American) a form of Jamaria.

Jamisha (American) a form of Jami.

Jamison BG (English) child of James.

Jamiya (English) a form of Jami.

Jammie (American) a form of Jami.

Jamonica (American) a combination of Jami + Monica.

Jamya (English) a form of Jami.

Jamylin (American) a form of Jamilynn.

Jan BG (English) a short form of Jane, Janet, Janice.

Jana (Hebrew) gracious, merciful. (Slavic) a form of Jane.

Janae (American) a form of Jane. (Hebrew) a form of Jana.

Janaé (American, Hebrew) a form of Janae.

Janai (American) a form of Janae.

Janaki (Hindi) mother.

Janalee (American) a combination of Jana + Lee.

Janalynn (American) a combination of Jana + Lynn.

Janan (Arabic) heart; soul.

Janay, Janaye (American) forms of Jane. (Hebrew, Arabic) forms of Janna.

Janaya (American) a form of Jane. (Hebrew, Arabic) a form of Janna.

Jane (Hebrew) God is gracious. Janea, Janee **(American) forms of Janae.**

Janecia (Hebrew, English) a form of Janice.

Janeen (French) a form of Janine.

Janeisha (American) a form of Janessa.

Janel, Janell, Jannell, Jannelle (French) forms of Janelle.

Janelle (French) a form of Jane.

Janelly, Janely (French) forms of Janelle.

Janese (Hebrew) a form of Janis. (English) a form of Jane.

Janesha (American) a form of Janessa.

Janessa (American) a form of Jane.

Janet (English) a form of Jane.

Janeth (English) a form of Janet.

85

Janett, Janette, Jannet, Jannette (French) forms of Janet.

Janetta (French) a form of Janet.

Janey, Jani, Janie, Jany (English) familiar forms of Jane.

Jania (Hebrew) a form of Jana. (Slavic) a form of Jane.

Janica (Hebrew) a form of Jane.

Janice (Hebrew) God is gracious. (English) a familiar form of Jane.

Janick (Slavic) a short form of Janica.

Janiece (Hebrew, English) a form of Janice.

Janik (Slavic) a short form of Janika.

Janika (Slavic) a form of Jane.

Janina (French) a form of Jane.

Janine (French) a form of Jane.

Janiqua (French) a form of Jane.

Janique (French) a form of Jane.

Janis GB (Hebrew, English) a form of Janice.

Janise (Hebrew, English) a form of Janice.

Janisha (American) a form of Janessa.

Janita (American) a form of Juanita. .

Janiya (American) a combination of Jan or Jane + Mariah.

Janna (Arabic) harvest of fruit. (Hebrew) a short form of Johana.

Jannah (Hebrew, English) a form of Janna.

Jannali (Australian) moon.

Jannick (Slavic) a form of Janick.

Jannie (English) a familiar form of Jan, Jane.

Japonica (Latin) from Japan. Botany: an ornamental shrub with red flowers native to Japan.

Jaquana (American) a combination of Jacqueline + Anna.

Jaquelen, Jaquelin, Jaqueline, Jaquelyn (French) forms of Jacqueline.

Jaquetta (French) a form of Jacqui.

Jaquiline (French) a form of Jacqueline.

Jaquinda (Spanish) a form of Jacinda.

Jaquita (French) a form of Jacqui.

Jardena (French, Spanish) garden. (Hebrew) a form of Jordan.

Jarian (American) a combination of Jane + Marian.

Jarita (Arabic) earthen water jug.

Jarmilla (Slavic) a form of Yarmilla.

Jarnila (Arabic) beautiful.

Jarvia (German) skilled with a spear.

Jarvinia (German) intelligent; keen as a spear.

Jas BG (American) a short form of Jasmine.

Jasa (Polish) a form of Jane.

Jasey (Polish) a form of Jane.

Jasia (Polish) a form of Jane.

Jaskiran (Sikh) a form of Jaskaran

Jasleen (Latin) a form of Jocelyn.

Jaslyn (Latin) a form of Jocelyn.

Jasma (Persian) a short form of Jasmine.

Jasmain, Jasmaine (Persian) forms of Jasmine.

Jasman (Persian) a form of Jasmine.

Jasmarie (American) a combination of Jasmine + Marie.

Jasmeen (Persian) a form of Jasmine.

Jasmeet BG (Persian) a form of Jasmine.

Jasmin (Persian) a form of Jasmine.

Jasmina (Persian) a form of Jasmine.

Jasmine ✵ (Persian) jasmine flower. **Jasmyn, Jasmyne, Jassmine** (Persian) forms of Jasmine.

Jasone (Basque) assumption.

Jasper BG (French) red, yellow, or brown ornamental stone.

Jaspreet BG (Punjabi) virtuous.

Jassi (Persian) a familiar form of Jasmine.

Jatara (American) a combination of Jane + Tara.

Javán (Hebrew) from Greece.

Javana (Malay) from Java.

Javiera (Spanish) owner of a new house.

Javon BG (Malay) a short form of Javana.

Javona, Javonna (Malay) forms of Javana.

Jaya (Hindi) victory.

Jayanna (American) a combination of Jaye + Anna.

Jayce BG (American) a form of Jacey.

Jaycee, Jayci, Jaycie (American) forms of Jacey.

Jayda (Spanish) a form of Jada.

Jayde GB (Spanish) a form of Jade.

Jaydee (American) a combination of the initials J. + D.

Jayden BG (Spanish) a form of Jade.

Jaydon BG (Spanish) a form of Jayden.

Jaye BG (Latin) jaybird.

Jayla (American) a short form of Jayleen.

Jaylee GB (American) a familiar form of Jaylyn.

Jayleen, Jaylene (American) forms of Jaylyn.

Jaylen BG (American) a form of Jaylyn.

Jaylin GB (American) a form of Jaylyn.

Jaylyn BG (American) a combination of Jaye + Lynn. Jaylynn **(American) a combination of Jaye + Lynn.**

Jayme GB (English) a form of Jami.

Jaymee, Jaymi, Jaymie (English) forms of Jami.

Jayna (Hebrew) a form of Jane.

Jayne (Hindi) victorious. (English) a form of Jane.

Jaynee, Jaynie (English) familiar forms of Jayne.

Jazlyn, Jazlynn, Jazzlyn (American) combinations of Jazman + Lynn.

Jazman, Jazmen, Jazmin, Jazmyn (Persian) forms of Jasmine.

Jazmín (Arabic) a form of Jasmine.

Jazz BG (American) jazz.

Jean BG (Scottish) God is gracious.

Jeana, Jeanna (Scottish) forms of Jean.

Jeanelle (American) a form of Jenell.

Jeanetta (French) a form of Jean.

Jeanette, Jeannett, Jeannette (French) forms of Jean.

Jeanie, Jeannie (Scottish) familiar forms of Jean.

Jeanine, Jeannine, Jenine (Scottish) forms of Jean.

Jeanne (Scottish) a form of Jean.

Jelani BG (Russian) a form of Jelena.

Jelena (Russian) a form of Helen.

Jelisa (American) a combination of Jean + Lisa.

Jelissa (American) a form of Jelisa.

Jem GB (Hebrew) a short form of Jemima.

Jemila (Arabic) a form of Jamila.

Jemima (Hebrew) dove.

Jemina, Jenima (Hebrew) forms of Jemima.

Jemma (Hebrew) a short form of Jemima. (English) a form of Gema.

Jena, Jennah (Arabic) forms of Jenna.

Jenae, Jenay (American, Hebrew) forms of Janae. (Arabic) forms of Jenna.

Jenara (Latin) dedicated to the god Janus.

Jenaya (American, Hebrew) a form of Janae. (Arabic) a form of Jenna.

Jendaya (Zimbabwean) thankful.

Jendayi (Egyptian) a form of Jendaya.

Jeneleah (American) a combination of Jenny + Leah.

Jenell, Jenelle, Jennelle (American) combinations of Jenny + Nell.

Jenessa (American) a form of Jenisa.

Jenette (French) a form of Jean.

Jeneva (French) a form of Geneva.

Jeni, Jenni, Jennie (Welsh) familiar forms of Jennifer.

Jenica, Jenika, Jennica, Jennicah (Romanian) forms of Jane.

Jenice, Jenise (Hebrew) forms of Janice.

Jenifer, Jeniffer, Jenniffer (Welsh) forms of Jennifer.

Jenilee, Jennilee (American) combinations of Jeni + Lee. .

Jenisa (American) a combination of Jennifer + Nisa.

Jenka (Czech) a form of Jane.

Jenna (Arabic) small bird. (Welsh) a short form of Jennifer.

Jenna-Lee, Jennalee (American) combinations of Jenna + Lee.

Jennafer (Welsh) a form of Jennifer.

Jennifer (Welsh) white wave; white phantom. A form of Guinevere.

Jennilyn, Jennilynn (American) combinations of Jeni + Lynn.

Jenny (Welsh) a familiar form of Jennifer.

Jenny Lee (American) a combination of Jenny + Lee

Jennyfer (Welsh) a form of Jennifer.

Jensen GB (Scandinavian) a form of Janson

Jensine (Welsh) a form of Jeni.

Jeraldine (English) a form of Geraldine.

Jeremia (Hebrew) God will uplift.

Jereni **(Russian) a form of Irene.**

Jeri, Jerri, Jerrie (American) short forms of Jeraldine. Jerica, Jericka, Jerika, Jerrica.

Jerrika (American) combinations of Jeri + Erica.

Jerilyn (American) a combination of Jeri + Lynn.

Jermaine BG (French) a form of Germaine.

Jermeka (French) a form of Jermaine.

Jeroma (Latin) holy.

Jerónima (Greek) a form of Jeroma.

Jerusalem (Hebrew) vision of peace.

Geography: Jerusalem is a holy city in Israel.

Jerusalén (Spanish) a form of Jerusalem.

Jerusha (Hebrew) inheritance.

Jesenia, Jessenia (Arabic) flower.

Jesi, Jessye (Hebrew) forms of Jessie.

Jesica, Jesika, Jessicca, Jessika (Hebrew) forms of Jessica.

Jésica (Slavic) a form of Jessica.

Jessa (American) a short form of Jessalyn, Jessamine, Jessica.

Jessalyn (American) a combination of Jessica + Lynn.

Jessamine (French) a form of Jasmine.

Jesse BG (Hebrew) a form of Jessie.

Jesseca (Hebrew) a form of Jessica.

Jessi GB (Hebrew) a form of Jessie.

Jessica (Hebrew) wealthy. Literature: a name perhaps invented by Shakespeare for a character in his play *The Merchant of Venice*

Jessica-Lynn (American) a combination of Jessica + Lynn.

Jessie GB (Hebrew) a short form of Jessica. (Scottish) a form of Janet.

Jessilyn (American) a form of Jessalyn.

Jesslyn (American) a short form of Jessalyn.

Jessy BG (Hebrew) a short form of Jessica. (Scottish) a form of Janet.

Jessyca, Jessyka (Hebrew) forms of Jessica.

Jesus BG (Hebrew) God is my salvation. A form of Joshua. Bible: son of Mary and Joseph, believed by Christians to be the Son of God.

Jesusa (Spanish) a form of Jesus.

Jésusa (Spanish) a form of Jesus.

Jetta (English) jet black mineral. (American) a familiar form of Jevette.

Jevette (American) a combination of Jean + Yvette.

Jewel (French) precious gem.

Jewelana (American) a combination of Jewel + Anna.

Jewell (French) a form of Jewel.

Jezabel (Hebrew) a form of Jezebel.

Jezebel (Hebrew) unexalted; impure. Bible: the wife of King Ahab.

Jianna (Italian) a form of Giana.

Jibon (Hindi) life.

Jill (English) a short form of Jillian.

Jillaine (Latin) a form of Jillian.

Jillanna (Latin) a form of Jillian.

Jilleen (Irish) a form of Jillian.

Jilli (Australian) today.

Jillian (Latin) youthful.

Jimena (Hebrew, American) a form of Jimi.

Jimi BG (Hebrew) supplanter, substitute.

Jimisha (American) a combination of Jimi + Aisha.

Jin BG (Japanese) tender. (American) a short form of Ginny, Jinny.

Jina GB (Swahili) baby with a name. (Italian) a form of Gina.

Jinny (Scottish) a familiar form of Jenny. (American) a familiar form of Virginia.

Jira (African) related by blood.

Jirakee (Australian) waterfall, cascade.

Jirina (Czech) a form of Georgia.

Jizelle (American) a form of Giselle.

Jo GB (American) a short form of Joana, Jolene, Josephine.

Joan GB (Hebrew) God is gracious. History: Joan of Arc was a fifteenth-century heroine and resistance fighter.

Joana, Joanna (English) forms of Joan

Joanie, Joannie, Joanny, Joany (Hebrew) familiar forms of Joan.

Joann, Joanne (English) forms of Joan.

Joaquina (Hebrew) God will establish.

Joba (Hebrew) a form of Joby.

Jobeth (English) a combination of Jo + Beth.

Jobina (Hebrew) a form of Joby.

Joby BG (Hebrew) afflicted. (English) a familiar form of Jobeth.

Jocacia (American) a combination of Joy + Acacia.

Jocelin, Joceline, Jocelyne, Jocelynn (Latin) forms of Jocelyn.

Jocelín, Joselín (Latin) forms of Jocelyn.

Jocelyn (Latin) joyous. .

Joclyn (Latin) a short form of Jocelyn.

Jocosa, Jocose (Latin) jubilant.

Jodee, Jodi, Jodie (American) familiar forms of Judith.

Jodiann (American) a combination of Jodi (see Jodee) + Ann.

Jody BG (American) a familiar form of Judith.

Joelle (Hebrew) God is willing.

Joelynn (American) a combination of Joelle + Lynn.

Joey BG (American) a familiar form of Jo.

Johana, Johanna, Johannah (German) forms of Joana.

Johanie, Johannie, Johanny (Hebrew) forms of Joanie.

Johanne (German) a short form of Johana. A form of Joann.

Johna, Johnna (American) forms of Joana, Johana.

Johnae (American) a form of Janae.

Johnesha (American) a form of Johnnessa.

Johnetta (American) a form of Jonita.

Johnisha (American) a form of Johnnessa.

Johnnessa (American) a combination of Johna + Nessa.

Johnnie BG (Hebrew) a form of Joanie.

Joi, Joie (Latin) forms of Joy.

Jokia (Swahili) beautiful robe.

Jolan (Hungarian) violet blossom.

Jolanda (Greek) a form of Yolanda. **Jolee** (French) a form of Jolie.

Joleen, Joline (English) forms of Jolene.

Jolena (Hebrew) a form of Jolene.

Jolene (Hebrew) God will add, God will increase. (English) a form of Josephine.

Jolie (French) pretty.

Jolisa (American) a combination of Jo + Lisa.

Jolyane (English) a form of Jolene.

Jolyn, Jolynn (American) combinations of Jo + Lynn.

Jona (Hebrew) a short form of Jonina.

Jonae (American, Hebrew) a form of Janae. A form of Jona.

Jonatha (Hebrew) a form of Jonathan.

Jonathan BG (Hebrew) gift of God. Bible: the son of King Saul who became a loyal friend of David.

Jonell, Jonelle (American) combinations of Joan + Elle.

Jonesha (American) a form of Jonatha.

Joni (American) a familiar form of Joan.

Jonika (American) a form of Janika.

Jonina (Hebrew) dove.

Jonisha (American) a form of Jonatha.

Jonita (Hebrew) a form of Jonina.

Jonna (American) a form of Joana, Johana.

Jonni, Jonnie (American) familiar forms of Joan.

Jonquil (Latin, English) Botany: an ornamental plant with fragrant yellow flowers.

Jontel (American) a form of Johna.

Jora GB (Hebrew) autumn rain.

Jordain, Jordane (Hebrew) forms of Jordan.

Jordan BG (Hebrew) descending.

Jordana, Jordanna (Hebrew) forms of Jordan.

Jordann, Jordanne, Jordyne, Jordynn (Hebrew) forms of Jordan.

Jorden BG (Hebrew) a form of Jordan.

Jordin, Jordyn GB (Hebrew) forms of Jordan.

Jordon BG (Hebrew) a form of Jordan.

Jorgelina (Greek) she who works well in the countryside.

Jori, Jorie (Hebrew) familiar forms of Jordan.

Joriann (American) a combination of Jori + Ann.

Jorja (American) a form of Georgia.

Jory BG (Hebrew) a familiar form of Jordan.

Josafata (Hebrew) God will judge.

Josalyn, Jossalin (Latin) forms of Jocelyn.

Joscelin, Joscelyn (Latin) forms of Jocelyn.

Jose BG (Spanish) a form of Joseph.

Josee, Josée (American) familiar forms of Josephine.

Josefina (Spanish) a form of Josephine.

Joselin, Joseline, Joselyn, Joselyne, Josselyn (Latin) forms of Jocelyn.

Joselle (American) a form of Jizelle.

Joseph BG (Hebrew) God will add, God will increase. Bible: in the Old Testament, the son of Jacob who came to rule Egypt; in the New Testament, the husband of Mary.

Josepha (German) a form of Josephine.

Josephina (French) a form of Josephine.

Josephine (French) a form of Joseph.

Josette (French) a familiar form of Josephine.

Josey GB (Hebrew) a familiar form of Josephine.

Joshann (American) a combination of Joshlyn + Ann.

Joshelle (American) a combination of Joshlyn + Elle.

Joshlyn (Latin) a form of Jocelyn. (Hebrew) a form of Joshua.

Joshua BG (Hebrew) God is my salvation. Bible: led

the Israelites into the Promised Land.

Josi, Josie, Jossie (Hebrew) familiar forms of Josephine.

Josiane, Josiann, Josianne (American) combinations of Josie (see Josi) + Ann.

Josilin, Josilyn (Latin) forms of Jocelyn.

Joslin, Joslyn, Joslynn (Latin) short forms of Jocelyn.

Jossline (Latin) a form of Jocelyn.

Josune (Spanish) a form of Jesus.

Jourdan GB (Hebrew) a form of Jordan.

Journey (English) travel or trip.

Jovana (Latin) a form of Jovanna.

Jovanna (Latin) majestic. (Italian) a form of Giovanna. Mythology: Jove, also known as Jupiter, was the supreme Roman god.

Jovannie (Italian) a familiar form of Jovanna.

Jovi (Latin) a short form of Jovita.

Joviana (Latin) a form of Jovanna.

Jovina (Latin) a form of Jovanna.

Jovita (Latin) jovial.

Joxepa (Hebrew) a form of Josefina.

Joy (Latin) joyous.

Joya (Latin) a form of Joy.

Joyann, Joyanne (American) combinations of Joy + Ann.

Joyce (Latin) joyous. A short form of Joycelyn.

Joycelyn (American) a form of Jocelyn.

Joyceta (Spanish) a form of Joyce.

Joylyn (American) a combination of Joy + Lynn.

Jozephine (French) a form of Josephine.

Jozie (Hebrew) a familiar form of Josephine.

Juana (Spanish) a short form of Juanita.

Juana del Pilar (Spanish) Juana of the pillar.

Juandalyn (Spanish) a form of Juanita.

Juaneta (Spanish) a form of Juana.

Juanita (Spanish) a form of Jane, Joan.

Jubilee (Latin) joyful celebration.

Juci (Hungarian) a form of Judy.

Jucunda (Latin) pleasant.

Judine (Hebrew) a form of Judith.

Judith (Hebrew) praised. Mythology: the slayer of Holofernes, according to ancient Jewish legend.

Judy (Hebrew) a familiar form of Judith.

Judyann (American) a combination of Judy + Ann.

Jula (Polish) a form of Julia.

Julee (English) a form of Julie.

Julene (Basque) a form of Julia. .

Julia ★ (Latin) youthful. .

Julian BG (English) a form of Julia.

Juliana (Czech, Spanish) a form of Julia.

Juliane, Juliann, Julianne (English) forms of Julia.

Julianna (Hungarian) a form of Julia. Julie **(English) a form of Julia.**

Julie Ann, Julie Anne, Julieann (American) combinations of Julie + Ann.

Julieanna (American) a form of Juliana.

Julienne (English) a form of Julia.

Juliet, Juliette (French) forms of Julia.

Julieta (French) a form of Julia.

Julisa, Julissa (Latin) forms of Julia.

Julita (Spanish) a form of Julia.

Jullian BG (English) a form of Julia.

Jumaris (American) a combination of Julie + Maris.

Jun BG (Chinese) truthful.

June (Latin) born in the sixth month.

Junee (Latin) a familiar form of June.

Juniper (English) Botany: an evergreen shrub or tree that belongs to the pine family.

Juno (Latin) queen. Mythology: the supreme Roman goddess.

Jupita (Latin) Mythology: Jupiter is the supreme Roman god and the husband of Juno. Astronomy: Jupiter is the largest planet in the solar system and the fifth planet from the sun.

Jurisa (Slavic) storm.

Jurnee (American) a form of Journey.

Justa (Latin) a short form of Justina, Justine.

Justice GB (Latin) a form of Justin.

Justin BG (Latin) just, righteous.

Justina (Italian) a form of Justine. .

Justine (Latin) a form of Justin.

Justiniana (Spanish) a form of Justine.

Justis BG (Latin) a form of Justice.

Justise, Justyce (Latin) forms of Justice.

Justus BG (Latin) a form of Justice.

Justyna (Italian) a form of Justine.

Justyne (Latin) a form of Justine.

Juvencia (Latin) a form of Juventina.

Juventa (Greek) a form of Juventina.

Juventina (Latin) youth.

Jyllian (Latin) a form of Jillian.

K

Ka'la (Arabic) a form of Kala.

Kacee, Kaci, Kacie (Irish, American) forms of Kacey.

Kacey GB (Irish) brave. (American) a form of Casey. A combination of the initials K. + C.

Kachina (Native American) sacred dancer.

Kacia (Greek) a short form of Acacia.

Kacy GB (Irish) brave. (American) a form of Casey. A combination of the initials K. + C.

Kadedra (American) a combination of Kady + Dedra.

Kadee, Kadi, Kadie (English) forms of Kady.

Kadeejah (Arabic) a form of Kadijah.

Kadeesha (American) a form of Kadesha.

Kadeidra (American) a form of Kadedra.

Kadeija (Arabic) a form of Kadijah.

Kadeisha (American) a form of Kadesha.

Kadeja, Kadejah (Arabic) forms of Kadijah.

Kadelyn (American) a combination of Kady + Lynn.

Kadesha (American) a combination of Kady + Aisha.

Kadeshia (American) a form of Kadesha.

Kadesia (American) a form of Kadesha.

Kadija (Arabic) a form of Kadijah.

Kadijah (Arabic) trustworthy.

Kadisha (American) a form of Kadesha.

Kady (English) a form of Katy. A combination of the initials K. + D.

Kae (Greek, Teutonic, Latin) a form of Kay.

Kaedé (Japanese) maple leaf.

Kaela (Hebrew, Arabic) beloved, sweetheart. A short form of Kalila, Kelila.

Kaelee, Kaeleigh, Kaeley, Kaeli, Kaelie, Kaely (American) forms of Kaela.

Kaelen BG (American) a form of Kaelyn.

Kaelin BG (American) a form of Kaelyn.

Kaelyn (American) a combination of Kae + Lynn.

Kaelynn (American) a form of Kaelyn.

Kaetlyn (Irish) a form of Kaitlin.

Kaferine (Greek) a form of Katherine.

Kafleen (Irish) a form of Kathleen.

Kagami (Japanese) mirror.

Kahla (Arabic) a form of Kala.

Kahli (American) a form of Kalee.

Kahsha (Native American) fur robe.

Kai BG (Hawaiian) sea. (Hopi, Navajo) willow tree.

Kaia (Greek) earth.

Kaija (Greek) a form of Kaia.

Kaila (Hebrew) laurel; crown.

Kailah (Hebrew) a form of Kaila.

Kailani (Hawaiian) sky. .

Kaile, Kailee, Kaileigh, Kailey, Kailie, Kaily (American) familiar forms of Kaila. Forms of Kaylee.

Kaileen (American) a form of Kaitlin.

Kailen GB (American) a form of Kaitlin.

Kaili GB (American) a familiar form of Kaila. A form of Kaylee.

Kaimana (Hawaiian) diamond.

Kaimi (Hawaiian) seeker.

Kaira (Greek) a form of Kairos. (Greek, Danish) a form of Kara.

Kairos (Greek) opportunity.

Kaisa (Swedish) pure.

Kaisha (American) a short form of Kaishawn.

Kaishawn (American) a combination of Kai + Shawna.

Kaitlan, Kaitlen, Kaitlinn, Kaitlyne,

Kaitlynn, Kaitlynne (Irish) forms of Kaitlin.

Kaitland (Irish) a form of Caitlin.

Kaitlin (Irish) pure.

Kaitlyn (Irish) a form of Kaitlin.

Kaiya (Japanese) forgiveness. (Aboriginal) a type of spear.

Kala GB (Arabic) a short form of Kalila. A form of Cala.

Kalah, Kalla (Arabic) forms of Kala.

Kalama BG (Hawaiian) torch.

Kalan BG (American) a form of Kaelyn, Kaylyn. (Hawaiian) a short form of Kalani. (Slavic) a form of Kallan.

Kalani GB (Hawaiian) chieftain; sky.

Kalare (Latin, Basque) bright; clear.

Kalasia (Tongan) graceful.

Kalauni (Tongan) crown.

Kalea GB (Hawaiian) bright; clear.

Kalee, Kaleigh, Kaley, Kalie, Kally, Kaly (American) forms of Calee, Kaylee. (Sanskrit, Hawaiian) forms of Kali. (Greek) forms of Kalli. (Arabic) familiar forms of Kalila.

Kaleen, Kalene
(Hawaiian) short forms of
Kalena.

Kaleena (Hawaiian) a form
of Kalena. (Slavic) a form
of Kalina.

Kalei (Hawaiian) flower
wreath.

Kalen BG (Slavic) a form of
Kallan.

Kalena (Hawaiian) pure.

Kalere (Swahili) short
woman.

Kali GB (Hindi) the black
one. (Hawaiian)
hesitating. Religion: a
form of the Hindu
goddess Devi. Kalia,

Kaliah (Hawaiian) forms of
Kalea.

Kalid (Arabic) a form of
Khalida.

Kalida (Spanish) a form of
Calida.

Kalifa (Somali) chaste;
holy.

Kalila (Arabic) beloved,
sweetheart.

Kalin BG (Slavic, Hawaiian)
a short form of Kalina.
(American) a form of
Kaelyn, Kaylyn.

Kalina (Slavic) flower.
(Hawaiian) a form of
Karen.

Kalinda (Hindi) sun.

Kalisa (American) a
combination of Kate +
Lisa.

Kalisha (American) a
combination of Kate +
Aisha.

Kaliska (Moquelumnan)
coyote chasing deer.

Kalissa (American) a form
of Kalisa.

Kalista, Kallista (Greek)
forms of Calista.

Kallan (Slavic) stream,
river.

Kalle BG (Finnish) a form
of Carol.

Kalli, Kallie (Greek) forms
of Calie. Familiar forms of
Kalista, Kalliope,
Kalliyan.

Kalliope (Greek) a form of
Calliope.

Kalliyan (Cambodian)
best.

Kallolee (Hindi) happy.

Kaloni (Tongan) fragrant;
perfume.

Kalonice (Greek) beauty's
victory.

Kaltha (English) marigold,
yellow flower.

Kaluwa (Swahili) forgotten
one.

Kalyca (Greek) rosebud. .

Kalyn GB (American) a
form of Kaylyn.

Kalynn (American) a form
of Kaylyn.

Kama (Sanskrit) loved one.
Religion: the Hindu god
of love.

Kamala (Hindi) lotus.

Kamalei (Hawaiian)
beloved child.

Kamali (Rhodesian) spirit
guide; protector.

Kamalynn, Kamalynne
(American) combinations
of Kama + Lynn.

Kamara (Swahili) a short
form of Kamaria.

Kamari BG (Swahili) a
short form of Kamaria.

Kamaria (Swahili)
moonlight.

Kamata (Moquelumnan)
gambler.

Kamballa (Australian)
young woman.

Kambria (Latin) a form of
Cambria.

Kamea (Hawaiian) one
and only; precious.

Kameke (Swahili) blind.

Kameko (Japanese) turtle
child. Mythology: the
turtle symbolizes
longevity.

Kameli (Hawaiian) honey.

Kamelia (Italian) a form of
Camelia.

Kameron BG (American) a
form of Cameron.

Kameryn (American) a
form of Cameron.

Kami GB (Japanese) divine
aura. (Italian, North

African) a short form of Kamila, Kamilah.

Kamie (Italian, North African, Japanese) a form of Kami.

Kamila (Slavic) a form of Camila. .

Kamilah (North African) perfect.

Kamille (Slavic) a short form of Kamila.

Kamiya (Hawaiian) a form of Kamea.

Kamri **(American) a short form of Kameron.** Kamry **(American) a form of Kamri.**

Kamryn GB (American) a short form of Kameron.

Kanani (Hawaiian) beautiful.

Kanda (Native American) magical power.

Kandace, Kandice (Greek) glittering white; glowing. (American) forms of Candace, Candice.

Kandi (American) a familiar form of Kandace.

Kandis, Kandyce (Greek, American) forms of Kandace.

Kandra (American) a form of Kendra.

Kane BG (Japanese) two right hands.

Kaneesha (American) a form of Keneisha.

Kaneisha (American) a form of Keneisha.

Kaneli (Tongan) canary yellow.

Kanene (Swahili) a little important thing.

Kanesha (American) a form of Keneisha.

Kani (Hawaiian) sound.

Kanika (Mwera) black cloth.

Kanisha (American) a form of Keneisha.

Kaniva (Tongan) Milky Way, universe, galaxy.

Kaniya (Hindi, Tai) a form of Kanya.

Kannitha (Cambodian) angel.

Kanoa BG (Hawaiian) free.

Kanya GB (Hindi) virgin. (Tai) young lady. Religion: a form of the Hindu goddess Devi.

Kapri (American) a form of Capri.

Kapua (Hawaiian) blossom.

Kapuki (Swahili) first-born daughter.

Kara (Greek, Danish) pure.

Karah (Greek, Danish) a form of Kara. (Irish, Italian) a form of Cara.

Karalana (English) a combination of Kara + Lana.

Karalee (English) a combination of Kara + Lee.

Karalyn (English) a form of Karalynn. (American) a form of Karolyn.

Karalynn (English) a combination of Kara + Lynn.

Kareela (Australian) southern wind.

Kareema (Arabic) a form of Karimah.

Kareen (Scandinavian) a short form of Karena. A form of Karin.

Kareena (Scandinavian) a form of Karena.

Karel BG (American) a form of Carol.

Karelle (American) a form of Carol.

Karely (American) a familiar form of Karel.

Karen (Greek) pure. **Karena** (Scandinavian) a form of Karen.

Karenza (Cornish) loving, affectionate. .

Karessa (French) a form of Caressa.

Karey GB (Greek, Danish) a form of Kari.

Kari (Greek) pure. (Danish) a form of

Caroline, Katherine.
Karia (Greek, Danish) a
form of Kari.

Kariane, Kariann,
Karianne (American)
combinations of Kari +
Ann.
Karida (Arabic)
untouched, pure.
Karie, Kary (Greek,
Danish) forms of Kari.
Karilyn, Karilynn
(American) combinations
of Kari + Lynn.
Karima (Arabic) a form of
Karimah.
Karimah (Arabic)
generous.
Karin (Scandinavian) a
form of Karen.
Karina (Russian) a form of
Karen.
Karine (Russian) a form of
Karen.
Karis (Greek) graceful.
Karisa, Karissa, Karrisa
(Greek) forms of Carissa.
Karishma (American) a
form of Karisma.
Karisma (Greek) divinely
favored.

Karla (German) a form of
Carla. (Slavic) a short
form of Karoline.

Karlee, Karleigh, Karli,
Karlie (American) forms
of Karley.

Karleen, Karlene
(American) forms of
Karla.
Karlena (American) a form
of Karleen.
Karley, Karly (Latin) little
and strong. (American)
forms of Carly.
Karlotte (American) a
form of Charlotte.
Karlyn (American) a form
of Karla.
Karma (Hindi) fate,
destiny; action.
Karmaine (French) a form
of Charmaine.
Karmel BG (Hebrew) a
form of Carmela.
Karmen (Latin) song.
Karmiti (Bantu) tree.
Karniela (Greek) cornel
tree. (Latin) horn colored.

Karol BG (Slavic) a form of
Carol.

Karol Ann, Karolane,
Karolann, Karolanne
(American) combinations
of Karol + Ann.
Karolina (Slavic) a form of
Carolina.
Karoline (Slavic) a form of
Caroline.
Karoll (Slavic) a form of
Carol.
Karolyn (American) a
form of Carolyn.
Karon BG (American) a
form of Karen.

Karra (Greek, Danish) a
form of Kara.
Karrah (Greek, Danish,
Irish, Italian) a form of
Karah.
Karri, Karrie (American)
forms of Carrie.

Karsen BG (English) child
of Kar. A form of Carson.

Karson BG (English) child
of Kar. A form of Carson.
Karsyn (English) child of
Kar. A form of Carson.
Karuna (Hindi) merciful.
Karyn (American) a form
of Karen.
Karyna (American) a form
of Karina.
Karyssa (Greek) a form of
Carissa.
Kasa (Hopi) fur robe.
Kasandra, Kassandra,
Kassandre (Greek)
forms of Cassandra.
Kasaundra, Kassaundra
(Greek) forms of
Kasandra.
Kasen BG (Danish) a form
of Katherine.
Kasey GB (Irish) brave.
(American) a form of
Casey, Kacey.
Kasha (Native American) a
form of Kahsha.
(American) a form of
Kashawna.

Kashawna (American) a combination of Kate + Shawna.

Kashmere (Sanskrit) a form of Kashmir.

Kashmir (Sanskrit) Geography: a region located between India and Pakistan.

Kasi (Hindi) from the holy city.

Kasia (Polish) a form of Katherine.

Kasidy (Irish) a form of Kassidy.

Kasie (Irish, American) a form of Kasey. (Hindi) a form of Kasi.

Kasimira (Slavic) a form of Casimira.

Kasinda (Umbundu) our last baby.

Kasondra, Kassondra (Greek) forms of Cassandra.

Kassey (American) a form of Kassi. (Irish, American) a form of Kasey.

Kassi, Kassie, Kassy (American) familiar forms of Kasandra, Kassidy.

Kassia (Polish) a form of Kasia. (American) a form of Kassi.

Kassidee, Kassidi (Irish, American) forms of Kassidy.

Kassidy GB (Irish) clever. (American) a form of Cassidy.

Katalina (Irish) a form of Caitlin.

Katarina (Czech) a form of Katherine.

Katarzyna (Czech) a form of Katherine.

Kate (Greek) pure. (English) a short form of Katherine.

Kate-Lynn (American) a combination of Kate + Lynn.

Katee, Katey (English) familiar forms of Kate, Katherine. Kateland **(Irish) a form of Caitlin.**

Katelee (American) a combination of Kate + Lee.

Katelin (Irish) a form of Caitlin.

Katelyn (Irish) a form of Katelin.

Katerina (Slavic) a form of Katherine.

Katerine (Slavic) a form of Katherine.

Katharina (Greek) a form of Katharine.

Katharine, Katharyn (Greek) forms of Katherine.

Katherin, Katheryn, Katheryne (Greek) forms of Katherine.

Katherina (Greek) a form of Katherine.

Katherine ⭐ (Greek) pure.

Kathi, Kathy (English) familiar forms of Katherine, Kathleen. Kathia,

Kathya (English) forms of Kathi.

Kathleen (Irish) a form of Katherine.

Kathlyn (Irish) a form of Kathleen.

Kathrin, Kathrine (Greek) forms of Katherine.

Kathrina (Danish) a form of Katherine.

Kathryn, Kathryne, Kathrynn (English) forms of Katherine.

Kati (Estonian) a familiar form of Kate.

Katia, Katya (Russian) forms of Katherine.

Katie (English) a familiar form of Kate.

Katie-Lynn (American) a combination of Katie + Lynn.

Katilyn (Irish) a form of Katlyn.

Katina (English, Russian) a form of Katherine.

Katixa (Basque) a form of Catalina.

Katja (Estonian) a form of Kate.

Katlin, Katlyne, Katlynn (Greek, Irish) forms of Katlyn.

Katlyn (Greek) pure. (Irish) a form of Katelin.

Katreen, Katrin, Katrine (English) forms of Katherine.

Katrena (German) a form of Katrina.

Katrice (German) a form of Katrina.

Katriel GB (Hebrew) God is my crown.

Katrina (German) a form of Katherine

Katrinelle (American) a combination of Katrina + Elle.

Katryna (German) a form of Katrina.

Kattie, Katty (English) familiar forms of Kate.

Katy (English) a familiar form of Kate.

Kaulana (Hawaiian) famous.

Kaveri (Hindi) Geography: a sacred river in India.

Kavindra (Hindi) poet.

Kavita (Indian) a poem.

Kawena (Hawaiian) glow.

Kay GB (Greek) rejoicer. (Teutonic) a fortified place. (Latin) merry. A short form of Katherine. Caye, Kaye

Kaya (Hopi) wise child. (Japanese) resting place.

Kayanna (American) a combination of Kay + Anna.

Kayce, Kaycee, Kayci, Kaycie, Kaysie (American) combinations of the initials K. + C.

Kaydee (American) a combination of the initials K. + D.

Kayden BG (American) a form of Kaydee.

Kayla (Arabic, Hebrew) laurel; crown. A form of Kaela, Kaila.

Kaylah (Arabic, Hebrew) a form of Kayla.

Kaylan GB (Hebrew) a form of Kayleen.

Kaylani (Hawaiian) a form of Kailani, Keilana.

Kayle GB (American) a form of Kaylee.

Kaylea (Hawaiian) a form of Kalea. (Arabic, Hebrew) a form of Kayla. Kayleah

Kaylee ⭐ (American) a form of Kayla.

Kayleen, Kaylene (Hebrew) beloved, sweetheart. Forms of Kayla.

Kayleigh, Kayley, Kayli, Kaylie (American) forms of Kaylee.

Kaylen GB (Hebrew) a form of Kayleen.

Kaylena (Hebrew) a form of Kayleen.

Kaylia (Arabic, Hebrew) a form of Kayla. (American) a form of Kaylee.

Kaylin GB (American) a form of Kaylyn.

Kaylon BG (American) a form of Kaylyn.

Kaylyn, Kaylynn, Kaylynne (American) combinations of Kay + Lynn. Kayte,

Kaytie (English) forms of Katy.

Kaytlin, Kaytlyn (Irish) forms of Kaitlin.

Kc BG (American) a combination of the initials K. + C.

KC BG (American) a combination of the initials K. + C.

Keagan BG (Irish) a form of Keegan.

Keaira, Keairra (Irish) forms of Keara.

Keala (Hawaiian) path.

Keana, Keanna (German) bold; sharp. (Irish) beautiful.

Keandra (American) a form of Kenda.

Keanu BG (German, Irish) a form of Keana.

Keara (Irish) dark; black.

Kearra (Irish) a form of Keara.

Kearsten, Kearstin, Kearston (Greek) forms of Kirsten.

Keasha (African) a form of Keisha.

Keaton BG (English) where hawks fly.

Kecia (American) a form of Keshia.

Keegan BG (Irish) little; fiery.

Keeley GB (Irish) a form of Kelly.

Keelin, Keelyn (Irish) forms of Kellyn.

Keely (Irish) a form of Kelly.

Keena (Irish) brave.

Keera (Irish) a form of Keara. (Persian, Latin) a form of Kira. (Greek) a form of Kyra.

Keesha (American) a form of Keisha.

Kei (Japanese) reverent.

Keiana, Keianna (Irish) forms of Keana. (American) forms of Kiana.

Keiara, Keiarra (Irish) forms of Keara.

Keiki (Hawaiian) child.

Keiko (Japanese) happy child.

Keila, Keilah (Arabic, Hebrew) forms of Kayla.

Keilana (Hawaiian) gloriously calm.

Keilani (Hawaiian) glorious chief.

Keily (Irish) a form of Keeley, Kiley.

Keiona, Keionna (Irish) forms of Keana.

Keiosha (American) a form of Keesha.

Keira, Keirra (Irish) forms of Keara.

Keirsten, Keirstin, Keirstyn (Greek) forms of Kirsten.

Keisha (African) favorite.

Keita (Scottish) woods; enclosed place.

Kekona (Hawaiian) second-born child.

Kela (Arabic, Hebrew) a form of Kayla.

Kelby BG (German) farm by the spring.

Kelcee, Kelci, Kelcie, Kelcy (Scottish) forms of Kelsey.

Kelcey GB (Scottish) a form of Kelsey.

Kele BG (Hopi) sparrow hawk.

Kelemon (Welsh) child of Kei.

Keli GB (Irish) a form of Kelly.

Kelia (Irish) a form of Kelly.

Kelila (Hebrew) crown, laurel.

Kellan BG (Irish) a form of Kellyn.

Kellee, Kelleigh, Kelli, Kellie (Irish) forms of Kelly.

Kellen BG (Irish) a form of Kellyn.

Kelley GB (Irish) a form of Kelly.

Kellsey, Kellsie, Kelsea, Kelsee, Kelsei, Kelsi, Kelsie, Kelsy (Scandinavian, Scottish, English) forms of Kelsey.

Kelly GB (Irish) brave warrior.

Kelly Ann, Kelly Anne, Kellyanne (Irish) combinations of Kelly + Ann.

Kellyn, Kellynn (Irish) combinations of Kelly + Lynn.

Kelsa (Scandinavian, Scottish, English) a short form of Kelsey.

Kelsey GB (Scandinavian, Scottish) ship island. (English) a form of Chelsea.

Kemberly (English) a form of Kimberly.

Kena, Kenna (Irish) short forms of Kennice.

Kenadee, Kenadi, Kennadi, Kennady (Irish) forms of Kennedy.

Kenda (English) water baby. (Dakota) magical power.

Kendahl (English) a form of Kendall.

Kendal 🇬🇧 (English) a form of Kendall.

Kendall 🇬🇧 (English) ruler of the valley.

Kendalyn (American) a form of Kendellyn.

Kendel 🇧🇬 (English) a form of Kendall.

Kendell 🇧🇬 (English) a form of Kendall.

Kendellyn (American) a combination of Kendall + Lynn.

Kendra (English) a form of Kenda.

Kendria (English) a form of Kenda.

Kendyl, Kendyll (English) forms of Kendall.

Kcncdi, Kcnnedi, Kennedie (Irish) forms of Kennedy.

Keneisha (American) a combination of the prefix Ken + Aisha.

Kenenza (English) a form of Kennice.

Kenesha (American) a form of Keneisha.

Kenia, Kennia (Hebrew) forms of Kenya.

Kenise (English) a form of Kennice.

Kenisha, Kennisha (American) forms of Keneisha.

Kenley 🇧🇬 (English) royal meadow.

Kennedy ✨
🇧🇬 (Irish) helmeted chief. History: John F. Kennedy was the thirty-fifth U.S. president.

Kenni (English) a familiar form of Kennice.

Kennice (English) beautiful.

Kensley (English, Scottish) a combination of Kenley + Kenzie.

Kenya 🇬🇧 (Hebrew) animal horn. Geography: a country in Africa.

Kenyana (Hebrew) a form of Kenya.

Kenyata (American) a form of Kenya.

Kenyatta 🇬🇧 (American) a form of Kenyata.

Kenyetta (American) a form of Kenya.

Kenzi (Scottish, Irish) a form of Kenzie.

Kenzie 🇬🇧 (Scottish) light skinned. (Irish) a short form of Mackenzie.

Keona, Keonna (Irish) forms of Keana.

Keondra (American) a form of Kenda.

Keoni 🇧🇬 (Irish) a form of Keana.

Keosha (American) a short form of Keneisha.

Kera, Kerra (Hindi) short forms of Kerani.
Kerah

Kerani (Hindi) sacred bells.

Keren (Hebrew) animal's horn.

Kerensa (Cornish) a form of Karenza.

Keri, Kerri, Kerrie (Irish) forms of Kerry.

Keriann, Kerrianne (Irish) combinations of Keri + Ann.

Kerielle, Kerrielle (American) combinations of Keri + Elle.

Kerrin (Hebrew) a form of Keren.

Kerry 🇬🇧 (Irish) dark haired. Geography: a county in Ireland.

Kersten, Kerstin, Kerstyn (Scandinavian) forms of Kirsten.

Kerstina (Scandinavian) a form of Kristina.

Kesare (Latin) long haired. (Russian) a form of Caesar Kesha **(American) a form of Keisha.**

Keshara (American) a form of Keisha.

Keshawna (American) a form of Keisha.

Keshet (Hebrew) rainbow.

Keshia (American) a form of Keisha. A short form of Keneisha.

Kesi (Swahili) born during difficult times.

Kesia (African) favorite.

Kesley (Scandinavian, Scottish) a form of Kelsey.

Kessie (Ashanti) chubby baby.

Ketifa (Arabic) flower.

Ketina (Hebrew) girl.

Kevina (Irish) a form of Kevyn.
Kevinah

Kevyn 🅱🅶 (Irish) beautiful.

Keyana, Keyanna (American) forms of Kiana.

Keyandra (American) a form of Kiana.

Keyara, Keyarra (Irish) forms of Kiara.

Keyera, Keyerra (Irish) forms of Kiara.

Keyla (Arabic, Hebrew) a form of Kayla.
Keylah

Keyona, Keyonna (American) forms of Kiana.
Keyonnie

Keyonda (American) a form of Kiana.

Keyondra (American) a form of Kiana.

Keyonia (American) a form of Kiana.

Keyosha (American) a form of Keisha.

Keysha (American) a form of Keisha.

Kezia (Hebrew) a form of Keziah.
Kezzia

Keziah (Hebrew) cinnamon-like spice. Bible: one of the daughters of Job.

Khadeeja (Arabic) a form of Khadijah.

Khadeja, Khadejah (Arabic) forms of Khadijah.

Khadija (Arabic) a form of Khadijah.

Khadijah (Arabic) trustworthy. History: Muhammed's first wife.

Khalia, Khaliah (Arabic) forms of Khalida.

Khalida (Arabic) immortal, everlasting.

Khalilah (Arabic) a form of Kalila.

Khaliyah (Arabic) a form of Khalida.

Khayla (Arabic, Hebrew) a form of Kayla.

Khepri (Egyptian) emerging sun.

Khiana (American) a form of Kiana.

Khimberly (English) a form of Kimberly.

Khloe ⭐ (Greek) a form of Chloe.

Khrisha (American, Czech) a form of Khrissa.

Khrissa (American) a form of Chrissa. (Czech) a form of Krista.

Khristina (Russian, Scandinavian) a form of Kristina, Christina.

Khristine (Scandinavian) a form of Christine.

Ki 🅱🅶 (Korean) arisen.

Kia (African) season's beginning. (American) a short form of Kiana.

Kiah (African, American) a form of Kia.

Kiahna (American) a form of Kiana.

Kiaira (Irish) a form of Kiara.

Kiana (American) a combination of the prefix Ki + Ana.

Kiandra (American) a form of Kiana.

Kiani (American) a form of Kiana.

Kianna (American) a form of Kiana.

Kiara (Irish) little and dark.

Kiaria (Japanese) fortunate.

Kiarra (Irish) a form of Kiara. (Japanese) a form of Kiaria.

Kiauna (American) a form of Kiana.
Kiaundra

Kieanna (American) a form of Kiana.

Kieara (Irish) a form of Kiara.

Kiele 🇬🇧 (Hawaiian) gardenia; fragrant blossom.

Kiera, Kierra (Irish) forms of Kerry.
Kierea

Kieran 🅱🇬 (Irish) little and dark; little Keir. A form of Kerry. (Hindi) a form of Kiran.

Kiersten, Kierstin, Kierston, Kierstyn (Scandinavian) forms of Kirsten.

Kiesha (American) a form of Keisha.

Kigva (Welsh) Mythology: wife of Partholon's son.

Kiki 🇬🇧 (Spanish) a familiar form of names ending in "queta."

Kiku (Japanese) chrysanthemum.

Kilee (Irish) a form of Kiley.

Kiley 🇬🇧 (Irish) attractive; from the straits. .

Kilia (Hawaiian) heaven.

Kim 🇬🇧 (Vietnamese) needle. (English) a short form of Kimberly.

Kimalina (American) a combination of Kim + Lina.

Kimana (Shoshone) butterfly.

Kimani 🅱🇬 (Shoshone) a form of Kimana.

Kimbalee (English) a form of Kimberly.

Kimber (English) a short form of Kimberly.

Kimberlee, Kimberley, Kimberli, Kimberlie (English) forms of Kimberly.

Kimberlin, Kimberlyn, Kimberlynn (English) forms of Kimberly.

Kimberly (English) chief, ruler.

Kimi (Japanese) righteous.

Kimiko (Japanese) righteous child.

Kimmie, Kimmy (English) familiar forms of Kimberly.

Kimora (American) a combination of Kim + Mora.

Kina (Hawaiian) from China. (Irish) wise.

Kindra (English) a form of Kendra.

Kineisha (American) a form of Keneisha.

Kineta (Greek) energetic.

Kini 🇬🇧 (Hawaiian) a form of Jean.

Kinley (Irish) fair-haired Viking.

Kinsey 🇬🇧 (English) offspring; relative.

Kinsley (American) a form of Kinsey.

Kinza (American) a form of Kinsey.

Kinzie (Scottish, Irish) a form of Kenzie. (English) a form of Kinsey.

Kioko (Japanese) happy child.

Kiona (Native American) brown hills.

Kionna (Native American) a form of Kiona.

Kip 🅱🇬 (English) pointed hill.

Kipa (Indigenous) young girl.

Kira (Persian) sun. (Latin) light.

Kiran 🇬🇧 (Hindi) ray of light.

Kiranjit (Hindi) a form of Kiran.

Kiranjot (Hindi) a form of Kiran.

Kirby 🅱🇬 (Scandinavian) church village. (English) cottage by the water.

Kiri (Cambodian) mountain. (Maori) tree bark.

Kiriann, Kirianne (American) combinations of Kiri + Ann.

Kirilina (American) a combination of Kiri + Lina.

Kirima (Eskimo) hill.

Kirsi (Hindi) amaranth blossoms.

Kirsta (Scandinavian) a form of Kirsten.

Kirstan, Kirstin, Kirstyn (Greek, Scandinavian) forms of Kirsten.

Kirsten (Greek) Christian; anointed. (Scandinavian) a form of Christine.

Kirsti, Kirstie, Kirsty (Greek, Scandinavian) familiar forms of Kirsten.

Kirstina (Scandinavian) a form of Kristina.

Kisa (Russian) kitten.

Kisha (African) a form of Keisha. (Russian) a form of Kisa.

Kishi (Japanese) long and happy life.
Kishee, Kishey, Kishie, Kishy

Kismet (Arabic) lot, fate; fortune.

Kissa (Ugandan) born after twins.

Kita (Japanese) north.

Kitra (Hebrew) crowned.

Kitty (Greek) a familiar form of Katherine.

Kiwa (Japanese) borderline.

Kiya, Kiyah (American) short forms of Kiyana.

Kiyana, Kiyanna (American) forms of Kiana.

Kizzy (American) a familiar form of Keziah.

Klaire (French) a form of Clair.
Klair

Klara (Hungarian) a form of Clara.

Klarise (German) a form of Klarissa.

Klarissa (German) clear, bright. (Italian) a form of Clarissa.

Klarita (Spanish) a form of Clarita.

Klaudia (American) a form of Claudia.

Klementine (Latin) a form of Clementine.

Kloe (American) a form of Chloe.

Kloris (Greek) a form of Chloris.

Kodi BG (American) a form of Codi.

Kodie BG (American) a form of Codi.

Kody BG (American) a form of Codi.

Koemi (Japanese) smiling.

Koffi (Swahili) born on Friday.

Koko (Japanese) stork. .

Kolbi (American) a form of Colby.

Kolby BG (American) a form of Colby.

Kolette (Greek, French) a form of Colette.

Koleyn (Australian) winter.

Kolfinnia (Scandinavian) white.

Kolina (Swedish) a form of Katherine.

Kolleen (Swedish) a form of Kolina. (Irish) a form of Colleen.

Kolora (Australian) lake.

Komal (Hindi, Indian) delicate.

Kona BG (Hawaiian) lady. (Hindi) angular.

Konrada (German) brave counselor.

Konstance (Latin) a form of Constance.

Kontxexi (Basque) a form of Conchita.

Kora (Greek) a form of Cora.

Koral (American) a form of Coral.

Kordelia (Latin, Welsh) a form of Cordelia.

Koren (Greek) a form of Karen, Kora, Korin.

Koretta (Greek) a familiar form of Kora.

Korey BG (American) a familiar form of Korina.

Kori, Korie GB (American) familiar forms of Korina.

Korin, Korine, Korinne, Korrin, Koryn (Greek) short forms of Korina.

Korina (Greek) a form of Corina.

Kornelia (Latin) a form of Cornelia.

Korri (American) a familiar form of Korina.

Kortina (American) a combination of Kora + Tina.

Kortnee, Kortni, Kortnie (English) forms of Courtney.

Kortney GB (English) a form of Courtney.

Kory BG (American) a familiar form of Korina.

Kosma (Greek) order; universe.

Kosta (Latin) a short form of Constance.

Koto (Japanese) harp.

Kourtnee, Kourtnei, Kourtney, Kourtni, Kourtnie (American) forms of Courtney.

Krin (Indigenous) star.

Kris BG (American) a short form of Kristine. A form of Chris.

Krisandra (Greek) a form of Cassandra.

Krishna BG (Hindi) delightful, pleasurable. Religion: one of the human incarnations of the Hindu god Vishnu.

Krissa (American, Czech) a form of Khrissa.

Krissy (American) a familiar form of Kris.

Krista (Czech) a form of Christina. a

Kristabel (Latin, French) a form of Christabel.

Kristain (Greek) a form of Kristen.

Kristal, Kristel, Kristelle (Latin) forms of Crystal.

Kristalyn (American) a form of Krystalyn.

Kristan (Greek) a form of Kristen.

Kristen (Greek) Christian; anointed. (Scandinavian) a form of Christine.

Kristena (Greek, Scandinavian) a form of Kristina.

Kristi, Kristie (Scandinavian) short forms of Kristine.

Kristian BG (Greek) Christian; anointed. A form of Christian.

Kristiana, Kristianna (Greek) forms of Kristian.

Kristin (Scandinavian) a form of Kristen.

Kristina (Greek) Christian; anointed. (Scandinavian) a form of Christina.

Kristine (Scandinavian) a form of Christine.

Kriston BG (Greek) a form of Kristen.

Kristy (American) a familiar form of Kristine, Krystal.

Kristyn (Greek) a form of Kristen.

Kristyna (Greek, Scandinavian) a form of Kristina.

Krysta (Polish) a form of Krista.
Krystah, Krystka

Krystal (American) clear, brilliant glass.

Krystalee (American) a combination of Krystal + Lee.

Krystalyn, Krystalynn (American) combinations of Krystal + Lynn.

Krystan, Krysten (Greek) forms of Kristen.

Krystel, Krystelle (Latin) forms of Krystal.
Krystele, Krystell, Krystella

Krystian BG (Greek) a form of Christian.

Krystiana (Greek) a form of Krystian.

105

Krystin, Krystyn (Czech) forms of Kristin.

Krystina (Greek) a form of Kristina.

Krystine (Scandinavian) a form of Kristina. (Czech) a form of Krystin.

Krystle (American) a form of Krystal.

Krystyna (Greek) a form of Kristina.

Kudio (Swahili) born on Monday.

Kuma (Japanese) bear. (Tongan) mouse.

Kumari (Sanskrit) woman.

Kumberlin (Australian) sweet.

Kumi (Japanese) braid.

Kumiko (Japanese) girl with braids.

Kumuda (Sanskrit) lotus flower.

Kunani (Hawaiian) beautiful.

Kuniko (Japanese) child from the country.

Kunto (Twi) third-born.

Kuri (Japanese) chestnut.

Kusa (Hindi) God's grass.

Kuyen (Mapuche) moon.

Kwanita (Zuni) a form of Juanita.

Kwashi (Swahili) born on Sunday.

Kwau (Swahili) born on Thursday.

Kya (African) diamond in the sky. (American) a form of Kia.

Kyah (African, American) a form of Kya.

Kyana, Kyanna (American) forms of Kiana.

Kyara (Irish) a form of Kiara.

Kyera, Kyerra (Irish) forms of Kiara.

Kyla (Irish) lovely. (Yiddish) crown; laurel.

Kylah (Irish, Yiddish) a form of Kyla.

Kyle BG (Irish) attractive.

Kylea, Kylee, Kyleigh, Kyley, Kyli (West Australian Aboriginal, Irish) forms of Kylie.

Kyleen, Kylene (Irish) forms of Kyle.

Kyler BG (English) a form of Kyle.
Kylar, Kylor

Kylie ✴ (West Australian Aboriginal) curled stick; boomerang. (Irish) a familiar form of Kyle.

Kylynn (Irish) a form of Kyle.
Kylenn, Kylynne

Kym (Vietnamese, English) a form of Kim.

Kymber (English) a form of Kimber.

Kymberlee, Kymberli, Kymberly (English) forms of Kimberly.

Kymberlyn (English) a form of Kimberlin.

Kyndal (English) a form of Kendall.

Kyndall GB (English) a form of Kendall.

Kyndra (English) a form of Kendra.

Kynthia (Greek) a form of Cynthia.

Kyoko (Japanese) mirror.

Kyra (Greek) noble. A form of Cyrilla. Kyrene **(Greek) noble.**

Kyrie (Cambodian, Maori) a form of Kiri. (Greek) a familiar form of Kyra.

Kyrsten, Kyrstin, Kyrstyn (Greek, Scandinavian) forms of Kirsten.

L

La Cienega (Spanish) the marsh.

La Reina, La-Reina (Spanish) the queen.

Labreana (American) a combination of the prefix La + Breana.

Labrenda (American) a combination of the prefix La + Brenda.

Lace, Lacee, Laci, Lacie (Greek, Latin) forms of Lacey.

Lacey (Latin) cheerful. (Greek) a familiar form of Larissa.

Lachandra (American) a combination of the prefix La + Chandra.

Lachlanina (Scottish) land of lakes.

Lacole (Italian) a form of Nicole.

Lacrecia (Latin) a form of Lucretia.

Lacy GB (Latin) cheerful. (Greek) a familiar form of Larissa.

Lada (Russian) Mythology: the Slavic goddess of beauty.

Ladaisha (American) a form of Ladasha.

Ladan (American) a short form of Ladana.

Ladana (American) a combination of the prefix La + Dana.

Ladanica (American) a combination of the prefix La + Danica.

Ladasha (American) a combination of the prefix La + Dasha.

Ladawna (American) a combination of the prefix La + Dawna.

Ladeidra (American) a combination of the prefix La + Deidra.

Ladivina (American) a combination of the prefix La + Divinia.

Ladonna (American) a combination of the prefix La + Donna.

Laela (Arabic, Hebrew) a form of Leila.

Laeticia, Laetitia (Latin) forms of Leticia.

Laflora (American) a combination of the prefix La + Flora.

Lahela (Hawaiian) a form of Rachel.
Lahelah

Laia (Greek) a form of Lalia.

Laica (Greek) pure; secular.

Laila (Arabic) a form of Leila.

Lailaka (Tongan) lilac.

Laina (French) a form of Laine. (English) a form of Lane.

Laine BG (French) a short form of Elaine. **Lainey** (French) a familiar form of Elaine.

Laione (Tongan) lion.

Lais (Greek) one who is friendly with everyone.

Lajessica (American) a combination of the prefix La + Jessica.

Lajila (Hindi) shy; coy.

Lajuana (American) a combination of the prefix La + Juana.

Lajuliet, Lajuliette (American) combinations of the prefix La + Juliet.

Laka (Hawaiian) attractive; seductive; tame.

Mythology: the goddess of the hula.

Lakaya (American) a form of Lakayla.

Lakayla (American) a combination of the prefix La + Kayla.

Lakeisha (American) a combination of the prefix La + Keisha**Laken, Lakin, Lakyn** (American) short forms of Lakendra.

Lakendra (American) a combination of the prefix La + Kendra.

Lakenya (American) a combination of the prefix La + Kenya.

Lakesha (American) a form of Lakeisha.

Lakeshia (American) a form of Lakeisha.

Laketa (American) a combination of the prefix La + Keita.

Lakeya (Hindi) a form of Lakya.

Lakia (Arabic) found treasure.

Lakiesha (American) a form of Lakeisha.

Lakisha (American) a form of Lakeisha.

Lakita (American) a form of Laketa.

Lakiya (Hindi) a form of Lakya.
Lakieya

Lakkari (Australian) honeysuckle tree.

Lakmé (Hindi) born in milk.

Lakota BG (Dakota) a tribal name.

Lakresha (American) a form of Lucretia.

Lakya (Hindi) born on Thursday.

Lala (Slavic) tulip.

Lalasa (Hindi) love.

Laleh (Persian) tulip.

Lali (Spanish) a form of Lulani.

Lalirra (Australian) chatty.

Lalita (Greek) talkative. (Sanskrit) charming; candid.

Lallie (English) babbler.

Lama (German) a short form of Lamberta.

Lamani BG (Tongan) lemon.

Lamberta (German) bright land.

Lamesha (American) a combination of the prefix La + Mesha.

Lamia (German) a short form of Lamberta.

Lamis (Arabic) soft to the touch.

Lamonica (American) a combination of the prefix La + Monica.

Lamya (Arabic) dark lipped.

Lan (Vietnamese) flower.

Lana (Latin) woolly. (Irish) attractive, peaceful. A short form of Alana, Elana. (Hawaiian) floating; bouyant.

Lanae (Latin, Irish, Hawaiian) a form of Lana.

Lanca (Latin) blessed one.

Landa (Spanish) reference to the Virgin Mary.

Landeberta (Latin) a form of Lamberta.

Landelina (German) patriot.

Landon BG (English) open, grassy meadow.

Landra (German, Spanish) counselor.

Landrada (Spanish) a form of Landra.

Landyn (English) a form of Landon, London.

Lane BG (English) narrow road

Laneisha (American) a combination of the prefix La + Keneisha.

Lanelle (French) a combination of **Lane + Elle.**

Lanesha (American) a form of Laneisha.

Lanette (Welsh, French) a form of Linette.

Laney (English) a familiar form of Lane.

Langley GB (English) long meadow.

Lani GB (Hawaiian) sky; heaven. A short form of

'Aulani, Atlanta, Laulani, Leilani, Lulani.

Lanie (English) a form of Laney. (Hawaiian) a form of Lani.

Lanisha (American) a form of Laneisha.

Lanna (Latin, Irish, Hawaiian) a form of Lana.

Lantha (Greek) purple flower.

Laodamia (Greek) she who leads her community.

Laodicea (Greek) she who is fair with her community.

Laporsha (American) a combination of the prefix La + Porsha.

Laqueena (American) a combination of the prefix La + Queenie.

Laquesha (American) a form of Laquisha.

Laquinta (American) a combination of the prefix La + Quintana.

Laquisha (American) a combination of the prefix La + Queisha.

Laquita (American) a combination of the prefix La + Queta.

Lara (Greek) cheerful. (Latin) shining; famous. Mythology: a Roman nymph. A short form of Laraine, Larissa, Laura.

Larae (Greek, Latin) a form of Lara.

Laraina (Latin) a form of Lorraine.

Laraine (Latin) a form of Lorraine.

Laramie GB (French) tears of love. Geography: a town in Wyoming on the Overland Trail.

Laren (Latin) a form of Laraine. (Greek) a short form of Larina.

Lari (Latin) a familiar form of Lara. A short form of names starting with "Lari."

Larianna (American) a combination of Lari + Anna.

Laricia (Latin) a form of Laura.

Lariel (Hebrew) God's lioness.

Larina (Greek) sea gull.

Larisa, Larrisa, Larrissa (Greek) forms of Larissa.

Larisha (Greek) a form of Larissa.

Larissa (Greek) cheerful. **Lark** (English) skylark.

Larlene (Irish) promise.

Larmina (Persian) blue sky.

Larnelle (Latin) high degree.

Larunda, Laurinda, Laurita (Spanish) forms of Laura.

Laryssa (Greek) a form of Larissa.

Lasha (American) a form of Lashae.

Lashae, Lashai, Lashay, Lashea (American) combinations of the prefix La + Shay.

Lashana (American) a combination of the prefix La + Shana.

Lashanda (American) a combination of the prefix La + Shanda.

Lashaun BG (American) a short form of Lashawna.

Lashawn BG (American) a short form of Lashawna.

Lashawna (American) a combination of the prefix La + Shawna.

Lashawnda (American) a form of Lashonda.

Lashaya (American) a form of Lasha.

Lashon GB (American) a short form of Lashawna.

Lashonda (American) a combination of the prefix La + Shonda.

Lashondra (American) a form of Lashonda.

Lassie (Irish) young girl.

Latanya (American) a combination of the prefix La + Tanya.

Latara (American) a combination of the prefix La + Tara.

Lataree (Japanese) bent branch.

Latasha (American) a **combination of the prefix La + Tasha.**

Latashia (American) a form of Latasha.

Latavia (American) a combination of the prefix La + Tavia.

Lateasha (American) a form of Leticia, Latisha.

Lateefah **(Arabic) pleasant. (Hebrew) pat, caress.**

Lateesha (American) a form of Leticia, Latisha.

Lateisha (American) a form of Leticia, Latisha.

Latesha (American) a form of Leticia.

Lateshia (American) a form of Leticia.

Latia (American) a combination of the prefix La + Tia.

Laticia (Latin) a form of Leticia.

Latifah (Arabic, Hebrew) a form of Lateefah.

Latika (Hindi) elegant.

Lalina (American) a combination of the prefix La + Tina.

Latisha (Latin) joy. (American) a combination of the prefix La + Tisha.

Latona (Latin) Mythology: the powerful goddess who bore Apollo and Diana.

Latonia (Latin, American) a form of Latonya.

Latonya (American) a combination of the prefix La + Tonya. (Latin) a form of Latona.

Latoria (American) a combination of the prefix La + Tori.

Latosha (American) a combination of the prefix La + Tosha.

Latoya (American) a combination of the prefix La + Toya.

Latrice (American) a combination of the prefix La + Trice.

Latricia, Latrisha (American) combinations of the prefix La + Tricia.

Laudelina (Latin) deserves laud.

Laulani (Hawaiian) heavenly tree branch.

Laumalie (Tongan) lively, full of spirit.

Laura (Latin) crowned with laurel.

Lauralee (American) a combination of Laura + Lee. (German) a form of Lorelei.

Lauralyn (American) a combination of Laura + Lynn.

Lauran, Laurin (English) forms of Lauren.

Laure (Italian) a form of Laura.

Laureanne (English) a short form of Laurianna. (American) a form of Laurie Ann.

Laurel (Latin) laurel tree.

Laurelei (German) a form of Lorelei. (American) a form of Lauralee.

Lauren ⭐ (English) a form of Laura.

Laurence GB (Latin) crowned with laurel.

Lauretta (English) a form of Loretta.

Lauriane, Laurianne (English) short forms of Laurianna. (American) forms of Laurie Ann.

Laurianna (English) a combination of Laurie + Anna.

Laurie GB (English) a familiar form of Laura.

Laurie Ann, Laurie Anne (American) combinations of Laurie + Ann.

Laurissa (Greek) a form of Larissa.
Laurissah

Laury (English) a familiar form of Laura.
Lawrey, Lawry, Lawrya, Lawryah

Lauryn (English) a familiar form of Laura.

Lavani (Tongan) necklace.

Lave BG (Italian) lava. (English) lady. (Tongan) touch.

Laveda (Latin) cleansed, purified.

Lavelle BG (Latin) cleansing.

Lavena (Irish, French) joy. (Latin) a form of Lavina.

Lavender (Latin) bluish violet, purple. Botany: a plant with clusters of pale purple flowers.

Laveni (Tongan) lavender; light purple.

Lavenita (Tongan) lavender fragrance.

Laverne (Latin) springtime. (French) grove of alder trees.

Laviana (Latin) a form of Lavina.

Lavina (Latin) purified; woman of Rome.

Lavinia (Latin) a form of Lavina.

Lavonna (American) a combination of the prefix La + Yvonne.

Lavonne (American) a short form of Lavonna.

Lawan (Tai) pretty.

Lawanda (American) a combination of the prefix La + Wanda.

Lawren (American) a form of Lauren.

Layan (Iranian) bright; shining.

Layce (American) a form of Lacey.

Layla ✷ (Hebrew, Arabic) a form of Leila.

Layne 🅱🅶 (French) a form of Laine.

Layney (French) a familiar form of Elaine.

Lazalea (Greek) eagle ruler.

Le 🅱🅶 (Vietnamese) pearl.

Lea (Hawaiian) Mythology: the goddess of canoe makers. (Hebrew) a form of Leah.

Lea Marie (American) a combination of Lea + Marie.

Leah ✷ (Hebrew) weary. Bible: the first wife of Jacob.

Leala (French) faithful, loyal.

Lean, Leann, Leanne (English) forms of Leeann, Lian.

Leana, Leanna, Leeanna (English) forms of Liana.

Leandra (Latin) like a lioness.

Leanore (Greek) a form of Eleanor. (English) a form of Helen.

Lece (Latin) a form of Lacey.

Lecia (Latin) a short form of Felecia.

Leda (Greek) lady. Mythology: the queen of Sparta and the mother of Helen of Troy.

Ledicia (Latin) great joy.

Lee 🅱🅶 (Chinese) plum. (Irish) poetic. (English) meadow. A short form of Ashley, Leah.
Ly

Leea (American) a form of Leah.
Leeah

Leeann, Leeanne (English) combinations of Lee + Ann. Forms of Lian.

Leeba (Yiddish) beloved.

Leena (Estonian) a form of Helen. (Greek, Latin, Arabic) a form of Lina.

Leesa (Hebrew, English) a form of Leeza, Lisa.

Leesha (American) a form of Lecia.

Leewan (Australian) wind.

Leeza (Hebrew) a short form of Aleeza. (English) a form of Lisa, Liza.

Lefitray (Mapuche) speed of sound.

Leflay (Mapuche) lethargic woman.

Legarre (Spanish) reference to the Virgin Mary.

Lei 🅱🅶 (Hawaiian) a familiar form of Leilani.

Leia (Hebrew) a form of Leah. (Spanish, Tamil) a form of Leya.
Leiah

Leif 🅱🅶 (Scandinavian) beloved.
Leaf, Leaff, Leiff, Leyf, Leyff

Leigh (English) a form of Lee.

Leigha (English) a form of Leah.

Leighann, Leighanne (English) forms of Leeann.

Leighanna (English) a form of Liana.

Leighton (English) Geography: Leighton is the name of numerous towns in the United Kingdom, Australia, and the United States.

Leiko (Japanese) arrogant.

Leila (Hebrew) dark beauty; night. (Arabic) born at nightLeilah **(Hebrew, Arabic) a form of Leila.**

Leilani (Hawaiian) heavenly flower; heavenly child.

Leira (Basque) reference to the Virgin Mary.

Leisa (Hebrew, English) a form of Lisa.

Leisha (American) a form of Leticia.

Lekasha (American) a form of Lakeisha.

Lekeisha (American) a form of Lakeisha.

Lela (French) a form of Leala. (Hebrew, Arabic) a form of Leila.

Leli (Swiss) a form of Magdalen.

Lelia (Greek) fair speech. (Hebrew, Arabic) a form of Leila.

Lelica (Latin) talkative.

Lelya (Russian) a form of Helen.

Lemana (Australian) oak tree.

Lemuela (Hebrew) devoted to God.

Lena (Hebrew) dwelling or lodging. (Latin) temptress. (Norwegian) illustrious. (Greek) a short form of Eleanor. Music: Lena Horne, a well-known African American singer and actress.

Lenci (Hungarian) a form of Helen.

Lene (German) a form of Helen.

Leneisha (American) a combination of the prefix Le + Keneisha.

Lenia (German) a form of Leona.

Lenis (Latin) soft; silky.

Lenita (Latin) gentle.

Lennon BG (English) dear one. Music: John Lennon was a popular singer/songwriter.

Lenora (Greek, Russian) a form of Eleanor.

Lenore (Greek, Russian) a form of Eleanor.

Leocadia, Leocadía (Greek) shining; white.

Leocricia (Greek) she who judges her village well.

Leola (Latin) lioness.

Leolina (Welsh) a form of Leola.

Leoma (English) brilliant.

Leona (German) brave as a lioness.

Leonarda (German) brave as a lioness.

Leoncia (Latin) a form of Leonarda.

Leondra (German) a form of Leonarda.

Leónida (Greek) a form of Leonarda.

Leonie **(German) a familiar form of Leona.**

Leonila (Latin) a form of Leonarda.

Leonilda (German) fighter.

Leonna (German) a form of Leona.

Leonor, Leonore (Greek) forms of Eleanor.

Leontine (Latin) like a lioness.

Leopolda (German) princess of the village.

Leora (Hebrew) light. (Greek) a familiar form of Eleanor.

Leotie (Native American) prairie flower.

Lepati (Tongan) leopard.

Lera (Russian) a short form of Valera.

Lesbia (Greek) native of the Greek island of Lesbos.

Leslee, Lesleigh, Lesli, Lesly, Leslye (Scottish) forms of Lesley.

Lesley (Scottish) gray fortress.

Leslie ✹ GB (Scottish) a form of Lesley.

Leta (Latin) glad. (Swahili) bringer. (Greek) a short form of Aleta.

Letha (Greek) forgetful; oblivion.

Leticia (Latin) joy. **Letifa** (Arabic) a form of Lateefah.

Letisha (Latin) a form of Leticia.

Letitia (Latin) a form of Leticia.

Letty (English) a familiar form of Leticia.

Levana (Hebrew) moon; white. (Latin) risen. Mythology: the goddess of newborn babies.

Levani (Fijian) anointed with oil.

Levania (Latin) rising sun.

Levia (Hebrew) joined, attached.

Levina (Latin) flash of lightning.

Levita, Levyna (English) twinkle, sparkle.

Levona (Hebrew) spice; incense.

Lewana (Hebrew) a form of Levana.

Lexandra (Greek) a short form of Alexandra.

Lexi, Lexie, Lexy (Greek) familiar forms of Alexandra.
Leksi,

Lexia (Greek) a familiar form of Alexandra.

Lexis, Lexxus (Greek) short forms of Alexius, Alexis.

Lexus GB (Greek) a short form of Alexius, Alexis.

Leya (Spanish) loyal. (Tamil) the constellation Leo.

Leyla (Hebrew, Arabic) a form of Leila. (Spanish, Tamil) a form of Leya.

Leyna (Estonian, Greek, Latin, Arabic) a form of Leena.
Leynah

Lia (Greek) bringer of good news. (Hebrew, Dutch, Italian) dependent.

Lía (Hebrew) a form of Leah.

Liama (English) determined guardian.

Lian GB (Chinese) graceful willow. (Latin) a short form of Gillian, Lillian.

Liana, Lianna (Latin) youth. (French) bound, wrapped up; tree covered with vines. (English) meadow. (Hebrew) short forms of Eliana.

Liane, Lianne (Hebrew) short forms of Eliane. (English) forms of Lian.

Libby (Hebrew) a familiar form of Elizabeth.

Libera, Líbera (Latin) she who bestows abundance.

Liberada, Liberata, Liberdade (Latin) forms of Liberty.

Liberia, Liberta (Spanish) forms of Liberty.

Libertad (Latin) she who acts in good faith.

Liberty **(Latin) free.**

Libia (Latin) comes from the desert.

Libitina (Latin) she who is wanted.

Libna (Latin) whiteness.

Liboria (Latin) free.

Lican (Mapuche) flint.

Licia (Greek) a short form of Alicia.

Lida (Greek) happy. (Slavic) loved by people. (Latin) a short form of Alida, Elita.

Lide (Latin, Basque) life.

Lidia (Greek) a form of Lydia.

Lidía, Lídia, Lydía (Greek) forms of Lydia.

Liduvina (German) friend of the village.

Lien (Chinese) lotus.

Liesabet (German) a short form of Elizabeth.

Liese (German) a familiar form of Elise, Elizabeth.
Liesa, Liesah, Lieschen, Lise

Liesel (German) a familiar form of Elizabeth.

Liesha (Arabic) a form of Aisha.

Ligia (Greek) clear voiced; whistling.

Lígia (Portuguese) a form of Ligia.

Lila (Arabic) night. (Hindi) free will of God. (Persian) lilac. A short form of Dalila, Delilah, Lillian.

Lilac (Sanskrit) lilac; blue purple.

Lilah (Arabic, Hindi, Persian) a form of Lila.

Lili, Lillie (Latin, Arabic) forms of Lilly.

Lilí (English) a form of Alicia.

Lilia **(Persian) a form of Lila.**

Lilian, Liliane (Latin) forms of Lillian.

Lilián (Spanish) a form of Lillian.

Lílian (Portuguese) a form of Lillian.

Liliana, Lilliana, Lillianna (Latin) forms of Lillian.

Lilibeth (English) a combination of Lilly + Beth.

Lilis (Hebrew) a form of Lilith.

Lilit (Hebrew) patriot.

Lilith (Arabic) of the night; night demon. Mythology: the first wife of Adam, according to ancient Jewish legends.

Lillian ✸ (Latin) lily flower.

Lilly (Latin, Arabic) a familiar form of Lilith, Lillian, Lillyann.

Lillyann (English) a combination of Lilly + Ann. (Latin) a form of Lillian.

Lillybelle, Lilybelle (English) combinations of Lilly + Belle.

Lillybet, Lilybet (English) combinations of Lilly + Elizabeth.

Lilvina (Latin, German) friend of the iris.

Lily ✸ (Latin, Arabic) a form of Lilly.

Limber (Tiv) joyful.

Lin GB (Chinese) beautiful jade. (English) a form of Lynn.

Lina (Greek) light. (Arabic) tender. (Latin) a form of Lena.

Linda (Spanish) pretty.

Linden BG (English) linden-tree hill.

Lindsay GB (English) a form of Lindsey.

Lindsee, Lindsi, Lindsie, Lindsy (English) forms of Lindsey.

Lindsey GB (English) linden-tree island; camp near the stream.

Lindy (Spanish) a familiar form of Linda.

Linette (Welsh) idol. (French) bird.

Ling (Chinese) delicate, dainty.

Linh (Chinese, English) a form of Lin.

Linley GB (English) flax meadow.

Linnea (Scandinavian) lime tree. Botany: the national flower of Sweden.

Linsey, Linzee, Linzy (English) forms of Lindsey.

Lioba (German) beloved, valued.

Liolya (Russian) a form of Helen.

Liona (German) a form of Leona.

Lionetta (Latin) small lioness.

Liora (Hebrew) light.

Lirit (Hebrew) poetic; lyrical, musical.

Liron BG **(Hebrew) my song.**

Lis (French) lily.

Lisa (Hebrew) consecrated to God. (English) a short form of Elizabeth.

Lisa Marie (American) a combination of Lisa + Marie.

Lisandra (Greek) a form of Lysandra.

Lisann, Lisanne (American) combinations of Lisa + Ann.

Lisavet (Hebrew) a form of Elizabeth.

Lisbet (English) a short form of Elizabeth.

Lisbeth (English) a short form of Elizabeth.

Lis (German) a form of Lisa.

Lise (German) a form of Lisa.

Liset, Lisette, Lisset, Lissette (French) forms of Lisa. (English) familiar forms of Elise, Elizabeth.

Liseth (French, English) a form of Liset.

Lisha (Arabic) darkness before midnight. (Hebrew) a short form of Alisha, Elisha, Ilisha.

Lissa (Greek) honey bee. A short form of Elissa, Elizabeth, Melissa, Millicent.

Lissie (American) a familiar form of Alison, Elise, Elizabeth.

Lita (Latin) a familiar form of names ending in "lita."

Litonya (Moquelumnan) darting hummingbird.

Liuba (Russian) a form of Caridad.

Liv (Latin) a short form of Livia, Olivia.
Lyv

Livana (Hebrew) a form of Levana.

Livia (Hebrew) crown. A familiar form of Olivia. (Latin) olive.

Liviya (Hebrew) brave lioness; royal crown.

Livona (Hebrew) a form of Levona.

Liyah (Hebrew) a form of Leah.
Liya

Liz (English) a short form of Elizabeth.

Liza (American) a short form of Elizabeth.

Lizabeta (Russian) a form of Elizabeth.

Lizabeth (English) a short form of Elizabeth. **Lizbet** (English) a short form of Elizabeth.

Lizbeth (English) a short form of Elizabeth.
Lyzbeth

Lizet, Lizett, Lizette, Lizzet, Lizzette (French) forms of Liset.

Lizeth (French) a form of Liset.

Lizina (Latvian) a familiar form of Elizabeth.

Lizzie, Lizzy (American) familiar forms of Elizabeth.
Lizy

Llanquipan (Mapuche) fallen branch; solitary lioness.

Llanquiray (Mapuche) fallen flower.

Lledó (Catalan) hackberry tree.

Llesenia (Spanish) Television: the female lead in a 1970s soap opera.

Llian (Welsh) linen.

Lluvia (Spanish) rain.

Locaia (Greek) white roses.

Lodema, Lodima, Lodyma (English) guide.

Logan 🆖 (Irish) meadow.

Loida, Loída (Greek) example of faith and piousness.

Loila (Australian) sky.

Lois (German) famous warrior.

Lokalia (Hawaiian) garland of roses.

Lola (Spanish) a familiar form of Carlotta, Dolores, Louise.

Lolita (Spanish) sorrowful. A familiar form of Lola.

Lolly (English) sweet; candy. A familiar form of Laura.

Lolotea (Zuni) a form of Dorothy.

Lomasi (Native American) pretty flower.

Lona (Latin) lioness. (English) solitary. (German) a short form of Leona.

London ⭐ 🆖 (English) fortress of the moon. Geography: the capital of the United Kingdom.

Loni (American) a form of Lona.

Lonlee (English) a form of Lona.

Lonna (Latin, German, English) a form of Lona.

Lora (Latin) crowned with laurel. (American) a form of Laura.

Loraine (Latin) a form of Lorraine.

Lorda (Spanish) a form of Lourdes.

Lore (Basque) flower. (Latin) a short form of Flora.

Lorea (Basque) grove; light.

Loreal (German) a form of Lorelei.

Lorelei (German) alluring. Mythology: the siren of the Rhine River who lured sailors to their deaths.

Loreley (German) a form of Lorelei.

Lorelle (American) a form of Laurel.

Loren GB (American) a form of Lauren.

Lorena (English) a form of Lauren.

Lorene (American) a form of Lauren.

Lorenza BG (Latin) a form of Laura.

Loreto (Spanish) forest.

Loretta (English) a familiar form of Laura.

Lori (Latin) crowned with laurel. (French) a short form of Lorraine. (American) a familiar form of Laura.

Loriann, Lorianne (American) combinations of Lori + Ann.

Loric (Latin) armor.

Lorie, Lorrie, Lory (Latin, French, American) forms of Lori.

Lorielle (American) a combination of Lori + Elle.

Lorikeet (Australian) beautiful, colorful bird.

Lorin GB (American) a form of Lauren.

Lorinda (Spanish) a form of Laura.

Loris BG (Latin) thong. (Dutch) clown. (Greek) a short form of Chloris.

Lorissa (Greek, Latin, Dutch) a form of Loris. A form of Larissa.

Lorna (Latin) crowned with laurel. Literature: probably coined by Richard Blackmore in his novel *Lorna Doone*.

Lorraine (Latin) sorrowful. (French) from Lorraine, a former province of France.

Loryn (American) a form of Lauren.

Lotte (German) a short form of Charlotte.

Lottie (German) a familiar form of Charlotte.

Lotus (Greek) lotus.

Lou BG (American) a short form of Louise, Luella.
Lu

Louam (Ethiopian) sleep well.

Louisa (English) a familiar form of Louise. Literature: Louisa May Alcott was an American writer and reformer best known for her novel *Little Women*.

Louise (German) famous warrior.

Lourdes (French) from Lourdes, France. Religion: a place where the Virgin Mary was said to have appeared.

Louvaine (English) Louise's vanity.

Love (English) love, kindness, charity.

Lovely (English) lovely.

Lovinia (Latin) a form of Lavina.

Lovisa (German) a form of Louisa.

Lowri (Welsh) a form of Laura.

Lúa (Latin) moon.

Luann (Hebrew, German) graceful woman warrior. (Hawaiian) happy; relaxed. (American) a combination of Louise + Ann.

Luanna (German) a form of Luann.

Lubiana (Slavic) a form of Luvena.

Lubov (Russian) love.

Luca BG (Italian) a form of Lucy.

Lucelia (Spanish) a combination of Luz + Celia.

Lucena (Spanish) a form of Lucy.

Lucerne (Latin) lamp; circle of light. Geography: the Lake of Lucerne is in Switzerland.

Lucero (Latin) a form of Lucerne.

Lucetta (English) a familiar form of Lucy.

Lucette (French) a form of Lucy.

Lucha (Spanish) a form of Luisa.

Luci, Lucie (French) familiar forms of Lucy.

Lucia (Italian, Spanish) a form of Lucy.

Lucía (Latin) a form of Lucy.

Lúcia (Portuguese) a form of Lucy.

Luciana (Italian, Spanish) a form of Lucy.

Lucienne (French) a form of Lucy.

Lucila (English) a form of Lucille.

Lucille (English) a familiar form of Lucy.

Lucinda (Latin) a form of Lucy.

Lucindee (Latin) a familiar form of Lucinda.

Lucine (Arabic) moon. (Basque) a form of Lucy.

Lucita (Spanish) a form of Lucy.

Lucky BG (American) fortunate.

Lucretia (Latin) rich; rewarded.

Lucrezia (Italian) a form of Lucretia. History: Lucrezia Borgia was the Duchess of Ferrara and a patron of learning and the arts.

Lucy (Latin) light; bringer of light.

Ludmilla (Slavic) loved by the people. **Ludovica** (German) a form of Louise.

Luella (English) elf. (German) a familiar form of Louise.

Luisa (Spanish) a form of Louisa.

Luísa (Germanic) a form of Luisa.

Luisina (Teutonic) a form of Luisa.

Luján (Spanish) Geography: a city in Argentina.

Lulani BG (Polynesian) highest point of heaven.

Lulie (English) sleepy.

Lulu (Arabic) pearl. (English) soothing, comforting. (Native American) hare. (German) a familiar form of Louise, Luella.

Lulú (French) a form of Luisa.

Luminosa (Latin) she who illuminates.

Luna (Latin) moon.

Lundy GB (Scottish) grove by the island.

Lupa (Latin) a form of Lupe.

Lupe (Latin) wolf. (Spanish) a short form of Guadalupe.

Lupine (Latin) like a wolf.

Lupita (Latin) a form of Lupe.

Lur (Spanish) earth.

Lurdes (Portuguese, Spanish) a form of Lourdes.

Lurleen, Lurlene (Scandinavian) war horn. (German) forms of Lorelei.

Lusa (Finnish) a form of Elizabeth.
Lusah, Lussa, Lussah

Lusela (Moquelumnan) like a bear swinging its foot when licking it.

Lutana (Australian) moon.

Lutgarda (German) she who protects her village.

Lutrudis (German) strength of the village.

Luvena (Latin, English) little; beloved.

Luyu BG (Moquelumnan) like a pecking bird.

Luz (Spanish) light. Religion: *Nuestra Señora de Luz*—Our Lady of the

Light—is another name for the Virgin Mary.

Luzmaria (Spanish) a combination of Luz + Maria.

Luzmila (Slavic) loved by the village.

Ly (French) a short form of Lyla.

Lycoris (Greek) twilight.

Lyda (Greek) a short form of Lydia.

Lydia ✶ (Greek) from Lydia, an ancient land in Asia. (Arabic) strife.

Lyla (French) island. (English) a form of Lyle (Arabic, Hindi, Persian) a form of Lila.

Lynae, Lynnae (English) forms of Lynn.

Lynda (Spanish) pretty. (American) a form of Linda.

Lyndee, Lyndi, Lyndie (Spanish) familiar forms of Lynda.

Lyndell (English) a form of Lynelle.

Lyndsay, Lyndsee, Lyndsey, Lyndsie, Lyndsy (American) forms of Lindsey.

Lynelle (English) pretty.

Lynette (Welsh) idol. (English) a form of Linette.

Lynlee (English) a form of Lynn.

Lynn GB (English) waterfall; pool below a waterfall.

Lynna (Greek, Latin, Arabic) a form of Lina.

Lynne (English) waterfall; pool below a waterfall.

Lynnea (Scandinavian) a form of Linnea.

Lynnell (English) a form of Lynelle.

Lynnette (Welsh, English) a form of Lynette.

Lynsey, Lynsie, Lynzee, Lynzie (American) forms of Lindsey.

Lyonella (French) lion cub.

Lyra (Greek) lyre player.

Lyric GB (Greek) songlike; words of a song.

Lyris (Greek) lyre player.

Lysa (Hebrew, English) a form of Lisa.

Lysandra (Greek) liberator.

Lysandre (Greek) a form of Lysandra.

Lysann, Lysanne (American) combinations of Lysandra + Ann.

Lysette (French, English) a form of Liset.

Lyssa (Greek) a form of Lissa.

Lyzabeth (English) a short form of Elizabeth.

M

Ma Kayla (American) a form of Michaela.

Mab (Irish) joyous. (Welsh) baby. Literature: queen of the fairies.

Mabbina (Irish) a form of Mabel.

Mabel (Latin) lovable. A short form of Amabel.

Mabella (English) a form of Mabel.

Mabelle (French) a form of Mabel.

Mac Kenzie (Irish) a form of Mackenzie.

Macaela (Hebrew) a form of Michaela.

Macarena (Spanish) she who carries the sword; name for the Virgin Mary.

Macaria (Greek) happy.
Macariah, Macarya, Macaryah

Macawi (Dakota) generous; motherly.

Macayla (American) a form of Michaela.

Macee, Macey, Maci, Macie (Polish) familiar forms of Macia.

Machaela (Hebrew) a form of Michaela.

Machiko (Japanese) fortunate child.

Macia (Polish) a form of Miriam.

Maciela (Latin) very slender.

Mackayla (American) a form of Michaela.

Mackenna (American) a form of Mackenzie.

Mackensie, Mackenzi (American) forms of Mackenzie.

Mackenzie ⭐ (Irish) child of the wise leader

Mackenzy BG (American) a form of Mackenzie.

Mackinsey (Irish) a form of Mackenzie.

Macra (Greek) she who grows.

Macrina, Macronia (Greek) forms of Macra.

Macuilxóchitl (Nahuatl) five flowers.

Macy GB (Polish) a familiar form of Macia.

Mada (English) a short form of Madaline, Magdalen.

Madalaine (English) a form of Madeline.

Madaline (English) a form of Madeline.

Madalyn, Madalynn (Greek) forms of Madeline.

Maddie (English) a familiar form of Madeline.

Maddisen, Maddison, Madisen, Madisson, Madisyn (English) forms of Madison.

Maddox BG (Welsh, English) benefactor's child.

Madeira (Spanish) sweet wine.

Madelaine, Madeleine, Madeliene (French) forms of Madeline.

Madelena (English) a form of Madeline.

Madelene, Madelin (Greek, English) forms of Madeline.

Madeline ⭐ (Greek) high tower.

Madelón (Spanish) a form of Madeline.

Madelyn ⭐ (Greek, English) a form of Madeline.

Madena, Madina (Greek) forms of Madeline.

Madge (Greek) a familiar form of Madeline, Margaret.

Madhubala (Hindi) little girl of honey.

Madia (Greek) a form of Madeline.

Madilyn, Madilynn (Greek) forms of Madeline.

Madison ⭐ (English) good; child of Maud.

Madlaberta (German) brilliant work.

Madlyn (Greek, English) a form of Madeline.

Madolyn (Greek) a form of Madeline.

Madonna (Latin) my lady.

Madra (Spanish) a form of Madrona.

Madrona (Spanish) mother.

Madysen, Madyson (English) forms of Madison.

Mae (English) a form of May. History: Mae Jemison was the first African American woman in space.

Maegan, Maegen, Maeghan (Irish) forms of Megan.

Maeko (Japanese) honest child.

Maeve (Irish) joyous. Mythology: a legendary Celtic queen.

Magali, Magalie, Magaly (Hebrew) from the high tower.

Magalí (Spanish) a form of Magali.

Magan, Maghan (Greek) forms of Megan.

Magda (Czech, Polish, Russian) a form of Magdalen.

Magdalen (Greek) high tower. Bible: Magdala was the home of Saint Mary Magdalen.

Magdalén (Spanish) a form of Magdalen.

Magdalena (Greek) a form of Magdalen.

Magdalene (Greek) a form of Magdalen.

Magen GB (Greek) a form of Megan.

Magena (Native American) coming moon.

Maggi, Maggy (English) forms of Maggie.

Maggie (Greek) pearl. (English) a familiar form of Magdalen, Margaret.

Magina (Latin) magician.

Magna (Latin) great.

Magnolia (Latin) flowering tree.

Maha (Iranian) crystal. (Arabic) wild cow; cow's eyes.

Mahal (Filipino) love.

Mahala (Arabic) fat; marrow; tender. (Native American) powerful woman.

Mahalia (American) a form of Mahala.

Maharene (Ethiopian) forgive us.

Mahayla (American) a form of Mahala.

Mahesa BG (Hindi) great lord. Religion: a name for the Hindu god Shiva.

Mahila (Sanskrit) woman.

Mahina (Hawaiian) moon glow.

Mahira (Hebrew) energetic.

Mahlí (Hebrew) astute.

Mahogany (Spanish) rich; strong.

Mahogony (Spanish) a form of Mahogany.

Mahuitzic (Nahuatl) honored, glorious.

Mahuizoh (Nahuatl) glorious person.

Mai (Japanese) brightness. (Vietnamese) flower. (Navajo) coyote.

Maia (Greek) mother; nurse. (English) kinswoman; maiden. Mythology: the loveliest of the Pleiades, the seven daughters of Atlas, and the mother of Hermes.

Maiah (Greek, English) a form of Maia.

Maiara (Tupi) wise.

Maida (English) maiden. (Greek) a short form of Madeline.

Maigan (American) a form of Megan.

Maija (Finnish) a form of Mary.

Maika (Hebrew) a familiar form of Michaela.

Maili (Polynesian) gentle breeze.

Maimi (Japanese) smiling truth.

Maira (Irish) a form of Mary.

Maire (Irish) a form of Mary.

Mairghread (Irish, Scottish) a form of Margaret.

Mairi (Irish) a form of Mary.

Maisey, Maisie (Scottish) familiar forms of Margaret.

Maisha (Arabic) walking with a proud, swinging gait.

Maison BG (Arabic) a form of Maysun.

Maita (Spanish) a form of Martha.

Maitana, Maitea, Maiten, Maitena (Spanish) forms of Maite.

Maitane (English) a form of Maite.

Maite (Spanish) lovable. A combination of Maria + Teresa. A form of Maita.

Maitland GB (American) a form of Maitlyn.

Maitlyn (American) a combination of Maita + Lynn.

Maiya (Greek) a form of Maia.

Maja (Arabic) a short form of Majidah.

Majalí (Hebrew) astute.

Majesta (Latin) majestic.

Majidah (Arabic) splendid.

Majorie (Greek, Scottish) a form of Marjorie.

Makaela (American) a form of Michaela.

Makaila (American) a form of Michaela.

Makala (Hawaiian) myrtle. (Hebrew) a form of Michaela.

Makana (Hawaiian) gift, present.
Makanah, Makanna, Makannah

Makani 🅱🅶 (Hawaiian) wind.

Makara (Hindi) Astrology: another name for the zodiac sign Capricorn.

Makayla (American) a form of Michaela.

Makaylee (American) a form of Michaela.

Makeda (Ethiopian) beautiful.

Makell (American) a short form of Makaela, Makala, Makayla.

Makena, Makenna (American) forms of Mackenna.

Makensie, Makenzee, Makenzi (American) forms of Mackenzie.

Makenzie 🅶🅱 (American) a form of Mackenzie.

Makia, Makiah (Hopi) forms of Makyah Makyla **(American) a form of Michaela.**

Makylah

Mala (Greek) a short form of Magdalen.
Malee, Mali

Malachie (Hebrew) angel of God.

Malaika (African) angel.

Malaina (French) a form of Malena.

Malají (Hebrew) my messenger.

Malak (Hungarian) a form of Malika.

Malana (Hawaiian) bouyant, light.

Malanie (Greek) a form of Melanie.

Malaya (Filipino) free.

Malaysia (Malay) Geography: Southeast Asian country near Thailand and Vietnam.

Malea, Maleah (Filipino) forms of Malaya. (Hawaiian, Zuni, Spanish) forms of Malia.

Maleeka (Hungarian) a form of Malika.

Maleena (Hebrew, English, Native American, Russian) a form of Malina.

Malcka (Hungarian) a form of Malika.

Malena (Swedish) a familiar form of Magdalen.

Malerie (French) a form of Mallory.
Mallerie

Malfreda (German) peaceful worker.

Malha (Hebrew) queen.

Mali (Tai) jasmine flower. (Tongan) sweet. (Hungarian) a short form of Malika.

Malia (Hawaiian, Zuni) a form of Mary. (Spanish) a form of Maria.

Maliah (Hawaiian, Zuni, Spanish) a form of Malia.

Malika (Hungarian) industrious. (Arabic) queen.

Malikah (Hungarian) a form of Malika.

Malina (Hebrew) tower. (Native American) soothing. (Russian) raspberry.

Malinalxochitl (Nahuatl) grass flower.

Malinda (Greek) a form of Melinda.

Malini (Hindi) gardener.

Malisa, Malissa (Greek) forms of Melissa.

Maliyah (Hawaiian, Zuni, Spanish) a form of Malia.

Malka (Hebrew) queen.
Malkah, Malkl, Malkia, Malkiah, Malkya, Malkyah

Malki (Hebrew) a form of Malka.

Mallalai (Pashto) beautiful.

Malley (American) a familiar form of Mallory.
Mallee, Malli, Mallie, Mally, Maly

Mallori, Mallorie, Malori, Malorie, Malory (French) forms of Mallory.

Mallory GB (German) army counselor. (French) unlucky.

Malú (Spanish) a combination of Maria + Luisa.

Maluhia (Hawaiian) peaceful.

Malulani (Hawaiian) under a peaceful sky.

Malva (English) a form of Melba.
Malvah, Malvi, Malvy

Malvina (Scottish) a form of Melvina. Literature: a name created by the eighteenth-century Romantic poet James Macpherson.

Malyssa (Greek) a form of Melissa.

Mamen (Hebrew) a form of Carmen.

Mamie (American) a familiar form of Margaret.

Mamo BG (Hawaiian) saffron flower; yellow bird.

Mana (Hawaiian) psychic; sensitive.

Manal (Hawaiian) a form of Mana.

Manar (Arabic) guiding light.

Manara, Manayra

Manauia (Nahuatl) defend.

Manda (Spanish) woman warrior. (Latin) a short form of Amanda.

Mandara (Hindi) calm.
Mandarah

Mandee, Mandi, Mandie (Latin) forms of Mandy.

Mandeep BG (Punjabi) enlightened.

Mandisa (Xhosa) sweet.

Mandy (Latin) lovable. A familiar form of Amanda, Manda, Melinda.
Mandey

Manela (Catalan) a form of Manuela.

Manette (French) a form of Mary.

Mangena (Hebrew) song, melody.

Mani (Chinese) a mantra repeated in Tibetan Buddhist prayer to impart understanding.

Manilla (Australian) meandering, **winding river.**

Manisha (Indian) intellect.

Manjot BG (Indian) light of the mind.
Manjyot

Manka (Polish, Russian) a form of Mary.
Mankah

Manoela, Manoli (Hebrew) forms of Manuela.

Manola (Spanish) a form of Manuela.

Manon (French) a familiar form of Marie.

Manón (Spanish) a form of María.

Manpreet GB (Punjabi) mind full of love.
Manpret, Manprit

Manque (Mapuche) condor; woman of unyielding character.

Mansi (Hopi) plucked flower.

Manuela (Spanish) a form of Emmanuelle.

Manya (Russian) a form of Mary.

Mar (Spanish) sea.

Mara (Hebrew) melody. (Greek) a short form of Amara. (Slavic) a form of Mary.

Marabel (English) a form of Maribel.

Marah (Greek, Hebrew, Slavic) a form of Mara.

Maranda (Latin) a form of Miranda.
Marandah

Maravillas (Latin) admiration.

Maraya (Hebrew) a form of Mariah.

Marcedes (American) a form of Mercedes.

Marcela (Latin) a form of Marcella.

Marcelen (English) a form of Marcella.

Marceliana (Latin) a form of Marcela.

Marcelina (English) a form of Marcella.

Marcella (Latin) martial, warlike. Mythology: Mars was the god of war.

Marcelle (French) a form of Marcella.

Marcena (Latin) a form of Marcella, Marcia.

Marchelle (American) a form of Marcelle.

Marci, Marcie, Marcy (English) familiar forms of Marcella, Marcia.

Marcia (Latin) martial, warlike.

Márcia (Portuguese) a form of Marcia.

Marciann (American) a combination of Marci + Ann.

Marcilynn (American) a combination of Marci + Lynn.

Marcionila (Latin) a form of Marcia.

Mardella (English) meadow near a lake.

Marden BG (English) from the meadow with a pool.

Mardi (French) born on Tuesday. (Aramaic) a familiar form of Martha.

Mare (Irish) a form of Mary.

Mareena (Latin) a form of Marina.

Marelda (German) renowned warrior.

Maren GB (Latin) sea. (Aramaic) a form of Mary.

Marena (Latin) a form of Marina.

Maresa, Maressa (Latin) forms of Marisa.

Maretta (English) a familiar form of Margaret.

Margaret (Greek) pearl. History: Margaret Hilda Thatcher served as British prime minister. ,

Margarete (German) a form of Margaret.

Margaretha (German) a form of Margaret.
Margareth, Margarethe

Margarit (Greek) a form of Margaret.

Margarita (Italian, Spanish) a form of Margaret.

Margaux (French) a form of Margaret.
Margeaux

Marge (English) a short form of Margaret, Marjorie.

Margery (English) a form of Margaret.

Margie (English) a familiar form of Marge, Margaret.

Margit (Hungarian) a form of Margaret.

Margo, Margot (French) forms of Margaret.

Margret (German) a form of Margaret.

Margryta (Lithuanian) a form of Margaret.

Marguerite (French) a form of Margaret.

Mari (Japanese) ball. (Spanish) a form of Mary.

Maria (Hebrew) bitter; sea of bitterness. (Italian, Spanish) a form of Mary.

María (Hebrew) a form of Maria.

María de la Concepción (Spanish) Mary of the conception.

María de la Paz (Spanish) Mary of peace.

María de las Nieves (Spanish) Mary of the snows.

María de las Victorias (Spanish) victorious Mary.

María de los Angeles (Spanish) angelic Mary.

María de los Milagros (Spanish) miraculous Mary.

María del Mar (Spanish) Mary of the sea.

María Inmaculada (Spanish) Immaculate Mary.

María José (Latin) a combination of María + José.

María Noel (Latin) a combination of María + Noel.

Mariaelena (Italian) a combination of Maria + Elena.
Maria Elena

Mariah, Marriah (Hebrew) forms of Mary.

Mariam (Hebrew) a form of Miriam.

Mariama (Hebrew) a form of Mariam.

Marian GB (English) a form of Mary Ann.

Marián (Spanish) a short form of Mariana.

Mariana, Marianna (Spanish) forms of Marian.

Mariane, Mariann, Marianne (English) forms of Mary Ann.

Marianela (Spanish) a combination of Mariana + Estela.

Mariángeles (Spanish) a combination of María + Ángeles.

Maribel (French) beautiful. (English) a combination of Maria + Bel.

Maribeth (American) a form of Mary Beth.
Maribette, Mariebeth

Marica (Italian) a form of Marice. (Dutch, Slavic) a form of Marika.

Maricarmen (American) a form of Marycarmen.

Marice (Italian) a form of Mary.

Maricela (Latin) a form of Marcella.

Maricruz (Spanish) a combination of María + Cruz.

Maridel (English) a form of Maribel.

Marie (French) a form of Mary.
Maree, Marrie

Marie Andree (French) a combination of Marie + Andree.

Marie Ann, Marie Anne (American) **combinations of Marie + Ann.**

Marie Chantal (French) a combination of Marie + Chantal.

Marie Christi (American) a combination of Marie + Christi.

Marie Clair, Marie Claire (American) combinations of Marie + Clair.

Marie Claude (French) a combination of Marie + Claude.

Marie Elaine (American) a combination of Marie + Elaine.

Marie Eve, Marie-Eve (American) combinations of Marie + Eve.

Marie Frances (French) a combination of Marie + Frances.

Marie Helene (American) a combination of Marie + Helene.

Marie Jeanne (American) a combination of Marie + Jeanne.

Marie Joelle (French) a combination of Marie + Joelle.

Marie Josee (French) a combination of Marie + Josee.

Marie Kim (American) a combination of Marie + Kim.

Marie Laurence (French) a combination of Marie + Laurence.

Marie Lou (American) a combination of Marie + Lou.

Marie Louise (American) a combination of Marie + Louise.

Marie Maud, Marie Maude (American) combinations of Marie + Maud.
Marie-Maud, Marie-Maude

Marie Michele, Marie Michell (American)

combinations of Marie + Michele.

Marie Noelle (American) a combination of Marie + Noelle.

Marie Pascale (French) a combination of Marie + Pascale.

Marie Philippa (French) a combination of Marie + Philippa.

Marie Pier, Marie Pierre, Marie-Pier (French) combinations of Marie + Pier.

Marie Soleil (Spanish) a combination of Marie + Soleil (see Solana).

Marie Sophie (French) a combination of Marie + Sophie.
Marie-Sophie

Mariel, Marielle **(German, Dutch) forms of Mary.**

Mariela, Mariella (German, Dutch) forms of Mary.

Marielena (German, Dutch) a form of Mary.

Marietta (Italian) a familiar form of Marie.

Marieve (American) a combination of Mary + Eve.

Marigold (English) Mary's gold. Botany: a plant with yellow or orange flowers.

Mariha (Hebrew, Italian, Spanish) a form of Maria.

Marija (Hebrew, Italian, Spanish) a form of Maria.

Marika (Dutch, Slavic) a form of Mary.

Mariko (Japanese) circle.

Marilee, Marilie, Marily (American) combinations of Mary + Lee. See Marilín **(Spanish) a combination of Maria + Linda.**

Marilla (Hebrew, German) a form of Mary.

Marilou, Marilu (American) forms of Marylou.

Marilú (Spanish) a combination of María + Luz.

Marilyn (Hebrew) Mary's line or descendants.

Marilyne, Marilynn (Hebrew) forms of Marilyn.
Marilynne, Marrilynn, Marrilynne

Marin GB (Latin, Aramaic) a form of Maren.

Marina (Latin) sea. Mariña **(Latin) a form of Marina.**

Marinda (Latin) a form of Marina.

Marine, Maryn (Latin, Aramaic) forms of Maren.

Marinés (Spanish) a combination of María + Inés.

Marini (Swahili) healthy; pretty.

Marinna (Latin) a form of Marina.

Mariola (Italian) a form of María.

Marion GB **(French) a form of Mary.**

Marión, Mariona (Spanish) forms of Marion.

Mariposa (Spanish) butterfly.

Maris (Latin) sea. (Greek) a short form of Amaris, Damaris. **Marisa** (Latin) sea.
Mariesa, Marisah

Marisabel (Spanish) a combination of María + Isabel.

Marisabela (Spanish) a combination of María + Isabela.

Marisel (Spanish) a form of Marisabel.

Marisela (Latin) a form of Marisa.

Marisha (Russian) a familiar form of Mary.

Marisol (Spanish) sunny sea.

Marissa (Latin) a form of Maris, Marisa.

Marit (Aramaic) lady.

Marita (Spanish) a form of Marisa. (Aramaic) a form of Marit.

Maritsa (Arabic) a form of Maritza.

Maritxu (Basque) a familiar form of Maria.

Maritza (Arabic) blessed.

Mariya, Mariyah (Hebrew, Italian, Spanish) forms of Maria. (Arabic) forms of Mariyan.

Mariyan (Arabic) purity.
Mariyana, Mariyanna

Mariza (Latin) a form of Marisa.

Marja (Finnish) a form of Maria.

Marjan (Persian) coral. (Polish) a form of Mary.

Marjie (Scottish) a familiar form of Marjorie.
Marje, Marjey, Marji, Marjy

Marjolaine (French) marjoram.

Marjorie (Greek) a familiar form of Margaret. (Scottish) a form of Mary.

Markayla (American) a combination of Mary + Kayla.

Markeisha (English) a combination of Mary + Keisha.

Markell 🅱🅶 (Latin) a form of Mark

Markelle (Latin) a form of Mark **Markesha** (English) a form of Markeisha.

Markeshia (English) a form of Markeisha.

Marketa (Czech) a form of Markita.
Markete, Marketta, Markette

Marki (Latin) a form of Markie.

Markia (Latin) a form of Markie.

Markie (Latin) martial, warlike.

Markisha (English) a form of Markeisha.

Markita (Czech) a form of Margaret.

Marla (English) a short form of Marlena, Marlene.
Marlah

Marlaina (English) a form of Marlena.
Marlainna

Marlana (English) a form of Marlena.

Marlayna (English) a form of Marlena.

Marlee, Marleigh, Marlie, Marly (English) forms of Marlene.
Marlea, Marleah, Marli

Marleen (Greek, Slavic) a form of Marlene.
Marleene

Marlen (Greek, Slavic) a form of Marlene.

Marlena (German) a form of Marlene.

Marlene (Greek) high tower. (Slavic) a form of Magdalen.

Marleny (Greek, Slavic) a familiar form of Marlene.

Marley 🇬🇧 (English) a form of Marlene.

Marlin 🅱🅶 (Greek, Slavic) a form of Marlene.

Marlina (Greek, Slavic) a form of Marlena.
Marlinah, Marlinda

Marlis (English) a short form of Marlisa.

Marlisa (English) a combination of Maria + Lisa.
Marlissa, Marlysa, Marlyssa

Marlo 🅱🅶 (English) a form of Mary.

Marlyn (Hebrew) a short form of Marilyn. (Greek, Slavic) a form of Marlene.

Marmara (Greek) sparkling, shining.

Marmarah, Marmee

Marni, Marnie (Hebrew) short forms of Marnina.

Marnina (Hebrew) rejoice.

Marnisha (Hebrew) a form of Marnina.

Maroula (Greek) a form of Mary.
Maroulah, Maroulla, Maroullah

Marquesa (Spanish) she who works with a hammer.

Marquesha (American) a form of Markeisha.

Marquetta (Spanish) a form of Marcia.
Marquet, Marqueta, Marquete, Marquette

Marquilla (Spanish) bitter.

Marquis 🆚 (French) a form of Marquise.

Marquise 🆚 (French) noblewoman.

Marquisha (American) a form of Marquise.
Marquiesha, Marquisia

Marquita, Marquitta (Spanish) forms of Marcia.

Marrisa, Marrissa (Latin) forms of Marisa.
Marrisah, Marrissia

Marsala (Italian) from Marseilles, France.

Marsha (English) a form of Marcia.

Marshae, Marshay (English) forms of Marsha.

Marta (English) a short form of Martha, Martina.

Martha (Aramaic) lady; sorrowful. Bible: a friend of Jesus.

Marti 🆖 (English) a familiar form of Martha, Martina.

Martia (Latin) a form of Marcia.

Martina (Latin) martial, warlike.

Martine (Latin) a form of Martina.

Martiniana (Latin) a form of Martina.

Martirio (Spanish) martyrdom.

Martisha (Latin) a form of Martina.

Martiza (Arabic) blessed.

Marty 🆚 (English) a familiar form of Martha, Martina.

Maru (Japanese) round.
Maroo

Maruca (Spanish) a form of Mary.
Mariucca, Maruja, Maruka

Maruska, Marusya (Russian) tart.

Marva (Hebrew) sweet sage.
Marvah

Marvella (French) marvelous.

Marvina (English) lover of the sea.

Mary (Hebrew) bitter; sea of bitterness. Bible: the mother of Jesus.

Mary Ann, Maryan, Maryann, Maryanne (English) combinations of Mary + Ann.

Mary Beth, Marybeth (American) combinations of Mary + Beth.
Mareabeth, Mareebeth

Mary Kate, Mary-Kate, Marykate (American) combinations of Mary + Kate.

Mary Katherine (American) a combination of Mary + Katherine.

Mary Margaret, Mary-Margaret (American) combinations of Mary + Margaret.

Marya (Arabic) purity; bright whiteness.

Maryah (Arabic) a form of Marya.

Maryam (Hebrew) a form of Miriam.

Marycarmen (American) a combination of Mary + Carmen.

Maryellen (American) a combination of Mary + Ellen.

Maryjane (American) a combination of Mary + Jane.

Maryjo (American) a combination of Mary + Jo.

Marylene (Hebrew) a form of Marylin.
Marylina, Maryline

Marylin (Hebrew) a form of Marilyn.

Marylou (American) a combination of Mary + Lou.

Marysa, Maryse, Maryssa (Latin) forms of Marisa.

Masada (Hebrew) strong foundation, support.

Masago (Japanese) sands of time.

Masani (Luganda) gap toothed.

Masha (Russian) a form of Mary.

Mashika (Swahili) born during the rainy season.

Masiel (English) a form of Massiel.

Mason BG (Arabic) a form of Maysun.

Massiel (Hebrew) she who comes down from the stars.

Mastidia (Greek) whip.

Matahari (Indonesian) light of the day.

Matana (Hebrew) gift.

Mathena (Hebrew) gift of God.

Mathieu BG (French) a form of Matthew.

Mathilde (German) a form of Matilda.

Matilda (German) powerful battler.

Matrika (Hindi) mother. Religion: a name for the Hindu goddess Shakti in the form of the letters of the alphabet.

Matrona (Latin) mother.

Matsuko (Japanese) pine tree.

Mattea (Hebrew) gift of God.

Matthew BG (Hebrew) gift of God. Bible: author of the Gospel of Matthew.

Mattie (English) a familiar form of Martha, Matilda.

Mattison BG (English) a form of Madison.

Matty BG (English) a familiar form of Martha, Matilda.

Matusha (Spanish) a form of Matilda.

Matxalen (Basque) a form of Magdalena.

Maud, Maude (English) short forms of Madeline, Matilda.

Mauli BG (Tongan) a New Zealander of Pacific Island descent, also known as a Maori.

Maura (Irish) dark. A form of Mary, Maureen.
Maureen (French) dark. (Irish) a form of Mary. .

Maurelle (French) dark; elfin.

Maurise (French) dark skinned; moor; marshland.

Maurissa (French) a form of Maurise.

Mausi (Native American) plucked flower.

Mauve (French) violet colored.

Maverick BG (American) independent.

Mavia (Irish) happy.
Maviah, Mavie, Mavya, Mavyah

Mavis (French) thrush, songbird.

Maxie (English) a familiar form of Maxine.

Máxima, Máximina (Latin) forms of Maxine.

Maxime BG (Latin) a form of Maxine.

Maximiana (Spanish) a form of Máxima.

Maximiliana (Latin) eldest of all.

Maxine (Latin) greatest.

May (Latin) great. (Arabic) discerning. (English) flower; month of May

Maya ★ (Hindi) God's creative power. (Greek) mother; grandmother. (Latin) great. A form of Maia.
Mayam, Mya

Mayah (Hindi, Greek, Latin) a form of Maya.

Maybeline (Latin) a familiar form of Mabel.

Maybell (Latin) a form of Mabel.

Maycee (Scottish) a form of Maisey.

Maygan, Maygen (Irish) forms of Megan.

Maylyn (American) a combination of May + Lynn.

Mayola (Latin) a form of May.

Mayoree (Tai) beautiful.

Mayra (Australian) spring wind. (Tai) a form of Mayoree.
Mayrah

Maysa (Arabic) walks with a proud stride.

Maysun (Arabic) beautiful.

Mayte (Spanish) a form of Maite.

Mazel (Hebrew) lucky.
Mazal, Mazala, Mazalah, Mazela, Mazella, Mazelle

Mc Kenna, Mckena (American) forms of Mackenna.

Mc Kenzie, McKenzie 🇧🇬 (Irish) forms of Mackenzie.

Mckaela (American) a form of Michaela.

Mckaila (American) a form of Michaela.

Mckala (American) a form of Michaela.

Mckayla (American) a form of Michaela.

Mckaylee (American) a form of Michaela.

Mckell (American) a form of Makell.
Mckelle

Mckenna 🇬🇧 (American) a form of Mackenna.

Mckenzie 🇬🇧 (Irish) a form of Mackenzie.

Mckinley 🇧🇬 (Scottish) child of the learned ruler.

Mckinzie (American) a form of Mackenzie.

Mead 🇧🇬 (Greek) honey wine.

Meade (Greek) honey wine.

Meadow (English) meadow.

Meagan, Meagen (Irish) forms of Megan.

Meaghan (Welsh) a form of Megan.

Meara (Irish) mirthful.

Mecatl (Nahuatl) rope; lineage.

Mecha (Latin) a form of Mercedes.

Mechelle (French) a form of Michelle.

Meda (Native American) prophet; priestess.

Medea (Greek) ruling. (Latin) middle. Mythology: a sorceress who helped Jason get the Golden Fleece.

Medina (Arabic) History: the site of Muhammad's tomb.

Medora (Greek) mother's gift. Literature: a character in Lord Byron's poem *The Corsair*.

Meena (Hindi) blue semiprecious stone; bird. (Greek, German, Dutch) a form of Mena.

Meera (Hebrew) a form of Meira.

Meg (English) a short form of Margaret, Megan.

Megan (Greek) pearl; great. (Irish) a form of Margaret.

Megane, Megann, Meganne, Megen, Meggan (Irish) forms of Megan.

Megara (Greek) first. Mythology: Heracles's first wife.

Megean (American) a form of Megan.

Meggie, Meggy (English) familiar forms of Margaret, Megan.

Megha (Welsh) a short form of Meghan.

Meghan, Meghann (Welsh) forms of Megan.

Mehadi (Hindi) flower.

Mehira (Hebrew) speedy; energetic.

Mehitabel (Hebrew) benefited by trusting God.

Mehri (Persian) kind; lovable; sunny.

Mei (Hawaiian) great. (Chinese) a short form of Meiying.

Meira (Hebrew) light.

Meit (Burmese) affectionate.

Meiying (Chinese) beautiful flower.

Mejorana (Spanish) marjoram.

Meka 🇬🇧 (Hebrew) a familiar form of Michaela.

Mekayla (American) a form of Michaela.

Mekenzie (American) a form of Mackenzie.

Mel 🇧🇬 (Portuguese, Spanish) sweet as honey.
Mell

Mela (Hindi) religious service. (Polish) a form of Melanie.

Melaida (Spanish) a form of Melissa.

Melaina (Latin, Greek) a form of Melina.

Melana (Russian) a form of Melanie.

Melaney, Melani, Melannie, Melany (Greek) forms of Melanie.

Melanie ⭐ (Greek) dark skinned.

Melantha (Greek) dark flower.
Melanthe

Melba (Greek) soft; slender. (Latin) mallow flower.

Mele (Hawaiian) song; poem.

Melea, Meleah (German) forms of Melia.

Melecent (English) a form of Millicent.

Melecia (Greek) studious woman.

Meleni (Tongan) melon.

Melesse (Ethiopian) eternal.

Melia (German) a short form of Amelia.

Melibea (Greek) she who takes care of the oxen.

Melicent (English) a form of Millicent.

Melina (Latin) canary yellow. (Greek) a short form of Melinda.

Melinda (Greek) honey.

Meliora (Latin) better.

Mellisa, Mellissa (Greek) forms of Melissa.

Melisande (French) a form of Melissa, Millicent.

Melissa ⭐ (Greek) honey bee

Melita (Greek) a form of Melissa. (Spanish) a short form of Carmelita.

Melitina (Latin) a form of Melinda.

Melitona (Greek) she who was born in Malta.

Melly (American) a familiar form of names beginning with "Mel."

Melodía (Greek) a form of Melody.

Melodie (Greek) a form of Melody.

Melody (Greek) melody. .

Melonie (American) a form of Melanie.

Melosa (Spanish) sweet; tender.

Melosia (Spanish) sweet.

Melrose (American) a combination of Melanie + Rose.

Melusina (Greek) a form of Melissa.

Melvina (Irish) armored chief. .

Melyna (Latin, Greek) a form of Melina.

Melynda (Greek) a form of Melinda.

Melyne (Greek) a short form of Melinda.

Melyssa (Greek) a form of Melissa.

Mena (German, Dutch) strong. (Greek) a short form of Philomena. History: Menes is believed to be the first king of Egypt.

Mendi (Basque) a form of Mary.

Menodora (Greek) gift of Mene, the moon goddess.

Menora (Hebrew) candleholder. Religion: a menorah is a special nine-branched candleholder used during the holiday of Hanukkah.

Meranda, Merranda (Latin) forms of Miranda.

Mérane (French) a form of Mary.

Mercades (Latin, Spanish) a form of Mercedes.

Mercé (Spanish) a short form of Mercedes.

Mercede (Latin, Spanish) a form of Mercedes.

Mercedes (Latin) reward, payment. (Spanish) merciful.

Mercedez (Latin, Spanish) a form of Mercedes.
Mercedeez

Merces (Latin) mercies.

Mercia (English) a form of Marcia. History: an ancient British kingdom.

Mercilla (English) a form of Mercy.

Mercuria (Greek) refers to the Greek god Mercury.

Mercy (English) compassionate, merciful. .

Meredith (Welsh) protector of the sea.

Meri (Finnish) sea. (Irish) a short form of Meriel.

Meria (African) rebellious.

Meriah (Hebrew) a form of Mariah. (African) a form of Meria.

Meridith (Welsh) a form of Meredith.

Meriel (Irish) shining sea.

Merilyn (English) a combination of Merry + Lynn.

Merina (Latin) a form of Marina. (Australian) a form of Merrina.

Merinda (Australian) beautiful.

Merisa, Merissa (Latin) forms of Marisa.

Merite (Latin) deserving.

Merle BG (Latin, French) blackbird.

Merpati (Indonesian) dove.

Merrilee (American) a combination of Merry + Lee. ,

Merrina (Australian) grass seed.

Merritt BG (Latin) a form of Merite.

Merry (English) cheerful, happy. A familiar form of Mercy, Meredith.

Mertysa (English) famous.

Merudina (German) famous, notable.

Meruvina (German) famous victory.

Meryl (German) famous. (Irish) shining sea. A form of Meriel, Muriel.

Mesalina (Italian) History: Messalina was a Roman empress.

Mesha (Hindi) another name for the zodiac sign Aries.

Mesi (Egyptian) water.

Meskhenet (Egyptian) destiny.

Messalina (Latin) she who has an insatiable appetite.

Messina (Latin) middle child. (African) spoiler.

Meta (German) a short form of Margaret.

Metodia (Greek) methodical woman.

Metrodora (Greek) gift of the city.

Meztli (Nahuatl) moon.

Mhairie (Scottish) a form of Mary.

Mia ★ (Italian) mine. A familiar form of Michaela, Michelle.

Mía (Spanish) a form of Maria.

Miah (Italian) a form of Mia.

Mica (Hebrew) a form of Micah.

Micaela (Hebrew) a form of Michaela.

Micah BG (Hebrew) a form of Michael. Bible: one of the Old Testament prophets.

Micaiah BG (Hebrew) a form of Micah.

Micaila (Hebrew) a form of Michaela.

Micala (Hebrew) a form of Michaela.

Micayla (Hebrew) a form of Michaela.
Micayle, Micaylee

Micha GB (Hebrew) a form of Micah.

Michael BG (Hebrew) who is like God?

Michaela, Michaella (Hebrew) forms of Michael.

Michaila (Hebrew) a form of Michaela.

Michal BG (Hebrew) a form of Michael. (Italian) a form of Michele.

Michala, Michalla (Hebrew) forms of Michaela.

Michayla (Hebrew) a form of Michaela.

Micheala (Hebrew) a form of Michaela.
Michealia

Michel BG (Italian) a form of Michele. (French) a form of Michelle.

Michela (Hebrew) a form of Michala. (Italian) a form of Michele.

Michele GB (Italian) a form of Michelle.

Michelina (Italian) a form of Michaela.

Micheline (Italian) a form of Michelina.

Michell (Italian) a form of Michelle.

Michelle (French) who is like God? **Michi** (Japanese) righteous way.

Michiko (Japanese) righteous child.

Mickaela (Hebrew) a form of Michaela.
Mickael

Mickala (Hebrew) a form of Michaela.

Mickayla (Hebrew) a form of Michaela.

Mickenzie GB (American) a form of Mackenzie.

Micki (American) a familiar form of Michaela.

Micol, Milca, **Milcal** (Hebrew) she who is queen.

Midori (Japanese) green.

Mieko (Japanese) prosperous.
Mieke, Myeko

Mielikki (Finnish) pleasing.

Miette (French) small; sweet.

Migdana (Hebrew) present.

Migina (Omaha) new moon.

Mignon (French) dainty, petite; graceful.

Mignonette (French) flower.

Miguela (Spanish) a form of Michaela.
Micquel, Miguelina, Miguelita

Mika GB (Japanese) new moon. (Russian) God's child. (Native American) wise raccoon. (Hebrew) a form of Micah. (Latin) a form of Dominica.

Mikaela (Hebrew) a form of Michaela.

Mikah BG (Hebrew, Japanese, Russian, Native American) a form of Mika.

Mikaila (American) a form of Michaela.

Mikal BG (Hebrew) a short form of Michael, Michaela.

Mikala, Mikalah (Hebrew) forms of Michaela.

Mikayla (American) a form of Michaela.

Mikel BG (Hebrew) a short form of Michael, Michaela.

Mikela (Hebrew) a form of Michaela.

Mikelena (Danish) a form of Michaela.

Mikelle (Hebrew) a short form of Michael, Michaela.

Mikenna (American) a form of Mackenna.

Mikenzie (American) a form of Mackenzie.

Mikesha (American) a form of Michaela.

Mikhaela (American) a form of Michaela.
Mikhalea, Mikhelle

Mikhaila (American) a form of Michaela.

Mikhala (American) a form of Michaela.

Mikhayla (American) a form of Michaela.

Miki GB (Japanese) flower stem.

Mikia (Japanese) a form of Miki.

Mikka (Hebrew, Japanese, Russian, Native American) a form of Mika.

Mikki (Japanese) a form of Miki.

Mikyla (American) a form of Michaela.

Mila ☆ (Russian) dear one. (Italian, Slavic) a

short form of Camila,
Ludmilla.

Milada (Czech) my love.

Milagres (Latin) a form of
Milagros.

Milagros (Spanish)
miracle.

Milan GB (Italian) from
Milan, Italy.

Milana (Italian) from
Milan, Italy. (Russian) a
form of Melana.

Milba, Milva (German)
kind protector.

Milburga, Milburgues
(German) pleasant city.

Mildereda, Mildreda
(German) forms of
Mildred.

Mildred (English) gentle
counselor.

Milena (Greek, Hebrew,
Russian) a form of
Ludmilla, Magdalen,
Melanie.

Milenka (Russian) my
small one.

Mileta (German) generous,
merciful.

Milgita (German) pleasant
woman.

Milia (German)
industrious. A short form
of Amelia, Emily.

Miliani (Hawaiian)
caress.

Mililani BG (Hawaiian)
heavenly caress.

Milissa (Greek) a form of
Melissa.

Milka (Czech) a form of
Amelia.

Millaray (Mapuche)
golden, fragrant flower.

Millicent (English)
industrious. (Greek) a
form of Melissa. , .

Millie, Milly (English)
familiar forms of Amelia,
Camille, Emily, Kamila,
Melissa, Mildred,
Millicent.

Mima (Burmese) woman.

Mimi (French) a familiar
form of Miriam.

Mina (German) love.
(Persian) blue sky.
(Arabic) harbor.
(Japanese) south. A short
form of names ending in
"mina."

Minal (Native American)
fruit.

Minda (Hindi) knowledge.

Mindi, Mindy (Greek)
familiar forms of
Melinda.

Mine (Japanese) peak;
mountain range.

Minerva (Latin) wise.
Mythology: the goddess of
wisdom.

Minette (French) faithful
defender.

Minia (German) great;
strong.

Minikin (Dutch) dear,
darling.

Minka (Polish) a short
form of Wilhelmina.

Minkie (Australian)
daylight.

Minna (German) a short
form of Wilhelmina.

Minnehaha (Native
American) laughing
water; waterfall.

Minnie (American) a
familiar form of Mina,
Minerva, Minna,
Wilhelmina.

Minore (Australian) white
blossom.

Minowa (Native American)
singer.

Minta (Latin) mint, minty.

Minya (Osage) older sister.

Mio (Japanese) three times
as strong.

Mío (Spanish) mine.

Miquela (Spanish) a form
of Michaela.

Mira (Latin) wonderful.
(Spanish) look, gaze. A
short form of Almira,
Amira, Marabel, Mirabel,
Miranda.

Mirabel (Latin) beautiful.

Miracle GB (Latin) wonder,
marvel.

Mirah (Latin, Spanish) a
form of Mira.

Mirana (Spanish) a form of
Miranda.

Miranda (Latin) strange;
wonderful; admirable.
Literature: the heroine of

Shakespeare's *The
Tempest.*

Mirari (Spanish) miracle.

Mireia (Spanish) a form of
Mireya.

Mireille (Hebrew) God
spoke. (Latin) wonderful.

Mirella (German, Irish) a
form of Meryl. (Hebrew,
Latin) a form of Mireille.

Miren (Hebrew) bitter.

Mirena (Hawaiian)
beloved.

Mireya (Hebrew) a form of
Mireille.

Miri (Gypsy) a short form
of Miriam.
Myri, Myry

Miriah (Hebrew) a form of
Mireille. (Gypsy) a form
of Miriam.

Miriam (Hebrew) bitter;
sea of bitterness. Bible:
the original form of Mary.

Míriam (Hebrew) a form
of Miriam.

Mirian (Hebrew) a form of
Miriam.

Mirna (Irish) polite.
(Slavic) peaceful.

Mirranda (Latin) a form of
Miranda.

Mirrin (Australian) cloud.

Mirta, Mirtha (Greek)
crown of myrtle.

Mirya (French) a form of
Mira.

Miryam (Hebrew) a form
of Miriam.

Misericordia (Spanish)
mercy.

Misha GB (Russian) a form
of Michaela.

Missy (English) a familiar
form of Melissa,
Millicent.

Misti, Mistie (English)
forms of Misty.

Misty (English) shrouded
by mist.

Mitra (Hindi) Religion: god
of daylight. (Persian)
angel.

Mituna (Moquelumnan)
like a fish wrapped up in
leaves.

Mitzi, Mitzy (German)
forms of Mary, Miriam.

Miwa (Japanese) wise eyes.

Mixcóatl (Nahuatl) serpent
of the sky.

Miya (Japanese) temple.
Miyana, Miyanna

Miyah (Japanese) a form of
Miya.

Miyaoaxochitl (Nahuatl)
maize tassel flower.

Miyo (Japanese) beautiful
generation.

Miyoko (Japanese)
beautiful generation's
child.

Miyuki (Japanese) snow.

Mizquixaual (Nahuatl)
mesquite face paint.

Moana (Hawaiian) ocean;
fragrance.

Mocha (Arabic) chocolate-
flavored coffee.

Modesta (Italian, Spanish)
a form of Modesty.

Modestine (French) a
form of Modesty.

Modesty (Latin) modest.

Moema (Tupi) sweet.

Moesha (American) a
short form of Monisha.
Moeisha, Moeysha

Mohala (Hawaiian) flowers
in bloom.
Moala, Mohalah

Mohini (Sanskrit)
enchantress.

Moira (Irish) great. A form
of Mary.

Molara (Basque) a form of
Mary.

Molarah, Molarra, Molarrah

Moledina (Australian)
creek.

Moli (Tongan) orange.

Molli, Mollie (Irish) forms
of Molly.

Molly (Irish) a familiar
form of Mary.

Momoztli (Nahuatl) altar.

Mona GB (Irish) noble.
(Greek) a short form of
Monica, Ramona,
Rimona.

Monae (American) a form
of Monet.

Monegunda (German)
overprotective.

Moneisha (American) a
form of Monisha.

Monesa (German)
protection.

Monet (French) Art: Claude Monet was a leading French impressionist remembered for his paintings of water lilies.

Monica (Greek) solitary. (Latin) advisor.

Mónica (Greek) a form of Monica.

Monifa (Yoruba) I have my luck.

Monika (German) a form of Monica.

Moniqua (French) a form of Monica.

Monique (French) a form of Monica.

Monisha (American) a combination of Monica + Aisha.
Monesha, Monishia

Monita (Spanish) noble.

Monroe (Gaelic) from the red marsh.

Monserrat, Montserrat (Catalan) serrated mountain. Geography: an island in the Caribbean

Montana GB (Spanish) mountain. Geography: a U.S. state.

Monteen (French) a form of Montana.

Montgomery BG (English) rich man's mountain.

Monti (Spanish) a familiar form of Montana. (English) a short form of Montgomery.

Moona (English) moon. (Australian) plenty.

Mora (Spanish) blueberry.

Moraima (Latin) she who is beautiful as the blueberry tree.

Moree (Australian) water.

Morela (Polish) apricot.

Morena (Irish) a form of Maureen.

Morgan GB (Welsh) seashore. Literature: Morgan le Fay was the half-sister of King Arthur.

Morganda (Spanish) a form of Morgan.

Morgane, Morgann, Morganne, Morghan, Morgyn (Welsh) forms of Morgan.

Morgen GB (Welsh) a form of Morgan.

Moriah (Hebrew) God is my teacher. (French) dark skinned. Bible: the mountain on which the Temple of Solomon was built.

Morie (Japanese) bay.

Morina (Irish) mermaid.

Morit (Hebrew) teacher.

Morowa (Akan) queen.

Morrin (Irish) long-haired.

Morrisa (Latin) dark skinned; moor; marshland.

Moselle (Hebrew) drawn from the water. (French) a white wine.

Mosi BG (Swahili) first-born.

Mosina (Hebrew) a form of Moselle.

Moswen BG (Tswana) white.

Mouna (Arabic) wish, desire.
, Mounia

Moyolehuani (Nahuatl) enamored one.

Moztla (Nahuatl) tomorrow.

Mrena (Slavic) white eyes.

Mucamutara (Egyptian) born during the war.

Mumtaz (Arabic) distinguished.

Muna (Greek, Irish) a form of Mona. (Arabic) a form of Mouna.

Munira (Arabic) she who is the source of light.

Mura (Japanese) village.

Muriel (Arabic) myrrh. (Irish) shining sea. A form of Mary. **Murphy** BG (Irish) sea warrior.

Muse (Greek) inspiration. Mythology: the Muses were nine Greek goddesses of the arts and sciences.

Musetta (French) little bagpipe.

Mushira (Arabic) counselor.

Musidora (Greek) beautiful muse.

Musika (Tongan) music.

Muslimah (Arabic) devout believer.

My (Burmese) a short form of Mya.

Mya (Burmese) emerald. (Italian) a form of Mia.

Myah (Burmese, Italian) a form of Mya.

Mycah (Hebrew) a form of Micah.
Myca

Mychaela (American) a form of Michaela.

Myeisha (American) a form of Moesha.

Myesha (American) a form of Moesha.

Myeshia (American) a form of Moesha.

Myia (Burmese, Italian) a form of Mya.
Myiah

Myiesha (American) a form of Moesha.

Myisha (American) a form of Moesha.

Myka (Hebrew, Japanese, Russian, Native American) a form of Mika.

Mykaela (American) a form of Michaela.

Mykaila (American) a form of Michaela.

Mykala (American) a form of Michaela.

Mykayla (American) a form of Michaela.

Mykel BG (American) a form of Michael.

Myla (English) merciful.

Mylene (Greek) dark.

Myra (Latin) fragrant ointment.

Myranda (Latin) a form of Miranda.

Myriah (Hebrew, Gypsy) a form of Miriah.

Myriam (American) a form of Miriam.

Myrissa (American) a form of Marisa.

Myrna (Irish) beloved.

Myrtle (Greek) evergreen shrub.

Myune (Australian) clear water.

N

Nabila (Arabic) born to nobility.

Nacha (Latin) a form of Ignacia.

Nachine (Spanish) hot, fiery.

Nada GB (Arabic) a form of Nadda.

Nadal (Catalan) a form of Natividad.

Nadda (Arabic) generous; dewy.

Nadeen, Nadine (French, Slavic) forms of Nadia.

Nadette (French) a short form of Bernadette.

Nadia (French, Slavic) hopeful.

Nadía (Egyptian) one who received the call of God.

Nadira (Arabic) rare, precious.

Nadiyah (French, Slavic) a form of Nadia.
Nadiya

Nadja, Nadya (French, Slavic) forms of Nadia.

Nadyenka (Russian) a form of Nadia.

Naeva (French) a form of Eve.

Nafisa (Arabic) a form of Nafisah.

Nafisah **(Arabic) precious thing; gem.**

Nafuna **(Luganda) born feet first.**

Nagida (Hebrew) noble; prosperous.
Nagda, Nagdah, Nageeda, Nagyda

Nahama (Hebrew) sweetness.

Nahid (Persian) Mythology: another name for Venus, the goddess of love and beauty.

Nahimana (Dakota) mystic.

Nahir (Arabic) clear; bright.

Nahla (Arabic) honeybee [hard "H" sound]; a drink of water [soft "H" sound].

Nahuatl (Nahuatl) four waters; the Nahuatl language.

Nahum (Hebrew) consolation.

Naiara (Spanish) reference to the Virgin Mary.

Naida (Greek) water nymph.

Naila (Arabic) successful.

Nailah GB (Arabic) a form of Naila.

Naima (Arabic) comfort; peace. (Indian) belonging to one.

Nairi (Armenian) land of rivers. History: a name for ancient Armenia.

Naís (Spanish) a form of Inés.

Naiya (Greek) a form of Naida.
Naia, Naiyana, Naya

Naja, Najah (Greek) forms of Naida. (Arabic) short forms of Najam, Najila.

Najam (Arabic) star.

Najee BG (Arabic) a form of Naji Najila **(Arabic) brilliant eyes.**

Najla (Arabic) a short form of Najila.

Najma (Arabic) a form of Najam.

Nakayla (American) a form of Nicole.

Nakea (Arabic) a form of Nakia.

Nakeia (Arabic) a foirm of Nakia.

Nakeisha (American) a combination of the prefix Na + Keisha.

Nakeita (American) a form of Nikita.

Nakesha (American) a form of Nakeisha.

Nakeya (Arabic) a form of Nakia.

Nakia GB (Arabic) pure.

Nakiah (Arabic) a form of Nakia.

Nakiesha (American) a form of Nakeisha.

Nakisha (American) a form of Nakeisha.

Nakita (American) a form of Nikita.

Nakiya (Arabic) a form of Nakia.
Nakiyah

Nala (Tanzanian) queen.

Nalani (Hawaiian) calm as the heavens.

Nalda (Spanish) strong.

Nalleli (Spanish) a form of Najla.

—ambi (Guarani) curative herb.

Nami (Japanese) wave.

Nan (German) a short form of Fernanda. (English) a form of Ann.

Nana BG (Hawaiian) spring.

Naná (Greek) she who is very young.

Nanci (English) a form of Nancy.

Nancy (English) gracious. A familiar form of Nan.

Nandalia (Australian) fire.

Nanette (French) a form of Nancy.

Nani (Greek) charming. (Hawaiian) beautiful.

Nanon (French) a form of Ann.

Nantilde (German) daring in combat.

Naolin (Spanish) Mythology: the Aztec sun god.

Naomi ✸ (Hebrew) pleasant, beautiful. Bible: Ruth's mother-in-law.

Naomí (Hebrew) a form of Naomi.

Naomie, Naomy (Hebrew) forms of Naomi.

Napea (Latin) from the valleys.

Nara (Greek) happy. (English) north. (Japanese) oak.

Narcissa (Greek) daffodil. Mythology: Narcissus was the youth who fell in love with his own reflection.

Narda (Latin) fervently devoted.

Narelle (Australian) woman from the sea.

Nari (Japanese) thunder.

Narissa (Greek) a form of Narcissa, Nerissa.

Narmada (Hindi) pleasure giver.

Naroa (Basque) tranquil, peaceful.

Nashawna (American) a combination of the prefix Na + Shawna.

Nashota (Native American) double; second-born twin.

Nasrin (Muslim, Arabic) wild rose.

Nastasia (Greek) a form of Anastasia.

Nastassja (Greek) a form of Nastasia.

Nasya (Hebrew) miracle.

Nata (Sanskrit) dancer. (Latin) swimmer. (Native American) speaker; creator. (Polish, Russian) a form of Natalie.

Natacha (Russian) a form of Natasha.

Natachia, Natacia, Naticha

Natalee, Natali, Nataly (Latin) forms of Natalie.

Natalí (Spanish) a form of Natalie.

Natalia (Russian) a form of Natalie. ,

Natália (Hungarian, Portuguese) a form of Natalie.

Natalie ⭐ (Latin) born on Christmas day.

Nataline (Latin) a form of Natalie.

Natalle (French) a form of Natalie.
Natale

Natalya (Russian) a form of Natalia.

Natane (Arapaho) daughter.

Natania (Hebrew) gift of God.

Natara (Arabic) sacrifice.

Natascha (Russian) a form of Natasha.

Natasha (Russian) a form of Natalie. ,

Natashia (Russian) a form of Natasha.

Natasia, Natassia (Greek) forms of Nastasia.

Natassja (Greek) a form of Nastasia.

Natesa (Hindi) cosmic dancer. Religion: another name for the Hindu god Shiva.

Natesha (Russian) a form of Natasha.

Nathalia (Latin) a form of Natalie.

Nathália (Portuguese) a form of Natalie.

Nathalie, Nathaly (Latin) forms of Natalie.

Nathifa (Egyptian) pure.

Natie (English) a familiar form of Natalie.

Natisha (Russian) a form of Natasha.

Natividad (Spanish) a form of Natividade.

Natividade (Latin) birth, nativity.

Natori **(Arabic) a form of Natara.**

Natosha (Russian) a form of Natasha.

Nature (Latin) nature; essence; life.

Naudia (French, Slavic) a form of Nadia.

Naunet (Egyptian) Mythology: goddess of the underworld.

Nava (Hebrew) beautiful; pleasant.

Navdeep BG (Sikh) new light.
Navdip

Naveen BG (Hindi) a form of Navin **Naveena** (Indian) new.

Navit (Hebrew) a form of Nava.
Navita, Navitah, Navyt, Navyta, Navytah

Nayara (Basque) swallow.

Nayeli, Nayelly, Nayely (Irish) forms of Neila.

Nayila (Arabic) a form of Najla.

Nazarena (Hebrew) a form of Nazareth.

Nazaret (Spanish) a form of Nazareth.

Nazareth (Hebrew) Religion: Jesus' birthplace.

Nazaria (Spanish) dedicated to God.

Neala (Irish) a form of Neila.

Nebthet (Egyptian) a form of Nephthys.

Necahual (Nahuatl) survivor; left behind.

Necana, Necane (Spanish) sorrows.

Necha (Spanish) a form of Agnes.

Neci BG (Hungarian) fiery, intense.

Necole (French) a form of Nicole.

Neda **(Slavic) born on Sunday.**

Nedda (English) prosperous guardian.

Neelam (Indian) sapphire.

Neely (Irish) a familiar form of Nelia.

Neema BG (Swahili) born during prosperous times.

Neena (Spanish) a form of Nina.

Neera (Greek) young one.

Nefertari (Egyptian) most beautiful. History: an Egyptian queen.

Neftali, Neftalí (Hebrew) she who fights and is victorious.

Neha (Indian) rain.

Neida (Slavic) a form of Neda.

Neila (Irish) champion.

Neisha (Scandinavian, American) a form of Niesha.

Nekeisha (American) a form of Nakeisha.

Nekia (Arabic) a form of Nakia.

Nelia (Spanish) yellow. (Latin) a familiar form of Cornelia.

Nelida, Nélida (Greek, Hebrew, Spanish) forms of Eleanor.

Nell (Greek) a form of Nelle. (English) a short form of Nellie.

Nelle (Greek) stone.

Nelli (Nahuatl) truth.

Nellie GB (English) a familiar form of Cornelia, Eleanor, Helen, Prunella.

Nellwyn (English) Nellie's friend.

Nelly (English) a familiar form of Cornelia, Eleanor, Helen, Prunella.

Nemesia (Greek) she who administers justice.

Nena (Spanish) a form of Nina.

Nenet (Egyptian) born near the sea.

Nenetl (Nahuatl) doll.

Neola (Greek) youthful.

Neoma (Greek) new moon.

Neomisia (Greek) beginning of the month.

Nephthys (Egyptian) mistress of the house.

Mythology: the goddess of the underworld.

Nerea (Spanish) mine.

Nereida (Greek) a form of Nerine.

Nereyda (Greek) a form of Nerine.

Neriah (Hebrew) lamp of God.

Nerine (Greek) sea nymph.

Nerissa (Greek) sea nymph. **Nerys** (Welsh) lady.

Nesha (Greek) a form of Nessa.

Nessa (Scandinavian) promontory. (Greek) a short form of Agnes.

Nessie (Greek) a familiar form of Agnes, Nessa, Vanessa.

Neta (Hebrew) plant, shrub.

Netanya (Hebrew) a form of Nathaniel

Netis (Native American) trustworthy.

Nettie (French) a familiar form of Annette, Antoinette, Nanette.

Neva (Spanish) snow. (English) new. Geography: a river in Russia.

Nevada GB (Spanish) snow. Geography: a western U.S. state.

Nevaeh (American) "heaven" spelled backwards.

Neve (Hebrew) life.

Neves (Portuguese) a form of Nieves.

Nevina (Irish) worshipper of the saint.

Neylan (Turkish) fulfilled wish.

Neysa (Greek, Scandinavian) a form of Nessa.

Neza (Slavic) a form of Agnes.

Ngoc (Vietnamese) jade.

Nguyen BG (Vietnamese) a form of Ngu

Nia (Irish) a familiar form of Neila. Mythology: Nia Ben Aur was a legendary Welsh woman.

Niabi (Osage) fawn.

Niam (Irish) bright.

Niamh (Irish) a form of Niam.

Nicanora (Spanish) victorious army.

Nicasia (Greek) triumphant woman.

Nicerata (Greek) worth of victories.

Niceta (Spanish) victorious one.

Nichelle (American) a combination of Nicole + Michelle. Culture: Nichelle Nichols was the first African American

woman featured in a television drama (*Star Trek*).

Nichol, Nichole, Nicholle (French) forms of Nicole.

Nicholas BG (French) victorious people.

Nicholette (French) a form of Nicole.

Nicki, Nickie (French) familiar forms of Nicole.

Nickole **(French) a form of Nicole.**

Nicky BG (French) a familiar form of Nicole.

Nicola GB (Italian) a form of Nicole.

Nicolas BG (French) a form of Nicholas.

Nicolasa (Spanish) a form of Nicole.

Nicole **(French) a form of Nicholas.** Nicolette, Nicollette **(French) forms of Nicole.**

Nicolina (French) a form of Nicoline.

Nicoline (French) a familiar form of Nicole.

Nicolle (French) a form of Nicole.

Nidia (Latin) nest.

Nidía (Greek) a form of Nidia.

Niesha (American) pure. (Scandinavian) a form of Nissa.

Nieves (Latin) refers to the Virgin Mary.

Nige (Latin) dark night.

Nija, Nijah (Latin) forms of Nige.

Nika GB (Russian) belonging to God.

Nikayla (American) a form of Nicole.

Nike BG (Greek) victorious. Mythology: the goddess of victory.

Nikelle **(American) a form of Nicole.**
Nikeille, Nikel, Nikela, Nikelie

Niki GB (Russian) a short form of Nikita. (American) a familiar form of Nicole.

Nikia, Nikkia (Arabic) forms of Nakia. (Russian, American) forms of Niki, Nikki.

Nikita GB (Russian) victorious people.

Nikki GB (American) a familiar form of Nicole.

Nikkita (Russian) a form of Nikita.

Nikkole, Nikole (French) forms of Nicole.

Nikolaevna (Russian) on the side of God.

Nikolette (French) a form of Nicole.

Nikolina (French) a form of Nicole.

Nila GB (Latin) Geography: the Nile River in Africa. (Irish) a form of Neila.

Nilda (Spanish) a short form of Brunhilda.

Nima BG (Hebrew) thread. (Arabic) blessing.

Nimia (Latin) she who is ambitious.

Nina (Spanish) girl. (Native American) mighty. (Hebrew) a familiar form of Hannah.

Ninette (French) small.

Ninfa (Greek) young wife.

Ninfodora (Greek) gift of the nymphs.

Niní (French) a form of Virginia.

Niñita (Russian) victory of the community.

Ninon **(French) a form of Nina.**

Ninoska (Russian) a form of Nina.

Niobe (Greek) she who rejuvenates.

Nirali (Hebrew) a form of Nirel.

Niranjana (Sanskrit) night of the full moon.

Nirel (Hebrew) light of God.

Nirveli (Hindi) water child.

Nisa (Arabic) woman.
Nisah, Nysa, Nysah

Nisha (American) a form of Niesha, Nissa.

Nishi (Japanese) west.

Nissa (Hebrew) sign, emblem. (Scandinavian) friendly elf; brownie.

Nita (Hebrew) planter. (Choctaw) bear. (Spanish) a short form of Anita, Juanita.

Nitara (Hindi) deeply rooted.

Nitasha (American) a form of Natasha.

Nitsa (Greek) a form of Helen.

Nituna (Native American) daughter.

Nitza (Hebrew) flower bud.

Nixie (German) water sprite.

Niya, Niyah (Irish) forms of Nia.
Niyana, Niyia

Nizana (Hebrew) a form of Nitza.

Noah BG (Hebrew) peaceful, restful. Bible: the patriarch who built the ark to survive the Flood.

Nochtli (Nahuatl) prickly pear fruit.

Noe, Noé (Hebrew) forms of Noah.

Noel BG (Latin) Christmas.

Noelani (Hawaiian) beautiful one from heaven. (Latin) a form of Noel.

Noelia (Latin) a form of Noel.

Noeline (Latin) a form of Noel.

Noella (French) a form of Noelle.

Noelle (French) Christmas.

Noely (Latin) a form of Noel.

Noemi, Noemie, Noemy (Hebrew) forms of Naomi.

Noemí (Hebrew) a form of Naomi.

Noga (Hebrew) morning light.

Noheli, Nohely (Latin) forms of Noel.
Nohal

Nohemi (Hebrew) a form of Naomi.

Nokomis (Dakota) moon daughter.

Nola (Latin) small bell. (Irish) famous; noble. A short form of Fionnula.

Nolana (Irish) a form of Nola.

Noleta (Latin) unwilling.

Nollie BG (English) a familiar form of Magnolia.

Noma (Hawaiian) a form of Norma.

Nominanda (Latin) she who will be elected.

Nona (Latin) ninth.

Noor GB (Aramaic) a form of Nura.

Nora ✴ (Greek) light. A familiar form of Eleanor, Honora, Leonor.

Norah (Greek) a form of Nora.

Norberta (Scandinavian) brilliant hero.

Nordica (Scandinavian) from the north.

Noreen (Irish) a form of Eleanor, Nora. (Latin) a familiar form of Norma.

Norell (Scandinavian) from the north.

Nori (Japanese) law, tradition.

Norleen (Irish) honest.

Notburga (German) protected beauty.

Nour GB (Aramaic) a short form of Nura.

Nova (Latin) new. A short form of Novella, Novia. (Hopi) butterfly chaser. Astronomy: a star that releases bright bursts of energy.

Novella (Latin) newcomer.

Novia (Spanish) sweetheart.

Noxochicoztli (Nahuatl) my necklace of flowers.

Nu (Burmese) tender. (Vietnamese) girl.

Nuala **(Irish) a short form of Fionnula.**
Nualah, Nula

Nubia (Egyptian) mother of a nation.

Nuela (Spanish) a form of Amelia.

Numa, Numas (Greek) she who establishes laws.

Numeria (Latin) she who enumerates.

Numilla (Australian) scout, lookout.

Nuna (Native American) land.

Nuncia (Latin) she who announces.

Nunciata (Latin) messenger.

Nunila (Spanish) ninth daughter.

Nunilona (Latin) a form of Nunila.

Nur (Aramaic) a short form of Nura.

Nura (Aramaic) light.

Nuria (Aramaic) the Lord's light.

Núria (Basque) buried deep among the hills.

Nuru BG (Swahili) daylight.

Nusi **(Hungarian) a form of Hannah.**

Nuwa (Chinese) mother goddess. Mythology: another name for Nü-gua, the creator of mankind.

Nya, Nyah (Irish) forms of Nia.

Nyasia (Greek) a form of Nyssa.

Nycole (French) a form of Nicole.

Nydia (Latin) nest.

Nydía (Greek) a form of Nydia.

Nyeisha (American) a form of Niesha.

Nyesha (American) a form of Niesha.
Nyeshia

Nyia (Irish) a form of Nia.

Nykia (Arabic) a form of Nakia.
Nykiah

Nyla (Latin, Irish) a form of Nila.

Nyoko (Japanese) gem, treasure.
Nioko

Nyomi (Hebrew) a form of Naomi.

Nyree (Maori) sea.

Nyssa (Greek) beginning.

Nyusha (Russian) a form of Agnes.

Nyx (Greek) night.

O

O'shea BG (Irish) a form of O'Shea.

O'Shea BG (Irish) child of Shea.

Oakley BG (English) from the oak meadow.

Oba BG (Yoruba) chief, ruler.

Obdulia (Latin) she who takes away sadness and pain.

Obelia (Greek) needle.

Ocean BG (Greek) ocean.

Oceana (Greek) ocean. Mythology: Oceanus was the god of the ocean.

Oceane (Greek) a form of Ocean.

Ocilia (Greek) a form of Othelia.

Octavia (Latin) eighth. .

Octaviana (Spanish) a form of Octavia.

Odanda (Spanish) famous land.

Odda (Scandinavian) rich.

Ode BG (Nigerian) born during travels.

Odeda (Hebrew) strong; courageous.

Odele (Greek) melody, song.

Odelette (French) a form of Odele.

Odelia (Greek) ode; melodic. (Hebrew) I will praise God. (French) wealthy. **Odella** (English) wood hill.

Odera (Hebrew) plough.

Odessa (Greek) odyssey, long voyage.

Odetta (German, French) a form of Odelia.

Odette (German, French) a form of Odelia.

Odina (Algonquin) mountain.

Ofelia (Greek) a form of Ophelia.

Ofélia (Portuguese) a form of Ophelia.

Ofira (Hebrew) gold.

Ofra (Hebrew) a form of Aphra.

Ogin (Native American) wild rose.
Ogina, Ogyn, Ogyna, Ogynah

Ohanna (Hebrew) God's gracious gift.

Ohtli (Nahuatl) road.

Oihane (Spanish) from the forest.

Okalani (Hawaiian) heaven.

Oki (Japanese) middle of the ocean.

Oksana (Latin) a form of Osanna.

Oksanochka (Russian) praises of God.

Ola GB (Scandinavian) ancestor. (Greek) a short form of Olesia.

Olalla (Greek) sweetly spoken.

Olathe (Native American) beautiful.

Olaya (Greek) she who speaks well.

Oldina (Australian) snow.

Oleander (Latin) Botany: a poisonous evergreen shrub with fragrant white, rose, or purple flowers.

Olechka (Russian) a form of Helga.

Oleda (Spanish) a form of Alida. **Olen** BG (Russian) deer.

Olena (Russian) a form of Helen.

Olesia (Greek) a form of Alexandra.

Oletha (Scandinavian) nimble.

Olethea (Latin) truthful.

Olga (Scandinavian) holy.

Olia (Russian) a form of Olga.

Oliana (Polynesian) oleander.

Olimpe (French) a form of Olympia.

Olimpíades (Greek) a form of Olympia.

Olina (Hawaiian) filled with happiness.
Olinah, Olyna, Olynah

Olinda (Latin) scented. (Spanish) protector of property. (Greek) a form of Yolanda.

Olisa (Ibo) God.

Olive **(Latin) olive tree.**

Oliveria (Latin) affectionate.

Olivia ☆ (Latin) a form of Olive. (English) a form of Olga.

Ollie BG (English) a familiar form of Olivia.

Olwen (Welsh) white footprint.

Olympia (Greek) heavenly.

Olympie (German) a form of Olympia.

143

Olyvia (Latin) a form of Olivia.

Oma (Hebrew) reverent. (German) grandmother. (Arabic) highest.

Omaira (Arabic) red.

Omega (Greek) last, final, end. Linguistics: the last letter in the Greek alphabet.

Ona (Latin, Irish) a form of Oona. (English) river.

Onatah (Iroquoian) daughter of the earth and the corn spirit.

Onawa (Native American) wide awake.

Ondine (Latin) a form of Undine.

Ondrea (Czech) a form of Andrea.

Oneida (Native American) eagerly awaited.

Oneisha (American) a form of Onesha.

Onella (Hungarian) a form of Helen.
Onela, Onelah, Onellah

Onesha (American) a combination of Ondrea + Aisha.

Onésima (Latin) she who is burdened.

Onfalia (Egyptian) she who does good deeds.

Oni (Yoruba) born on holy ground.
Onee, Oney, Onie, Onnie, Ony

Onike (Tongan) onyx.
Onika, Onikah, Onikee

Onila (Latin) a form of Petronella.

Onofledis (German) she who shows her sword.

Onora (Latin) a form of Honora.

Ontario 🄱🄶 (Native American) beautiful lake. Geography: a province and a lake in Canada.

Onyx (Greek) onyx.

Oona (Latin, Irish) a form of Una.

Opa (Choctaw) owl. (German) grandfather.

Opal (Hindi) precious stone.

Opalina (Hindi) a form of Opal.

Opeli (Tongan) opal.

Ophelia (Greek) helper. Literature: Hamlet's love interest in the Shakespearean play *Hamlet*.

Ophelie (Greek) a form of Ophelia.
Ophellie, Ophelly, Ophely

Oportuna (Latin) opportune.

Oprah (Hebrew) a form of Orpah.
Ophra, Ophrah, Opra

Ora (Latin) prayer. (Spanish) gold. (English) seacoast. (Greek) a form of Aura.

Orabella (Latin) a form of Arabella.

Oraida (Arabic) eloquent.

Oralee (Hebrew) the Lord is my light.

Oralia (French) a form of Aurelia.

Oran 🄱🄶 (Irish) queen.

Orana (Australian) welcome.

Orane (French) rising.

Orazia (Italian) keeper of time.

Orea (Greek) mountains.

Orela (Latin) announcement from the gods; oracle.

Orenda (Iroquoian) magical power.

Oretha (Greek) a form of Aretha.

Orfelina (Italian) orphan.

Orfilia (German) female wolf.

Oriana (Latin) dawn, sunrise. (Irish) golden.

Oriel (Latin) fire. (French) golden; angel of destiny.

Oriella (Irish) fair; white skinned.

Orieta (Spanish) a form of Oriana.

Orina (Russian) a form of Irene.

Orinda (Hebrew) pine tree. (Irish) light skinned, white.

Orino (Japanese) worker's field.

Oriole (Latin) golden; black-and-orange bird.

Orla (Irish) golden woman.

Orlanda (German) famous throughout the land.

Orlena (Latin) golden.

Orlenda (Russian) eagle.

Orli (Hebrew) light.

Ormanda (Latin) noble. (German) mariner.

Ornat (Irish) green.

Ornella (Latin) she who is like an ash tree.

Ornice (Hebrew) cedar tree. (Irish) pale; olive colored.

Orofrigia (Greek, Spanish) Phrygian gold. Geography: Phrygia was an ancient region in Asia Minor.

Orosia (Greek) a form of Eurosia.

Orpah (Hebrew) runaway. Orquidea **(Spanish) orchid.**

Orquídea (Italian) beautiful as a flower.

Orsa (Latin) a short form of Orseline. **Orseline** (Latin) bearlike. (Greek) a form of Ursula.

Ortensia (Italian) a form of Hortense.

Orva (French) golden; worthy. (English) brave friend.

Orwina (Hebrew) boar friend.

Osane (Spanish) health.

Osanna (Latin) praise the Lord.

Osen (Japanese) one thousand.

Oseye (Benin) merry.

Osita (Spanish) divinely strong.

Osma (English) divine protector.

Oswalda (English) God's power; God's crest.

Otavia (Italian) a form of Octavia.

Othelia (Spanish) rich.
Othilia

Otilie (Czech) lucky heroine.

Otylia (Polish) rich.

Ovia (Latin, Danish) egg.

Ovidia, Ovidía (German) she who takes care of the sheep.

Owena (Welsh) born to nobility; young warrior.

Oya 🅱🅶 (Moquelumnan) called forth.

Oz 🅱🅶 (Hebrew) strength.

Ozara (Hebrew) treasure, wealth.

Ozera (Hebrew) helpful. (Russian) lake.

P

Pabla (Spanish) a form of Paula.

Paca (Spanish) a short form of Pancha.

Paciana (Latin) peaceful woman.

Pacífica (Spanish) peaceful.

Pacomia (Greek) large woman.

Padget 🅱🅶 (French) a form of Page.

Padma (Hindi) lotus.

Padmani (Sri Lankan) blossom, flower.

Pagan 🅶🅱 (Latin) from the country.

Page 🅶🅱 (French) young assistant.

Paige (English) young child.

Paisley ✬ (Scottish) patterned fabric first made in Paisley, Scotland.

Paiton (English) warrior's town.

Paka (Swahili) kitten.

Pakuna (Moquelumnan) deer bounding while running downhill.

Pala (Native American) water.

Palaciada, Palaciata (Greek) mansion.

Paladia (Spanish) a form of Palas.

Palas (Greek) a form of Pallas.

Palba (Basque) blond.

Palila (Polynesian) bird.

Palixena (Greek) she who returns from the foreign land.

Pallas (Greek) wise. Mythology: another name for Athena, the goddess of wisdom.

Palma (Latin) palm tree.

Palmela (Greek) a form of Pamela.

Palmer BG (Spanish) a short form of Palmira.

Palmera, Palmiera (Spanish) forms of palm tree.

Palmira (Spanish) a form of Palma.

Paloma (Spanish) dove.

Pamela (Greek) honey.

Pana (Native American) partridge.

Panambi (Guarani) butterfly.

Pancha (Spanish) free; from France.

Panchali (Sanskrit) princess from Panchala, a former country in what is now India.

Pancracia (Greek) all-powerful.

Pandita (Hindi) scholar.

Pandora (Greek) all-gifted. Mythology: a woman who opened a box out of curiosity and released evil into the world.

Pánfila (Greek) friend of all.

Pansofia (Greek) wise, knowledgeable.

Pansy (Greek) flower; fragrant. (French) thoughtful.

Panthea (Greek) all the gods.

Panya (Swahili) mouse; tiny baby. (Russian) a familiar form of Stephanie.

Panyin (Fante) older twin.

Paola (Italian) a form of Paula.

Papan (Nahuatl) flag.

Papina (Moquelumnan) vine growing on an oak tree.

Paquita (Spanish) a form of Frances.

Paradise (Persian) the garden of Eden.

Paramita (Sanskrit) virtuous; perfect.

Parasha, Parashie (Russian) born on Good Friday.

Pari (Persian) fairy eagle.

Paris GB (French) Geography: the capital of France. Mythology: the Trojan prince who started the Trojan War by abducting Helen.

Parisa (French) a form of Paris.

Parker BG (English) park keeper.

Parmenia (Greek) constant, faithful.

Parmenias (Spanish) a form of Parmenia.

Parnel (French) a form of Pernella.

Parris GB (French) a form of Paris.

Partenia (Greek) she who is as pure as a virgin.

Parthenia (Greek) virginal.

Parvati (Sanskrit) mountain climber.

Parveen (Indian) star.

Parveneh (Persian) butterfly.

Pascale (French) born on Easter or Passover.

Pascasia (Greek) Easter.

Pascua, Pascualina (Hebrew) forms of Pascale.

Pascuala (Spanish) a form of Pascale.

Pascuas (Hebrew) sacrificed for the good of the village.

Pasha BG (Greek) sea.

Pasifiki (Tongan) Pacific Ocean.

Passion (Latin) passion.

Pastora (German) shepherd.

Pasua (Swahili) born by cesarean section.

Pat BG (Latin) a short form of Patricia, Patsy.

Patam (Sanskrit) city.

Patamon BG (Native American) raging.

Pati (Moquelumnan) fish baskets made of willow branches.

Patia (Gypsy, Spanish) leaf. (Latin, English) a familiar form of Patience, Patricia.

Patience (English) patient.

Patli (Nahuatl) medicine.

Patra (Greek, Latin) a form of Petra.

Patrice GB (French) a form of Patricia.

Patricia (Latin) noblewoman.

Patrisha (Latin) a form of Patricia.

Patrizia (Italian) a form of Patricia.

Patrocinio (Spanish) sponsorship.

Patrycja (American) a form of Patricia.

Patsy (Latin) a familiar form of Patricia.

Patty (English) a familiar form of Patricia.

Paula (Latin) small.
Paulette (Latin) a familiar form of Paula.

Paulie (Latin) a familiar form of Paula.

Paulina (Slavic) a form of Paula.

Pauline (French) a form of Paula.

Paun (Indigenous) cloud.

Pavla (Czech, Russian) a form of Paula.

Paxton BG (Latin) peaceful town.

Payal (Indian) anklet, foot ornament.

Payge (English) a form of Paige.

Payten (Irish) a form of Patricia.

Payton GB (Irish) a form of Patricia.

Paz GB (Spanish) peace.

Pazi (Ponca) yellow bird.

Pazia (Hebrew) golden.

Peace (English) peaceful.

Pearl (Latin) jewel.

Peata (Maori) bringer of joy.

Pedra (Portuguese) rock.

Pedrina (Spanish) a form of Pedra.

Peggy (Greek) a familiar form of Margaret.

Peighton (Irish) a form of Patricia.

Peke (Hawaiian) a form of Bertha.

Pela (Polish) a short form of Penelope.

Pelagia (Greek) sea.

Pelipa (Zuni) a form of Philippa.

Pemba (Bambara) the power that controls all life.

Penda (Swahili) loved.

Penelope ✴ (Greek) weaver. Mythology: the clever and loyal wife of Odysseus, a Greek hero.

Penélope (Greek) a form of Penelope.

Peñen (Indigenous) promise.

Peni (Carrier) mind.

Peninah (Hebrew) pearl.

Pennie, Penny (Greek) familiar forms of Penelope, Peninah.

Penthea (Greek) fifth-born; mourner.

Peony (Greek) flower.

Pepita (Spanish) a familiar form of Josephine.

Pepper (Latin) condiment from the pepper plant.

Perah (Hebrew) flower.

Perdita (Latin) lost. Literature: a character in Shakespeare's play *The Winter's Tale*.

Peregrina (Latin) pilgrim, traveler.

Perfecta (Spanish) flawless.

Peri (Greek) mountain dweller. (Persian) fairy or elf.

Peridot (French) yellow-green gem.

Perilla (Latin) Botany: an ornamental plant with leaves often used in cooking.

Perla (Latin) a form of Pearl.

Perlie (Latin) a familiar form of Pearl.

Perlita (Italian) pearl.

Pernella (Greek, French) rock. (Latin) a short form of Petronella.

Perpetua (Spanish) perpetual.

Perri (Greek, Latin) small rock; traveler. (French) pear tree. (Welsh) child of Harry. (English) a form of Perry.

Perry BG (English) a familiar form of Peregrine, Peter **Parry, Perey, Perrey, Perrye, Pery**

Persephone (Greek) Mythology: the goddess of the underworld.

Perseveranda (Latin) she who perseveres.

Pérsida (Latin) a form of Persis.

Persis (Latin) from Persia.

Peta (Blackfoot) golden eagle.

Petra (Greek, Latin) small rock. A short form of Petronella.

Petrina (Greek) a form of Petronella.

Petrisse (German) a form of Petronella.

Petronella (Greek) small rock. (Latin) of the Roman clan Petronius.

Petronila (Latin) a form of Petronella.

Petula (Latin) seeker.
Petulah

Petunia (Native American) flower.

Peyeche (Mapuche) unforgettable woman.

Peyton ⭐

GB (Irish) a form of Patricia.

Phaedra (Greek) bright.

Phallon (Irish) a form of Fallon.

Phebe (Greek) a form of Phoebe.

Phelia (Greek) immortal and wise.

Phemie (Scottish) a short form of Euphemia.

Pheodora (Greek, Russian) a form of Feodora.

Philana (Greek) lover of mankind.

Philantha (Greek) lover of flowers.

Philberta (English) brilliant.

Philicia (Latin) a form of Phylicia.

Philippa (Greek) lover of horses.

Philomela (Greek) lover of songs.

Philomena (Greek) love song; loved one. Religion: a first-century saint.

Philyra (Greek) lover of music.

Phoebe (Greek) shining.

Phoenix BG (Latin) phoenix, a legendary bird.

Photina (Greek) a form of Fotina.

Phoung (Vietnamese) phoenix.

Phylicia (Latin) fortunate; happy. (Greek) a form of Felicia.

Phyllida (Greek) a form of Phyllis.

Phyllis (Greek) green bough.

Pia (Italian) devout.

Pía (Latin) a form of Pia.

Piedad (Spanish) devoted; pious.
Piedada

Piedade (Latin) pity.

Piencia (Latin) a form of Pía.

Pier (French) a form of Petra.

Pier Ann (American) a combination of Pier + Ann.

Pierce BG (English) a form of Petra.

Pila (Italian) a form of Pilar.

Pilar GB (Spanish) pillar, column.

Pili (Spanish) a form of Pilar.

Pililani (Hawaiian) close to heaven.

Pilmayquen (Araucanian) swallow.

Pimpinela (Latin) fickle one.

Ping (Chinese) duckweed. (Vietnamese) peaceful.

Pinga (Eskimo) Mythology: the goddess of game and the hunt.

Pink (American) the color pink.

Pinterry (Australian) star.

Piper ✿ (English) pipe player.
Pipper, Pyper

Pipina (Hebrew) a form of Josefina.

Pippa (English) a short form of Philippa.

Pippi (French) rosy cheeked.

Piro (Mapuche) snows.

Piscina (Italian) water.

Pita (African) fourth daughter.

Pitrel (Mapuche) small woman.

Piula (Catalan) a form of Paula.

Piuque (Araucanian) heart.

Pixie (English) mischievous fairy.

Placencia (Latin) pleasant woman.

Plácida (Latin) a form of Placida.

Placidia **(Latin) serene.**

Platona (Greek) broad shouldered.

Pleasance (French) pleasant.
Pleasence

Plena (Latin) abundant; complete.

Pocahontas (Native American) playful.

Poeta (Italian) poetry.

Polibia (Greek) full of life.

Policarpa (Greek) fertile.

Polidora (Greek) generous woman.

Polimnia (Greek) many hymns. Mythology: Polyhymnia is one of the Muses.

Polixena (Greek) a form of Polyxena.

Polla (Arabic) poppy.

Polly (Latin) a familiar form of Paula, Pauline**.**

Pollyanna (English) a combination of Polly + Anna. Literature: an overly optimistic heroine created by Eleanor Porter.

Poloma (Choctaw) bow.

Polyxena (Greek) welcoming.

Pomona (Latin) apple. Mythology: the goddess of fruit and fruit trees.

Pompeya (Latin) lavish.

Pompilia (Latin) fifth daughter.

Pomposa (Latin) lavish, magnificent.

Ponciana (Greek) blouse.

Poni **(African) second daughter.**

Pooja (Indian) worship.

Poonam (Indian) merit; full moon.
Punam

Poppy (Latin) poppy flower.

Pora, Poria (Hebrew) fruitful.

Porcha (Latin) a form of Portia.

Porche (Latin) a form of Portia.

Porchia (Latin) a form of Portia.

Porfiria (Greek) purple.

Porscha (German) a form of Portia.

Porsche (German) a form of Portia.

Porsha (Latin) a form of Portia.

Porter 🅑🅖 (Latin) gatekeeper.

Portia (Latin) offering. Literature: the heroine of Shakespeare's play *The Merchant of Venice*.

Posy (English) flower, small bunch of flowers.

Potamia, Potamiena (Greek) she who lives on the river.

Potenciana (Latin) powerful.

Prairie (French) prairie.

Praxedes, Práxedes (Greek) she who has firm intentions.

Preciosa (Latin) a form of Precious.

Precious (French) precious; dear.

Premilla (Sanskrit) loving girl.

Prepedigna (Greek) worthy.

Presencia (Spanish) presence.

Presentación (Latin) presentation.

Presley GB (English) priest's meadow.

Presta (Spanish) hurry, quick.

Pricilla (Latin) a form of Priscilla.

Prima (Latin) first, beginning; first child.

Primavera (Italian, Spanish) spring.

Primitiva (Latin) a form of Prima.

Primrose (English) primrose flower.

Princess (English) daughter of royalty.

Prisca (Latin) a short form of Priscilla.

Priscila (Latin) a form of Priscilla.

Prisciliana (English) a form of Prisca.

Priscilla (Latin) ancient.

Prissy (Latin) a familiar form of Priscilla.

Priya (Hindi) beloved; sweet natured.

Priyanka (Indian) dear one.
Priyasha

Procopia (Latin) declared leader.

Promise (Latin) promise, pledge.

Proserpina (Greek) Mythology: the queen of the underworld.

Prospera (Latin) prosperous.

Próspera (Greek) a form of Prospera.

Providencia (Spanish) providence, destiny.

Pru (Latin) a short form of Prudence.

Prudence (Latin) cautious; discreet.

Prudenciana (Spanish) a form of Prudence.

Prudy (Latin) a familiar form of Prudence.
Prudee, Prudi, Prudie

Prunella (Latin) brown; little plum.

Psyche (Greek) soul. Mythology: a beautiful mortal loved by Eros, the Greek god of love.

Pua (Hawaiian) **flower.**

Puakea (Hawaiian) white flower.

Pualani (Hawaiian) heavenly flower.

Publia (Latin) from the village.

Pudenciana (Latin) a form of Prudenciana.

Puebla (Spanish) Geography: a city in Mexico.

Puja (Indian) worship.

Pulqueria (Latin) pretty.

Purificación (Spanish) purification.

Purísima (Spanish) pure.

Purity (English) purity.

Pusina (Latin) child.

Pyralis (Greek) fire.

Pyrena (Greek) fiery.

Pythia (Greek) prophet.

Q

Qadesh (Egyptian) Mythology: an Egyptian goddess.

Qadira (Arabic) powerful.

Qamra (Arabic) moon.

Qiana (American) a form of Quiana.

Qitarah (Arabic) fragrant.

Quaashie BG (Ewe) born on Sunday.
Quashi, Quashie, Quashy

Quadeisha (American) a combination of Qadira + Aisha.

Quaneisha (American) a combination of the prefix Qu + Niesha.

Quanesha (American) a form of Quaneisha.

Quanika (American) a combination of the prefix Qu + Nika.

Quanisha (American) a form of Quaneisha.

Quarralia (Australian) star.

Quartilla (Latin) fourth.

Qubilah (Arabic) agreeable.

Queen (English) queen.

Queenie (English) a form of Queen.

Queisha (American) a short form of Quaneisha.

Quelidonia (Greek) swallow.

Quelita (American) a combination of Queen + Lita.

Quella (English) quiet, pacify.
Quela, Quele, Quellah, Quelle

Quenby BG (Scandinavian) feminine.

Quenisha (American) a combination of Queen + Aisha.

Quenna (English) a form of Queen.

Queralt (Celtic) high rock.

Querida (Spanish) dear; beloved.

Querima, **Querina** (Arabic) the generous one.

Quesara (Latin) youthful.

Quesare (Spanish) long-haired.

Questa (French) searcher.

Queta (Spanish) a short form of names ending in "queta" or "quetta."

Quetromán (Mapuche) restrained soul.

Quetzalxochitl (Nahuatl) precious flower; queen.

Quiana, Quianna (American) combinations of the prefix Qu + Anna.

Quíbele (Turkish) Mythology: another name for Cybele, the goddess mother.

Quieta (English) quiet.

Quiliana (Spanish) substantial; productive.

Quilla (Incan) Mythology: Mama Quilla was the goddess of the moon.

Quillen (Spanish) woman of the heights.

Quillén (Araucanian) tear.

Quimey (Mapuche) beautiful.

Quinby (Scandinavian) queen's estate.

Quincey BG (Irish) a form of Quincy.

Quincy BG (Irish) fifth.

Quinella (Latin) a form of Quintana.

Quinesburga (Anglo-Saxon) royal strength.

Quinesha (American) a form of Quenisha.

Quinetta (Latin) a form of Quintana.

Quinisha (American) a form of Quenisha.

Quinn BG (German, English) queen.

Quinshawna (American) a combination of Quinn + Shawna.

Quintana (Latin) fifth. (English) queen's lawn.

Quintessa (Latin) essence.

Quintilia (Latin) she who was born in the fifth month.

Quintiliana (Spanish) a form of Quintilia.

Quintina (Latin) a form of Quintana.

Quintrell (American) a combination of Quinn + Trella.

Quintruy (Mapuche) investigator.

Quintuqueo (Mapuche) she who searches for wisdom.

Quinturay (Mapuche) she who has a flower.

Quionia (Greek) she who is fertile.

Quirina (Latin) she who carries the lance.

Quirita (Latin) citizen.

Quisa (Egyptian) sister of twins.

Quisilinda (Scandinavian) sweet arrow.

Quitcrie (Latin, French) tranquil.

Qwanisha (American) a form of Quaneisha.

R

Ráa (Spanish) a form of Ria.

Raanana (Hebrew) fresh; luxuriant.

Rabecca (Hebrew) a form of Rebecca.

Rabi BG (Arabic) breeze.
Raby

Rabia (Arabic) a form of Rabi.
Rabiah, Rabya, Rabyah

Rachael (Hebrew) a form of Rachel.

Rachal (Hebrew) a form of Rachel.

Racheal (Hebrew) a form of Rachel.

Rachel (Hebrew) female sheep. Bible: the second wife of Jacob. ,

Rachele, Rachell, Rachelle (French) forms of Rachel.

Racquel (French) a form of Rachel.

Radegunda (German) battle counselor.

Radella (German) counselor.

Radeyah (Arabic) content, satisfied.

Radhika (Indian) beloved. (Swahili) agreeable.

Radiante (Latin) radiant.

Radinka (Slavic) full of life; happy, glad.

Radmilla (Slavic) worker for the people.

Rae (English) doe. (Hebrew) a short form of Rachel.

Raeann, Raeanne (American) combinations of Rae + Ann.

Raeanna (American) a combination of Rae + Anna.

Raeca (Spanish) beautiful; unique.

Raechel, Raechelle (Hebrew) forms of Rachel.

Raeden (Japanese) Mythology: Raiden was the god of thunder and lightning.

Raegan **(Irish) a form of Reagan.**

Raelene (American) a combination of Rae + Lee.

Raelyn, Raelynn (American) forms of Raelene.

Raena (German) a form of Raina.

Raetruda (German) powerful advice.

Raeven (English) a form of Raven.

Rafa (Arabic) happy; prosperous.

Rafaela (Hebrew) a form of Raphaela.

Rafaelle GB (French) a form of Raphaelle.

Ragan, Ragen (Irish) forms of Reagan.

Ragine (English) a form of Regina.

Ragnild (Scandinavian) battle counsel.

Raheem BG (Punjabi) compassionate God.

Rahel (German) a form of Rachel.
Rahela, Rahil

Ráidah **(Arabic) leader.**

Raimunda (Spanish) a form of Ramona.

Rain (Latin) a short form of Regina. A form of Raina, Rane.

Raina (German) mighty. (English) a short form of Regina.

Rainbow (English) rainbow.

Raine GB (Latin) a short form of Regina. A form of Raina, Rane.

Rainee, Rainy (Latin) familiar forms of Regina.

Rainelle (English) a combination of Raina + Elle.

Rainey GB (Latin) a familiar form of Regina.

Raingarda (German) prudent defender.

Raini GB (Latin) a familiar form of Regina.

Raisa (Russian) a form of Rose.

Raizel (Yiddish) a form of Rose.

Raja GB (Arabic) hopeful.

Rajah (Arabic) a form of Raja.

Rajani (Hindi) evening.

Rajel (Hebrew) bee.

Raku (Japanese) pleasure.

Raleigh BG (Irish) a form of Riley.

Raley (Irish) a form of Riley.

Rama (Hebrew) lofty, exalted. (Hindi) godlike. Religion: an incarnation of the Hindu god Vishnu.
Ramah

Raman (Spanish) a form of Ramona.

Ramandeep GB (Sikh) covered by the light of the Lord's love.

Ramira (Spanish) judicious.

Ramla (Swahili) fortuneteller.
Ramlah

Ramona (Spanish) mighty; wise protector. **Ramosa** (Latin) branch.

Ramsey BG (English) ram's island.

Ramya (Hindi) beautiful, elegant.

Ran (Japanese) water lily. (Scandinavian) destroyer. Mythology: the Norse sea goddess who destroys.

Rana (Sanskrit) royal. (Arabic) gaze, look.

Ranait (Irish) graceful; prosperous.

Randa (Arabic) tree.
Randah

Randall BG **(English) protected.**

Randee, Randi, Randie (English) familiar forms of Miranda, Randall.

Randy BG (English) a familiar form of Miranda, Randall.

Rane (Scandinavian) queen.

Raneisha (American) a combination of Rae + Aisha.

Ranesha (American) a form of Raneisha.

Rangi (Maori) sky.

Rani GB (Sanskrit) queen. (Hebrew) joyful. A short form of Kerani.

Rania (Sanskrit, Hebrew) a form of Rani.

Ranielle (American) a combination of Rani + Elle.
Rannielle, Rannyelle, Ranyelle

Ranisha (American) a form of Raneisha.

Ranita (Hebrew) song; joyful.

Raniyah (Arabic) gazing.

Ranya (Sanskrit, Hebrew) a form of Rani. (Arabic) a short form of Raniyah.

Rapa (Hawaiian) moonbeam.

Raphaela (Hebrew) healed by God.

Raphaelle (French) a form of Raphaela.

Raquel, Raquelle (French) forms of Rachel.

Raquilda (German) a form of Radegunda.

Raquildis (German) fighting princess.

Rasha (Arabic) young gazelle.

Rashanda (American) a form of Rashawna.

Rashawn BG (American) a short form of Rashawna.

Rashawna (American) a combination of the prefix Ra + Shawna.

Rashawnda (American) a form of Rashawna.

Rasheda (Swahili) a form of Rashida.

Rashel, Rashell, Rashelle (American) forms of Rachel.

Rashida GB (Swahili, Turkish) righteous.

Rashieka (Arabic) descended from royalty.

Rashonda (American) a form of Rashawna.

Rasia (Greek) rose.

Ratana (Tai) crystal.

Rathtyen (Welsh) child of Clememyl.

Ratri (Hindi) night. Religion: the goddess of the night.

Ratrudis (German) faithful counselor.

Raula (French) wolf counselor.

Raveen (English) a form of Raven.

Raveena (English) a form of Raven.

Raven GB (English) blackbird.

Ravin, Ravyn (English) forms of Raven.

Ravon BG (English) a form of Raven.

Rawan (Gypsy) a form of Rawnie.

Rawnie (Gypsy) fine lady.

Raya (Hebrew) friend.

Rayan BG **(American) a form of Raeann.**

Rayann, Rayanne (American) forms of Raeann.

Rayanna (American) a form of Raeanna.

Raychel, Raychelle (Hebrew) forms of Rachel.

Rayelle (American) a form of Raylyn.

Rayén (Araucanian, Mapuche) flower.

Raylee (American) a familiar form of Raylyn.

Rayleen, Raylene (American) forms of Raylyn.

Raylyn, Raylynn (American) combinations of Rae + Lyn.

Raymonde (German) wise protector.

Rayna (Scandinavian) mighty. (Yiddish) pure, clean. (English) king's advisor. (French) a familiar form of Lorraine.

Rayne GB (Scandinavian, Yiddish, French) a form of Rane, Rayna.

Raynisha (American) a form of Raneisha.

Rayonna (American) a form of Raeanna.

Rayven (English) a form of Raven.

Rayya (Arabic) thirsty no longer.

Razi BG (Aramaic) secretive.

Raziya (Swahili) agreeable.

Rea (Greek) poppy flower.

Reagan GB (Irish) little ruler.

Real (Spanish) real, true.

Reanna (German, English) a form of Raina. (American) a form of Raeann.

Reanne (American) a form of Raeann, Reanna.

Reba (Hebrew) fourth-born child. A short form of Rebecca.

Rebbecca, Rebeca, Rebeccah (Hebrew) forms of Rebecca.

Rebecca (Hebrew) tied, bound. Bible: the wife of Isaac.

Rebecka, Rebeckah (Hebrew) forms of Rebecca.

Rebekah, Rebekka, Rebekkah (Hebrew) forms of Rebecca.

Rebi (Hebrew) a familiar form of Rebecca.

Redempta (Latin) redemption.

Reed BG (English) a form of Reid.

Reem (Arabic) a short form of Rima.

Reema, Reemah (Arabic) forms of Rima.

Reena (Greek) peaceful. (English) a form of Rina. (Hebrew) a form of Rinah.

Reese GB (Welsh) a form of Rhys. Movies: Reese Witherspoon is a popular movie star.

Reet (Estonian) a form of Margaret.

Refugio (Latin) refuge.

Regan GB **(Irish) a form of Reagan.**

Reganne (Irish) a form of Reagan.

Regenfrida (German) peaceful advice.

Reggie BG (English) a familiar form of Regina.

Reghan (Irish) a form of Reagan.

Regina (Latin) queen. (English) king's advisor. Geography: the capital of Saskatchewan. Regine **(Latin) a form of Regina.**

Regla (Spanish) rule.
Régula (Latin) small king.
Rei GB (Japanese) polite, well behaved.
Reia, Reya, Reyes (Spanish) forms of Reina.
Reid BG (English) redhead.
Reiko (Japanese) grateful.
Reilly BG (Irish) a form of Riley.
Reina (Spanish) a short form of Regina. Rekha **(Hindi) thin line.**

Relinda (German) kind-hearted princess.
Remedios (Spanish) remedy.
Remei (Catalan) a form of Remedios.
Remi BG (French) from Rheims, France.
Remigia (Latin) rower.
Remington BG **(English) raven estate.**
Remy BG **(French) a form of Remi.**
Ren (Japanese) arranger; water lily; lotus.
Rena (Hebrew) song; joy. A familiar form of Irene, Regina, Renata, Sabrina, Serena.

Renae (French) a form of Renée.
Renata (French) a form of Renée.
Rene BG (Greek) a short form of Irene, Renée.
Renea (French) a form of Renée.
Renee (French) a form of Renée.
Renée (French) born again.
Reneisha (American) a form of Raneisha.
Renelle (French) a form of Renée.
Renell
Renesha (American) a form of Raneisha.
Renisha (American) a form of Raneisha.
Renita (French) a form of Renata.
Rennie (English) a familiar form of Renata.
Reparada (Latin) renewed.
Reseda (Spanish) fragrant mignonette blossom.
Reshawna (American) a combination of the prefix Re + Shawna.
Resi **(German) a familiar form of Theresa.**
Restituta (Latin) restitution.
Reta (African) shaken.
Retha (Greek) a short form of Aretha.
Reubena (Hebrew) behold a child.

Reva (Latin) revived. (Hebrew) rain; one-fourth. A form of Reba, Riva.
Reveca, Reveka (Slavic) forms of Rebecca, Rebekah.
Revocata (Latin) call again.
Rewuri (Australian) spring.
Rexanne (American) queen.
Reyhan BG (Turkish) sweet-smelling flower.
Reyna (Greek) peaceful. (English) a form of Reina.
Reynalda (German) king's advisor.
Réz BG (Latin, Hungarian) copper-colored hair.
Reza BG (Czech) a form of Theresa.
Rhea (Greek) brook, stream. Mythology: the mother of Zeus.
Rheanna (Greek) a form of Rhea.
Rheannon (Welsh) a form of Rhiannon.
Rhedyn (Welsh) fern.
Rhian (Welsh) a short form of Rhiannon.
Rhiana, Rhianna (Greek) forms of Rheanna. (Welsh) forms of Rhian. (Arabic) forms of Rihana.
Rhiannon (Welsh) witch; nymph; goddess.

Rhoda (Greek) from Rhodes, Greece.

Rhodelia (Greek) rosy.

Rhody (Greek) rose.

Rhona (Scottish) powerful, mighty. (English) king's advisor.

Rhonda (Welsh) grand.

Rhonwyn (Irish) a form of Bronwyn.

Rhyan BG (Welsh) a form of Rhian.
Rhyane, Rhyann, Rhyanne

Rhyanna (Greek) a form of Rheanna.

Ria (Spanish) river.

Rian GB (Welsh) a form of Rhian.

Riana, Rianna (Irish) short forms of Briana. (Arabic) forms of Rihana.

Riane, Rianne (Welsh) forms of Rhian.

Rica (Spanish) a short form of Erica, Frederica, Ricarda. .

Ricadonna (Italian) a combination of Ricarda + Donna.

Ricarda (Spanish) rich and powerful ruler.

Ricci (American) a familiar form of Erica, Frederica, Ricarda.

Richa (Spanish) a form of Rica.

Richael (Irish) saint.

Richelle (German, French) a form of Ricarda.

Rickelle (American) a form of Raquel.

Ricki GB (American) a familiar form of Erica, Frederica, Ricarda.

Rickia (American) a form of Ricki.
Rickina, Rickita, Rikia, Rikita, Rikkia

Rickie BG (American) a familiar form of Erica, Frederica, Ricarda.

Rickma (Hebrew) woven.

Ricquel (American) a form of Raquel.

Rictruda (German) powerful strength.

Rida BG (Arabic) favored by God.

Rigel (Spanish) foot. Astronomy: one of the stars in the constellation Orion.

Rigoberta (German) brilliant advisor.

Rihana (Arabic) sweet basil.

Rika (Swedish) ruler.

Riki GB (American) a familiar form of Erica, Frederica, Ricarda.

Rikki GB (American) a familiar form of Erica, Frederica, Ricarda.

Rilee, Rileigh (Irish) forms of Riley.

Riley ⭐

GB (Irish) valiant.

Rilla (German) small brook.

Rim (Arabic) a short form of Rima.

Rima (Arabic) white antelope.

Rimona (Hebrew) pomegranate.

Rin (Japanese) park. Geography: a Japanese village.

Rina (English) a short form of names ending in "rina." (Hebrew) a form of Rena, Rinah.

Rinah (Hebrew) joyful.

Rio BG (Spanish) river. Geography: Rio de Janeiro is a seaport in Brazil.
Ryo

Río (Spanish) a form of Rio.

Riona (Irish) saint.

Risa (Latin) laughter.

Risha (Hindi) Vrishabha is another name for the zodiac sign Taurus.

Rishona (Hebrew) first.
Rishina, Rishon, Rishonah, Ryshona, Ryshonah

Rissa (Greek) a short form of Nerissa.

Rita (Sanskrit) brave; honest. (Greek) a short form of Margarita.

Ritsa (Greek) a familiar form of Alexandra.

Riva (French) river bank. (Hebrew) a short form of Rebecca. .

Rivalea (American) a combination of Riva + Lea.

River 🅱🅶 (Latin, French) stream, water.

Rivka (Hebrew) a short form of Rebecca.

Riza (Greek) a form of Theresa.

Roanna (American) a form of Rosana.

Robbi (English) a familiar form of Roberta.

Robbie 🅱🅶 (English) a familiar form of Roberta.

Robert 🅱🅶 (English) famous brilliance.

Roberta (English) a form of Robert. ,

Robin 🅶🅱 (English) robin. A form of Roberta.

Robinette (English) a familiar form of Robin.

Robustiana (Latin) well-built woman.

Robyn (English) a form of Robin.

Robynn (English) a form of Robin.

Rochel (Hebrew, French) a form of Rochelle.

Rochelle (French) large stone. (Hebrew) a form of Rachel.

Rochely (Latin) a form of Rochelle.

Rocio (Spanish) dewdrops.

Roderica (German) famous ruler.

Roderiga, Rodriga (Spanish) forms of Roderica.

Rodia (Greek) rose.

Rodnae (English) island clearing.

Rodneisha (American) a combination of Rodnae + Aisha.

Rodnesha (American) a form of Rodneisha.

Rodnisha (American) a form of Rodneisha.

Rogaciana (Latin) forgiving woman.

Rogelia (Teutonic) beautiful one.

Rohana (Hindi) sandalwood. (American) a combination of Rose + Hannah.

Rohini (Hindi) woman.

Roisin (Irish) a short form of Roisina.

Roisina (Irish) rose.

Roja (Spanish) red.

Rolanda (German) famous throughout the land.

Roldana (Spanish) a form of Rolanda.

Rolene (German) a form of Rolanda.

Rolonda (German) a form of Rolanda.

Roma (Latin) from Rome.

Romaine (French) from Rome.

Romelda (German) Roman fighter.

Romelia (Hebrew) God's beloved one.

Romero (Spanish) romero plant.

Romia (Hebrew) praised.

Romola (Latin) a form of Roma.

Romualda (German) glorious governess.

Rómula (Spanish) possessor of great strength.

Romy 🅶🅱 (French) a familiar form of Romaine. (English) a familiar form of Rosemary.

Rona, Ronna (Scandinavian) short forms of Ronalda.

Ronaele (Greek) the name Eleanor spelled backwards.

Ronalda (Scottish) powerful, mighty. (English) king's advisor.

Ronda (Welsh) a form of Rhonda.

Rondelle (French) short poem.

Roneisha (American) a combination of Rhonda + Aisha.

Ronelle (Welsh) a form of Rhonda, Ronda.

Ronesha (American) a form of Roneisha.
Ronnesha

Roneshia (American) a form of Roneisha.

Roni GB (American) a familiar form of Veronica and names beginning with "Ron."

Ronica, Ronika, Ronique (Latin) short forms of Veronica.

Ronisha, Ronnisha (American) forms of Roneisha.

Ronli (Hebrew) joyful.

Ronnette (Welsh) a familiar form of Rhonda, Ronda.

Ronni (American) a familiar form of Veronica and names beginning with "Ron."

Ronnie, Ronny BG (American) familiar forms of Veronica and names beginning with "Ron."

Roquelia (German) war cry.

Roquelina (Latin) a form of Rochelle.

Rori (Irish) famous brilliance; famous ruler.

Rory BG (Irish) famous brilliance; famous ruler.

Ros (English) a short form of Rosalind, Rosalyn.

Rosa (Italian, Spanish) a form of Rose. History: Rosa Parks inspired the American Civil Rights movement by refusing to give up her bus seat to a white man in Montgomery, Alabama. Rosa de Lima (Spanish) Rose from Lima, the capital of Peru.

Rosabel (French) beautiful rose.

Rosalba (Latin) white rose.

Rosalee, Rosalie (English) forms of Rosalind.

Rosalia (English) a form of Rosalind.

Rosalía (Spanish) a form of Rosalia.

Rosalín, Roselín (Spanish) forms of Rosalyn.

Rosalina (Spanish) a form of Rosalind.

Rosalind (Spanish) fair rose.

Rosalinda (Spanish) a form of Rosalind.

Rosalva (Latin) a form of Rosalba.

Rosalyn (Spanish) a form of Rosalind.

Rosamaria (English) a form of Rose Marie.

Rosamaría (Spanish) a form of Rosamaria.

Rosamond (German) famous guardian.

Rosamund (Spanish) a form of Rosamond.

Rosana, Rosanna, Roseanna (English) combinations of Rose + Anna.

Rosangelica (American) a combination of Rose + Angelica.

Rosanne, Roseann, Roseanne (English) combinations of Rose + Ann.

Rosario GB (Filipino, Spanish) rosary.

Rosaura (Filipino, Spanish) a form of Rosario.

Rose (Latin) rose.

Rose Marie, Rosemarie (English) combinations of Rose + Marie.

Roselani (Hawaiian) heavenly rose.

Roseline, Roselyn (Spanish) forms of Rosalind.

Rosella (Latin) a form of Rose.

Rosemary (English) a combination of Rose + Mary.

Rosemonde (French) a form of Rosamond.

Rosenda (German) excellent lady.

Roser (Catalan) a form of Rosario.

Rosetta (Italian) a form of Rose.

Roshan 🅱🅶 (Sanskrit) shining light.

Roshawna (American) a combination of Rose + Shawna.

Roshni (Indian) brighteners.

Roshonda (American) a form of Roshawna.

Roshunda (American) a form of Roshawna.

Rosicler (French) a combination of Rosa + Clara.

Rosie, Rosy (English) familiar forms of Rosalind, Rosana, Rose.

Rosilda (German) horse-riding warrior.

Rosina (English) a familiar form of Rose.

Rosinda, Rosuinda (Teutonic) famous warrior.

Rosio (Spanish) a form of Rosie.

Rosita (Spanish) a familiar form of Rose.

Roslyn (Scottish) a form of Rossalyn.

Rosmarí (Spanish) a form of Rosamaría.

Rosmira (German) a form of Rosilda.

Rosó (Catalan) a form of Rosario.

Rosoínda (Latin) a form of Rosa.

Rossalyn (Scottish) cape; promontory.

Rósula (Latin) a form of Rosa.

Rosura (Latin) golden rose.

Roswinda (Germanic) a form of Rosinda.

Rotrauda (Germanic) celebrated counselor.

Rowan 🅱🅶 (English) tree with red berries. (Welsh) a form of Rowena.

Rowena (Welsh) fair-haired. (English) famous friend. Literature: Ivanhoe's love interest in Sir Walter Scott's novel *Ivanhoe*.

Roxana, Roxanna (Persian) forms of Roxann.

Roxane (Persian) a form of Roxann.

Roxann, Roxanne (Persian) sunrise. Literature: Roxanne is the heroine of Edmond Rostand's play *Cyrano de Bergerac*.

Roxie, Roxy (Persian) familiar forms of Roxann.
Roxi

Roya (English) a short form of Royanna.

Royale **(English) royal.**

Royanna (English) queenly, royal.

Roz (English) a short form of Rosalind, Rosalyn.

Roza (Slavic) a form of Rosa.

Rozelle (Latin) a form of Rose.

Rozene (Native American) rose blossom.

Ruana (Spanish) poncho.

Ruba (French) a form of Ruby.

Rubena (Hebrew) a form of Reubena.

Rubi (French) a form of Ruby.

Rubí (Latin) a form of Ruby.

Ruby ⭐ (French) precious stone.

Ruchi **(Hindi) one who wishes to please.**
Ruchee, Ruchey, Ruchie, Ruchy

Rudecinda (Spanish) a form of Rosenda.

Rudee (German) a short form of Rudolfa.

Rudelle (American) a combination of Rudee + Elle.

Rudolfa (German) famous wolf.

Rudra (Hindi) Religion: another name for the Hindu god Shiva.

Rue (German) famous. (French) street. (English) regretful; strong-scented herbs.

Ruel **(English) path.**

Rufa (Latin) a form of Ruffina.

Ruffina (Italian) redhead.

Rui (Japanese) affectionate.

Rukan (Arabic) steady; confident.

Rula (Latin, English) ruler.

Rumer (English) gypsy.

Runa (Norwegian) secret; flowing.
Runah, Rune, Runna, Runnah, Runne

Ruperta (Spanish) a form of Roberta.

Rupinder (Sanskrit) beautiful.

Ruri (Japanese) emerald.

Rusalka (Czech) wood nymph. (Russian) mermaid.

Russhell (French) redhead; fox colored.

Rusti (English) redhead.

Rústica (Latin) country dweller, rustic.

Rut (Hebrew) a form of Ruth.

Rute (Portuguese) a form of Ruth.

Ruth (Hebrew) friendship. Bible: daughter-in-law of Naomi.

Ruthann (American) a combination of Ruth + Ann.

Ruthie (Hebrew) a familiar form of Ruth.
Ruthey, Ruthi, Ruthy

Rutilda (German) strong because of her fame.

Rutilia (German) she who shines brightly.

Ruza (Czech) rose.

Ryan 🅱🅶 (Irish) little ruler.

Ryane, Ryanne (Irish) forms of Ryan.

Ryann (Irish) little ruler.

Ryanna (Irish) a form of Ryan.

Ryba (Czech) fish.

Rylan 🅱🅶 (English) land where rye is grown.

Rylee 🅶🅱 (Irish) valiant. Ryleigh **(Irish) a form of Rylee.**

Ryley 🅱🅶 (Irish) a form of Rylee.

Rylie 🅶🅱 (Irish) a form of Rylee.

Ryo 🅱🅶 (Japanese) dragon.

S

Saarah (Arabic) princess.

Saba (Arabic) morning. (Greek) a form of Sheba.

Sabana (Latin) a form of Savannah.

Sabelia (Spanish) a form of Sabina.

Sabi (Arabic) young girl.

Sabina (Latin) a form of Sabine.

Sabine (Latin) History: the Sabine were a tribe in ancient Italy.

Sabiniana (Latin) a form of Sabina.

Sabiya (Arabic) morning; eastern wind.

Sable (English) sable; sleek.

Sabra (Hebrew) thorny cactus fruit. (Arabic) resting. History: a name for native-born Israelis, who were said to be hard on the outside and soft and sweet on the inside.

Sabreen (English) a short form of Sabreena.

Sabreena (English) a form of Sabrina.

Sabrena (English) a form of Sabrina.

Sabria (Hebrew, Arabic) a form of Sabra.

Sabrina (Latin) boundary line. (English) princess. (Hebrew) a familiar form of Sabra. Sabrine (Latin, Hebrew) a short form of Sabrina.

Sabryna (English) a form of Sabrina.

Sacha 🅱🅶 (Russian) a form of Sasha.

Sachi (Japanese) blessed; lucky.

Sacnite (Mayan) white flower.

Sacramento (Latin) consecrated. Geography: the capital of California.

Sada (Japanese) chaste. (English) a form of Sadie.

Sadaf (Indian) pearl. (Iranian) seashell.

Sade (Hebrew) a form of Chadee, Sarah, Shardae.

Sadé (Hebrew) a form of Sade.

Sadee (Hebrew) a form of Sade, Sadie.

Sadella (American) a combination of Sade + Ella.

Sadhana (Hindi) devoted.

Sadi (Hebrew) a form of Sadie. (Arabic) a short form of Sadiya.

Sadia (Arabic) a form of Sadiya.

Sadie ✦ (Hebrew) a familiar form of Sarah.

Sadira (Persian) lotus tree. (Arabic) star.

Sadiya (Arabic) lucky, fortunate.

Sadzi (Carrier) sunny disposition.

Safa (Arabic) pure.
Safah, Saffa, Saffah

Saffi (Danish) wise.

Saffron (English) Botany: a plant with purple or white flowers whose orange stigmas are used as a spice.

Safia (Arabic) a form of Safiya.

Safiya (Arabic) pure; serene; best friend.

Safo (Greek) she who sees with clarity.

Sagara (Hindi) ocean.

Sage GB (English) wise. Botany: an herb used as a seasoning.

Sagrario (Spanish) tabernacle.

Sahar, Saher (Arabic) short forms of Sahara.

Sahara (Arabic) desert; wilderness.

Sahra (Hebrew) a form of Sarah.

Sai (Japanese) talented.

Saida (Arabic) happy; fortunate. (Hebrew) a form of Sarah.

Saída (Arabic) a form of Saida.

Saige GB (English) a form of Sage.

Saira (Hebrew) a form of Sara.

Sakaë (Japanese) prosperous.

Sakari (Hindi) sweet.

Saki (Japanese) cloak; rice wine.

Sakina (Indian) friend. (Muslim) tranquility, calmness.

Sakti (Hindi) energy, power.

Sakuna (Native American) bird.

Sakura (Japanese) cherry blossom; wealthy; prosperous.

Sala (Hindi) sala tree. Religion: the sacred tree under which Buddha died.

Salaberga, Solaberga (German) she who defends the sacrifice.

Salali (Cherokee) squirrel.

Salama (Arabic) peaceful.

Salbatora (Spanish) a form of Salvadora.

Saleena (French) a form of Salina.

Salem GB (Arabic) a form of Salím

Salena (French) a form of Salina.

Salette (English) a form of Sally.

Salima (Arabic) safe and sound; healthy.

Salina (French) solemn, dignified.

Salinas (Spanish) salt mine.

Salliann (English) a combination of Sally + Ann.

Sallie (English) a form of Sally.

Sally (English) princess. History: Sally Ride, an American astronaut, became the first U.S. woman in space.,

Salma (Arabic) a form of Salima.

Salome (Hebrew)

Salud (Spanish) a form of Salustiana.

Salustiana (Latin) healthy.

Salvadora (Spanish) savior.

Salvatora (Italian) a form of Salvadora.

Salvia (Spanish) healthy; saved. (Latin) a form of Sage.

Samah (Hebrew, Arabic) a form of Sami.

Samala (Hebrew) asked of God.

Samanatha (Aramaic, Hebrew) a form of Samantha.

Samanfa (Hebrew) a form of Samantha.

Samanta (Hebrew) a form of Samantha.

Samantha ✦ (Aramaic) listener. (Hebrew) told by God. .

Samara (Latin) elm-tree seed.

Samarah (Latin) a form of Samara.

Samaria (Latin) a form of Samara.

Samatha (Hebrew) a form of Samantha.

Sameera (Hindi) a form of Samira.

Sameh (Hebrew) listener. (Arabic) forgiving.

Sami BG (Arabic) praised. (Hebrew) a short form of Samantha, Samuela.

Samia (Arabic) exalted.

Samina (Hindi) happiness. (English) a form of Sami.

Samira (Arabic) entertaining.

Samiya (Arabic) a form of Samia.

Sammantha (Aramaic, Hebrew) a form of Samantha.

Sammi (Hebrew) a familiar form of Samantha, Samuel, Samuela. (Arabic) a form of Sami.

Sammie BG (Hebrew) a familiar form of Samantha, Samuel, Samuela. (Arabic) a form of Sami.

Sammy BG (Hebrew) a familiar form of Samantha, Samuel, Samuela. (Arabic) a form of Sami.

Samone (Hebrew) a form of Simone.

Samuel BG (Hebrew) heard God; asked of God. Bible: a famous Old Testament prophet and judge.

Samuela (Hebrew) a form of Samuel.

Samuelle (Hebrew) a form of Samuel.

Sana (Arabic) mountaintop; splendid; brilliant.

Sancia (Spanish) holy, sacred.

Sandeep BG (Punjabi) enlightened.

Sandi (Greek) a familiar form of SandraSandía **(Spanish) watermelon.**

Sandra (Greek) defender of mankind. A short form of Cassandra. History: Sandra Day O'Connor was the first woman appointed to the U.S. Supreme Court.

Sandrea (Greek) a form of Sandra.

Sandrica (Greek) a form of Sandra.

Sandrine (Greek) a form of Alexandra.

Sandy GB (Greek) a familiar form of Cassandra, Sandra.

Sanne (Hebrew, Dutch) lily.

Santana GB (Spanish) saint.

Santanna (Spanish) a form of Santana.

Santina (Spanish) little saint. .

Sanura (Swahili) kitten.

Sanuye (Moquelumnan) red clouds at sunset.

Sanya (Sanskrit) born on Saturday.

Sanyu BG (Luganda) happiness.

Sapata (Native American) dancing bear.

Saphire (Greek) a form of Sapphire.

Sapphira (Hebrew) a form of Sapphire.

Sapphire (Greek) blue gemstone.

Saqui (Mapuche) chosen one; kind soul.

Sara (Hebrew) a form of Sarah.

Sara Eve, Sarah Eve (American) combinations of Sarah + Eve.

Sara Jane, Sarah Jane (American) combinations of Sarah + Jane.

Sara Maude, Sarah Maud, Sarah Maude (American) combinations of Sarah + Maud.

Sarafina (Hebrew) a form of Serafina.

Sarah ⭐ (Hebrew) princess. Bible: the wife of Abraham and mother of Isaac.

Sarah Ann, Sarah Anne (American) combinations of Sarah + Ann.

Sarah Jeanne (American) a combination of Sarah + Jeanne.

Sarah Marie (American) a combination of Sarah + Marie.

Sarahi (Hebrew) a form of Sarah.

Sarai, Saray (Hebrew) forms of Sarah.

Saralyn (American) a combination of Sarah + Lynn.

Saree (Arabic) noble. (Hebrew) a familiar form of Sarah.

Sarena (Hebrew) a form of Sarina.

Sarha (Hebrew) a form of Sarah.

Sari (Hebrew, Arabic) a form of Saree.

Saria, Sariah (Hebrew) forms of Sarah.

Sarika (Hebrew) a familiar form of Sarah. .

Sarila (Turkish) waterfall.

Sarina (Hebrew) a familiar form of Sarah.

Sarita (Hebrew) a familiar form of Sarah.

Sarolta (Hungarian) a form of Sarah.

Sarotte (French) a form of Sarah.

Sarra, Sarrah (Hebrew) forms of Sara.

Sasa (Japanese) assistant. (Hungarian) a form of Sarah, Sasha.

Sasha GB (Russian) defender of mankind.

Saskia, Sasquia (Teutonic) one who carries a knife.

Sass (Irish) Saxon.

Sata (Spanish) princess.

Satara (American) a combination of Sarah + Tara.

Satin (French) smooth, shiny.

Satinka (Native American) sacred dancer.

Sato (Japanese) sugar.

Saturia (Latin) she who has it all.

Saturniana (Latin) healthy.

Saturnina (Spanish) gift of Saturn.

Saula (Greek) desired woman.

Saundra (English) a form of Sandra, Sondra.

Saura (Hindi) sun worshiper.

Savana, Savanah, Savanna (Spanish) forms of Savannah.

Savannah ⭐ (Spanish) treeless plain. See also

Saveria (Teutonic) from the new house.

Savhanna (Spanish) a form of Savannah.

Savina (Latin) a form of Sabina.

Sawa (Japanese) swamp. (Moquelumnan) stone.
Sawah

Sawyer BG (English) wood worker.
Sawyar, Sawyor

Sayde, Saydee (Hebrew) forms of Sadie.

163

Sayén (Mapuche) sweet woman.

Saylor (American) a form of Sailor.

Sayo (Japanese) born at night.

Sayra (Hebrew) a form of Sarah.

Scarlet (English) a form of Scarlett.

Scarlett ⭐ (English) bright red. Literature: Scarlett O'Hara is the heroine of Margaret Mitchell's novel *Gone with the Wind.*

Schyler GB (Dutch) sheltering.

Scotti (Scottish) from Scotland.

Scout (French) scout. Literature: Scout is a protagonist in Harper Lee's *To Kill a Mockingbird.*

Seaira, Seairra (Irish, Spanish) forms of Sierra.

Sealtiel (Hebrew) my desire is God.

Sean BG (Hebrew, Irish) God is gracious.

Seana, Seanna (Irish) forms of Jane, Sean.

Searra (Irish, Spanish) a form of Sierra.

Sebastiane (Greek) venerable. (Latin) revered. (French) a form of Sebastian

Seble (Ethiopian) autumn.

Sebrina (English) a form of Sabrina.

Secilia (Latin) a form of Cecilia.

Secret (Latin) secret.

Secunda (Latin) second.

Secundila (Latin) a form of Secundina.

Secundina (Latin) second daughter.

Seda (Armenian) forest voices.

Sedna (Eskimo) well-fed. Mythology: the goddess of sea animals.

Sedofa (Latin) silk.

Sedona (French) a form of Sidonie.

Seelia (English) a form of Sheila.

Seema (Greek) sprout. (Afghan) sky; profile.

Sefa (Swiss) a familiar form of Josefina.

Séfora (Hebrew) like a small bird.

Segene (German) victorious.

Segismunda (German) victorious protector.

Segunda (Spanish) a form of Secundina.

Seina (Basque) innocent.

Seirra (Irish) a form of Sierra.

Sejal (Indian) river water.

Seki (Japanese) wonderful.

Sela, Selah (English) short forms of Selena.

Selam (Ethiopian) peaceful.

Selda (German) a short form of Griselda. (Yiddish) a form of Zelda.

Selena (Greek) a form of Selene. See also **Selene** (Greek) moon. Mythology: Selene was the goddess of the moon.

Seleste (Latin) a form of Celeste.

Selestina (Latin) a form of Celestina.

Selia (Latin) a short form of Cecilia.

Selima (Hebrew) peaceful.

Selin (Greek) a short form of Selina.

Selina (Greek) a form of Celina, Selena.

Selma (German) divine protector. (Irish) fair, just. (Scandinavian) divinely protected. (Arabic) secure.

Selva (Latin) a form of Silvana.

Sema (Turkish) heaven; divine omen.

Semaj BG (Turkish) a form of Sema.

Semele (Latin) once.

Seminaris, Semíramis (Assyrian) she who lives harmoniously with the doves.

Sempronia (Spanish) a form of Semproniana.

Semproniana (Latin) eternal.

Sena (Greek) a short form of Selena. (Spanish) a short form of Senalda.

Senalda (Spanish) sign.

Seneca (Iroquoian) a tribal name.

Senia (Greek) a form of Xenia.

Senona (Spanish) lively.

Senorina (Latin) aged.

Sephora (English) a form of Séfora.

September (Latin) born in the ninth month.

Septima (Latin) seventh.

Sequoia (Cherokee) giant redwood tree.

Sequoya, Sequoyah (Cherokee) forms of Sequoia.

Sera, Serah (American) forms of Sarah.
Serra

Serafia (Spanish) a form of Seraphina.

Serafín (Hebrew) a form of Seraphina.

Serafina (Hebrew) burning; ardent. Bible: seraphim are an order of angels.

Seraphyne (French) a form of Serafina.

Serén (Welsh) star.

Serena (Latin) peaceful.

Serene (French) a form of Serena.

Serenela (Spanish) a form of Seren.

Serenity ✰ (Latin) peaceful.

Sergia (Greek) attendant.

Serica (Greek) silky smooth.

Serilda (Greek) armed warrior woman.

Serina (Latin) a form of Serena.

Serita (Hebrew) a form of Sarita.

Serotina (Latin) dusk.

Servanda, Sevanda (Latin) she who must be saved and protected.

Servia (Latin) daughter of those who serve the Lord.

Severa (Spanish) severe.

Severina (Italian, Portuguese, Croatian, German, Ancient Roman) severe.

Sevilla (Spanish) from Seville, Spain.

Sexburgis (German) shelter of the victorious one.

Shaba (Spanish) rose.

Shada (Native American) pelican.

Shaday (American) a form of Sade.

Shade BG (English) shade.

Shadia (Native American) a form of Shada.

Shadow BG (English) shadow.

Shadrika (American) a combination of the prefix Sha + Rika.

Shae GB (Irish) a form of Shea.

Shae-Lynn, Shaelyn, Shaelynn (Irish) forms of Shea.

Shaela (Irish) a form of Sheila.

Shaelee (Irish) a form of Shea.

Shaena (Irish) a form of Shaina.

Shafira (Swahili) distinguished.

Shahar (Arabic) moonlit.

Shahina (Arabic) falcon.

Shahira (Arabic) famous.

Shahla (Afghan) beautiful eyes.

Shai BG (Irish) a form of Shea.

Shaianne (Cheyenne) a form of Cheyenne.

Shaila (Latin) a form of Sheila.

Shailee (Irish) a form of Shea.

Shailyn, Shailynn (Irish) forms of Shea.

Shaina (Yiddish) beautiful.

Shajuana (American) a combination of the prefix Sha + Juanita.

Shaka BG (Hindi) a form of Shakti. A short form of names beginning with "Shak."

Shakala (Arabic) a form of Shakila.

Shakara, Shakarah (American) combinations of the prefix Sha + Kara.

Shakari (American) a form of Shakara.

Shakayla (Arabic) a form of Shakila.

Shakeena (American) a combination of the prefix Sha + Keena.

Shakeita (American) a combination of the prefix Sha + Keita.

Shakela (Arabic) a form of Shakila.

Shakera, Shakerra (Arabic) forms of Shakira.

Shakeria, Shakerria (Arabic) forms of Shakira.

Shakeya (American) a form of Shakia.

Shakia (American) a combination of the prefix Sha + Kia.

Shakiera (Arabic) a form of Shakira.

Shakila (Arabic) pretty.

Shakima (African) beautiful one.

Shakira (Arabic) thankful.

Shakirra (Arabic) a form of Shakira.

Shakita (American) a form of Shakeita.

Shakti (Hindi) energy, power. Religion: a form of the Hindu goddess Devi.

Shakyra (Arabic) a form of Shakira.

Shalana (American) a combination of the prefix Sha + Lana.

Shalanda (American) a form of Shalana.

Shalayna (American) a form of Shalana.

Shaleah (American) a combination of the prefix Sha + Leah.

Shalee (American) a form of Shaleah.

Shaleen, Shalene (American) short forms of Shalena.

Shaleisha (American) a combination of the prefix Sha + Aisha.

Shalena (American) a combination of the prefix Sha + Lena.

Shalini (American) a form of Shalena.

Shalisa (American) a combination of the prefix Sha + Lisa.

Shalita (American) a combination of the prefix Sha + Lita.

Shalon (American) a short form of Shalona.

Shalona (American) a combination of the prefix Sha + Lona.

Shalonda (American) a combination of the prefix Sha + Ondine.

Shalyn, Shalynn, Shalynne (American) combinations of the prefix Sha + Lynn.

Shamara (Arabic) ready for battle.

Shamari BG (Arabic) a form of Shamara.

Shamaria (Arabic) a form of Shamara.

Shameka (American) a combination of the prefix Sha + Meka.

Shamia (American) a combination of the prefix Sha + Mia.

Shamika (American) a combination of the prefix Sha + Mika.

Shamira (Hebrew) precious stone.

Shamiya (American) a form of Shamia.

Shamyra (Hebrew) a form of Shamira.

Shana (Hebrew) God is gracious. (Irish) a form of Jane.

Shanae, Shanea (Irish) forms of Shana.

Shanaya (American) a form of Shania.

Shanda (American) a form of Chanda, Shana.

Shandi (English) a familiar form of Shana.

Shandra (American) a form of Shanda.

Shandria (American) a form of Shandra.

Shandrika (American) a form of Shandria.

Shane 🅱🇬 (Irish) a form of Shana.

Shanece (American) a form of Shanice.

Shanee (Irish) a familiar form of Shane. (Swahili) a form of Shany.

Shaneice (American) a form of Shanice.

Shaneika (American) a form of Shanika.

Shaneisha (American) a combination of the prefix Sha + Aisha.

Shaneka (American) a form of Shanika.

Shanel, Shanell, Shanelle, Shannel (American) forms of Chanel.

Shanequa (American) a form of Shanika.

Shanese (American) a form of Shanice.

Shaneta (American) a combination of the prefix Sha + Neta.

Shani 🇬🇧 (Swahili) a form of Shany.

Shania, Shaniah, Shaniya (American) forms of Shana.

Shanice (American) a form of Janice. **Shanida** (American) a combination of the prefix Sha + Ida.

Shanie (Irish) a form of Shane. (Swahili) a form of Shany.

Shaniece (American) a form of Shanice.

Shanika (American) a combination of the prefix Sha + Nika.

Shaniqua, Shanique (American) forms of Shanika.

Shanise (American) a form of Shanice.

Shanita (American) a combination of the prefix Sha + Nita.

Shanley 🇬🇧 (Irish) hero's child.

Shanna, Shannah (Irish) forms of Shana, Shannon.

Shannen, Shanon (Irish) forms of Shannon.

Shannon 🇬🇧 (Irish) small and wise.

Shanny (Swahili) a form of Shany.

Shanta (French) a form of Chantal**.**

Shantae 🇬🇧 (French) a form of Chantal.

Shantal (American) a form of Shantel.

Shantana (American) a form of Santana.

Shantara (American) a combination of the prefix Sha + Tara.

Shante (French) a form of Chantal.

Shanté (French) a form of Chantal.

Shanteca (American) a combination of the prefix Sha + Teca.

Shantel, Shantell, Shantelle (American) song.

Shanteria, Shanterria (American) forms of Shantara.

Shantesa (American) a combination of the prefix Sha + Tess.

Shanti (American) a short form of Shantia.

Shantia (American) a combination of the prefix Sha + Tia.

Shantille (American) a form of Chantilly.

Shantina (American) a combination of the prefix Sha + Tina.,

Shantora (American) a combination of the prefix Sha + Tory.

Shantoria (American) a form of Shantora.

Shantrell (American) a form of Shantel.

Shantrice (American) a combination of the prefix Sha + Trice.

Shany (Swahili) marvelous, wonderful.

Shanyce (American) a form of Shanice.

Shappa (Native American) red thunder.

Shaquan BG (American) a short form of Shaquanda.

Shaquana, Shaquanna (American) forms of Shaquanda.

Shaquanda (American) a combination of the prefix Sha + Wanda.

Shaquandey (American) a form of Shaquanda.

Shaqueita (American) a form of Shakeita.

Shaquetta (American) a form of Shakeita.

Shaquia (American) a short form of Shakila.

Shaquila, Shaquilla (American) forms of Shakila.

Shaquille BG (American) a form of Shakila.

Shaquira (American) a form of Shakira.

Shaquita, Shaquitta (American) forms of Shakeita.

Shara (Hebrew) a short form of Sharon.

Sharai (Hebrew) princess.

Sharan (Hindi) protector.

Sharda (Punjabi, Yoruba, Arabic) a form of Shardae.

Shardae, Sharday (Punjabi) charity. (Yoruba) honored by royalty. (Arabic) runaway. Forms of Chardae.

Sharee (English) a form of Shari.

Sharen (English) a form of Sharon.

Shari (French) beloved, dearest. (Hungarian) a form of Sarah.

Shariah (French, Hungarian) a form of Shari.

Shariann, Sharianne (English) combinations of Shari + Ann.

Sharice (French) a form of Cherice.

Sharik (African) child of God.

Sharina (English) a form of Sharon.

Sharissa (American) a form of Sharice.

Sharita (French) a familiar form of Shari. (American) a form of Charity.

Sharla (French) a short form of Sharlene, Sharlotte.

Sharleen (French) a form of Sharlene.

Sharlene (French) little and strong.

Sharlotte (American) a form of Charlotte.

Sharma (American) a short form of Sharmaine.

Sharmaine (American) a form of Charmaine.

Sharna (Hebrew) a form of Sharon.

Sharnell (American) a form of Sharon.

Sharnice (American) a form of Sharon.

Sharolyn (American) a combination of Sharon + Lynn.

Sharon (Hebrew) desert plain. A form of Sharai.

Sharonda (Hebrew) a form of Sharon.

Sharron GB (English) a form of Sharon.

Sharrona (Hebrew) a form of Sharon.

Shatara (Hindi) umbrella. (Arabic) good; industrious. (American) a combination of Sharon + Tara.

Shateria (American) a form of Shatara.

Shaterra (American) a form of Shatara.

Shatoria (American) a combination of the prefix Sha + Tory.

Shatoya (American) a form of Shatoria.

Shaun BG (Irish) a form of Sean.

Shauna (Hebrew, Irish) a form of Shana.

Shaunda (Irish) a form of Shauna. **Shaunice** (Irish) a form of Shauna.

Shaunna (Hebrew, Irish) a form of Shauna.

Shaunta (Irish) a form of Shauna.

Shauntae (Irish) a form of Shaunta.

Shauntel (American) song.

Shaunya (Hebrew, Irish) a form of Shauna.

Shavon GB (American) a combination of the prefix Sha + Yvonne.

Shavonda (American) a form of Shavon.

Shavonna (American) a form of Shavon.

Shavonne (American) a combination of the prefix Sha + Yvonne.

Shawana, Shawanna (American) combinations of the prefix Sha + Wanda.

Shawn BG (Irish) a form of Sean.

Shawna (Hebrew, Irish) a form of Shana, Shawn.

Shawnda (Irish) a form of Shawna. **Shawndelle** (Irish) a form of Shawna.

Shawnee (Irish) a form of Shawna.

Shawnika (American) a combination of Shawna + Nika.

Shawnna (Hebrew, Irish) a form of Shawna.

Shawnta GB (Irish) a form of Shawna.

Shawntel (American) song.

Shay BG (Irish) a form of Shea.

Shaya (Irish) a form of Shay.

Shayann, Shayanne (Irish) combinations of Shay + Ann.

Shaye GB (Irish) a form of Shea.

Shayla, Shaylah (Irish) forms of Shay.

Shaylee, Shayli, Shaylie (Irish) forms of Shea.

Shayleen, Shaylene (Irish) forms of Shea.

Shaylen, Shaylin, Shaylyn, Shaylynn (Irish) forms of Shealyn.

Shayna (Hebrew) beautiful.

Shayne BG (Hebrew) a form of Shayna. (Irish) a form of Shane.

Shea GB (Irish) fairy palace.

Shealyn (Irish) a form of Shea.

Sheba (Hebrew) a short form of Bathsheba. Geography: an ancient country of south Arabia.

Sheena (Hebrew) God is gracious. (Irish) a form of Jane.

Sheila (Latin) blind. (Irish) a form of Cecelia.

Shelbe, Shelbee, Shelbey, Shelbi, Shelbie, Shellbie, Shellby (English) forms of Shelby.

Shelby GB (English) ledge estate.

Sheldon BG (English) farm on the ledge.

Shelee (English) a form of Shelley.

Shelia (Latin, Irish) a form of Sheila.

Shelisa (American) a combination of Shelley + Lisa.

Shelley GB (English) meadow on the ledge. (French) a familiar form of MichelleShellie, Shelly (English) meadow on the ledge. (French) familiar forms of Michelle.

Shelsea (American) a form of Chelsea.

Shena (Irish) a form of Sheena.

Shenae (Irish) a form of Sheena.

Shenandoa (Algonquin) beautiful star.

Shenell, Shenelle (American) forms of Shanel.

Shenice, Shenise (American) forms of Shanice.Shenika, Sheniqua (American) forms of Shanika, Shena.

Shera (Aramaic) light.

Sheralee (American) a combination of Shera + Lee.

Sheree (French) beloved, dearest.

Shereen (French) a form of Sheree.

Sherell, Sherelle,
Sherrell (French) forms
of Cherelle, Sheryl.

Sheri, Sherie, Sherri,
Sherrie (French) forms
of Sherry.

Sherian, Sheriann
(American) combinations
of Sheri + Ann.

Sherica (Punjabi, Arabic) a
form of Sherika.

Sherice (French) a form of
Cherice.

Sheridan GB (Irish) wild.

Sherika (Punjabi) relative.
(Arabic) easterner.

Sherilyn (American) a
form of Sherylyn.

Sherissa **(French) a form**
of Sherry, Sheryl.

Sherita (French) a form of
Sherry, Sheryl. **Sherleen**
(French, English) a form
of Sheryl, Shirley.

Sherley (English) a form of
Shirley.

Shermaine (American) a
form of Sharmaine.

Sherron (Hebrew) a form
of Sharon.

Sherry (French) beloved,
dearest. A familiar form
of Sheryl.

Sheryl (French) beloved. A
familiar form of Shirley.

Sherylyn (American) a
combination of Sheryl +
Lynn.

Shevonne (American) a
combination of the prefix
She + Yvonne.

Sheyanne, Sheyenne
(Cheyenne) forms of
Cheyenne.

Shi (Japanese) a short form
of Shika.

Shian, Shiane, Shiann,
Shianne (Cheyenne)
forms of Cheyenne.

Shiana, Shianna
(Cheyenne) forms of
Cheyenne.

Shifra (Hebrew) beautiful.

Shika (Japanese) gentle
deer.

Shikha (Japanese) a form
of Shika.

Shilah (Latin, Irish) a form
of Sheila.

Shilo BG (Hebrew) a form of
Shiloh.

Shiloh GB (Hebrew) God's
gift. Bible: a sanctuary for
the Israelites where the
Ark of the Covenant was
kept.

Shilpa (Indian) well
proportioned.

Shina (Japanese) virtuous,
good; wealthy. (Chinese)
a form of China.

Shino (Japanese) bamboo
stalk.

Shinobu (Japanese) to
support.

Shiquita (American) a
form of Chiquita.

Shira (Hebrew) song.

Shirin (Persian) charming,
sweet.

Shirlene (English) a form
of Shirley.

Shirley (English) bright
meadow.

Shivani (Hindi) life and
death.

Shizu (Japanese) silent.

Shona (Irish) a form of
Jane. A form of Shana,
Shauna, Shawna.

Shonda (Irish) a form of
Shona.

Shonna (Irish) a form of
Shona.

Shonta (Irish) a form of
Shona.

Shontae (Irish) a form of
Shonta.

Shontavia (Irish) a form of
Shonta.

Shonte (Irish) a form of
Shonta.

Shontel, Shontell
(American) forms of
Shantel.

Shontia (American) a form
of Shantia.

Shoshana (Hebrew) a
form of Susan.

Shreya (Indian) better.

Shu (Chinese) kind, gentle.

Shug (American) a short
form of Sugar.

Shula (Arabic) flaming,
bright.

Shulamith (Hebrew)
peaceful.

Shunta (Irish) a form of Shonta.

Shura (Russian) a form of Alexandra.

Shy, Shye (Cheyenne) short forms of Shyan.

Shyan, Shyann, Shyanne, Shyenne (Cheyenne) forms of Cheyenne. Shyanna (Cheyenne) a form of Cheyenne.

Shyla (English) a form of Sheila.

Shylo (Hebrew) a form of Shilo.

Shyra (Hebrew) a form of Shira.

Sianna (Irish) a form of Seana.

Siara, Siarra (Irish) forms of Sierra.
Siarah, Siarrah

Sibeta (Moquelumnan) finding a fish under a rock.

Sibila, Sibilia, Sibilina (Greek) forms of Sybil.

Sibley (English) sibling; friendly. (Greek) a form of Sybil.

Sidnee, Sidnie (French) forms of Sydney.

Sidney GB (French) a form of Sydney.

Sidonia (Hebrew) enticing.

Sidonie (French) from Saint-Denis, France.

Sidra (Latin) star child.
Sidrah, Sidras

Siena, Sienna (American) forms of Ciana.

Siera, Sierrah (Irish) forms of Sierra.

Sierra ✰ Irish) black. (Spanish) saw toothed. Geography: any rugged range of mountains that, when viewed from a distance, has a jagged profile.

Sigfreda (German) victorious peace

Siglinda (Germanic) protective victory.

Sigmunda (German) victorious protector.

Signe (Latin) sign, signal. (Scandinavian) a short form of Sigourney.

Sigolena (Scandinavian) gentle victory.

Sigourney (English) victorious conquerer.

Sigrada (German) famous because of the victory.

Sigrid (Scandinavian) victorious counselor.

Sihu (Native American) flower; bush.

Siko (African) crying baby.

Silenia (Latin) belongs to the earthly gods.

Silvana (Latin) a form of Sylvana.

Silver (English) a precious metal.

Silveria, Silvina (Spanish) forms of Selva.

Silvia (Latin) a form of Sylvia.
Silivia, Silva, Silvya

Simcha BG (Hebrew) joyful.

Simona (Hebrew, French) a form of Simone.

Simone (Hebrew) she heard. (French) a form of Simon

Simran GB (Sikh) absorbed in God.

Sina BG (Irish) a form of Seana.

Sinclair GB (French) a form of Sinclaire.

Sinclaire (French) prayer.

Sinclética (Greek) she who is invited.

Sindy (American) a form of Cindy.

Sinead (Irish) a form of Jane.

Sinforiana (Greek) a form of Sinforosa.

Sinforosa (Latin) full of misfortunes.

Sinovia, Sinya (Russian) foreign.

Sintiques, Síntiques (Greek) fortunate.

Siobhan (Irish) a form of Joan.

Sión (Latin) a form of Asunción.

Sira (Latin) she who comes from Syria.

Sirena (Greek) enchanter. Mythology: Sirens were sea nymphs whose singing enchanted sailors and made them crash their ships into nearby rocks.

Siri (Scandinavian) a short form of Sigrid.

Sisika (Native American) songbird.

Sissy (American) a familiar form of Cecelia.

Sita (Hindi) a form of Shakti.
Sitah, Sitha

Sitara (Sanskrit) morning star.
Sitarah, Sithara

Siti (Swahili) respected woman.

Sky BG (Arabic, Dutch) a form of Skye.
Skky

Skye GB (Arabic) water giver. (Dutch) a short form of Skyler. Geography: an island in the Inner Hebrides, Scotland.

Skyla (Dutch) a form of Skyler.

Skylar ☆ (Dutch) a form of Skyler.

Skyler BG (Dutch) sheltering.

Skyy (Arabic, Dutch) a form of Skye.

Sloan BG (Irish) a form of Sloane.

Sloane (Irish) warrior.

Socorro (Spanish) helper.

Sofia ☆ (Greek) a form of Sophia.

Sofía (Greek) a form of Sofia.

Sofie (Greek) a form of Sofia.
Soffi, Sofi

Sol (Latin) sun.

Solada (Tai) listener.

Solana (Spanish) sunshine.

Solange (French) dignified.

Soledad (Spanish) solitary.

Soledada (Spanish) a form of Soledad.

Solenne (French) solemn, dignified.

Solita (Latin) alone.

Solomon BG (Hebrew) peaceful.

Soma (Hindi) lunar.

Somer (English, Arabic) a form of Sommer.

Sommer (English) summer; summoner. (Arabic) black.

Somoche (Mapuche) distinguished woman.

Sondra (Greek) defender of mankind.

Sonia (Russian, Slavic) a form of Sonya.

Sonja (Scandinavian) a form of Sonya.

Sonora (Spanish) pleasant sounding.

Sonsoles (Spanish) they are suns.

Sonya (Greek) wise. (Russian, Slavic) a form of Sophia.

Sook (Korean) pure.

Sopatra (Greek) father's savior.

Sopheary (Cambodian) beautiful girl.

Sophia ☆ (Greek) wise.

Sophie ☆ (Greek) a familiar form of Sophia

Sophronia (Greek) wise; sensible.
Soffrona, Sofronia

Sora (Native American) chirping songbird.

Soraya (Persian) princess.
Suraya

Sorne (Basque) a form of Concepción.

Sorrel GB (French) reddish brown. Botany: a plant whose leaves are used as salad greens.

Sorya (Spanish) she who is eloquent.

Soso (Native American) tree squirrel dining on pine nuts; chubby-cheeked baby.

Sotera (Greek) savior.

Soterraña (Spanish) burier; burial site.

Souzan (Persian) burning fire.

Spencer, Spenser BG (English) dispenser of provisions.

Speranza (Italian) a form of Esperanza.

Spica (Latin) ear of wheat. Astronomy: a star in the constellation Virgo.

Spring (English) springtime.

Stacee, Staci, Stacie (Greek) forms of Stacey.

Stacey GB (Greek) resurrection. (Irish) a short form of Anastasia, Eustacia, Natasha.

Stacia, Stasia (English) short forms of Anastasia.

Stacy GB (Greek) resurrection. (Irish) a short form of Anastasia, Eustacia, Natasha.

Star (English) star.

Starla (English) a form of Star.

Starleen (English) a form of Star.

Starley (English) a familiar form of Star.

Starling BG (English) bird.

Starlyn (English) a form of Star.

Starr GB (English) star.

Stasha (Greek, Russian) a form of Stasya.
Stashia

Stasya (Greek) a familiar form of Anastasia. (Russian) a form of Stacey.

Stefani, Stefanie, Stefany, Steffani, Steffanie, Steffany (Greek) forms of Stephanie.

Stefania (Greek) a form of Stephanie.

Stefanía (Greek) a form of Stephanie.

Steffi (Greek) a familiar form of Stefani, Stephanie.

Stella ✰ (Latin) star. (French) a familiar form of Estelle.

Stella Maris (Hispanic) star of the sea.

Stepania (Russian) a form of Stephanie.

Stephaine (Greek) a form of Stephanie.

Stephani, Stephannie, Stephany (Greek) forms of Stephanie.

Stephania (Greek) a form of Stephanie.

Stephanie (Greek) crowned.

Stephene (Greek) a form of Stephanie.

Stephenie (Greek) a form of Stephanie.

Stephine (Greek) a form of Stephanie.

Stephney (Greek) a form of Stephanie.

Sterling BG (English) valuable; silver penny.

Stevi (Greek) a familiar form of Stephanie.

Stevie GB (Greek) a familiar form of Stephanie.

Stina (German) a short form of Christina.

Stockard (English) stockyard.

Storm BG (English) storm.

Stormi, Stormie (English) forms of Stormy.

Stormy (English) impetuous by nature.

Su (Chinese) revive, resurrect.

Suchin (Tai) beautiful thought.

Sue (Hebrew) a short form of Susan, Susana.

Sueann (American) a combination of Sue + Ann.

Sueanna (American) a combination of Sue + Anna.

Suela (Spanish) consolation.

Sugar (American) sweet as sugar.

Sugi (Japanese) cedar tree.

Suke (Hawaiian) a form of Susan.

Sukey (Hawaiian) a familiar form of Susan.

Sukhdeep (Sikh) light of peace and bliss.

Suki (Japanese) loved one. (Moquelumnan) eagle-eyed.
Sukie

Sula (Icelandic) large sea bird. (Greek, Hebrew) a short form of Shulamith, Ursula.

Sulamita (Hebrew) peaceful woman.

Suleika (Arabic) most beautiful woman.

Suletu (Moquelumnan) soaring bird.

Sulia (Latin) a form of Julia.

Sullivan BG (Irish) black eyed.

Sulpicia (Latin) Literature: a woman poet from ancient Rome.

Sulwen (Welsh) bright as the sun.

Suma (English) born in the summertime.

Sumalee (Tai) beautiful flower.

Sumati (Hindi) unity.

Sumaya (American) a combination of Sue + Maya.

Sumer (English) a form of Summer.

Sumi (Japanese) elegant, refined.

Summer (English) summertime. **Sun** (Korean) obedient.

Sun-Hi (Korean) good; joyful.

Sunday (Latin) born on the first day of the week.

Sunee (Tai) good.

Suni (Zuni) native; member of our tribe.

Suniva (Latin) radiant; enlightened.

Sunki (Hopi) swift.

Sunny BG (English) bright, cheerful.

Sunshine (English) sunshine.

Surata (Pakistani) blessed joy.

Suri (Todas) pointy nose.

Surya BG (Sanskrit) Mythology: a sun god.

Susammi (French) a combination of Susan + Aimee.

Susan (Hebrew) lily. Susana, Susanna, Susannah (Hebrew) forms of Susan

Susanita (Spanish) a familiar form of Susana.

Susanne (Hebrew) a form of Susan.

Suse (Hawaiian) a form of Susan.

Susette (French) a familiar form of Susan, Susana.

Susie (American) a familiar form of Susan, Susana.

Susima (Greek) elected.

Sutton (American) Geography: Sutton Place is a posh neighborhood in Manhattan.

Suyapa (Spanish) Geography: a village in Honduras.

Suzan (English) a form of Susan.

Suzana, Suzanna, Suzannah (Hebrew) forms of Susan.

Suzanne (English) a form of Susan.

Suzette (French) a form of Susan.

Suzie (American) a familiar form of Susan, Susana.

Suzu (Japanese) little bell.

Suzuki (Japanese) bell tree.

Svetlana (Russian) bright light.

SyÀ (Chinese) summer.

Sybella (English) a form of Sybil.

Sybil (Greek) prophet. Mythology: sibyls were oracles who relayed the messages of the gods.

Sydne, Sydnee, Sydnei, Sydni, Sydnie (French) forms of Sydney.

Sydney (French) from Saint-Denis, France.

Syerra (Irish, Spanish) a form of Sierra.

Sying BG (Chinese) star.

Sylvana (Latin) forest.

Sylvia (Latin) forest. Literature: Sylvia Plath was a well-known American poet.

Sylviann, Sylvianne (American) combinations of Sylvia + Ann.

Sylvie (Latin) a familiar form of Sylvia.

Sylwia (Latin) a form of Sylvia.

Symantha (American) a form of Samantha.

Symone (Hebrew) a form of Simone.

Symphony (Greek) symphony, harmonious sound.

Synthia (Greek) a form of Cynthia.

Syreeta (Hindi) good traditions. (Arabic)

Syrena (Greek) a form of Sirena.

T

T'keyah (American) a form of Takia.

Tabatha, Tabbatha (Greek, Aramaic) forms of Tabitha.

Tabbitha (Greek, Aramaic) a form of Tabitha.

Tabby (English) a familiar form of Tabitha.

Tabea (Swahili) a form of Tabia.

Tabetha (Greek, Aramaic) a form of Tabitha.

Tabia (Swahili) talented.

Tabina (Arabic) follower of Muhammad.

Tabitha (Greek, Aramaic) gazelle.

Tabora (Arabic) plays a small drum.

Tabytha (Greek, Aramaic) a form of Tabitha.
Tabbytha

Tacey (English) a familiar form of Tacita.

Taci (Zuni) washtub. (English) a form of Tacey.

Tacita (Latin) silent.

Tácita (Latin) a form of Tacita.

Taddea (Greek) a form of Thaddea.

Tadita (Omaha) runner.

Taelar, Taeler, Taelor (English) forms of Taylor.

Taesha (Latin) a form of Tisha. (American) a combination of the prefix Ta + Aisha.

Taffline (Welsh) beloved.

Taffy GB (Welsh) a familiar form of Taffline.

Tafne (Egyptian) Mythology: the goddess of light.

Tahira (Arabic) virginal, pure.

Tahiti (Polynesian) rising sun. Geography: an island in the southern Pacific Ocean.

Tahlia (Greek, Hebrew) a form of Talia.

Tai BG (Vietnamese) weather; prosperous; talented.

Taija (Hindi) a form of Taja.

Tailer, Tailor (English) forms of Taylor.

Taima GB (Native American) clash of thunder.

Taimani (Tongan) diamonds.

Taipa (Moquelumnan) flying quail.

Taira (Aramaic, Irish, Arabic) a form of Tara.

Tais (Greek) bound.

Taisha (American) a form of Taesha.

Taite (English) cheerful.

Taja (Hindi) crown.
Tahai, Tajae, Teja, Tejah, Tejal

Tajah (Hindi) a form of Taja.

Taka (Japanese) honored.
Takah

Takala (Hopi) corn tassel.

Takara (Japanese) treasure.

Takayla (American) a combination of the prefix Ta + Kayla.

Takeia (Arabic) a form of Takia.

Takeisha (American) a combination of the prefix Ta + Keisha.

Takenya (Hebrew) animal horn. (Moquelumnan) falcon. (American) a combination of the prefix Ta + Kenya.

Takeria (American) a form of Takira.

Takesha (American) a form of Takeisha.

Takeya (Arabic) a form of Takia.

Taki (Japanese) waterfall.

Takia (Arabic) worshiper.

Takila (American) a form of Tequila.

Takira (American) a combination of the prefix Ta + Kira.

Takisha (American) a form of Takeisha.

Takiya, Takiyah (Arabic) forms of Takia.

Tala (Native American) stalking wolf.

Talasi (Hopi) corn tassel.

Talaya (American) a form of Talia.
Talayah, Talayia

Talea, Taleah (American) forms of Talia.

Taleebin (Australian) young.

Taleisha (American) a combination of Talia + Aisha.

Talena (American) a combination of the prefix Ta + Lena.

Talesha (American) a form of Taleisha.

Talia (Greek) blooming. (Hebrew) dew from heaven. (Latin, French) birthday. A short form of Natalie.

Talía (Greek) a form of Talia.

Taliah (Greek, Hebrew, Latin, French) a form of Talia.

Talina (American) a combination of Talia + Lina.

Talisa, Talissa (English) forms of Tallis.

Talisha (American) a form of Taleisha. (English) a form of Talisa.
Talishia

Talitha (Arabic) young girl.

Taliyah (Greek) a form of Talia.

Talley (French) a familiar form of Talia.

Tallis BG (French, English) forest.

Tallulah (Choctaw) leaping water.

Talma (Native American) thunder.

Talman BG (Hebrew) to injure, oppress.

Talon BG (French, English) claw, nail.

Talor GB (Hebrew) dew.

Talya (Greek) a form of Talia.

Tam BG (Vietnamese) heart.

Tama (Japanese) jewel.
Tamaa, Tamah, Tamaiah, Tamala, Tema

Tamaira (American) a form of Tamara.
Tamairah

Tamaka (Japanese) bracelet.

Tamanna (Hindi) desire.

Tamar GB (Russian) History: a twelfth-century Georgian queen. (Hebrew) a short form of Tamara.

Tamara (Hebrew) palm tree,

Tamarah, Tamarra (Hebrew) forms of Tamara.

Tamaria (Hebrew) a form of Tamara.

Tamassa (Hebrew) a form of Thomasina.

Tamaya (Quechua) in the center.

Tameisha (American) a form of Tamesha.

Tameka (Aramaic) twin.

Tamekia (Aramaic) a form of Tameka.

Tamela (American) a form of Tamila.

Tamera (Hebrew) a form of Tamara.

Tamesha (American) a combination of the prefix Ta + Mesha.

Tameshia (American) a form of Tamesha.

Tami, Tammi, Tammie (English) forms of Tammy.

Tamia (Hebrew, English) a form of Tammy.

Tamika (Japanese) a form of Tamiko.

Tamiko (Japanese) child of the people.

Tamila (American) a combination of the prefix Ta + Mila.

Tamira (Hebrew) a form of Tamara.

Tamisha (American) a form of Tamesha.

Tamiya (Hebrew, English) a form of Tammy.

Tammy (English) twin. (Hebrew) a familiar form of Tamara.

Tamra (Hebrew) a short form of Tamara.

Tamrika (American) a combination of Tammy + Erika.

Tamsin (English) a short form of Thomasina.

Tamyra (Hebrew) a form of Tamara.

Tana, Tanna (Slavic) short forms of Tanya.

Tanaya (Russian, Slavic) a form of Tanya.

Tandra (English) a form of Tandy.

Tandy (English) team.

Tanea (Russian, Slavic) a form of Tanya.

Tanechka, Tanichka (Russian) forms of Tania.

Taneesha (American) a form of Tanesha.

Taneisha (American) a form of Tanesha.

Tanesha (American) a combination of the prefix Ta + Nesha.

Taneya (Russian, Slavic) a form of Tanya.

Tangela (American) a combination of the prefix Ta + Angela.

Tangi, Tangie (American) short forms of Tangia.

Tangia (American) a form of Tangela.

Tani GB (Japanese) valley. (Slavic) stand of glory. A familiar form of Tania.

Tania (Russian, Slavic) fairy queen.

Taniel GB (American) a combination of Tania + Danielle.

Taniesha (American) a form of Tanesha.

Tanika, Taniqua (American) forms of Tania.

Tanis (Slavic) a form of Tania, Tanya.

Tanisha (American) a combination of the prefix Ta + Nisha.

Tanissa (American) a combination of the prefix Tania + Nissa.

Tanita (American) a combination of the prefix Ta + Nita.

Tanith (Phoenician) Mythology: Tanit is the goddess of love.

Taniya (Russian, Slavic) a form of Tania, Tanya.

Tanja (American) a short form of Tangela.

Tanner BG (English) leather worker, tanner. Tannor

Tannis GB (Slavic) a form of Tania, Tanya.

Tansy (Greek) immortal. (Latin) tenacious, persistent.

Tanya (Russian, Slavic) fairy queen.

Tao (Chinese, Vietnamese) peach.

Tara (Aramaic) throw; carry. (Irish) rocky hill. (Arabic) a measurement.

Tarah, Tarra, Tarrah (Irish) forms of Tara.

Taralyn (American) a form of Teralyn.

Taran BG (Persian) a short form of Taraneh. (Irish) a form of Tara.

Taraneh (Persian) melody.

Tararia (Spanish) a form of Teresa.

Tarati (Maori) God's gift.

Tarbula (Arabic) square, block.

Tarcisia (Greek) valiant.

Taree GB (Japanese) arching branch.

Tareixa (Galician) wild animal.

Tari (Irish) a familiar form of Tara.

Tarian (Welsh) coat of arms.

Tarika (Hindi) star.

Tarin, Tarryn (Irish) forms of Tara.

Tarissa (American) a combination of Tara + Rissa.

Tarne (Scandinavian) lake in the mountains. (Australian) salty water.

Tarsicia (Latin) she who was born in Tarso, the Turkish city where St. Paul was born.

Társila (Greek) valiant.

Tarsilia (Greek) basket weaver.

Taryn GB (Irish) a form of Tara.

Tasarla (Gypsy) dawn.

Taseem (Indian) salute of praise.

Tasha (Greek) born on Christmas day. (Russian) a short form of Natasha.

Tashana (American) a combination of the prefix Ta + Shana.

Tashara (American) a combination of the prefix Ta + Shara.

Tashauna (American) a form of Tashawna.

Tashawna (American) a combination of the prefix Ta + Shawna.

Tashay (Greek, Russian) a form of Tasha.

Tasheena (American) a combination of the prefix Ta + Sheena.

Tashelle (American) a combination of the prefix Ta + Shelley.

Tashena (American) a form of Tasheena.

Tashi (Hausa) a bird in flight. (Slavic) a form of Tasha.

Tashia (Slavic, Hausa) a form of Tashi.

Tashiana (American) a form of Tashana.

Tasia (Slavic) a familiar form of Tasha.

Tasmin (English) a short form of Thomasina.

Tassie (English) a familiar form of Tasmin.

Tassos (Greek) a form of Theresa.

Tata (Russian) a familiar form of Tatiana.

Tate BG (English) a short form of Tatum. A form of Taite, Tata.

Tatiana (Slavic) fairy queen.

Tatianna (Slavic) a form of Tatiana.

Tatiyana (Slavic) a form of Tatiana.

Tatjana (Slavic) a form of Tatiana.

Tatum GB (English) cheerful.

Tatyana, Tatyanna (Slavic) forms of Tatiana.

Taura (Latin) bull. Astrology: Taurus is a sign of the zodiac.

Tauri (English) a form of Tory.

Tavia (Latin) a short form of Octavia.

Tavie (Scottish) twin.

Tawana, Tawanna (American) combinations of the prefix Ta + Wanda.

Tawia (African) born after twins. (Polish) a form of Tavia.

Tawnee, Tawney, Tawni, Tawnie (English) forms of Tawny.

Tawny (Gypsy) little one. (English) brownish yellow, tan.

Tawnya (American) a combination of Tawny + Tonya.

Taya (English) a short form of Taylor.

Tayana (English) a form of Taya.

Tayanita (Cherokee) beaver.

Taye (English) a short form of Taylor.

Tay

Tayla (English) a short form of Taylor.

Taylar, Taylore, Taylour, Taylre (English) forms of Taylor.

Tayler GB (English) a form of Taylor.

Taylor ⭐ GB (English) tailor.

Tazu (Japanese) stork; longevity.

Tea (Spanish) a short form of Dorothy.

Teagan GB (Welsh) beautiful, attractive.

Teah (Greek, Spanish) a form of Tia.

Teaira, Teairra (Latin) forms of Tiara.

Teal (English) river duck; blue green.

Teala (English) a form of Teal. (American) combinations of the prefix Te + Anna. Forms of Tiana.

Teara, Tearra (Latin) forms of Tiara.

Teasha (Latin, American) a form of Taesha.

Teca (Hungarian) a form of Theresa.

Tecla (Greek) God's fame.

Tecusa (Latin) covered, hidden.

Teda (Greek) a form of Teodora.

Teddi, Tedi (Greek) familiar forms of Theodora.

Tedra (Greek) a short form of Theodora.

Tedya (Russian) a form of Teodora.

Teela (English) a form of Teala.

Teena (Spanish, American) a form of Tina.

Teesha (Latin) a form of Tisha.

Tegan GB (Welsh) a form of Teagan.

Tehya (Hindi) a form of Taja.

Teia (Greek, Spanish) a form of Tia.

Teicuih (Nahuatl) younger sister.

Teila (English) a form of Teala.

Teira, Teirra (Latin) forms of Tiara.

Teisha (Latin, American) a form of Taesha.

Tejana (Spanish) Texan.

Tekia (Arabic) a form of Takia.

Teleri (Welsh) child of Paul.

Telisha (American) a form of Taleisha.

Telmao (Greek) loving with her fellow people.

Temira (Hebrew) tall.

Temis (Greek) she who establishes order and justice.

Tempany (Australian) a form of Tempest.

Temperance (French) moderation or restraint.

Tempest GB (French) stormy.

Tempestt (French) a form of Tempest.

Tenesha (American) a form of Tenisha.

Tenestina (Greek) bandage.

Tenille, Tennille (American) combinations of the prefix Te + Nellie.

Tenise (Slavic) a form of Tanis.

Tenisha (American) a combination of the prefix Te + Nisha.

Tenley (English) Dennis' field.

Teo (Greek) a short form of Teodora.

Teoctistes (Greek) created by God.

Teodelina, Teodolinda (German) she who loves her village.

Teodequilda (German) warrior of her village.

Teodomira (Spanish) important woman in the village.

Teodora (Czech) a form of Theodora.

Teodota (Greek) a form of Teodora.

Teofania, Teofanía (Greek) forms of Theophania.

Teófila (Greek) a form of Theophilia.

Teolinda (German) a short form of Teodelinda.

Teona, Teonna (Greek) forms of Tiana.

Teopista, Teopistes (Greek) dignity of God.

Teorítgida (Greek) converted to God.

Teotista (Greek) drunk with the love of God.

Teoxihuitl (Nahuatl) turquoise; precious and divine.

Tepin (Nahuatl) little one.

Tequila (Spanish) a kind of liquor.

Tequilla (Spanish) a form of Tequila.

Tera, Terah, Terra, Terrah (Latin) earth. (Japanese) swift arrow. (American) forms of Tara.

Teralyn (American) a combination of Teri + Lynn.

Terceira, Tercera, Terciera (Spanish) born third.

Teresa (Greek) a form of Theresa.

Terese (Greek) a form of Teresa.

Teresina (Italian) a form of Teresa.

Teresinha (Portuguese) a form of Teresa.

Teresita (Spanish) a form of Teresa.

Teressa (Greek) a form of Teresa.

Teri, Terri, Terrie (Greek) familiar forms of Theresa.

Teria, Terria (Irish) forms of Tera. (Greek) forms of Teri.

Terica, Terrica, Terricka (American) combinations of Teri + Erica.

Terika, Terrika (American) forms of Terica.

Terpsícore (Greek) she who enjoys dancing.

Terrelle BG (German) thunder ruler.

Terrene (Latin) smooth.

Terriana, Terrianna (American) combinations of Teri + Anna.

Terriann (American) a combination of Teri + Ann.

Terrin BG (Latin) a form of Terrene.

Terriona (American) a form of Terriana.

Terrwyn (Welsh) valiant.

Terry BG (Greek) a familiar form of Theresa.

Terry-Lynn (American) a combination of Teri + Lynn.

Terryn, Teryn (Latin) forms of Terrene.

Tersea (Greek) a form of Teresa.

Tertia (Latin) third.

Tesa (Greek) a form of Tessa.

Tesha (Latin, American) a form of Taesha, Tisha.

Tesia, Tessia (Greek) forms of Tessa.

Tesira (Greek) founder.

Tesla (American) a unit of magnetic flux density, named after its creator, Nikola Tesla, a Croatian-born physicist.

Tess (Greek) a short form of Quintessa, Theresa.

Tessa (Greek) reaper.

Tessie (Greek) a familiar form of Theresa.

Tessla (American) a form of Tesla.

Tetis (Greek) nurse for the new mother.

Tetsu (Japanese) strong as iron.

Tetty (English) a familiar form of Elizabeth.

Teuicui (Nahuatl) younger sister.

Tevy (Cambodian) angel.

Teya (English) a form of Taya. (Greek, Spanish) a form of Tia.

Teyacapan (Nahuatl) first born.

Teyana, Teyanna (American) forms of Teana.

Teylor (English) a form of Taylor.

Teyona (American) a form of Teana.

Thaddea (Greek) courageous. (Latin) praiser.

Thais (Greek) a form of Tais.
Thays

Thaís (Greek) bond.

Thalassa (Greek) sea, ocean.

Thalia (Greek) a form of Talia. Mythology: the Muse of comedy.

Thamara (Hebrew) a form of Tamara.

Thana (Arabic) happy occasion.

Thandie BG (Zulu) beloved.

Thanh BG (Vietnamese) bright blue. (Punjabi) good place.

Thania (Arabic) a form of Thana.

Thao (Vietnamese) respectful of parents.

Thea (Greek) goddess. A short form of Althea.

Theadora (Greek) a form of Theodora.

Thelma (Greek) willful.

Thema (African) queen.

Theodora (Greek) gift of God.

Theodosia (Greek) a form of Theodora.

Theone (Greek) gift of God.

Theophania (Greek) God's appearance.

Theophila (Greek) loved by God.

Theresa (Greek) reaper.

Therese (Greek) a form of Theresa.

Thérèse (French) a form of Teresa.

Theta (Greek) Linguistics: a letter in the Greek alphabet.

Thetis (Greek) disposed. Mythology: the mother of Achilles.

Thi (Vietnamese) poem.

Thirza (Hebrew) pleasant.

Thomasina (Hebrew) twin.

Thora (Scandinavian) thunder.

Thordis (Scandinavian) Thor's spirit.

Thrina (Greek) a form of Trina.

Thu (Vietnamese) autumn; poem.

Thuy (Vietnamese) gentle.

Tia (Greek) princess. (Spanish) aunt.

Tía (Spanish, Greek) a form of Tia.

Tiaira (Latin) a form of Tiara.

Tiana, Tianna (Greek) princess. (Latin) short forms of Tatiana.

Tiani (Greek, Latin) a form of Tiana.

Tiara (Latin) crowned.

Tiare (Latin) a form of Tiara.

Tiarra (Latin) a form of Tiara.

Tiauna (Greek) a form of Tiana.

Tiberia (Latin) Geography: the Tiber River in Italy.

Tiburcia (Spanish) born in the place of pleasures.

Tichina (American) a combination of the prefix Ti + China.

Ticiana (Latin) valiant defender.

Tida (Tai) daughter.

Tieara (Latin) a form of Tiara.

Tiera, Tierra (Latin) forms of Tiara.

Tierney GB (Irish) noble.

Tiesha (Latin) a form of Tisha.

Tifani, Tiffaney, Tiffani, Tiffanie (Latin) forms of Tiffany.

Tifara (Hebrew) happy.

Tiff (Latin) a short form of Tiffany.

Tiffany (Latin) trinity. (Greek) a short form of Theophania

Tiffini (Latin) a form of Tiffany.

Tiffney (Latin) a form of Tiffany.

Tiffy (Latin) a familiar form of Tiffany.

Tigris (Irish) tiger. Geography: a river in southwest Asia that flows from Turkey, through Iraq, to the Euphrates River.

Tijuana (Spanish) Geography: a border town in Mexico.

Tikvah (Hebrew) hope.

Tilda (German) a short form of Matilda.

Tillie (German) a familiar form of Matilda.

Timara (Hebrew) a form of Tamara.

Timber (English) wood.

Timeka (Aramaic) a form of Tameka.

Timesha (American) a form of Tamesha.

Timi (English) a familiar form of Timothea.

Timia (English) a form of Timi.

Timotea (Greek) a form of Timothea.

Timothea (English) honoring God.

Tina (Spanish, American) a short form of Augustine, Martina, Christina, Valentina.

Tinble (English) sound bells make.

Tíndara (Greek) she who is willing to love.

Tinesha (American) a combination of the prefix Ti + Niesha.

Tinisha (American) a form of Tenisha.

Tinley (American) Geography: Tinley Park is a town in Illinois.

Tiona, Tionna (American) forms of Tiana.

Tiphanie (Latin) a form of Tiffany.

Tiponya (Native American) great horned owl.

Tipper (Irish) water pourer. (Native American) a short form of Tiponya.

Tippi (Greek) a familiar form of Xanthippe.

Tira (Hindi) arrow.

Tirranna (Australian) stream of water.

Tirtha (Hindi) ford.

Tirza (Hebrew) pleasant.

Tirzah (Hebrew) a form of Tirza.

Tisa (Swahili) ninth-born.

Tish (Latin) a short form of Tisha.

Tisha (Latin) joy. A short form of Leticia.

Tita (Greek) giant. (Spanish) a short form of names ending in "tita." A form of Titus

Titania (Greek) giant. Mythology: the Titans were a race of giants.

Titiana (Greek) a form of Titania.

Tivona (Hebrew) nature lover.

Tiwa (Zuni) onion.

Tiyana, Tiyanna (English) forms of Tayana. (Greek) forms of Tiana.

Tj BG (American) a form of TJ.

TJ BG (American) a combination of the initials T. + J.

Tkeyah (American) a form of Takia.

Tlachinolli (Nahuatl) fire.

Tlaco (Nahuatl) a short form of Tlacoehua.

Tlacoehua (Nahuatl) middle one.

Tlacotl (Nahuatl) osier twig.

Tlahutli (Nahuatl) sir.

Tlalli (Nahuatl) earth.

Tlanextli (Nahuatl) radiance; majesty.

Tlazohtzin (Nahuatl) one who is loved.

Tlexictli (Nahuatl) fire navel.

Tobi GB (Hebrew) God is good.

Tocarra (American) a combination of the prefix To + Cara.

Toinette (French) a short form of Antoinette.

Toki (Japanese) hopeful.

Tokoni BG (Tongan) helpful.

Tola (Polish) a form of Toinette.

Toltecatl, Toltecatli (Nahuatl) artist.

Tomi GB (Japanese) rich.

Tomiko (Japanese) wealthy.

Tommi (Hebrew) a short form of Thomasina.

Tommie 🅱🄶 (Hebrew) a short form of Thomasina.

Tomo (Japanese) intelligent.

Tonalnan (Nahuatl) mother of light.

Tonatzin (Nahuatl) goddess of the earth.

Toneisha (American) a combination of the prefix To + Niesha.

Tonesha (American) a form of Toneisha.

Toni 🄶🄱 (Greek) flourishing. (Latin) praiseworthy.

Tonia (Latin, Slavic) a form of Toni, Tonya.

Tonie (Greek, Latin) a form of Toni.

Tonisha (American) a form of Toneisha.

Tonneli (Swiss) a form of Toni.

Tonya (Slavic) fairy queen.

Topaz (Latin) golden yellow gem.

Topsy (English) on top. Literature: a slave in Harriet Beecher Stowe's novel *Uncle Tom's Cabin*.

Tora (Japanese) tiger.

Torcuata (Latin) adorned.

Toree, Torie, Torri (English) forms of Tori, Tory.

Toreth (Welsh) abundant.

Torey 🅱🄶 (English) a form of Tori, Tory.

Tori 🄶🄱 (Japanese) bird. (English) a form of Tory.

Toria (English) a form of Tori, Tory.

Toriana (English) a form of Tori.

Toribia (Latin) a form of Tránsito.

Torilyn (English) a combination of Tori + Lynn.

Torlan (Welsh) comes from the river.

Torrey 🅱🄶 (English) a form of Tori, Tory.

Torrie 🄶🄱 (English) a form of Tori, Tory.

Tory 🅱🄶 (English) victorious. (Latin) a short form of Victoria.

Tosca, Toscana (Latin) native of Tuscany, a region in Italy.

Tosha (Punjabi) armaments. (Polish) a familiar form of Antonia. (Russian) a form of Tasha.

Toshi (Japanese) mirror image.

Toski (Hopi) squashed bug.

Totsi (Hopi) moccasins.

Tottie (English) a familiar form of Charlotte.

Tova (Hebrew) a form of Tovah.

Tovah (Hebrew) good.

Toya (Spanish) a form of Tory.

Tracey 🄶🄱 (Latin) warrior. (Greek) a familiar form of Theresa.

Traci, Tracie (Latin) forms of Tracey.

Tracy 🄶🄱 (Latin) warrior. (Greek) a familiar form of Theresa.

Tralena (Latin) a combination of Tracey + Lena.

Tranesha (American) a combination of the prefix Tra + Niesha.

Trang (Vietnamese) intelligent, knowledgeable; beautiful.

Tranquila, Tranquilla (Spanish) forms of Tranquilina.

Tranquilina (Latin) tranquil.

Tránsito (Latin) she who moves on to another life.

Trashawn 🅱🄶 (American) a combination of the prefix Tra + Shawn.

Trava (Czech) spring grasses.

Traviata (Italian) straying.

Treasure (Latin) treasure, wealth; valuable.

Trella (Spanish) a familiar form of Estelle.

Tresha (Greek) a form of Theresa.

Tressa (Greek) a short form of Theresa.

Treva (Irish, Welsh) a short form of Trevina.

Trevina (Irish) prudent. (Welsh) homestead.

Trevona (Irish) a form of Trevina.

Triana (Latin) third. (Greek) a form of Trina.

Trice (Greek) a short form of Theresa.

Tricia (Latin) a form of Trisha.

Trifena (Greek) delicate.

Trifina, Trifonia (Greek) fun.

Trifosa (Greek) she who delights in God.

Trilby (English) soft hat.

Trina (Greek) pure.

Trindade, Trinidad (Latin) forms of Trinity.

Trini 🇬🇧 (Greek) a form of Trina.

Trinity 🇬🇧 (Latin) triad. Religion: the Father, the Son, and the Holy Spirit.

Tripaileo (Mapuche) passionate woman.

Trish (Latin) a short form of Beatrice, Trisha.

Trisha (Latin) noblewoman. (Hindi) thirsty.

Trissa (Latin) a familiar form of Patricia.

Trista (Latin) a short form of Tristan.

Tristabelle (English) a combination of Tristan + Belle.

Tristan 🇧🇬 (Latin) bold.

Tristen 🇧🇬 (Latin) a form of Tristan.

Tristian 🇧🇬 (Irish) a short form of Tristianna.

Tristianna (Irish) a combination of Tristan + Anna.

Tristin 🇧🇬 (Latin) a form of Tristan.

Triston 🇧🇬 (Latin) a form of Tristan.

Tristyn 🇧🇬 (Latin) a form of Tristan.

Trixie (American) a familiar form of Beatrice.

Troy 🇧🇬 (Irish) foot soldier. (French) curly haired. (English) water.

Troya (Irish) a form of Troy.

Trudel (Dutch) a form of Trudy.

Trudy (German) a familiar form of Gertrude.

Trycia (Latin) a form of Trisha.

Tryna (Greek) a form of Trina.

Tryne (Dutch) pure.

Trynel (Bavarian) a form of Katherine.

Trystan 🇧🇬 (Latin) a form of Tristan.

Trystyn (Latin) a form of Tristan.

Tsigana (Hungarian) a form of Zigana.

Tu 🇧🇬 (Chinese) jade.

Tuesday (English) born on the third day of the week.

Tuhina (Hindi) snow.

Tula (Teutonic) a form of Gertrudes.

Tulip (French) tulip flower.

Tullia (Irish) peaceful, quiet.

Tully 🇧🇬 (Irish) at peace with God.

Tulsi (Hindi) basil, a sacred Hindu herb.

Tura (Catalan) ox.

Turquoise (French) blue-green semi-precious stone.

Tusa (Zuni) prairie dog.

Tusnelda (German) she who fights giants.

Tuyen 🇬🇧 (Vietnamese) angel.

Tuyet (Vietnamese) snow.

Twyla (English) woven of double thread.

Ty 🇧🇬 (English) a short form of Tyler.

Tyana, Tyanna (Greek) forms of Tiana. (American) combinations of Ty + Anna.

Tyann (Greek, American) a short form of Tyana.

Tyasia (American) a form of Tyesha.

Tyeesha (American) a form of Tyesha.

Tyeisha (American) a form of Tyesha.

Tyesha (American) a combination of Ty + Aisha.

Tyeshia (American) a form of Tyesha.

Tyfany (American) a short form of Tiffany.

Tyiesha (American) a form of Tyesha.

Tykeisha (American) a form of Takeisha.

Tykera (American) a form of Takira.

Tykeria (American) a form of Tykera.

Tykia (American) a form of Takia.

Tylar 🅱🄶 (English) a form of Tyler.

Tyler 🅱🄶 **(English) tailor.**

Tylor 🅱🄶 (English) a form of Tyler.

Tyna (Czech) a short form of Kristina.

Tyne (English) river.

Tyneisha (American) a form of Tynesha.

Tynesha (American) a combination of Ty + Niesha.

Tyneshia (American) a form of Tynesha.

Tynisha (American) a form of Tynesha.

Tyonna (American) a form of Tiana.

Tyra (Scandinavian) battler. Mythology: Tyr was the god of war. A form of Thora. (Hindi) a form of Tira.

Tyrah (Scandinavian, Hindi) a form of Tyra.

Tyree 🅱🄶 (Scandinavian, Hindi) a form of Tyra.

Tyshanna (American) a combination of Ty + Shawna.

Tytiana, Tytianna (Greek) forms of Titania.

U

U (Korean) gentle.

Ualani (Hawaiian) rain from heaven.

Ubaldina (Teutonic) audacious; intelligent.

Udalrica (Scandinavian) rich country.

Udele (English) prosperous.

Ugolina (German) bright mind; bright spirit.

Ujana (Breton) noble; exellent. (African) youth.

Ula (Irish) sea jewel. (Scandinavian) wealthy. (Spanish) a short form of Eulalia.

Ulalia (Greek) sweet; soft-spoken.

Ulani (Polynesian) cheerful.

Ulima (Arabic) astute; wise.

Ulla (German, Swedish) willful. (Latin) a short form of Ursula.

Ulrica (German) wolf ruler; ruler of all. .

Ultima (Latin) last, endmost, farthest.

Ululani (Hawaiian) heavenly inspiration.

Ulva (German) wolf.

Uma (Hindi) mother. Religion: another name for the Hindu goddess Devi.

Umay (Turkish) hopeful.

Umbelina (Latin) she who gives protective shade.

Umeko (Japanese) plum-blossom child; patient.

Umiko (Japanese) child of the sea.

Una (Latin) one; united. (Hopi) good memory. (Irish) a form of Agnes.

Undine (Latin) little wave. Mythology: the undines were water spirits.

Unice (English) a form of Eunice.

Unika 🄶🄱 (American) a form of Unique.

Uniqua (Latin) a form of Uniquc.

Unique 🄶🄱 (Latin) only one.

Unity 🄶🄱 (English) unity.

Unn (Norwegian) she who is loved.

Unna (German) woman.

Unnea (Scandinavian) linden tree.

Urania (Greek) heavenly. Mythology: the Muse of astronomy.

Urbana (Latin) city dweller.

Uri 🅱🅶 (Hebrew) my light.

Uriana (Greek) heaven; the unknown.

Uriel (Hebrew) light of God.

Urika (Omaha) useful to everyone.

Urit (Hebrew) bright.

Urith (German) worthy.

Urola (Russian) a form of Ursula.

Urraca (German) magpie.

Ursa (Greek) a short form of Ursula. (Latin) a form of Orsa.

Ursicina (Latin) bear meat.

Ursina (Latin) a form of Ursula.

Ursula (Greek) little bear.

Usha (Hindi) sunrise.

Ushi (Chinese) ox. Astrology: a sign of the Chinese zodiac.

Usoa (Spanish) dove.

Uta (German) rich. (Japanese) poem.

Utano (Japanese) field of songs.

Utina (Native American) woman of my country.

Uxía (Greek) born from a good family.

Uxue (Basque) dove.

Uzza (Arabic) strong.

Uzzia (Hebrew) God is my strength.

V

Valene (Latin) a short form of Valentina.

Valentia (Italian) a form of Valentina.

Valentina (Latin) strong. History: Valentina Tereshkova, a Soviet cosmonaut, was the first woman in space.

Valera (Russian) a form of Valerie.

Valeria (Latin) a form of Valerie.

Valéria (Hungarian, Portuguese) a form of Valerie.

Valerie (Latin) strong.

Valery (Latin) a form of Valerie.

Valeska (Slavic) glorious ruler.

Valkiria (German) Mythology: the Valkyries were Norse handmaidens who carried warriors' souls to Valhalla.

Valli (Latin) a familiar form of Valentina, Valerie. Botany: a plant native to India.

Vallia (Spanish) strong protector.

Valma (Finnish) loyal defender.

Valonia (Latin) shadow valley.

Valora (Latin) a form of Valerie.

Valorie (Latin) a form of Valerie.

Valtruda (German) strong dynasty.

Van 🅱🅶 (Greek) a short form of Vanessa.

Vanda 🅶🅱 (German) a form of Wanda.

Vandani (Hindi) worthy, honorable.

Vanesa, Vannesa, Vannessa (Greek) forms of Vanessa.

Vanessa (Greek) butterfly. Literature: a name invented by Jonathan Swift as a nickname for Esther Vanhomrigh.

Vanetta (English) a form of Vanessa.

Vani (Hindi) voice. (Italian) a form of Ann.

Vania (Russian) a familiar form of Anna.

Vanity (English) vain.

Vanna (Cambodian) golden. (Greek) a short form of Vanessa.

Vanora (Welsh) white wave.

Vantrice (American) a combination of the prefix Van + Trice.

Vanya BG (Russian) a familiar form of Anna.

Vara (Scandinavian) careful.

Varana (Hindi) river.

Varda (Hebrew) rose.

Vardina (Hebrew) a form of Varda.

Varina (English) thorn.

Varinia (Roman, Spanish) versatile.

Varvara (Slavic) a form of Barbara.

Vashti (Persian) lovely. Bible: the wife of Ahasuerus, king of Persia.

Vasilisa, Vasillisa (Russian) royal.

Vassy (Persian) beautiful.

Vasya (Russian) royal.

Veanna (American) a combination of the prefix Ve + Anna.

Veda (Sanskrit) sacred lore; knowledge. Religion: the Vedas are the sacred writings of Hinduism.

Vedette (Italian) sentry; scout. (French) movie star.

Vedis (German) spirit from the forest.

Vega (Arabic) falling star.

Velda (German) a form of Valda.

Velia (Latin) concealed.

Velika (Slavic) great, wondrous.

Velinda (American) a combination of the prefix Ve + Linda.

Velma (German) a familiar form of Vilhelmina.

Velvet (English) velvety.

Venancia (Latin) hunter.

Venecia (Italian) from Venice, Italy.

Veneranda (Latin) worthy of veneration.

Venessa (Latin) a form of Vanessa.

Venetia (Italian) a form of Venecia.

Venezia (Italian) a form of Venecia.

Venice (Italian) from Venice, Italy.

Venidle (German) flag of the warrior.

Ventana (Spanish) window.

Ventura (Spanish) good fortune.

Venus (Latin) love. Mythology: the goddess of love and beauty.

Venustiana (Latin) a form of Venus.

Vera (Latin) true. (Slavic) faith. A short form of Elvera, Veronica.

Veradis (Latin) truthful.

Verbena (Latin) sacred plants.

Verda (Latin) young, fresh.

Verdad (Spanish) truthful.

Verdianna (American) a combination of Verda + Anna.

Veredigna (Latin) she who has earned great honors for her dignity.

Verena (Latin) truthful. A familiar form of Vera, Verna.

Verenice (Latin) a form of Veronica.

Veridiana (Latin) truthful.

Verity (Latin) truthful.

Verlene (Latin) a combination of Veronica + Lena.

Verna (Latin) springtime. (French) a familiar form of Laverne.

Vernice (Latin) a form of Bernice, Verna.

Vernisha (Latin) a form of Vernice.

Veronic (Latin) a short form of Veronica.

Veronica (Latin) true image.

Verónica (Spanish) a form of Veronica.

Verônica (Portuguese) a form of Veronica.

Veronika (Latin) a form of Veronica.

Veronique, Véronique
(French) forms of
Veronica.

Vespasiana (Latin)
Vespera (Latin) evening
star.

Vesta (Latin) keeper of the
house. Mythology: the
goddess of the home.

Veta (Slavic) a familiar
form of Elizabeth.

Vevila (Irish) melodious
voice.

Vevina (Irish) pleasant,
sweet.

Vi (Latin, French) a short
form of Viola, Violet.

Vianca (Spanish) a form of
Bianca.

Vianey, Vianney
(American) familiar
forms of Vianna.

Vianna (American) a
combination of Vi +
Anna.

Vica (Hungarian) a form of
Eve.

Vicka, Vika (Latin)
familiar forms of Victoria.

Vicki, Vickie, Vicky
(Latin) familiar forms of
Victoria.

Victoria ☆ (Latin)
victorious. **Victorine**
(Latin) a form of Victoria.

Victory (Latin) victory.

Vida (Sanskrit) a form of
Veda. (Hebrew) a short
form of Davida.

Vidal 🅱🅶 (Latin) life.

Vidalina (Spanish) a form
of Vidal.

Vidonia (Portuguese)
branch of a vine.

Vienna (Latin) Geography:
the capital of Austria.

Vigilia (Latin) wakeful,
watching.

Vignette (French) small
vine.

Vikki (Latin) a familiar
form of Victoria.

   Viktoria (Latin) a form
of Victoria.

Vila (Latin) from a house in
the country.

Vilana (Latin) inhabitant
of a small village.

Vilhelmina (German) a
form of Wilhelmina.

Villette (French) small
town.

Vilma (German) a short
form of Vilhelmina.

Vina (Hindi) Religion: a
musical instrument
played by the Hindu
goddess of wisdom.
(Spanish) vineyard.
(Hebrew) a short form of
Davina. (English) a short
form of Alvina

Vincent 🅱🅶 (Latin) victor,
conqueror.

Vincentia (Latin) a form of
Vincent.

Vinia (Latin) wine.

Viñita (Spanish) a form of
Vina.

Viola (Latin) violet;
stringed instrument in
the violin family.
Literature: the heroine of
Shakespeare's play
Twelfth Night.

Violet ☆ (French) Botany:
a plant with purplish blue
flowers.

Violeta, Violetta (French)
forms of Violet.

Virgilia (Latin) rod bearer,
staff bearer.

Virginia (Latin) pure,
virginal. Literature:
Virginia Woolf was a well-
known British writer.

Virginie (French) a form of
Virginia.

Viridiana (Latin) a form of
Viridis.

Viridis (Latin) green.

Virtudes (Latin) blessed
spirit.

Virtue (Latin) virtuous.

Virxinia (Latin) pure.

Visia (Latin) strength,
vigor.

Visitación (Latin) refers to
the Virgin Mary visiting
Saint Elizabeth.

Vita (Latin) life.

Vitalia (Latin) a form of Vita.

Vitoria, Vittoria (Spanish, Italian) forms of Victoria.

Vitória (Portuguese) a form of Victoria.

Viv (Latin) a short form of Vivian.
Vive, Vyv

Viva (Latin) a short form of Aviva, Vivian.

Vivalda (Latin) alive; brave in battle.

Viveca (Scandinavian) a form of Vivian.

Vivian ✴ (Latin) full of life.

Viviana, Vivianna (Latin) forms of Vivian.

Viviane, Vivianne, Vivien (Latin) forms of Vivian.

Voleta (Greek) veiled.

Volupia (Greek) voluptuous woman.

Vondra (Czech) loving woman.

Voneisha (American) a combination of Yvonne + Aisha.

Vonna (French) a form of Yvonne.

Vonny (French) a familiar form of Yvonne.

Vontricia (American) a combination of Yvonne + Tricia.

Vorsila (Greek) a form of Ursula.

Vulpine (English) like a fox.

Vy (Latin, French) a form of Vi.

Vyoma (Hindi) sky.

W

Wadd (Arabic) beloved.

Wahalla (Scandinavian) immortal.

Waheeda (Arabic) one and only.

Wainani (Hawaiian) beautiful water.

Wakana (Japanese) plant.

Wakanda (Dakota) magical power.

Wakeisha (American) a combination of the prefix Wa + Keisha.

Walad (Arabic) newborn.

Walda (German) powerful; famous.

Waleria (Polish) a form of Valerie.

Walker 🇧🇬 (English) cloth; walker.

Wallis 🇬🇧 (English) from Wales.

Wanda (German) wanderer.

Wandie (German) a familiar form of Wanda.

Waneta (Native American) charger.

Wanetta (English) pale face.

Wanika (Hawaiian) a form of Juanita.

Warda (German) guardian.

Washi (Japanese) eagle.

Wasila (English) healthy.

Wattan (Japanese) homeland.

Wauna (Moquelumnan) snow geese honking.

Wava (Slavic) a form of Barbara.

Waverly 🇬🇧 (English) quaking aspen-tree meadow.

Wayca (Aboriginal) sauce.

Wayna (Quechua) young.

Waynesha (American) a combination of Waynette + Niesha.

Waynette (English) wagon maker.

Wednesday (Latin, English) born on the fourth day of the week.

Weeko (Dakota) pretty girl.

Wehilani (Hawaiian) heavenly adornment.

Wenda (Welsh) a form of Wendy.

Wendelle (English) wanderer.

Wendi (Welsh) a form of Wendy.

Wendy (Welsh) white; light skinned. A familiar form of Gwendolyn, Wanda.

Wera (Polish) a form of Vera.

Wereburga (Germanic) protector of the army.

Weronika (Polish) a form of Veronica.

Wesisa (Musoga) foolish.

Weslee (English) a form of Wesley.

Wesley ⃞BG (English) western meadow.

Whaley (English) whale meadow.

Whisper (English, German) whisper.

Whitley ⃞GB (English) white field.

Whitnee, Whitni, Whitnie, Whittney (English) forms of Whitney.

Whitney ⃞GB (English) white island.

Whoopi (English) happy; excited.

Wicktoria (Polish) a form of Victoria.

Wila (Hawaiian) loyal, faithful.

Wilda (German) untamed. (English) willow.

Wileen (English) a short form of Wilhelmina.

Wilhelmina (German) a form of Wilhelm

Wilikinia (Hawaiian) a form of Virginia.

Willa (German) a short form of Wilhelmina, William.

Willabelle (American) a combination of Willa + Belle.

Willette (English) a familiar form of Wilhelmina, Willa, William.

William ⃞BG (English) determined guardian.

Willie ⃞BG (English) a familiar form of Wilhelmina, William.

Willow (English) willow tree.

Wilma (German) a short form of Wilhelmina.

Wilona (English) desired.

Win ⃞BG (German) a short form of Winifred**Winda** (Swahili) hunter.

Windy (English) windy.

Winefrida, Winifreda (Germanic) forms of Winifred.

Winema (Moquelumnan) woman chief.

Wing ⃞GB (Chinese) glory.

Winifred (German) peaceful friend. (Welsh) a form of Guinevere.

Winna (African) friend.

Winnie (English) a familiar form of Edwina, Gwyneth, Winifred, Winona, Wynne. History: Winnie Mandela kept the anti-aparteid movement alive in South Africa while her then-husband, Nelson Mandela, was imprisoned. Literature: the lovable bear in A. A. Milne's children's story *Winnie-the-Pooh*.

Winola (German) charming friend.

Winona (Lakota) oldest daughter.

Wira (Polish) a form of Elvira.

Wisia (Polish) a form of Victoria.

Wren ⃞BG (English) wren, songbird.

Wulfilde (Germanic) one who fights with the wolves.

Wyanet (Native American) legendary beauty.

Wynne (Welsh) white, light skinned. A short form of Blodwyn, Guinevere, Gwyneth.

Wynonna (Lakota) a form of Winona.

Wynter (English) a form of Winter.

Wyoming (Native American) Geography: a western U.S. state.

X

Xabrina (Latin) a form of Sabrina.

Xalbadora, Xalvadora (Spanish) forms of Salvadora.

Xalina (French) a form of Salina.

Xamantha (Hebrew) a form of Samantha.

Xami (Hebrew) a form of Sami.

Xamuela (Hebrew) a form of Samuela.

Xana (Greek) a form of Xanthe.

Xandi (Greek) a form of Sandi.

Xandra (Greek) a form of Sandra. (Spanish) a short form of Alexandra.

Xandria (Greek, Spanish) a form of Xandra.

Xàndria (Catalan) a form of Alexandria.

Xandrine (Greek) a form of Sandrine.

Xanthe (Greek) yellow, blond.

Xanthippe (Greek) a form of Xanthe. History: Socrates's wife.

Xantina (Spanish) a form of Santina.

Xara (Hebrew) a form of Sarah.

Xarika (Hebrew) a form of Sarika.

Xarina (Hebrew) a form of Sarina.

Xavier 🅱🅶 (Arabic) bright. (Basque) owner of the new house.

Xaviera (Basque, Arabic) a form of Xavier.

Xela (Quiché) my mountain home.

Xema (Latin) precious.

Xena (Greek) a form of Xenia.

Xenia (Greek) hospitable.

Xenobia (Greek) a form of Cenobia.

Xenosa (Greek) stanger.

Xerena (Latin) a form of Serena.

Xesca (Catalan) a form of Francesca.

Xevera, Xeveria (Spanish) forms of Xavier.

Xiang (Chinese) fragrant.

Xihuitl (Nahuatl) year; comet.

Xilda (Celtic) tribute.

Xiloxoch (Nahuatl) calliandra flower.

Xima (Catalan) a form of Joaquina.

Ximena (Spanish) a form of Simone.

Xiomara (Teutonic) glorious forest.

Xipil (Nahuatl) noble of the fire.

Xirena (Greek) a form of Sirena.

Xita (Catalan) a form of Conchita.

Xitlali (Nahuatl) a form of Citlali.

Xiu Mei (Chinese) beautiful plum.

Xiuhcoatl (Nahuatl) fire serpent.

Xiuhtonal (Nahuatl) precious light.

Xoana (Hebrew) God is compassionate and merciful.

Xochicotzin (Nahuatl) little necklace of flowers.

Xochilt (Nahuatl) a form of Xochitl.

Xochiquetzal (Nahuatl) most beautiful flower.

Xochitl (Nahuatl) place of many flowers.

Xochiyotl (Nahuatl) heart of a gentle flower.

Xoco (Nahuatl) youngest sister.

Xocotzin (Nahuatl) youngest daughter.

Xocoyotl (Nahuatl) youngest child.

Xosefa (Hebrew) seated by God.

Xuan (Vietnamese) spring.

Xuxa (Portuguese) a familiar form of Susanna.

Xyleena (Greek) forest dweller

Xylia (Greek) a form of Sylvia.

Xylona (Greek) a form of Xyleena.

Xylophia (Greek) forest lover.

Y

Yachne (Hebrew) hospitable.

Yadira (Hebrew) friend.

Yadra (Spanish) mother.

Yael GB (Hebrew) strength of God. Beautiful.

Yahaira (Hebrew) a form of Yakira.

Yaíza (Guanche) rainbow.

Yajaira (Hebrew) a form of Yakira.

Yakira (Hebrew) precious; dear.

Yalanda (Greek) a form of Yolanda.

Yalena (Greek, Russian) a form of Helen. **Yaletha** (American) a form of Oletha.

Yamary (American) a combination of the prefix Ya + Mary.

Yamelia (American) a form of Amelia.

Yamila (Arabic) a form of Jamila.

Yamilet (Arabic) a form of Jamila.

Yamileta (Germanic) a form of Yamilet.

Yaminah (Arabic) right, proper.

Yaminta (Native American) mint, minty.

Yamka (Hopi) blossom.

Yamuna (Hindi) sacred river.

Yana BG (Slavic) a form of Jana.

Yanaba (Navajo) brave.

Yanamaría (Slavic) bitter grace.

Yaneli, Yanely (American) combinations of the prefix Ya + Nellie.

Yanet (American) a form of Janet.

Yaneta (Russian) a form of Jeannette.

Yaneth (American) a form of Janet.

Yáng (Chinese) sun.

Yani (Australian) peaceful. (Hebrew) a short form of Yannis.

Yannis (Hebrew) gift of God.

Yaotl (Nahuatl) war; warrior.

Yara (Iranian) courage.

Yareli, Yarely (American) forms of Oralee.

Yaretzi (Nahuatl) you will always be loved.

Yarina (Slavic) a form of Irene.

Yaritza (American) a combination of Yana + Ritsa.

Yarkona (Hebrew) green.

Yarmilla (Slavic) market trader.

Yasemin (Persian) a form of Yasmin.

Yashira (Afghan) humble; takes it easy. (Arabic) wealthy.

Yasmeen, Yasmen (Persian) forms of Yasmin.

Yasmin, Yasmine (Persian) jasmine flower.

Yasmín, Yazmín (Persian) forms of Yasmin.

Yasmina (Persian) a form of Yasmin.

Yasu (Japanese) resting, calm.

Yasú (Japanese) calm.

Yayauhqui (Nahuatl) black smoking mirror.

Yayoi (Japanese) spring.

Yazmin, Yazmine (Persian) forms of Yasmin.

Yecenia (Arabic) a form of Yesenia.

Yedida (Hebrew) dear friend.

Yegane (Persian) incomparable beauty.

Yehudit (Hebrew) a form of Judith.

Yei (Japanese) flourishing.

Yeira (Hebrew) light.

Yekaterina (Russian) a form of Katherine.

Yelena (Russian) a form of Helen, Jelena

Yelisabeta (Russian) a form of Elizabeth.

Yemena (Arabic) from Yemen.

Yen (Chinese) yearning; desirous.

Yenay (Chinese) she who loves.

Yenene (Native American) shaman.

Yenifer (Welsh) a form of Jennifer.

Yeo (Korean) mild.

Yepa (Native American) snow girl.

Yeruti (Guarani) turtledove.

Yesenia (Arabic) flower.

Yesica, Yessica (Hebrew) forms of Jessica.

Yésica (Hebrew) a form of Jessica.

Yesim (Turkish) jade.

Yessenia (Arabic) a form of Yesenia.

Yetta (English) a short form of Henrietta.

Yeva (Ukrainian) a form of Eve.

Yevgenia (Russian) a form of Eugenia.

Yexalén (Indigenous) star.

Yiesha (Arabic, Swahili) a form of Aisha.

Yildiz (Turkish) star.

Yín (Chinese) silver.

Ynés, Ynéz (Spanish) forms of Ines, Inez.

Ynez (Spanish) a form of Agnes.

Yoana, Yoanna (Hebrew) forms of Joana.

Yocasta (Greek) a form of Yolanda.

Yocceline (Latin) a form of Jocelyn.

Yocelin, Yocelyn (Latin) forms of Jocelyn.

Yoconda (Italian) happy and jovial.

Yohana (Hebrew) a form of Joana.

Yoi (Japanese) born in the evening.

Yoki (Hopi) bluebird.

Yoko (Japanese) good girl.

Yolanda (Greek) violet flower.

Yole (Greek) a form of Yolanda.

Yolencia (Greek) a form of Yolie.

Yolie (Greek) a familiar form of Yolanda.

Yolihuani (Nahuatl) source of life.

Yolonda (Greek) a form of Yolanda.

Yolotli (Nahuatl) heart.

Yoloxochitl, Yoloxóhitl (Nahuatl) flower of the heart.

Yoltzin (Nahuatl) small heart.

Yoluta (Native American) summer flower.

Yolyamanitzin (Nahuatl) just; tender and considerate person.

Yomara (American) a combination of Yolanda + Tamara.

Yomaris (Spanish) I am the sun.

Yon (Burmese) rabbit. (Korean) lotus blossom.

Yone (Greek) a form of Yolanda.

Yoné (Japanese) wealth; rice.

Yonie (Hebrew) a familiar form of Yonina.

Yonina (Hebrew) a form of Jonina.

Yonita (Hebrew) a form of Jonita.

Yoomee (Coos) star.

Yordana (Basque) descendant.

Yori (Japanese) reliable.

Yoselin, Yoseline, Yoselyn (Latin) forms of Jocelyn.

Yosepha (Hebrew) a form of Josephine.

Yoshi (Japanese) good; respectful.

Yovela (Hebrew) joyful heart; rejoicer.

Yoyotli (Nahuatl) bell of the tree.

Yris (Greek) a form of Iris.

Ysabel (Spanish) a form of Isabel.

Ysann, Ysanne (American) combinations of Ysabel + Ann.

Ysbail (Welsh) to trip.

Ysbaíl (Welsh) spoiled.

Yseult (German) ice rule. (Irish) fair; light skinned. (Welsh) a form of Isolde.

Yu BG (Chinese) universe.
Yue

Yuana (Spanish) a form of Juana.

Yudelle (English) a form of Udele.

Yudita (Russian) a form of Judith.

Yuki BG (Japanese) snow.

Yulene (Basque) a form of Julia.

Yulia (Russian) a form of Julia.

Yuliana (Spanish) a form of Juliana.

Yuliya (Russian) a form of Julia.

Yuri GB (Japanese) lily.

Yvanna (Slavic) a form of Ivana.

Yvette (French) a familiar form of Yvonne.

Yvonne (French) young archer. (Scandinavian) yew wood; bow wood.

Z

Zaba (Hebrew) she who offers a sacrifice to God.

Zabrina (American) a form of Sabrina.

Zacharie BG (Hebrew) God remembered.

Zachary BG (Hebrew) a form of Zacharie.

Zada (Arabic) fortunate, prosperous.

Zafina (Arabic) victorious.

Zafirah (Arabic) successful; victorious.

Zahar (Hebrew) daybreak; dawn.

Zahara (Swahili) a form of Zahra.

Zahavah (Hebrew) golden.

Zahra (Swahili) flower. (Arabic) white.

Zaida (Arabic) a form of Zada.

Zaída (Arabic) a form of Zada.

Zaidee (Arabic) rich.

Zaina (Spanish, English) a form of Zanna.

Zainab (Iranian) child of Ali.

Zainabu (Swahili) beautiful.

Zaira (Hebrew) a form of Zara.

Zaire BG (Hebrew) a short form of Zara.

Zakelina (Russian) a form of Zacharie.

Zakia GB (Swahili) smart. (Arabic) chaste.

Zakira (Hebrew) a form of Zacharie.

Zakiya (Arabic) a form of Zakia.

Zali (Polish) a form of Sara.

Zalika (Swahili) born to royalty.

Zalina (French) a form of Salina.

Zaltana (Native American) high mountain.

Zamantha (Hebrew) a form of Samantha.

Zami (Hebrew) a form of Sami.

Zamuela (Hebrew) a form of Samuela.

Zana (Spanish, English) a form of Zanna.

Zandi (Greek) a form of Sandi.

Zandra (Greek) a form of Sandra.

Zandria (Greek) a form of Zandra.

Zandrine (Greek) a form of Sandrine.

Zaneta (Spanish) a form of Jane.

Zaniyah (Arabic) beautiful.

Zanna (Spanish) a form of Jane. (English) a short form of Susanna.

Zanthe (Greek) a form of Xanthe.

Zantina (Spanish) a form of Santina.

Zara, Zarah (Hebrew) forms of Sarah, Zora.

Zari (Hebrew) a form of Zara.

Zaria (Hebrew) a form of Zara.

Zarifa (Arabic) successful.

Zarika (Hebrew) a form of Sarika.

Zarina (Hebrew) a form of Sarina.

Zarita (Spanish) a form of Sarah.

Zariyah (American) a combination of Mariah + Z.

Zasha (Russian) a form of Sasha.

Zavannah (Spanish) a form of Savannah.

Zaviera (Spanish) a form of Xaviera.

Zavrina (English) a form of Sabrina.

Zawati (Swahili) gift.

Zayit BG (Hebrew) olive.
Zayita

Zayna (Arabic) a form of Zaynah.

Zaynab (Iranian) a form of Zainab.

Zaynah (Arabic) beautiful.

Zayra (Hebrew) a form of Zara.

Zaza (Hebrew) golden.

Zea (Latin) grain. **Zebina** (Greek) hunter's dart.

Zecharia BG (Hebrew) a form of Zachariah
Zedislava (German) glory, honor.

Zefiryn (Polish) a form of Zephyr.

Zeina (Greek, Ethiopian, Persian) a form of Zena.

Zeinab (Somali) good.

Zelda (Yiddish) gray haired. (German) a short form of Griselda.

Zelena (Greek) a form of Selena.

Zelene (English) sunshine.

Zelia (Spanish) sunshine.

Zelizi (Basque) a form of Sheila.

Zelma (German) a form of Selma.

Zelmira (Arabic) brilliant one.

Zeltzin (Nahuatl) delicate.

Zemirah (Hebrew) song of joy.

Zena (Ethiopian) news. (Persian) woman. (Greek) a form of Xenia.

Zenadia (Greek) she who is dedicated to God.

Zenaida (Greek) white-winged dove.

Zenaide (Greek) a form of Zenaida.

Zenda GB (Persian) sacred; feminine.

Zendaya (Shona) to give thanks.

Zenia (Greek, Ethiopian, Persian) a form of Zena.

Zenobia (Greek) sign, symbol. History: a queen who ruled the city of Palmyra in ancient Syria.

Zeonchka (Russian) comes from Zeus.

Zephania (Greek) a form of Stephanie.

Zephanie (Greek) a form of Stephanie.

Zephrine (English) breeze.

Zephyr BG (Greek) west wind.
Zephra, Zephria, Zephyer

Zera (Hebrew) seeds.

Zerdali (Turkish) wild apricot.

Zerena (Latin) a form of Serena.

Zerlina (Latin, Spanish) beautiful dawn. Music: a character in Mozart's opera *Don Giovanni*.

Zerrin (Turkish) golden.

Zeta (English) rose. Linguistics: a letter in the Greek alphabet.

Zetta (Portuguese) rose.

Zhana (Slavic) a form of Jane.

Zhane (Slavic) a form of Jane.

Zhané (Slavic) a form of Jane.

Zhen (Chinese) chaste.
Zen, Zenn, Zhena

Zi (Chinese) beautiful; with grace.

Zia GB (Latin) grain. (Arabic) light.

Ziang (Chinese) a form of Xiang.

Zidanelia (Greek) she who is God's judge.

Zigana (Hungarian) gypsy girl.

Zihna (Hopi) one who spins tops.

Zilia (Greek) a form of Sylvia.

Zilla (Hebrew) shadow.

Zilpah (Hebrew) dignified. Bible: Jacob's wife.

Zilya (Russian) a form of Theresa.

Zimena (Spanish) a form of Simone.

Zimra 🅱🅶 (Hebrew) song of praise.

Zina (African) secret spirit. (English) hospitable. (Greek) a form of Zena.

Zinerva (Italian) fair, light-haired.

Zinnia (Latin) Botany: a plant with beautiful, colorful flowers.

Zion 🅱🅶 (Hebrew) Bible: name of the fort that David conquered, which became synonymous with Jerusalem and the Holy Land.

Zipporah (Hebrew) bird. Bible: Moses' wife.

Zirina (Greek) a form of Sirena.

Zita (Spanish) rose. (Arabic) mistress. A short form of names ending in "sita" or "zita."

Ziva (Hebrew) bright; radiant.

Zizi (Hungarian) a familiar form of Elizabeth.

Zoa (Greek) a form of Zoe.

Zobeida (Arabic) pleasant as cream.

Zocha (Polish) a form of Sophie.
Zochah

Zoe ✨ (Greek) life.

Zoey ✨ (Greek) a form of Zoe.

Zofia (Slavic) a form of Sophia.

Zohar 🅱🅶 (Hebrew) shining, brilliant.

Zohra (Hebrew) blossom.

Zohreh (Persian) happy.

Zoie (Greek) a form of Zoe.

Zoila (Italian) a form of Zola.

Zola 🅶🅱 (Italian) piece of earth.

Zona (Latin) belt, sash.

Zondra (Greek) a form of Zandra.

Zora (Slavic) aurora; dawn. Zoraida (Arabic) she who is eloquent.

Zorina (Slavic) golden.

Zósima (Greek) vital, vigorous.

Zoya (Slavic) a form of Zoe.

Zsa Zsa (Hungarian) a familiar form of Susan.

Zsofia (Hungarian) a form of Sofia.

Zsuzsanna (Hungarian) a form of Susanna.

Zubaida (Arabic) excellent.

Zubaidah (Arabic) excellent.

Zudora (Sanskrit) laborer.

Zulecia, Zuleica, Zuleyca (Arabic) plump, chubby.

Zuleika (Arabic) brilliant.

Zuleima (Arabic) a form of Zulima.

Zulema (Arabic) a form of Zulima.

Zuleyma (Arabic) a form of Zulima.

Zulima (Arabic) a form of Salama.

Zulma (Arabic) healthy and vigorous woman.

Zulmara (Spanish) a form of Zulma.

Zuly (Arabic) a short form of Zulma.

Zurafa (Arabic) lovely.

Zuri (Basque) white; light skinned. (Swahili) beautiful.

Zurina, Zurine (Basque) white.

Zurisaday (Arabic) over the earth.

Zusa (Czech, Polish) a form of Susan.

Zuwena (Swahili) good.

Zyanya (Zapotec) always.

196

Zylina (Greek) a form of Xyleena.

.

Zytka (Polish) rose

Boys

A

'**Aziz** (Arabic) strong.
Azizz

Aabha (Indian) light.

Aabharan (Indian) jewel.

Aabheer, Aabher, Abheer (Indian) cowherd.

Aacharya, Acharya (Indian) teacher.

Aadarsh (Indian) one who has principles.

Aadesh (Indian) command; message.

Aadhishankar (Indian) another name for Sri Shankaracharya, founder of Adwaitha philosophy.

Aadhunik (Indian) modern; new.

Aadi (Indian) first; most important.

Aadinath (Indian) God, supreme ruler of the universe, the first god.

Aaditey (Indian) son of Aditi.

Aafreen (Indian) encouragement.

Aagney (Indian) son of the fire god.

Aahlaad (Indian) delight.

Aahlaadith (Indian) joyous person.

Aahwaanith (Indian) one who has been invited; wanted.

Aakaash, Aakash, Akaash, Akash (Indian) the sky; vast like the sky.

Aakanksh (Indian) desire.

Aakar (Indian) form, shape.

Aakash (Hindi) a form of Akash.

Aalam (Indian) ruler, king.

Aalap (Indian) musical prelude.

Aalok (Indian) cry of victory.

Aamir (Hebrew, Punjabi, Arabic) a form of Amir.

Aamod (Indian) pleasant.

Aandaleeb (Indian) bulbul bird.

Aaran (Hebrew) a form of Aaron. (Scottish) a form of Arran.

Aarav (Sanskrit) peaceful.

Aaron ✬
BG (Hebrew) enlightened. (Arabic) messenger. Bible: the brother of Moses and the first high priest.

Aarón (Hebrew) a form of Aaron.

Aaronjames (American) a combination of Aaron + James.
Aaron James, Aaron-James

Aarron, Aaryn (Hebrew, Arabic) forms of Aaron.

Aashish (Indian) blessings.

Abaco (Hebrew) abacus.

Aban (Persian) Mythology: a figure associated with water and the arts.

Abasi (Swahili) stern.

Abban (Latin) white.

Abbas (Arabic) lion.

Abbey GB (Hebrew) a familiar form of Abe.

Abbón (Hebrew) a form of Abbott.

Abbott (Hebrew) father; abbot.

Abbud (Arabic) devoted.

Abd-El-Kader (Arabic) servant of the powerful.

Abda (Hebrew) servant of God.

Abdalongo (Hebrew) servant of Elon.

Abdecalas (Hebrew) server of a dog.

Abdénago (Hebrew) Abdenago is the Babylonian name for Azarilts, one of the three companions of the prophet Daniel.

Abderico (Hebrew) rich and powerful servant.

Abdi (African) my servant.

Abdías (Hebrew) God's servant.

Abdiel (Hebrew) I serve God.

Abdikarim (Somali) slave of God.

Abdirahman (Arabic) a form of Abdulrahman.

Abdiraxman (Somali) servant of divine grace.

Abdón (Hebrew) servant of God; the very helpful man.

Abdul (Arabic) servant.

Abdulaziz (Arabic) servant of the Mighty**.**

Abdullah (Arabic) servant of Allah.

Abdullahi (Arabic) a form of Adullah.

Abdulmalik (Arabic) servant of the Master.

Abdulrahman (Arabic) servant of the Merciful.

Abe (Hebrew) a short form of Abel, Abraham. (German) a short form of Abelard.
Ab, Abb, Abbe

Abebe (Amharic) one who has flourished, thrived.

Abel (Hebrew) breath. (Assyrian) meadow. (German) a short form of Abelard. Bible: Adam and Eve's second son.

Abelard (German) noble; resolute.

Abelardo (Spanish) a form of Abelard.

Abercio (Greek) first son.

Abernethy (Scottish) river's beginning.

Abi (Turkish) older brother.

Abiah (Hebrew) God is my father.

Abibo (Hebrew) beloved.

Abibón (Hebrew) a form of Abibo.

Abidan (Hebrew) father of judgment.

Abie (Hebrew) a familiar form of Abraham.

Abiel (Hebrew) a form of Abiah.

Abihú (Hebrew) he is my father.

Abilio (Latin) expert; able.

Abimael (Hebrew) my father is God.

Abir (Hebrew) strong.

Abiram (Hebrew) my father is great.

Abisha (Hebrew) gift of God.

Ableberto (Germanic) brilliant strength.

Abner (Hebrew) father of light. Bible: the commander of Saul's army.

Abo (Hebrew) father.

Abraam (Hebrew) a form of Abraham.

Abrafo (Ghanaian) warrior.

Abraham (Hebrew) father of many nations. Bible: the first Hebrew patriarch.

Abrahan (Spanish) a form of Abraham.

Abram (Hebrew) a short form of Abraham.

Abrúnculo (Latin) shattered; devastated.

Absalom (Hebrew) father of peace. Bible: the rebellious third son of King David. **Absalón** (Hebrew) a form of Absalom.

Abubakar (Egyptian) noble.

Abudemio (Latin) one who speaks in a sweet, refined way.

Abundancio (Latin) rich, affluent.

Abundio (Latin) he who has a lot of property.

Acab (Hebrew) uncle.

Acacio (Greek) honorable.

Acañir (Mapuche) freed fox.

Acapana (Quechua) lightning; swirl of wind, small hurricane.

Acar (Turkish) bright.

Acario (Greek) without grace.

Ácatl (Nahuatl) giant reed.

Acayo (Greek) out of step; ill-timed.

Accas (Hebrew) winding.

Ace (Latin) unity.

Acel (French) nobility.

Acesto (Greek) one who can fix; useful.

Achachic (Aymara) ancestor; grandfather.

Achcauhtli (Nahuatl) leader.

Achic (Quechua) luminous, resplendent.

Achilles (Greek) Mythology: a hero of the Trojan War. Literature: the hero of Homer's epic poem *Iliad*.

Acilino (Spanish) sharp.

Acindino (Greek) out of danger, safe.

Acisclo (Latin) a pick used to work on rocks.

Ackerley (English) meadow of oak trees.

Ackley (English) a form of Ackerley.

Aconcauac (Quechua) stone sentinel.

Acton (English) oak-tree settlement.

Acucio (Latin) sharp; shrewd.

Acursio (Latin) he who heads toward God.

Adabaldo (German) noble and bold.

Adacio (Latin) determined; active.

Adael (Hebrew) eternity of God.

Adahy (Cherokee) in the woods.
Adahi

Adair GB (Scottish) oak-tree ford.

Adalbaro (Greek) the combatant of nobility.

Adalbergo (German) village.

Adalberón (Spanish) a form of Adalbergo.

Adalberto (Italian, Spanish, Portuguese) a form of Alberto.

Adalgiso, Adalvino (Greek) the lance of nobility.

Adalhardo (Scandinavian) noble and strong.

Adalrico (Greek) noble chief of his lineage.

Adam ✦ (Phoenician) man; mankind. (Hebrew) earth; man of the red earth. Bible: the first man created by God.

Adám (Hebrew) a form of Adam.

Adamec (Czech) a form of Adam.

Adamnán (Hebrew) a form of Adan.

Adamson (Hebrew) son of Adam.

Adan (Irish) a form of Aidan.
Adian, Adun

Adar GB **(Syrian) ruler; prince. (Hebrew) noble; exalted.**

Adarius (American) a combination of Adam + Darius.

Adaucto (Latin) increase.

Adauto (Roman) increased.

Addam (Phoenician, Hebrew) a form of Adam.

Addison BG (English) son of Adam.

Addo (Ghanaian) king of the path.

Addy GB (Hebrew) a familiar form of Adam,

Adlai. (German) a familiar form of Adelard.

Ade (Yoruba) royal.

Adeel (Arabic) a form of Adil.

Adel (German) a short form of Adelard.

Adelard (German) noble; courageous.

Adelardo (Greek) the daring prince.

Adelelmo, Adelmo (German) noble protector.

Adelfo (Greek) male friend.

Adelgario (German) noble lance.

Adelino (Greek) the daring prince.

Adelio (Spanish) father of the noble prince.

Adelmaro (Greek) distinguished because of his lineage.

Adelric (German) noble ruler.

Ademar, Ademaro, Adhemar, Adimar (German) he whose battles have made him distinguished; celebrated and famous combatant.

Aden (Arabic) Geography: a region in southern Yemen. (Irish) a form of Aidan.

Aderito (German) strong and powerful.

Adham (Arabic) black.

Adhelmar (Greek) ennobled by his battles.

Adiel (Hebrew) he was adorned by God.

Adif (Hebrew) the preferred one.

Adil **(Arabic) just; wise.**

Adilón (Spanish) noble.

Adin (Hebrew) pleasant.
Addin, Addyn, Adyn

Adín (Hebrew) a form of Adin.

Adino (Hebrew) adorned.

Adiosdado (Latin) given by God.

Adir (Hebrew) majestic; noble.
Adeer

Adirán (Latin) from the Adriatic Sea.

Adisa (Ghanaian) one who teaches us.

Adison 🆋 (English) a form of Addison.

Aditya (Hindi) sun.

Adiv (Hebrew) pleasant; gentle.

Adjatay (Cameroon) prince.

Adjutor (Latin) one who helps.

Adlai (Hebrew) my ornament.

Adler (German) eagle.

Adli (Turkish) just; wise.

Admiel (Hebrew) land of God.

Admon (Hebrew) peony.

Adnan (Arabic) pleasant.

Adney (English) noble's island.

Ado (Hebrew) beauty.

Adofo (Ghanaian) one who loves us.

Adolf (German) noble wolf. History: Adolf Hitler's German army was defeated in World War II.

Adolfo (Spanish) a form of Adolf.

Adolph (German) a form of Adolf.

Adolphus (French) a form of Adolf.

Adom (Akan) help from God.

Adon (Hebrew) Lord. (Greek) a short form of Adonis.

Adón (Hebrew) a form of Adon.

Adonai (Hebrew) my Lord.

Adonías (Hebrew) God is my Lord.

Adonis (Greek) highly attractive. Mythology: the attractive youth loved by Aphrodite.

Adrian ✨

🆋 (Greek) rich. (Latin) dark. (Swedish) a short form of Hadrian.

Adrián (Latin) a form of Adrian.

Adriano (Italian) a form of Adrian.

Adriel (Hebrew) member of God's flock.

Adrien 🆋 (French) a form of Adrian.

Adrik (Russian) a form of Adrian.

Adrodato (Germanic) daring father.

Adulfo (Germanic) of noble heritage.

Adwin (Ghanaian) creative.

Adyuto, Adyutor (Latin) one who helps.

Aeneas (Greek) praised. (Scottish) a form of Angus. Literature: the Trojan hero of Vergil's epic poem *Aeneid*.

Afework (Ethiopian) one who speaks of pleasing things.

Afonso (German) prepared for combat.

Afram (African) Geography: a river in Ghana, Africa.

Áfrico (Greek) left to the sun.

Afrodisio (Greek) amorous.

Afton 🆬 (English) from Afton, England.
Affton, Aftan, Aften, Aftin, Aftyn

Aftonio (Greek) one who does not have jealousy.

Agabio (Greek) of much life, vigor.

Ágabos (Greek) magnificent.

Agacio (Greek) good.

Agamemnon (Greek) resolute. Mythology: the king of Mycenae who led the Greeks in the Trojan War.

Agamenón (Greek) a form of Agamemnon.

Ágape (Latin) love.

Agapito (Hebrew) the beloved one.

Agar (Hebrew) he who escaped.

Agatángel (Greek) good angel.

Agatodoro (Greek) worthy of admiration.

Agatón (Greek) the victor.

Agatónico (Greek) good victory.

Agatopo (Greek) nice scenery.

Agatópode, Agatópodis (Greek) good feet.

Agberto (German) famous for the sword.

Agenor (Greek) the strong man.

Agento (Latin) efficient; active.

Ageo (Hebrew) having a festive character, makes people happy.

Agerico (Latin) powerful sword.

Agesislao (Greek) leader of villages.

Agila (Teutonic) he who possesses combat support.

Agilberto (German) famous sword from combat.

Agileo (German) spade of a fighter.

Agilulfo (German) spear of the warrior.

Agliberto (German) a form of Agilberto.

Agnelo (Latin) reference to the lamb of God.

Agni (Hindi) Religion: the Hindu fire god.

Agoardo (German) strong sword.

Agobardo (German) strong spear.

Agofredo (German) spear that brings peace.

Agomar (German) distinguished sword.

Agostino (Italian) a form of Augustine.

Agresto (Latin) rugged, rustic.

Agrícola (Latin) farmer.

Agrippa (Latin) born feet first. History: the commander of the Roman fleet that defeated Mark Antony and Cleopatra at Actium.

Agu (Ibo) leopard.

Aguinaldo (Germanic) one who rules by the sword.

Agur (Hebrew) accumulation.

Agús (Spanish) a form of Agustín.

Agustin (Latin) a form of Augustine.

Agustín (Latin) a form of Agustin.

Agustine (Latin) a form of Augustine.

Ahab (Hebrew) father's brother. Literature: the captain of the *Pequod* in Herman Melville's novel *Moby-Dick*.

Ahanu (Native American) laughter.

Aharon (Hebrew, Arabic) a form of Aaron.

Ahdik (Native American) caribou; reindeer.

Ahearn (Scottish) lord of the horses. (English) heron.

Ahir (Turkish) last.

Ahkeem (Hebrew) a form of Akeem.

Ahmad (Arabic) most highly praised.

Ahmed (Swahili) praiseworthy.

Ahsan (Arabic) charitable.

Ahuatzi (Nahuatl) small oak.

Ahuiliztli (Nahuatl) joy.

Ahuv (Hebrew) loved.

Ahuviá (Hebrew) loved by God.

Aicardo (German) strong sword.

Aidan BG (Irish) fiery.

Aidano (Teutonic) he who distinguishes himself.

Aiden ☀

🅱🅶 (Irish) a form of Aidan.

Aiken (English) made of oak.

Aimario (German) strong lineage.

Aimery (French) a form of Emery.

Aimon (French) house. (Irish) a form of Eamon.

Aindrea (Irish) a form of Andrew.

Aingeru (Basque) angel.

Ainsley 🅶🅱 (Scottish) my own meadow.

Aitalas (Greek) eternally young.

Aitor (Basque) father.

Aizik (Russian) a form of Isaac.

Aj (Punjabi, American) a form of Ajay.

Ajab (Hebrew) uncle.

Ajala (Yoruba) potter.

Aján (Hebrew) problem.

Ajay (Punjabi) victorious; undefeatable. (American) a combination of the initials A. + J.

Ajidan (Hebrew) my brother judges.

Ajiel (Hebrew) my brother is God.

Ajiezer (Hebrew) my brother is help.

Ajimán (Hebrew) my brother is manna.

Ajiram (Hebrew) my brother exalted.

Ajishar (Hebrew) my brother sings.

Ajit (Sanskrit) unconquerable.

Ajitov (Hebrew) my brother is good.

Ajshalom (Hebrew) brother of peace.

Akar (Turkish) flowing stream.

Akash (Hindi) sky.

Akbar (Arabic) great.

Akecheta (Sioux) warrior.

Akeem (Hebrew) a short form of Joachim.

Akemi (Japanese) dawn.
Akemee, Akemie, Akemy

Akhil **(Arabic) a form of Akil.**

Akia (African) first born.

Akiiki (Egyptian) friendly.

Akil (Arabic) intelligent. (Greek) a form of Achilles.

Akili 🅱🅶 (Greek) a form of Achilles. (Arabic) a form of Akil.

Akim (Hebrew) a short form of Joachim.

Akins (Yoruba) brave.

Akinsanya (Nigerian) courage for the rematch.

Akintunde (Nigerian) courageous return.

Akinyemi (Nigerian) destined to be a warrior.

Akio (Japanese) bright.

Akira 🅶🅱 (Japanese) intelligent.

Akiva (Hebrew) a form of Jacob.

Akmal (Arabic) perfect.

Akram (Arabic) most generous.

Aksel (Norwegian) father of peace.
Aksell

Akshat (Sanskrit) unable to be injured.

Akshay **(American) a form of Akash.**

Akule **(Native American) he looks up.**
Akul

Al (Irish) a short form of Alan, Albert, Alexander.

Alaa 🅶🅱 (Arabic) a short form of Aladdin.

Alacrino (Latin) alive; outgoing.

Aladdin (Arabic) height of faith. Literature: the hero of a story in the *Arabian Nights*.

Alain (French) a form of Alan.

Alaire (French) joyful.

Alam (Arabic) universe.

Alan (Irish) handsome; peaceful.

Alán (Celtic) a form of Alan.

Alante, Allante, Allanté (Spanish) forms of Alan.

Alardo (Greek) the courageous prince.

Alaric (German) ruler of all.

Alastair (Scottish) a form of Alexander.

Alba (Latin) town on the white hill.

Alban (Latin) from Alba, Italy.

Albano (Germanic) a form of Alban.

Alberic (German) smart; wise ruler.

Alberico (German) a form of Alberic.

Albern (German) noble; courageous.

Alberón (German) noble bear.

Albert (German, French) noble and bright.

Alberte (German) a form of Albert.

Alberto (Italian) a form of Albert.

Albie, Alby (German, French) familiar forms of Albert.

Albin (Latin) a form of Alvin.

Albion (Latin) white cliffs. Geography: a reference to the white cliffs in Dover, England.

Albón (German, Spanish) brave ruler.

Albuino (German) powerful; noble home.

Alcandor (Greek) manly; strong.

Alceo (Greek) man of great strength and vigor.

Alcibiades (Greek) generous and violent.

Alcibíades (Greek) strong and valiant man.

Alcides (Greek) strong and vigorous.

Alcott (English) old cottage.

Alcuino (Teutonic) friend of sacred places, friend of the temple.

Aldair (German, English) a form of Alder.

Aldano (Celtic) noble; full of experience, experienced man.

Aldeberto (German) famous leader.

Aldebrando (German) governs with the sword.

Aldelmo (German) old helmet.

Aldemar (German) famous for nobility.

Alden 🅱🅶 (English) old; wise protector.

Alder (German, English) alder tree.

Alderidge (English) alder ridge.

Aldetrudis (Germanic) strong leader.

Aldino (Celtic) noble, full of experience.

Aldis (English) old house. (German) a form of Aldous.

Aldo (Italian) old; elder. (German) a short form of Aldous.

Aldobrando (Germanic) ancient sword.

Aldous (German) a form of Alden.

Aldred (English) old; wise counselor.

Aldrich (English) wise counselor.

Aldwin (English) old friend.

Alec, Aleck, Alek (Greek) short forms of Alexander.

Aleczander (Greek) a form of Alexander.

Alefrido (Germanic) total peace.

Aleixo (Greek) defender.

Alejandrino (Spanish) a form of Alexander.

Alejandro (Spanish) a form of Alexander.

Alejándro (Spanish) a form of Alejandro.

Alejo (Greek) he who protects and defends.

Aleksandar, Aleksander, Aleksandr (Greek) forms of Alexander.

Aleksei (Russian) a short form of Alexander.

Alekzander (Greek) a form of Alexander.

Alem (Arabic) wise.

Alen, Allan, Allen (Irish) forms of Alan.

Aleo (German) governor.

Aleric (German) a form of Alaric.

Aleron (Latin) winged.

Alerón (French) a form of Aleron.

Alesio (Italian) a form of Alejo.

Alessandro (Italian) a form of Alexander.

Alex 🇧🇬 (Greek) a short form of Alexander.

Alexandar, Alexandr (Greek) forms of Alexander.

Alexander ⭐

🇧🇬 (Greek) defender of mankind. History: Alexander the Great was the conqueror of the civilized world.

Alexandre 🇧🇬 (French) a form of Alexander.

Alexandro (Greek) a form of Alexander.

Alexandros (Greek) a form of Alexander.

Alexei (Russian) a form of Aleksei. (Greek) a short form of Alexander.

Alexi 🇬🇧 (Greek) a short form of Alexander.

Alexis 🇬🇧 (Greek) a short form of Alexander.

Alexsander (Greek) a form of Alexander.

Alexy (Greek) a short form of Alexander.

Alexzander (Greek) a form of Alexander.

Aleydis (Teutonic) born into a noble family.

Alfa (African) leader.

Alferio (Greek) saint who suffered a great disease and promised to become a monk if cured.

Alfie 🇧🇬 (English) a familiar form of Alfred.

Alfio (Greek) he who has a white complexion.

Al**fonso, Alfonzo** (Italian, Spanish) forms of Alphonse.

Alford (English) old river ford.

Alfred (English) elf counselor; wise counselor. **Alfredo** (Italian, Spanish) a form of Alfred.

Alger (German) noble spearman. (English) a short form of Algernon. **Algerico** (German) a form of Algerio.

Algerio (German) noble governor prepared for combat.

Algernon (English) bearded, wearing a moustache.

Algie (English) a familiar form of Algernon.

Algis (German) spear.

Algiso (Greek) the lance of nobility.

Algrenon (French) beard.

Ali 🇧🇬 (Arabic) greatest. (Swahili) exalted.

Alí (Arabic) a form of Ali.

Alic (Greek) a short form of Alexander.

Alicio (Greek) truth.

Alijah (Hebrew) a form of Elijah.

Alim (Arabic) scholar. A form of Alem.

Alîm (Arabic) wise.

Alinando (German) daring ruler.

Alipio (Greek) he who suffering does not affect.

Alisander (Greek) a form of Alexander.

Alistair (English) a **form of Alexander.**

Alix 🇬🇧 (Greek) a short form of Alixander.

Alixander (Greek) a form of Alexander.

Aliz (Hebrew) happy.

Alladin (Arabic) nobility of faith.

Allambee (Australian) quiet place.

Allard (English) noble, brave.

Allison 🇬🇧 (English) Alice's son.

Allister (English) a form of Alistair.

Almagor (Hebrew) indestructible.

Almano (German) famous for nobility.

Almanzor (Arabic) triumphant.

Almaquio (Greek) foreign combatant.

Almárico (German) rich family; powerful.

Almeric (German) powerful ruler.

Almodis (Germanic) totally spirited.

Almon (Hebrew) widower.

Aloín (French) noble friend.

Alois (German) a short form of Aloysius.

Aloisio (Spanish) a form of Louis.

Alok (Sanskrit) victorious cry.

Alon **(Hebrew) oak.**
Allon, Alonn

Alón (Hebrew) a form of Alon.

Alonso, Alonzo (Spanish) forms of Alphonse.

Alonza BG (Spanish) a form of Alphonse.

Aloyoshenka, Aloysha (Russian) defender of humanity.

Aloysius (German) a form of Louis.

Alpha (African) leader.

Alphonse (German) noble and eager.

Alphonso (Italian) a form of Alphonse.

Alpin (Irish) attractive.

Alpiniano (Swiss) belongs to the Alps mountains.

Alquimio (Greek) strong.

Alredo (German) advice from the governor.

Alroy (Spanish) king.

Alston (English) noble's settlement.

Altair BG (Greek) star. (Arabic) flying eagle.

Alterio (Greek) like a starry night.

Altman (German) old man.

Alton (English) old town.
Alten

Alucio (Latin) he is lucid and illustrious.

Aluín (French) noble friend.

Alula (Latin) winged, swift.

Alva BG (Hebrew) sublime.

Alvan (German) a form of Alvin.

Alvar (English) army of elves.

Àlvar, Álvaro (Spanish) forms of Alvaro.

Alvaro (Spanish) just; wise.

Alvern (Latin) spring.

Alvero (Germanic) completely prudent.

Alví (German) friend.

Alvin (Latin) white; light skinned. (German) friend to all; noble friend; friend of elves.

Alvino (Spanish) a form of Alvin.

Alvis (Scandinavian) all-knowing.

Alwin **(German) a form of Alvin.**

Amable (Latin) one who loves; nice.

Amadeo (Italian) a form of Amadeus.

Amadeus (Latin) loves God. Music: Wolfgang Amadeus Mozart was a famous eighteenth-century Austrian composer.

Amado (Spanish) a form of Amadeus.

Amador (Spanish) a form of Amadeus.

Amal GB (Hebrew) worker. (Arabic) hopeful.

Amalio (Greek) a man who is carefree.

Aman BG (Arabic) a short form of Amani.

Amancio (Latin) he who loves God.

Amanda GB (Latin) lovable.

Amandeep BG (Punjabi) light of peace.

Amando (French) a form of Amadeus.

Amani GB (Arabic) believer. (Yoruba) strength; builder.

Amanpreet BG (Punjabi) a form of Amandeep.

Amar (Punjabi) immortal. (Arabic) builder.

Amaranto (Greek) he who does not slow down.

Amari 🅱🅶 (Punjabi, Arabic) a form of Amar.

Amaru (Quechua) sacred serpent.

Amaruquispe (Quechua) free, like the Amaru.

Amarutopac (Quechua) glorious, majestic Amaru.

Amaruyupanqui (Quechua) he who honors Amaru.

Amato (French) loved.

Amauri, Amaury (French) name of a count.

Amazu (Nigerian) no one knows everything.

Ambar 🅶🅱 (Sanskrit) sky.

Amber 🅶🅱 (French) amber. (Sanskrit) a form of Ambar.

Amberto (German) brilliant work.

Ambico (Latin) one who is ambitious.

Ambroise (French) a form of Ambrose.

Ambrose (Greek) immortal.

Ameen (Hebrew, Arabic, Hindi) a form of Amin.

Ameer (Hebrew) a form of Amir.

Amelio (Teutonic) very hard worker, energetic.

Amenhotep (Egyptian) name of a count.

Amenophis (Egyptian) name of the pharaoh.

Amenra (Egyptian) personification of the universe's power.

Amer (Hebrew) a form of Amir.

Américo (Germanic) the prince in action.

Amerigo (Teutonic) industrious. History: Amerigo Vespucci was the Italian explorer for whom America is named.

Ames (French) friend.

Amfiloquio (Greek) distinguished sword.

Amfión (Greek) argumentative.

Ami (Hebrew) the builder.

Amiano (Hebrew) a form of Amon.

Amicus (English, Latin) beloved friend.

Amiel (Hebrew) God of my people.

Amiezer (Hebrew) my community is helped.

Amijai (Hebrew) my community is alive.

Amílcar (Punic) he who governs the city.

Amin (Hebrew, Arabic) trustworthy; honest. (Hindi) faithful.

Amín (Arabic) a form of Amin.

Amine (Hebrew, Arabic, Hindi) a form of Amin.

Amintor (Greek) the protector.

Amior (Hebrew) my community is light.

Amir (Hebrew) proclaimed. (Punjabi) wealthy; king's minister. (Arabic) prince.

Amiram (Hebrew) my community is lifted high.

Amish (Sanskrit) honest.

Amishalom (Hebrew) my community is peace.

Amishar (Hebrew) my community sings.

Amistad (Spanish) friendship.

Amit (Punjabi) unfriendly. (Arabic) highly praised.

Amitai (Hebrew) my truth.

Ammar (Punjabi, Arabic) a form of Amar.

Ammâr (Arabic) builder.

Ammon (Egyptian) hidden. Mythology: the ancient god associated with reproduction.

Amnas (Greek, Latin) young lamb.

Amnicado (Latin) one who lives close to the river.

Amol **(Hindi) priceless, valuable.**

Amoldo (Spanish) power of an eagle.

Amon (Hebrew) trustworthy; faithful.

Amón (Hebrew) a form of Amon.

Amory (German) a form of Emory.

Amos (Hebrew) burdened, troubled. Bible: an Old Testament prophet.
Amose, Amous

Amós (Hebrew) a form of Amos.

Amoxtli (Nahuatl) book.

Amparo (Latin) to prepare oneself.

Ampelio (Greek) he who makes wine from his own grapes.

Ampelos (Greek) a satyr and good friend of Dionysus.

Ampliato (Latin) illustrious.

Ampodio (Greek) well-behaved.

Amram (Hebrew) mighty nation.

Amrit BG (Sanskrit) nectar. (Punjabi, Arabic) a form of Amit.

Amritpal (Sikh) protector of the Lord's nectar.

Amsi (Egyptian) embodiment of the power of the universe.

Amsu (Egyptian) embodiment of reproduction.

Amuillan (Mapuche) he who warmly serves others.

An BG (Chinese, Vietnamese) peaceful.

Anacario (Greek) not without grace.

Anacleto (Greek) he who was called upon.

Anaías (Hebrew) the Lord answers.

Anakin (American) Movies: Anakin Skywalker became Darth Vader in Star Wars.

Anan, Anán (Hebrew) cloudy.

Anand (Hindi) blissful.

Ananías (Hebrew) he who has the grace of God.

Anantas (Hindi) infinite.

Anas (Greek) a short form of Anastasius.

Anastario, Anastasón (Greek) forms of Anastasios.

Anastasios (Greek) a form of Anastasius.

Anastasius (Greek) resurrection.

Anasvindo (German) strength of God.

Anatalón (Greek) one who grows and flourishes.

Anatole (Greek) east.

Anatolii (Russian) what comes from the east.

Anayantzin (Basque) small.

Anbesa, Anbessa (Spanish) governor of Spain.

Anca (Quechua) black eagle.

Ancasmayu (Quechua) blue like the river.

Ancaspoma, Ancaspuma (Quechua) bluish puma.

Ancavil (Mapuche) identical mythological being.

Ancavilo (Mapuche) snake's body.

Anchali (Taos) painter.

Ancil (French) of nobility.

Ancuguiyca (Quechua) having sacred resistance.

Anders (Swedish) a form of Andrew.

Anderson (Swedish) son of Andrew.

Andomarro (German) notable God.

Andoni (Greek) a form of Anthony.

Andonios (Greek) a form of Anthony.

Andoquino (Greek) without comparison.

Andor (Hungarian) a form of Andrew, Anthony.

Andra GB (French) a form of Andrew.

Andrae (French) a form of Andrew.

András (Hungarian) a form of Andrew.

Andre, André (French) forms of Andrew.

Andrea GB (Greek) a form of Andrew.

Andreas (Greek) a form of Andrew.

Andrei, Andrey (Bulgarian, Romanian,

Russian) forms of Andrew.

Andreo (Greek) manly.

Andres, Andrez (Spanish) forms of Andrew.

Andrew ☆ (Greek) strong; manly; courageous. Bible: one of the Twelve Apostles.

Andrian (Greek) a form of Andrew.

Androcles (Greek) man covered with glory.

Andrónico (German) victorious man.

Andros (Polish) sea. Mythology: the god of the sea.

Andru, Andrue (Greek) forms of Andrew.

Andrzej (Polish) a form of Andrew.

Andy (Greek) a short form of Andrew.

Anecto (Greek) tolerable.

Anesio (Greek) a form of Anisio.

Aneurin (Welsh) honorable; gold.

Anfernee (Greek) a form of Anthony.

Anfión (Greek) Mythology: Amphion is the son of Antiope and Jupiter.

Anfos (Catalan) a form of Alfonso.

Angel ☆

Bɢ (Greek) angel. (Latin) messenger.

Ángel (Greek) a form of Angel.

Angelino (Latin) messenger.

Angelo (Italian) a form of Angel.

Ángelo (Spanish) a form of Angelo.

Angilberto (Teutonic) a combination of Ángel and Alberto.

Angulo (German) lance.

Angus (Scottish) exceptional; outstanding. Mythology: Angus Og was the Celtic god of youth, love, and beauty.

Anh ɢʙ (Vietnamese) peace; safety.

Aniano (Greek) he who is sad and upset.

Anías (Hebrew) God answers.

Anibal (Phoenician) a form of Hannibal.

Aníbal (Punic) a form of Anibal.

Anicet, Aniceto (Greek) invincible man of great strength.

Anil (Hindi) wind god.

Aniol (Catalan) a form of Aniano.

Anîs (Arabic) intimate friend.

Anish (Greek) a form of Annas.

Anisio (Greek) reliable.

Anka ɢʙ (Turkish) phoenix.

Anker (Danish) a form of Andrew.
Ankor, Ankur

Annan (Scottish) brook. (Swahili) fourth-born son.

Annas (Greek) gift from God.

Anno (German) a familiar form of Johann.

Anoki (Native **American) actor.**

Anón (Latin) yearly.

Anoop (Sikh) beauty.

Anpu (Egyptian) God of death.

Ansaldo (German) he who represents God.

Ansano (Latin) ear.

Ansbaldo (Germanic) peaceful God.

Ansberto (German) brilliant God.

Ansejiso (German) lance.

Ansel (French) follower of a nobleman.

Anselm (German) divine protector.

Anselmo (Italian) a form of Anselm.

Anserico (German) rich in God.

Ansfrido (German) peaceful God.

Ansis (Latvian) a form of Janis.

Ansley GB (Scottish) a form of Ainsley.

Anson (German) divine. (English) Anne's son.

Ansovino (German) friend of God.

Anta (Quechua) copper-like

Antal **(Hungarian) a form of Anthony.**

Antares (Greek) giant, red star. Astronomy: the brightest star in the constellation Scorpio.

Antauaya (Quechua) copper-colored meadow.

Antavas (Lithuanian) a form of Anthony.

Antavious **(Lithuanian) a form of Antavas.**
Antavius

Antay (Quechua) copper-colored.

Ante (Lithuanian) a short form of Antavas.
Antae, Anteo

Antelmo (Germanic) protector of the homeland.

Antem (Germanic) giant who wears a helmet.

Antenor (Greek) he who is a fighter.

Anteros (Greek) god of mutual love.

Anthany (Latin, Greek) a form of Anthony.

Anthoney, Anthonie (Latin, Greek) forms of Anthony.

Anthony ⭐

BG (Latin) praiseworthy. (Greek) flourishing.
  Antico (Latin) old; venerable.

Antidio (Greek) one who radiates God in his actions.

Antígono (Greek) he who stands out amongst all of his fellow men.

Antilaf (Mapuche) happy day.

Antimo (Greek) flourishing.

Antininan (Quechua) copper-colored, like fire.

Antinko (Russian) invaluable.

Antinógenes (Greek) a saint.

Antioco (Greek) he who commands the chariot in the fight against the enemy.

Antíoco (Greek) firm; liberator.

Antione (French) a form of Anthony.

Antipan (Mapuche) sunny branch of a clear brown color.

Antipas (Greek) he is the enemy of all, in opposition to everyone.

Antivil (Mapuche) sunny snake.

Antjuan (Spanish) a form of Anthony.

Antoan (Vietnamese) safe, secure.

Antoine (French) a form of Anthony.

Antolín (Greek) flourishing, beautiful like a flower.

Anton (Slavic) a form of Anthony.

Antón (Spanish) a form of Antonio.

Antone (Slavic) a form of Anthony.

Antoni (Latin) a form of Anthony.

Antonino (Italian) a form of Anthony.

Antonio (Italian) a form of Anthony. **Antonios** (Italian) a form of Anthony.

Antonius (Italian) a form of Anthony.

Antony (Latin) a form of Anthony.

Antonyo (Italian) a form of Antonio.

Antosha (Russian) invaluable.

Antoshika (Catalan) a form of Antonio.

Antti (Finnish) manly.

Antu (Indigenous) salt.

Antwain, Antwane (Arabic) forms of Antwan.

Antwan, Antwaun, Antwoine, Antwon,

Antwone (Arabic) forms of Anthony.

Anubis (Egyptian) god of death.

Anum (Egyptian) fifth birth.

Anwar (Arabic) luminous.

Anxo (Greek) messenger.

Anyaypoma,
  Anyaypuma (Quechua) he who roars and becomes angry like the puma.

Aparicio (Latin) he who refers to the appearances of the Virgin in different stages.

Apeles (Greek) he who is in a sacred place.

Apelio (Greek) of clear skin.

Aperio (Greek) wild pig.

Apfiano (Greek) a form of Apfías.

Apfías (Greek) youthful term for father.

Apiatan (Kiowa) wooden lance.

Apo, Apu (Quechua) chief; he who moves forward.

Apodemio (Greek) one who travels far from his country.

Apolinar (Greek) a form of Apollo.
Apolinario

Apólito (Latin) dedicated to the god Apollo.

Apollo (Greek) manly. Mythology: the god of prophecy, healing, music, poetry, and light.

Apolodoro (Greek) the skill of Apollo.

Aprión (Greek) convincing.

Apro (Greek) a form of Aperio.

Apronio (Greek) a form of Aperio.

Apucachi (Quechua) salty.

Apucatequil,
  Apucatiquil (Quechua) God of lightning.

Apumaita (Quechua) where are you, master?

Apurimac (Quechua) eloquent master.

Apuyurac (Quechua) white chief.

Aquías (Hebrew) brother of God.

Aquila GB (Latin, Spanish) eagle.

Ara BG (Syrian) a form of Aram.

Arador (Latin) farmer; laborer.

Arafat (Arabic) mountain of recognition.

Araldo (Spanish) a form of Harold.

Aram (Syrian) high, exalted.

Aramis (French) Literature: one of the title characters in Alexandre

Dumas's novel *The Three Musketeers.*

Aran (Tai) forest. (Danish) a form of Aren. (Hebrew, Scottish) a form of Arran.

Arapey (Indigenous) aquatic plant that forms floating islands.

Arbel (Hebrew) divine night.

Arbogastro (French) inheriting guest.

Arcadio (Spanish) a form of Archibald.

Arcángel (Greek) the prince of all angels.

Archard (French) powerful.

Archenbaud (French) courageous.

Archer **(English) bowman.**

Archibald (German) bold.
  Archie (German, English) a familiar form of Archer, Archibald.

Arconcio (Greek) one who governs.

Ardal (Irish) a form of Arnold.

Ardalión (Greek) Ardalion was a martyr who professed Christ while performing on stage.

Ardell (Latin) eager; industrious.
Ardel

Arden GB (Latin) ardent; fiery.

Ardley (English) ardent meadow.

Ardon (Hebrew) bronzed.

Arecio (Latin) the god of war.

Arelí (Hebrew) lion of God.

Aren (Danish) eagle; ruler. (Hebrew, Arabic) a form of Aaron.

Aretas (Arabic) metal forger.

Aretino **(Greek, Italian) victorious.**

Argar (Greek) shining; gleaming.

Argénides (Greek) white.

Argenis (Greek) he who has a great whiteness.

Argentino, Argento (Latin) shines like silver.

Argimiro (Greek) careful, vigilant.

Argimundo (German) defending army.

Argus (Danish) watchful, vigilant.

Argyle (Irish) from Ireland.

Ari BG (Hebrew) a short form of Ariel. (Greek) a short form of Aristotle.

Arian BG (Greek) a form of Arion.

Ariano (Greek) a form of Arian.

Aric, Arick, Arik (Scandinavian) forms of Eric. (German) forms of Richard.

Arie BG (Greek, Hebrew) a form of Ari. (Greek, Latin) a form of Aries.

Ariel GB (Hebrew) lion of God. Bible: another name for Jerusalem. Literature: the name of a sprite in the Shakespearean play *The Tempest*.

Aries GB (Latin) ram. Astrology: the first sign of the zodiac.

Arif (Arabic) knowledgeable.

Arin BG (Hebrew, Arabic) a form of Aaron. (Danish) a form of Aren.

Arion (Greek) enchanted. (Hebrew) melodious.

Aristarco (Greek) the best of the princes.

Aristeo (Greek) the outstanding one, the most significant one.

Aristides (Greek) son of the best.

Arístides (Greek) a form of Aristides.

Aristión (Greek) selective person.

Aristóbulo (Greek) the greatest and best counselor, he who gives very good advice.

Aristofanes (Greek) the best, the optimum.

Aristónico (Greek) perfect victory.

Aristóteles (Greek) the best; the most optimistic.

Aristotle (Greek) best; wise. History: a third-century b.c. philosopher who tutored Alexander the Great.

Arjun (Hindi) white; milk colored.

Arkady (Russian) a form of Archibald.

Arkin (Norwegian) son of the eternal king.

Arledge (English) lake with the hares.

Arlen (Irish) pledge.

Arley (English) a short form of Harley.

Arlo (Spanish) barberry. (English) fortified hill. A form of Harlow. **(**German) a form of Charles.

Armaan (Persian) a form of Arman.

Arman (Persian) desire, goal.

Armand (Latin, German) a form of Herman.

Armando (Spanish) a form of Armand.

Armani BG (Hungarian) sly. (Hebrew) a form of Armon.

Armelio (Greek) union.

Armen, Armin (Hebrew) forms of Armon.

Armengol (German) ready for combat.

Armentario (Greek) herder of livestock.

Armentaro (Latin) winner.

Armogastes (German) guest of the eagle.

Armon (Hebrew) high fortress, stronghold.

Armond (Latin, German) a form of Armand.

Armstrong (English) strong arm. History: astronaut Neil Armstrong was the commander of Apollo 11 and the first person to walk on the moon.

Arnaldo (Spanish) a form of Arnold.

Arnau (Catalan) a form of Arnaldo.

Arnaud (French) a form of Arnold.

Arnav (Sanskrit) ocean.

Arne (German) a form of Arnold.

Arnette ᴮᴳ (English) little eagle.

Arniano (Latin) lamb.

Arnie (German) a familiar form of Arnold.

Arno (German) a short form of Arnold. (Czech) a short form of Ernest.

Arnold (German) eagle ruler.

Arnoldo (Spanish) a form of Arnold.

Arnon **(Hebrew) rushing river.**

Arnulfo (German) a form of Arnold.

Aron, Arron **(Hebrew) forms of Aaron. (Danish) forms of Aren.**

Aroon **(Tai) dawn.**

Arquelao (Greek) governor of his village.

Arquimedes (Greek) he who has profound thoughts.

Arquímedes (Greek) deep thinker.

Arquipo (Greek) horse-breaker.

Arran (Scottish) island dweller. Geography: an island off the west coast of Scotland. (Hebrew) a form of Aaron.

Arrigo (Italian) a form of Harry.
Alrigo, Arrighetto

Arrio **(Spanish) warlike.**

Arsalan (Pakistani) lion of the mountain.

Arsenio (Greek) masculine; virile. History: Saint Arsenius was a teacher in the Roman Empire.

Arsha (Persian) venerable.

Art (English) a short form of Arthur.

Artemio (Spanish) a form of Artemus.

Artemón (Greek) consecrated by the goddess Artemis.

Artemus (Greek) gift of Artemis. Mythology:

Artemis was the goddess of the hunt and the moon.

Arthur (Irish) noble; lofty hill. (Scottish) bear. (English) rock. (Icelandic) follower of Thor. **Artie** (English) a familiar form of Arthur.

Artis ᴮᴳ (English) a form of Artie.

Artur (Italian) a form of Arthur.

Arturo (Italian) a form of Arthur.

Artzi (Hebrew) my land.

Arun (Cambodian, Hindi) sun.

Arundel (English) eagle valley.

Arve (Norwegian) heir, inheritor.

Arvel (Welsh) wept over.

Arvid (Hebrew) wanderer. (Norwegian) eagle tree.

Arvin (German) friend of the people; friend of the army.

Arvind (Hebrew, Norwegian) a form of Arvid. (German) a form of Arvin.

Arya (Hebrew) a form of Aria.

Aryan (Greek) a form of Arion.

Aryeh (Hebrew) lion.

Aryn GB (Hebrew, Arabic) a form of Aaron. (Danish) a form of Aren.

Asa BG (Hebrew) physician, healer. (Yoruba) falcon.

Asad (Arabic) a form of Asád. (Turkish) a form of Azad.

Asád (Arabic) lion.

Asadel (Arabic) prosperous.

Asaf (Hebrew) the one chosen by God.

Asafo (Spanish) Yahweh has chosen.

Asaiá (Hebrew) God did it.

Asante (African) thank you.

Ascensión (Spanish) alludes to the ascension of Jesus Christ to heaven.

Ascot (English) eastern cottage; style of necktie. Geography: a village near London and the site of the Royal Ascot horseraces.

Asdrúbal (Punic) he who is protected by God.

Asedio (Latin) stable.

Asgard (Scandinavian) court of the gods.

Ash (Hebrew) ash tree.

Ashanti GB **(Swahili) from a tribe in West Africa.**

Ashburn (English) from the ash-tree stream.

Ashby (Scandinavian) ash-tree farm. (Hebrew) a form of Ash.

Asher ✦ (Hebrew) happy; blessed.

Ashford (English) ash-tree ford.

Ashley GB (English) ash-tree meadow.

Ashon (Swahili) seventh-born son.

Ashraf (Arabic) most honorable.

Ashten GB (English) a form of Ashton.

Ashtin GB (English) a form of Ashton.

Ashton ✦ BG (English) ash-tree settlement.

Ashur (Swahili) Mythology: the principal Assyrian deity.

Ashwani (Hindi) first. Religion: the first of the twenty-seven galaxies revolving around the moon.

Ashwin (Hindi) star.

Asiel (Hebrew) created by God.
Asyel

Asif (Arabic) forgiveness.

Asker (Turkish) soldier.

Aspacio, Aspasio (Greek) welcome.

Aspen GB (English) aspen tree.

Asprén, Asprenio (Latin) hard; rough.

Aster (Greek) a form of Asterio.

Asterio (Greek) mythical figure that was thrown

into the sea because of his escape from Zeus.

Astío (Latin) one who belongs.

Astley (Greek) starry field.

Asto, Astu (Quechua) bird of the Andes.

Astolfo (Greek) he who helps with his lance.

Aston **(English) eastern town.**

Astuguaraca (Quechua) he who hunts Astus with a sling.

Aswad (Arabic) dark skinned, black.

Aswaldo (Germanic) lance of the leader.

Ata **(Fante) twin.**

Atahualpa (Quechua) bird of fortune.

Atalas, Ataleno, Atalo (Greek) young; energetic.

Atanasio, Atansasio (Greek) immortal.

Atau (Quechua) fortunate.

Atauaipa (Quechua) bird of fortune.

Atauanca (Quechua) fortunate eagle.

Atauchi (Quechua) he who makes us good fortunes.

Ataulfo (Germanic) noble warrior.

Âtef (Arabic) nice.

Atek (Polish) a form of Tanek.

Atenodoro (Greek) gift of wisdom.

Atenógenes (Greek) descendent of Atenas.

Athan (Greek) immortal.

Atherton (English) town by a spring.

Athol (Scottish) from Ireland.

Ático (Greek) top floor; loft.

Atid (Tai) sun.
Atyd

Atif (Arabic) caring.

Atkins (English) from the home of the relatives.

Atl (Nahuatl) water.

Atlas (Greek) lifted; carried. Mythology: Atlas was forced by Zeus to carry the heavens on his shoulders as a punishment for his share of the war of the Titans.

Atley (English) meadow.

Atoc, Atuc (Quechua) sly as a fox.

Atocuaman (Quechua) he who possesses the strength of a falcon and the shrewdness of a fox.

Atón (Egyptian) sundial.

Atonatihu (Nahuatl) sun of water.

Atsu (Egyptian) twins.

Atticus (Latin) from Attica, a region outside Athens.

Attila (Gothic) little father. History: the Hun leader who invaded the Roman Empire.

Atu (Ghanaian) born on Sunday.

Atur (Hebrew) crowned.

Atwater (English) at the water's edge.

Atwell (English) at the well.

Atwood (English) at the forest.

Atworth (English) at the farmstead.

Atzel (Hebrew) noble, generous.

Auberon (German) a form of Oberon.

Aubrey GB (German) noble; bearlike. (French) a familiar form of Auberon. **Auburn** GB (Latin) reddish brown.

Audacto (Latin) bold.

Audas (Latin) valiant, bold.

Auden (English) old friend.

Audie (German) noble; strong. (English) a familiar form of Edward.

Audífaz (Latin) hatred and acts.

Audomaro (Greek) famous because of his riches.

Audon (French) old; rich.

Audric (English) wise ruler.

Audun (Scandinavian) deserted, desolate.

Augie (Latin) a familiar form of August.
Auggie, Augy

Augurio (Latin) name of priests specializing in understanding divine will through the flight and sounds of birds.

August BG (Latin) a short form of Augustine, Augustus.

Augustin (Latin) a form of Augustine.

Augustine BG (Latin) majestic. Religion: Saint Augustine was the first archbishop of Canterbury.

Augustus (Latin) majestic; venerable. History: an honorary title given to the first Roman emperor, Octavius Caesar.

Aukai (Hawaiian) seafarer.

Aundre (Greek) a form of Andre.

Auqui (Quechua) master, prince.

Auquipuma (Quechua) prince who is as strong as a puma.

Auquitupac (Quechua) glorious prince.

Auquiyupanqui (Quechua) he who honors his masters.

Aurek (Polish) golden haired.

Aurelia (Latin) gold.

Aureliano (Latin) a form of Aurelius.

Aurelio (Latin) a short form of Aurelius.

Aurelius (Latin) golden. History: Marcus Aurelius was a second-century a.d. philosopher and emperor of Rome.

Auremundo (Germanic) old army.

Áureo (Latin) golden.

Aurick **(German) protecting ruler.**

Auriville (French) one who comes from the city of gold.

Auspicio (Latin) protector.

Austen 🅱🅶 (Latin) a short form of Augustine.

Austin ✨

🅱🅶 (Latin) a short form of Augustine.

Austín (Latin) a form of Austin.

Auston (Latin) a short form of Augustine.

Austyn 🅱🅶 (Latin) a short form of Augustine.

Autónomo (Greek) one who values himself.

Auxano (Greek) one who grows.

Auxencio (Greek) a form of Auxano.

Auxibio (Greek) powerful; alive.

Auxilio (Latin) he who saves, who brings help.

Avdel (Hebrew) servant of God.

Avel (Greek) breath.

Avelino (Latin) he who was born in Avella, Italy.

Avenall, Aveneil, Avenelle (French) lives close to the oat field.

Avent (French) born during Advent.

Averill (French) born in April.

Avertano (Latin) one who moves away.

Avery 🇬🇧 (English) a form of Aubrey.

Avi (Hebrew) God is my father.
Avian, Avidan, Avidor, Avie, Aviel, Avion, Avy

Aviezri (Hebrew) my father is my help.

Avimael (Hebrew) my father is of divine origin.

Avimelej (Hebrew) my father is king.

Avinatán (Hebrew) my father provided for me.

Aviramv (Hebrew) my father is lifted up.

Aviraz (Hebrew) father of the secret.

Avishajar (Hebrew) father of the morning.

Avitio, Avito (Latin) from grandfather.

Avitzedek (Hebrew) father of justice.

Aviv (Hebrew) youth; springtime.

Avner (Hebrew) a form of Abner.

Avraham (Hebrew) a form of Abraham.

Avram (Hebrew) a form of Abraham, Abram.

Avshalom (Hebrew) father of peace. **Awan** (Native American) somebody.

Awar (Lebanese) the brightest.

Axel (Latin) axe. (German) small oak tree; source of life. (Scandinavian) a form of Absalom.

Axl (Latin, German, Scandinavian) a form of Axel.

Axton (English) from the town near the ash trees.

Ayaan (Arabic) gift of God.

Ayar (Quechua) wild quinoa.

Ayden ✨ **(Irish) a form of Aidan. (Turkish) a form of Aydin.**

Aydin **(Turkish) intelligent.**

Ayers (English) heir to a fortune.

Ayinde (Yoruba) we gave praise and he came.

Aylmer (English) a form of Elmer.

Aylwin (English) noble friends.

Ayman, Aymon (French) forms of Raymond.

Aymán (Lebanese) skillful.

Aymil (Greek) a form of Emil.

Ayo (Yoruba) happiness.

Ayraldo (Germanic) noble, honorable.

Ayub (Arabic) penitent.

Ayyûb (Arabic) a form of Job.

Azad (Turkish) free.

Azadanes (Hebrew) strong.

Azades (Hebrew) a form of Azadanes

Azael (Hebrew) made from God.

Azahar (Arabic) alludes to the flower of the orange tree.

Azái (Hebrew) strong.

Azanías (Hebrew) God hears him.

Azare (Hebrew) God helped.

Azarias, Azarías (Hebrew) the Lord sustains me.

Azariel (Hebrew) he who has control over the waters.

Azas (Hebrew) strong.

Azazael (Hebrew) name of an evil spirit.

Azazel (Hebrew) cancerous spirit.

Azeca (Hebrew) strong

Azeem (Arabic) a form of Azim.

Azekel (Angolan) praise from God.

Azhar (Arabic) luminous.

Azi (Nigerian) youth.

Azikiwe (African) full of vigor.

Azim (Arabic) defender.

Azîm (Arabic) a form of Azim.

Azizi (Swahili) precious.

Azriel (Hebrew) God is my aid.

Azul (Arabic) the color of the sky without clouds.

Azuriah (Hebrew) aided by God.

Azzâm (Arabic) resolved, decided.

B

Baal (Chaldean) he who dominates a territory.

Babatunde (Nigerian) father has returned.

Bábilas (Hebrew) mouth of God.

Babu (African) grandfather.

Baco (Greek) he who creates disturbances.

Badal (Indian) cloud; rain.

Baden (German) bather.

Badilón (Spanish) bold, courageous.

Badri, Badrinath (Indian) other names for the Hindu god Vishnu.

Badrick (English) axe ruler.
Badric, Badrik, Badryc, Badryck, Badryk

Badriprasad, Bhadriprasad (Indian) Bhadri's gift.

Badru (Swahili) born from a full moon.

Badu (Ghanaian) tenth born.

Baez (Welsh) boar.

Bahir (Arabic) brilliant, dazzling.

Bahram (Persian) ancient king.

Bahubali (Indian) son of the first Tirthankar, a type of Jain god.

Bahuleya (Indian) another name for the Hindu god Kartikeya.

Bail (English) a form of Vail.

Bailey GB (French) bailiff, steward.

Bain (Irish) a short form of Bainbridge.

Bainbridge (Irish) fair bridge.

Baird (Irish) traveling minstrel, bard; poet.

Bajrang (Indian) another name for the Hindu monkey god Hanuman.

Bakari BG (Swahili) noble promise.

Baker (English) baker. **Bal** (Sanskrit) child born with lots of hair.

Balaaditya (Indian) young sun.

Balachandra (Indian) young moon.

Balagopal, Balagovind, Balakrishna, Balgopal

(Indian) the Hindu god Krishna as a baby.

Balaji (Indian) another name for the Hindu god Vishnu.

Balamani (Indian) young jewel.

Balamohan (Indian) one who is attractive; the Hindu god Krishna as a youth.

Balaraj, Balbir, Baldev, Balvinder, Balvindra, Balwant (Indian) strong.

Balaram (Indian) brother of the Hindu god Krishna.

Balasi (Basque) flat footed.

Balbino (Latin) he who mumbles.

Balbo (Latin) stammerer.

Baldemar (German) bold; famous.

Balder (Scandinavian) bald. Mythology: the Norse god of light, summer, purity, and innocence.

Balderico (German) a form of Baldemar.

Baldomero (German) a form of Baldemar.

Baldomlano (German) governor.

Baldovín (Spanish) a form of Balduino.

Baldric (German) brave ruler.

Balduino (Germanic) the valiant friend.

Baldwin (German) bold friend.

Balfour (Scottish) pastureland.

Balin (Hindi) mighty soldier.

Ballard **(German) brave; strong.**

Balraj (Hindi) strongest.

Balsemio (Latin) balm.

Baltazar (Greek) a form of Balthasar.

Balthasar (Greek) God save the king. Bible: one of the three wise men who bore gifts for the infant Jesus.

Banan (Irish) white.

Banbihari (Indian) another name for the Hindu god Krishna.

Bancroft (English) bean field.

Bandarido (Latin) flag.

Bandhu (Indian) friend.

Bandhul (Indian) pleasing.

Bandi BG (Hungarian) a form of Andrew.

Bandit (German) outlaw, robber.

Bane (Hawaiian) a form of Bartholomew.

Banner (Scottish, English) flag bearer.

Banning (Irish) small and fair.

Bao GB (Chinese) treasure.

Baptist (Greek) baptised.

Baradine (Australian) small kangaroo.

Barak (Hebrew) lightning bolt. Bible: the valiant warrior who helped Deborah.

Baram (Hebrew) son of the people.

Baran (Russian) ram.

Barasa (Kikuyu) meeting place.

Barbaciano (Latin) full of hair.

Barclay (Scottish, English) birch-tree meadow.y

Bard (Irish) a form of Baird.

Barden (English) barley valley.

Bardolf (German) bright wolf.

Bardrick (Teutonic) axe ruler.

Bareh (Lebanese) able.

Baris (Turkish) peaceful.

Barker (English) lumberjack; advertiser at a carnival.

Barlaán (Hebrew) son of the community.

Barlow (English) bare hillside.

Barnabas (Greek, Hebrew, Aramaic, Latin) son of the missionary. Bible: Christian apostle and companion of Paul on his first missionary journey.

Barnabás (Hebrew) a form of Barnabas.

Barnabe (French) a form of Barnabas.

Barnaby (English) a form of Barnabas.

Barnard (French) a form of Bernard.

Barnes (English) bear; son of Barnett.

Barnett (English) nobleman; leader.

Barney (English) a familiar form of Barnabas, Barnett.

Barnum (German) barn; storage place. (English) baron's home.

Baron (German, English) nobleman, baron.

Baroncio (Latin) clumsy.

Barret (German) a form of Barrett.

Barric (English) grain farm.

Barrington (English) fenced town. Geography: a town in England.

Barron (German, English) a form of Baron.

Barry (Welsh) son of Harry. (Irish) spear, marksman. (French) gate, fence.

Barsabás, Bársabas (Hebrew) son of the time away.

Bart (Hebrew) a short form of Bartholomew, Barton.

Bartel (German) a form of Bartholomew.

Bartelemy (French) a form of Barthelemy.

Barthelemy (French) a form of Bartholomew.

Bartholomew (Hebrew) son of Talmaí. Bible: one of the Twelve Apostles.

Bartlet (English) a form of Bartholomew.

Bartley (English) barley meadow.

Barto (Spanish) a form of Bartholomew.

Barton (English) barley town; Bart's town.

Bartram (English) a form of Bertram.

Baruc, Baruj (Hebrew) he who is blessed by God.

Baruch (Hebrew) blessed.

Baruti (Egyptian) teacher.

Basam (Arabic) smiling.

Basiano (Latin) short and stout.

Basil (Greek, Latin) royal, kingly. Religion: a saint and founder of monasteries. Botany: an herb often used in cooking.

Basile (French) a form of Basil.

Basílides (Greek) son of the king.

Basilio (Greek, Latin) a form of Basil.

Basir (Turkish) intelligent, discerning.

Basistha (Indian) an ancient Indian sage.

Bassett (English) little person.

Bastet (Egyptian) cat.

Bastien (German) a short form of Sebastian.

Basudha (Indian) earth.

Bat (English) a short form of Bartholomew.

Batildis (Germanic) intrepid revolutionary.

Baudilio (Teutonic) he who is brave and valiant.

Baul (Gypsy) snail.

Bauterio (Germanic) heroic army.

Bautista (Greek) he who baptizes.

Bavol (Gypsy) wind; air.

Baxter (English) a form of Baker.

Bay (Vietnamese) seventh son. (French) chestnut brown color; evergreen tree. (English) howler.

Bayard (English) reddish brown hair.

Baylee GB (French) a form of Bailey.

Bayley GB (French) a form of Bailey.

Baylor (American) a private university in Texas.

Bayron (German, English) a form of Baron.

Beacan (Irish) small.

Beacher (English) beech trees.

Beagan (Irish) small.

Beale (French) a form of Beau.

Beaman (English) beekeeper.

Beamer (English) trumpet player.

Beasley (English) field of peas.

Beato (Latin) happy; blessed.

Beattie (Latin) blessed; happy; bringer of joy.

Beau (French) handsome.

Beaufort (French) beautiful fort.

Beaumont (French) beautiful mountain.

Beauregard (French) handsome; beautiful; well regarded.

Beaver (English) beaver.

Bebe BG (Spanish) baby.

Beck (English, Scandinavian) brook.

Beckham (English) from the Beck home. Sports: David Beckham is a popular British soccer star.

Beda (Teutonic) he who orders and provides for.

Bede (English) prayer. Religion: the patron saint of lectors.

Bedir (Turkish) full moon.

Bee BG (American) the letter B.

Beethoven (German) Music: Ludwig van Beethoven was a German musical genius.

Beinvenido (Spanish) welcome.

Bejay (American) a combination of Beau + Jay.

Bekele (Ethiopian) he has grown.

Bela BG (Czech) white. (Hungarian) bright.

Belal (Czech, Hungarian) a form of Bela.

Belarmino (Germanic) having beautiful armor.

Belden (French, English) pretty valley.

Belen GB (Greek) arrow.

Belén (Hebrew) house of bread.

Beli (Welsh) white.

Belino (Latin) man of war.

Belisario (Greek) he who shoots arrows skillfully.

Bell (French) handsome. (English) bell ringer.

Bellamy (French) beautiful friend.

Bello (African) helper or promoter of Islam.

Belmiro (Portuguese) good-looking; attractive.

Beltane (French) classic name.

Belveder (Italian) beautiful.

Bem (Tiv) peace.
Behm

Bemabé (Spanish) son of comfort.

Bembé (Spanish) prophet.

Ben (Hebrew) a short form of Benjamin.
Behn, Benio, Benn

Ben Zion (Hebrew) son of Zion.

Ben-ami (Hebrew) son of my people.
Baram, Barami

Benaiá (Hebrew) God has built.

Benedict (Latin) blessed.

Benedicto (Spanish) a form of Benedict.

Benedikt (German, Slavic) a form of Benedict.

Benedito (Latin) a form of Benedict.

Benevento (Latin) welcome.

Bengt (Scandinavian) a form of Benedict.

Beniam (Ethiopian) a form of Benjamin.

Benicio (Latin) riding friend.

Benigno (Latin) the prodigal son; he who does good deeds.

Benildo (Teutonic) fights against bears.

Benincasa (Arabic) child of Qasim.

Benito (Italian) a form of Benedict. History: Benito Mussolini led Italy during World War II.

Benjamen (Hebrew) a form of Benjamin.

Benjamin ✴ (Hebrew) son of my right hand.

Benjamín (Hebrew) a form of Benjamin.

Benjiman (Hebrew) a form of Benjamin.

Benjiro (Japanese) enjoys peace.

Benjy (Hebrew) a familiar form of Benjamin.

Bennett BG (Latin) little blessed one.

Bennie, Benny (Hebrew) familiar forms of Benjamin.

Beno (Hebrew) son. (Mwera) band member.

Benoit (French) a form of Benedict.

Benoni (Hebrew) son of my sorrow. Bible: Benoni was the son of Jacob and Rachel.

Benson (Hebrew) son of Ben. A short form of Ben Zion.

Bentivolio (Latin) I love you; I desire you.

Bentley (English) moor; coarse grass meadow.

Bento (Latin) well-named.

Benton (English) Ben's town; town on the moors.

Benxamín (Hebrew) a form of Benjamin.

Benzi (Hebrew) a familiar form of Ben Zion.

Beppe (Italian) a form of Joseph.
Bepe, Beppy

Ber (English) boundary. (Yiddish) bear.

Beraco (Celtic) bear.

Berardo (Germanic) a form of Bernard.

Bercario (German) prince of the army.

Beredei (Russian) a form of Hubert.

Beregiso (Germanic) blade of the bear.

Berengario (Germanic) blade of the warrior.

Berenger (French) courageous as a bear.

Berenguer (Teutonic) a form of Berenger.

Berg (German) mountain.

Bergen (German, Scandinavian) hill dweller.

Berger (French) shepherd.

Bergren (Scandinavian) mountain stream.

Berhanu (Ethiopian) your light.

Berk (Turkish) solid; rugged.

Berkeley (English) a form of Barclay.

Berkley BG (English) a form of Barclay.

Berl (German) a form of Burl.

Berlyn (German) boundary line.

Bermo (Greek) from Thesalia, a region in Greece.

Bermudo (German) valiant bear; warrior.

Bern (German) a short form of Bernard.

Bernabe (French) a form of Barnabas.

Bernal (German) strong as a bear.

Bernaldino (German) strong bear.

Bernard (German) brave as a bear. **Bernardino** (Spanish) a form of Bernard.

Bernardo (Spanish) a form of Bernard.

Bernbe (Spanish) a form of Barnaby.

Bernd (German) a form of Bernardo.

Bernie (German) a familiar form of Bernard.

Bernón (German, Spanish) bear.

Bernstein (German) amber stone.

Berry BG (English) berry; grape.

Bersh (Gypsy) one year.

Bert (German, English) bright, shining. A short form of Berthold, Berton, Bertram, Bertrand, Egbert, Filbert.

Bertadio (German) a form of Burton.

Bertario (Germanic) brilliant army.

Berthold (German) bright; illustrious; brilliant ruler.

Bertie (English) a familiar form of Bert, Egbert.

Bertil (Scandinavian) bright; hero.

Bertín (Spanish) distinguished friend.

Bertino (German) brilliant; famous.

Berto (Spanish) a short form of Alberto.

Bertoldi (Italian) a form of Berthold.

Bertoldo (Germanic) the splendid boss.

Berton (English) bright settlement; fortified town.

Bertram (German) bright; illustrious. (English) bright raven. **Bertrán** (Spanish) a form of Bertram.

Bertrand (German) bright shield.

Bertualdo (German) community; illustrious leader.

Bertuino (German) brilliant.

Bertulfo (Teutonic) the warrior who shines.

Berwick (English) barley farm.

Berwyn [BG] (Welsh) white head.

Besa (Greek) man of the valley.

Besarión (Greek) the walker.

Besín (Greek) relative of Bessa.

Betel, Betue (Hebrew) house of God.

Betsabé (Hebrew) oath of God.

Beval (English) like the wind.

Beverly [GB] (English) beaver meadow.

Bevis (French) from Beauvais, France; bull.

Bhagwandas (Hindi) servant of God.

Bibiano (Spanish) small man.

Bickford (English) axe-man's ford.

Bieito, Bieto (Latin) well-named.

Bienvenido (Filipino) welcome.

Bijan (Persian) ancient hero.

Bilal (Arabic) chosen.

Bill (German) a short form of William.

Billie [GB] (German) a familiar form of Bill, William.

Billy [BG] (German) a familiar form of Bill, William.

Binah (Hebrew) understanding; wise.

Bing (German) kettle-shaped hollow.

Binh (Vietnamese) peaceful.

Binkentios (Greek) a form of Vincent.

Binky (English) a familiar form of Bancroft, Vincent.

Birch (English) white; shining; birch tree.

Birger (Norwegian) rescued.

Birin (Australian) cliff.

Birino (Latin) reddish.

Birkey (English) island with birch trees.

Birkitt **(English) birch-tree coast.**

Birley (English) meadow with the cow barn.

Birney (English) island with a brook.

Birtle (English) hill with birds.

Bishop (Greek) overseer. (English) bishop.

Bjorn (Scandinavian) a form of Bernard.

Blackburn (Scottish) black brook.

Blade (English) knife, sword.

Bladimir (Russian) a form of Vladimir.
Bladimer

Bladimiro (Slavic) prince of peace.

Blain (Irish, English) a form of Blaine.

Blaine BG (Irish) thin, lean. (English) river source.

Blair BG (Irish) plain, field. (Welsh) place.

Blaise BG (French) a form of Blaze.

Blaize (French) a form of Blaze.

Blake ☆
BG (English) attractive; dark.

Blakely BG (English) dark meadow.

Blanco (Spanish) light skinned; white; blond.

Blandino (Latin) he who is flattered.

Blane (Irish) a form of Blaine.

Blas (French) a form of Blaze.

Blasco (Latin) of a pale color.

Blayke (English) a form of Blake.

Blayne BG (Irish) a form of Blaine.

Blayze (French) a form of Blaze.

Blaze (Latin) stammerer. (English) flame; trail mark made on a tree.

Bliss GB (English) blissful; joyful.

Blondel (French) blond.

Bly (Native American) high.

Bo BG (English) a form of Beau, Beauregard.

(German) a form of Bogart.

Boaz (Hebrew) swift; strong.

Bob (English) a short form of Robert.

Bobbie GB (English) a familiar form of Bob, Robert.

Bobby (English) a familiar form of Bob, Robert.

Bobek (Czech) a form of Bob, Robert.

Bobo (Ghanaian) born on a Tuesday.

Bode, Bodie (American) familiar forms of Boden and Bodhi.

Boden (Scandinavian) sheltered. (French) messenger, herald.

Bodhi (Sanskrit) enlightened.

Bodil BG (Norwegian) mighty ruler.

Bodua **(Akan) animal's tail.**

Boecio (Greek) he who helps; the defender, who goes into battle ready.

Bogart (German) strong as a bow. (Irish, Welsh) bog, marshland.

Bohdan (Ukrainian) a form of Donald.

Boleslao (Slavic) the most glorious of the glorious.

Bolívar (Basque) mill of the shore.

Bolodenka (Russian) calm.

Bolton (English) from the manor farm.

Bomani (Egyptian) warrior.

Bonaro (Italian, Spanish) friend.

Bonaventure (Italian) good luck.

Bond (English) tiller of the soil.

Bonfilio, Bonfilo (Latin) good son.

Boni (Latin) man of decency.

Boniface (Latin) do-gooder.

Bonifaci (French) a form of Boniface.

Bonito (Latin) worthy.

Bono, Bonoso (Latin) man of decency.

Booker (English) bookmaker; book lover; Bible lover.

Boone (Latin, French) good. History: Daniel Boone was an American pioneer.

Booth (English) hut. (Scandinavian) temporary dwelling.

Borak (Arabic) lightning. Mythology: the horse that carried Muhammad to seventh heaven.

Borden (French) cottage. (English) valley of the boar; boar's den.

Boreas (Greek) the north wind.

Borg (Scandinavian) castle.

Boris (Slavic) battler, warrior. Religion: the patron saint of Moscow, princes, and Russia.

Borís (Russian) a form of Boris.

Borka (Russian) fighter.

Boseda (Tiv) born on Saturday.

Bosley (English) grove of trees.

Boston (English) Botwulf's stone. Geography: the largest city in Massachusetts.

Boswell (English) boar enclosure by the stream.

Botan (Japanese) blossom, bud.

Boulus (Arabic) a form of Pablo.

Bourey (Cambodian) country.

Bourne (Latin, French) boundary. (English) brook, stream.

Boutros (Arabic) a form of Peter.

Bowen (Welsh) son of Owen.

Bowie (Irish) yellow haired. History: James Bowie was an American-born Mexican colonist who died during the defense of the Alamo.

Boy (French) a short form of Boyce.

Boyce (French) woods, forest.

Boyd (Scottish) yellow haired.

Brad (English) a short form of Bradford, Bradley.

Bradburn (English) broad stream.

Braden (English) broad valley.

Bradey (Irish, English) a form of Brady.

Bradford (English) broad river crossing.

Bradlee, Bradly (English) forms of Bradley.

Bradley BG (English) broad meadow.

Bradon (English) broad hill.

Bradshaw (English) broad forest.

Brady BG (Irish) spirited. (English) broad island.

Bradyn (English) a form of Braden.

Braedan, Braedyn (English) forms of Braden.

Braeden BG (English) a form of Braden.

Braedon (English) a form of Bradon.

Bragi (Scandinavian) poet. Mythology: the god of poetry, eloquence, and song.

Braham (Hindi) creator.

Braiden (English) a form of Braden.

Braidon (English) a form of Bradon.

Brainard (English) bold raven; prince.

Bram (Scottish) bramble, brushwood. (Hebrew) a short form of Abraham, Abram.

Bramwell (English) bramble spring.

Branch (Latin) paw; claw; tree branch.

Brand (English) firebrand; sword. A short form of Brandon.

Brandan (English) a form of Brandon.

Brandán (Celtic) a form of Brandan.

Brandeis (Czech) dweller on a burned clearing.

Branden BG (English) beacon valley.

Brandin (English) a form of Branden.

Brando (English) a form of Brand.

Brandon ☆ BG (English) beacon hill.

Brandt (English) a form of Brant.

Brandyn (English) a form of Branden, Brandon.

Brannen, Brannon (Irish) forms of Brandon.

Bransen (English) a form of Branson.

Branson (English) son of Brandon, Brant. A form of Bronson.

Brant (English) proud.

Brantley, Brantly (English) forms of Brant.

Branton (English) Brant's town.

Brasil (Irish) brave; strong in conflict.

Braulio (Italian) a form of Brawley.

Brawley (English) meadow on the hillside.

Braxton BG (English) Brock's town.

Brayan (Irish, Scottish) a form of Brian.

Brayden (English) a form of Braden.

Braydon (English) a form of Bradon.

Braylon (American) a combination of Braydon + Lynn.

Brayson (American) a name that sounds like Mason and Jason.

Brayton (English) a form of Brighton. (Scottish) a form of Bret.

Breck BG (Irish) freckled.

Brede (Scandinavian) iceberg, glacier.

Brencis (Latvian) a form of Lawrence.

Brendan (Irish) little raven. (English) sword.

Brenden, Brendin (Irish) forms of Brendan.

Brendon (English) a form of Brandon. (Irish, English) a form of Brendan.

Brendyn (Irish, English) a form of Brendan.

Brenen, Brennen, Brennon (English, Irish) forms of Brendan.

Brennan BG (English, Irish) a form of Brendan.

Brenner (English, Irish) a form of Brendan.

Brent (English) a short form of Brenton.

Brenten (English) a form of Brenton.

Brentley (English) a form of Brantley.

Brenton (English) steep hill.

Breogán (Spanish) indicative of family or origin.

Breon, Breyon (Irish, Scottish) forms of Brian.

Bret BG (Scottish) from Great Britain.

Breton, Bretton (Scottish) forms of Bret.

Brett BG (Scottish) from Great Britain.

Brewster (English) brewer.

Brian ☆ (Irish, Scottish) strong; virtuous; honorable. History: Brian Boru was an eleventh-century Irish king and national hero.

Briar BG (French) heather.

Briccio, Bricio (Celtic) strength.

Brice BG (Welsh) alert; ambitious. (English) son of Rice.

Brick (English) bridge.

Bridgely (English) meadow near a bridge.

Bridger (English) bridge builder.

Brien (Irish, Scottish) a form of Brian.

Brigham (English) covered bridge. (French) troops, brigade.

Brighton BG (English) bright town.

Brigliadoro (French) classic name.

Brinley (English) tawny.

Brion (Irish, Scottish) a form of Brian.

Brishan (Gypsy) born during a rain.

Brit (Scottish) a form of Bret. **Britanic** (Catalan) a form of Bruno.

Briton BG (Scottish) a form of Britton.

Britt BG (Scottish) a form of Bret.

Brittan BG (Scottish) a form of Britton.

Britten BG (Scottish) a form of Britton.

Britton 🅱🅶 (Scottish) from Great Britain.

Britvaldo (Germanic) leader of the British.

Broc (English) a form of Brock.

Brocardo (Breton) armed warrior.

Brock **(English) badger.**

Brockton (English) a form of Brock.

Brod (English) a short form of Broderick.

Broden (Irish) a form of Brody. (English) a form of Brod.

Broderick (Welsh) son of the famous ruler. (English) broad ridge.

Brodie 🅱🅶 (Irish) a form of Brody.

Brodrick (Welsh, English) a form of Broderick.

Brody ✲ (Irish) ditch; canal builder.

Brogan 🅱🅶 (Irish) a heavy work shoe.

Bromley (English) brushwood meadow.

Bron (Afrikaans) source.

Bronislaw (Polish) weapon of glory.

Bronson (English) son of Brown.

Brooks 🅱🅶 (English) son of Brook.

Brown (English) brown; bear.

Bru (Catalan) a form of Bruno.

Bruce (French) brushwood thicket; woods.

Brunelle (French) black hair.

Bruno (German, Italian) brown haired; brown skinned.

Brutus (Latin) coarse, stupid. History: a Roman general who conspired to assassinate Julius Caesar.

Bryan (Irish) a form of Brian.

Bryant (Irish) a form of Bryan.

Bryar, Bryer (French) forms of Briar.

Bryce 🅱🅶 (Welsh) a form of Brice.

Bryden, Brydon (English) forms of Braden.

Bryn 🅶🅱 (Welsh) mountain. (German, English) a form of Bryon.

Brynmor (Welsh) big mountain.

Bryon (German) cottage. (English) bear.

Brys (French) comes from Brys.

Brysen (Welsh) a form of Bryson.

Bryson (Welsh) son of Brice.

Bryton (English) a form of Brighton.

Bubba (German) a boy.

Buck (German, English) male deer.

Buckley (English) deer meadow.

Buckminster (English) preacher.

Bucolo (Greek) voyeur.

Bud (English) herald, messenger.

Buddy (American) a familiar form of Bud.

Buell (German) hill dweller. (English) bull.

Buenaventura (Latin) he who predicts happiness.

Buford (English) ford near the castle.

Buinton, Buintón (Spanish) born fifth.

Bundy (English) free.

Bunyan (Australian) home of pigeons.

Burbank (English) from the castle on a slope.

Burcardo (Germanic) daring protector; the defender of the fortress.

Burcet (French) comes from the stronghold.

Burdan (English) birch valley.

Burdett (French) small shield.

Burford (English) birch ford.

Burgess (English) town dweller; shopkeeper.

Burian (Ukrainian) lives near weeds.

Burke (German, French) fortress, castle.

Burl (English) cup bearer; wine servant; knot in a tree. (German) a short form of Berlyn.

Burleigh (English) meadow with knotted tree trunks.

Burne (English) brook.

Burnell (French) small; brown haired.

Burnett (English) burned nettle.

Burney (English) island with a brook. A familiar form of Rayburn.

Burr (Swedish) youth. (English) prickly plant.

Burrell (French) purple skin.

Burril (Australian) wallaby.

Burris (English) town dweller.

Burt (English) a form of Bert. A short form of Burton.

Burton (English) fortified town.

Busby (Scottish) village in the thicket; tall military hat made of fur.

Buster (American) hitter, puncher.

Butch (American) a short form of Butcher.

Butcher (English) butcher.

Butrus (Arabic) a form of Peter.

Buz (Hebrew) rebelliousness; disdain.

Buzz (Scottish) a short form of Busby.

Bwana (Swahili) gentleman.

Byford (English) by the ford.

Byram (English) cattle yard.

Byran (French, English) a form of Byron.

Byrd (English) birdlike.

Byrne (English) a form of Burne.

Byron (French) cottage. (English) barn.

C

Cable (French, English) rope maker.

Cachayauri (Quechua) hard as a shard of copper.

Cadao (Vietnamese) folksong.

Cadby (English) warrior's settlement.

Caddock (Welsh) eager for war.

Cade (Welsh) a short form of Cadell.

Cadell (Welsh) battler.

Caden (American) a form of Kadin.

Cadman (Irish) warrior.

Cadmar (Irish) brave warrior.

Cadmus (Greek) from the east. Mythology: a Phoenician prince who founded Thebes and introduced writing to the Greeks.

Caelan (Scottish) a form of Nicholas.

Caesar (Latin) long-haired. History: a title for Roman emperors.

Caesear (Latin) a form of Caesar.

Cagnoaldo (German) illustrious.

Cahil (Turkish) young, naive.

Cai 🇧🇬 (Welsh) a form of Gaius.

Caiden (American) a form of Kadin.

Caifas (Assyrian) man of little energy.

Cain (Hebrew) spear; gatherer. Bible: Adam and Eve's oldest son.

Caín (Hebrew) a form of Cain.

Cainán (Hebrew) blacksmith.

Caine (Hebrew) a form of Cain.

Cairn (Welsh) landmark made of a mound of stones.

Cairo (Arabic) Geography: the capital of Egypt.

Caitan (Latin) a form of Caín.

Caitán (Galician) a form of Cayetano.

Caiya (Quechua) close, nearby.

Cal (Latin) a short form of Calvert, Calvin.

Calan (Scottish) a form of Caelan. (Australian) a form of Callan.

Calánico (Greek) blend of to yell and victory.

Caldeolo (Latin) hot.

Calder (Welsh, English) brook, stream.

Caldwell (English) cold well.

Cale (Hebrew) a short form of Caleb.

Caleb ☆ (Hebrew) dog; faithful. (Arabic) bold, brave. Bible: one of the twelve spies sent by Moses.

Calen, Calin (Scottish) forms of Caelan.

Calean

Calepodio (Greek) he who has beautiful feet.

Caley 🇬🇧 (Irish) a familiar form of Calan, Caleb.

Calfumil (Mapuche) glazed ceramic tile, brilliant blue.

Calhoun (Irish) narrow woods. (Scottish) warrior.

Calib (Hebrew, Arabic) a form of Caleb.

Calícrates (Greek) excellent government.

Calígula (Latin) he who wears sandals.

Calimaco, Calímaco (Greek) excellent fighter.

Calimerino (Greek) a form of Calimero.

Calimerio (Greek) he who ushers in a beautiful day.

Calimero (Greek) beautiful body.

Calinico, Calínico (Greek) he who secures a beautiful victory.

Calistenes (Greek) beautiful and strong.

Calisto, Calixto (Greek) the best and the most beautiful.

Calistrato, Calístrato (Greek) he who commands a great army.

Calistro (Galician) a form of Calisto.

Calixtrato (Greek) a form of Calisto.

Callahan (Irish) descendant of Ceallachen.

Callan 🇬🇧 (Australian) sparrow hawk. (Scottish) a form of Caelan.

Callen (Scottish) a form of Caelan. (Australian, Scottish) a form of Callan.

Callis (Latin) chalice, goblet.

Callum (Irish) dove.

Calminio (Latin) calmed.

Calócero (Greek) well traveled.

Calogero (Greek) the wise one.

Calros (German) free man.

Calum (Irish) a form of Callum.

Calvert (English) calf herder.

Calvin (Latin) bald.

Calvucura (Mapuche) blue stone.

Cam 🇧🇬 (Gypsy) beloved. (Scottish) a short form of Cameron. (Latin, French, Scottish) a short form of Campbell.

Camara (West African) teacher.

Camaron (Scottish) a form of Cameron.

Camden ☆
🇧🇬 (Scottish) winding valley.

Cameren (Scottish) a form of Cameron.

Cameron ☆

🇧🇬 (Scottish) crooked nose. **Camille** 🇬🇧 (French) young ceremonial attendant.

Camilo (Latin) child born to freedom; noble.

Campbell 🇧🇬 (Latin, French) beautiful field. (Scottish) crooked mouth.

229

Camren, Camrin, Camron (Scottish) short forms of Cameron.

Camryn GB (Scottish) a short form of Cameron.

Canaan (French) a form of Cannon. History: an ancient region between the Jordan River and the Mediterranean.

Cancio (Latin) founder of the city of Anzio.

Candide (Latin) pure; sincere.

Candido (Latin) a form of Candide.

Cándido (Latin) a form of Candido.

Canión (Latin) dog.

Cannon (French) church official; large gun. ,

Canon (French) a form of Cannon.

Cantidio (Latin) song.

Canute (Latin) white haired. (Scandinavian) knot. History: a Danish king who became king of England after 1016.

Canuto (Latin) a form of Canute.

Canyon (Latin) canyon.

Capac, Capah (Quechua) rich in kindness.

Capacuari (Quechua) kind-hearted master and untamable like the Vicuna.

Capaquiupanqui (Quechua) he who honors his master.

Capitón (Latin) big head.

Cappi (Gypsy) good fortune.

Caprasio (Latin) regarding the goat.

Caquia (Quechua) thunder.

Car (Irish) a short form of Carney.

Caralampio (Greek) to shine with happiness.

Caralipo (Greek) saddened heart.

Carden (French) wool comber. (Irish) from the black fortress.

Carey BG (Greek) pure. (Welsh) castle; rocky island.

Carilao (Greek) grace of the community.

Carim (Arabic) generous.

Carino (Greek) smiley; friendly.

Carión (Greek) beautiful; graceful.

Carísimo (Latin) loved; appreciated.

Caritón (Greek) person that loves.

Carl (German, English) a short form of Carlton. A form of Charles.

Carleton (English) a form of Carlton.

Carlin BG (Irish) little champion.

Carlisle (English) Carl's island.

Carlito (Spanish) a familiar form of Carlos.

Carlo (Italian) a form of Carl, Charles.

Carlomagno (Spanish) Charles the great.

Carlomán (Germanic) one who lives.

Carlos (Spanish) a form of Carl, Charles.

Carlton (English) Carl's town.

Carlyle BG (English) a form of Carlisle.

Carmel GB (Hebrew) vineyard, garden.

Carmelo (Hebrew) a form of Carmel.

Carmen GB (Latin, Italian) a form of Carmine.

Carmichael (Scottish) follower of Michael.

Carmine BG (Latin) song; crimson. (Italian) a form of Carmel.

Carnelius (Greek, Latin) a form of Cornelius.

Carnell (English) defender of the castle. (French) a form of Cornell.

Carney (Irish) victorious. (Scottish) fighter.

Carolas (French) strong.

Carpo (Greek) valuable fruit.

Carpóforo (Greek) he who carries nuts and dried fruit.

Carponio (Greek) a form of Carpo.

Carr (Scandinavian) marsh.

Carrick (Irish) rock.

Carrington ⒷⒼ (Welsh) rocky town.

Carroll (Irish) champion. (German) a form of Carl.

Carsen (English) a form of Carson.

Carson ⒷⒼ (English) son of Carr.

Carsten (Greek) a form of Karsten.

Carter ☆ ⒷⒼ (English) cart driver.

Carterio (Greek) solid, sensible.

Cartland (English) cart builder's island.

Cartwright (English) cart builder.

Caruamayu (Quechua) yellow river.

Carvell (French, English) village on the marsh.

Carver (English) wood-carver; sculptor.

Cary ⒷⒼ (Welsh) a form of Carey. (German, Irish) a form of Carroll.

Casandro (Greek) the hero's brother.

Case (Irish) a short form of Casey. (English) a short form of Casimir.

Caseareo (Italian) a form of Caesar.

Casey ⒷⒼ (Irish) brave.

Cash (Latin) vain. (Slavic) a short form of Casimir.

Cashlin (Irish) little castle.

Casiano (Latin) he who is equipped with a helmet.

Casildo (Arabic) the youth that carries the lance.

Casimir (Slavic) peacemaker.

Casiodoro (Greek) gift from a friend.

Cason, Kason (American) a form of caisson (French), a chest or vehicle that transports ammunition.

Casper (Persian) treasurer. (German) imperial.

Cass ⒷⒼ (Irish, Persian) a short form of Casper, Cassidy.

Cassidy ⒼⒷ (Irish) clever; curly haired.

Cassius (Latin, French) box; protective cover.

Casta (Spanish) pure.

Castiel (Hebrew) shield of God.

Castle (Latin) castle.

Casto (Greek) pure, clean; honest.

Castor (Greek) beaver. Astrology: one of the twins in the constellation Gemini. Mythology: one of the patron saints of mariners.

Cástor (Greek) a form of Castor.

Castrense (Latin) castle.

Cataldo (Greek) outstanding in war.

Catari (Aymara) serpent.

Catequil, Catiquil (Quechua) ray of light.

Cater (English) caterer.

Cathal (Irish) strong; wise.

Cathmor (Irish) great fighter.

Catlin ⒼⒷ (Irish) a form of Caitlin **Cato** (Latin) knowledgeable, wise.

Catricura (Mapuche) cut stone.

Catuilla (Quechua) ray of light.

Catulino, Catulo (Latin) little dog.

Cauac (Quechua) sentinel, he who guards.

Cauachi (Quechua) he who makes us attentive, vigilant.

Cauana (Quechua) he who is in a place where all can be seen.

Cautaro (Araucanian) daring and enterprising.

Cavan (Irish) handsome.

Cavell (French) small and active.

231

Cavin (Irish) a form of Cavan.

Cawley (Scottish) ancient. (English) cow meadow.

Cayden (American) a form of Caden.
Cayde, Caydin

Cayetano (Latin) he who is from Gaeta, an ancient Italian city in the Lazio region.

Caylan (Scottish) a form of Caelan.

Cayo (Latin) happy and fun.

Cayua (Quechua) he who follows.

Cazzie (American) a familiar form of Cassius.

Ceadas (Anglo-Saxon) battle.

Ceasar (Latin) a form of Caesar.

Ceasario (Italian) a form of Caesar.

Cecil (Latin) blind.

Cecilio (Latin) a form of Cecil.

Cedar BG (Latin) a kind of evergreen conifer.

Cederic (English) a form of Cedric.

Cedric (English) battle chieftain.

Cedrick, Cedrik (English) forms of Cedric.

Cedro (Spanish) strong gift.

Ceejay (American) a combination of the initials C. + J.

Cefas (Hebrew) rock.

Ceferino (Greek) he who caresses like the wind.

Celedonio, Celonio (Latin) he who is like the swallow.

Celerino (Latin) fast.

Celestino (Latin) a form of Celestine.

Celso (Italian, Spanish, Portuguese) tall.

Cemal (Arabic) attractive.

Cencio (Italian) a form of Vicente.

Cenerico (German) bold; rich and powerful.

Cenobio (Latin) he who rejects the strangers.

Censurio (Latin) critic.

Cephas (Latin) small rock. Bible: the term used by Jesus to describe Peter.

Cepos (Egyptian) pharaoh.

Cerano (Greek) thunder.

Cerdic (Welsh) beloved.

Cerek (Polish) lordly. (Greek) a form of Cyril.

Cerni (Catalan) a form of Saturno.

Cesar (Spanish) a form of Caesar.

Cesáreo (Latin) relating to Caesar.

Cesarión (Latin) Caesar's follower.

Cesidio (Latin) blue.

Ceslao (Greek) one who is with the community.

Cestmir (Czech) fortress.

Cezar (Slavic) a form of Caesar.

Chace (French) a form of Chase.

Chad (English) warrior. A short form of Chadwick. Geography: a country in north-central Africa.

Chadd (English) a form of Chad.

Chadrick (German) mighty warrior.

Chadwick (English) warrior's town.

Chafulumisa (Egyptian) quickly.

Chago (Spanish) a form of Jacob.

Chaicu (Aymara) he who has great strength to fling stones.

Chaim (Hebrew) life.

Chaise (French) a form of Chase.

Chaitanya (Indian) consciousness.

Chakir (Arabic) the chosen one.

Chakor (Indian) a bird enamored of the moon.

Chakrapani (Indian) another name for the Hindu god Vishnu.

Chakshu (Indian) eye.

Chal (Gypsy) boy; son.

Chale (Spanish) strong and youthful.

Chalmers (Scottish) son of the lord.

Chalten (Tehuelche) bluish.

Cham (Vietnamese) hard worker.

Chaman, Chamanlal (Indian) garden.

Chambi (Aymara) he who brings good news.

Chambigüiyca, Champigüiyca (Aymara) beam of sunlight.

Champak (Indian) flower.

Champi (Aymara) he who brings good news.

Chan 🆂🅶 (Sanskrit) shining. (English) a form of Chauncey. (Spanish) a form of Juan.

Chanan (Hebrew) cloud.

Chance 🆂🅶 (English) a short form of Chancellor, Chauncey.

Chancellor (English) record keeper.

Chancelor (English) a form of Chancellor.

Chancey 🆂🅶 (English) a familiar form of Chancellor, Chauncey.

Chanchal (Indian) restless.

Chandak, Chandra, Chandrabhan, Chandrakanta, Chandrakishore, Chandrakumar,

Chandran, Chandranath (Indian) moon.

Chander (Hindi) moon.

Chandler 🆂🅶 (English) candle maker.

Chandrachur (Indian) another name for the Hindu god Shiva.

Chandrahas (Indian) bow of the Hindu god Shiva.

Chandrak (Indian) peacock feather.

Chandramohan (Indian) attractive like the moon.

Chandraraj (Indian) moonbeam.

Chandrashekhar (Indian) one who holds moon in his hair knot; another name for the Hindu god Shiva.

Chandresh (Indian) lord of the moon.

Chane (Swahili) dependable.

Chaney 🆂🅶 (French) oak.

Chanler (French) a form of Chandler.

Channing 🆂🅶 (English) wise. (French) canon; church official.

Chanse (English) a form of Chance.

Chante 🆂🅶 (French) singer.

Chanten (Galician) colored blue.

Chantz (English) a form of Chance.

Chanz, Chanze

Chapal (Indian) quick.

Chapin (French) scholar.

Chapman (English) merchant.

Chappel, Chappell (French) one who comes from the chapel.

Charan (Indian) feet.

Charanjeet, Charanjit (Indian) one who has won over the lord.

Charanjiv (Hindi) long lived.

Charif (Lebanese) honest.

Charles ⭐ (German) farmer. (English) strong and manly. **Charleston** (English) a form of Carlton.

Charley 🆂🅶 (German, English) a familiar form of Charles.

Charlie 🆂🅶 (German, English) a familiar form of Charles.

Charlton (English) a form of Carlton.

Charly 🆂🅶 (German, English) a familiar form of Charles.

Charro (Spanish) cowboy.

Chas (English) a familiar

Chase ⭐ 🆂🅶 (French) hunter.

Chasen, Chason (French) forms of Chase.

Chaska (Sioux) first-born son.

Chatha (African) ending.

233

Chatham (English) warrior's home.

Chatuluka (Egyptian) to divert.

Chaturbhuj (Indian) strong; broad-shouldered.

Chauar (Quechua) fiber, rope.

Chauki (Lebanese) my wishes, desires.

Chauncey (English) chancellor; church official.

Chauncy (English) a form of Chauncey.

Chaupi (Quechua) he who is in the middle of everything.

Chavez (Hispanic) a surname used as a first name.

Chávez (Spanish) a form of Chavez.

Chavis (Hispanic) a form of Chavez.
Chivass

Chayanne (Cheyenne) a form of Cheyenne.

Chayce, Chayse (French) forms of Chase.

Chayton (Lakota) falcon.

Chaz, Chazz (English) familiar forms of Charles.

Che, Ché (Spanish) familiar forms of Jose. History: Ernesto "Che" Guevara was a revolutionary who fought at Fidel Castro's side in Cuba.

Checha (Spanish) a familiar form of Jacob.

Cheche (Spanish) a familiar form of Joseph.

Chee (Chinese, Nigerian) a form of Chi.

Cheikh (African) to learn.

Chen (Chinese) great, tremendous.

Chenche (Spanish) conquer.

Chencho (Spanish) a familiar form of Lawrence.

Cheney (French) from the oak forest.

Chenzira (Egyptian) born on a trip.

Chepe (Spanish) a familiar form of Joseph.

Cherokee GB (Cherokee) people of a different speech.

Chesmu (Native American) gritty.

Chester (English) a short form of Rochester.

Cheston (English) a form of Chester.

Chet (English) a short form of Chester.

Chetan (Indian) consciousness; life.

Chetana (Indian) consciousness.

Cheung (Chinese) good luck.

Chevalier (French) horseman, knight.

Chevy (French) a familiar form of Chevalier. Geography: Chevy Chase is a town in Maryland. Culture: a short form of Chevrolet, an American automobile company.

Cheyenne GB (Cheyenne) a tribal name.

Cheyne (French) a form of Chaney.

Chhandak (Indian) charioteer of Buddha.

Chi BG (Chinese) younger generation. (Nigerian) personal guardian angel.

Chicahua (Nahuatl) strong.

Chican (Quechua) unique.

Chicho (Spanish) a form of Chico.

Chick (English) a familiar form of Charles.

Chico (Spanish) boy.

Chidambar (Indian) one whose heart is as big as the sky.

Chidananda (Indian) the Hindu god Shiva.

Chik (Gypsy) earth.

Chike (Ibo) God's power.

Chiko (Japanese) arrow; pledge.

Chilo (Spanish) a familiar form of Francisco.

Chilton (English) farm by the spring.

Chim (Vietnamese) bird.

Chimalli (Nahuatl) shield.

Chincolef (Mapuche) swift squad; rapid.

Chinmay, Chinmayananda (Indian) blissful.

Chintamani (Indian) philosopher's stone.

Chinua (Ibo) God's blessing.

Chioke (Ibo) gift of God.

Chip (English) a familiar form of Charles.

Chipahua (Nahuatl) clean.

Chipper (English) a form of Chip.

Chippia **(Australian) duck.**

Chirag (Indian) lamp.

Chiram (Hebrew) exalted; noble.

Chiranjeev, Chirantan, Chirayu (Indian) immortal.

Chisisi (Egyptian) secret.

Chitrabhanu (Indian) fire.

Chitraksh (Indian) beautiful-eyed.

Chitral (Indian) variegated.

Chitrarath (Indian) the sun.

Chitrasen (Indian) a king of the Gandharvas, Hindu spirits of the air, forests, and mountains.

Chitta (Indian) mind.

Chittaranjan (Indian) joy of the inner mind.

Chittaswarup (Indian) the supreme spirit.

Chittesh (Indian) lord of the soul.

Choque, Chuqui (Quechua) lance.

Chorche (Aragonese) a form of George.

Chris 🅱🅶 (Greek) a short form of Christian, Christopher.

Christain 🅱🅶 (Greek) a form of Christian.

Christan 🅱🅶 (Greek) a form of Christian.

Christapher (Greek) a form of Christopher.

Christen, Christin 🅶🅱 (Greek) forms of Christian.

Christian ✨

🅱🅶 (Greek) follower of Christ; anointed.
Christien (Greek) a form of Christian.

Christofer, Christoffer (Greek) forms of Christopher.

Christoff (Russian) a form of Christopher.

Christoper (Greek) a form of Christopher.

Christoph (French) a form of Christopher.

Christophe 🅱🅶 (French) a form of Christopher.

Christopher ✨

🅱🅶 (Greek) Christ-bearer. Religion: the patron saint of travelers.

Christophoros (Greek) a form of Christopher.

Christos (Greek) a form of Christopher.

Chrysander (Greek) golden.

Chucho (Hebrew) a familiar form of Jesus.

Chuck (American) a familiar form of Charles.

Chucri (Lebanese) my grace.

Chudamani (Indian) jewel adorned by the gods.

Chui (Swahili) leopard.

Chul (Korean) firm.

Chuma (Ibo) having many beads, wealthy. (Swahili) iron.

Chuminga (Spanish) a familiar form of Dominic.

Chumo (Spanish) a familiar form of Thomas.

Chun 🅱🅶 (Chinese) spring.

Chung (Chinese) intelligent.

Chuquigüaman (Quechua) dancing falcon; golden falcon.

Chuquigüiyca (Quechua) sacred dance.

Chuquilla (Quechua) ray of light, golden light.

Churchill (English) church on the hill. History: Sir

Winston Churchill served as British prime minister and won a Nobel Prize for literature.

Chuscu (Quechua) fourth son.

Chuya (Quechua) clear as water, pure.

Cian 🇧🇬 (Irish) ancient.

Ciaran (Irish) black; little.

Cibardo (German) strong offering.

Cibrán, Cibrao (Latin) inhabitant of Chipre.

Cicero (Latin) chickpea. History: a famous Roman orator, philosopher, and statesman.

Cid (Spanish) lord. History: title for Rodrigo Díaz de Vivar, an eleventh-century Spanish soldier and national hero.

Cidro (Spanish) strong gift.

Cilistro (Galician) a form of Celestino.

Cindeo (Greek) one who escapes danger.

Cipactli (Nahuatl) crocodile.

Cipactonal (Nahuatl) production of the day.

Ciqala (Dakota) little.

Cireneo, Cirineo (Greek) native from Cyrene.

Ciriaco, Ciríaco (Greek) Lord.

Cirilo, Cirrillo (Italian) forms of Cyril.

Ciro (Italian) a form of Cyril. (Persian) a form of Cyrus. (Latin) a form of Cicero.

Cisco (Spanish) a short form of Francisco.

Citino (Latin) quick to act.

Citlali (Nahuatl) star.

Clancey (Irish) a form of Clancy.

Clancy 🇧🇬 (Irish) redheaded fighter.

Clare 🇬🇧 (Latin) a short form of Clarence.

Clarence (Latin) clear; victorious.

Clarencio (Latin) a form of Clarence.

Clark (French) cleric; scholar.

Claro (Latin) he who is clean and transparent.

Clateo (Greek) honored.

Claude 🇧🇬 (Latin, French) lame.

Claudino (Italian) a form of Claudio.

Claudio (Italian) a form of Claude.

Claudius (German, Dutch) a form of Claude.

Claus (German) a short form of Nicholas. **Clay** (English) clay pit. A short form of Clayborne, Clayton.

Clayborne (English) brook near the clay pit.

Clayton (English) town built on clay.

Cleandro (Greek) glorious man.

Cleary (Irish) learned.

Cleavon (English) cliff.

Clem (Latin) a short form of Clement.

Clemence 🇬🇧 (French) a form of Clement.

Clemencio (Italian) a form of Clemence.

Clement (Latin) merciful. Bible: a coworker of Paul. **Clemente** (Italian, Spanish) a form of Clement.

Cleo 🇧🇬 (Greek) a form of Clio **Cleóbulo** (Greek) glorious counselor.

Cleofas (Greek) he is the glory of his father.

Cleómaco (Greek) he who fights gloriously.

Cleómenes (Greek) glorious courage.

Cleon (Greek) famous.

Cleónico (Greek) a form of Cleon.

Cleto (Greek) he was chosen to fight.

Cletus (Greek) illustrious. History: a Roman pope and martyr.

Cleve (English) a short form of Cleveland. A form of Clive.

Cleveland (English) land of cliffs.

Clicerio (Greek) sweet.

Cliff (English) a short form of Clifford, Clifton.

Clifford (English) cliff at the river crossing.

Clifton (English) cliff town.

Climaco, Clímaco (Greek) he who climbs the ladder.

Clímene (Greek) famous, celebrated.

Clint (English) a short form of Clinton.

Clinton (English) hill town.

Clio (Greek) one who celebrates.

Clitarco (Greek) wing of the army.

Clive (English) a form of Cliff.

Clodio (German) glorious.

Clodoaldo (Teutonic) illustrious captain.

Clodomiro (Germanic) he of illustrious fame.

Clodoveo (Spanish) famous warrior.

Clodulfo (Germanic) glory.

Clorindo (Greek) he who is like the grass.

Clotario (Gothic) a form of Lotario.

Clove (Spanish) a nail.

Clovis (German) famous soldier. **Cluny** (Irish) meadow.

Clyde (Welsh) warm. (Scottish) Geography: a river in Scotland.

Coady (English) a form of Cody.

Coatl (Nahuatl) snake.

Cobi, Coby **(Hebrew) familiar forms of Jacob.**

Coburn (English) meeting of streams.

Cochise (Apache) hardwood. History: a famous Chiricahua Apache leader.

Coco GB (French) a familiar form of Jacques.

Codey (English) a form of Cody.

Codi BG (English) a form of Cody.

Codie BG (English) a form of Cody.

Cody BG (English) cushion. History: William "Buffalo Bill" Cody was an American frontier scout who toured America and Europe with his Wild West show. **Coffie** (Ewe) born on Friday.

Cohen (Hebrew) priest.

Coique, Cuiycui (Quechua) silver.

Coiquiyoc (Quechua) he who is rich with silver.

Cola (Italian) a familiar form of Nicholas, Nicola.

Colar (French) a form of Nicholas.

Colbert (English) famous seafarer.

Colbey (English) a form of Colby.

Colby BG (English) dark; dark haired.

Cole (Latin) cabbage farmer. (English) a short form of Colbert, Coleman. (Greek) a short form of Nicholas.

Coleman (Latin) cabbage farmer. (English) coal miner.

Colen, Colyn (Greek, Irish) forms of Colin.

Coley (Greek, Latin, English) a familiar form of Cole. (English) a form of Colley.

Colin (Irish) young cub. (Greek) a short form of Nicholas.

Colla, Culla (Quechua) eminent, excellent.

Collacapac, Collatupac, Cullacapac, Cullatupac (Quechua) eminent and kind-hearted lord.

Collana, Cullana (Quechua) the best.

Collen (Scottish) a form of Collin.

Colley (English) black haired; swarthy.

Collier (English) miner.

Collin (Scottish) a form of Colin, Collins.

Collins (Greek) son of Colin. (Irish) holly.

Colman (Latin, English) a form of Coleman.

Colombino (Latin) dove.

Colon (Latin) he has the beauty of a dove.

Colón (Spanish) a form of Colon.

Colson (Greek, English) son of Nicholas.

Colt (English) young horse; frisky. A short form of Colbert, Colter, Colton.

Coltan, Colten, Coltin, Coltyn (English) forms of Colton.

Colter (English) herd of colts.

Colton ☆ (English) coal town.

Columba 🆖 (Latin) dove.

Columbo (Latin) a form of Columba.

Colwyn (Welsh) Geography: a river in Wales.

Coman (Arabic) noble. (Irish) bent.

Coñalef (Mapuche) rapid; agile.

Conall (Irish) high, mighty.

Conan (Irish) praised; exalted. (Scottish) wise.

Conary (Irish) a form of Conan.

Concordio (Latin) harmony; union.

Condel (Celtic) intrepid.

Congal (Celtic) tall.

Coni (Quechua) warm.

Coniraya, Cuñiraya (Quechua) heat from the sun.

Conlan (Irish) hero.

Conley (Irish) a form of Conlan.

Connar (Irish) a form of Connor.

Connell (Irish) a form of Conall.

Conner 🆖 (Irish) a form of Connor.

Connie 🆖 (English, Irish) a familiar form of Conan, Conrad, Constantine, Conway.

Connor ☆ 🆖 (Scottish) wise. (Irish) a form of Conan.

Cono (Mapuche) ringdove.

Conón (Greek) dust.

Conor (Irish) a form of Connor.

Conrad (German) brave counselor.

Conrado (Spanish) a form of Conrad.

Conroy (Irish) wise.
Conroi, Conry, Roy

Constable (Latin) established

Constancio (Latin) the perseverant one.

Constant (Latin) a short form of Constantine.

Constantine (Latin) firm, constant. History: Constantine the Great was the Roman emperor who adopted the Christian faith **Constantino** (Latin) a form of Constantine.

Consuelo (Spanish) consolation.

Contardo (Teutonic) he who is daring and valiant.

Conun-Huenu (Mapuche) entrance to the sky; elevated hill.

Conway (Irish) hound of the plain.

Cook (English) cook.

Cooper ☆

🆖 **(English) barrel maker.** Copres **(Greek) gentile from Atenas.**

Corban, Corben (Latin) forms of Corbin.

Corbett (Latin) raven.

Corbin 🆖 (Latin) raven.

Corbiniano (Latin) raven, crow.

Corby (Latin) a familiar form of Corbett, Corbin.

Corcoran (Irish) ruddy.

Cord (French) a short form of Cordell, Cordero.

Cordarius (Spanish) a form of Cordero.

Cordaro (Spanish) a form of Cordero.

Cordel (French) a form of Cordell.

Cordell (French) rope maker.

Cordero (Spanish) little lamb.

Córdulo (Latin) heart.

Corentino (Latin) he who helps.

Corey GB (Irish) hollow.

Cori GB (Irish) a form of Corey.

Corie GB (Irish) a form of Corey.

Coriguaman (Quechua) golden falcon.

Corin BG (Irish) a form of Corrin.

Coriñaui, Curiñaui (Quechua) he who has eyes that are the color gold.

Coripoma (Quechua) golden puma.

Corliss BG (English) cheerful; goodhearted.

Cormac (Irish) raven's son. History: a third-century king of Ireland who was a great lawmaker.

Cornelius (Greek) cornel tree. (Latin) horn colored. **Cornell** (French) a form of Cornelius.

Cornwallis (English) from Cornwall.

Corona (Latin) crown.

Corpus (Latin) body.

Corradeo (Italian) bold.

Corrado (Italian) a form of Conrad.

Corrigan (Irish) spearman.

Corrin GB (Irish) spear carrier.

Corry (Latin) a form of Corey.

Cort (German) bold. (Scandinavian) short. (English) a short form of Courtney.

Cortez (Spanish) conqueror. History: Hernando Cortés was a Spanish conquistador who conquered Aztec Mexico.

Cortland (English) a form of Courtland.

Cortney GB (English) a form of Courtney.

Corwin (English) heart's companion; heart's delight.

Cory BG (Latin) a form of Corey. (French) a familiar form of Cornell. (Greek) a short form of Corydon.

Corydon (Greek) helmet, crest.

Cosgrove (Irish) victor, champion.

Cósima (Greek) gifted; adorned.

Cosimus (Italian) a form of Cosme.

Cosino (Greek) name of a Greek family.

Cosme (Greek) a form of Cosmo.

Cosmo (Greek) orderly; harmonious; universe.

Cosnoaldo (German) daring ruler.

Costa (Greek) a short form of Constantine.

Cótido (Latin) every day.

Coty (French) slope, hillside.

Coulter (English) a form of Colter.

Courtland (English) court's land.

Courtney GB (English) court.

Cowan (Irish) hillside hollow.

Coy (English) woods.

Coyahue (Mapuche) meeting place for speaking and debating.

Coyle (Irish) leader in battle.

Coyne (French) modest.

Coyotl (Nahuatl) coyote.

Craddock (Welsh) love.

Craig (Irish, Scottish) crag; steep rock.

Cramer (English) full.

Crandall (English) crane's valley.

Cranc (English) crane.

Cranston (English) crane's town.

Cratón (Greek) he who rules.

Crawford (English) ford where crows fly.

Creed (Latin) belief.

Creighton (English) town near the rocks. (Welsh) a form of Crichton.

Crepin (French) a form of Crispin.

Crescencio (Latin) he who constantly increases his virtue.

Crescente (Latin) growing.

Cretien (French) Christian.

Crevan (Irish) fox.
Creven, Crevin, Crevon, Crevyn

Crew (English) people who work together on a job, a boat, or an airplane.

Crichton (Welsh) from the town on the hill.

Cripín, Cripo (Latin) forms of Crispin.

Crisantemo (Latin) the plant of the golden flowers.

Crisanto (Greek) golden flower.

Crisiant **(Welsh) crystal.**

Crisipo (Greek) golden horse.

Crisoforo (Greek) he who wears gold.

Crisóforo (Greek) he who gives advice that has value.

Crisógono (Greek) of golden roots; creator of richness.

Crisol (Latin) cross; light.

Crisologo (Greek) he who says words that are like gold.

Crisólogo (Greek) a form of Crisologo.

Crisostomo, Crisóstomo (Greek) mouth of gold.

Crisóteles (Greek) one who has golden aims.

Crispin (Latin) curly haired.

Crispín (Latin) a form of Crispin.

Cristian 🇧🇬 (Greek) a form of Christian.

Cristián (Latin) Christian, he who follows Christ.

Cristo (Greek) a form of Cristopher.

Cristobal (Greek) a form of Christopher.

Cristódulo (Greek) slave of Christ.

Cristofer (Greek) a form of Christopher.

Cristoforo (Italian) a form of Christopher.

Cristopher (Greek) a form of Christopher.

Cristovo (Greek) Christ's servant.

Crofton (Irish) town with cottages.

Cromacio (Greek) colored; adorned.

Cromwell (English) crooked spring, winding spring.

Crónidas (Greek) time.

Crosby (Scandinavian) shrine of the cross.

Crosley (English) meadow of the cross.

Crowther (English) fiddler.

Cruz (Portuguese, Spanish) cross.

Crystek (Polish) a form of Christian.

Crystian (Polish) a form of Christian.

Cuadrado (Latin) complete; square.

Cuadrato (Latin) square; medium height.

Cuahutémoc (Nahuatl) eagle that falls.

Cualli (Nahuatl) good.

Cuartio, Cuarto (Spanish) born fourth.

Cuasimodo (Latin) he who is childlike.

Cuauhtemoc (Nahuatl) descending eagle.

Cuba (Spanish) tub. Geography: the largest island country in the Caribbean.

Cuetlachtli (Nahuatl) wolf.

Cuetzpalli (Nahuatl) lizard

Cuirpuma (Quechua) golden puma.

Cuixtli (Nahuatl) kite.

Cullan (Irish) a form of Cullen.

Cullen (Irish) handsome.

Culley (Irish) woods.

Culmacio (Latin) elevated; important.

Culver (English) dove.

Cuminao (Mapuche) crimson glow.

Cumya (Quechua) thunder.

Cunac (Quechua) counselor.

Cuñi (Quechua) warm.

Cunibaldo (Greek) of noble birth.

Cuniberto (Teutonic) he who stands apart from the other noble gentlemen.

Cunningham (Irish) village of the milk pail.

Cuntur (Quechua) condor.

Cunturcanqui, Cunturchaua (Quechua) he who has all the virtues of a condor.

Cunturi (Aymara) representative of the gods.

Cunturpoma, Cunturpuma (Quechua) powerful as the puma and the condor.

Cunturuari (Quechua) untamable and savage like the vicuna and the condor.

Cunturumi (Quechua) strong as the stone and the condor.

Curamil (Mapuche) brilliant stone of gold and silver.

Curi (Quechua) golden.

Curiguaman (Quechua) golden falcon.

Curileo (Mapuche) black river.

Curiman (Mapuche) black condor.

Curipan (Mapuche) stinging nettle.

Curran 🅱🅶 (Irish) hero.

Currito (Spanish) a form of Curtis.

Curro (Spanish) a form of Curtis.

Curry (Irish) a familiar form of Curran.

Curt (Latin) a short form of Courtney, Curtis. **Curtis** (Latin) enclosure. (French) courteous.

Curtiss (Latin, French) a form of Curtis.

Cusi (Quechua) prosperous man.

Cusiguaman (Quechua) happy falcon.

Cusiguaypa (Quechua) happy rooster.

Cusiñaui (Quechua) smiling, with happy eyes.

Cusipoma, Cusipuma (Quechua) happy puma.

Cusirimachi (Qucchua) he who fills us with happy words.

Cusiyupanqui (Quechua) honored and fortunate.

Custodio (Latin) guardian spirit.

Cutberto (German) famous for knowledge.

Cuthbert (English) brilliant.

Cutler (English) knife maker.

Cutmano (Anglo-Saxon) the man who is famous.

Cutter (English) tailor.

Cuycusi (Quechua) he who moves happily.

Cuyquiyuc (Quechua) he who is rich with silver.

Cuyuc (Quechua) he who is restless.

Cuyuchi (Quechua) he who makes us move.

Cy (Persian) a short form of Cyrus.

Cyle (Irish) a form of Kyle.

Cynan (Welsh) chief.

Cyprian (Latin) from the island of Cyprus.

Cyrano (Greek) from Cyrene, an ancient city in North Africa. Literature: *Cyrano de Bergerac* is a play by Edmond Rostand about a great guardsman and poet whose large nose prevented him from pursuing the woman he loved.

Cyril (Greek) lordly.

Cyrus (Persian) sun. Historial: Cyrus the Great was a king in ancient Persia

D

D Andre (American) a form of Deandre.

D'andre (American) a form of Dandre, Deandre.

D'angelo (American) a form of Dangelo, Deangelo.

D'ante (American) a form of Dante.

D'anthony (American) a form of Deanthony.

D'arcy (American, French) a form of Darcy.

D'juan, Djuan (American) forms of Dajuan, Dejuan.

D'marco (American) a form of Damarco, Demarco.

D'marcus (American) a form of Damarcus, Demarcus.

D'quan (American) a form of Daquan, Dequan.

D'vonte (American) a form of Davonte, Devonte.

Da Quan, Da'quan (American) forms of Daquan.

Da'shawn (American) a form of Dashawn.

Da'ûd (Arabic) a form of David.

Da'von (American) a form of Davon.

Dabeet (Indian) warrior.

Dabi (Basque) a form of David.

Dabir (Arabic) tutor.

Dacey GB (Latin) from Dacia, an area now in Romania. (Irish) southerner.

Dacoda (Dakota) a form of Dakota.

Dacota, Dacotah (Dakota) forms of Dakota.

Dada (Yoruba) curly haired.

Dadas (Greek) torch.

Dadio (Greek) a form of Dada.

Daegan (Irish) black haired.

Daegel (English) from Daegel, England.

Daelen (English) a form of Dale.

Daemon (Greek) a form of Damian. (Greek, Latin) a form of Damon.

Daequan (American) a form of Daquan.

Daeshawn (American) a combination of the prefix Da + Shawn.

Daevon (American) a form of Davon.

Dafydd (Welsh) a form of David.

Dag (Scandinavian) day; bright.

Dagan (Hebrew) corn; grain.

Dagoberto (Germanic) he who shines like the sun.

Dagwood (English) shining forest.

Dai GB (Japanese) big.
Dae, Dai, Daie, Daye

Daimian (Greek) a form of Damian.

Daimon (Greek, Latin) a form of Damon.

Dain (Scandinavian) a form of Dana. (English) a form of Dane.

Daiquan (American) a form of Daquan.

Daivon (American) a form of Davon.

Dajon (American) a form of Dajuan.

Dajuan (American) a combination of the prefix Da + Juan.

Dakarai (Shona) happy.

Dakari (Shona) a form of Dakarai.

Dakoda BG (Dakota) a form of Dakota.

Dakota GB (Dakota) friend; partner; tribal name.

Dakotah BG (Dakota) a form of Dakota.

Daksh (Hindi) efficient.

Dalal (Sanskrit) broker.

Dalan, Dalen, Dalon, Dalyn (English) forms of Dale.

Dalbert (English) bright, shining.

Dale BG (English) dale, valley.

Daley (Irish) assembly. (English) a familiar form of Dale.

Dalin (English) a form of Dallin.

Dallan, Dallen (English) forms of Dalan, Dallin.

Dallas 🅱🅶 (Scottish) valley of the water; resting place. Geography: a town in Scotland; a city in Texas.

Dallin, Dallyn (English) pride's people.

Dallis 🅱🅶 (Scottish) a form of Dallas.

Dallon (English) a form of Dallan, Dalston.

Dalmacio (Latin) from Dalmatia.

Dalman (Australian) bountiful place.

Dalmazio (Italian) a form of Dalmacio.

Dalmiro (Germanic) the illustrious one.

Dalphin (French) dolphin.

Dalston (English) Daegel's place.

Dalton 🅱🅶 (English) town in the valley.

Dalvin (English) a form of Delvin.

Dalziel (Scottish) small field.

Damain (Greek) a form of Damian.

Daman, Damen, Damin (Greek, Latin) forms of Damon.

Damani (Greek) a form of Damian.

Damar (American) a short form of Damarcus, Damario.

Damarco (American) a form of Damarcus. (Italian) a form of Demarco.

Damarcus (American) a combination of the prefix Da + Marcus. A form of Demarcus.

Damario (Greek) gentle. (American) a combination of the prefix Da + Mario.

Damarius (Greek, American) a form of Damario.

Damarkus (American) a form of Damarcus.

Damaso, Dámaso (Greek) skillful horse-breaker.

Damein (Greek) a form of Damian.

Dameion, Dameon (Greek) forms of Damian.

Damek (Slavic) a form of Adam.

Dametri (Greek) a form of Dametrius, Demetrius.

Dametrius (Greek) a form of Demetrius.

Damian (Greek) tamer; soother.

Damien, Damion (Greek) forms of Damian. Religion: Father Damien ministered to the leper colony on the Hawaiian island Molokai.

Damocles, Damócles (Greek) gives glory to his village.

Damodar (Indian) another name for the Hindu god Ganapati.

Damon (Greek) constant, loyal. (Latin) spirit, demon.

Damond, Damone, Damonta (Greek, Latin) forms of Damon.

Damonte (Greek, Latin) a form of Damon.

Dan (Vietnamese) yes. (Hebrew) a short form of Daniel.

Dana 🅶🅱 (Scandinavian) from Denmark.

Dandin (Hindi) holy man.

Dandre (French) a combination of the prefix De + Andre.

Dandré (French) a form of Dandre.

Dane (English) from Denmark. **Danek** (Polish) a form of Daniel.

Danforth (English) a form of Daniel.

Dang (Italian) a short form of Deangelo.

Dangelo (Italian) a form of Deangelo.

Daniachew (Ethiopian) you will be judged.

Danial (Hebrew) a form of Daniel.

Danick, Danik, Dannick (Slavic) familiar forms of Daniel.

Daniel ⭐

BG (Hebrew) God is my judge. Bible: a Hebrew prophet. **Danilo** (Slavic) a form of Daniel.

Danior (Gypsy) born with teeth.

Danish (English) from Denmark.

Danladi (Hausa) born on Sunday.

Dannie, Danny, Dany (Hebrew) familiar forms of Daniel.

Danniel (Hebrew) a form of Daniel.

Danno (Japanese) gathering in the meadow. (Hebrew) a familiar form of Daniel.

Dannon (American) a form of Danno.

Dano (Czech) a form of Daniel.

Danso (Ghanaian) trustworthy; reliable.

Dantae (Latin) a form of Dante.

Dante, Danté (Latin) lasting, enduring.

Dantel (Latin) a form of Dante.

Danton (American) a form of Deanthony.

Dantrell (American) a combination of Dante + Darell.

Danyel GB (Hebrew) a form of Daniel.

Danzel (Cornish) a form of Denzell.

Daoud (Arabic) a form of Daniel, David.

Daquan (American) a combination of the prefix Da + Quan.

Daquane (American) a form of Daquan.

Daquarius (American) a form of Daquan.

Daquon (American) a form of Daquan.

Dar (Hebrew) pearl.

Dara GB (Cambodian) stars.

Daran, Darin, Darrin, Darron, Darryn (Irish, English) forms of Darren.

Darby GB (Irish) free. (English) deer park.

Darcy GB (Irish) dark. (French) from Arcy, France.

Dardo (Greek) astute and skillful.

Dareh (Persian) wealthy.

Darek, Darick, Darik, Darrick (German) forms of Derek.

Darell, Darrel (English) forms of Darrell.

Daren (Hausa) born at night. (Irish, English) a form of Darren.

Dareon (Irish, English) a form of Darren.

Darian BG (Irish, English) a form of Darren.

Dariel BG (French) a form of Darrell.

Darien BG (Irish, English) a form of Darren.

Dario (Spanish) affluent.

Darío (Spanish) a form of Dario.

Darion BG (Irish, English) a form of Darren.

Darious, Darrious, Darrius (Greek) forms of Darius.

Daris, Darris (Greek) short forms of Darius.

Darius (Greek) wealthy.

Darkon (English) dark.

Darnel (English) a form of Darnell.

Darnell (English) hidden place.

Darnelle BG (English) a form of Darnell.

Daron BG (Irish, English) a form of Darren.

Darpan (Indian) mirror.

Darrell (French) darling, beloved; grove of oak trees.

Darren (Irish) great. (English) small; rocky hill.

Darrian BG (Irish, English) a form of Darren.

Darrien 🅱🅶 (Irish, English) a form of Darren.

Darrion 🅱🅶 (Irish, English) a form of Darren.

Darryl, Daryle (French) forms of Darrell.

Darshan (Sanskrit) philosophy; seeing clearly.

Darton (English) deer town.

Darvell (English) eagle town.

Darvin (English) a form of Darwin.

Darwin (English) dear friend. History: Charles Darwin was the British naturalist who established the theory of evolution.

Darwishi (Egyptian) saint.

Daryl 🅱🅶 (French) a form of Darrell.

Daryn 🅱🅶 (Irish, English) a form of Darren.

Dasan (Pomo) leader of the bird clan.

Dasean, Dashaun, Dashon (American) forms of Dashawn, Deshawn.

Dasharath (Indian) father of the Hindu god Rama.

Dasharathi (Indian) another name for the Hindu god Rama.

Dashawn 🅱🅶 (American) a combination of the prefix Da + Shawn.

Dashiell (English) a form of the French surname de Cheil.

Dasio (Latin) baron.

Dat (Vietnamese) accomplished.

Dativo (Latin) term from Roman law, applied to educators.

Dato (Latin) a form of Donato.

Dauid (Swahili) a form of David.

Daulton (English) a form of Dalton.

Daunte (Spanish) a form of Dante.

Davante, Davanté (American) forms of Davonte.

Davaris (American) a combination of Dave + Darius.

Davaughn (American) a combination of the prefix Da + Vaughn.

Dave (Hebrew) a short form of David, Davis.

Daven (Hebrew) a form of David. (Scandinavian) a form of Davin.

Daveon (American) a form of Davin.

Davet (French) loved.

Davey, Davy **(Hebrew) familiar forms of David.**

Davian, Davion (American) forms of Davin.

David ☆

🅱🅶 (Hebrew) beloved. Bible: the second king of Israel. **David Alexander** (American) a combination of David + Alexander.

Davidia (Hebrew) a form of David.

Davidson (Welsh) a form of Davis.

Davin (Scandinavian) brilliant Finn.

Davis (Welsh) son of David.

Davon 🅱🅶 (American) a form of Davin.

Davonta (American) a form of Davonte.

Davontae, Davontay, Davonté (American) forms of Davonte.

Davonte (American) a combination of Davon + the suffix Te.

Dawan (American) a form of Dajuan, Davin.

Dawid (Polish) a form of David.

Dawit (Ethiopian) a form of David.

Dawson (English) son of David.

Dawûd (Arabic) a form of David.

Dax (French, English) water.

Daxton (French) from the town of Dax.

Day (English) a form of Daniel.

Daylan 🄱🄶 (American) a form of Dalan, Dillon.

Daylen, Daylon (American) forms of Dalan, Dillon.

Daylin 🄱🄶 (American) a form of Dalan, Dillon.

Daymian (Greek) a form of Damian.

Daymon (Greek, Latin) a form of Damon.

Daymond (Greek, Latin) a form of Damon.

Dayne (Scandinavian) a form of Dane.

Dayquan (American) a form of Daquan.

Dayshawn (American) a form of Dashawn.

Dayton 🄱🄶 (English) day town; bright, sunny town.

Daytona 🄱🄶 (English) a form of Dayton.

Dayvon (American) a form of Davin.

De (Chinese) virtuous.

De Andre, Deandré, Déandre (American) forms of Deandre.

De Marcus, Démarcus (American) forms of Demarcus.

De Vante, Devanté, Dévante (American) forms of Devante.

Deacon (Greek) one who serves.
Deakin, Deicon, Deke, Deycon

Dean (French) leader. (English) valley.

Deandra 🄶🄱 (French) a form of Deandre.

Deandre (French) a combination of the prefix De + Andre.

Deangelo (Italian) a combination of the prefix De + Angelo.

Déangelo (American) a form of Deangelo.

Deante, Deanté (Latin) forms of Dante, Deonte.

Deanthony (Italian) a combination of the prefix De + Anthony.

Déanthony (American) a form of Deanthony.

Dearborn (English) deer brook.

Deaundre (French) a form of Deandre.

Deaven (Hindi, Irish) a form of Deven.

Debashis (Indian) benediction of God.

Decarlos (Spanish) a combination of the prefix De + Carlos.

Decha (Tai) strong.

Decimus (Latin) tenth.

Decio (Latin) tenth.

Declan (Irish) man of prayer. Religion: Saint Declan was a fifth-century Irish bishop.

Decoroso (Latin) he is practical.

Dédalo (Greek) industrious and skillful artisan.

Dedric (German) a form of Dedrick.

Dedrick (German) ruler of the people. **Deems** (English) judge's child.

Deenabandhu (Indian) friend of the poor.

Deep (Indian) lamp.

Deepak (Hindi) a form of Dipak.

Deepan (Indian) lighting up.

Deepankar, Deepesh (Indian) lord of light.

Deependu, Deeptendu (Indian) bright moon.

Deepit (Indian) lighted.

Deeptanshu (Indian) sun.

Deeptiman, Deeptimoy (Indian) lustrous.

Deicola, Deícola (Latin) he who cultivates a relationship with God.

Deion (Greek) a form of Deon, Dion.

Deiondre (American) a form of Deandre.

Deionte (American) a form of Deontae.

Dejon 🄱🄶 (American) a form of Dejuan.

Déjon (American) a form of Dejuan.

Dejuan (American) a combination of the prefix De + Juan.

Dekel (Hebrew, Arabic) palm tree, date tree.

Dekota (Dakota) a form of Dakota.

Del (English) a short form of Delbert, Delvin, Delwin.

Delaiá (Hebrew) God has liberated me.

Delaney GB (Irish) descendant of the challenger.

Delano (French) nut tree. (Irish) dark.

Delbert (English) bright as day. **Delfín** (Greek) the playful one with a graceful and beautiful form.

Delfino (Latin) dolphin.

Délì (Chinese) virtuous.

Dell (English) small valley. A short form of Udell.

Delling (Scandinavian) scintillating.

Delmar BG (Latin) sea.

Delmon (French) mountain.

Delon (American) a form of Dillon.

Delroy (French) belonging to the king. **Delshawn** (American) a combination of Del + Shawn.

Delsin (Native American) he is so.

Delton (English) a form of Dalton.

Delvin (English) proud friend; friend from the valley.

Delvon (English) a form of Delvin.

Delvonte (American) a form of Delvon.

Delwin (English) a form of Delvin.

Deman (Dutch) man.

Demarco (Italian) a combination of the prefix De + Marco.

Demarcus (American) a combination of the prefix De + Marcus.

Demarea (Italian) a form of Demario.

Demario (Italian) a combination of the prefix De + Mario.

Demarion (Italian) a form of Demario.

Demarious (Italian) a form of Demario.

Demarius (American) a combination of the prefix De + Marius.

Demarko (Italian) a form of Demarco.

Demarkus (Italian, American) a form of Demarco, Demarcus.

Demarquis (American) a combination of the prefix De + Marquis.

Dembe (Luganda) peaceful.

Demetre, Demetri (Greek) short forms of Demetrius.

Demetric, Demetrick (Greek) forms of Demetrius.

Demetrice (Greek) a form of Demetrius.

Demetrio (Greek) a form of Demetrius.

Demetrios (Greek) a form of Demetrius.

Demetrious (Greek) a form of Demetrius.

Demetris (Greek) a short form of Demetrius.

Demetrius (Greek) lover of the earth. Mythology: a follower of Demeter, the goddess of the harvest.

Demetruis (Greek) a form of Demetrius.

Demian (Greek) he who emerged from the village.

Demián (Spanish) a form of Damian.

Demichael (American) a combination of the prefix De + Michael.

Demissie (Ethiopian) destructor.

Demitri (Greek) a short form of Demetrius.

Demitrius (Greek) a form of Demetrius.

Demócrito (Greek) arbiter of the village.

Demófilo (Greek) friend of the community.

Demon (Greek) demon.

Demond (Irish) a short form of Desmond.

Demondre (American) a form of Demond.

Demont (French) mountain.

Demonta (American) a form of Demont.

Demontae, Demonte, Demonté (American) forms of Demont.

Demontre (American) a form of Demont.

Demorris (American) a combination of the prefix De + Morris.

Demos (Greek) people.

Demóstenes (Greek) the strength of the village.

Demothi (Native American) talks while walking.

Dempsey (Irish) proud.

Dempster (English) one who judges.

Denham (English) village in the valley.
Denhem

Denholm (Scottish) Geography: a town in Scotland.

Denis 🅱🅶 (Greek) a form of Dennis.

Denís (Greek) a form of Denis.

Deniz, Dennys (Greek) forms of Dennis.

Denley (English) meadow; valley.

Denman (English) man from the valley.

Dennis (Greek) Mythology: a follower of Dionysus, the god of wine.

Dennison (English) son of Dennis. **Denny** (Greek) a familiar form of Dennis.

Denton (English) happy home.

Denver 🅱🅶 (English) green valley. Geography: the capital of Colorado.

Denzel, Denzil (Cornish) forms of Denzell.

Denzell (Cornish) Geography: a location in Cornwall, England.

Deocaro (Latin) loved by God.

Deodato (Latin) he who serves God.

Deon 🅱🅶 (Greek) a form of Dennis. **Deondra** 🅶🅱 (French) a form of Deandre.

Deondre, Deondré (French) forms of Deandre.

Deonta, Deontá (American) forms of Deontae.

Deontae (American) a combination of the prefix De + Dontae.

Deontay, Deonte, Deonté, Déonte (American) forms of Deontae.

Deontrae, Deontray, Deontre (American) forms of Deontae.

Dequan (American) a combination of the prefix De + Quan.

Déquan (American) a form of Dequan.

Dequante (American) a form of Dequan.

Dequavius (American) a form of Dequan.

Dereck, Deric, Derick, Derik, Derreck, Derrek, Derric, Derrick, Derrik, Deryck, Deryk (German) forms of Derek.

Derek (German) a short form of Theodoric.

Derion, Derrian, Derrion (Irish, English) forms of Darren.

Derius, Derrius (Greek) forms of Darius.

Dermot (Irish) free from envy. (English) free. (Hebrew) a short form of Jeremiah.

Deron (Hebrew) bird; freedom. (American) a combination of the prefix De + Ron.

Deror (Hebrew) lover of freedom.

Derrell (French) a form of Darrell.

Derren (Irish, English) a form of Darren.

Derron (Irish, English) a form of Darren. (Hebrew, American) a form of Deron.

Derry BG (Irish) redhead. Geography: a city in Northern Ireland.

Derryl (French) a form of Darryl.

Derward (English) deer keeper.

Derwin (English) a form of Darwin.

Deseado (Spanish) a form of Desiderio.

Desean (American) a combination of the prefix De + Sean.

Désean (American) a form of Desean.

Deshane (American) a combination of the prefix De + Shane.

Deshaun (American) a combination of the prefix De + Shaun.

Déshaun (American) a form of Deshaun.

Deshawn BG (American) a combination of the prefix De + Shawn.

Déshawn (American) a form of Deshawn.

Deshea (American) a combination of the prefix De + Shea.

Déshì (Chinese) virtuous.

Deshon (American) a form of Deshawn.

Deshun (American) a form of Deshon.

Desi BG (Latin) desiring. (Irish) a short form of Desmond.

Desiderato (Spanish) a form of Desiderio.

Desiderio (Spanish) desired.

Desierto (Latin) wild.

Desire (French) wish.

Desmon (Irish) a form of Desmond.

Desmond (Irish) from south Munster.

Desta (Ethiopian) happiness.

Destin BG (French) destiny, fate.

Destry (American) a form of Destin.

Detrick (German) a form of Dedrick.

Deuce (Latin) two; devil.

Deusdedit (Latin) God has given to him.

Dev Kumar (Indian) son of gods.

Devabrata (Indian) another name for Bhisma, a hero of the Indian epic poem *Mahabharata*.

Devadas (Indian) follower of God.

Devajyoti (Indian) brightness of the lord.

Devak (Indian) divine.

Devan BG (Irish) a form of Devin.

Devanta (American) a form of Devante.

Devante (American) a combination of Devan + the suffix Te.

Devaughn (American) a form of Devin.

Devaun (American) a form of Devaughn.

Devayne (American) a form of Dewayne.

Devdutta (Indian) king.

Deven (Hindi) for God. (Irish) a form of Devin.

Devendra (Indian) another name for the Hindu god Indra.

Deveon (American) a form of Devon.

Deverell (English) riverbank.

Devesh, Deveshwar (Indian) other names for the Hindu god Shiva.

Devin BG (Irish) poet.

Devine (Latin) divine. (Irish) ox.

Devion (American) a form of Devon.

Devlin (Irish) brave, fierce.

Devlyn (Irish) a form of Devlin.

Devon BG (American) a form of Davon. (Irish) a form of Devin.

Dévon, Devonne (American) forms of Davon. (Irish) forms of Devin.

Devone (Irish, American) a form of Devon.

Devonta (American) a combination of Devon + the suffix Ta.

Devontá, Dévonta (American) forms of Devonta.

Devontae, Devontay, Devonté (American) forms of Devonte.

Devonte (American) a combination of Devon + the suffix Te.

Devoto (Latin) dedicated.

Devyn BG (Irish) a form of Devin.

Dewan (American) a form of Dejuan, Dewayne.

Dewayne (American) a combination of the prefix De + Wayne. (Irish) a form of Dwayne.

Dewei (Chinese) highly virtuous.

Dewey (Welsh) prized.

DeWitt (Flemish) blond.

Dexter (Latin) dexterous, adroit. (English) fabric dyer.

Deyonte (American) a form of Deontae.

Dezmon (Irish) a form of Desmond.

Dezmond (Irish) a form of Desmond.
Dezmand, Dezmund

Día (West African) champion.

Diadelfo (Greek) brother of Zeus.

Diamante, Diamonte (Spanish) forms of Diamond.

Diamond GB (English) brilliant gem; bright guardian.

Diandre (French) a form of Deandre.

Diante, Dianté (American) forms of Deontae.

Dick (German) a short form of Frederick, Richard.

Dickran (Armenian) History: an ancient Armenian king.

Dickson **(English) son of Dick.**

Dictino (Greek) goddess of the ocean.

Dídac (Catalan) a form of Diego.

Diderot (Spanish) a form of Desiderio.

Didi (Hebrew) a familiar form of Jedidiah, Yedidya.

Didier (French) desired, longed for.

Didimo, Dídimo (Greek) twin brother.

Diedrich **(German) a form of Dedrick, Dietrich.**

Diego (Spanish) a form of Jacob, James.

Dietbald (German) a form of Theobald.

Dieter (German) army of the people.

Dietrich (German) a form of Dedrick.

Digby (Irish) ditch town; dike town.

Digno (Latin) worthy of the best.

Diji (Nigerian) farmer.

Dijon (French) Geography: a city in France. (American) a form of Dejon.

Dilan, Dillen, Dillyn (Irish) forms of Dillon.

Dillan BG (Irish) a form of Dillon.

Dillian BG (Irish) a form of Dillon.

Dillion (Irish) a form of Dillon.

Dillon (Irish) loyal, faithful.

Dilwyn (Welsh) shady place.

Dima (Russian) a familiar form of Vladimir.

Dimano (Latin) to lose.

Dimas (Greek) loyal comrade.

Dimitri (Russian) a short form of Demetrius.

Dimitrios (Greek) a form of Demetrius.

Dimitrius (Greek) a form of Demetrius.

Dingbang (Chinese) protector of the country.

Dinh (Vietnamese) calm, peaceful.

Dinís (Greek) devoted to Dionysus.

Dino (German) little sword. (Italian) a form of Dean.

Dinos (Greek) a familiar form of Constantine, Konstantin.

Dinsmore (Irish) fortified hill.

Dioclecio (Greek) a form of Diocles.

Diocles (Greek) glory of God.

Diogenes (Greek) honest. History: an ancient philosopher who searched with a lantern in daylight for an honest man.

Diógenes (Greek) a form of Diogenes.

Diogo (Galician) a form of Diego.

Diomedes (Greek) thoughts of God.

Diómedes (Greek) he who trusts in God's protection.

Dion (Greek) a short form of Dennis, Dionysus.

Dión (Greek) a form of Dion.

Diondre (French) a form of Deandre.

Dione (American) a form of Dion.

Dionicio (Spanish) a form of Dionysus.

Dionne GB (American) a form of Dion.

Dionta (American) a form of Deontae.

Diontae, Diontay, Dionte, Dionté (American) forms of Deontae.

Dionysus (Greek) celebration. Mythology: the god of wine.

Dioscórides (Greek) relative of Dioscoro.

Dioscoro, Dióscoro (Latin) he who is of the Lord.

Dipak (Hindi) little lamp. Religion: another name for the Hindu god Kama.

Diquan (American) a combination of the prefix Di + Quan.

Dirk (German) a short form of Derek, Theodoric.

Disibodo (German) bold wise one.

Dixon (English) son of Dick.

Dmitri, Dmitry (Russian) forms of Dimitri.

Doane (English) low, rolling hills.

Dob (English) a familiar form of Robert.

Dobry (Polish) good.

Doherty (Irish) harmful.

Dolan (Irish) dark haired.

Dolf, Dolph (German) short forms of Adolf, Adolph, Rudolf, Rudolph.

Dom (Latin) a short form of Dominic.

Domanic (Latin) a form of Dominic.

Doménech (Catalan) a form of Domingo.

Domenic, Domenick (Latin) forms of Dominic.

Domenico (Italian) a form of Dominic.

Dominador (Latin) to want to be loved.

Domingo (Spanish) born on Sunday.

Dominic ✶ (Latin) belonging to the Lord.

Dominick, Dominik (Latin) forms of Dominic.

Dominique GB (French) a form of Dominic.

Domokos (Hungarian) a form of Dominic.

Domonic, Domonick (Latin) forms of Dominic.

Don (Scottish) a short form of Donald.

Donahue (Irish) dark warrior.

Donal (Irish) a form of Donald.

Donald (Scottish) world leader; proud ruler.

Donaldo (Spanish) a form of Donald.

Donardo (Celtic) a form of Donald.

Donatien (French) gift.

Donato (Italian) gift.

Donavan, Donavin, Donavon (Irish) forms of Donovan.

Dondre, Dondré (American) forms of Deandre.

Donell (Irish) a form **Dong** (Vietnamese) easterner.

Donivan (Irish) a form of Donovan.

Donkor (Akan) humble.

Donnell (Irish) brave; dark.

Donnelly (Irish) a form of Donnell.

Donnie, Donny (Irish) familiar forms of Donald.

Donovan (Irish) dark warrior.

Donovon (Irish) a form of Donovan.

Donta (American) a form of Dante.

Dontae, Dontay, Donte, Donté (Latin) forms of Dante.

Dontarious, Dontarius (American) forms of Dontae.

Dontavious, Dontavius (American) forms of Dontae.

Dontavis (American) a form of Dontae.

Dontez (American) a form of Dontae.

Dontray, Dontre (American) forms of Dontrell.

Dontrell (American) a form of Dantrell.

Donyell (Irish) a form of Donnell.
Donyel

Donzell (Cornish) a form of Denzell.

Dooley (Irish) dark hero.

Dor (Hebrew) generation.

Doran (Greek, Hebrew) gift. (Irish) stranger; exile.

Dorcas (Hebrew) gazelle.

Dorian 🅱🅶 (Greek) from Doris, Greece.

Dorien, Dorion, Dorrian (Greek) forms of Dorian.

Doroteo (Greek) gift of God.

Dorrell (Scottish) king's doorkeeper. **Dosio** (Latin) rich.

Dositeo (Greek) God's possession.

Dotan (Hebrew) law.

Doug (Scottish) a short form of Dougal, Douglas.

Dougal (Scottish) dark stranger. **Douglas** (Scottish) dark river, dark stream.

Douglass (Scottish) a form of Douglas.
Duglass

Dov (Yiddish) bear. (Hebrew) a familiar form of David.

Dovev (Hebrew) whisper.

Dovid (Hebrew, Yiddish) a form of Dov.

Dow (Irish) dark haired.

Doyle (Irish) a form of Dougal.

Drago (Italian) a form of Drake.

Drake (English) dragon; owner of the inn with the dragon trademark.

Draper (English) fabric maker.

Draven (American) a combination of the letter D + Raven.

Dre (American) a short form of Andre, Deandre.

Dreng (Norwegian) hired hand; brave.

Drequan (American) a combination of Drew + Quan.

Dréquan (American) a form of Drequan.

Dreshawn (American) a combination of Drew + Shawn.

Drevon (American) a form of Draven.

Drew BG (Welsh) wise. (English) a short form of Andrew.

Drey (American) a form of Dre.

Driscoll (Irish) interpreter.

Dru (English) a form of Drew.

Drue BG (English) a form of Drew.

Drummond (Scottish) druid's mountain.

Drury (French) loving. Geography: Drury Lane is a street in London's theater district.

Dryden (English) dry valley.

Duane (Irish) a form of Dwayne.

Duardo (Spanish) prosperous guardian.

Duardos (Galician) a form of Eduardo.

Duarte (Portuguese) rich guard.
Duart

Dubham (Irish) black.

Dubric (English) dark ruler.

Duc (Vietnamese) moral.

Duce (Latin) leader, commander.

Dudd (English) a short form of Dudley.

Dudley (English) common field.

Duer (Scottish) heroic.

Duff (Scottish) dark.

Dugan (Irish) dark.

Duilio (Latin) ready to fight.

Dujuan (American) a form of Dajuan, Dejuan.

Duke (French) leader; duke.

Dukker (Gypsy) fortuneteller.
Duker

Dulani (Nguni) cutting.

Dulcidio (Latin) sweet.

Dumaka (Ibo) helping hand.

Duman (Turkish) misty, smoky.

Duncan (Scottish) brown warrior. Literature: King Duncan was Macbeth's victim in Shakespeare's play *Macbeth*.

Dunham (Scottish) brown.

Dunixi (Basque) a form of Dionysus.

Dunley (English) hilly meadow.

Dunlop (Scottish) muddy hill.

Dunmore (Scottish) fortress on the hill.

Dunn (Scottish) a short form of Duncan.

Dunstan (English) brownstone fortress.

Dunstano (English) a form of Dunstan.

Dunton (English) hill town.

Dur (Hebrew) stacked up. (English) a short form of Durwin.

Duran (Latin) a form of Durant.

Durand (Latin) a form of Durant.

Durando (Latin) a form of Durand.

Durant (Latin) enduring.

Durell (Scottish, English) king's doorkeeper.

Durko (Czech) a form of George.

Duron (Hebrew, American) a form of Deron.

Durrell (Scottish, English) a form of Durell.

Durriken (Gypsy) fortuneteller.

Durril (Gypsy) gooseberry.

Durward (English) gatekeeper.

Durwin (English) a form of Darwin.

Dusan (Czech) lively, spirited. (Slavic) a form of Daniel.

Dushawn (American) a combination of the prefix Du + Shawn.

Dustan, Dusten, Duston, Dustyn (German, English) forms of Dustin.

Dustin BG (German) valiant fighter. (English) brown rock quarry.

Dusty BG (English) a familiar form of Dustin.

253

Dutch (Dutch) from the Netherlands; from Germany.

Duval (French) a combination of the prefix Du + Val.

Duy (Vietnamese) a form of Duc.

Dwan (American) a form of Dajuan. (Irish) a form of Dwayne.

Dwaun (American) a form of Dajuan.

Dwayne (Irish) dark.

Dwight (English) a form of DeWitt.

Dyami (Native American) soaring eagle.

Dyer (English) fabric dyer.

Dyke (English) dike; ditch. Dike

Dylan ☆

🅱️🅶 (Welsh) sea. Dylin, Dyllan, Dyllon,

Dylon (Welsh) forms of Dylan.

Dyonis (Greek) a form of Dionicio.

Dyre (Norwegian) dear heart.

Dyson (English) a short form of Dennison.

Dzigbode (Ghanaian) patience.

E

Ea (Irish) a form of Hugh.

Eabrizio (Italian) artisan.

Eabroni (Italian) blacksmith.

Eachan (Irish) horseman.

Eadberto (Teutonic) outstanding for his riches.

Eagan (Irish) very mighty.

Eamon, Eamonn (Irish) forms of Edmond, Edmund.

Ean (English) a form of Ian.

Earl (Irish) pledge. (English) nobleman.

Earnest (English) a form of Ernest.

Easton ☆ (English) eastern town.

Eaton (English) estate on the river.

Eb (Hebrew) a short form of Ebenezer.

Eben (Hebrew) rock.

Ebenezer (Hebrew) foundation stone. Literature: Ebenezer Scrooge is a miserly character in Charles Dickens's *A Christmas Carol.*

Eber (German) a short form of Eberhard.

Eberhard (German) courageous as a boar.

Ebner (English) a form of Abner.

Ebo (Fante) born on Tuesday.

Ebon (Hebrew) a form of Eben.

Ecio (Latin) possessor of great strength.

Eco (Greek) sound, resonance.

Ed (English) a short form of Edgar, Edsel, Edward.

Edan (Scottish) fire.

Edbert (English) wealthy; bright.

Edberto (Germanic) he whose blade makes him shine.

Edco (Greek) he who blows with force.

Eddie (English) a familiar form of Edgar, Edsel, Edward.

Eddy 🅱️🅶 (English) a familiar form of Edgar, Edsel, Edward.

Edel (German) noble.

Edelberto (German) a form of Edelbert.

Edelio (Greek) person who always remains young.

Edelmiro (Germanic) celebrated for the nobility that he represents.

Eden 🅶🅱️ (Hebrew) delightful. Bible: the garden that was first home to Adam and Eve.

Eder (Hebrew) flock.

Edgar (English) successful spearman. **Edgard** (English) a form of Edgar.

Edgardo (Spanish) a form of Edgar.

Edgerrin (American) a form of Edgar.

Edik (Slavic) a familiar form of Edward.

Edilio (Greek) he who is like a statue.

Edin (Hebrew) a form of Eden.

Edipo (Greek) he who has swollen feet.

Edison (English) son of Edward.

Edmond (English) a form of Edmund.

Edmund (English) prosperous protector.

Edmundo (Spanish) a form of Edmund.

Edo (Czech) a form of Edward.

Edoardo (Italian) a form of Edward.

Edorta (Basque) a form of Edward.

Edouard (French) a form of Edward.

Edric (English) prosperous ruler.

Edsel (English) rich man's house.

Edson (English) a short form of Edison.

Eduard (Spanish) a form of Edward.

Eduardo (Spanish) a form of Edward.

Edur (Basque) snow.

Edvar (Czech) a form of Eduardo.

Edward (English) prosperous guardian.

Edwardo (Italian) a form of Edward.

Edwin (English) prosperous friend.

Effiom (African) crocodile.

Efrain (Hebrew) fruitful.

Efraín (Hebrew) a form of Efrain.

Efrat (Hebrew) honored.

Efreín, Efrén (Spanish) forms of Efraín.

Efrem (Hebrew) a short form of Ephraim.

Efren (Hebrew) a form of Efrain, Ephraim.

Egan (Irish) ardent, fiery.

Egbert (English) bright sword.

Egecatl (Nahuatl) wind serpent.

Egerton (English) Edgar's town.

Egidio (Greek) he who carries the goatskin sword in battle.

Egil (Norwegian) awe inspiring.

Eginhard (German) power of the sword.

Egisto (Greek) raised on goat's milk.

Egon (German) formidable.

Egor (Russian) a form of George.

Ehren (German) honorable.

Eian, Eion (Irish) forms of Ean, Ian.

Eikki (Finnish) ever powerful.
Eiki

Einar (Scandinavian) individualist.

Eitan (Hebrew) a form of Ethan.

Ejau (Ateso) we have received.

Ekalavya (Indian) renowned for his devotion to his guru.

Ekambar (Indian) sky.

Ekanath (Indian) king.

Ekewaka (Hawaiian) a form of Edward.

Ekon (Nigerian) strong.

Ekram (Indian) honor.

Eladio (Greek) he who came from Greece.

Elam (Hebrew) highlands.

Elan (Hebrew) tree. (Native American) friendly.

Elbert (English) a form of Albert.

Elbio (Celtic) he who comes from the mountain.

Elchanan (Hebrew) a form of John.

Elden (English) a form of Alden, Aldous.

Elder (English) dweller near the elder trees.

Eldon (English) holy hill. A form of Elton.

Eldred (English) a form of Aldred.

Eldridge (English) a form of Aldrich.

Eldwin (English) a form of Aldwin.

Eleazar (Hebrew) God has helped.

Eleazaro (Hebrew) a form of Eleazar.

Elek (Hungarian) a form of Alec, Alex.

Elenio (Greek) he who shines like the sun.

Eleodoro (Greek) he who comes from the sun.

Eleuia (Nahuatl) wish.

Eleuterio (Greek) he who enjoys liberty for being honest.

Elfego (Germanic) spirit of the air.

Elger (German) a form of Alger.

Elgin (English) noble; white.

Eli ⭐

BG (Hebrew) uplifted. A short form of Elijah, Elisha. Bible: the high priest who trained the prophet Samuel.

Elia GB (Zuni) a short form of Elijah.

Eliahu (Hebrew) a form of Elijah.

Elian (English) a form of Elijah.

Elián (Greek) sunshine.

Elias (Greek) a form of Elijah.

Elías (Greek) a form of Elias.

Eliazar (Hebrew) a form of Eleazar.

Elido (Greek) native of Elida.

Elie (Hebrew) a form of Eli.

Eliecer (Hebrew) God is his constant aid.

Eliezer (Hebrew) a form of Eleazar.

Elifelet (Hebrew) God is my liberation.

Eligio (Latin) he who has been elected by God.

Elihu (Hebrew) a short form of Eliyahu.

Elihú (Hebrew) a form of Elihu.

Elijah ⭐

BG (Hebrew) a form of Eliyahu. Bible: a Hebrew prophet. **Elijha** (Hebrew) a form of Elijah.

Elika (Hawaiian) a form of Eric.

Elimu (African) knowledge.

Elio (Zuni) a form of Elia. (English) a form of Elliot.

Eliot (English) a form of Elliot.

Elisandro (Greek) liberator of men.

Eliseo (Hebrew) a form of Elisha.

Elisha BG (Hebrew) God is my salvation. Bible: a Hebrew prophet, successor to Elijah.

Eliyahu (Hebrew) the Lord is my God.

Elkan (Hebrew) God is jealous.

Elki (Moquelumnan) hanging over the top.

Ellard (German) sacred; brave.

Ellery BG (English) from a surname derived from the name Hilary.

Elliot, Elliott BG (English) forms of Eli, Elijah.

Ellis BG (English) a form of Elias.

Ellison GB (English) son of Ellis.

Ellsworth **(English) nobleman's estate.**

Elman **(German) like an elm tree.**

Elmer **(English) noble; famous.**

Elmo (Greek) lovable, friendly. (Italian) guardian. (Latin) a familiar form of Anselm. (English) a form of Elmer.

Elmore (English) moor where the elm trees grow.

Eloi (Hebrew) a form of Eli.

Elon (Spanish) a short form of Elonzo.

Elonzo (Spanish) a form of Alonso.

Eloy (Latin) chosen. (Hebrew) a form of Eli.

Elpidio (Greek) he who has hopes.

Elrad (Hebrew) God rules.

Elroy (French) a form of Delroy, Leroy.

Elsdon (English) nobleman's hill.

Elston (English) noble's town.

Elsu (Native American) swooping, soaring falcon.

Elsworth (English) noble's estate.

Elton (English) old town.

Eluney (Mapuche) gift.

Elvern (Latin) a form of Alvern.

Elvin (English) a form of Alvin.

Elvio (Spanish) light skinned; blond.

Elvío (Spanish) a form of Elvio.

Elvis (Scandinavian) wise.

Elvy (English) elfin warrior.

Elwell (English) old well.
Elwel

Elwood (English) old forest.

Ely (Hebrew) a form of Eli. Geography: a region of England with extensive drained bogs.

Elzeario (Hebrew) God has helped.

Eman BG (Czech) a form of Emmanuel.

Emanuel (Hebrew) a form of Emmanuel.

Emerenciano (Latin) deserving.

Emerson GB (German, English) son of Emery.

Emery GB (German) industrious leader.

Emesto (Spanish) serious.

Emeterio (Greek) he who deserves affection.

Emigdio (Greek) he who has brown skin.

Emil (Latin) flatterer. (German) industrious.

Emila (Greek) a form of Emilio.

Emile BG (French) a form of Emil.

Émile (French) a form of Emil.

Emiliano (Italian) a form of Emil.

Emilien (Latin) friendly; industrious.

Emilio (Italian, Spanish) a form of Emil.

Emillen (Latin) a form of Emilien.

Emir (Arabic) chief, commander.

Emlyn (Welsh) waterfall.

Emmanuel (Hebrew) God is with us.

Emmet, Emmitt (German, English) forms of Emmett.

Emmett (German) industrious; strong. (English) ant. History: Robert Emmett was an Irish patriot.

Emory GB (German) a form of Emery.

Emre (Turkish) brother.

Emrick (German) a form of Emery.

Emry (Welsh) honorable.

Enan (Welsh) hammer.

Enapay (Sioux) brave appearance; he appears.

Endre (Hungarian) a form of Andrew.

Enea (Italian) ninth born.

Eneas (Greek) a form of Aeneas.

Engelbert (German) bright as an angel.

Engelberto (Germanic) a form of Engelbert.

Enio (Spanish) the second divinity of war.

Enli (Dene) that dog over there.

Enmanuel (Hebrew) a form of Emmanuel.

Ennis (Greek) mine. (Scottish) a form of Angus.

Enoc (Hebrew) a form of Enoch.

Enoch (Hebrew) dedicated, consecrated. Bible: the father of Methuselah.

Enol (Asturian) referring to Lake Enol.

Enos (Hebrew) man.

Enric, Enrick (Romanian) forms of Henry.

Enrico (Italian) a form of Henry.

Enright (Irish) son of the attacker.

Enrikos (Greek) a form of Henry.

Enrique, Enrrique (Spanish) forms of **Henry.**

Enver (Turkish) bright; handsome.

Enyeto (Native American) walks like a bear.

Enzi (Swahili) powerful.

Enzo (Italian) a form of Enrico.

Eoin (Welsh) a form of Evan.

Ephraim (Hebrew) fruitful. Bible: the second son of Joseph.

Epicuro (Greek) he who helps.

Epifanio (Greek) he who gives off brilliance.

Epimaco (Greek) easy to attack.

Epulef (Mapuche) two quick trips.

Eraclio (Greek) a form of Hercules.

Erán (Hebrew) vigilant.

Erasmo (Greek) a form of Erasmus.

Erasmus (Greek) lovable.

Erasto (East African) man of peace.

Erastus (Greek) beloved.

Erato (Greek) kind, pleasant.

Erbert (German) a short form of Herbert.

Ercole (Italian) splendid gift.

Erek, Erik (Scandinavian) forms of Eric.

Erhard (German) strong; resolute.

Eri (Teutonic) vigilant.

Eriberto (Italian) a form of Herbert.

Eric (Scandinavian) ruler of all. (English) brave ruler. (German) a short form of Frederick. History: Eric the Red was a Norwegian explorer who founded Greenland's first colony.

Erich (Czech, German) a form of Eric.

Erick, Errick (English) forms of Eric.

Erickson (English) son of Eric.

Erikur (Icelandic) a form of Erek, Eric.

Eriq (American) a form of Eric.

Erland (English) nobleman's land.

Erling (English) nobleman's son.

Ermanno (Italian) a form of Herman.

Ermano (Spanish) a form of Herman.

Ermelindo (Teutonic) offers sacrifices to God.

Ermenegildo (German) strong warrior.

Ermengaldo (Germanic) dwelling of strength.

Ermengol (Catalan) a form of Armengol.

Ermino (Spanish) a form of Erminoldo.

Erminoldo (Germanic) government of strength.

Ernest (English) earnest, sincere.

Ernesto (Spanish) a form of Ernest.

Ernie (English) a familiar form of Ernest.

Erno (Hungarian) a form of Ernest.

Ernst (German) a form of Ernest.

Erol (Turkish) strong, courageous.

Eron, Erron (Irish) forms of Erin.

Erón (Spanish) a form of Aaron.

Eros (Greek) love, desire. Mythology: Eros was the god of love.

Errando (Basque) bold.

Errol (Latin) wanderer. (English) a form of Earl.

Erroman (Basque) from Rome.

Erskine (Scottish) high cliff. (English) from Ireland.

Ervin, Erwin (English) sea friend. Forms of Irving, Irwin.

Ervine (English) a form of Irving.

Ervino (Germanic) he who is consistent with honors.

Eryk (Scandinavian) a

Esau (Hebrew) rough; hairy. Bible: Jacob's twin brother.

Esaú, Esav (Hebrew) forms of Esau.

Esben (Scandinavian) god.

Esbern **(Danish) holy bear.**

Escipion, Escipión (Latin) man who uses a cane.

Escolástico (Latin) the man who teaches all that he knows.

Escubillón (Latin) one who is in the main seat.

Esculapio (Greek) the doctor.

Esdras, Esdrás (Hebrew) forms of Ezra.

Esequiel (Hebrew) a form of Ezekiel.

Eshkol (Hebrew) grape clusters.

Eshwar (Indian) another name for the Hindu god Shiva.

Esidore (Greek) a form of Isidore.

Eskil (Norwegian) god vessel.

Esleban (Hebrew) bearer of children.

Esmond (English) rich protector.

Esopo (Greek) he who brings good luck.

Espartaco (Greek) he who plants.

Espen (Danish) bear of the gods.

Espiridión (Greek) breadbasket.

Essâm (Arabic) shelter.

Essien (African) sixth-born son.

Estanislao (Slavic) the glory of his village.

Estanislau (Slavic) glory.

Este (Italian) east.

Esteban, Estéban (Spanish) forms of Stephen.

Estebe (Basque) a form of Stephen.

Estéfan, Estévan, Estévon (Spanish) forms of Estevan.

Estevan, Esteven (Spanish) forms of Stephen.

Estevao (Spanish) a form of Stephen.

Esteve (Catalan) a form of Estevan.

Estevo (Greek) a form of Estevan.

Estraton (Greek) man of the army.

Estuardo (Spanish) a form of Edward.

Etalpalli (Nahuatl) wing.

Etel (Germanic) noble.

Etelberto (Spanish) a form of Adalberto.

Eterio (Greek) as clean and pure as heaven.

Ethan ✮ (Hebrew) strong; firm.

Ethán (Hebrew) a form of Ethan.

Ethen (Hebrew) a form of Ethan.

Etienne 🅱🅖 (French) a form of Stephen.

Étienne (French) a form of Stephen.

Ettore (Italian) steadfast.

Etu (Native American) sunny.

Eubulo (Greek) good counselor.

Eucario (Greek) gracious, generous.

Eucarpo (Greek) he who bears good fruit.

Euclid (Greek) intelligent. History: the founder of Euclidean geometry.

Euclides (Greek) a form of Euclid.

Eudaldo (German) famous leader.

Eudoro (Greek) beautiful gift.

Eudoxio (Greek) he who is famous.

Eufemio (Greek) he who has a good reputation.

Eufrasio (Greek) he who uses words well.

Eufronio (Greek) having a good mind.

Eugen (German) a form of Eugene.

Eugene (Greek) born to nobility.

Eugène (French) a form of Eugenio.

Eugenio (Spanish) a form of Eugene.

Euladio (Greek) one who is pious.

Eulalio (Greek) good speaker.

Eulises (Latin) a form of Ulysses.

Eulogio (Greek) he who speaks well.

Eumenio (Greek) opportune, favorable.

Euniciano (Spanish) happy victory.

Euno (Greek) intellect.

Eupilo (Greek) warmly welcomed.

Euprepio (Greek) decent; comfortable.

Eupsiquio (Greek) having a good soul.

Euquerio (Greek) sure handed.

Eurico (Germanic) the prince to whom all pay homage.

Eusebio (Greek) with good feelings.

Eusiquio (Greek) a form of Eupsiquio.

Eustace (Greek) productive. (Latin) stable, calm.

Eustacio (Greek) healthy and strong.

Eustaquio (Greek) he who has many heads of wheat.

Eustasio (Greek) healthy and strong.

Eustoquio (Greek) good marksman.

Eustorgio (Greek) well loved.

Eustrato (Greek) good soldier.

Eutiquio (Greek) fortunate.

Eutrapio (Greek) changing, transforming.

Euxenio (Greek) born into nobility.

Evan ⭐

🅱🅶 (Irish) young warrior. (English) a form of John.

Evander (Greek) benevolent ruler; preacher.

Evando (Greek) considered a good man.

Evangelino (Greek) he who brings glad tidings.

Evangelos (Greek) a form of Andrew.

Evans (Irish, English) a form of Evan.

Evarado (Spanish) hardy, brave.

Evaristo (Greek) the excellent one.

Evelio (Hebrew) he who gives life.

Evelyn 🅶🅱 (English) hazelnut.

Evencio (Latin) successful.

Ever (English) boar. A short form of Everett, Everley, Everton. (German) a short form of Everardo.

Everardo (German) strong as a boar. A form of Eberhard.

Everett 🅱🅶 (English) a form of Eberhard.

Everette (English) a form of Eberhard.

Everley (English) boar meadow.

Everton (English) boar town.

Evgenii (Russian) a form of Evgeny.

Evgeny (Russian) a form of Eugene.

Evin, Evon, Evyn (Irish) forms of Evan.

Evodio (Greek) he who follows a good road.

Ewald (German) always powerful. (English) powerful lawman.

Ewan (Scottish) a form of Eugene, Evan.

Ewert (English) ewe herder, shepherd.

Ewing (English) friend of the law.

Exavier (Basque) a form of Xavier.

Exequiel (Hebrew) God is my strength.

Expedito (Latin) unencumbered.

Expósito (Latin) abandoned.

Exuperancio (Latin) he who is outstanding.

Exuperio (Latin) he who exceeds expectations.

Eyén (Araucanian) God.

Eynstein (Norse) stone island.

Eyota BG (Native American) great.

Ezekiel (Hebrew) strength of God. Bible: a Hebrew prophet.

Ezequias (Hebrew) Yahweh is my strength.

Ezequías (Hebrew) has divine power.

Ezequiel (Hebrew) a form of Ezekiel.

Ezer (Hebrew) a form of Ezra.

Ezio (Latin) he who has a nose like an eagle.

Ezra (Hebrew) helper; strong. Bible: a Jewish priest who led the Jews back to Jerusalem.

Eztli (Nahuatl) blood.

Ezven (Czech) a form of Eugene.

F

Faas (Scandinavian) wise counselor.

Faber (German) a form of Fabian.

Fabian (Latin) bean grower.

Fabián (Spanish) a form of Fabian.

Fabiano (Italian) a form of Fabian.

Fabien (Latin) a form of Fabian.

Fabio (Latin) a form of Fabian. (Italian) a short form of Fabiano.

Fabrice (Italian) a form of Fabrizio.

Fabrizio (Italian) craftsman.

Fabron (French) little blacksmith; apprentice.

Facundo (Latin) he who makes convincing arguments.

Fâdel (Arabic) generous.

Fadey (Ukrainian) a form of Thaddeus.

Fadi (Arabic) redeemer.

Fadil (Arabic) generous.

Fadrique (Spanish) a form of Federico.

Fagan (Irish) little fiery one.

Fahd (Arabic) lynx.

Fai (Chinese) beginning.

Fairfax (English) blond.

Faisal (Arabic) decisive.

Fakhir (Arabic) excellent.

Fakih (Arabic) thinker; reader of the Koran.

Falak (Indian) sky.

Falco (Latin) falconer.

Falguni (Indian) born in the Hindu month of Falgun.

Falito (Italian) a familiar form of Rafael, Raphael.

Falkner (English) trainer of falcons.

Fane (English) joyful, glad.

Fanibhusan (Indian) another name for the Hindu god Shiva.

Fanindra, Fanish (Indian) other names for the Hindu serpent god Shesh.

Fanishwar (Indian) lord of serpents.

Fantino (Latin) innocent.

Fanuco (Spanish) free.

Fanuel (Hebrew) vision of God.

Faraji (Swahili) consolation.

Faraón (Egyptian) pharaoh.

Faraz (Arabic) a form of Faris.

Farhad, Farhat (Indian) happiness.

Farid (Arabic) unique.

Faris (Arabic) horseman. (Irish) a form of Ferris.

Fâris (Arabic) a form of Faris.

Farlane (English) far lane.

Farley (English) bull meadow; sheep meadow.

Farnell (English) fern-covered hill.

Farnham (English) field of ferns.

Farnley (English) fern meadow.

Faroh (Latin) a form **of Pharaoh.**

Farokh, Farukh (Indian) power of discrimination.

Farold (English) mighty traveler.

Faron (English) a form of Faren

Farón (Spanish) pharaoh.

Farquhar (Scottish) dear.

Farr (English) traveler.

Farrar (English) blacksmith.

Farrell (Irish) heroic; courageous.

Farrow (English) piglet.

Farruco (Spanish) a form of Francis, Francisco.

Faruq (Arabic) honest.

Faste (Norwegian) firm.

Fateh (Indian) victory.

Fath (Arabic) victor.

Fatik (Indian) crystal.

Fatin (Arabic) clever.

Fâtin (Arabic) a form of Fatin.

Fauac (Quechua) he who flies.

Fauacuaipa (Quechua) rooster in flight.

Faust (Latin) lucky, fortunate. History: the sixteenth-century German necromancer who inspired many legends.

Faustino (Italian) a form of Faust.

Fausto (Italian) a form of Faust.

Favian (Latin) understanding.

Fawwâz, Fawzî (Arabic) successful.

Faxon BG (German) long-haired.

Fazio (Italian) good worker.

Febe, Febo (Latin) he who shines.

Federico (Italian, Spanish) a form of Frederick.

Fedro (Greek) the splendid man.

Fedyenka (Russian) gift of God.

Feivel (Yiddish) God aids.

Feliciano (Italian) a form of Felix.

Feliks (Russian) a form of Felix.

Felipe (Spanish) a form of Philip.

Felippo (Italian) a form of Philip.

Felisardo (Latin) valiant and skillful man.

Felix (Latin) fortunate; happy. **Félix** (Latin) a form of Felix.

Felix Antoine (Latin, French) a combination of Felix + Antoine.

Felix Olivier (Latin, French) a combination of Felix +Olivier.

Felton (English) field town.

Fenton (English) marshland farm.

Fenuku (Egyptian) born late.

Fenyang (Egyptian) conqueror.

Feo (Spanish) ugly.

Feodor (Slavic) a form of Theodore.

Feoras (Greek) smooth rock.

Ferd (German) horse.

Ferdinand (German) daring, adventurous.

Ferdinando (Italian) a form of Ferdinand.

Ferenc (Hungarian) a form of Francis.

Fergus (Irish) strong; manly.

Fermin (French, Spanish) firm, strong.

Fermín (Spanish) a form of Fermin.

Fernán (Spanish) a form of Fernando.

Fernando (Spanish) a form of Ferdinand.

Feroz (Persian) fortunate.

Ferran (Arabic) baker.

Ferrand (French) iron-gray hair.

Ferrell (Irish) a form of Farrell.

Ferreolo (Latin) referring to iron.

Ferris (Irish) a form of Peter.

Festus (Latin) happy.

Feta-plom (Mapuche) high and large plain.

Fhakîr (Arabic) proud; excellent.

Fiacro (Latin) the soldier.

Fico (Spanish) a familiar form of Frederick.

Fidel (Latin) faithful.
History: Fidel Castro was the Cuban revolutionary who overthrew a dictatorship in 1959 and established a communist regime in Cuba.

Fidencio (Latin) trusting; fearless.

Fidias (Greek) unhurried, calm.

Field (English) a short form of Fielding.

Fielding (English) field; field worker.

Fife (Scottish) from Fife, Scotland.

Fil (Polish) a form of Phil.

Filadelfo, Filademo (Greek) man who loves his brothers.

Filbert (English) brilliant.

Filberte (French) a form of Filbert.

Fileas (Greek) he who loves deeply.

Filebert (Catalan) a form of Filiberto.

Filelio (Latin) he who is trustworthy.

Filemón (Greek) horse lover.

Filiberto (Spanish) a form of Filbert.

Filip (Greek) a form of Philip.

Fillipp (Russian) a form of Philip.

Filmore (English) famous.

Filón (Greek) philosophical friend.

Filya (Russian) a form of Philip.

Findlay (Irish) a form of Finlay.

Fineas (Irish) a form of Phineas.

Finian (Irish) light skinned; white.

Finlay (Irish) blond-haired soldier.

Finn (German) from Finland. (Irish) blond haired; light skinned. A short form of Finlay. (Norwegian) from the Lapland.

Finnegan (Irish) light skinned; white.

Fintan (Irish) from Finn's town.

Fiorello (Italian) little flower.

Firas (Arabic) persistent.

Firdaus (Indian) paradise.

Firman (French) firm; strong.

Firmino (Latin) firm, sure.

Firmo (Latin) morally and physically firm.

Firth (English) woodland.

Fischel (Yiddish) a form of Philip.

Fischer (English) a form of Fisher.

Fisher (English) fisherman.

Fiske (English) fisherman.

Fitch (English) weasel, ermine.

Fito (Spanish) a form of Adolfo.

Fitz (English) son.

Fitzgerald (English) son of Gerald.

Fitzhugh (English) son of Hugh.

Fitzpatrick (English) son of Patrick.

Fitzroy (Irish) son of Roy.

Fiz (Latin) happy; fertile.

Flaminio (Spanish) Religion: Marcantonio Flaminio coauthored one of the most important texts of the Italian Reformation.

Flann (Irish) redhead.

Flavian (Latin) blond, yellow haired.

Flaviano (Latin) a form of Flavian.

Flavio (Italian) a form of Flavian.

Fleming (English) from Denmark; from Flanders.

Fletcher (English) arrow featherer, arrow maker.

Flint (English) stream; flint stone.

Flip (Spanish) a short form of Felipe. (American) a short form of Philip.

Floreal (Latin) alludes to the eighth month of the French Revolution.

Florencio (Italian) a form of Florent.

Florent (French) flowering.

Florente (Latin) a form of Florent.

Florentino (Italian) a form of Florent.

Florian 🇧🇬 (Latin) flowering, blooming.

Florián (Latin) a form of Florian.

Floriano (Spanish) a form of Florian.

Floriberto (Germanic) brilliant master.

Florio (Spanish) a form of Florián.

Floro (Spanish) flower.

Florus (French) flowers.

Flósculo (Latin) wildflower.

Floyd (English) a form of Lloyd.

Flurry (English) flourishing, blooming.

Flynn (Irish) son of the red-haired man.

Focas (Greek) habitant of Focida.

Focio (Latin) illuminated, shining.

Fodjour (Ghanaian) fourth born.

Folco (Catalan) man who belongs to the community.

Folke (German) a form of Volker.

Foluke 🇧🇬 (Yoruba) given to God.

Foma (Bulgarian, Russian) a form of Thomas.

Fonso (German, Italian) a short form of Alphonso.

Fontaine (French) fountain.

Fonzie (German) a familiar form of Alphonse.

Forbes (Irish) prosperous.

Ford (English) a short form of names ending in "ford."

Fordel (Gypsy) forgiving.

Fordon (German) destroyer.

Forest (French) a form of Forrest.

Forester (English) forest guardian.

Formerio (Latin) beauty.

Forrest 🇧🇬 (French) forest; woodsman.

Fortino (Italian) fortunate, lucky.

Fortune (French) fortunate, lucky.

Foster (Latin) a short form of Forester.

Fouad (Lebanese) heart.

Fowler (English) trapper of wildfowl.

Fraco (Spanish) weak.

Fran 🇬🇧 (Latin) a short form of Francis.

Francesco (Italian) a form of Francis.

Franchot (French) a form of Francis.

Francis BG (Latin) free; from France. Religion: Saint Francis of Assisi was the founder of the Franciscan order.

Francisco (Portuguese, Spanish) a form of Francis.

Franco (Latin) a short form of Francis.

Francois, François (French) forms of Francis.

Frank (English) a short form of Francis, Franklin.

Frankie BG (English) a familiar form of Frank.

Franklin (English) free landowner.

Franklyn (English) a form of Franklin.

Franky (English) a familiar form of Frank.

Frans (Swedish) a form of Francis.

Fransisco (Portuguese, Spanish) a form of Francis.

Frantisek (Czech) a form of Francis.

Frantz, Franz (German) forms of Francis.

Fraser (French) strawberry. **(English) curly haired.**

Fraterno (Latin) relating to the brother.

Frayne (French) dweller at the ash tree. (English) stranger.

Frazer, Frazier (French, English) forms of Fraser.

Fred (German) a short form of Alfred, Frederick, Manfred.

Freddie BG (German) a familiar form of Frederick.

Freddrick, Fredrick (German) forms of Frederick.

Freddy, Fredi, Fredy (German) familiar forms of Frederick.

Frederic, Frederik (German) forms of Frederick.

Frederick (German) peaceful ruler.

Frederico (Spanish) a form of Frederick.

Frederique GB (French) a form of Frederick.

Fredo (Spanish) a form of Fred.

Freeborn (English) child of freedom.

Freeman (English) free.

Fremont (German) free; noble protector.

Frenchc (Catalan) a form of Francisco.

Fresco (Spanish) fresh.

Frewin (English) free; noble friend.

Frey (English) lord. (Scandinavian) Mythology: the Norse god who dispenses peace and prosperity.

Frick (English) bold.

Fridmund (German) peaceful guardian.

Fridolf (English) peaceful wolf.

Fridolino (Teutonic) he who loves peace.

Friedrich (German) a form of Frederick.

Frisco (Spanish) a short form of Francisco.

Fritz (German) a familiar form of Frederick.

Froberto (Spanish) a form of Roberto.

Frode (Norwegian) wise.

Froilan, Froilán (Teutonic) rich and beloved young master.

Fronton (Latin) he who thinks.

Fructuoso (Latin) he who bears much fruit.

Frumencio (Latin) he who provides wheat.

Frutos (Latin) fertile.

Fu'ad (Arabic) heart.

Fuad (Lebanese) heart.

Fulberto (Germanic) he who shines.

Fulbright (German) very bright.

Fulco (Spanish) village.

Fulgencio (Latin) he who shines and stands out.

Fuller (English) cloth thickener.

Fulton (English) field near town.

Fulvio (Latin) he who has reddish hair.

Funsani (Egyptian) request.

Funsoni (Nguni) requested.

Fyfe (Scottish) a form of Fife.

Fynn (Ghanaian) Geography: another name for the Offin River in Ghana.

Fyodor (Russian) a form of Theodore.

G

Gabby (American) a familiar form of Gabriel.

Gabe (Hebrew) a short form of Gabriel.

Gabela (Swiss) a form of Gabriel.

Gabino (American) a form of Gabriel.

Gábor (Hungarian) God is my strength.

Gabrial (Hebrew) a form of Gabriel.

Gabriel ⭐

BG (Hebrew) devoted to God. Bible: the angel of the Annunciation.

Gabriele GB (Hebrew) a form of Gabriel.

Gabriell GB (Hebrew) a form of Gabriel.

Gabrielle GB (Hebrew) a form of Gabriel.

Gabrielli (Italian) a form of Gabriel.

Gabrio (Spanish) a form of Gabriel.

Gabryel (Hebrew) a form of Gabriel.

Gadi (Arabic) God is my fortune.

Gael (Irish) Gaelic-speaking Celt. (Greek) a form of Gale.

Gaetan (Italian) from Gaeta, a region in southern Italy.

Gagan (Sikh) sky.

Gagandeep BG (Sikh) sky's light.

Gage BG (French) pledge.

Gahiji (Egyptian) hunter.

Gaige (French) a form of Gage.

Gair (Irish) small.

Gaius (Latin) rejoicer.

Gajanand, Ganapati (Indian) other names for the Hindu god Ganesh.

Gaje (French) a form of Gage.

Gajendra (Indian) king of elephants.

Gálatas (Greek) white as milk.

Galbraith (Irish) Scotsman in Ireland.

Gale (Greek) a short form of Galen.

Galeaso (Latin) he who is protected by the helmet.

Galen BG (Greek) healer; calm. (Irish) little and lively.

Galeno (Spanish) illuminated child. (Greek, Irish) a form of Galen.

Galileo (Hebrew) he who comes from Galilee.

Gallagher (Irish) eager helper.

Galloway (Irish) Scotsman in Ireland.

Galo (Latin) native of Galilee.

Galt (Norwegian) high ground.

Galton (English) owner of a rented estate.

Galvin (Irish) sparrow.

Gamal (Arabic) camel.

Gamaliel (Hebrew) God is your reward.

Gamble (Scandinavian) old.

Gamelberto (Germanic) distinguished because of his age.

Gamlyn (Scandinavian) small elder.

Gan (Chinese) daring, adventurous. (Vietnamese) near.

Gandharva (Indian) celestial musician.

Gandhik (Indian) fragrant.

Gandolfo (Germanic) valiant warrior.

Ganesh (Indian) Hindu god with an elephant's head, son of the god Shiva and goddess Parvati.

Gangesh, Gaurinath (Indian) other names for the Hindu god Shiva.

Gangeya (Indian) of the Ganges River.

Gangol (Indian) precious.

Ganimedes (Spanish) the most beautiful of the mortals.

Gannon (Irish) light skinned, white.

Ganya BG (Zulu) clever.

Gar (English) a short form of Gareth, Garnett, Garrett, Garvin.

Garai (Egyptian) stable.

Garcia (Spanish) mighty with a spear.

García (Spanish) a form of Garcia.

Garcilaso (Spanish) a form of García.

Gardner **(English) gardener.**

Garek (Polish) a form of Edgar.

Garak, Garok

Garen, Garin, Garren, Garrin (English) forms of Garry.

Garet, Garett, Garret (Irish) forms of Garrett.

Gareth (Welsh) gentle. (Irish) a form of Garrett.

Garfield (English) field of spears; battlefield.

Garibaldo (Germanic) he who is bold with a lance.

Garion (English) a form of Garry.

Garland BG (French) wreath of flowers; prize. (English) land of spears; battleground.

Garman (English) spearman.

Garner (French) army guard, sentry.

Garnet BG (Latin, English) a form of Garnett.

Garnett (Latin) pomegranate seed; garnet stone. (English) armed with a spear.

Garnock (Welsh) dweller by the alder river.

Garoa (Basque) dew.

Garrad (English) a form of Garrett, Gerard. **Garrett** (Irish) brave spearman. **Garrick** (English) oak spear.

Garrison (English) Garry's son. (French) troops stationed at a fort; garrison.

Garroway (English) spear fighter.

Garraway

Garry (English) a form of Gary.

Garson (English) son of Gar.

Garth (Scandinavian) garden, gardener. (Welsh) a short form of Gareth.

Garthe

Garvey (Irish) rough peace. (French) a form of Gervaise.

Garvin (English) comrade in battle.

Garwood (English) evergreen forest. **Gary** (German) mighty spearman. (English) a familiar form of Gerald.

Gaspar (French) a form of Casper.

Gaston (French) from Gascony, France.

Gastón (French) a form of Gaston.

Gaudencio, Gaudioso (Latin) he who is happy and content.

Gauge (French) a form of Gage.

Gausberto (Germanic) the Gothic brightness.

Gautam (Indian) another name for Buddha.

Gaute (Norwegian) great.

Gautier (French) a form of Walter.

Gaven, Gavyn (Welsh) forms of Gavin.

Gavin (Welsh) white hawk.

Gavino (Italian) a form of Gavin.

Gavriel (Hebrew) man of God.

Gavril (Russian) a form of Gavriel. (Hebrew) a form of Gabriel.

Gavrilovich (Russian) a form of Gavril.

Gawain (Welsh) a form of Gavin.

Gaylen, Gaylon (Greek) forms of Galen.

Gaylord (French) merry lord; jailer.

Gaynor (Irish) son of the fair-skinned man.

Geary (English) variable, changeable.

Geb (Egyptian) land of God.

Gedeon (Bulgarian, French) a form of Gideon.

Gedeón (Hebrew) a form of Gedeon.

Geet (Indian) song.

Geffrey (English) a form of Geoffrey.

Gelasio (Greek) cheerful and happy.

Gellert (Hungarian) a form of Gerald.

Gemelo (Latin) fraternal twin.

Geminiano (Latin) identical twin.

Genadio (Greek) lineage.

Genardo (German) of strong lineage.

Genaro (Latin) consecrated to God.

Genciano (Latin) family.

Gencio (Latin) he who loves family.

Gene (Greek) a short form of Eugene.

Genek (Polish) a form of Gene.

Gener (Catalan) January.

Generos, Generoso (Spanish) generous.

Genesis GB (Greek) beginning, origin.

Geno (Italian) a form of John. A short form of Genovese.

Genovese (Italian) from Genoa, Italy.

Gent (English) gentleman.

Gentry BG (English) a form of Gent.

Genty (Irish, English) snow.

Geoff (English) a short form of Geoffrey.

Geoffery (English) a form of Geoffrey.

Geoffrey (English) a form of Jeffrey. **Geordan** (Scottish) a form of Gordon.

Geordie (Scottish) a form of George.

Georg (Scandinavian) a form of George.

George (Greek) farmer. **Georges** (French) a form of George.

Georgio (Italian) a form of George.

Georgios (Greek) a form of George.

Georgy (Greek) a familiar form of George.

Geovani, Geovanni, Geovanny, Geovany (Italian) forms of Giovanni.

Geraint (English) old.

Gerald (German) mighty spearman.

Geraldo (Italian, Spanish) a form of Gerald.

Gerard (English) brave spearman.

Gerardo (Spanish) a form of Gerard.

Gerasimo (Greek) award, recompense.

Géraud (French) a form of Gerard.

Gerbrando (Germanic) sword.

Gerek (Polish) a form of Gerald, Gerard.

Geremia (Hebrew) exalted by God. (Italian) a form of Jeremiah.

Geremiah (Italian) a form of Jeremiah.

Geremy (English) a form of Jeremy.

Gerhard (German) a form of Gerard.

Gerik (Polish) a form of Edgar.

Gerino (German) lance.

Germain (French) from Germany. (English) sprout, bud. **Germaine** BG (French, English) a form of Germain.

German (French, English) a form of Germain.

Germán (French) a form of German.

Germana (Latin) ready for action.

Germinal (Latin) he who sprouts.

Geroldo (Germanic) the commander of the lance.

Gerome (English) a form of Jerome.

Geroncio (Greek) little old man.

Geronimo (Greek, Italian) a form of Jerome. History: a famous Apache chief.

Gerónimo (Greek) a form of Geronimo.

Gerrit (Irish) a form of Garrett. (Dutch) a form of Gerald. (English) a form of Gerard.

Gerrod (English) a form of Garrad.

Gerry (English) a familiar form of Gerald, Gerard.

Gershom (Hebrew) exiled. (Yiddish) stranger in exile.

Gershón (Hebrew) a form of Gershom.

Gerson (English) son of Gar. (Hebrew, Yiddish) a form of Gershom.

Gert (German, Danish) fighter.

Gervaise BG (French) honorable.

Gerwin (Welsh) fair love.

Gesualdo (Germanic) the prisoner of the king.

Getachew (African) your teacher.

Geteye (African) his teacher.

Gethin **(Welsh) dusky.**

Getulio (Latin) he who came from Getulia.

Gevork (Armenian) a form of George.

Ghalib (Indian) excellent.

Ghâlib (Arabic) a form of Victor.

Ghanashyam, Giridari, Giridhar (Indian) other names for the Hindu god Krishna.

Ghazi (Arabic) conqueror.

Ghedi (Somali) traveler.

Ghilchrist (Irish) servant of Christ.

Ghislain (French) pledge.

Gi (Korean) brave.

Gia GB (Vietnamese) family.

Giacinto (Portuguese, Spanish) a form of Jacinto.

Giacomo (Italian) a form of Jacob.

Gian (Italian) a form of Giovanni, John.

Giancarlo (Italian) a combination of Gian + Carlo.

Gianfranco (Italian) a combination of Gian + Franco.

Gianluca (Italian) a combination of Gian + Luca.

Gianmarco (Italian) a combination of Gian + Marco.

Gianni (Italian) a form of Johnie.

Gianpaolo (Italian) a combination of Gian + Paolo.

Gib (English) a short form of Gilbert.

Gibert (Catalan) a form of Gilberto.

Gibor (Hebrew) powerful.

Gibson (English) son of Gilbert.

Gideon (Hebrew) tree cutter. Bible: the judge who defeated the Midianites.

Gidon (Hebrew) a form of Gideon.

Gifford **(English) bold giver.**

Gig (English) horse-drawn carriage.

Gil (Greek) shield bearer. (Hebrew) happy. (English) a short form of Ghilchrist, Gilbert.

Gilad (Arabic) camel hump; from Giladi, Saudi Arabia.

Gilamu (Basque) a form of William.

Gillen, Gylamu

Gilbert (English) brilliant pledge; trustworthy. **Gilberto** (Spanish) a form of Gilbert.

Gilby (Scandinavian) hostage's estate. (Irish) blond boy.

Gilchrist (Irish) a form of Ghilchrist.

Gildardo (German) good.

Gildo (Spanish) a form of Hermenegildo.

Gilen (Basque, German) illustrious pledge.

Giles (French) goatskin shield.

Gillean (Irish) Bible: Saint John's servant.

Gillermo (Spanish) resolute protector.

Gilles (French) a form of Giles.

Gillespie (Irish) son of the bishop's servant.

Gillett (French) young Gilbert.

Gilmer (English) famous hostage.

Gilmore (Irish) devoted to the Virgin Mary.

Gilon (Hebrew) circle.

Gilroy (Irish) devoted to the king.

Gines (Greek) he who produces life.

Ginés (Greek) a form of Genesis.

Gino (Greek) a familiar form of Eugene. (Italian) a short form of names ending in "gene," "gino."

Giona (Italian) a form of Jonah.

Giordano (Italian) a form of Jordan.

Giorgio (Italian) a form of George.

Giorgos (Greek) a form of George.

Giosia (Italian) a form of Joshua.

Giotto (Italian) a form of Geoffrey.

Giovani, Giovanny, Giovany (Italian) forms of Giovanni.

Giovanni BG (Italian) a form of John.

Gipsy (English) wanderer.

Giri (Indian) mountain.

Girik, Girilal, Girindra, Girish (Indian) other names for the Hindu god Shiva.

Giriraj (Indian) lord of the mountains.

Girvin (Irish) small; tough.

Gisberto (Germanic) he who shines in battle with his sword.

Gitano (Spanish) gypsy.

Giuliano (Italian) a form of Julius.

Giulio (Italian) a form of Julius.

Giuseppe (Italian) a form of Joseph.

Giustino (Italian) a form of Justin.

Givon (Hebrew) hill; heights.

Gladwin (English) cheerful.

Glanville (English) village with oak trees.

Glasson (Scottish) from Glasgow, Scotland.

Glen, Glenn (Irish) short forms of Glendon.

Glendon (Scottish) fortress in the glen.

Glendower (Welsh) from Glyndwr, Wales.

Glenrowan (Irish) valley with rowan trees.

Glenton (Scottish) valley town.

Glenville (Irish) village in the glen.

Glyn, Glynn (Welsh) forms of Glen.

Godardo (German) a form of Goddard.

Goddard (German) divinely firm.

Godeardo (German) a form of Gotardo.

Godfredo (Spanish) friend of God.

Godfrey (Irish) God's peace. (German) a form of Jeffrey.

Godwin (English) friend of God.

Goel (Hebrew) redeemer.

Gogo (African) like a grandfather.

Gokul (Indian) place where the Hindu god Krishna was brought up.

Golden (English) a form of Goldwin.

Goldwin (English) golden friend.

Goliard (Spanish) the rebel.

Goliat (Hebrew) he who lives his life making pilgrimages.

Goliath (Hebrew) exiled. Bible: the giant Philistine whom David slew with a slingshot.

Gomda (Kiowa) wind.

Gomer (Hebrew) completed, finished. (English) famous battle.

Gomez (Spanish) man.

Gontrán (German, Spanish) famous warrior.

Gonza (Rutooro) love.

Gonzalo (Spanish) wolf.

Gopal (Indian) protector of cows; another name for the Hindu god Krishna.

Gopesh (Indian) another name for the Hindu god Krishna.

Gopichand (Indian) name of a king.

Gorakh (Indian) cowherd.

Goran (Greek) a form of George.

Gordon (English) triangular-shaped hill.

Gordy (English) a familiar form of Gordon.

Gore (English) triangular-shaped land; wedge-shaped land.

Gorge (Latin) gorge. (Greek) a form of George.

Gorgonio (Greek) the violent one.

Gorman **(Irish) small; blue eyed.**

Goro (Japanese) fifth.

Gosheven (Native American) great leaper.

Gosvino (Teutonic) friend of God.

Gotardo (Germanic) he who is valiant because of the strength God gives him.

Gottfried (German) a form of Geoffrey, Godfrey.

Gotzon (German) a form of Angel.

Govert (Dutch) heavenly peace.

Gower (Welsh) pure.

Gowon (Tiv) rainmaker.

Goyo (Spanish) a form of Gerardo.

Gozol (Hebrew) soaring bird.

Gracia (Latin) nice; welcome.

Gracián (Latin) the possessor of grace.

Graciano (Latin) the one recognized by God.

Grady (Irish) noble; illustrious.

Graeme (Scottish) a form of Graham.

Graham (English) grand home.

Granger (French) farmer.

Grant 🅱🅶 (English) a short form of Grantland.

Grantland (English) great plains.

Grantley (English) great meadow.

Granville (French) large village.

Grato (Latin) the one recognized by God.

Grau (Spanish) a form of Gerardo.

Gray (English) gray haired.

Grayden (English) gray haired.

Graydon (English) gray hill.

Grayson ⭐

🅱🅶 (English) bailiff's son.

Greeley (English) gray meadow.

Greenwood (English) green forest.

Greg, Gregg (Latin) short forms of Gregory.

Greggory (Latin) a form of Gregory.

Gregor (Scottish) a form of Gregory.

Gregorio (Italian, Portuguese) a form of Gregory.

Gregorios

Gregory (Latin) vigilant watchman.

Gresham (English) village in the pasture.

Grey (English) a form of Gray.

Greyson (English) a form of Grayson.

Griffen (Latin) a form of Griffin.

Griffin (Latin) hooked nose.

Griffith (Welsh) fierce chief; ruddy.

Grigor (Bulgarian) a form of Gregory.

Grigori (Bulgarian) a form of Gregory.

Grigorii (Russian) a form of Gregory.

Grimoaldo (Spanish) confessor.

Grimshaw (English) dark woods.

Grisha **(Russian) a form of Gregory.**

Grysha

Griswold (German, French) gray forest.

Grosvener (French) big hunter.

Grosvenor (French) great hunter.

Grover (English) grove.

Guacraya (Quechua) strong and brave like a bull.

Guadalberto (Germanic) he is all powerful.

Guaina (Quechua) young.

Guala (German) governor.

Gualberto (Spanish) a form of Walter.

Gualtiero (Italian) a form of Walter.

Guaman (Quechua) falcon.

Guamanachachi (Quechua) he who has valorous ancestors like the falcon.

Guamancapac (Quechua) lord falcon.

Guamancaranca (Quechua) he who fights like a thousand falcons.

Guamanchaua (Quechua) cruel as a falcon.

Guamanchuri (Quechua) son of the falcon.

Guamanpuma (Quechua) strong and powerful as a puma and a falcon.

Guamantiupac (Quechua) glorious falcon.

Guamanyana (Quechua) black falcon.

Guamanyurac (Quechua) white falcon.

Guamay (Quechua) young, fresh.

Guanca, Guancar (Quechua) rock; summit.

Guanpú (Aymara) born in a festive time.

Guari (Quechua) savage, untamable.

Guarino (Teutonic) he who defends well.

Guariruna (Quechua) untamed and wild man.

Guarititu, Guartito (Quechua) untamed and difficult to handle.

Guascar (Quechua) he of the chain, rope, or bindweed.

Guaual (Quechua) myrtle.

Guayasamin (Quechua) happy white bird in flight.

Guayau (Quechua) royal willow.

Guaynacapac (Quechua) young master.

Guaynarimac (Quechua) young speaker.

Guaynay (Quechua) my youngster.

Guaypa, Guaypaya (Quechua) rooster; creator.

Guayra (Quechua) fast as the wind.

Guayua (Aymara) restless; mischievous.

Guglielmo (Italian) a form of William.

Guido (Italian) a form of Guy.

Guifford (French) chubby cheeks.

Guifré (Catalan) a form of Wilfredo.

Guilford (English) ford with yellow flowers.

Guilherme (Portuguese) a form of William.

Güillac (Quechua) he who warns.

Guillaume (French) a form of William.

Guillerme (German) a form of William.

Guillermo (Spanish) a form of William.

Guillerrmo

Guir (Irish) beige.

Güiracocha, Güiracucha (Quechua) sea foam.

Güisa (Quechua) prophet.

Güiuyac (Quechua) brilliant, luminous.

Güiyca (Quechua) sacred.

Güiycauaman (Quechua) sacred falcon.

Gumaro (Germanic) army of men; disciplined man.

Gumersindo (Germanic) the excellent man.

Gundelberto (Teutonic) he who shines in battle.

Gundislavo (German) joy; strength.

Gunnar (Scandinavian) a form of Gunther.

Gunner (English) soldier with a gun. (Scandinavian) a form of Gunther.

Gunter (Scandinavian) a form of Gunther.

Gunther (Scandinavian) battle army; warrior.

Guotin (Chinese) polite; strong leader.

Gurdeep (Sikh) lamp of the guru.

Gurion (Hebrew) young lion.

Gurjot (Sikh) light of the guru.

Gurpreet BG (Sikh) devoted to the guru; devoted to the Prophet.

Gurveer (Sikh) guru's warrior.

Gurvir (Sikh) a form of Gurveer.

Gus (Scandinavian) a short form of Angus, Augustine, Gustave.

Gustaf (Swedish) a form of Gustave.

Gustave (Scandinavian) staff of the Goths. History: Gustavus Adolphus was a king of Sweden.

Gustavo (Italian, Spanish) a form of Gustave.

Guthrie (German) war hero. (Irish) windy place.

Gutierre (Spanish) a form of Walter.

Guy (Hebrew) valley.
(German) warrior.
(French) guide.

Guyapi (Native American)
candid.

Guyllaume (French) a
form of William.

Guzman, Guzmán
(Gothic) good man; man
of God.

Gwayne (Welsh) a form of
Gawain.

Gwidon (Polish) life.

Gwilym (Welsh) a form of
William.

Gwyn GB (Welsh) fair;
blessed.

Gyasi (Akan) marvelous
baby.

Gyorgy (Russian) a form of
George.

Gyula (Hungarian) youth.

H

Habacuc (Hebrew)
embrace.
Habib (Arabic) beloved.
Habîb (Hebrew) a form of
Habib.
Habid (Arabic) the
appreciated one.

Hacan (Quechua) brilliant,
splendorous.
Hacanpoma,
Hacanpuma (Quechua)
brilliant puma.
Hackett (German, French)
little wood cutter.
Hackman (German,
French) wood cutter.
Haddad (Arabic)
blacksmith.
Haddâd (Arabic) a form of
Haddad.
Hadden (English) heather-
covered hill.
Haden (English) a form of
Hadden.
Hadi (Arabic) guiding to
the right.
Hadley GB (English)
heather-covered meadow.
Hadrian (Latin, Swedish)
dark.
Hadrián (Latin) a form of
Hadrian.
Hadulfo (Germanic) the
combat wolf.
Hadwin (English) friend in
a time of war.
Hafiz (Indian) protected.
Hagan (German) strong
defense.
Hagar GB (Hebrew)
forsaken; stranger.
Hagen (Irish) young,
youthful.
Hagley (English) enclosed
meadow.
Hagop (Armenian) a form
of James.

Hagos (Ethiopian) happy.
Hahnee (Native American)
beggar.
Hai (Vietnamese) sea.
Haidar (Arabic) lion.
Haiden BG (English) a
form of Hayden.
Haider (Arabic) a form of
Haidar.
Haig (English) enclosed
with hedges.
Hayg
Hailama (Hawaiian)
famous brother.
Haines (English) from the
vine-covered cottage.
Haji (Swahili) born during
the pilgrimage to Mecca.
Hajjâj (Arabic) traveler.
Hakan (Native American)
fiery.
Hakeem (Arabic) a form of
Hakim.
Hakim (Arabic) wise.
(Ethiopian) doctor.
Hakîm (Arabic) a form of
Hakim.
Hakizimana (Egyptian)
salvation of God.
Hakon (Scandinavian) of
Nordic ancestry.
Hal (English) a short form
of Halden, Hall, Harold.
Halbert (English) shining
hero.
Halcyon (Greek) tranquil,
peaceful; kingfisher.
Mythology: the kingfisher
bird was supposed to
have the power to calm

the wind and the waves while nesting near the sea.

Halden (Scandinavian) half-Danish.

Hale (English) a short form of Haley. (Hawaiian) a form of Harry.

Halen (Swedish) hall.

Haley GB (Irish) ingenious.

Halford (English) valley ford.

Hali GB (Greek) sea.

Halian (Zuni) young.

Halifax (English) holy field.

Halil (Turkish) dear friend.

Halim (Arabic) mild, gentle.

Hall (English) manor, hall.

Hallam (English) valley.

Hallan (English) dweller at the hall; dweller at the manor.

Halley GB (English) meadow near the hall; holy.

Halliwell (English) holy well.

Hallward (English) hall guard.

Halsey GB (English) Hal's island.

Halstead (English) manor grounds.

Halton (English) estate on the hill.

Halvor (Norwegian) rock; protector.

Ham (Hebrew) hot. Bible: one of Noah's sons.

Hamal (Arabic) lamb. Astronomy: a bright star in the constellation of Aries.

Hamar (Scandinavian) hammer.

Hamdân (Arabic) praised.

Hamed (Arabic) a form of Hamid.

Hamid (Arabic) praised.
Hamîd (Arabic) a form of Hamid.

Hamidi (Kenyan) admired.

Hamill (English) scarred.

Hamilton (English) proud estate.

Hamir (Indian) a raga, an ancient form of Hindu devotional music.

Hamish (Scottish) a form of Jacob, James.

Hamisi (Swahili) born on Thursday.

Hamlet (German, French) little village; home. Literature: one of Shakespeare's tragic heroes.

Hamlin (German, French) loves his home.

Hammet (English, Scandinavian) village.

Hammond (English) village.

Hampton (English) Geography: a town in England.

Hamza (Arabic) powerful.

Hamzah (Arabic) a form of Hamza.

Hanale (Hawaiian) a form of Henry.

Hanan GB (Hebrew) grace.

Hanbal (Arabic) pure. History: Ahmad Ibn Hanbal founded an Islamic school of thought.

Handel (German, English) a form of John. Music: George Frideric Handel was a German composer whose works include *Messiah* and *Water Music*.

Hanford (English) high ford.

Hani (Lebanese) happy.

Hâni (Arabic) happy, satisfied.

Hanif (Arabic) true believer.

Hanisi (Swahili) born on Thursday.

Hank (American) a familiar form of Henry.

Hanley (English) high meadow.

Hannes (Finnish) a form of John.

Hannibal (Phoenician) grace of God. History: a famous Carthaginian general who fought the Romans.

Hanno (German) a short form of Johann.

Hans (Scandinavian) a form of John.

Hansel (Scandinavian) a form of Hans.

Hansen (Scandinavian) son of Hans.

Hansh (Hindi) god; godlike.

Hanson (Scandinavian) a form of Hansen.

Hanuman, Hanumant (Indian) the Hindu monkey god.

Hanus (Czech) a form of John.

Haoa (Hawaiian) a form of Howard.

Hapi (Egyptian) god of the Nile.

Hapu (Egyptian) pharaoh.

Hara GB (Hindi) seizer. Religion: another name for the Hindu god Shiva.

Harald (Scandinavian) a form of Harold.

Harb (Arabic) warrior.

Harbin (German, French) little bright warrior.

Harcourt (French) fortified dwelling.

Hardeep (Punjabi) a form of Harpreet.

Harden (English) valley of the hares.

Hardik (Indian) heartfelt.

Harding (English) brave; hardy.

Hardwin (English) brave friend.

Hardy (German) bold, daring.

Harekrishna, Haresh, Harigopal, Harkrishna (Indian) other names for the Hindu god Krishna.

Harel (Hebrew) mountain of God.

Harendra, Harishankar (Indian) other names for the Hindu god Shiva.

Harford (English) ford of the hares.

Hargrove (English) grove of the hares.

Hari (Hindi) tawny.

Haridas (Indian) servant of the Hindu god Krishna.

Harihar, Harinarayan, Hariom (Indian) other names for the Hindu god Vishnu.

Hariprasad (Indian) blessed by the Hindu god Krishna.

Hariram (Indian) another name for the Hindu god Rama.

Haris (English) a form of Harris.

Harishchandra (Indian) charitable; a king of the Surya dynasty, 1435–1523.

Haritbaran (Indian) green.

Harith (Arabic) cultivator.

Harjot BG (Sikh) light of God.

Harkin (Irish) dark red.

Harlan (English) hare's land; army land.

Harland (English) a form of Harlan.

Harley GB (English) hare's meadow; army meadow.

Harlow (English) hare's hill; army hill.

Harman, Harmon (English) forms of Herman.

Harmendra (Indian) moon.

Harmodio (Greek) convenient.

Harold (Scandinavian) army ruler. **Haroon** (Arabic) a form of Haroun.

Haroun (Arabic) lofty; exalted.

Harper GB (English) harp player.

Harpreet GB (Punjabi) loves God, devoted to God.

Harrington (English) Harry's town.

Harris (English) a short form of Harrison.

Harrison (English) son of Harry.

Harrod (Hebrew) hero; conqueror.

Harry (English) a familiar form of Harold, Henry.

Harsh (Indian) happiness.

Harshad (Indian) giver of joy.

Harshavardhan (Indian) creator of joy.

Harshil, Harshit, Harshita (Indian) joyful.

Hart (English) a short form of Hartley.

Hartley (English) deer meadow.

Hartman (German) hard; strong.

Hartwell (English) deer well.

Hartwig (German) strong advisor.

Hartwood (English) deer forest.

Hârûn (Arabic) a form of Aaron.

Harvey (German) army warrior.

Harvir (Sikh) God's warrior.

Hasaan, Hasan (Arabic) forms of Hassan.

Hasad (Turkish) reaper, harvester.

Hasani (Swahili) handsome.

Hashim (Arabic) destroyer of evil.

Hashîm (Arabic) a form of Hashim.

Hasin (Hindi) laughing.

Haskel (Hebrew) a form of Ezekiel.

Haslett (English) hazel-tree land.

Hassan (Arabic) handsome.

Hassân (Arabic) a form of Hassan.

Hassel (German, English) witches' corner.

Hastin (Hindi) elephant.

Hastings (Latin) spear. (English) house council.

Hastu (Quechua) bird of the Andes.

Hatim (Arabic) judge.

Hatuntupac (Quechua) magnificent, great and majestic.

Hauk (Norwegian) hawk.

Havelock (Norwegian) sea battler.

Haven GB (Dutch, English) harbor, port; safe place.

Havgan (Irish) white.

Havika (Hawaiian) a form of David.

Hawk (English) hawk.

Hawley (English) hedged meadow.

Hawthorne (English) hawthorn tree.

Hayden BG (English) hedged valley.

Haydn, Haydon (English) forms of Hayden.

Hayes (English) hedged valley.

Hayward (English) guardian of the hedged area.

Haywood (English) hedged forest.

Hazen (Hindi) a form of Hasin.

Haziel (Hebrew) vision of God.

Hearn (Scottish, English) a short form of Ahearn.

Heath (English) heath.

Heathcliff (English) cliff near the heath. Literature: the hero of Emily Brontë's novel *Wuthering Heights*.

Heaton (English) high place.

Heber (Hebrew) ally, partner.

Hector (Greek) steadfast. Mythology: the greatest hero of the Trojan War in Homer's epic poem *Iliad*.

Héctor (Greek) a form of Hector.

Hedley (English) heather-filled meadow.

Hedwig BG (German) fighter.

Hedwyn (Welsh) friend of peace and blessings. (English) a form of Hadwin.

Hegesipo (Greek) horse rider.

Heh (Egyptian) god of the immeasurable.

Heinrich (German) a form of Henry.

Heinz (German) a familiar form of Henry.

Héitor (Spanish) a form of Hector.

Helaku BG (Native American) sunny day.

Heldrado (Germanic) counselor of warriors.

Helge (Russian) holy.

Heli (Hebrew) he who offers himself to God.

Helio (Greek) Mythology: Helios was the sun god.

Heliodoro (Greek) gift of the sun god.

Heliogabalo (Syrian) he who adores the sun.

Helki BG (Moquelumnan) touching.

Helmer (German) warrior's wrath.

Helmut (German) courageous.

Helué (Arabic) sweet.

Heman (Hebrew) faithful.

Henderson (Scottish, English) son of Henry.

Hendrick (Dutch) a form of Henry.

Heniek (Polish) a form of Henry.

Henley (English) high meadow.

Henning (German) a form of Hendrick, Henry.

Henoch (Yiddish) initiator.

Henri (French) a form of Henry.

Henrick (Dutch) a form of Henry.

Henrique (Portuguese) a form of Henry.

Henry ✸ (German) ruler of the household.

Heracleos, Heraclio (Greek) belonging to Hercules.

Heracles, Hércules (Greek) forms of Hercules.

Heraclito, Heráclito (Greek) he who is drawn to the sacred.

Heraldo (Spanish) a form of Harold.

Herb (German) a short form of Herbert.

Herbert (German) glorious soldier.

Herculano (Latin) belonging to Hercules.

Hercules (Latin) glorious gift. Mythology: a Greek hero of fabulous strength, renowned for his twelve labors.

Heriberto (Spanish) a form of Herbert.

Hermagoras (Greek) disciple of Hermes.

Hermalindo, Hermelindo (German) he who is like a shield of strength.

Herman (Latin) noble. (German) soldier.

Hermán (Germanic) a form of Herman.

Hermenegildo (Germanic) he who offers sacrifices to God.

Hermes (Greek) messenger. Mythology: the divine herald of Greek mythology.

Hermilo (Greek) little Hermes.

Hermócrates (Greek) powerful like Hermes.

Hermógenes (Greek) sent from Hermes.

Hermolao (Greek) messenger of God.

Hermoso (Latin) with shape.

Hernan (German) peacemaker.

Hernán (Spanish) a form of Hernan.

Hernández (Spanish) a form of Ferdinand.

Hernando (Spanish) a form of Ferdinand.

Herodes (Greek) the fire dragon.

Herodías (Greek) leader.

Herodoto (Greek) the sacred talent.

Heródoto (Greek) the divine talent.

Herón, Heros (Latin) hero.

Herrick (German) war ruler.

Herschel (Hebrew) a form of Hershel.

Hersh (Hebrew) a short form of Hershel.

Hershel (Hebrew) deer.

Hertz (Yiddish) my strife.

Heru (Egyptian) god of the sun.

Hervé **(French) a form of Harvey.**

Hesiquio (Greek) tranquil.

Hesperia (Greek) one who follows the star of the first evening performance.

Hesperos (Greek) evening star.

Hesutu (Moquelumnan) picking up a yellow jacket's nest.

Hew (Welsh) a form of Hugh.

Hewitt (German, French) little smart one.

Hewson (English) son of Hugh.

Hezekiah (Hebrew) God gives strength.

Hiamovi (Cheyenne) high chief.

Hiawatha 🅱🅶 (Iraquoian) river maker. History: the Onondagan leader credited with organizing the Iroquois confederacy.

Hibah 🇬🇧 (Arabic) gift.

Hidalgo (Spanish) noble one.

Hideaki (Japanese) smart, clever.

Hieremias (Greek) God will uplift.

Hieronymos (Greek) a form of Jerome. Art: Hieronymus Bosch was a fifteenth-century Dutch painter.

Hieu (Vietnamese) respectful.

Higinio (Greek) he who has good health.

Hilal (Arabic) new moon.

Hilâl (Arabic) a form of Hilal.

Hilaria, Hilarión (Latin) happy, content.

Hilario (Spanish) a form of Hilary.

Hilary 🇬🇧 **(Latin) cheerful.** Hildebrand **(German) battle sword.**

Hildemaro (Germanic) famous in combat.

Hilderic (German) warrior; fortress.

Hillel (Hebrew) greatly praised. Religion: Rabbi Hillel originated the Talmud.

Hilliard (German) brave warrior.

Hilmar (Swedish) famous noble.

Hilton (English) town on a hill.

Hinto (Dakota) blue.

Hinun (Native American) spirit of the storm.

Hipacio (Spanish) confessor.

Hipócrates (Greek) powerful because of his cavalry.

Hipolito (Spanish) a form of Hippolyte.

Hipólito (Greek) a form of Hipolito.

Hippolyte (Greek) horseman.

Hiram (Hebrew) noblest; exalted.

Hiromasa (Japanese) fair, just.

Hiroshi **(Japanese) generous.**

Hishâm (Arabic) generosity.

Hisoka (Japanese) secretive, reserved.

Hiu (Hawaiian) a form of Hugh.

Hixinio (Greek) vigorous.

Ho (Chinese) good.

Hoang (Vietnamese) finished.

Hobart (German) Bart's hill. A form of Hubert.

Hobert (German) Bert's hill.

Hobie (German) a short form of Hobart, Hobert.

Hobson (English) son of Robert.

Hoc (Vietnamese) studious.

Hod (Hebrew) a short form of Hodgson.

Hodgson (English) son of Roger.

Hoffman (German) influential.

Hogan (Irish) youth.

Holbrook (English) brook in the hollow.

Holden (English) hollow in the valley.

Holic (Czech) barber.

Holland GB (French) Geography: a former province of the Netherlands.

Holleb (Polish) dove.

Hollis BG (English) grove of holly trees.

Holmes (English) river islands.

Holt (English) forest.

Homar (Greek) a form of Homer.

Homer (Greek) hostage; pledge; security. Literature: a renowned Greek epic poet.

Homero (Spanish) a form of Homer.

Hondo (Shona) warrior.

Honesto (Filipino) honest.

Honi (Hebrew) gracious.

Honok (Polish) a form of Henry.

Honon (Moquelumnan) bear.

Honorato (Spanish) honorable.

Honoré (Latin) honored.

Honovi BG (Native American) strong.

Honza (Czech) a form of John.

Hop (Chinese) agreeable.

Horace (Latin) keeper of the hours. Literature: a famous Roman lyric poet and satirist.

Horacio (Latin) a form of Horace.

Horado (Spanish) timekeeper.

Horangel (Greek) the messenger from the mountain.

Horatio (Latin) clan name. (Persian) the great wise one.

Horst (German) dense grove, thicket.

Hortencio, Hortensio (Latin) he who has a garden and loves it.

Horton (English) garden estate.

Horus (Egyptian) god of the sky.

Hosa (Arapaho) young crow.

Hosea (Hebrew) salvation. Bible: a Hebrew prophet.

Hospicio (Spanish) he who is accommodating.

Hotah (Lakota) white.

Hototo (Native American) whistler.

Houghton (English) settlement on the headland.

Houston (English) hill town. Geography: a city in Texas.

Howard (English) watchman. **Howe** (German) high.

Howell (Welsh) remarkable.

Howi BG (Moquelumnan) turtledove.

Howie (English) a familiar form of Howard, Howland.

Howin (Chinese) loyal swallow.

Howland (English) hilly land.

Hoyt (Irish) mind; spirit.

Hu (Chinese) tiger.

Huaiquilaf (Mapuche) good, straight lance.

Huapi (Mapuche) island.

Hubbard (German) a form of Hubert.

Hubert (German) bright mind; bright spirit. **Huberto** (Spanish) a form of Hubert.

Hubie (English) a familiar form of Hubert.

Hucsuncu (Quechua) he who has only one love.

Hud (Arabic) Religion: a Muslim prophet.

Hudson ✨ (English) son of Hud.

Huechacura (Mapuche) sharp rock; peak.

Huemac (Nahuatl) name of a Toltec king.

Huenchulaf (Mapuche) healthy man.

Huenchuleo (Mapuche) brave, handsome river.

Huenchuman (Mapuche) proud, male condor.

Huenchumilla (Mapuche) ascending light.

Huenchuñir (Mapuche) male fox.

Huentemil (Mapuche) light from above.

Huenu (Araucanian) heaven.

Huenuhueque (Mapuche) lamb from heaven.

Huenullan (Mapuche) heavenly altar.

Huenuman (Mapuche) condor from the sky.

Huenupan (Mapuche) branch from heaven.

Huey (English) a familiar form of Hugh.

Hueypín (Mapuche) broken, odd land.

Hugh (English) a short form of Hubert.

Hugo (Latin) a form of Hugh.

Hugolino (Germanic) he who has spirit and intelligence.

Hugues (French) a form of Hugh.

Huichacura (Mapuche) rock with just one ridge.

Huichahue (Mapuche) battlefield.

Huichalef (Mapuche) he who runs on just one side.

Huichañir (Mapuche) fox from another region.

Huidaleo (Mapuche) branch in the river.

Huinculche (Mapuche) people that live on the hill.

Huircalaf (Mapuche) cry of joy.

Huircaleo (Mapuche) whisper of the river.

Huitzilli (Nahuatl) hummingbird.

Hulbert (German) brilliant grace.
e,

Huldá (Hebrew) valiant.

Hullen (Mapuche) spring.

Humam (Arabic) courageous; generous.

Humbaldo (Germanic) daring as a lion cub.

Humbert (German) brilliant strength.
Humberto (Portuguese) a form of Humbert.

Humphrey (German) peaceful strength. **Hung** (Vietnamese) brave.

Hunt (English) a short form of names beginning with "Hunt."

Hunter ☆
BG (English) hunter.

Huntington (English) hunting estate.

Huntley (English) hunter's meadow.

Hurley (Irish) sea tide.

Hurst (English) a form of Horst.

Husai (Hebrew) the hurried one.

Husam (Arabic) sword.

Husamettin (Turkish) sharp sword.

Huslu (Native American) hairy bear.

Hussain, Hussien (Arabic) forms of Hussein.

Hussein (Arabic) little; handsome.

Huston (English) a form of Houston.

Hutchinson (English) son of the hutch dweller.

Hute (Native American) star.

Hutton (English) house on the jutting ledge.

Huxley (English) Hugh's meadow.

Huy (Vietnamese) glorious.

Hy (Vietnamese) hopeful. (English) a short form of Hyman.

Hyacinthe (French) hyacinth.

Hyatt (English) high gate.

Hyde (English) cache; measure of land equal to 120 acres; animal hide.

Hyder (English) tanner, preparer of animal hides for tanning.

Hyman (English) a form of Chaim.

Hyrum (Hebrew) a form of Hiram.

Hyun-Ki (Korean) wise.

Hyun-Shik (Korean) clever.

I

'Imâd, 'Imad Al-Dîn (Arabic) support; pillar.

'Isà-Eisà (Arabic) a form of Jesus.

'Issâm (Arabic) shelter.

Iadón (Hebrew) thankful.

Iago (Spanish, Welsh) a form of Jacob, James. Literature: the villain in Shakespeare's *Othello*.

Iain (Scottish) a form of Ian.

Iajín (Hebrew) God establishes.

Iakobos (Greek) a form of Jacob.

Iakona (Hawaiian) healer.

Ialeel (Hebrew) waiting for God.

Iamín (Hebrew) right hand.

Ian ⚝

⒝⒢ (Scottish) a form of John.

Ianos (Czech) a form of John.

Iazeel (Hebrew) contributions of God.

Ib (Phoenician, Danish) oath of Baal.

Iban (Basque) a form of John.

Ibán (German) glorious.

Iber, Ibérico, Iberio, Ibero, Ibi (Latin) native of Iberia.

Ibon (Basque) a form of Ivor.

Ibrahim (Hausa) my father is exalted. (Arabic) a form of Abraham.

Ibrahîm (Arabic) a form of Ibrahim.

Ibsen (German) archer's son. Literature: Henrik Ibsen was a nineteenth-century Norwegian poet and playwright whose works influenced the development of modern drama.

Icabod (Hebrew) without glory.

Ícaro (Greek) image.

Iccauhtli (Nahuatl) younger brother.

Ichabod (Hebrew) glory is gone. Literature: Ichabod Crane is the main character of Washington Irving's story "The Legend of Sleepy Hollow."

Ichiro (Japanese) born first.

Ichtaca (Nahuatl) secret.

Icnoyotl (Nahuatl) friendship.

Iden (English) pasture in the wood.

Idi (Swahili) born during the Idd festival.

Idogbe (Egyptian) brother of twins.

Idris (Welsh) eager lord. (Arabic) Religion: a Muslim prophet.

Idrîs (Arabic) a form of Idris.

Idumeo (Latin) red.

Iedidiá (Hebrew) loved by God.

Iejiel (Hebrew) God lives.

Iestyn (Welsh) a form of Justin.

Igashu (Native American) wanderer; seeker.

Iggy (Latin) a familiar form of Ignatius.

Ignacio (Italian) a form of Ignatius.

Ignado (Spanish) fiery or ardent.

Ignatius (Latin) fiery, ardent. Religion: Saint Ignatius of Loyola founded the Jesuit order.

Igor (Russian) a form of Inger, Ingvar.

Iham (Indian) expected.

Ihit (Indian) prize; honor.

Ihsan (Turkish) compassionate.

Ihsân (Turkish) a form of Ihsan.

Ihuicatl (Nahuatl) sky.

Ike (Hebrew) a familiar form of Isaac. History:

the nickname of the thirty-fourth U.S. president Dwight D. Eisenhower.

Iker (Basque) visitation.

Ilan (Hebrew) tree. (Basque) youth.

Ilari (Basque) a form of Hilary.

Ilbert (German) distinguished fighter.

Ildefonso (German) totally prepared for combat.

Ilhicamina (Nahuatl) he shoots arrows at the sky.

Ilhuitl (Nahuatl) day.

Ilias (Greek) a form of Elijah.

Ilidio (Latin) troop.

Illan (Basque, Latin) youth.

Illayuc (Quechua) luminous.

Ilom (Ibo) my enemies are many.

Iluminado (Latin) he who receives the inspiration of God.

Ilya (Russian) a form of Elijah.

Ilyas (Greek) a form of Elijah.

Imad (Arabic) supportive; mainstay.

Iman 𝔾𝔹 (Hebrew) a short form of Immanuel.

Imani 𝔾𝔹 (Hebrew) a short form of Immanuel.

Imaran (Indian) strong.

Imbert (German) poet.

Immanuel (Hebrew) a form of Emmanuel.

Imran (Arabic) host.

Imre (Hungarian) a form of Emery.

Imrich (Czech) a form of Emery.

Imtiaz (Indian) power of discrimination.

Inalef (Mapuche) the swift reinforcement.

Inay (Hindi) god; godlike.

Inca (Quechua) prince.

Incaurco, Incaurcu (Quechua) hill; Inca god.

Ince (Hungarian) innocent.

Incencio (Spanish) white.

Incendio (Spanish) fire.

Indalecio (Arabic) the same as the master.

Inder (Hindi) god; godlike.

Indiana 𝔹𝔾 (Hindi) from India.

Indíbil (Spanish) he who is very black.

Indivar (Indian) blue lotus.

Indrajeet (Indian) conqueror.

Indrakanta (Indian) another name for the Hindu god Indra.

Indraneel (Indian) sapphire.

Indro (Spanish) the victor.

Indubhushan (Indian) the moon

Induhasan, Indukanta, Indushekhar (Indian) like a moon.

Indulal (Indian) moon's luster.

Inek (Welsh) a form of Irvin.

Inés (Greek) pure.

Ing (Scandinavian) a short form of Ingmar.

Ingelbert (German) a form of Engelbert.

Inger (Scandinavian) son's army.

Inglis (Scottish) English.

Ingmar (Scandinavian) famous son.

Ingram (English) angel.

Ingvar (Scandinavian) Ing's soldier.

Ini-Herit (Egyptian) he who returns from far away.

Inigo (Basque) a form of Ignatius.

Íñigo (Basque) a form of Inigo.

Iniko (Ibo) born during bad times.

Inir (Welsh) honorable.

Innis (Irish) island.

Innocenzio (Italian) innocent.

Intekhab (Indian) chosen.

Inteus (Native American) proud; unashamed.

Inti (Aymara) he who is bold.

Intiauqui (Quechua) sun prince.

Intichurin (Quechua) child of the sun.

Intiguaman (Quechua) sun falcon.

Intiyafa (Quechua) ray of sunlight.

Ioakim (Russian) a form of Joachim.

Ioan (Greek, Bulgarian, Romanian) a form of John.

Ioannis (Greek, Bulgarian, Romanian) a form of Ioan.

Iojanán (Hebrew) God is merciful.

Iokepa (Hawaiian) a form of Joseph.

Iokia (Hawaiian) healed by God.

Iolo (Welsh) the Lord is worthy.

Ionakana (Hawaiian) a form of Jonathan.

Iorgos (Greek) a form of George.

Iosef (Hebrew) a form of Iosif.

Iosif (Greek, Russian) a form of Joseph.

Iosua (Romanian) a form of Joshua.

Ipyana (Nyakyusa) graceful.

Iqbal (Indian) desire.

Ira BG (Hebrew) watchful.

Iram (English) bright.

Ireneo, Irineo (Greek) the lover of peace.

Irfan (Arabic) thankfulness.

Irmin **(German) strong.**

Irshaad (Indian) signal.

Irumba (Rutooro) born after twins.

Irv (Irish, Welsh, English) a short form of Irvin, Irving.

Irvin (Irish, Welsh, English) a short form of Irving.

Irving (Irish) handsome. (Welsh) white river. (English) sea friend.

Irwin (English) a form of Irving. **Isa** BG (Hebrew) a form of Isaiah. (Arabic) a form of Jesus.

Isaac (Hebrew) he will laugh. Bible: the son of Abraham and Sarah.

Isaak (Hebrew) a form of Isaac.

Isac, Isacc, Issac (Hebrew) forms of Isaac.

Isacar (Hebrew) he was given for a favor.

Isacio (Greek) equality.

Isadoro (Spanish) gift of Isis.

Isai, Isaih (Hebrew) forms of Isaiah.

Isaiah (Hebrew) God is my salvation. Bible: a Hebrew prophet.

Isaias (Hebrew) a form of Isaiah.

Isaías (Hebrew) a form of Isaias.

Isam (Arabic) safeguard.

Isamu (Japanese) courageous.

Isar (Indian) eminent; another name for the Hindu god Shiva.

Isarno (Germanic) eagle of iron.

Isas (Japanese) meritorious.

Iscay (Quechua) second child.

Iscaycuari (Quechua) doubly savage and untamable.

Isekemu (Native American) slow-moving creek.

Isham (English) home of the iron one.

Ishan (Hindi) direction.

Ishaq (Arabic) a form of Isaac.

Ishâq (Arabic) a form of Ishaq.

Ishboshet (Hebrew) man of shame.

Ishmael (Hebrew) God will hear. Literature: the narrator of Herman Melville's novel *Moby-Dick*.

Ishmerai (Hebrew) God takes care.

Ishrat (Indian) affection.

Ishwar (Indian) God.

Isiah, Issiah (Hebrew) forms of Isaiah.

Isidore (Greek) gift of Isis.

Isidoro (Greek) a form of Isidore.

Isidro (Greek) a form of Isidore.

Iskander (Afghan) a form of Alexander.

Iskinder (Ethiopian) a form of Alexander.

Islam (Arabic) submission; the religion of Muhammad.

Isma'îl (Arabic) a form of Ismael.

Ismael, Ismail (Arabic) forms of Ishmael.
Ismal, Ismale, Ismeil, Ismiel

Isocrates (Greek) he who can do as much as the next man.

Isócrates (Greek) one who shares power with the same legal authority.

Isod (Hebrew) God fights and prevails.

Isra'îl (Arabic) a form of Israel.

Israel (Hebrew) prince of God; wrestled with God. History: the nation of Israel took its name from the name given Jacob after he wrestled with the angel of the Lord.

Isreal (Hebrew) a form of Israel.

Issa (Swahili) God is our salvation.

Issmat (Lebanese) infallible.

Istu (Native American) sugar pine.

István (Hungarian) a form of Stephen.

Itaete (Guarani) blade.

Italo (Latin) he came from the land that is between the seas.

Ithamat (Hebrew) a form of Ittamar.

Ithel (Welsh) generous lord.

Itotia (Nahuatl) dance.

Ittamar (Hebrew) island of palms.

Ittmar (Hebrew) a form of Ittamar.

Itzak (Hebrew) a form of Isaac, Yitzchak.

Itzjac (Hebrew) reason for joy.

Itztli (Nahuatl) obsidian knife.

Iuitl (Nahuatl) feather.

Iukini (Hawaiian) a form of Eugene.

Iustin (Bulgarian, Russian) a form of Justin.

Ivan, Ivann (Russian) forms of John.

Ivana (Catalan) a form of Ivo.

Ivanhoe (Hebrew) God's tiller. Literature: *Ivanhoe*

is a historical romance by Sir Walter Scott.

Ivar (Scandinavian) a form of Ivor. **Ives** (English) young archer.

Ivo (German) yew wood; bow wood.

Ivor (Scandinavian) a form of Ivo.

Ivory GB (Latin) made of ivory.

Iwan (Polish) a form of John.

Ixtli (Nahuatl) face.

Iyafa, Iyapa (Quechua) lightning.

Iyapo (Yoruba) many trials; many obstacles.

Iyapoma, Iyapuma, Iyaticsi (Quechua) puma of light.

Iyapu (Quechua) lightning.

Iyatecsi (Quechua) eternal light.

Iye (Native American) smoke.

Izaac (Czech) a form of Izak.

Izak (Czech) a form of Isaac.

Izar (Basque) star.

Izhar (Indian) submission.

Izod (Irish) light haired.

Izzy (Hebrew) a familiar form of Isaac, Isidore, Israel.

J

J (American) an initial used as a first name.

J. (American) a form of J.

J'quan (American) a form of Jaquan.

Ja BG (Korean) attractive, magnetic.

Ja'far (Sanskrit) little stream.

Ja'juan (American) a form of Jajuan.

Ja'marcus (American) a form of Jamarcus.

Ja'quan (American) a form of Jaquan.

Ja'von (American) a form of Javan.

Jaali (Swahili) powerful.

Jaan (Estonian) a form of Christian. (Dutch, Slavic) a form of Jan.

Jaap (Dutch) a form of Jim.

Jabari (Swahili) fearless, brave.

Jabbar (Arabic) fixer.

Jabel (Hebrew) like the arrow that flies.

Jâber (Arabic) comforter.

Jabez (Hebrew) born in pain.

Jabin (Hebrew) God has created.

Jabín (Hebrew) a form of Jabin.

Jabir (Arabic) consoler, comforter.

Jabril (Arabic) a form of Jibril.

Jabulani (Shona) happy.

Jacan (Hebrew) trouble.

Jacari (American) a form of Jacorey.

Jaccob (Hebrew) a form of Jacob.

Jace ✩ (American) a combination of the initials J. + C.

Jacek (American) a form of Jace.

Jacen (Greek) a form of Jason.

Jacey GB (American) a form of Jace.

Jacinto (Portuguese, Spanish) hyacinth.

Jack ✩ (American) a familiar form of Jacob, John.

Jackie BG (American) a familiar form of Jack.

Jackson ✩
BG (English) son of Jack.

Jacky (American) a familiar form of Jack.

Jaco (Portuguese) a form of Jacob.

Jacob ✩
BG (Hebrew) supplanter, substitute. Bible: son of Isaac, brother of Esau.

Jacobe, Jacoby (Hebrew) forms of Jacob.

Jacoberto (Germanic) famous.

Jacobi BG (Hebrew) a form of Jacob.

Jacobo (Hebrew) a form of Jacob.

Jacobson (English) son of Jacob.

Jacolby (Hebrew) a form of Jacob.

Jacorey (American) a combination of Jacob + Corey.

Jacory (American) a form of Jacorey.

Jacquan (French) a form of Jacques.

Jacque (French) a form of Jacob.

Jacquel (French) a form of Jacques.

Jacques (French) a form of Jacob, James. Jacquez,

Jaquez (French) forms of Jacques.

Jacy GB (Tupi-Guarani) moon. (American) a form of Jace.

Jad (Hebrew) a short form of Jadon. (American) a short form of Jadrien.

Jadarius (American) a combination of the prefix Ja + Darius.

Jaden BG (Hebrew) a form of Jadon.

Jadiel (Spanish) a form of Jehudiel; (Hebrew) a form of Yehudiel; he who praises God.

Jadon (Hebrew) God has heard.

Jadrien (American) a combination of Jay + Adrien.

Jadyn GB (Hebrew) a form of Jadon.

Jae BG (French, English) a form of Jay.

Jae-Hwa (Korean) rich, prosperous.

Jaeden, Jaedon (Hebrew) forms of Jadon.

Jaegar (German) hunter.

Jael GB (Hebrew) mountain goat.

Jaelen, Jaelin, Jaelon (American) forms of Jalen.

Jafar (Sanskrit) a form of Ja'far.

Jafet (Hebrew) enlargement.

Jag, Jagat (Indian) the universe.

Jagadbandu (Indian) another name for the Hindu god Krishna.

Jagadish (Indian) lord of the universe.

Jaganmay (Indian) spread over the universe.

Jagannath (Indian) another name for the Hindu god Vishnu.

Jagdeep (Sikh) the lamp of the world.

Jagger (English) carter.

Jagjeevan (Indian) worldly life.

Jagmeet (Sikh) friend of the world.

Jago (English) a form of Jacob, James.

Jaguar (Spanish) jaguar.

Jahan (Indian) the world.

Jahi (Swahili) dignified.

Jahleel (Hindi) a form of Jalil.

Jahlil (Hindi) a form of Jalil.

Jahmal (Arabic) a form of Jamal.

Jahmar (American) a form of Jamar.

Jahvon (Hebrew) a form of Javan.

Jai BG (Tai) heart.
Jaie, Jaii

Jaichand (Indian) victory of the moon.

Jaidayal (Indian) victory of kindness.

Jaiden BG (Hebrew) a form of Jadon.

Jaidev (Indian) victory of God.

Jaigopal, Jaikrishna (Indian) victory of the Hindu god Krishna.

Jailen (American) a form of Jalen.

Jaime BG (Spanish) a form of Jacob, James.

Jaimini (Indian) an ancient Hindu philosopher.

Jainarayan, Jaiwant (Indian) victory.

Jaipal (Indian) another name for the Hindu god Brahma.

Jaiquan (American) a form of Jaquan.

Jair (Spanish) a form of Jairo.

Jaír (Spanish) a form of Jair.

Jairaj (Indian) lord of victory.

Jairo (Spanish) God enlightens.

Jairus (American) a form of Jairo.

Jaisal (Indian) famous folk.

Jaison (Greek) a form of Jason.

Jaisukh (Indian) joy of winning.

Jaivon (Hebrew) a form of Javan.

Jaja (Ibo) honored.

Jajuan (American) a combination of the prefix Ja + Juan.

Jakari (American) a form of Jacorey.

Jake ☆ (Hebrew) a short form of Jacob.

Jakeb, Jakeob, Jakob, Jakub (Hebrew) forms of Jacob.

Jakeem (Arabic) uplifted.

Jakome (Basque) a form of James.

Jal (Gypsy) wanderer.

Jalâl (Arabic) glorious.

Jalan, Jalin, Jalon (American) forms of Jalen.

Jaleel (Hindi) a form of Jalil.
Jaleell, Jaleil, Jalel

Jaleen (American) a form of Jalen.

Jalen BG **(American) a combination of the prefix Ja + Len.**
Jalend, Jallen

Jalendu (Indian) moon in the water.

Jalene BG (American) a form of Jalen.

Jalil (Hindi) revered.

Jalisat (Arabic) he who receives little, gives more.

Jalyn GB (American) a form of Jalen.

Jam (American) a short form of Jamal, Jamar.

Jamaal, Jamahl, Jamall, Jamaul (Arabic) forms of Jamal.

Jamaine (Arabic) a form of Germain.

Jamal (Arabic) handsome**Jamâl** (Arabic) a form of Jamal.

Jamale (Arabic) a form of Jamal.

Jamar (American) a form of Jamal.

Jamarcus (American) a combination of the prefix Ja + Marcus.

Jamare (American) a form of Jamario.

Jamaree, Jamari (American) forms of Jamario.

Jamarion (American) a combination of the prefix Ja + Marion

Jamario (American) a combination of the prefix Ja + Mario.

Jamarious, Jamarius (American) forms of Jamario.

Jamaris (American) a form of Jamario.

Jamarkus (American) a combination of the prefix Ja + Markus.

Jamarquis (American) a combination of the prefix Ja + Marquis.

Jameel (Arabic) a form of Jamal.

Jamel, Jamell (Arabic) forms of Jamal.

Jamen, Jamon (Hebrew) forms of Jamin.

James ☀ BG (Hebrew) supplanter, substitute. (English) a form of Jacob. Bible: James the Great and James the Less were two of the Twelve Apostles.

Jameson (English) son of James.

Jamey GB (English) a familiar form of James.

Jamez (Hebrew) a form of James.

Jamie GB (English) a familiar form of James.

Jamieson (English) a form of Jamison.

Jamil (Arabic) a form of Jamal.

Jamin (Hebrew) favored.

Jamir (American) a form of Jamar.

Jamison BG (English) son of James.

Jamond (American) a combination of James + Raymond.

Jamor (American) a form of Jamal.

Jamsheed (Persian) from Persia.

Jan BG (Dutch, Slavic) a form of John.

Janco (Czech) a form of John.

Jando (Spanish) a form of Alexander.

Janeil (American) a combination of the prefix Ja + Neil.

Janek (Polish) a form of John.

Janina (Hebrew) grace.

Janis GB (Latvian) a form of John.

Janne (Finnish) a form of John.

János (Hungarian) a form of John.

Jansen (Scandinavian) a form of Janson.

Janson (Scandinavian) son of Jan.

Jantzen (Scandinavian) a form of Janson.

Janus (Latin) gate, passageway; born in January. Mythology: the Roman god of beginnings and endings.

Janvier (French) a form of Jenaro.

Japa (Indian) chanting.

Japendra, Japesh (Indian) lord of chants; other names for the Hindu god Shiva.

Japheth (Hebrew) handsome. (Arabic) abundant. Bible: a son of Noah.

Jaquan (American) a combination of the prefix Ja + Quan.

Jaquarius (American) a combination of Jaquan + Darius.

Jaquavious, Jaquavius (American) forms of Jaquavis.

Jaquavis (American) a form of Jaquan.

Jaquawn, Jaquon (American) forms of Jaquan.

Jarad, Jarid, Jarod, Jarrad, Jarred, Jarrid, Jarrod, Jarryd, Jaryd (Hebrew) forms of Jared.

Jarah (Hebrew) sweet as honey.

Jaran, Jaren, Jarin, Jarren, Jarron, Jaryn (Hebrew) forms of Jaron.

Jardan (French) garden. (Hebrew) a form of Jordan.

Jareb (Hebrew) contending.

Jared (Hebrew) a form of Jordan.

Jarek (Slavic) born in January.

Jarel, Jarell (Scandinavian) forms of Gerald.

Jaret, Jarett, Jarret (English) forms of Jarrett.

Jareth (American) a combination of Jared + Gareth.

Jarius, Jarrius (American) forms of Jairo.

Jarl (Scandinavian) earl, nobleman.

Jarlath (Latin) in control.

Jarmal (Arabic) a form of Jamal.

Jarman (German) from Germany.

Jarmarcus (American) a form of Jamarcus.

Jarom (Latin) a form of Jerome.

Jaron (Hebrew) he will sing; he will cry out.

Jaroslav (Czech) glory of spring.

Jarrell (English) a form of Gerald.

Jarreth (American) a form of Jareth.

Jarrett (English) a form of Garrett, Jared.

Jarvis (German) skilled with a spear.

Jas BG (English) a familiar form of James. (Polish) a form of John.

Jasbeer (Indian) victorious hero.

Jasdeep (Sikh) the lamp radiating God's glories.

Jase (Greek) a short form of Jason.

Jasen, Jasson (Greek) forms of Jason.

Jasha (Russian) a familiar form of Jacob, James.

Jashawn (American) a combination of the prefix Ja + Shawn.

Jashua (Hebrew) a form of Joshua.

Jaskaran (Sikh) sings praises to the Lord.

Jaskarn (Sikh) a form of Jaskaran.

Jasmeet BG (Sikh) friend of the Lord. (Persian) a form of Jasmin.

Jason ★ (Greek) healer. Mythology: the hero who led the Argonauts in search of the Golden Fleece.

Jasón (Greek) a form of Jason.

Jaspal (Punjabi) living a virtuous lifestyle.

Jasper BG (French) brown, red, or yellow ornamental stone. (English) a form of Casper.

Jaspreet BG (Punjabi) virtuous.

Jaswant (Indian) famous.

Jathan (Greek) a form of Jason.

Jatinra (Hindi) great Brahmin sage.

Jaume (Catalan) a form of Jaime.

Javan (Hebrew) Bible: son of Japheth.

Javante (American) **a form of Javan.**

Javar (American) a form of Jarvis.

Javari (American) a form of Jarvis.

Javarious, Javarius (American) forms of Javar.

Javaris (English) a form of Javar.

Javas (Sanskrit) quick, swift.

Javaughn (American) a form of Javan.

Javen, Javin (Hebrew) forms of Javan.

Javeon (American) a form of Javan.

Javian, Javion (American) forms of Javan.

Javier (Spanish) owner of a new house. **Javiero** (Spanish) a form of Javier.

Javilá (Hebrew) strip of sand.

Javon BG (Hebrew) a form of Javan.

Javone (Hebrew) a form of Javan.

Javonta (American) a form of Javan.

Javontae, Javontay, Javonte, Javonté (American) forms of Javan.

Jawad (Arabic) openhanded, generous.

Jawan, Jawaun, Jawon, Jawuan (American) forms of Jajuan.

Jawara (African) peace and love.

Jawhar (Arabic) jewel; essence.

Jaxon ★ (English) a form of Jackson.

Jaxson ★ (English) a form of Jackson.

Jaxton (American) Jack's town

Jay (French) blue jay. (English) a short form of James, Jason.
Jai, Jave, Jeays, Jeyes

Jayanti (Hindi) sacred anniversary.

Jayce BG (American) a combination of the initials J. + C.

Jaycob (Hebrew) a form of Jacob.

Jayde GB (American) a combination of the initials J. + D.

Jayden ★
BG (Hebrew) a form of Jadon. (American) a form of Jayde.

Jaydon BG (Hebrew) a form of Jadon.

Jaye BG (French, English) a form of Jay.

Jaylan, Jayln, Jaylon (American) forms of Jaylen.

Jayland (American) a form of Jaylen.

Jaylee GB (American) a combination of Jay + Lee.

Jaylen BG (American) a combination of Jay + Len. A form of Jaylee.

Jaylin GB (American) a form of Jaylen.

Jaylyn BG (American) a form of Jaylen.

292

Jayme GB (English) a form of Jamey.

Jaymes, Jaymz (English) forms of James.

Jayquan (American) a combination of Jay + Quan.

, **Jayro** (Spanish) a form of Jairo.

Jaysen, Jayson (Greek) forms of Jason.

Jayshawn (American) a combination of Jay + Shawn. A form of Jaysen.

Jayvon (American) a form of Javon.

Jaz (American) a form of Jazz.

Jazael (Hebrew) perceives God.

Jazz BG (American) jazz.

Jean BG (French) a form of John.

Jean Benoit (French) a combination of Jean + Benoit.

Jean Christoph (French) a combination of Jean + Christoph.

Jean Daniel (French) a combination of Jean + Daniel.

Jean David (French) a combination of Jean + David.

Jean Denis (French) a combination of Jean + Denis.

Jean Felix (French) a combination of Jean + Felix.

Jean Francois, Jean-Francois (French) combinations of Jean + Francois.

Jean Gabriel (French) a combination of Jean + Gabriel.

Jean Luc, Jean-Luc, Jeanluc (French) combinations of Jean + Luc.

Jean Marc, Jean-Marc (French) combinations of Jean + Marc.

Jean Michel (French) a combination of Jean + Michel.

Jean Nicholas (French) a combination of Jean + Nicholas.

Jean Pascal (French) a combination of Jean + Pascal.

Jean Philip, Jean Philippe, Jean-Philippe (French) combinations of Jean + Philip.

Jean Samuel (French) a combination of Jean + Samuel.

Jean Sebastien (French) a combination of Jean + Sebastien.

Jean Simon (French) a combination of Jean +Simon.

Jean-Claude (French) a combination of Jean + Claude.

Jean-Paul, Jeanpaul (French) combinations of Jean + Paul.

Jean-Pierre, Jeanpierre (French) combinations of Jean + Pierre.

Jeb **(Hebrew) a short form of Jebediah.**

Jebediah (Hebrew) a form of Jedidiah.

Jed (Hebrew) a short form of Jedidiah. (Arabic) hand.

Jediah (Hebrew) hand of God.

Jedidiah (Hebrew) friend of God, beloved of God.

Jedrek (Polish) strong; manly.

Jeff (English) a short form of Jefferson, Jeffrey. A familiar form of Geoffrey.

Jefferey, Jeffery (English) forms of Jeffrey.

Jefferson (English) son of Jeff. History: Thomas Jefferson was the third U.S. president.

Jefford (English) Jeff's ford.

Jeffrey (English) divinely peaceful. .

Jeffry (English) a form of Jeffrey.

Jehan (French) a form of John.

Jehová (Hebrew) I am what I am.

Jehu (Hebrew) God lives. Bible: a military commander and king of Israel.

Jela (Swahili) father that has suffered during birth.

Jelani BG (Swahili) mighty.

Jem GB (English) a short form of James, Jeremiah.

Jemal (Arabic) a form of Jamal.

Jemel (Arabic) a form of Jamal.

Jemond (French) worldly.
, **Jenaro** (Latin) born in January.

Jenkin (Flemish) little John.

Jenö (Hungarian) a form of Eugene.
Jenoe

Jenofonte (Greek) he who comes from another country and is eloquent.

Jens (Danish) a form of John.

Jensen GB (Scandinavian) a form of Janson.

Jensi (Hungarian) born to nobility. (Danish) a familiar form of Jens.

Jeovanni (Italian) a form of Giovanni.

Jequan (American) a combination of the prefix Je + Quan.

Jerad, Jered, Jerid, Jerod, Jerrad, Jerred, Jerrid, Jerrod (Hebrew) forms of Jared.

Jerahmy (Hebrew) a form of Jeremy.

Jerald, Jerold, Jerrold (English) forms of Gerald.

Jerall (English) a form of Gerald.

Jeramey, Jeramie, Jeramy (Hebrew) forms of Jeremy.

Jeramiah (Hebrew) a form of Jeremiah.

Jerard (French) a form of Gerard.

Jerardo (Spanish) a form of Gerard.

Jere (Hebrew) a short form of Jeremiah, Jeremy.
Jeré,

Jerel, Jerell, Jerrell (English) forms of Gerald.

Jereme, Jeremey, Jeremi, Jeremie, Jérémie (English) forms of Jeremy.

Jeremiah ★ (Hebrew) God will uplift. Bible: a Hebrew prophet.

Jeremias (Hebrew) a form of Jeremiah.

Jeremías (Hebrew) a form of Jeremias.

Jeremiel (Hebrew) God lifts me up.

Jeremy (English) a form of Jeremiah.

Jeriah (Hebrew) Jehovah has seen.

Jeric, Jerick (Arabic) short forms of Jericho. (American) forms of Jerrick.

Jericho (Arabic) city of the moon. Bible: a city conquered by Joshua.

Jerico (Arabic) a short form of Jericho.

Jérico (Spanish) a form of Jericho.

Jerimiah (Hebrew) a form of Jeremiah.

Jermain (French, English) a form of Jermaine.

Jermaine BG (French) a form of Germain. (English) sprout, bud.

Jermal (Arabic) a form of Jamal.

Jérme (French) a form of Jerome.

Jermel, Jermell (Arabic) forms of Jamal.

Jermey (English) a form of Jeremy.

Jermiah (Hebrew) a form of Jeremiah.

Jerney (Slavic) a form of Bartholomew.

Jerolin (Basque, Latin) holy.

Jerome (Latin) holy.
Jeromy (Latin) a form of Jerome.

Jeron, Jerrin, Jerron (English) forms of Jerome.

Jeronimo (Greek, Italian) a form of Jerome.

Jerónimo (Spanish) a form of Jeronimo.

Jerret, Jerrett (Hebrew) forms of Jarrett.

Jerrick (American) a combination of Jerry + Derric.

Jerry (German) mighty spearman. (English) a familiar form of Gerald, Gerard.

Jerusalén (Hebrew) peaceful place.

Jervis (English) a form of Gervaise, Jarvis.

Jerzy (Polish) a form of George.

Jesabel (Hebrew) oath of God.

Jesé (Hebrew) riches.

Jeshua (Hebrew) a form of Joshua.

Jess (Hebrew) a short form of Jesse.

Jesse BG (Hebrew) wealthy. Bible: the father of David.

Jessee, Jessey (Hebrew) forms of Jesse.

Jessi GB (Hebrew) a form of Jesse.

Jessie GB (Hebrew) a form of Jesse.

Jessy BG (Hebrew) a form of Jesse.

Jestin **(Welsh) a form of Justin.**

Jesualdo (Germanic) he who takes the lead.

Jesus BG (Hebrew) a form of Joshua. Bible: son of Mary and Joseph, believed by Christians to be the Son of God. su

Jesús (Hispanic) a form of Jesus.

Jethro (Hebrew) abundant. Bible: the father-in-law of Moses.

Jethró (Hebrew) a form of Jethro.

Jett (English) hard, black mineral. (Hebrew) a short form of Jethro.

Jevan (Hebrew) a form of Javan.

Jevin (Hebrew) a form of Javan.

Jevon (Hebrew) a form of Javan.

Jevonte (American) a form of Jevon.

Jezabel (Hebrew) oath of God.

Jhon (Hebrew) a form of John.

Jhonathan (Hebrew) a form of Jonathan.

Jhonny (Hebrew) a form of Johnie.

Jiang (Chinese) fire.

Jibade (Yoruba) born close to royalty.

Jibben (Gypsy) life.

Jibril (Arabic) archangel of Allah.

Jibrîl (Arabic) a form of Jibril.

Jihad (Arabic) struggle; holy war.

Jilt (Dutch) money.

Jim (Hebrew, English) a short form of James.

Jimbo (American) a familiar form of Jim.

Jimell (Arabic) a form of Jamel.

Jimeno (Spanish) a form of Simeón.

Jimi BG (English) a form of Jimmy.

Jimiyu (Abaluhya) born in the dry season.

Jimmie (English) a form of Jimmy.

Jimmy (English) a familiar form of Jim.

Jimmy Lee (American) a combination of Jimmy + Lee.

Jimoh (Swahili) born on Friday.

Jin BG (Chinese) gold.

Jina GB (Swahili) name.

Jinan (Arabic) garden.

Jindra (Czech) a form of Harold.

Jing-Quo (Chinese) ruler of the country.

Jiovanni (Italian) a form of Giovanni.

Jirair (Armenian) strong; hard working.

Jiri (Czech) a form of George.

Jiro (Japanese) second son.

Jivin (Hindi) life giver.

Jjiri (Zimbabwe) wild fruits of the jungle.

Jo GB (Hebrew, Japanese) a form of Joe.

Joab (Hebrew) God is father.

Joachim (Hebrew) God will establish. ,

Joan GB (German) a form of Johann.

Joao, João (Portuguese) forms of John.

Joaquim (Portuguese) a form of Joachim.

Joaquin, Joaquín (Spanish) forms of Joachim.

Job (Hebrew) afflicted. Bible: a righteous man whose faith in God survived the test of many afflictions.

Joben (Japanese) enjoys cleanliness.

Jobo (Spanish) a familiar form of Joseph.

Joby BG (Hebrew) a familiar form of Job.

Jock (American) a familiar form of Jacob. A form of Jack.

Jocquez (French) a form of Jacquez.

Jocqui (French) a form of Jacque.

Jocundo (Latin) pleasant, festive.

Jodan (Hebrew) a combination of Jo + Dan.

Jody BG (Hebrew) a familiar form of Joseph.

Joe (Hebrew) a short form of Joseph.
Jow

Joel (Hebrew) God is willing. Bible: an Old Testament Hebrew prophet.

Joeseph, Joesph (Hebrew) forms of Joseph.

Joey BG (Hebrew) a familiar form of Joe, Joseph.

Johan (German) a form of Johann.

Johann (German) a form of John.

Johannes (German) a form of Johann.

Johathan (Hebrew) a form of Jonathan.

John ☆ (Hebrew) God is gracious. Bible: the name honoring John the Baptist and John the Evangelist.

John Paul, John-Paul, Johnpaul (American) combinations of John + Paul.

John-Michael, Johnmichael (American) combinations of John + Michael.

John-Robert (American) a combination of John + Robert.

Johnathan, Johnathen, Johnathon (Hebrew) forms of Jonathan.

Johnie, Johnny, Johny (Hebrew) familiar forms of John.

Johnnie BG (Hebrew) a familiar form of John.

Johnpatrick (American) a combination of John + Patick.

Johnson (English) son of John.

Johntavius (American) a form of John.

Johnthan (Hebrew) a form of Jonathan.

Joji (Japanese) a form of George.

Jojo (Fante) born on Monday.

Jokim (Basque) a form of Joachim.

Jolon (Native American) valley of the dead oaks.

Jomar (American) a form of Jamar.

296

Jomei (Japanese) spreads light.

Jomo (African) farmer.

Jon (Hebrew) a form of John. A short form of Jonathan.

Jon-Michael (American) a combination of Jon + Michael.

Jon-Pierre (American) a combination of Jon + Pierre.

Jonah (Hebrew) dove. Bible: an Old Testament prophet who was swallowed by a large fish.

Jonas (Hebrew) he accomplishes. (Lithuanian) a form of John.

Jonás (Hebrew) a form of Jonas.

Jonatan **(Hebrew) a form of Jonathan.**

Jonathan ⭐

🅱🅶 (Hebrew) gift of God. Bible: the son of King Saul who became a loyal friend of David.

Jonathen, Jonathon, Jonnathan (Hebrew) forms of Jonathan.

Jones (Welsh) son of John.

Jonothan (Hebrew) a form of Jonathan.

Jontae (French) a combination of Jon + the suffix Tae.

Jontavious (American) a form of Jon.

Jontay, Jonte (American) forms of Jontae.

Jonthan (Hebrew) a form of Jonathan.

Joop **(Dutch) a familiar form of Joseph.**

Joost (Dutch) just.

Joquin (Spanish) a form of Joaquin.

Jora 🅶🅱 (Hebrew) teacher.

Joram (Hebrew) Jehovah is exalted.

Jordan ⭐

🅱🅶 (Hebrew) descending. J

Jordán (Hebrew) a form of Jordan.

Jorden 🅱🅶 (Hebrew) a form of Jordan.

Jordi, Jordie, Jordy (Hebrew) familiar forms of Jordan.

Jordin, Jordyn 🅶🅱 (Hebrew) forms of Jordan.

Jordon 🅱🅶 (Hebrew) a form of Jordan.

Jorell (American) he saves. Literature: a name inspired by the fictional character Jor-El, Superman's father.

Jorey (Hebrew) a familiar form of Jordan.

Jörg (German) a form of George.

Jorge, Jorje (Spanish) forms of George.

Jorgeluis (Spanish) a combination of Jorge + Luis.

Jorgen (Danish) a form of George.

Joris (Dutch) a form of George.

Jörn (German) a familiar form of Gregory.

Jorrín (Spanish) a form of George.

Jory 🅱🅶 (Hebrew) a familiar form of Jordan.

Josafat (Hebrew) God's judgment.

Jose ⭐ 🅱🅶 (Spanish) a form of Joseph. **José** (Spanish) a form of Joseph.

Josealfredo (Spanish) a combination of Jose + Alfredo.

Joseantonio (Spanish) a combination of Jose + Antonio.

Josef (German, Portuguese, Czech, Scandinavian) a form of Joseph.

Joseguadalup (Spanish) a combination of Jose + Guadalupe.

Joseluis (Spanish) a combination of Jose + Luis.

Josemanuel (Spanish) a combination of Jose + Manuel.

Joseph ☆

BG (Hebrew) God will add, God will increase. Bible: in the Old Testament, the son of Jacob who came to rule Egypt; in the New Testament, the husband of Mary.

Josey GB (Spanish) a form of Joseph.

Josh (Hebrew) a short form of Joshua.

Josha (Hindi) satisfied.

Joshawa (Hebrew) a form of Joshua.

Joshi (Swahili) galloping.

Joshua ☆

BG (Hebrew) God is my salvation. Bible: led the Israelites into the Promised Land.

Joshuah (Hebrew) a form of Joshua.

Joshue (Hebrew) a form of Joshua.

Josiah ☆ (Hebrew) fire of the Lord.

Josias (Hebrew) a form of Josiah.

Josías (Spanish) a form of Josias.

Joss (Chinese) luck; fate.

Josue (Hebrew) a form of Joshua.

Josué (Spanish) a form of Josue.

Jotham (Hebrew) may God complete. Bible: a king of Judah.

Jourdan GB (Hebrew) a form of Jordan.

Jovan (Latin) Jove-like, majestic. (Slavic) a form of John. Mythology: Jove, also known as Jupiter, was the supreme Roman deity.

Jovani, Jovanni, Jovanny, Jovany (Latin) forms of Jovan.

Jovante (American) a combination of Jovan + the suffix Te.

Jovon (Latin) a form of Jovan.

Jovonté (American) a combination of Jovon + the suffix Te.

Jozef (German, Portuguese, Czech, Scandinavian) a form of Josef.

Jr (Latin) a short form of Junior.

Juan ☆ **(Spanish) a form of John.** Juan Carlos, Juancarlos **(Spanish)**

combinations of Juan + Carlos.

Juanantonio (Spanish) a combination of Juan + Antonio.

Juandaniel (Spanish) a combination of Juan + Daniel.

Juanelo (Spanish) a form of Juan.

Juanito (Spanish) a form of Juan.

Juanjo (Spanish) a combination of Juan and José.

Juanjose (Spanish) a combination of Juan + Jose.

Juanma (Spanish) a combination of Juan and Manuel.

Juanmanuel (Spanish) a combination of Juan + Manuel.

Juaquin (Spanish) a form of Joaquin.

Jubal (Hebrew) ram's horn. Bible: a musician and a descendant of Cain.

Jucundo (Latin) happy, joyous one.

Judah (Hebrew) praised. Bible: the fourth of Jacob's sons.

Judas (Latin) a form of Judah. Bible: Judas Iscariot was the disciple who betrayed Jesus.

Judás (Hebrew) a form of Judas.

Judd (Hebrew) a short form of Judah.

Jude (Latin) a short form of Judah, Judas. Bible: one of the Twelve Apostles, author of "The Epistle of Jude."

Judson (English) son of Judd.

Juhana (Finnish) a form of John.

Jujuan (American) a form of Jajuan.

Juku (Estonian) a form of Richard.

Jules (French) a form of Julius.

Julian ☆
BG (Greek, Latin) a form of Julius.

Julián (Spanish) a form of Julian.

Juliano (Spanish) a form of Julian.

Julien (Latin) a form of Julian.

Julio (Hispanic) a form of Julius.

Juliocesar (Hispanic) a combination of Julio + Cesar.

Julis (Spanish) a form of Julius.

Julius (Greek, Latin) youthful, downy bearded. History: Julius Caesar was a great Roman

dictator. **Jullian** BG (Greek, Latin) a form of Julius.

Jumaane (Swahili) born on Tuesday.

Jumah (Arabic, Swahili) born on Friday, a holy day in the Islamic religion.

Jumoke (Yoruba) loved by everyone.

Jun BG (Chinese) truthful. (Japanese) obedient; pure.

Junior (Latin) young.

Júpiter (Latin) origin of light.

Jupp (German) a form of Joseph.

Juquan (Spanish) a form of Juaquin.

Jur (Czech) a form of George.

Jurgis (Lithuanian) a form of George.

Juro (Japanese) best wishes; long life.

Jurrien (Dutch) God will uplift.

Justan, Justen, Juston, Justyn (Latin) forms of Justin.

Justice GB (Latin) a form of Justis.

Justin ☆

BG (Latin) just, righteous. **J.**

ustiniano (Spanish) a form of Justino.

Justino (Spanish) a form of Justin.

Justis BG (French) just.

Justus BG (French) a form of Justis.

Jutta (Germanic) fair.

Juven, Juvencio, Juventino (Latin) one that represents youth.

Juvenal (Latin) young. Literature: a Roman satirist.

Juwan, Juwon (American) forms of Jajuan.

K

Ka'eo (Hawaiian) victorious.

Kabiito (Rutooro) born while foreigners are visiting.

Kabil (Turkish) a form of Cain.

Kabir (Hindi) History: an Indian mystic poet.

Kabonero (Runyankore) sign.

Kabonesa (Rutooro) difficult birth.

Kacey GB (Irish) a form of Casey. (American) a combination of the initials K. + C

Kacy GB (Irish, American) a form of Kacey.

Kadar (Arabic) powerful.

Kadarius (American) a combination of Kade + Darius.

Kade (Scottish) wetlands. (American) a combination of the initials K. + D.

Kadeem (Arabic) servant.

Kaden (Arabic) a form of Kadin.

Kadin (Arabic) friend, companion.

Kadîn (Arabic) a form of Kadin.

Kadir (Arabic) spring greening.

Kado (Japanese) gateway.

Kaeden (Arabic) a form of Kadin.

Kaelan, Kaelon (Irish) forms of Kellen.

Kaeleb (Hebrew) a form of Kaleb.

Kaelen ⏚ (Irish) a form of Kellen.

Kaelin ⏚ (Irish) a form of Kellen.

Kaemon (Japanese) joyful; right-handed.

Kaenan (Irish) a form of Keenan.

Kafele (Nguni) worth dying for.

Kaga (Native American) writer.

Kagan (Irish) a form of Keegan.

Kahale (Hawaiian) home.

Kahana (Hawaiian) priest.

Kahil (Turkish) young; inexperienced; naive.

Kahlil (Arabic) a form of Khalíl.

Kaholo (Hawaiian) runner.

Kahraman (Turkish) hero.

Kai ⏚ (Welsh) keeper of the keys. (Hawaiian) sea. (German) a form of Kay. (Danish) a form of Kaj.

Kaid (Scottish, American) a form of Kade.

Kaiden (Arabic) a form of Kadin.

Kailas (Indian) abode of the Hindu god Shiva.

Kailashchandra, Kailashnath (Indian) other names for the Hindu god Shiva.

Kailen ⏚ (Irish) a form of Kellen.

Kaili ⏚ (Hawaiian) Religion: a Hawaiian god.

Kain, Kaine (Welsh, Irish) forms of Kane.

Kainoa (Hawaiian) name.

Kaipo (Hawaiian) sweetheart.

Kairo (Arabic) a form of Cairo.

Kaiser (German) a form of Caesar.

Kaiven (American) a form of Kevin.

Kaj (Danish) earth.

Kajuan (American) a combination of the prefix Ka + Juan.

Kakar (Hindi) grass.

Kala ⏚ (Hindi) black; phase. (Hawaiian) sun.

Kalama ⏚ (Hawaiian) torch.

Kalameli (Tongan) caramel.

Kalan ⏚ (Hawaiian) a form of Kalani. (Irish) a form of Kalen.

Kalani ⏚ (Hawaiian) sky; chief.

Kalash (Indian) sacred pot.

Kale (Arabic) a short form of Kahlil. (Hawaiian) a familiar form of Carl.

Kalea ⏚ (Hawaiian) happy; joy.

Kaleb, Kalib, Kalob (Hebrew) forms of Caleb.

Kaled, Kalid (Arabic) immortal.

Kaleel (Arabic) a form of Khalíl.

Kalen ⏚ (Arabic, Hawaiian) a form of Kale. (Irish) a form of Kellen.

Kalevi (Finnish) hero.

Kali ⏚ (Arabic) a short form of Kalil. (Hawaiian) a form of Gary.

Kalicharan (Indian) devoted to the Hindu goddess Kali.

Kalil (Arabic) a form of Khalíl.

Kalin BG (Arabic, Hawaiian) a form of Kale. (Irish) a form of Kellen.

Kaliq (Arabic) a form of Khaliq.

Kalkin (Hindi) tenth. Religion: Kalki is the final incarnation of the Hindu god Vishnu.

Kalle BG (Scandinavian) a form of Carl. (Arabic, Hawaiian) a form of Kale.

Kallen, Kalon (Irish) forms of Kellen.

Kalmin (Scandinavian) manly, strong.

Kaloosh (Armenian) blessed event.

Kalvin (Latin) a form of Calvin.

Kalyan (Indian) welfare.

Kalyn GB (Irish) a form of Kellen.

Kamaka (Hawaiian) face.

Kamakani (Hawaiian) wind.

Kamal (Hindi) lotus. (Arabic) perfect, perfection.

Kamâl, Kamîl (Arabic) forms of Kamal.

Kamalakar, Kamalapati (Indian) other names for the Hindu god Vishnu.

Kamalesh (Indian) one with eyes like a lotus; another name for the Hindu god Vishnu.

Kamalnayan (Indian) one with eyes like a lotus.

Kamari BG (Swahili) a short form of Kamaria.

Kamau (Kikuyu) quiet warrior.

Kambod, Kambodi, Kamod (Indian) a raga, an ancient form of Hindu devotional music.

Kamden (Scottish) a form of Camden.

Kamel (Hindi, Arabic) a form of Kamal.

Kameron BG (Scottish) a form of Cameron.

Kamesh, Kameshwar, Kamraj, Kandarpa (Indian) the Hindu god of love.

Kami GB (Hindi) loving.

Kamil (Arabic) a form of Kamal.

Kamilo (Latin) a form of Camilo.

Kampbell (Scottish) a form of Campbell. Kambel, Kambell, Kamp

Kamran, Kamren, Kamron (Scottish) forms of Kameron.

Kamryn GB (Scottish) a form of Kameron.

Kamuela (Hawaiian) a form of Samuel.

Kamuhanda (Runyankore) born on the way to the hospital.

Kamukama (Runyankore) protected by God.

Kamuzu (Nguni) medicine.

Kamya (Luganda) born after twin brothers.

Kana (Japanese) powerful; capable. (Hawaiian) Mythology: a demigod.

Kanaan (Hindi) a form of Kannan.

Kanad (Indian) an ancient Indian sage.

Kanaiela (Hawaiian) a form of Daniel.

Kanchan (Indian) gold.

Kane BG (Welsh) beautiful. (Irish) tribute. (Japanese) golden. (Hawaiian) eastern sky. (English) a form of Keene.

Kanen (Hindi) a form of Kannan.

Kange (Lakota) raven.

Kanhaiya, Kanhaiyalal (Indian) other names for the Hindu god Krishna.

Kaniel (Hebrew) stalk, reed.

Kanishka (Indian) name of a king.

Kannan (Hindi) Religion: another name for the Hindu god Krishna. Kanan, Kanin, Kanine, Kannen

Kannon (Polynesian) free. (French) a form of Cannon.

Kanoa BG (Hawaiian) free.

Kantu (Hindi) happy.

Kanu (Swahili) wildcat.

Kanya GB (Australian) rock. (Hindi) virgin.

Kanyon (Latin) a form of Canyon.

Kaori (Japanese) strong.

Kapali (Hawaiian) cliff.

Kapeni (Malawian) knife.

Kaphiri (Egyptian) hill.

Kapila (Hindi) ancient prophet.

Kapono (Hawaiian) righteous.

Kappi (Gypsy) a form of Cappi.

Karan (Greek) a form of Karen **Kardal** (Arabic) mustard seed.
Karandal, Kardel, Kardell

Kare (Norwegian) enormous.

Kareb (Danish) pure; immaculate.

Kareem (Arabic) noble; distinguished.

Karel BG (Czech) a form of Carl.

Karey GB (Greek) a form of Carey.

Karif (Arabic) born in autumn.

Kariisa (Runyankore) herdsman.

Karim (Arabic) a form of Kareem.

Karl (German) a form of Carl.

Karlen (Latvian, Russian) a form of Carl.

Karlos (Spanish) a form of Carlos.

Karlton (English) a form of Carlton.

Karmel BG (Hebrew) a form of Carmel.

Karney (Irish) a form of Carney.

Karol BG (Czech, Polish) a form of Carl.

Karoly (French) strong and masculine.

Karon BG (Greek) a form of Karen.

Karr (Scandinavian) a form of Carr.

Karsen BG (English) a form of Carson.

Karson BG (English) a form of Carson.

Karsten (Greek) anointed.

Karu (Hindi) cousin.
Karun

Karutunda (Runyankore) little.

Karwana (Rutooro) born during wartime.

Kaseem (Arabic) divided.

Kaseko (Rhodesian) mocked, ridiculed.

Kasem (Tai) happiness.

Kasen BG (Basque) protected with a helmet.

Kasey GB (Irish) a form of Casey.

Kashawn (American) a combination of the prefix Ka + Shawn.

Kasib (Arabic) fertile.
Kasyb

Kasîb (Arabic) a form of Kasib.

Kasim (Arabic) a form of Kaseem.

Kasimir (Arabic) peace. (Slavic) a form of Casimir.

Kasiya (Nguni) separate.

Kason (Basque) a form of Kasen.

Kasper (Persian) treasurer. (German) a form of Casper.

Kass (German) blackbird.

Kasseem (Arabic) a form of Kaseem.

Kassidy GB (Irish) a form of Cassidy.

Kateb (Arabic) writer.

Kato (Runyankore) **Katriel** GB (Hebrew) crowned with God's glory. (Arabic) peace.

Katungi (Runyankore) rich.

Kaufman (German) merchant.

Kauri (Polynesian) tree.
of Kevin.

Kavanagh (Irish) Kavan's follower.

Kaveh (Persian) ancient hero.

Kaven, Kavin, Kavon (Irish) forms of Kavan.

Kavi (Hindi) poet.

Kawika (Hawaiian) a form of David.

Kay GB (Greek) rejoicing. (German) fortified place. Literature: one of King Arthur's knights of the Round Table.

Kayden ⭐

BG (Arabic) a form of Kadin.

Kayin (Nigerian) celebrated. (Yoruba) long-hoped-for child.

Kaylan **GB** (Irish) a form of Kellen.
Kaylyn, Kaylynn

Kayle **GB** (Hebrew) faithful dog. (Arabic) a short form of Kahlil. (Arabic, Hawaiian) a form of Kale.

Kayleb (Hebrew) a form of Caleb.

Kaylen **GB** (Irish) a form of Kellen.

Kaylin **GB** (Irish) a form of Kellen.

Kaylon **BG** (Irish) a form of Kellen.

Kayne (Hebrew) a form of Cain.

Kayode (Yoruba) he brought joy.

Kayonga (Runyankore) ash.

Kayvan, Kayvon (Irish) forms of Kavan.

Kazemde (Egyptian) ambassador.

Kazio (Polish) a form of Casimir, Kasimir. **Kazuo** (Japanese) man of peace.

Kc **BG** (American) a form of KC.

KC **BG** (American) a combination of the initials K. + C.

Keagan **BG** (Irish) a form of Keegan.

Keahi (Hawaiian) flames.

Keaka (Hawaiian) a form of Jack.

Kealoha (Hawaiian) fragrant.
Ke'ala, Kealohah

Kean (German, Irish, English) a form of Keane.

Keanan (Irish) a form of Keenan.

Keandre (American) a combination of the prefix Ke + Andre.

Kéandre (American) a form of Keandre.

Keane (German) bold; sharp. (Irish) handsome. (English) a form of Keene.

Keano (Irish) a form of Keanu.

Keanu **BG** (Hawaiian) cool breeze over the mountains (Irish) a form of Keenan.

Kearn (Irish) a short form of Kearney.

Kearney (Irish) a form of Carney.

Keary (Irish) a form of Kerry.

Keaton **BG** (English) where hawks fly.

Keaven (Irish) a form of Kevin.

Keawe (Hawaiian) strand.

Keb (Egyptian) earth. Mythology: an ancient earth god, also known as Geb.

Kedar (Hindi) mountain lord. (Arabic) powerful. Religion: another name for the Hindu god Shiva.

Keddy (Scottish) a form of Adam.

Kedem (Hebrew) ancient.

Kedric, Kedrick (English) forms of Cedric.

Keefe (Irish) handsome; loved.

Keegan **BG** (Irish) little; fiery.

Keelan (Irish) little; slender. A form of Kellen.

Keeley **GB** (Irish) handsome.

Keenan (Irish) little Keene.

Keene (German) bold; sharp. (English) smart. ,

Keenen, Keenon (Irish) forms of Keenan.

Kees (Dutch) a form of Kornelius.

Keevon (Irish) a form of Kevin.

Kegan (Irish) a form of Keegan.

Kehind (Yoruba) second-born twin.

Keifer, Keiffer (German) forms of Cooper.

Keigan (Irish) a form of Keegan.

Keiji (Japanese) cautious ruler.

Keilan (Irish) a form of Keelan.

Keiley (Irish) a form of Keeley.

Keion (Irish) a form of Keon.

Keir (Irish) a short form of Kieran.

Keiran (Irish) a form of Kieran.

Keitaro (Japanese) blessed.

Keith (Welsh) forest. (Scottish) battle place.

Keithen (Welsh, Scottish) a form of Keith.

Keivan (Irish) a form of Kevin.

Kejuan (American) a combination of the prefix Ke + Juan.

Kek (Egyptian) god of the darkness.

Kekapa (Hawaiian) tapa cloth.

Kekipi (Hawaiian) rebel.

Kekoa (Hawaiian) bold, courageous.
Kekoah

Kelan (Irish) a form of Keelan.

Kelby BG (German) farm by the spring. (English) a form of Kolby.

Kelcey GB (Scandinavian) a form of Kelsey.

Keldon (English) a form of Kelton.

Kele BG (Hopi) sparrow hawk. (Hawaiian) a form of Jerry.

Kelemen (Hungarian) gentle; kind.

Kelevi (Finnish) hero.

Keli GB (Hawaiian) a form of Terry.

Keli'i (Hawaiian) chief.

Kelile (Ethiopian) protected.

Kell (Scandinavian) spring.

Kellan BG (Irish) a form of Kellen.

Kellen BG (Irish) mighty warrior. A form of Kelly.

Keller (Irish) little companion.

Kelley GB (Irish) a form of Kelly.

Kelly GB (Irish) warrior.

Kelmen (Basque) merciful. n

Kelsey GB (Scandinavian) island of ships.

Kelson (English) a form of Kelton.

Kelton (English) keel town; port.

Kelvin (Irish, English) narrow river. Geography: a river in Scotland.

Kelwin (English) friend from the ridge.

Kemal (Turkish) highest honor.

Kemen (Basque) strong.

Kemp (English) fighter; champion.

Kempton (English) military town.

Ken (Japanese) one's own kind. (Scottish) a short form of Kendall, Kendrick, Kenneth.

Kenan (Irish) a form of Keenan.

Kenán (Hebrew) to acquire.

Kenaniá (Hebrew) God stabilizes.

Kenard (Irish) a form of Kennard.

Kenaz (Hebrew) bright.

Kendal GB (English) a form of Kendall.

Kendale (English) a form of Kendall.

Kendall GB (English) valley of the river Kent.

Kendarius (American) a combination of Ken + Darius.

Kendel BG (English) a form of Kendall.

Kendell BG (English) a form of Kendall.

Kendrell (English) a form of Kendall.

Kendrew (Scottish) a form of Andrew.

Kendric (Irish, Scottish) a form of Kendrick.

Kendrick (Irish) son of Henry. (Scottish) royal chieftain.

Kenji (Japanese) intelligent second son.

Kenley BG (English) royal meadow.

Kenn (Scottish) a form of Ken.

Kennan (Scottish) little Ken.

Kennard (Irish) brave chieftain.

Kennedy GB (Irish) helmeted chief. History: John F. Kennedy was the thirty-fifth U.S. president.

Kenneth (Irish) handsome. (English) royal oath.

Kennith (Irish, English) a form of Kenneth.

Kennon (Scottish) a form of Kennan.

Kenny (Scottish) a familiar form of **Kenneth.** (English) a form of Kenrick.

Kenrick (English) bold ruler; royal ruler.

Kent (Welsh) white; bright. (English) a short form of Kenton. Geography: a region in England.

Kentaro (Japanese) big boy.

Kenton (English) from Kent, England.

Kentrell (English) king's estate.

Kenward (English) brave; royal guardian.

Kenya GB (Hebrew) animal horn. (Russian) a form of Kenneth. Geography: a country in east-central Africa.

Kenyan (Irish) a form of Kenyon.

Kenyatta GB (American) a form of Kenya.

Kenyon (Irish) white haired, blond.

Kenzie GB (Scottish) wise leader.

Keoki (Hawaiian) a form of George.

Keola (Hawaiian) life.

Keon (Irish) a form of Ewan.

Keondre (American) a form of Keandre.

Keoni BG (Hawaiian) a form of John.

Keonta (American) a form of Keon.

Keontae, Keonte, Keonté (American) forms of Keon.

Kerbasi (Basque) warrior.

Kerel (Afrikaans) young.

Kerem (Turkish) noble; kind.

Kerey (Gypsy) homeward bound.

Kerman (Basque) from Germany.

Kermit (Irish) a form of Dermot.

Kern (Irish) a short form of Kieran.

Keron (Hebrew) a form of Keren **Kerr**

(Scandinavian) a form of Carr.

Kerrick (English) king's rule.

Kerry GB (Irish) dark; dark haired.

Kers (Todas) Botany: an Indian plant.

Kersen (Indonesian) cherry.

Kerstan (Dutch) a form of Christian.

Kervin (Irish, English) a form of Kerwin.

Kerwin (Irish) little; dark. (English) friend of the marshlands.

Kesar (Russian) a form of Caesar.
Kesare

Keshaun, Késhawn, Keshon (American) forms of Keshawn.

Keshawn (American) a combination of the prefix Ke + Shawn.

Keshun (American) a form of Keshawn.

Kesin (Hindi) long-haired beggar.

Kesse (Ashanti, Fante) chubby baby.

Kester (English) a form of Christopher.

Kestrel (English) falcon.

Keung (Chinese) universe.

Kevan, Keven, Kevon (Irish) forms of Kevin.

Kevin ⭐ (Irish) handsome.

Kevion (Irish) a form of Kevin.

Kevontae, Kevonte (American) forms of Kevin.

Kevyn 🇧🇬 (Irish) a form of Kevin.

Kewan, Kewon (American) forms of Kevin.

Key (English) key; protected.

Keyan, Keyon (Irish) forms of Keon.

Keynan (Irish) a form of Keenan.

Keyonta (American) a form of Keon.

Keyshawn (American) a combination of Key + Shawn.

Keyton (English) a form of Keaton.

Khachig (Armenian) small cross.

Khachik (Armenian) a form of Khachig.

Khaim (Russian) a form of Chaim.

Khaldun (Arabic) forever.

Khaldûn (Arabic) a form of Khaldun.

Khaled, Khalid, Khallid (Arabic) forms of Khälid.

Khaleel (Arabic) a form of Khalíl.

Khalfani (Swahili) born to lead.

Khalîd (Arabic) a form of Khälid.

Khälid (Arabic) eternal.

Khalil (Arabic) a form of Khalíl.

Khalíl (Arabic) friend.

Khalîl (Arabic) a form of Khalil.

Khaliq (Arabic) creative.

Khâliq (Arabic) a form of Khaliq.

Khamisi (Swahili) born on Thursday.

Khan (Turkish) prince.

Kharald (Russian) a form of Gerald.

Khayrî (Arabic) charitable.

Khayru (Arabic) benevolent.

Khentimentiu (Egyptian) god of death.

Khiry (Arabic) a form of Khayru.

Khnum (Egyptian) rising sun.

Khons (Egyptian) god of the moon.

Khoury **(Arabic) priest.**

Khrisna (Indian) the black one.

Khristian (Greek) a form of Christian, Kristian.

Khristopher (Greek) a form of Kristopher.

Khristos (Greek) a form of Christos.

Khûrî (Arabic) priest.

Ki 🇧🇬 (Korean) arisen.

Kian, Kion (Irish) forms of Keon.

Kibuuka (Luganda) brave warrior. Mythology: a Ganda warrior deity.

Kidd (English) child; young goat.

Kiefer, Kieffer (German) forms of Keifer.

Kiel (Irish) a form of Kyle.

Kiele 🇬🇧 (Hawaiian) gardenia.

Kienan (Irish) a form of Keenan.

Kier (Irish) a short form of Kieran.

Kieran 🇧🇬 (Irish) little and dark; little Keir.

Kieren, Kieron (Irish) forms of Kieran.

Kiernan (Irish) a form of Kieran.

Kiet (Tai) honor.

Kifeda (Luo) only boy among girls.

Kiho (Rutooro) born on a foggy day.

Kijika (Native American) quiet walker.

Kika (Hawaiian) a form of Keith.

Kiki 🇬🇧 (Spanish) a form of Henry.

Kile (Irish) a form of Kyle.

Kiley 🇬🇧 (Irish) a form of Kyle.

Killian (Irish) little Kelly.

Kim 🇬🇧 (English) a short form of Kimball.

Kimani 🇧🇬 (Shoshone) a form of Kimana

(**Kimball** (Greek) hollow vessel. (English) warrior chief.

Kimo (Hawaiian) a form of James.

Kimokeo (Hawaiian) a form of Timothy.

Kin (Japanese) golden.

Kincaid (Scottish) battle chief.

Kindin (Basque) fifth.

King (English) king. A short form of names beginning with "King."
Kyng

Kingsley (English) king's meadow.

Kingston (English) king's estate.

Kingswell (English) king's well.

Kini GB (Hawaiian) a short form of Iukini.

Kinnard (Irish) tall slope.

Kinsey GB (English) victorious royalty.

Kinton (Hindi) crowned.

Kioshi (Japanese) quiet.

Kip BG (English) a form of Kipp.

Kipp (English) pointed hill.

Kir (Bulgarian) a familiar form of Cyrus.

Kiral (Turkish) king; supreme leader.

Kiran GB (Sanskrit) beam of light.

Kirby BG (Scandinavian) church village. (English) cottage by the water.

Kiri (Cambodian) mountain.

Kirian (Irish) he who was born in a dark place.

Kiril (Slavic) a form of Cyril.

Kirios (Greek) the supreme being.

Kiritan (Hindi) wearing a crown.

Kirk (Scandinavian) church.

Kirkland (English) church land.

Kirkley (English) church meadow.

Kirklin (English) a form of Kirkland.

Kirkwell (English) church well; church spring.

Kirkwood (English) church forest.

Kirt (Latin, German, French) a form of Kurt.

Kirton (English) church town.

Kishan (American) a form of Keshawn.

Kistna (Hindi) sacred, holy. Geography: a sacred river in India.

Kistur (Gypsy) skillful rider.

Kit (Greek) a familiar form of Christian, Christopher, Kristopher.

Kito (Swahili) jewel; precious child.

Kitwana (Swahili) pledged to live.

Kiva (Hebrew) a short form of Akiva, Jacob.

Kiyoshi (Japanese) quiet; peaceful.

Kizza (Luganda) born after twins.

Kjell (Swedish) a form of Karl.

Klaus (German) a short form of Nicholas. A form of Claus.

Klay (English) a form of Clay.

Klayton (English) a form of Clayton.

Kleef (Dutch) cliff.

Klement **(Czech) a form of Clement.**

Kleng (Norwegian) claw.

Knight (English) armored knight.

Knoton (Native American) a form of Nodin.

Knowles (English) grassy slope.

Knox (English) hill.

Knute (Scandinavian) a form of Canute.

Kobi, Koby (Polish) familiar forms of Jacob.

Kodey (English) a form of Cody.

Kodi BG (English) a form of Cody.

Kodie BG (English) a form of Cody.

Kody BG (English) a form of Cody.

Kofi (Twi) born on Friday.

Kohana (Lakota) swift.

Kohl (English) a form of Cole.

Koi (Choctaw) panther. (Hawaiian) a form of Troy.

Kojo (Akan) born on Monday.

Koka (Hawaiian) Scotsman.

Kokayi (Shona) gathered together.

Kolby BG (English) a form of Colby.

Kole (English) a form of Cole.

Koleman (English) a form of Coleman.

Kolin, Kollin (English) forms of Colin.

Kolt (English) a short form of Koltan. A form of Colt.

Koltan, Kolten, Koltin, Kolton, Koltyn (English) forms of Colton.

Kolya (Russian) a familiar form of Nikolai, Nikolos.

Kona BG (Hawaiian) a form of Don.

Konane (Hawaiian) bright moonlight.

Kong (Chinese) glorious; sky.

Konner, Konnor (Irish) forms of Connar, Connor.

Kono (Moquelumnan) squirrel eating a pine nut.

Konrad (German) a form of Conrad.

Konstantin (German, Russian) a form of Constantine.

Konstantinos (Greek) a form of Constantine.

Kontar (Akan) only child.

Korb (German) basket.

Korbin (English) a form of Corbin.

Kordell (English) a form of Cordell.

Korey BG (Irish) a form of Corey, Kory.

Kori, Korie GB (Irish) forms of Corey, Kory.

Kornel (Latin) a form of Cornelius, Kornelius.
Soma

Kornelius (Latin) a form of Cornelius.

Korrigan (Irish) a form of Corrigan.

Kort (German, Dutch) a form of Cort, Kurt. (German) a form of Konrad.

Kortney GB (English) a form of Courtney.

Korudon (Greek) helmeted one.

Kory BG (Irish) a form of Corey.

Korydon (Greek) a form of Corydon.

Kosey (African) lion.

Kosmo (Greek) a form of Cosmo.

Kostas (Greek) a short form of Konstantin.

Kosti (Finnish) a form of Gustave.

Kosumi (Moquelumnan) spear fisher.

Koty (English) a form of Cody.

Koukalaka (Hawaiian) a form of Douglas.

Kourtland (English) a form of Courtland.

Kraig (Irish, Scottish) a form of Craig.

Kramer (English) a form of Cramer.

Krikor (Armenian) a form of Gregory.

Kris BG (Greek) a form of Chris. A short form of Kristian, Kristofer, Kristopher.

Krischan, Krishan (German) forms of Christian.

Krishna BG (Hindi) delightful, pleasurable. Religion: the eighth and principal avatar of the Hindu god Vishnu.

Krisiant (Welsh) a form of Crisiant.

Krispin (Latin) a form of Crispin.

Krister (Swedish) a form of Christian.

Kristian BG (Greek) a form of Christian, Khristian.

Kristjan (Estonian) a form of Christian, Khristian.

Kristo (Greek) a short form of Khristopher.

Kristofer, Kristoffer (Swedish) forms of Kristopher.

Kristoff (Greek) a short form of Kristofer, Kristopher.

Kriston [BG] (Greek) a form of Kristian.

Kristophe (French) a form of Kristopher.

Kristopher (Greek) a form of Christopher.

Kruz (Spanish) a form of Cruz.

Krystian [BG] (Polish) a form of Christian.

Krystopher (Greek) a form of Christopher.

Krzysztof (Polish) a form of Kristoff.

Kuba (Czech) a form of Jacob.

Kueng (Chinese) universe.

Kugonza (Rutooro) love.

Kuiril (Basque) lord.

Kullen (Irish) a form of Cullen.

Kumar (Sanskrit) prince.

Kunle (Yoruba) home filled with honors.

Kuper (Yiddish) copper.

Kurt (Latin, German, French) a short form of Kurtis. A form of Curt.

Kurtis (Latin, French) a form of Curtis.

Kuruk (Pawnee) bear.

Kuzih (Carrier) good speaker.

Kwabena (Akan) born on Tuesday.

Kwacha (Nguni) morning.

Kwako **(Akan) born on Wednesday.**

Kwam (Zuni) a form of John.

Kwame (Akan) born on Saturday.

Kwamé (Akan) a form of Kwame.

Kwan (Korean) strong.

Kwasi (Akan) born on Sunday. (Swahili) wealthy.

Kwayera (Nguni) dawn.

Kwende (Nguni) let's go.

Ky, Kye (Irish, Yiddish) short forms of Kyle.

Kyele (Irish) a form of Kyle.

Kylan, Kylen (Irish) forms of Kyle.

Kylar, Kylor (English) forms of Kyle.

Kyle [BG] (Irish) narrow piece of land; place where cattle graze. (Yiddish) crowned with laurels.

Kyler [BG] (English) a form of Kyle.

Kylle (Irish) a form of Kyle.

Kymani (Swahili) son of the great warrior; a man of integrity.

Kynan (Welsh) chief.
Kinan

Kyndall [GB] (English) a form of Kendall.

Kyne (English) royal.

Kyran, Kyren, Kyron (Irish) forms of Kieran. (Sanskrit) forms of Kiran.

Kyree (Cambodian, Maori, Greek) a form of Kyrie .

Kyrios (Greek) sir.

Kyros (Greek) master.

Kyson (English) son of Kay, Ky.

Kyven (American) a form of Kevin.

L

La'darius, Ladarrius (American) forms of Ladarius.

Laban (Hawaiian) white.

Labán (Hebrew) a form of Laban.

Labaron (American) a combination of the prefix La + Baron.

Labib (Arabic) sensible; intelligent.

Labîb (Arabic) a form of Labib.

Labrentsis (Russian) a form of Lawrence.

Lachlan (Scottish) land of lakes.

Lacy [GB] (Greek, Latin) cheerful.

Ladarian (American) a combination of the prefix La + Darian.

Ladarius (American) a combination of the prefix La + Darius.

Ladd (English) attendant.

Laderrick (American) a combination of the prefix La + Derric.

Ladio (Slavic) he who governs with glory.

Ladislav (Czech) a form of Walter.

Lado (Fante) second-born son.

Ladolfo, Landolf, Landolfo (Germanic) skillful as a wolf in the city.

Laertes (Greek) the rock-picker.

Lafayette (French) History: Marquis de Lafayette was a French soldier and politician who aided the American Revolution.

Lagan (Indian) appropriate time.

Lahual (Araucanian) larch tree.

Laidley (English) path along the marshy meadow.

Lain (English) a form of Lane.

Laine BG (English) a form of Lane.

Laird (Scottish) wealthy landowner.

Lais (Arabic) lion.

Laith (Scandinavian, English) a form of Latham.

Lajos (Hungarian) famous; holy.

Lajuan (American) a combination of the prefix La + Juan.

Lake (English) lake.

Lakeith (American) a combination of the prefix La + Keith.

Lakota BG (Dakota) a tribal name.

Lakshman (Indian) younger brother of the Hindu god Rama.

Lakshmibanta (Indian) fortunate.

Lakshmidhar, Lakshmigopal, Lakshmikanta, Lohitaksha, Loknath, Lokranjan (Indian) other names for the Hindu god Vishnu.

Lal (Hindi) beloved.

Lalit, Lalitkishore, Lalitkumar, Lalitmohan (Indian) beautiful.

Lalla (Spanish) well spoken.

Lamani BG (Tongan) lemon.

Lamarcus (American) a combination of the prefix La + Marcus.

Lamario (American) a form of Lamar.

Lamarr (German, French) a form of Lamar.

Lambert (German) bright land.

Lambodar (Indian) another name for the Hindu god Ganesh.

Lami (Tongan) hidden.

Lamon (French) a form of Lamond.

Lamond (French) world.

Lamont (Scandinavian) lawyer.

Lamonte (Scandinavian) a form of Lamont.

Lance (German) a short form of Lancelot.

Lancelin (French) servant.

Lancelot (French) attendant. Literature: the knight who loved King Arthur's wife, Queen Guinevere.

Landan, Landen, Landin (English) forms of Landon.

Landelino (Teutonic) he who is a friend of the earth.

Lander (Basque) lion man. (English) landowner.

Landerico (Teutonic) powerful in the region.

Landis (French) one who comes from the prairie.

Lando (Portuguese, Spanish) a short form of Orlando, Rolando.

Landon ⭐

LBG (English) open, grassy meadow. A form of Langdon.

Landrada (Teutonic) counselor in his village.

Landric (German) ruler of the land.

Landry (French, English) ruler.

Lane LBG (English) narrow road.

Lang (Scandinavian) tall man.

Langdon (English) long hill.

Langford (English) long ford.

Langi (Tongan) heaven.

Langley GB (English) long meadow.

Langston (English) long, narrow town.

Langundo (Native American) peaceful.

Lani GB (Hawaiian) heaven.

Lankesh (Indian) another name for the Hindu demon king Ravana.

Lanny (American) a familiar form of Laurence, Lawrence.

Lanu (Moquelumnan) running around the pole.

Lanz **(Italian) a form of Lance.**

Lao (Spanish) a short form of Stanislaus.

Lap (Vietnamese) independent.

Lapidos (Hebrew) torches.

Laquan (American) a combination of the prefix La + Quan.

Laquintin (American) a combination of the prefix La + Quinten.

Laramie GB (French) tears of love. Geography: a town in Wyoming on the Overland Trail.

Larenz (Italian, Spanish) a short form of Larenzo.

Larenzo (Italian, Spanish) a form of Lorenzo.

Larkin (Irish) rough; fierce.

Larnell (American) a combination of Larry + Darnell.

Laron (French) thief.

Larrimore (French) armorer.

Larry (Latin) a familiar form of Lawrence.

Lars (Scandinavian) a form of Lawrence.

Larson (Scandinavian) son of Lars.

LaSalle (French) hall.

Lash (Gypsy) a form of Louis.

Lashaun BG (American) a form of Lashawn.

Lashawn BG (American) a combination of the prefix La + Shawn.

Lashon GB (American) a form of Lashawn.

Lashone (American) a form of Lashawn.

Lasse (Finnish) a form of Nicholas.

László (Hungarian) famous ruler.

Latafat (Indian) elegance.

Lateef (Arabic) gentle; pleasant.

Latham (Scandinavian) barn. (English) district.
Lathe, Lay

Lathan (American) a combination of the prefix La + Nathan.

Lathrop (English) barn, farmstead.

Latîf (Arabic) friendly; pleasant.

Latimer (English) interpreter.

Latrell (American) a combination of the prefix La + Kentrell.

Laudalino (Portuguese) praised.

Laughlin (Irish) servant of Saint Secundinus.

Laurelino, Laurelito, Laurentino (Latin) winner.

Laurence GB (Latin) crowned with laurel. A form of Lawrence. See also

Laurencio (Spanish) a form of Laurence.

Laurens (Dutch) a form of Laurence.

Laurent (French) a form of Laurence.

Laurie [GB] (English) a familiar form of Laurence.

Lauris (Swedish) a form of Laurence.

Lauro (Filipino) a form of Laurence.

Lautaro (Araucanian) daring and enterprising.

Lav, Luv (Indian) son of the Hindu god Rama.

LaValle (French) valley.

Lavan (Hebrew) white.

Lavaughan (American) a form of Lavan.

Lave [BG] (Italian) lava. (English) lord.

Lavell (French) a form of LaValle.

Lavelle [BG] (French) a form of LaValle.

Lavi (Hebrew) lion.

Lavon (American) a form of Lavan.

Lavonte, Lavonté (American) forms of Lavon.

Lavrenti (Russian) a form of Lawrence.

Lawerence (Latin) a form of Lawrence.

Lawford (English) ford on the hill.

Lawler (Irish) soft-spoken.

Lawley (English) low meadow on a hill.

Lawrance (Latin) a form of Lawrence.

Lawrence (Latin) crowned with laurel.

Lawry (English) a familiar form of Lawrence.

Lawson (English) son of Lawrence.

Lawton (English) town on the hill.

Layne [BG] (English) a form of Lane.

Layton (English) a form of Leighton.

Lazar (Greek) a short form of Lazarus.

Lazaro (Italian) a form of Lazarus.

Lázaro (Italian) a form of Lazaro.

Lazarus (Greek) a form of Eleazar. Bible: Lazarus was raised from the dead by Jesus.

Le [BG] (Vietnamese) pearl.

Leal (Spanish) loyal and faithful worker.

Leander (Greek) lion-man; brave as a lion.

Leandre (French) a form of Leander.

Leandro (Spanish) a form of Leander.

Learco (Greek) judge of his village.

Leben (Yiddish) life.

Lebna (Ethiopian) spirit; heart.

Ledarius (American) a combination of the prefix Le + Darius.

Lee [BG] (English) a short form of Farley, Leonard, and names containing "lee."

Legend (Latin, French) a story, folktale, or myth.

Legget (French) a form of Leggett.

Leggett (French) one who is sent; delegate.

Lei [BG] (Chinese) thunder. (Hawaiian) a form of Ray.

Leib (Yiddish) roaring lion.

Leif [BG] (Scandinavian) beloved.

Leighton (English) meadow farm.

Leith (Scottish) broad river.

Leixandre (Galician) a form of Alejandro.

Lek (Tai) small.

Lekeke (Hawaiian) powerful ruler.

Leks (Estonian) a familiar form of Alexander.

Lel (Gypsy) taker.

Leland (English) meadowland; protected land.

Lelio (Latin) he who is talkative.

Lemar (French) a form of Lamar.

Lemuel (Hebrew) devoted to God.

Len (Hopi) flute. (German) a short form of Leonard.

Lencho (Spanish) a form of Lawrence.

Lenin (Russian) one who belongs to the river Lena.

Lennart (Swedish) a form of Leonard.

Lennie, Lenny (German) familiar forms of Leonard. (American) forms of Lanny.

Lenno (Native American) man.

Lennon BG (Irish) small cloak; cape.

Lennor (Gypsy) spring; summer.

Lennox (Scottish) with many elms.
Lennix, Lenox

Lenya (Russian) lion.

Leo ★ (Latin) lion. (German) a short form of Leon, Leopold.

Leobardo (Italian) a form of Leonard.

Leocadie (French) lion.

Leocadio (Greek) he who shines because of his whiteness.

Leodegrance (French) lion.

Leodoualdo, Leodovaldo (Teutonic) he who governs his village.

Leofrido (Teutonic) he who brings peace to his village.

Leon (Greek, German) a short form of Leonard, Napoleon.

León (Greek) a form of Leon.

Leonard (German) brave as a lion.

Leonardo (Italian) a form of Leonard.

Leonce (French) lion.

Leondre (American) a form of Leon.

Leonel (English) little lion.

Leonelo (Spanish) a form of Leonel.

Leonhard (German) a form of Leonard.

Leonid (Russian) a form of Leonard.

Leonidas (Greek) a form of Leonard.

Leónidas (Spanish) a form of León.

Leontino (German) strong as a lion.

Leopold (German) brave people.

Leopoldo (Italian) a form of Leopold.

Leor (Hebrew) my light.

Leovixildo (German) armed warrior.

Lequinton (American) a combination of the prefix Le + Quinten.

Lerenzo (Italian, Spanish) a form of Lorenzo.

Leron (French) round, circle. (American) a combination of the prefix Le + Ron.

Leroy (French) king. **Les** (Scottish, English) a short form of Leslie, Lester.

Lesharo (Pawnee) chief.

Leshawn (American) a combination of the prefix Le + Shawn.

Leslie GB (Scottish) gray fortress.

Lesmes (Teutonic) he whose nobility protects him.

Lester (Latin) chosen camp. (English) from Leicester, England.

Let (Catalan) a form of Leto.

Leto (Latin) he who is always happy.

Leuco (Greek) the luminous one.

Leuter (Galician) a form of Eleuterio.

Lev (Hebrew) heart. (Russian) a form of Leo. A short form of Leverett, Levi.

Levant (Latin) rising.

Leveni (Tongan) raven.

Leverett (French) young hare.

Levi ★ (Hebrew) joined in harmony. Bible: the third son of Jacob; Levites are the priestly tribe of the Israelites.

Levin (Hebrew) a form of Levi.

Levina (Hebrew) one who unites.

Levka, Levushka (Russian) lion.

Levon (American) a form of Lavon.

Levonte (American) a form of Levon.

Lew (English) a short form of Lewis.

Lewin (English) beloved friend.

Lewis (Welsh) a form of Llewellyn. (English) a form of Louis.

Lex (English) a short form of Alexander.

Lexus GB (Greek) a short form of Alexander.

Leyati (Moquelumnan) shape of an abalone shell.

Lí (Chinese) strong.

Lía (Spanish) an abbreviation of names that end with the suffix Lia.

Liam ⭐ (Irish) a form of William.

Lian GB (Irish) guardian. (Chinese) graceful willow.

Liang (Chinese) good, excellent.

Liban (Hawaiian) a form of Laban.

Libanio (Latin) tree of incense.

Líbano (Latin) white.

Liber (Latin) he who spreads abundance.

Liberal (Latin) the lover of liberty.

Liberato (Latin) the liberated one.

Liberio (Portuguese) liberation.

Libiac, Llipiac (Quechua) ray of light.

Libio, Livio (Latin) born in a dry place.

Licas (Greek) wolf.

Licerio (Greek) pertaining to light.

Licurgo (Greek) he who frightens off wolves.

Lidia (Greek) one who comes from Lidia.

Lidio (Greek, Portuguese) ancient.

Liem (Irish) a form of Liam.

Ligongo (Yao) who is this?

Lihue, Lihuel (Araucanian) life; existence.

Likeke (Hawaiian) a form of Richard.

Liko (Chinese) protected by Buddha. (Hawaiian) bud.

Lin GB (Burmese) bright. (English) a short form of Lyndon.

Linc (English) a short form of Lincoln.

Lincoln ⭐ (English) settlement by the pool. History: Abraham Lincoln was the sixteenth U.S. president.

Lindberg (German) mountain where linden grow.

Lindbert (German) a form of Lindberg.

Lindell (English) valley of the linden.

Linden BG (English) a form of Lyndon.

Lindley (English) linden field.

Lindon (English) a form of Lyndon.

Lindor (Latin) he who seduces.

Lindsay GB (English) a form of Lindsey.

Lindsey GB (English) linden island.

Linford (English) linden ford.

Linfred (German) peaceful, calm.

Linley GB (English) flax meadow.

Lino (Portuguese) a short form of Laudalino.

Linton (English) flax town.

Linu (Hindi) lily.

Linus (Greek) flaxen haired.

Linwood (English) flax wood.

Lio (Hawaiian) a form of Leo.

Lionel (French) lion cub.

Liron BG (Hebrew) my song.

Lisandro (Spanish) liberator.

Lisardo (Hebrew) defender of the faith.

314

Lisias, Lisístrato (Greek) liberator.

Lisimba (Yao) lion.

Lister (English) dyer.

Litton (English) town on the hill.

Liu (African) voice.

Liuz (Polish) light.

Livingston (English) Leif's town.

Liwanu (Moquelumnan) growling bear.

Llacsa (Quechua) he who is the color of bronze.

Llallaua (Aymara) magnificent.

Llancamil (Mapuche) shining stone.

Llancañir (Mapuche) fox that is pearl-colored.

Llanqui (Quechua) potter's clay.

Llarico, Llaricu (Aymara) indomitable.

Llashapoma, Llashapuma (Quechua) heavy puma; slow.

Llewellyn (Welsh) lionlike.

Lleyton (English) a form of Leighton.

Llipiac, Lloque, Lluqui (Quechua) left-handed, from the left side.

Lloqueyupanqui, Lluquiyupanqui (Quechua) left-handed; memorable.

Lloyd (Welsh) gray haired; holy.

Lobo (Spanish) wolf.

Lochan (Indian) eye.

Lochlain (Irish, Scottish) land of lakes.

Locke (English) forest.

Loe (Hawaiian) a form of Roy.

Logan ⭐

BG (Irish) meadow.

Logen (Irish) a form of Logan.

Lois (German) famous in battle.

Lok (Chinese) happy.

Lokela (Hawaiian) a form of Roger.

Lokesh (Indian) another name for the Hindu god Brahma.

Lokni (Moquelumnan) raining through the roof.

Lomán (Irish) bare. (Slavic) sensitive.

Lombard (Latin) long bearded fierce. (Spanish) a short form of Alonso, Leonard, Lonnie.

Lonan (Zuni) cloud.

Lonato (Native American) flint stone.

Loncopan (Mapuche) puma's head.

London GB (English) fortress of the moon. Geography: the capital of the United Kingdom.
Londen, Londyn, Lunden, Lundon

Long (Chinese) dragon. (Vietnamese) hair.

Longinos (Latin) long.

Lonnie, Lonny (German, Spanish) familiar forms of Alonso.

Lono (Hawaiian) Mythology: the god of learning and intellect.

Lonzo (German, Spanish) a short form of Alonso.

Lootah (Lakota) red.

Lopaka (Hawaiian) a form of Robert.

Lope (Latin) wolf.

Loran (American) a form of Lauren.

Loránd (Hungarian) a form of Roland.

Lóránt (Hungarian) a form of Lawrence.

Lorcan (Irish) little; fierce.

Lord (English) noble title.

Loren GB (Latin) a short form of Lawrence.

Lorenza BG (Italian, Spanish) a form of Lorenzo.

Lorenzo (Italian, Spanish) a form of Lawrence.

Loretto (Italian) a form of Lawrence.

Lorién (Aragonese) a form of Lorenzo.

Lorimer (Latin) harness maker.
Lorrimer, Lorrymer, Lorymer

Lorin GB (Latin) a short form of Lawrence.

Loring (German) son of the famous warrior.

Loris BG (Dutch) clown.

Loritz (Latin, Danish) laurel.

Lotario (Germanic) the distinguished warrior.

Lothar (German) a form of Luther.

Lou BG (German) a short form of Louis.

Loudon (German) low valley.

Louie (German) a familiar form of Louis.

Louis (German) famous warrior.

Louis Alexander (French) a combination of Louis + Alexander.

Louis Charles (French) a combination of Louis + Charles.

Louis David (French) a combination of Louis + David.

Louis Mathieu (French) a combination of Louis + Mathieu.

Louis Philipp (French) a combination of Louis + Philip.

Louis Xavier (French) a combination of Louis + Xavier.

Louvain (English) Lou's vanity. Geography: a city in Belgium.

Lovell (English) a form of Lowell.

Lowell (French) young wolf. (English) beloved.

Loyal (English) faithful, loyal.

Loyola (Latin) has a wolf on his shield.

Luano (Latin) fountain.

Lubomir (Polish) lover of peace.

Luboslaw (Polish) lover of glory.

Luc (French) a form of Luke.

Luca BG (Italian) a form of Lucius.

Lucas ⭐ (German, Irish, Danish, Dutch) a form of Lucius.

Lucero, Lucío (Spanish) bringer of light.

Lucian (Latin) a form of Lucius.

Luciano (Italian) a form of Lucian.

Lucien (French) a form of Lucius.

Lucífero, Lucila (Latin) he who gives light.

Lucio (Italian) a form of Lucius.

Lucius (Latin) light; bringer of light.

Lucky BG (American) fortunate. (Latin) a familiar form of Luke.

Lucrecio (Latin) twilight of dawn.

Lucus (German, Irish, Danish, Dutch) a form of Lucas.

Ludlow (English) prince's hill.

Ludovic, Ludovick (German) forms of Ludwig.

Ludwig (German) a form of Louis. Music: Ludwig van Beethoven was a famous nineteenth-century German composer.

Luftî (Arabic) friendly.

Lui (Hawaiian) a form of Louis.

Luigi (Italian) a form of Louis.

Luis ⭐ (Spanish) a form of Louis.

Luís, Luiz (Spanish) forms of Louis.

Luisalberto (Spanish) a combination of Luis + Alberto.

Luisangel (Spanish) a combination of Luis + Angel.

Luisantonio (Spanish) a combination of Luis + Antonio.

Luisenrique (Spanish) a combination of Luis + Enrique.

Luka (Italian) a form of Luke.

Lukas, Lukasz, Lukus (Greek, Czech, Swedish) forms of Luke.

Luke ⭐ (Latin) a form of Lucius. Bible: companion

of Saint Paul and author of the third Gospel of the New Testament.

Lukela (Hawaiian) a form of Russell.

Luken **(Basque) bringer of light.**

Luki (Basque) famous warrior.

Lukman (Arabic) prophet.

Lulani BG (Hawaiian) highest point in heaven.

Lumo (Ewe) born facedown.

Lundy GB (Scottish) grove by the island.

Lunn (Irish) warlike.

Lunt (Swedish) grove.

Lupercio (Latin) name given to people from Lupercus.

Luperco (Latin) he who frightens off wolves.

Luqmân (Arabic) prophet.

Lusila (Hindi) leader.

Lusio (Zuni) a form of Lucius.

Lusorio (Latin) he enjoys games.

Lutalo (Luganda) warrior.

Lutardo (Teutonic) he who is valiant in his village.

Lutfi (Arabic) kind, friendly.

Luther (German) famous warrior. History: Martin Luther was one of the central figures of the Reformation.

Lutherum (Gypsy) slumber.

Luyu BG (Moquelumnan) head shaker.

Luzige (Egyptian) lobster.

Lyall, Lyell (Scottish) loyal.

Lyle (French) island.

Lyman (English) meadow.

, **Lynch** (Irish) mariner.

Lyndal (English) valley of lime trees.

Lynden (English) a form of Lyndon.

Lyndon (English) linden hill. History: Lyndon B. Johnson was the thirty-sixth U.S. president.

Lynn GB (English) waterfall; brook. A short form of Lyndon. (Burmese, English) a form of Lin.

Lyonechka (Russian) lion.

Lyric GB (Latin, French) words to a song or poem.

Lyron (Hebrew) a form of Leron, Liron.

Lysander (Greek) liberator.

M

Ma'an (Arabic) benefit.

Ma'mûn (Arabic) reliable.

Maalik (Punjabi) a form of Málik.

Mac (Scottish) son.

Macabee (Hebrew) hammer.

Macadam (Scottish) son of Adam.

Macaire (French) a form of Macario.

Macalla (Australian) full moon.

Macallister (Irish) son of Alistair.

Macario (Spanish) a form of Makarios.

Macarthur (Irish) son of Arthur.

Macaulay (Scottish) son of righteousness.

Macbride (Scottish) son of a follower of Saint Brigid.

Maccoy (Irish) son of Hugh, Coy.

Maccrea (Irish) son of grace.

Macdonald (Scottish) son of Donald.

Macdougal (Scottish) son of Dougal.

Mace (French) club. (English) a short form of Macy, Mason.

Macedonio (Greek) he who triumphs and grows in stature.

Maceo (Spanish) a form of Mace.

Macèo (Italian) gift of God.

Macerio (Spanish) blessed.

Macfarlane (English) son of Farlane.

Macgregor (Scottish) son of Gregor.

Macharios (Greek)
blessed.
Macarius, Macharyos, Makarius

Machas (Polish) a form of
Michael.

Macián, Macías (Hebrew)
forms of Matias.

Maciel (Latin) very
slender.

Mack (Scottish) a short
form of names beginning
with "Mac" and "Mc."

Mackenzie GB (Irish) son
of Kenzie.

Mackenzy BG (Irish) a
form of Mackenzie.

Mackinley (Irish) a form
of Mackinnley.

Mackinnley (Irish) son of
the learned ruler.

Macklain (Irish) a form of
Maclean.
Macklaine, Macklane

Macklin (Scottish) a form
of Mack.

Maclean (Irish) son of
Leander.

Macmahon (Irish) son of
Mahon.

Macmurray (Irish) son of
Murray.

Macnair (Scottish) son of
the heir.

Maco (Hungarian) a form
of Emmanuel.
Macko, Mako

Macon (German, English)
maker.
Macan, Macen, Macin, Macun, Macyn

Macrobio (Greek) he who
enjoys a long life.

Macy GB (French)
Matthew's estate.

**Madangopal, Madhav,
Madhusudan** (Indian)
other names for the
Hindu god Krishna.

Maddock (Welsh)
generous.

Maddox BG (Welsh,
English) benefactor's son.

Madhar (Hindi) full of
intoxication; relating to
spring.

Madhavdas (Indian)
servant of the Hindu god
Krishna.

Madhu (Indian) honey.

**Madhuk, Madhukar,
Madhup** (Indian)
honeybee.

Madhukanta (Indian)
moon.

Madhur (Indian) sweet.

Madon **(Irish)**
charitable.
Madyn

Madongo (Luganda)
uncircumcised.

Madu (Ibo) people.

Mael (Celtic) prince.

Magan (Indian) engrossed.

Magar (Armenian) groom's
attendant.

Magee (Irish) son of Hugh.

Magen GB (Hebrew)
protector.

Magín (Latin) he who is
imaginative.

Magina (Latin) sage;
charmer.

Magnar (Norwegian)
strong; warrior.

Magno (Latin) great.

Magnus (Latin) great.

Magomu (Luganda)
younger of twins.

Maguire (Irish) son of the
beige one.

Mahabahu (Indian)
another name for Arjuna,
a warrior prince in the
Indian epic poem
Mahabharata.

**Mahadev, Mahesh,
Maheshwar** (Indian)
other names for the
Hindu god Shiva.

Mahammed (Arabic) a
form of Muhammad.

Mahaniya (Indian) worthy
of honor.

Mahavir (Indian) the
twenty-fourth and last
Tirthankar, a type of Jain
god; very courageous.

Mahdi (Arabic) guided to
the right path.

Mahendra (Indian)
another name for the
Hindu god Vishnu.

Maher (Arabic, Hebrew) a
form of Mahir.

Mâher (Arabic) a form of
Maher.

Mahesa BG (Hindi) great
lord. Religion: another
name for the Hindu god
Shiva.

Mahi'ai (Hawaiian) a form
of George.

Mahieu (French) gift of God.

Mahin (Indian) the earth.

Mahindra, Mahipal, Mahish (Indian) king.

Mahir (Arabic, Hebrew) excellent; industrious.

Mahkah (Lakota) earth.

Mahlí (Hebrew) astute; shrewd.

Mahmoud, Mahmúd (Arabic) forms of Muhammad.

Mahmud (Indian) another name for Muhammad, the founder of Islam.

Mahmûd (Arabic) a form of Mahmoud.

Mahoma (Arabic) worthy of being praised.

Mahomet (Arabic) a form of Muhammad.

Mahon (Irish) bear.

Mahpee (Lakota) sky.

Mahtab (Indian) moon.

Mahuizoh (Nahuatl) glorious person.

Maicu (Quechua) eagle.

Maidoc (Welsh) fortunate.

Mailhairer (French) unfortunate.

Maimun (Arabic) lucky.

Mainak (Indian) a mountain in the Himalayas.

Mainque (Mapuche) condor.

Maiqui (Quechua) tree.

Mairtin (Irish) a form of Martin.

Maison BG (French) house. A form of Mason.

Maitias (Irish) a form of Mathias.

Maitiú (Irish) a form of Matthew.

Maitland GB (English) meadowland.

Majed (Arabic) a form of Majid.

Majencio (Latin) he who becomes more famous.

Majid (Arabic) great, glorious.

Mâjid (Arabic) a form of Majid.

Major (Latin) greater; military rank.

Makaio (Hawaiian) a form of Matthew.

Makalani (Mwera) writer.

Makani BG (Hawaiian) wind.

Makarios (Greek) happy; blessed.

Makenzie GB (Irish) a form of Mackenzie.

Makhi (Greek) battle or struggle.

Makin (Arabic) strong.

Makis (Greek) a form of Michael.

Makoto (Japanese) sincere.

Maks (Hungarian) a form of Max.

Maksim (Russian) a form of Maximilian.

Maksym (Polish) a form of Maximilian.

Makyah (Hopi) eagle hunter.

Mal (Irish) a short form of names beginning with "Mal."

Malachi (Hebrew) angel of God. Bible: the last canonical Hebrew prophet.

Malachy (Irish) a form of Malachi.

Malají (Hebrew) my messenger.

Malajitm (Sanskrit) garland of victory.

Malakai (Hebrew) a form of Malachi.

Malaquias, Malaquías (Hebrew) God's messenger.

Malco, Malcon (Hebrew) he who is like a king.

Malcolm (Scottish) follower of Saint Columba, who Christianized North Scotland. (Arabic) dove.

Malcom (Scottish) a form of Malcolm.

Malden (English) meeting place in a pasture.

Maleek, Maliek, Malique (Arabic) forms of Málik.

Malek, Malik (Arabic) forms of Málik.

Maleko (Hawaiian) a form of Mark.

Málik (Punjabi) lord, master. (Arabic) a form of Malachi.

Mâlik (Arabic) a form of Malik.

Malin (English) strong, little warrior.

Malleville (French) comes from Malleville.

Mallory GB (German) army counselor. (French) wild duck.

Maloney (Irish) church going.

Malvern (Welsh) bare hill.

Malvin (Irish, English) a form of Melvin.

Mamani (Aymara) falcon.

Mamés (Greek) mother.

Mamo BG (Hawaiian) yellow flower; yellow bird.

Mampu (Araucanian) caress.

Man-Shik (Korean) deeply rooted.

Man-Young (Korean) ten thousand years of prosperity.

Manases, Manasés (Hebrew) he who forgets everything.

Manauia (Nahuatl) defend.

Manchu (Chinese) pure.

Mancio (Latin) he who foretells the future.

Manco (Peruvian) supreme leader. History: a sixteenth-century Incan king.

Mandala (Yao) flowers.

Mandeep BG (Punjabi) mind full of light.

Mandek (Polish) a form of Herman.

Mandel (German) almond.

Mander (Gypsy) from me.

Manés (Greek) craziness.

Manesio (Greek) a form of Manés.

Manford (English) small ford.

Manfred (English) man of peace.

Manger (French) stable.

Mango (Spanish) a familiar form of Emmanuel, Manuel.

Manheim (German) servant's home.

Manipi (Native American) living marvel.

Manius (Scottish) a form of Magnus.

Manjot BG (Indian) light of the mind.

Manley (English) hero's meadow.

Manlio (Latin) he who was born in the morning.

Mann (German) man.

Manneville (French) one who comes from the great state.

Manning (English) son of the hero.

Mannix (Irish) monk.

Manny (German, Spanish) a familiar form of Manuel.

Mano (Hawaiian) shark. (Spanish) a short form of Manuel.

Manoj (Sanskrit) cupid.

Manolito (Spanish) God is with us.

Manpreet GB (Punjabi) mind full of love.

Manque (Mapuche) condor.

Manquecura (Mapuche) refuge from the condor; two-colored rock.

Manquepan (Mapuche) the condor's branch.

Manric (Catalan) a form of Manrique.

Manrico (American) a combination of Mann + Enrico.

Manrique (Germanic) powerful leader.

Mansa (Swahili) king. History: a fourteenth-century king of Mali.
Mansah

Mansel (English) manse; house occupied by a clergyman.

Mansfield (English) field by the river; hero's field.

Manso (Latin) the delivered, trusted one.

Mansueto (Latin) he who is peaceful, docile.

Mansûr (Arabic) a form of Mansur.

Mansür (Arabic) divinely aided.

Mantel (French) designer.

Manton (English) man's town; hero's town.

Manu (Hindi) lawmaker. History: the reputed writer of the Hindi compendium of sacred laws and customs. (Hawaiian) bird. (Ghanaian) second-born son.

Manuel (Hebrew) a short form of Emmanuel.

Manville (French) worker's village. (English) hero's village.

Manzo (Japanese) third son.

Manzur (Arabic) the winner.

Maona (Winnebago) creator, earth maker.

Mapira (Yao) millet.

Marat (Indian) life-death-birth-giving cycle.

Marc (French) a form of Mark. (Latin) a short form of Marcus.

Marc Alexander (French) a combination of Marc + Alexander.

Marc Andre, Marc-Andre (French) combinations of Marc + Andre.

Marc Antoine, Marc-Antoine (French) combinations of Marc + Antoine.

Marc Etienne (French) a combination of Marc + Etienne.

Marc Olivier, Marc-Olivier (French) combinations of Marc + Olivier.

Marcanthony (American) a combination of Marc + Anthony.

Marcel, Marcell (French) forms of Marcellus.

Marceliano (Spanish) a form of Marcello.

Marcelino (Italian) a form of Marcellus.

Marcellis, Marcellous (Latin) forms of Marcellus.

Marcello, Marcelo (Italian) forms of Marcellus.

Marcellus (Latin) a familiar form of Marcus.

March (English) dweller by a boundary.

Marciano (Italian) a form of Martin.

Marcilka (Hungarian) a form of Marcellus.

Marcin (Polish) a form of Martin.

Marco (Italian) a form of Marcus. History: Marco Polo was a thirteenth-century Venetian traveler who explored Asia.

Marcoantonio (Italian) a combination of Marco + Antonio.

Marcos (Spanish) a form of Marcus.

Marcus (Latin) martial, warlike.

Marden BG (English) valley with a pool.

Mardonio (Persian) the male warrior.

Mardoqueo (Hebrew) he who adores the god of war.

Mâred (Arabic) rebel.

Marek (Slavic) a form of Marcus.

Maren GB (Basque) sea.

Mareo (Japanese) uncommon.

Margarito (Latin) pearl.

Marian GB (Polish) a form of Mark.

Mariano (Italian) a form of Mark. A form of Marion.

Marid (Arabic) rebellious.

Marin GB (French) sailor.

Marino (Italian) a form of Marin.

Marlo (Italian) a form of Marino.

Marion GB (French) bitter; sea of bitterness.

Marius (Latin) a form of Marin.

Mark (Latin) a form of Marcus. Bible: author of

the second Gospel in the New Testament.

Mark Anthony, Markanthony (Italian) combinations of Mark + Anthony.

Marke (Polish) a form of Mark.

Markel (Latin) a form of Mark.

Markell 🅱🅶 (Latin) a form of Mark.

Markes (Portuguese) a form of Marques.

Markese (French) a form of Marquis.

Markez (French) a form of Marquis.

Markham (English) homestead on the boundary.

Markis (French) a form of Marquis.

Marko (Latin) a form of Marco, Mark.

Markos (Spanish) a form of Marcos. (Latin) a form of Mark, Markus.

Markus (Latin) a form of Marcus.

Marland (English) lake land.

Marley 🅶🅱 (English) lake meadow.

Marlin 🅱🅶 (English) deep-sea fish.

Marlo 🅱🅶 (English) a form of Marlow.

Marlon (French) a form of Merlin.

Marlow (English) hill by the lake.

Marmion (French) small.

Marnin (Hebrew) singer; bringer of joy.

Maro (Japanese) myself.

Marón (Arabic) the male saint.

Marquan (American) a combination of Mark + Quan.

Marque (American) a form of Mark.

Marquel, Marquell (American) forms of Marcellus.

Marques (Portuguese) nobleman.

Marqués (Portuguese) a form of Marques.

Marquese (Portuguese) a form of Marques.

Marquez (Portuguese) a form of Marques.

Marquice (American) a form of Marquis.

Marquies (American) a form of Marquis.

Marquis 🅱🅶 (French) nobleman.

Marquise 🅱🅶 (French) nobleman.

Marquon (American) a combination of Mark + Quon.

Marqus (American) a form of Markus. (Portuguese) a form of Marques.

Marr (Spanish) divine. (Arabic) forbidden.

Mars (Latin) bold warrior. Mythology: the Roman god of war.

Marsalis (Italian) a form of Marcellus.

Marsden (English) marsh valley.

Marsh (English) swamp land. (French) a short form of Marshall.

Marshal (French) a form of Marshall.
Marschal, Marshel

Marshall **(French) caretaker of the horses; military title.**

Marshaun, Marshon (American) forms of Marshawn.

Marshawn (American) a combination of Mark + Shawn.

Marston (English) town by the marsh.

Martel (English) a form of Martell.

Martell (English) hammerer.

Marten (Dutch) a form of Martin.

Martese (Spanish) a form of Martez.

Martez (Spanish) a form of Martin.

Marti GB (Spanish) a form of Martin.

Martial (French) a form of Mark.

Martice (Spanish) a form of Martez.

Martin (Latin, French) a form of Martinus. History: Martin Luther King, Jr. led the Civil Rights movement and won the Nobel Peace Prize. **Martín** (Latin) a form of Martin.

Martinez (Spanish) a form of Martin.

Martínez (Spanish) a form of Martinez.

Martinho (Portuguese) a form of Martin.

Martino (Italian) a form of Martin.

Martiño (Spanish) a form of Martino.

Martins (Latvian) a form of Martin.

Martinus **(Latin) martial, warlike.**

Martir (Greek) he who gives a testament of faith.

Martirio (Latin) testimony.

Marty BG (Latin) a familiar form of Martin.

Martyn (Latin, French) a form of Martin.

Marut (Hindi) Religion: the Hindu god of the wind.

Marv (English) a short form of Marvin.

Marvel (Latin) marvel.

Marvell (Latin) a form of Marvel.

Marvin (English) lover of the sea.

Marwan (Arabic) history personage.

Marwood (English) forest pond.

Marzûq (Arabic) blessed by God.

Mas'ûd (Arabic) a form of Masud.

Masaccio (Italian) twin.

Masahiro (Japanese) broad-minded. Masahyro

Masamba **(Yao) leaves.** Masambah

Masao (Japanese) righteous.

Masato (Japanese) just.

Mashama (Shona) surprising.

Maska (Native American) powerful. (Russian) mask.

Maskini (Egyptian) poor.

Maslin **(French) little Thomas.**

Mason ⭐ BG (French) stone worker.

Masou (Native American) fire god.

Massey (English) twin.

Massimo (Italian) greatest.

Masud (Arabic, Swahili) fortunate.

Matai (Basque, Bulgarian) a form of Matthew. Máté, Matei

Matalino (Filipino) bright.

Matán (Hebrew) gift.

Matatías (Hebrew) gift of God.

Mateo, Matteo (Spanish) forms of Matthew.

Mateos (Hebrew) offered up to God.

Mateusz (Polish) a form of Matthew.

Mathe (German) a short form of Matthew.

Mather (English) powerful army.

Matheu (German) a form of Matthew.

Mathew (Hebrew) a form of Matthew.

Mathias, Matthias (German, Swedish) forms of Matthew.

Mathías (German) a form of Mathias.

Mathieu BG (French) a form of Matthew.

Mathis (German, Swedish) a form of Mathias.

Matias, Matías, Mattias (Spanish) forms of Mathias. Mattia

Matitiahu (Hebrew) given by God.

Matlal (Nahuatl) dark green; net.

Matlalihuitl (Nahuatl) blue-green feather.

Mato (Native American) brave.

Matope (Rhodesian) our last child.

Matoskah (Lakota) white bear.

Mats (Swedish) a familiar form of Matthew.

Matsimela (Egyptian) roots.

Matson (Hebrew) son of Matt.

Matt (Hebrew) a short form of Matthew.

Matteen (Afghan) disciplined; polite.

Matteus (Scandinavian) a form of Matthew.

Mattew (Hebrew) a form of Matthew.

Mattheus (Scandinavian) a form of Matthew.

Matthew ✴
BG (Hebrew) gift of God. Bible: author of the first Gospel of the New Testament.

Matthieu (French) a form of Matthew.

Mattison BG (Hebrew) a form of Matson.

Matty BG (Hebrew) a familiar form of Matthew.

Matus (Czech) a form of Mathias.

Matusalén (Hebrew) symbol of longevity.

Matvey (Russian) a form of Matthew.

Matyas (Polish) a form of Matthew.
Mátyás

Mauli BG (Hawaiian) a form of Maurice.

Maurice (Latin) dark skinned; moor; marshland. **Mauricio** (Spanish) a form of Maurice.

Mauritz (German) a form of Maurice.

Maurizio (Italian) a form of Maurice.

Mauro (Latin) a short form of Maurice.

Maury (Latin) a familiar form of Maurice.

Maverick BG (American) independent.

Mavilo (Latin) to not want.

Mawuli (Ewe) there is a God.

Max (Latin) a short form of Maximilian, Maxwell.
Maks, Maxe

Maxx (Latin) a form of Max.

Maxfield (English) Mack's field.

Maxi (Czech, Hungarian, Spanish) a familiar form of Maximilian, Maximo.

Maxim (Russian) a form of Maxime.

Maxime BG (French) most excellent.

Maximilian (Latin) greatest.

Maximiliano (Italian) a form of Maximilian.

Maximilien, Maximillian (Latin) forms of Maximilian.

Maximino (Italian) a form of Maximilian.

Maximo, Máximo (Spanish) forms of Maximilian.

Maximos (Greek) a form of Maximilian.

Maxton (American) Max's town.

Maxwell (English) great spring.

Maxy (English) a familiar form of Max, Maxwell.

Maxyme (French) a form of Maxime.

Mayer (Latin) a form of Magnus, Major. (Hebrew) a form of Meir.

Mayes (English) field.
Maies, Mays

Mayhew (English) a form of Matthew. (Latin) a form of Maximilian.

Maymûm (Arabic) fortunate.

Maynard (English) powerful; brave. .

Maynor (English) a form of Maynard.

Mayo (Irish) yew-tree plain. (English) a form of Mayes. Geography: a county in Ireland.
Maio

Mayon (Indian) person of black complexion. Religion: another name for the Indian god Mal.

Mayonga (Luganda) lake sailor.

Mayson (French) a form of Mason.

Mayta (Quechua) where are you?

Maytacuapac (Quechua) Oh, Lord, where are you?

Mayua (Quechua) violet, purple.

Mazatl (Nahuatl) deer.

Mazi (Ibo) sir.

Mazin (Arabic) proper.

Mbita (Swahili) born on a cold night.

Mbizi (Egyptian) water.

Mbwana (Swahili) master.

Mc Kenzie, McKenzie BG (Irish) forms of Mackenzie.

Mccoy (Irish) a form of Maccoy.

McGeorge (Scottish) son of George.

Mckade (Scottish) son of Kade.

Mckay (Scottish) son of Kay.

Mckenna GB (American) a form of Mackenzie.

Mckenzie GB (Irish) a form of Mackenzie.

Mckinley BG (Irish) a form of Mackinnley.

Mead BG (English) meadow.

Mecatl (Nahuatl) rope; lineage.

Medardo (Germanic) boldly powerful.

Medarno (Saxon) he who deserves to be honored.

Medgar (German) a form of Edgar.

Medín (Greek) rejecter, defender.

Medir (Greek) a form of Medín.

Medric (English) flourishing meadow.

Medwin (German) faithful friend.

Meginardo (Teutonic) he who is a strong leader.

Mehetabel (Hebrew) who God benefits.

Mehmet (Arabic) a form of Mahomet, Mohamet.

Mehrdad (Persian) gift of the sun.

Mehtar (Sanskrit) prince.

Meinhard (German) strong, firm.

Meinrad (German) strong counsel.

Meir (Hebrew) one who brightens, shines; enlightener. History: Golda Meir was the prime minister of Israel.

Meka GB (Hawaiian) eyes.

Mel BG (English, Irish) a familiar form of Melvin.

Melanio (Greek) having black skin.

Melbourne (English) mill stream.

Melchior (Hebrew) king.

Melchor (Hebrew) a form of Melchior.

Meldon (English) mill hill.

Meldrick (English) strong mill.

Melecio (Greek) careful and attentive.

Melibeo (Greek) he who takes care of the mentally handicapped.

Melino (Tongan) peace.

Meliso (Greek) bee.

Melito (Greek) sugary sweet; pleasant.

Meliton, Melitón (Greek) from the island of Malta.

Melivilu (Mapuche) four snakes.

Melquiades, Melquíades (Hebrew) Yahweh is my God.

Melrone (Irish) servant of Saint Ruadhan.

Melvern (Native American) great chief.

Melville (French) mill town. Literature: Herman Melville was a well-known nineteenth-century American writer.

Melvin (Irish) armored chief. (English) mill friend; council friend.

Memphis (Egyptian) one who comes from Memphis.

Menachem (Hebrew) comforter.

Menajem (Hebrew) comforting.

Menandro (Greek) he who remains a man.

Menas (Greek) related to the months.

Menassah (Hebrew) cause to forget.

Mendel (English) repairman.

Mendo (Spanish) a form of Hermenegildo.

Menelao (Greek) he who goes to the village to fight.

Menes (Egyptian) name of the king.

Mengesha (Ethiopian) kingdom.

Menico (Spanish) a short form of Domenico.

Mensah (Ewe) third son.

Mentor (Greek) the teacher.

Menz (German) a short form of Clement.

Mercer (English) storekeeper.

Mercurio (Latin) he who pays attention to business.

Mered (Hebrew) revolter.

Merion (Welsh) from Merion, Wales.
Merrion

Merivale (English) pleasant valley.

Merle 🅱🅶 (French) a short form of Merlin, Merrill.

Merlin (English) falcon. Literature: the magician who served as counselor in King Arthur's court.

Merlín (French) a form of Merlin.

Merlino (Spanish) a form of Merlín.

Merrick (English) ruler of the sea.

Merrill (Irish) bright sea. (French) famous.

Merritt 🅱🅶 (Latin, Irish) valuable; deserving.

Merton (English) sea town.

Merulo (Latin) he who is fine as a blackbird.

Merv (Irish) a short form of Mervin.
Merve

Merville (French) sea village.

Mervin (Irish) a form of Marvin.

Meshach (Hebrew) artist. Bible: one of Daniel's three friends who emerged unharmed from the fiery furnace of Babylon.

Meshulam (Hebrew) paid.

Messiah (Hebrew) the annointed one; a hoped-for savior.

Mesut (Turkish) happy.

Metikla (Moquelumnan) reaching a hand underwater to catch a fish.

Metrenco (Mapuche) still water.

Metrofanes (Greek) he who resembles his mother.

Mette (Greek, Danish) pearl.

Meulén (Mapuche) whirlwind.

Meurig (Welsh) a form of Maurice.

Meyer (German) farmer. (Hebrew) a form of Meir.

Meztli (Nahuatl) moon.

Mhina **(Swahili) delightful.**

Micael (Hebrew) a form of Michael.

Micah 🅱🅶 (Hebrew) a form of Michael. Bible: a Hebrew prophet.

Micaiah 🅱🅶 (Hebrew) a form of Micah.

Micha 🅶🅱 (Hebrew) a short form of Michael.

Michael ⭐

🅱🅶 (Hebrew) who is like God?

Michaelangel (American) a form of Michael + Angel.

Michail (Russian) a form of Michael.

Michal BG (Polish) a form of Michael.

Michale (Polish) a form of Michal.

Micheal (Irish) a form of Michael.

Michel BG (French) a form of Michael.

Michelangelo (Italian) a combination of Michael + Angelo. Art: Michelangelo Buonarroti was one of the greatest Renaissance painters.

Michele GB (Italian) a form of Michael.

Michio (Japanese) man with the strength of three thousand.

Mick (English) a short form of Michael, Mickey.

Mickael, Mickel (English) forms of Michael.

Mickenzie GB (Irish) a form of Mackenzie.

Mickey (Irish) a familiar form of Michael.

Micu (Hungarian) a form of Nick.

Midas (Greek) the fleeting and admirable business.

Migel (Portuguese, Spanish) a form of Miguel.

Miguel (Portuguese, Spanish) a form of Michael.

Miguelangel (Spanish) a combination of Miguel + Angel.

Mihail (Greek, Bulgarian, Romanian) a form of Mikhail.

Mijael, Mijaiá (Hebrew) who but God?

Mijaíl (Russian) a form of Miguel.

Mika GB (Ponca) raccoon. (Hebrew) a form of Micah. (Russian) a familiar form of Michael.

Mikael (Swedish) a form of Michael.

Mikáele (Hawaiian) a form of Michael.
Mikele

Mikah BG (Hebrew) a form of Micah. (Hebrew, Russian, Ponca) a form of Mika.

Mikail (Greek, Russian) a form of Mikhail.

Mikal BG (Hebrew) a form of Michael.

Mikasi (Omaha) coyote.

Mike (Hebrew) a short form of Michael.

Mikeal (Irish) a form of Michael.

Mikel BG (Basque) a form of Michael.

Mikelis (Latvian) a form of Michael.

Mikell (Basque) a form of Michael.

Mikey (Hebrew) a short form of Michael.

Mikhael (Greek, Russian) a form of Mikhail.

Mikhail (Greek, Russian) a form of Michael.

Miki GB (Japanese) tree.

Mikizli (Nahuatl) rest after hard work.

Mikkel (Norwegian) a form of Michael.

Mikko (Finnish) a form of Michael.

Mikolaj (Polish) a form of Nicholas.

Mikolas (Greek) a form of Nicholas.

Miksa (Hungarian) a form of Max.

Milagro (Spanish) miracle.

Milan GB (Italian) northerner. Geography: a city in northern Italy.

Milap (Native American) giving.

Milborough (English) middle borough.

Milburn (English) stream by the mill. A form of Melbourne.

Milcíades (Greek) he of reddish complexion.

Milek (Polish) a familiar form of Nicholas.

Miles (Greek) millstone. (Latin) soldier. (German) merciful. (English) a short form of Michael.

Milford (English) mill by the ford.

Mililani BG (Hawaiian) heavenly caress.

Milintica (Nahuatl) he is waving; fire.

Milko (German) a familiar form of Emil. (Czech) a form of Michael.

Millán (Latin) belonging to the Emilia family.

Millañir (Mapuche) silver fox.

Millard (Latin) caretaker of the mill.

Miller (English) miller; grain grinder.

Mills (English) mills.

Milo (German) a form of Miles. A familiar form of Emil.

Milos (Greek, Slavic) pleasant.

Miloslav (Czech) lover of glory.

Milt (English) a short form of Milton.

Milton (English) mill town.

Mimis (Greek) a familiar form of Demetrius.

Min (Burmese) king.

Mincho (Spanish) a form of Benjamin.

Minel (Spanish) a form of Manuel.

Miner (English) miner.

Minervino (Greek) a form of Minervo.

Minervo (Greek) power; young.

Mingan (Native American) gray wolf.

Mingo (Spanish) a short form of Domingo.

Minh (Vietnamese) bright.

Minkah (Akan) just, fair.

Minor (Latin) junior; younger.

Minoru (Japanese) fruitful.

Mío (Spanish) mine.

Mique (Spanish) a form of Mickey.

Miquel (Spanish) a form of Mique.

Miracle GB (Latin) miracle.

Mirco (Spanish) he who assures the peace.

Mirko (Slavic) glorious for having assured peace.

Miron (Polish) peace.

Miroslav (Czech) peace; glory.

Miroslavo (Slavic) a form of Miroslav.

Mirwais (Afghan) noble ruler.

Mirza (Persian) sir.

Misael, Missael (Hebrew) forms of Michael.

Misha GB (Russian) a short form of Michail.

Miska (Hungarian) a form of Michael.

Mister (English) mister.

Misu (Moquelumnan) rippling water.

Mitch (English) a short form of Mitchell.

Mitchel (English) a form of Mitchell.

Mitchell (English) a form of Michael.

Mitsos (Greek) a familiar form of Demetrius.

Mixel (Catalan) a form of Miguel.

Moctezuma (Nahuatl) prince of the austere gesture.

Modesto (Latin) modest.

Moe (English) a short form of Moses.

Mogens (Dutch) powerful.
Mogen

Mohamad, Mohamed, Mohammad, Mohammed (Arabic) forms of Muhammad.

Mohamet (Arabic) a form of Muhammad.

Mohamud (Arabic) a form of Muhammad.

Mohan (Hindi) delightful.

Moise (Portuguese, Spanish) a form of Moises.

Moises (Portuguese, Spanish) a form of Moses.

Moishe (Yiddish) a form of Moses.

Mojag (Native American) crying baby.

Moki (Australian) cloudy.

Molimo (Moquelumnan) bear going under shady trees.

Momoztli (Nahuatl) altar.

Momuso (Moquelumnan) yellow jackets crowded in their nests for the winter.

Mona GB (Moquelumnan) gathering jimsonweed seed.

Monahan (Irish) monk.

Mongo (Yoruba) famous.

Mónico (Latin) solitary.

Monitor (Latin) he who counsels.

Monolo (Spanish) a familiar form of Manuel.

Monroe (Irish) from the mount on the river Roe.

Montague (French) pointed mountain.

Montaigu (French) one who comes from the hill.

Montana GB (Spanish) mountain. Geography: a U.S. state.

Montaro (Japanese) big boy.

Monte (French) a form of Montague. (Spanish) a short form of Montgomery.

Montego (Spanish) mountainous.

Montel, Montell (American) forms of Montreal.

Montenegro (Spanish) black mountain.

Monterio (Japanese) a form of Montaro.

Montes, Móntez (Spanish) forms of Montez.

Montez (Spanish) dweller in the mountains.

Montgomery BG (English) rich man's mountain.

Month (Egyptian) god of Thebes.

Montre (French) show.

Montreal (French) royal mountain. Geography: a city in Quebec.

Montrel, Montrell (French) forms of Montreal.

Montrez (French) a form of Montre.

Montserrat (Catalan) upon the mountain range.

Montsho (Tswana) black.

Monty (English) a familiar form of Montgomery.

Moore (French) dark; moor; marshland.

Mordecai (Hebrew) martial, warlike. Bible: wise counselor to Queen Esther.

Mordechai (Hebrew) a form of Mordecai.

Mordred (Latin) painful. Literature: the bastard son of King Arthur.
, **Mordryd**

Morel (French) an edible mushroom.

Moreland (English) moor; marshland.

Morell (French) dark; from Morocco.

Morey (Greek) a familiar form of Moris. (Latin) a form of Morrie.

Morfeo (Greek) he who makes you see beautiful figures.

Morgan GB (Scottish) sea warrior.

Morgen GB (Scottish) a form of Morgan.

Morio (Japanese) forest.

Moris (Greek) son of the dark one. (English) a form of Morris.
Morey, Morisz, Moriz, Morys

Moritz (German) a form of Maurice, Morris.
Morisz

Morley (English) meadow by the moor.

Morrie (Latin) a familiar form of Maurice, Morse.
Morey, **Mori, Morie, Morri**

Morris (Latin) dark skinned; moor; marshland. (English) a form of Maurice.

Morse (English) son of Maurice.
Morresse, Morrison, Morrisson

Mort (French, English) a short form of Mordecai, Morten, Mortimer, Morton.

Morten (Norwegian) a form of Martin.

Mortimer (French) still water.

Morton (English) town near the moor.

Morven (Scottish) mariner.

Mose (Hebrew) a short form of Moses.

Mosegi (Egyptian) tailor.

Moses (Hebrew) drawn out of the water. (Egyptian) son, child. Bible: the Hebrew lawgiver who

brought the Ten
Commandments down
from Mount Sinai.

Moshe (Hebrew, Polish) a
form of Moses.

Moshé (Hebrew) a form of
Moshe.

Mosi BG (Swahili) first-
born.

Moss (Irish) a short form of
Maurice, Morris.
(English) a short form of
Moses.

Moswen BG (African) light
in color.

Motega (Native American)
new arrow.

Mouhamed (Arabic) a
form of Muhammad.

Mousa (Arabic) a form of
Moses.

Moyolehuani (Nahuatl)
enamored one.

Mozart (Italian)
breathless. Music:
Wolfgang Amadeus
Mozart was a famous
eighteenth-century
Austrian composer.

Moze (Lithuanian) a form
of Moses.

Mpasa (Nguni) mat.

Mposi (Nyakyusa)
blacksmith.

Mpoza (Luganda) tax
collector.

Msamaki (Egyptian) fish.

Msrah (Akan) sixth-born.

Mtima (Nguni) heart.

Mu'âdh (Arabic) protected.

Mû'awîyya (Arabic) young
fox.

Mu'tassim (Arabic)
adhered to faith.

Mu'tazz (Arabic) proud.

Muata (Moquelumnan)
yellow jackets in their
nest.
Mutah

Mubârak (Arabic) blessed.

Mucio (Latin) he who
endures silence.

Mufid (Arabic) useful.

Mugamba (Runyoro) talks
too much.

Mugisa (Rutooro) lucky.

Muhammad (Arabic)
praised. History: the
founder of the Islamic
religion.

Muhammed (Arabic) a
form of Muhammad.

Muhannad (Arabic)
sword.

Muhsin (Arabic)
beneficent; charitable.

Muhtadi (Arabic) rightly
guided.

Muir (Scottish) moor;
marshland.

Mujahid (Arabic) fighter in
the way of Allah.

Mujâhid (Arabic) a form of
Mujahid.

Mukasa (Luganda) God's
chief administrator.

Mukhtar (Arabic) chosen.
Mukhtaar

Mukhwana (Egyptian)
twins.

Mukul (Sanskrit) bud,
blossom; soul.

Mullu (Quechua) coral,
jewel.

Mulogo (Musoga) wizard.

Mun-Hee (Korean)
literate; shiny.

Mundan (Rhodesian)
garden.

Mundo (Spanish) a short
form of Edmundo.

Mundy **(Irish) from
Reamonn.**

Mungo (Scottish) amiable.

Munir (Arabic) brilliant;
shining.

Munny (Cambodian) wise.

Muntassir (Arabic)
victorious.

Muraco (Native American)
white moon.

Murali (Hindi) flute.
Religion: the instrument
the Hindu god Krishna is
usually depicted as
playing.

Murat (Turkish) wish come
true.

Murdock (Scottish)
wealthy sailor.

Murphy BG (Irish) sea
warrior.

Murray (Scottish) sailor.

Murtadi (Arabic) satisfied.

Murtagh (Irish) a form of
Murdock.

Musa (Swahili) child.

Mûsà (Arabic) a form of Moises.

Musád (Arabic) untied camel.

Mushin (Arabic) charitable.

Muslim (Egyptian) believer.

Musoke (Rukonjo) born while a rainbow was in the sky.

Mustafa (Arabic) chosen; royal.

Mustafá, Mustafà (Arabic) forms of Mustafa.

Mustapha (Arabic) a form of Mustafa.

Muti (Arabic) obedient.

Muwaffaq (Arabic) successful.

Mwaka (Luganda) born on New Year's Eve.

Mwamba (Nyakyusa) strong.

Mwanje (Luganda) leopard.

Mwinyi (Swahili) king.

Mwita (Swahili) summoner.

Mychael (American) a form of Michael.

Mychajlo (Latvian) a form of Michael.

Mychal (American) a form of Michael.

Myer (English) a form of Meir.

Mykal (American) a form of Michael.

Mykel 🅱🅶 (American) a form of Michael.

Myles (Latin) soldier. (German) a form of Miles.

Mylon (Italian) a form of Milan.

Mynor (Latin) a form of Minor.

Myo (Burmese) city.

Myron **(Greek) fragrant ointment. (Polish) a form of Miron.**

Myung-Dae (Korean) right; great.

Mzuzi (Swahili) inventive.

N

N'namdi (Ibo) his father's name lives on.

Naaman (Hebrew) pleasant.

Nabarun (Indian) morning sun.

Nabeel (Arabic) a form of Nabil.

Nabendu (Indian) new moon.

Nabhân, Nabîh (Arabic) worthy.

Nabhi (Indian) focus; the best.

Nabiha (Arabic) intelligent.

Nabil (Arabic) noble.

Nabor (Hebrew) the prophet's light.

Nabucodonosor (Chaldean) God protects my reign.

Nachiketa (Indian) an ancient Rishi, or Hindu sage; fire.

Nachman (Hebrew) a short form of Menachem.

Nada 🅶🅱 (Arabic) generous.

Nadav (Hebrew) generous; noble.

Nader (Afghan, Arabic) a form of Nadir.

Nadidah (Arabic) equal to anyone else.

Nadim (Arabic) friend.

Nadîm (Arabic) a form of Nadim.

Nadir (Afghan, Arabic) dear, rare.

Nadisu (Hindi) beautiful river.

Naeem (Arabic) benevolent.

Naftali (Hebrew) wreath.

Naftalí (Hebrew) a form of Naftali.

Nagendra, Nagesh (Indian) other names for the Hindu serpent god Sesh.

Nagid (Hebrew) ruler; prince.

Nahele (Hawaiian) forest.

Nahma (Native American) sturgeon.

Nahuatl (Nahuatl) four waters.

Nahuel (Araucanian) tiger.

Nahum (Hebrew) a form of Nachman.

Nahusha (Indian) a mythological king.

Naiara (Spanish) of the Virgin Mary.

Nailah GB (Arabic) successful.

Nairit (Indian) southwest.

Nairn (Scottish) river with alder trees.

Naishadh (Indian) another name for King Nala, a hero from the Indian epic poem *Mahabharata*.

Najee BG (Arabic) a form of Naji.

Naji (Arabic) safe.

Nâji (Arabic) a form of Naji.

Najíb (Arabic) born to nobility.

Najjâr (Arabic) carpenter.

Najm Al-Dîn (Arabic) star of faith.

Nakia GB (Arabic) pure.

Nakos (Arapaho) sage, wise.

Nakshatra (Indian) star.

Nakul (Indian) one of the Pandavas, descendents of King Pandu in the Indian epic poem *Mahabharata*.

Naldo (Spanish) a familiar form of Reginald.

Nalin (Indian) lotus.

Nalinaksha (Indian) one with eyes like a lotus.

Nalren (Dene) thawed out.

Nam (Vietnamese) scrape off.

Namacuix (Nahuatl) king.

Namaka (Hawaiian) eyes.

Namdev, Narahari (Indian) other names for the Hindu god Vishnu.

Namid (Ojibwa) star dancer.

Namir (Hebrew) leopard.

Namuncura, Namuncurá (Mapuche) foot of stone, strong foot.

Nana BG (Hawaiian) spring.

Nanak (Indian) Sikh guru.

—**ancuvilu** (Mapuche) snake that is the color of lead.

Nand (Indian) joyful.

Nandi (Indian) another name for the Hindu god Shiva; the bull of Shiva.

Nandin (Hindi) Religion: a servant of the Hindu god Shiva.

Nando (German) a familiar form of Ferdinand.

Nangila (Abaluhya) born while parents traveled.

Nangwaya (Mwera) don't mess with me.

Nansen (Swedish) son of Nancy.

Nantai (Navajo) chief.

Nantan (Apache) spokesman.

Naoko (Japanese) straight, honest.

Naolin (Spanish) sun god of the Mexican people.

Naotau (Indian) new.

Napayshni (Lakota) he does not flee; courageous.

Napier (Spanish) new city.

Napoleon (Greek) lion of the woodland. (Italian) from Naples, Italy. History: Napoleon Bonaparte was a famous nineteenth-century French emperor.

Napoleón (Greek) a form of Napoleon.

Naquan (American) a combination of the prefix Na + Quan.

Narain (Hindi) protector. Religion: another name for the Hindu god Vishnu.

Narasimha (Indian) an incarnation of the Hindu god Vishnu.

Narcisse (French) a form of Narcissus.

Narcissus (Greek) daffodil. Mythology: the youth who fell in love with his own reflection.

Nard (Persian) chess player.

Nardo (German) strong, hardy. (Spanish) a short form of Bernardo.

Narendra (Indian) king.

Naresh (Hindi) the king.

Narmer (Egyptian) name of the king.

Narno (Latin) he who was born in the Italian city of Narnia.

Narrie (Australian) bush fire.

Narses (Persian) what the two martyrs brought from Persia.

Narve (Dutch) healthy, strong.

Nash (English) Geography: Nash is the name of many towns in England and America.

Nashashuk (Fox, Sauk) loud thunder.

Nâshe (Arabic) counselor.

Nashoba (Choctaw) wolf.

Nasim (Persian) breeze; fresh air.

Nasîm (Persian) a form of Nasim.

Nasir (Arabic) a form of Nasser.

Nassar (Arabic) protector.

Nasser (Arabic) victorious.

Nat (English) a short form of Nathan, Nathaniel.
Natt, Natty

Natal (Spanish) a form of Noël.
Natale, Natalie, Natalino, Natalio, Nataly

Natalicio (Latin) day of birth.

Natan (Hebrew, Hungarian, Polish, Russian, Spanish) God has given.

Natán (Hebrew) a form of Natan.

Natanael (Hebrew) a form of Nathaniel.

Nate (Hebrew) a short form of Nathan, Nathaniel.

Natesh (Hindi) destroyer. Religion: another name for the Hindu god Shiva.

Nathan ☆ (Hebrew) a short form of Nathaniel. Bible: a prophet during the reigns of David and Solomon.

Nathanael (Hebrew) gift of God. Bible: one of the Twelve Apostles, also known as Bartholomew.

Nathaneal, Nathanial (Hebrew) forms of Nathanael.

Nathanie (Hebrew) a familiar form of Nathaniel.
Nathania, Nathanni

Nathaniel ☆ (Hebrew) a form of Nathanael.

Nathen, Nathon (Hebrew) forms of Nathan.

Natividad (Spanish) nativity.

Natlalihuitl (Nahuatl) blue-green feather or purple feather.

Natwar (Indian) another name for the Hindu god Krishna.

—aupac, —aupari (Quechua) firstborn.

—auque, —auqui (Quechua) before everyone.

Nav (Gypsy) name.

Naval (Latin) god of the sailing vessels.

Navaneet (Indian) butter.

Navarro (Spanish) plains.

Navdeep BG (Sikh) new light.

Naveen BG (Hindi) a form of Navin.

Navin (Hindi) new, novel.
Naven, Navyn

Navrang (Indian) beautiful.

Navroz (Indian) Parsi festival to celebrate the new year.

Nawat (Native American) left-handed.

Nawkaw (Winnebago) wood.

Nayan (Indian) eye.

Nayati (Native American) wrestler.

Nayi (Lebanese) saved.

Nayland (English) island dweller.

Nazareno (Hebrew) he who has separated himself from the rest.

Nazareth (Hebrew) born in Nazareth, Israel.

Nâzeh (Arabic) chaste.

Nazih (Arabic) pure, chaste.

Ndale (Nguni) trick.

Neal, Neel (Irish) forms of Neil.

Neandro (Greek) young and manly.

Neb-Er-Tcher (Egyptian) god of the universe.

Nebrido (Greek) graceful like the fawn.

Necalli (Nahuatl) battle.

Neci [BG] (Latin) a familiar form of Ignatius.

Nectario (Greek) he who sweetens life with nectar.

Nectarios (Greek) Religion: a saint in the Greek Orthodox Church.

Necuamatl (Nahuatl) king.

Neculman (Mapuche) swift condor.

Neculqueo (Mapuche) rapid speaker.

Ned (English) a familiar form of Edward, Edwin.

Neeladri (Indian) the Nilgiris, a mountainous region in India.

Neelambar (Indian) blue sky.

Neema [BG] (Swahili) born during prosperous times.

Nefertum (Egyptian) cultured in Memphis.

Neftalí (Hebrew) one who helps in the struggle.

Neguib (Arabic) famous.

Nehemiah (Hebrew) compassion of Jehovah. Bible: a Jewish leader.

Nehru (Hindi) canal.

Nehuén (Araucanian) strong.

Neil (Irish) champion.

Neka (Native American) wild goose.

Nekiron (Japanese) unsure.

Nelek (Polish) a form of Cornelius.

Nelius (Latin) a short form of Cornelius.

Nelli (Nahuatl) truth.

Nellie [GB] (English) a familiar form of Cornelius, Cornell, Nelson.

Nelo (Spanish) a form of Daniel.

Nels (Scandinavian) a form of Neil, Nelson.

Nelson (English) son of Neil.

Nemesia (Latin) punishment of the gods.

Nemesio (Spanish) just.

Nemo (Greek) glen, glade. (Hebrew) a short form of Nehemiah.

Nemorio (Latin) belongs to the sacred forest.

Nemuel (Hebrew) God's sea.

Nen (Egyptian) ancient waters.

Neo (Greek) new. (African) gift.

Neofito (Greek) he who began recently.

Neon (Greek) he who is strong.

Neopolo (Spanish) a form of Napoleon.

Nepomuceno (Slavic) he who gives his help.

Neptune (Latin) sea ruler. Mythology: the Roman god of the sea.

Neptuno (Latin) a form of Neptune.

Nereo (Greek) he who is the captain at sea.

Nereu (Catalan) a form of Nereo.

Neriá (Hebrew) light of God.

Nerio (Greek) sea traveler.

Nero (Latin, Spanish) stern. History: a cruel Roman emperor.

Neron (Spanish) strong.

Nerón (Spanish) a form of Neron.

Nerville (French, Irish) village by the sea.

Nery (Hebrew, Arabic) a form of Nuri.

Nesbit (English) nose-shaped bend in a river.

Nesto (Spanish) serious.

Nestor (Greek) traveler; wise.

Néstor (Greek) a form of Nestor.

Nestorio (Greek) a form of Nestor.

Nethaniel (Hebrew) a form of Nathaniel.

Neto (Spanish) a short form of Ernesto.

Netzahualcoyotl (Nahuatl) hungry coyote.

Neuveville (French) one who comes from the new city.

Nevada [GB] (Spanish) covered in snow. Geography: a U.S. state.

Nevan (Irish) holy.

Neville (French) new town.

Nevin (Irish) worshiper of the saint. (English) middle; herb.

Newbold (English) new tree.

Newell (English) new hall.
Newall, Newel, Newyle

Newland (English) new land.
Newlan

Newlin (Welsh) new lake.

Newman (English) newcomer.

Newton **(English) new town.**

Neyén (Araucanian) a smooth breath.

Neymar (Portuguese) Sports: Neymar da Silva Santos Junior is a Brazilian soccer star.

Nezahualcoyotl (Nahuatl) fasting coyote.

Nezahualpilli (Nahuatl) a prince who fasts.

Ngai (Vietnamese) herb.

Nghia (Vietnamese) forever.

Ngozi (Ibo) blessing.

Ngu (Vietnamese) sleep.

Nguyen BG (Vietnamese) a form of Ngu.

Nhean (Cambodian) self-knowledge.

Niall (Irish) a form of Neil. History: Niall of the Nine Hostages was a famous Irish king.

Nibal (Arabic) arrows.
Nibel, Nybal

Nibaw **(Native American) standing tall.**

Nicabar (Gypsy) stealthy.

Nicandro (Greek) he who is victorious among men.

Nicasio (Greek) the victorious one.

Nicco, Nico (Greek) short forms of Nicholas.

Niccolo, Nicolo (Italian) forms of Nicholas.

Níceas (Greek) he of the great victory.

Nicéforo (Greek) he who brings victory.

Nicetas, Niceto (Greek) victorious.

Nicho (Spanish) a form of Dennis.

Nicholai (Norwegian, Russian) a form of Nicholas.

Nicholas ✴

BG (Greek) victorious people. Religion: Nicholas of Myra is a patron saint of children.

Nicholaus (Greek) a form of Nicholas.

Nicholes, Nichols **(English) son of Nicholas.**

Nicholis (English) a form of Nicholes.

Nicholos (Greek) a form of Nicholas.

Nicholson (English) son of Nicholas.

Nick (English) a short form of Dominic, Nicholas.

Nickalas, Nickalus (Greek) forms of Nicholas.

Nicklaus, Nicklas (Greek) forms of Nicholas.

Nickolas, Nickolaus, Nickolis, Nickolus (Greek) forms of Nicholas.

Nicky BG (Greek) a familiar form of Nicholas.

Nicodemo (Greek) a form of Nicodemus.

Nicodemus **(Greek) conqueror of the people.**

Nicola GB **(Italian) a form of Nicholas.** Nicolaas, Nicolaus **(Italian) forms of Nicolas.**

Nicolai (Norwegian, Russian) a form of Nicholas.

Nicolas BG (Italian) a form of Nicolas.

Nicomedes (Greek) he who prepares the victories.

Nicón (Greek) the victorious one.

Nicostrato (Greek) the general who leads to victory.

—ielol (Mapuche) eye of the cave.

Niels (Danish) a form of Neil.

Nien (Vietnamese) year.
Nyen

Nigan (Native American) ahead.
Nigen

Nigel (Latin) dark night.

Niguel (Spanish) champion.

Nika GB (Yoruba) ferocious.

Nike BG (Greek) victorious.

Nikhil (Indian) a form of Nicholas.

Niki GB (Hungarian) a familiar form of Nicholas.

Nikita GB (Russian) a form of Nicholas.

Nikiti (Native American) round and smooth like an abalone shell.

Nikki GB (Hungarian) a familiar form of Nicholas.

Nikko, Niko (Hungarian) forms of Nicholas.
Nikoe, Nyko

Niklas (Latvian, Swedish) a form of Nicholas.

Nikola (Greek) a short form of Nicholas.

Nikolai (Estonian, Russian) a form of Nicholas.

Nikolaos (Greek) a form of Nicholas.

Nikolas, Nikolaus (Greek) forms of Nicholas.

Nikolos (Greek) a form of Nicholas. **Nil** (Russian) a form of Neil.

Nila GB (Hindi) blue.

Nile (Russian) a form of Nil.

Niles (English) son of Neil.

Nilo (Finnish) a form of Neil.

Nils (Swedish) a short form of Nicholas. (Danish) a form of Niels.

Nima BG (Hebrew) thread. (Arabic) blessing.

Nimrod (Hebrew) rebel. Bible: a great-grandson of Noah.

Ninacolla (Quechua) flame of fire.

Ninacuyuchi, Ninan (Quechua) he who stokes the fire.

Ninauari (Quechua) llama-like animal of fire.

Ninauíca (Quechua) sacred fire.

Nino (Spanish) a form of Niño.

Niño (Spanish) young child.

Niran (Tai) eternal.

Nishan (Armenian) cross, sign, mark.

Nissan (Hebrew) sign, omen; miracle.

Nitgardo (Germanic) fighter who maintains combative fire.

Nitis (Native American) friend.

Nixon (English) son of Nick.

Nizam (Arabic) leader.

Nkosi (Egyptian) rule.

Nkrumah (Egyptian) ninth born.

Nkunda (Runyankore) loves those who hate him.

Noach (Hebrew) a form of Noah.

Noah ☆
BG (Hebrew) peaceful, restful. Bible: the patriarch who built the ark to survive the Flood.

Noaj (Hebrew) a rest.

Noam (Hebrew) sweet; friend.

Noble (Latin) born to nobility.

Nochehuatl (Nahuatl) consistent.

Nochtli (Nahuatl) prickly pear fruit.

Nodin (Native American) wind.

Noe (Czech, French) a form of Noah.

Noé (Hebrew, Spanish) quiet, peaceful. **Noel** BG (French) a form of Noël.

Noël (French) day of Christ's birth.

Noelino (Spanish) a form of Natal.

Nohea (Hawaiian) handsome.

Nokonyu (Native American) katydid's nose.

Nolan ⭐ (Irish) famous; noble.

Nolasco (Hebrew) he who departs and forgets about promises.

Nolberto (Teutonic) a form of Norberto.

Nolen (Irish) a form of Nolan.

Nollie 🅱🅶 (Latin, Scandinavian) a familiar form of Oliver.

Nono (Latin) ninth born.

Noor 🅶🅱 (Sikh) divine light. (Aramaic) a form of Nura.

Nopaltzin (Nahuatl) cactus; king.

Norbert (Scandinavian) brilliant hero.

Norberto (Spanish) a form of Norbert.

Norman (French) Norseman. History: a name for the Scandinavians who settled in northern France in the tenth century, and who later conquered England in 1066.

Normando (Spanish) man of the north.

Norris (French) northerner. (English) Norman's horse.

Northcliff (English) northern cliff.

Northrop (English) north farm.

Norton (English) northern town.

Norville (French, English) northern town.

Norvin (English) northern friend.

Norward (English) protector of the north.

Norwood (English) northern woods.

Nostriano (Latin) he who is from our homeland.

Notaku (Moquelumnan) growing bear.

Notelmo (Teutonic) he who protects himself in combat with the helmet.

Nouel (French) almond.

Nour 🅶🅱 (Aramaic) a short form of Nura **Nowles** (English) a short form of Knowles.

Nsoah (Akan) seventh-born.

Numa (Arabic) pleasant.

Numair (Arabic) panther.

Nun (Egyptian) god of the ocean.

Nuncio (Italian) messenger.

Nuno (Basque) monk.

Nuri (Hebrew, Arabic) my fire.

Nuriel (Hebrew, Arabic) fire of the Lord.

Nuru 🅱🅶 (Swahili) born in daylight.

Nusair (Arabic) bird of prey.

Nwa (Nigerian) son.

Nwake (Nigerian) born on market day.

Nye (English) a familiar form of Aneurin, Nigel.

Nyle (English) island. (Irish) a form of Neil.

O

O'shea 🅱🅶 (Irish) a form of O'Shea.

O'neil (Irish) son of Neil.

O'shay, Oshay, Oshea (Irish) forms of O'Shea.

O'Shea 🅱🅶 (Irish) son of Shea.

Oakes (English) oak trees.

Oakley 🅱🅶 (English) oak-tree field.

Oalo (Spanish) a form of Paul.

Oba 🅱🅶 (Yoruba) king.

Obadele (Yoruba) king arrives at the house.

Obadiah (Hebrew) servant of God.

Obdulio (Latin) he who calms in sorrowful moments.

Obed (English) a short form of Obadiah.
_{Obad}

Oberon (German) noble; bearlike. Literature: the king of the fairies in the

337

Shakespearean play *A Midsummer Night's Dream*.

Obert (German) wealthy; bright.

Oberto (Germanic) a form of Adalberto.

Obie (English) a familiar form of Obadiah.

Ocan (Luo) hard times.

Ocean BG (Greek) a short form of Oceanus.

Oceanus (Greek) Mythology: a Titan who rules over the outer sea encircling the earth.

Ocotlán (Nahuatl) pine.

Octavio (Latin) eighth.
Octavious (Latin) forms of Octavio.

Octavis (Latin) a form of Octavio.

Odakota (Lakota) friendly.

Odd (Norwegian) point.

Ode BG (Benin) born along the road. (Irish, English) a short form of Odell.

Odeberto (Teutonic) he who shines because of his possessions.

Oded (Hebrew) encouraging.

Odell (Greek) ode, melody. (Irish) otter. (English) forested hill.

Oderico (Germanic) powerful in riches.

Odilón (Teutonic) owner of a bountiful inheritance.

Odin (Scandinavian) ruler. Mythology: the Norse god of wisdom and war.

Odín (Scandinavian) a form of Odin.

Odion (Benin) first of twins.
Odyon

Odo (Norwegian) a form of Otto.

Odoacro (German) he who watches over his inheritance.

Odolf (German) prosperous wolf.

Odom (Ghanaian) oak tree.

Odon (Hungarian) wealthy protector.

Odón (Hungarian) a form of Odon.

Odran (Irish) pale green.

Odwin (German) noble friend.

Odysseus (Greek) wrathful. Literature: the hero of Homer's epic poem *Odyssey*.

Ofer (Hebrew) young deer.

Ofir (Hebrew) ferocious.

Og (Aramaic) king. Bible: the king of Basham.

Ogaleesha (Lakota) red shirt.

Ogbay (Ethiopian) don't take him from me.

Ogbonna (Ibo) image of his father.

Ogden (English) oak valley. Literature: Ogden Nash was a twentieth-century American writer of light verse.

Ogilvie (Welsh) high.

Ogima (Ojibwa) chief.

Ogun (Nigerian) Mythology: the god of war.

Ohanko (Native American) restless.

Ohannes (Turkish) a form of John.

Ohanzee (Lakota) comforting shadow.

Ohin (African) chief.
Ohan, Ohyn

Ohitekah (Lakota) brave.
Ohiteka

Ohtli (Nahuatl) road.

Oisin (Irish) small deer.

Oistin (Irish) a form of Austin.

OJ (American) a combination of the initials O. + J.

Ojas (Indian) luster.

Ojo (Yoruba) difficult delivery.

Okapi (Swahili) an African animal related to the giraffe but having a short neck.

Oke (Hawaiian) a form of Oscar.

Okechuku (Ibo) God's gift.

Okeke (Ibo) born on market day.

Okie (American) from Oklahoma.

Oko (Ghanaian) older twin. (Yoruba) god of war.

Okorie (Ibo) a form of Okeke.

Okpara (Ibo) first son.

Okuth (Luo) born in a rain shower.

Ola GB (Yoruba) wealthy, rich.

Olaf (Scandinavian) ancestor. History: a patron saint and king of Norway.

Olaguer (Catalan) a form of Olegario.

Olajuwon (Yoruba) wealth and honor are God's gifts.

Olamina (Yoruba) this is my wealth.

Olatunji (Yoruba) honor reawakens.

Olav (Scandinavian) a form of Olaf.

Ole (Scandinavian) a familiar form of Olaf, Olav.

Oleg (Latvian, Russian) holy.

Olegario (Germanic) he who dominates with his strength and his lance.

Oleguer (Catalan) a form of Olegario.

Oleksandr (Russian) a form of Alexander.

Olen BG (Scandinavian) a form of Olaf.

(Scandinavian, English) a form of Olin.

Oleos (Spanish) holy oil used in church.

Olés (Polish) a familiar form of Alexander.

Olezka (Russian) saint.

Olimpíades (Greek) a form of Olympia

Olimpio (Greek) Mount Olympus.

Olimpo (Greek) sky.

Olin (English) holly. (Scandinavian) a form of Olaf.

Olindo (Italian) from Olinthos, Greece.

Oliver ⭐ (Latin) olive tree. (Scandinavian) kind; affectionate.

Olivero, Oliveros (Italian, Spanish) forms of Oliver.

Olivier (French) a form of Oliver.
Olier

Olivo (Latin) olive branch.

Oliwa (Hawaiian) a form of Oliver.
Olliva, Ollyva

Ollanta (Aymara) the warrior who sees everything from his watchtower.

Ollantay (Aymara) one who sees all.

Ollie BG (English) a familiar form of Oliver.

Ollin (Nahuatl) movement.

Olo (Spanish) a short form of Orlando, Rolando.

Olric (German) a form of Ulric.

Olubayo (Yoruba) highest joy.

Olufemi (Yoruba) wealth and honor favors me.

Olujimi (Yoruba) God gave me this.

Olushola (Yoruba) God has blessed me.

Om (Indian) the sacred syllable.

Omair (Arabic) a form of Omar.

Omar (Arabic) highest; follower of the Prophet. (Hebrew) reverent.

Omari (Swahili) a form of Omar.

Omarr (Arabic) a form of Omar.

Omer (Arabic) a form of Omar.

Omja (Indian) born of cosmic unity.

Omkar (Indian) the sound of the sacred syllable.

Omolara (Benin) child born at the right time.

Omprakash (Indian) light of God.

Omrao (Indian) king.

Omswaroop (Indian) manifestation of divinity.

On (Burmese) coconut. (Chinese) peace.

Onan (Turkish) prosperous.

Onani (African) quick look.

Onaona (Hawaiian) pleasant fragrance.

Ondro (Czech) a form of Andrew.

Onesíforo (Greek) he who bears much fruit.

Onésimo (Greek) he who is useful and worthwhile.

Onfroi (French) calm.

Onkar (Hindi) God in his entirety.

Onofrio (German) a form of Humphrey.

Onslow (English) enthusiast's hill.

Ontario BG (Native American) beautiful lake. Geography: a province and a lake in Canada.

Onufry (Polish) a form of Humphrey.

Onur (Turkish) honor.

Ophir (Hebrew) faithful. Bible: an Old Testament people and country.

Opio (Ateso) first of twin boys.

Optato (Latin) desired.

Oral (Latin) verbal; speaker.

Oran BG (Irish) green.

Orangel (Greek) the messenger from the mountain.

Oratio (Latin) a form of Horatio.

Orbán (Hungarian) born in the city.

Ordell (Latin) beginning.

Orel (Latin) listener. (Russian) eagle.

Oren (Hebrew) pine tree. (Irish) light skinned, white.

Orencio (Greek) examining judge.

Orestes (Greek) mountain man. Mythology: the son of the Greek leader Agamemnon.

Orfeo (Greek) he who has a good voice.

Ori (Hebrew) my light.

Orien (Latin) visitor from the east.

Orígenes (Greek) born into caring arms.

Orin (English) a form of Orrin.

Oriol (Latin) golden oriole.

Orion (Greek) son of fire. Mythology: a giant hunter who was killed by Artemis.

Orión (Greek) a form of Orion.

Orji (Ibo) mighty tree.

Orlán, Orlín (Spanish) renowned in the land. Forms of Roland.

Orlando (German) famous throughout the land. (Spanish) a form of Roland.

Orleans (Latin) golden.

Orman (German) mariner, seaman. (Scandinavian) serpent, worm.

Ormond (English) bear mountain; spear protector.

Oro (Spanish) golden.

Oroncio (Persian) runner.

Orono (Latin) a form of Oren.

Orosco (Greek) he who lives in the mountains.

Orpheus (Greek) Mythology: a fabulous musician.

Orrick (English) old oak tree.

Orrin (English) river.

Orris (Latin) a form of Horatio.

Orry (Latin) from the Orient.

Orsino (Italian) a form of Orson.

Orson (Latin) bearlike.

Orton (English) shore town.

Ortzi (Basque) sky.

Orunjan (Yoruba) born under the midday sun.

Orval (English) a form of Orville.

Orville (French) golden village. History: Orville Wright and his brother Wilbur were the first men to fly an airplane.

Orvin (English) spear friend.

Osahar (Benin) God hears.

Osayaba (Benin) God forgives.

Osaze (Benin) whom God likes.

Osbaldo (Spanish) a form of Oswald.

Osbert (English) divine; bright.

Osborn (Scandinavian) divine bear. (English) warrior of God.

Oscar (Scandinavian) divine spearman.

Óscar (Scandinavian) a form of Oscar.

Oseas, Osías (Hebrew) the Lord sustains me.

Osei (Fante) noble.

Osgood (English) divinely good.

Osip (Russian, Ukrainian) a form of Joseph, Yosef

Osiris (Egyptian) he who possesses a powerful vision.

Oskar (Scandinavian) a form of Oscar.

Osman (Turkish) ruler. (English) servant of God. A form of Osmond.

Osmán (Turkish) a form of Osman.

Osmar (English) divine; wonderful.

Osmara, Osmaro (Germanic) he who shines like the glory of God.

Osmond (English) divine protector.

Osorio (Slavic) the killer of wolves.

Osric (English) divine ruler.

Ostiano (Spanish) confessor.

Ostin (Latin) a form of Austin.

Osvaldo (Spanish) a form of Oswald.

Oswald (English) God's power; God's crest.

Oswaldo (Spanish) a form of Oswald.

Oswin (English) divine friend.

Osya (Russian) a familiar form of Osip.

Ota (Czech) prosperous.

Otadan (Native American) plentiful.

Otaktay (Lakota) kills many; strikes many.

Otek (Polish) a form of Otto.

Otello (Italian) a form of Othello.

Otelo (Spanish) a form of Otello.

Otem (Luo) born away from home.

Othello (Spanish) a form of Otto. Literature: the title character in the Shakespearean tragedy *Othello*.

Othman (German) wealthy.

Othmân (Arabic) name of one of the prophet's companions.

Othniel (Hebrew) strength of God.

Otilde (Teutonic) owner of a bountiful inheritance.

Otis (Greek) keen of hearing. (German) son of Otto.

Otniel, Otoniel (Hebrew) God is my strength.

Otoronco (Quechua) jaguar.

Ottah (Nigerian) thin baby.

Ottar (Norwegian) point warrior; fright warrior.

Ottmar (Turkish) a form of Osman.

Otto (German) rich.

Ottokar (German) happy warrior.

Otu (Native American) collecting seashells in a basket.

Oubastet (Egyptian) cat.

Ouray (Ute) arrow. Astrology: born under the sign of Sagittarius.

Ourson (French) small bear.

Oved (Hebrew) worshiper, follower.

Overton (English) high town.

Ovidio (Spanish) shepherd.

Owen ☆ (Irish) born to nobility; young warrior. (Welsh) a form of Evan.

Owney (Irish) elderly.

Oxford (English) place where oxen cross the river.

Oxley (English) ox meadow.

Oxton (English) ox town.

Oya BG (Moquelumnan) speaking of the jacksnipe.

Oystein (Norwegian) rock of happiness.

Oz BG (Hebrew) a short form of Osborn, Oswald.

Ozias (Hebrew) God's strength.

s

Oziel (Hebrew) he who has divine strength.

Ozturk (Turkish) pure; genuine Turk.

Ozuru (Japanese) stork.

Ozzie, Ozzy (English) familiar forms of Osborn, Oswald.

P

Paavan (Indian) purifier.

Paavo (Finnish) a form of Paul.

Pabel (Russian) a form of Paul.

Pabla (Spanish) a form of Paul.

Pablo (Spanish) a form of Paul.

Pace (English) a form of Pascal.

Pacey (English) a form of Pace.

Pachacutec, Pachacutic (Quechua) he who changes the world.

Pacho (Spanish) free.

Paciano (Latin) he who belongs to the peace.

Paciente (Latin) he who knows how to be patient.

Pacifico (Filipino) peaceful.

Pacífico (Filipino) a form of Pacifico.

Paco (Italian) pack. (Spanish) a familiar form of Francisco. (Native American) bald eagle.

Pacomio (Greek) he who is robust.

Paddy (Irish) a familiar form of Padraic, Patrick.

Paden (English) a form of Patton.

Padget BG (English) a form of Page.

Padman, Pankaj (Indian) lotus.

Padmanabha, Padmapati (Indian) other names for the Hindu god Vishnu.

Padraic (Irish) a form of Patrick.

Pafnucio (Greek) rich in merits.

Pagan GB (Latin) from the country.

Page GB (French) youthful assistant.

Pagiel (Hebrew) worshiping God.

Paien (French) name of the noble ones.

Paillalef (Mapuche) return quickly.

Painecura (Mapuche) iridescent stone.

Painevilu (Mapuche) iridescent snake.

Painter (Latin) artist, painter.

Paio (Latin) belonging to the sea.

Pakelika (Hawaiian) a form of Patrick.

Paki (African) witness.

Pakile (Hawaiian) royal.

Pal (Swedish) a form of Paul.

Pál (Hungarian) a form of Paul.

Palaina (Hawaiian) a form of Brian.

Palak (Indian) eyelash.

Palaki (Polynesian) black.

Palani (Hawaiian) a form of Frank.

Palash (Hindi) flowery tree.

Palashkusum (Indian) the flower of a Palash tree.

Palashranjan (Indian) beautiful like a Palash tree.

Palatino (Latin) he who comes from Mount Palatine.

Palban, Palbán, Palbén (Basque) blond.

Palben (Basque) blond.

Pallab (Indian) new leaves.

Palladin (Native American) fighter.

Palmacio (Latin) adorned with bordered palm leaves.

Palmer 🅱🅶 (English) palm-bearing pilgrim.

Palmiro (Latin) born on Palm Sunday.

Palti (Hebrew) God liberates.

Pampín (Latin) he who has the vigor of a sprouting plant.

Panas (Russian) immortal.

Panayiotis (Greek) a form of Peter.

Panchanan (Indian) another name for the Hindu god Shiva.

Pancho (Spanish) a familiar form of Francisco, Frank.

Pancracio (Greek) all powerful.

Pandhari, Panduranga (Indian) other names for Vithobha, an incarnation of the Hindu god Krishna.

Panfilo, Pánfilo (Greek) friend of all.

Panini (Indian) a great Sanskrit scholar-grammarian of ancient India.

Pannalal (Indian) emerald.

Panos (Greek) a form of Peter.
Pano

Pantaleón (Greek) all merciful.

Panteno (Greek) he who is worthy of all praise.

Panti (Quechua) species of brush.

Paolo (Italian) a form of Paul.

Papias (Greek) the venerable father.

Paquito (Spanish) a familiar form of Paco.

Parag (Indian) pollen.

Parakram (Indian) strength.

Param (Indian) the best.

Paramananda (Indian) superlative joy.

Paramesh (Hindi) greatest. Religion: another name for the Hindu god Shiva.

Paramhansa (Indian) supreme soul.

Paranjay (Indian) another name for the Hindu god Varun, lord of the waters.

Parantapa (Indian) conqueror; another name for Arjuna, a warrior prince in the Indian epic poem *Mahabharata*.

Parashar (Indian) an ancient Indian sage.

Parashuram (Indian) sixth incarnation of the Hindu god Vishnu.

Parasmani (Indian) touchstone.

Paravasu (Indian) an ancient Indian sage.

Pardeep **(Sikh) mystic light.**
Pardip

Pardulfo (Germanic) brave warrior.

Paresh (Indian) supreme lord.

Parfait (French) perfect.

Paris 🅶🅱 (Greek) lover. Geography: the capital of France. Mythology: the prince of Troy who started the Trojan War by abducting Helen.

París (Greek) a form of Paris.

Parish (English) a form of Parrish.

Parisio (Spanish) a form of Paris.

Pariuana (Quechua) Andean flamingo.

Park (Chinese) cypress tree. (English) a short form of Parker.

Parker ⭐ 🅱🅶 (English) park keeper.

Parkin (English) little Peter.

Parlan (Scottish) a form of Bartholomew.

Parménides, Parmenio (Greek) he who is a constant presence.

Parnell (French) little Peter. History: Charles Stewart Parnell was a famous Irish politician.

Parodio (Greek) he who imitates the singing.

Parr (English) cattle enclosure, barn.

Parris GB (Greek) a form of Paris.

Parrish (English) church district.

Parry (Welsh) son of Harry.

Partemio (Greek) having a pure and virginal appearance.

Parth (Irish) a short form of Parthalán.

Parthalán (Irish) plowman. .

Parthenios (Greek) virgin. Religion: a Greek Orthodox saint.

Pascal (French) born on Easter or Passover.

Pascua (Hebrew) in reference to Easter.

Pascual (Spanish) a form of Pascal.

Pasha BG (Russian) a form of Paul.

Pashenka (Russian) small.

Pasicrates (Greek) he who dominates everyone.

Pasquale (Italian) a form of Pascal.

Pastor (Latin) spiritual leader.

Pastora (Latin) a form of Pastor.

Pat BG (Native American) fish. (English) a short form of Patrick.

Patakusu (Moquelumnan) ant biting a person.

Patamon BG (Native American) raging.

Patek (Polish) a form of Patrick.

Paterio (Greek) he who was born in Pateria.

Paterno (Latin) belonging to the father.

Patli (Nahuatl) medicine.

Patric, Patrik, Patryk (Latin) forms of Patrick.

Patrice GB (French) a form of Patrick.

Patricio (Spanish) a form of Patrick.

Patrick ⭐ (Latin) nobleman. Religion: the patron saint of Ireland.

Patrido (Latin) noble.

Patrin (Gypsy) leaf trail.

Patrocinio (Latin) patronage.

Patterson (Irish) son of Pat.

Pattin (Gypsy) leaf. (English) a form of Patton.

Patton (English) warrior's town.

Patwin (Native American) man.

Patxi (Basque, Teutonic) free.

Paucar (Quechua) very refined, excellent.

Paucartupac (Quechua) majestic and excellent.

Paul (Latin) small. Bible: Saul, later renamed Paul, was the first to bring the teachings of Christ to the Gentiles.

Paúl (Latin) a form of Paul.

Pauli (Latin) a familiar form of Paul.

Paulin (German, Polish) a form of Paul.

Paulino (Spanish) a form of Paul.

Pauliño (Spanish) a form of Paul.

Paulinus **(Lithuanian) a form of Paul.**

Paulo (Portuguese, Swedish, Hawaiian) a form of Paul.

Pausidio (Greek) deliberate, calm man.

Pauyu (Aymara) he who finishes.

Pavel (Russian) a form of Paul.

Pavit (Hindi) pious, pure.

Pavla, Pavlov, Pavlusha, Pavlushka, Pavlushshenka, Pavlya (Russian) small.

Pawel (Polish) a form of Paul.

Pax (Latin) peaceful.

Paxton BG (Latin) peaceful town.

Payat (Native American) he is on his way.

Payden (English) a form of Payton.

Payne (Latin) from the country.

Payo (Galician) a short form of Pelayo.

Paytah (Lakota) fire.
Pay, Payta

Payton GB (English) a form of Patton.

Paz GB (Spanish) a form of Pax.

Pearce (English) a form of Pierce.

Pearson (English) son of Peter. **Peder** (Scandinavian) a form of Peter.

Pedro (Spanish) a form of Peter.

Peerless (American) incomparable, without a peer.

Peers (English) a form of Peter.

Peeter (Estonian) a form of Peter.

Pegaso (Greek) born next to the fountain.

Pehuen (Mapuche) nut.

Peirce (English) a form of Peter.

Pekelo (Hawaiian) a form of Peter.
Pekeio, Pekka

Pelagio, Pelayo (Greek) excellent sailor.

Peleke (Hawaiian) a form of Frederick.

Pelham (English) tannery town.

Pelí (Latin, Basque) happy.

Pell (English) parchment.

Pello (Greek, Basque) stone.

Pelope (Greek) having a brown complexion.

Pelton (English) town by a pool.

Pembroke (Welsh) headland. (French) wine dealer. (English) broken fence.

Pendle (English) hill.

Peniamina (Hawaiian) a form of Benjamin.

Penley (English) enclosed meadow.

Penn (Latin) pen, quill. (English) enclosure. (German) a short form of Penrod.

Penrod (German) famous commander.

Pepa (Czech) a familiar form of Joseph.

Pepe (Spanish) a familiar form of Jose.

Pepin (German) determined; petitioner. History: Pepin the Short was an eighth-century king of the Franks.

Peppe (Italian) a familiar form of Joseph.

Peppin (French) a form of Pepin.

Per (Swedish) a form of Peter.

Perben (Greek, Danish) stone.

Percival (French) pierce the valley. Literature: a knight of the Round Table who first appears in Chrétien de Troyes's poem about the quest for the Holy Grail.

Percy (French) a familiar form of Percival.

Pere (Catalan) a form of Pedro.

Peregrine (Latin) traveler; pilgrim; falcon.

Peregrino (Latin) a form of Peregrine.

Perfecto (Latin) without any defects.

Periandro (Greek) worries about men.

Pericles (Greek) just leader. History: an Athenian statesman.

Perico (Spanish) a form of Peter.

Perine (Latin) a short form of Peregrine.

Perkin (English) little Peter.

Pernell (French) a form of Parnell.

Perpetuo (Latin) having an unchanging goal.

Perrin (Latin) a short form of Peregrine.

Perry 🅱🅶 (English) a familiar form of Peregrine, Peter.

Perseo (Greek) the destroyer.

Perth (Scottish) thornbush thicket. Geography: a burgh in Scotland; a city in Australia.

Pervis (Latin) passage.

Pesach (Hebrew) spared. Religion: **another name for Passover.**

Petar (Greek) a form of Peter.

Pete (English) a short form of Peter.

Petenka (Russian) stone.

Peter (Greek, Latin) small rock. Bible: Simon, renamed Peter, was the leader of the Twelve Apostles. **Peterson** (English) son of Peter.

Petiri (Shona) where we are.

Peton (English) a form of Patton.

Petr (Bulgarian) a form of Peter.

Petras (Lithuanian) a form of Peter.

Petros (Greek) a form of Peter.

Petru (Romanian) a form of Peter.
Petrukas, Petruno, Petrus, Petruso

Petruos (Latin) firm as a rock.

Petter (Norwegian) a form of Peter.

Peverell (French) piper.

Peyo (Spanish) a form of Peter.

Peyton 🅶🅱 (English) a form of Patton, Payton.

Phalguni (Indian) born in the Hindu month of Falgun.

Pharaoh (Latin) ruler. History: a title for the ancient kings of Egypt.

Phelan (Irish) wolf.

Phelipe (Spanish) a form of Philip.

Phelix (Latin) a form of Felix.

Phelps (English) son of Phillip.

Phil (Greek) a short form of Philip, Phillip.

Philander (Greek) lover of mankind.

Philart (Greek) lover of virtue.

Philbert (English) a form of Filbert.

Philemon (Greek) kiss.

Philip (Greek) lover of horses. Bible: one of the Twelve Apostles.

Philipe, Philippe (French) forms of Philip.

Philipp (German) a form of Philip.

Phillip (Greek) a form of Philip.

Phillipos (Greek) a form of Phillip.

Philly (American) a familiar form of Philip, Phillip.
Phillie

Philo (Greek) love.

Phinean (Irish) a form of Finian.

Phineas (English) a form of Pinchas. **Phirun** (Cambodian) rain.

Phoenix 🅱🅶 (Latin) phoenix, a legendary bird.

Phuok (Vietnamese) good.

Pias (Gypsy) fun.

Pichi (Araucanian) small.

Pichiu (Quechua) baby bird.

Pichulman (Mapuche) the condor's feather.

Pichunlaf (Mapuche) lucky feather.

Pickford (English) ford at the peak.

Pickworth (English) wood cutter's estate.

Picton (English) town on the hill's peak.

Pier Alexander (French) a combination of Pierre + Alexander.

Pier Luc, Pierre Luc, Pierre-Luc (French) combinations of Pierre + Luc.

Pierce 🅱🅶 (English) a form of Peter.

Piero (Italian) a form of Peter.

Pierpont, Pierrepont (French) living underneath the stone bridge.

Pierre (French) a form of Peter.

Pierre Alexan (French) a combination of Pierre + Alexander.

Pierre Andre (French) a combination of Pierre + Andre.

Pierre Antoin (French) a combination of Pierre + Antoine.

Pierre Etienn (French) a combination of Pierre + Etienne.

Pierre Marc (French) a combination of Pierre + Marc.

Pierre Olivier (French) combinations of Pierre + Olivier.

Pierre Yves (French) a combination of Pierre + Yves.

Piers (English) a form of Peter. A form of Peers.

Pierson (English) son of Peter. **Pieter** (Dutch) a form of Peter.

Pietro (Italian) a form of Peter.

Pigmalion (Spanish) sculptor.

Pilar GB (Spanish) pillar.

Pilato (Latin) soldier armed with a lance.

Pilatos (Latin) he who is armed with a pick.

Pili (Swahili) second born.

Pilipo (Hawaiian) a form of Philip.

Pillan (Native American) supreme essence.

Pin (Vietnamese) faithful boy.

Pinchas (Hebrew) oracle. (Egyptian) dark skinned.

Pinito (Greek) inspired; very wise.

Pinjás (Hebrew) mouth of the serpent.

Pinky (American) a familiar form of Pinchas.

Pino (Italian) a form of Joseph.

Piñon (Tupi-Guarani) Mythology: the hunter who became the constellation Orion.

Pio (Latin) pious.

Pío (Latin) a form of Pio.

Piotr (Bulgarian) a form of Peter.

Pipino (German) a form of Pippin.

Pippin (German) father.

Piquichaqui (Quechua) light footed.

Piran (Irish) prayer. Religion: the patron saint of miners.

Pirrin (Australian) cave.

Pirro (Greek, Spanish) flaming hair.

Pista (Hungarian) a familiar form of István.

Pitágoras (Greek) he who is like a divine oracle.

Piti (Spanish) a form of Peter.

Pitin (Spanish) a form of Felix.

Pitney (English) island of the strong-willed man.

Pitt (English) pit, ditch.

Piuque (Araucanian) heart.

Piyco, Piycomayu, Piycu, Piycumayu (Quechua) red bird.

Placido (Spanish) serene.

Plácido (Spanish) a form of Placido.

Plato (Greek) broad shouldered. History: a famous Greek philosopher.

Platón (Greek) a form of Plato.

Platt (French) flatland.

Plauto, Plotino (Greek) he who has flat feet.

Plaxico (American) a form of Placido.

Plinio (Latin) he who has many skills.

Plubio (Greek) man of the sea.

Plutarco (Greek) rich prince.

Plutón (Greek) owner of many riches.

Po Sin (Chinese) grandfather elephant.

Pol (Swedish) a form of Paul.

Poldi (German) a familiar form of Leopold.

Poliano (Greek) he who suffers.

Policarpo (Greek) he who produces abundant fruit.

Policeto (Greek) he who caused much sorrow.

Polidoro (Greek) having virtues.

Poliecto (Greek) he who is very desired.

Polifemo (Greek) he who is spoken about a lot.

Polión (Greek) the powerful Lord who protects.

Pollard (German) close-cropped head.

Pollock (English) a form of Pollux. Art: American artist Jackson Pollock was a leader of abstract expressionism.

Pollux (Greek) crown. Astronomy: one of the stars in the constellation Gemini.

Polo (Tibetan) brave wanderer. (Greek) a short form of Apollo. Culture: a game played on horseback. History: Marco Polo was a thirteenth-century Venetian explorer who traveled throughout Asia.

Poma, Pomacana, Puma, Pumacana (Quechua) strong and powerful puma.

Pomacaua, Pumacaua (Quechua) he who guards with the quietness of a puma.

Pomagüiyca, Pumagüiyca (Quechua) sacred like the puma.

Pomalloque, Pumalluqui (Quechua) left-handed puma.

Pomauari, Pumauari (Quechua) indomitable as a vicuna and strong as a puma.

Pomayauri, Pumayauri (Quechua) copper-colored puma.

Pomeroy (French) apple orchard.

Pommeraie (French) a form of Pomeroy.

Pompeo (Greek) a form of Pompeyo.

Pompeyo (Greek) he who heads the procession.

Pomponio (Latin) the lover of grandeur and the open plains.

Ponce (Spanish) fifth. History: Juan Ponce de León of Spain searched for the Fountain of Youth in Florida.

Poncio (Greek) having come from the sea.

Ponpey (English) a form of Pompeyo.

Pony (Scottish) small horse.

Porcio (Latin) he who earns his living raising pigs.

Porfirio (Greek, Spanish) purple stone.

Porfiro (Greek) a form of Porfirio.

Porter BG (Latin) gatekeeper.

Poseidón (Greek) the owner of the waters.

Poshita (Sanskrit) cherished.

Posidio (Greek) he who is devoted to Poseidon.

Potenciano (Latin) he who dominates with his empire.

Poul (Danish) a form of Paul.

Pov (Gypsy) earth.

Powa (Native American) wealthy.

Powell (English) alert.

Prabhjot (Sikh) the light of God.

Prácido (Latin) tranquil, calm.

Pragnacio (Greek) he who is skillful and practical in business.

Pramad (Hindi) rejoicing.

Pravat (Tai) history.

Pravin (Hindi) capable.

Prem (Hindi) love.

Prentice (English) apprentice.

Prescott (English) priest's cottage.

Presidio (Latin) he who gives pleasant shelter.

Presley GB (English) priest's meadow. Music: Elvis Presley was an influential American rock 'n' roll singer.

Preston (English) priest's estate.

Pretextato (Latin) covered by a toga.

Prewitt (French) brave little one.

Priamo, Príamo (Greek) the rescued one.

Price (Welsh) son of the ardent one.
Pryce

Pricha (Tai) clever.

Priest (English) holy man. A short form of Preston.

Prilidiano, Prilidíano (Greek) he who remembers things from the past.

Primael (Latin) chosen first.

Primeiro (Italian) born first.

Primitivo (Latin) original.

Primo (Italian) first; premier quality.

Prince (Latin) chief; prince.

Princeton (English) princely town.

Prisco (Latin) old; from another time.

Probo (Latin) having moral conduct.

Proceso (Latin) he who moves forward.

Procopio (Greek) he who progresses.

Procoro (Greek) he who prospers.

Proctor **(Latin) official, administrator.**

Proculo (Latin) he who was born far from home.

Prokopios (Greek) declared leader.

Promaco (Greek) he who prepares for battle.

Prometeo (Greek) he who resembles God.

Prosper (Latin) fortunate.

Protasio, Protólico (Greek) preferred one.

Proteo (Greek) lord of the waves of the sea.

Proterio, Proto (Greek) he who precedes all the rest.

Prudenciano (Spanish) humble and honest.

Prudencio (Latin) he who works with sensitivity and modesty.

Prudens (German) a form of Prudencio.

Pryor (Latin) head of the monastery; prior.

Ptah (Egyptian) cultured by God in Memphis.

Publio (Latin) he who is popular.

Puchac (Quechua) leader.

Pueblo (Spanish) from the city.

Pulqueria (Latin) the beautiful one.

Pulqui (Araucanian) arrow.

Pumasonjo, Pumasuncu (Quechua) heart of a puma.

Pumeet (Sanskrit) pure.

Pupulo (Latin) the little boy.

Purdy (Hindi) recluse.

Puric (Quechua) walker.

Purvis **(French, English) providing food.**

Pusaki (Indigenous) fire.

Putnam (English) dweller by the pond.

Pyotr (Russian) a form of Peter.

Q

Qabic (Arabic) able.

Qabil (Arabic) able.

Qadim (Arabic) ancient.

Qadir (Arabic) powerful.

Qamar (Arabic) moon.

Qasim (Arabic) divider.

Qatadah (Indian) a hardwood tree.

Qays (Indian) firm.

Qeb (Egyptian) father of the earth.

Qi (Chinese) fine jade; outstanding; distinguished.

Qian (Chinese) thousand.

Qiang (Chinese) powerful.

Qiao (Chinese) pretty, handsome.

Qimat (Hindi) valuable.

Qin (Chinese) industrious.

Qing (Chinese) stainless.

Qing Yuan (Chinese) deep water; clear spring.

Qing-Yuan (Chinese) clear spring.

Qiong (Chinese) fine jade.

Qiu (Chinese) autumn.

Qu (Chinese) interest, delight.

Quaashie BG (Ewe) born on Sunday.

Quadarius (American) a combination of Quan + Darius.

Quade (Latin) fourth.

Quain (French) clever.

Quamaine (American) a combination of Quan + Jermaine.

Quan (Comanche) a short form of Quanah.

Quanah (Comanche) fragrant.

Quandre (American) a combination of Quan + Andre.

Quang (Vietnamese) clear; brilliant; good reputation.

Quant (Greek) how much?

Quantavious (American) a form of Quantavius.

Quantavius (American) a combination of Quan + Octavius.

Quantez (American) a form of Quant.

Quashawn (American) a combination of Quan + Shawn.

Quauhtli (Nahuatl) eagle.

Qudamah (Arabic) courage.

Que (Chinese) reliable.

Quenán (Hebrew) fixed.

Quenby BG (Scandinavian) a form of Quimby.

Quennell (French) small oak.

Quenten, Quenton (Latin) forms of Quentin.

Quenti, Quinti (Quechua) hummingbird.

Quentin (Latin) fifth. (English) queen's town.

Querubín (Hebrew) swift, young bull.

Quesnel (French) one who comes from the oak tree.

Quespi (Quechua) jewel, shiny like a diamond.

Quest (Latin) quest.

Queupulicán (Mapuche) white stone with a black stripe.

Queupumil (Mapuche) shining stone.

Quichuasamin (Quechua) he who brings fortune

and happiness to the Quechua village.

Quico (Spanish) a familiar form of many names.

Quidequeo (Mapuche) brilliant.

Quigley (Irish) maternal side.

Quillan (Irish) cub.

Quillén (Araucanian) tear.

Quillinchu, Quilliyicu (Quechua) sparrow hawk.

Quillon (Latin) sword.
Quilon, Quyllon, Quylon

Quimby (Scandinavian) woman's estate.

Quimey (Araucanian) pretty; beautiful.

Quin (Irish) a form of Quinn.

Quincey BG (French) a form of Quincy.

Quincy BG (French) fifth son's estate.

Quindarius (American) a combination of Quinn + Darius.

Quiñelef (Mapuche) quick race.

Quinlan (Irish) strong; well shaped.

Quinn BG (Irish) a short form of Quincy, Quinlan, Quinten.

Quintavious (American) a form of Quintavius.

Quintavis (American) a form of Quintavius.

Quintavius (American) a combination of Quinn + Octavius.

Quinten, Quintin, Quinton (Latin) forms of Quentin.

Quintilian (French) a form of Quintiliano.

Quintiliano (Spanish) a form of Quintilio.

Quintilio (Latin) he who was born in the fifth month.

Quintrilpe (Mapuche) place of organization.

Quintuillan (Mapuche) searching for the altar.

Quiqui (Spanish) a familiar form of Enrique.

Quiríaco (Greek) a form of Ciriaco.

Quirino (Latin) he who carries a lance.

Quispe, Quispi (Quechua) jewel.

Quispiyupanqui (Quechua) he who honors his liberty.

Quisu (Aymara) he who appreciates the value of things.

Quitin (Latin) a short form of Quinten.

Quito (Spanish) a short form of Quinten.

Qun (Chinese) the masses.

Quoc (Vietnamese) nation.

Quon (Chinese) bright.

Qutaybah (Indian) irritable, impatient.

Qutub (Indian) tall.

Quy (Vietnamese) precious.

R

Ra (Egyptian) sunshine.

Ra`Id (Arabic) leader.

Ra`Is (Arabic) boss.

Ra'shawn, Rashaan, Rashaun, Rashon (American) forms of Rashawn.

Raamah (Hebrew) thunder.

Raanan (Hebrew) fresh; luxuriant.

Rabah (Arabic) winner.

Rabel (Catalan) a form of Rafael.

Rabi BG (Arabic) breeze. (Scottish) famous.

Race (English) race.
Racee, Racel

Racham (Hebrew) compassionate.

Rachid (Lebanese) prudent.

Rad (English) advisor. (Slavic) happy.

Radbert (English) brilliant advisor.

Radburn (English) red brook; brook with reeds.

Radcliff (English) red cliff; cliff with reeds.

Radek (Czech) famous ruler.

Radford (English) red ford; ford with reeds.

Radhakanta (Indian) another name for the Hindu god Krishna.

Radhakrishna (Indian) the Hindu god Krishna and Radha, lover of Krishna.

Radhavallabh (Indian) beloved of Radha; another name for the Hindu god Krishna.

Radheshyam (Indian) another name for the Hindu god Krishna.

Radheya (Indian) another name for Karna, a hero in the Indian epic poem *Mahabharata*.

Radley (English) red meadow; meadow of reeds.

Radman (Slavic) joyful.

Radnor (English) red shore; shore with reeds.

Radomil (Slavic) happy peace.

Radoslaw (Polish) happy glory.

Radwan (Arabic) pleasant, delightful.

Raekwon, Raequan (American) forms of Raquan.

Raeshawn (American) a form of Rashawn.

Rafa (Hebrew) the giant.

Rafael (Spanish) a form of Raphael.

Rafaele, Raffaele
(Italian) forms of
Raphael.

Rafaelle 🆖 (French) a
form of Raphael.

Rafal (Polish) a form of
Raphael.

Rafat (Indian) elevation.

Rafe (English) a short form
of Rafferty, Ralph.

Rafer (Irish) a short form
of Rafferty.

Rafferty (Irish) rich,
prosperous.

Raffi (Hebrew, Arabic) a
form of Rafi.

Rafi (Arabic) exalted.
(Hebrew) a familiar form
of Raphael.

Rafiq (Arabic) friend.

Rafiq (Arabic) a form of
Rafiq.

**Raghav, Raghavendra,
Raghunandan,
Raghunath,
Raghupati, Raghuvir**
(Indian) other names for
the Hindu god Rama.

Raghib (Arabic) desirous.

Raghîb (Arabic) a form of
Raghib.

Raghnall (Irish) wise
power.

Raghu (Indian) family of
the Hindu god Rama.

Ragnar (Norwegian)
powerful army.

Rago (Hausa) ram.

Raguel (Hebrew)
everybody's friend.

Rahas (Indian) secret.

Raheem 🆖🅶 (Punjabi)
compassionate God.

Raheim (Punjabi) a form
of Raheem.

Rahim (Arabic) merciful.

Rahman (Arabic)
compassionate.

Rahsaan (American) a
form of Rashean.

Rahul (Arabic) traveler.

Raíd (Arabic) leader.

Raiden (Japanese)
Mythology: the thunder
god.

Railef (Mapuche) a flower
that is bedraggled
because of a strong wind.

Raimi (Quechua) party,
celebration.

Raimondo (Italian) a form
of Raymond.

Raimund (German) a form
of Raymond.

Raimundo **(Portuguese,
Spanish) a form of
Raymond.**

Raine 🆖 (English) lord;
wise.

Rainer (German)
counselor.

**Rainerio, Rainero,
Rainiero** (German)
forms of Rainer.

Rainey 🆖 (German) a
familiar form of Rainer.

Raini 🆖 ('Tupi-Guarani)
Religion: the god who
created the world.

Rainier (French) a form of
Rainer.

Rainieri (Italian) a form of
Rainer.

Raishawn (American) a
form of Rashawn.

Raj (Hindi) a short form of
Rajah.

Raja 🆖 (Hindi) a form of
Rajah.

Rajabu (Swahili) born in
the seventh month of the
Islamic calendar.

Rajah (Hindi) prince; chief.

Rajak (Hindi) cleansing.

Rajam (Indian) another
name for the Hindu
goddess Lakshmi.

Rajan (Hindi) a form of
Rajah.

Rajarshi, Rajrishi
(Indian) king's sage.

Rajas (Indian) mastery;
fame; pride.

Rajat (Indian) silver.

Rajatshubhra (Indian)
white as silver.

Rajdulari (Indian) dear
princess.

**Rajendra,
Rajendrakumar,
Rajendramohan,
Rajesh** (Indian) king.

Rajit (Indian) decorated.

Rakeem (Punjabi) a form
of Raheem.

Rakim (Arabic) a form of Rahim.

Rakin (Arabic) respectable.

Raktim (Hindi) bright red.

Raleigh 🅱🅶 (English) a form of Rawleigh.

Ralph (English) wolf counselor.

Ralphie (English) a familiar form of Ralph.

Ralston (English) Ralph's settlement.

Ram (Hindi) god; godlike. Religion: another name for the Hindu god Rama. (English) male sheep. A short form of Ramsey.

Ramadan (Arabic) ninth month in the Islamic calendar.

Ramanan (Hindi) god; godlike.

Ramandeep 🅶🅱 (Hindi) a form of Ramanan.

Rambert (German) strong; brilliant.

Rami (Hindi, English) a form of Ram. (Spanish) a short form of Ramiro.

Ramírez (Spanish) judicious.

Ramiro (Portuguese, Spanish) supreme judge.

Ramlal (Hindi) son of the god Ram.

Ramon, Ramón (Spanish) forms of Raymond.

Ramond (Dutch) a form of Raymond.

Ramone (Dutch) a form of Raymond.

Ramsden (English) valley of rams.

Ramsey 🅱🅶 (English) ram's island.

Ramy (Hindi, English) a form of Ram.

Ramzi (American) a form of Ramsey.

Rance (American) a familiar form of Laurence. (English) a short form of Ransom.

Rancul (Araucanian) plant from the grasslands whose leaves are used to make roofs for huts.

Rand (English) shield; warrior.

Randal, Randell (English) forms of Randall.

Randall 🅱🅶 (English) a form of Randolph.

Randeep (Sikh) battle lamp.

Randolph (English) shield wolf.

Randy 🅱🅶 (English) a familiar form of Rand, Randall, Randolph.

Ranen (Hebrew) joyful.

Ranger (French) forest keeper.

Rangle (American) cowboy.

Rangsey (Cambodian) seven kinds of colors.

Rangvald (Scandinavian) a form of Reynold.

Rani 🅶🅱 (Hebrew) my song; my joy.

Ranieri (Italian) a form of Ragnar.

Ranjan (Hindi) delighted; gladdened.

Rankin (English) small shield.

Ransford (English) raven's ford.

Ransley (English) raven's field.

Ransom (Latin) redeemer. (English) son of the shield.

Raoul (French) a form of Ralph, Rudolph.

Raphael (Hebrew) God has healed. Bible: one of the archangels. Art: a prominent painter of the Renaissance. , Raphiel, Rephael

Rapheal (Hebrew) a form of Raphael.

Rapier (French) blade-sharp.

Rapiman (Mapuche) the condor's vomit; indigestion.

Raquan (American) a combination of the prefix Ra + Quan.

Rashaad, Rashaud, Rashod (Arabic) forms of Rashad.

Rashad (Arabic) wise counselor.

Rashâd (Arabic) a form of Rashad.

Rashan (American) a form of Rashawn.

Rashard (American) a form of Richard.

Rashawn BG (American) a combination of the prefix Ra + Shawn.

Rashean (American) a combination of the prefix Ra + Sean.

Rasheed (Arabic) a form of Rashad.

Rasheen (American) a form of Rashean.

Rashid (Arabic) a form of Rashad.

Rashîd (Arabic) a form of Rashid.

Rashida GB (Swahili) righteous.

Rashidi (Swahili) wise counselor.

Rasmus (Greek, Danish) a short form of Erasmus.

Râteb (Arabic) administrator.

Rauel (Hebrew) friend of God.

Raul (French) a form of Ralph.

Raulas (Lithuanian) a form of Laurence.

Raulo (Lithuanian) a form of Laurence.

Raurac (Quechua) burning, ardent.

Raven GB (English) a short form of Ravenel.

Ravenel (English) raven.

Ravi (Hindi) sun.

Ravid (Hebrew) a form of Arvid.

Raviv (Hebrew) rain, dew.

Ravon BG (English) a form of Raven.

Rawdon (English) rough hill.

Rawleigh (English) deer meadow.

Rawlins (French) a form of Roland.

Ray (French) kingly, royal. (English) a short form of Rayburn, Raymond.

Rayan BG (Irish) a form of Ryan.

Rayburn (English) deer brook.

Rayce (English) a form of Race.

Rayden (Japanese) a form of Raiden.

Rayfield (English) stream in the field.

Rayford (English) stream ford.

Rayhan (Arabic) favored by God.

Rayi (Hebrew) my friend, my companion.

Raylan (American) Literature: Raylan Givens is a character in Elmore Leonard novels.

Raymán (Spanish) a form of Raymond.

Raymon (English) a form of Raymond.

Raymón (Spanish) a form of Raymon.

Raymond (English) mighty; wise protector.

Raymundo (Spanish) a form of Raymond. (Portuguese, Spanish) a form of Raimundo.

Raynaldo (Spanish) a form of Reynold.

Raynard (French) a form of Renard, Reynard.

Rayne GB (English) a form of Raine.

Rayner (German) a form of Rainer.

Raynor (Scandinavian) a form of Ragnar.

Rayquan (American) a combination of Ray + Quan.

Raysean, Rayshaun, Rayshon (American) forms of Rayshawn.

Rayshawn (American) a combination of Ray + Shawn.

Rayshod (American) a form of Rashad.

Rayvon (American) a form of Ravon.

Razi BG (Aramaic) my secret.

Raziel (Aramaic) a form of Razi.

Re (Egyptian) half day.

Read (English) a form of Reed, Reid.

Reading (English) son of the red wanderer.

Reagan 🅶🅱 (Irish) little king. History: Ronald Wilson Reagan was the fortieth U.S. president.

Real (Latin) real.

Rebel **(American) rebel.**

Recaredo (Teutonic) counsels his superiors.

Red (American) red, redhead.

Reda (Arabic) satisfied.

Redempto, Redento (Latin) redeemed.

Redford (English) red river crossing.

Redley (English) red meadow; meadow with reeds.

Redmond (German) protecting counselor. (English) a form of Raymond.

Redpath (English) red path.

Reece (Welsh) a form of Rhys.

Reed 🅱🅶 (English) a form of Reid.

Rees, Reese 🅶🅱 (Welsh) forms of Rhys.

Reeve (English) steward.

Reg (English) a short form of Reginald.

Regan 🅶🅱 (Irish) a form of Reagan.

Reggie 🅱🅶 (English) a familiar form of Reginald.

Reginal (English) a form of Reginald.

Reginald (English) king's advisor. A form of Reynold.

Regis (Latin) regal.

Regulo, Régulo (Latin) forms of Rex.

Rehema (Swahili) second-born.
Rehemah

Rei 🅶🅱 (Japanese) rule, law.

Reid 🅱🅶 (English) redhead.

Reidar (Norwegian) nest warrior.

Reilly 🅱🅶 (Irish) a form of Riley.

Reimunde (German) counselor and protector.

Reinaldo (Spanish) a form of Reynold.

Reinardo (Teutonic) valiant counselor.

Reinhart (German) a form of Reynard. (English) a form of Reynold.

Reinhold (Swedish) a form of Ragnar. (English) a form of Reynold.

Reku (Finnish) a form of Richard.

Remedio (Latin) medicine.

Remi 🅱🅶 (French) a form of Remy.

Rémi (French) a form of Remy.

Remigio (Latin) he who mans the oars.

Remington 🅱🅶 (English) raven estate.

Remo (Greek) the strong one.

Remus (Latin) speedy, quick. Mythology: Remus and his twin brother, Romulus, founded Rome.

Remy 🅱🅶 (French) from Rheims, France.

Renaldo (Spanish) a form of Reynold.

Renán (Irish) seal.

Renard (French) a form of Reynard.

Renardo (Italian) a form of Reynard.

Renato (Italian) reborn.

Renaud (French) a form of Reynard, Reynold.

Rendor (Hungarian) policeman.

Rene 🅱🅶 (French) a form of René.

René (French) reborn.

Renfred (English) lasting peace.

Renfrew (Welsh) raven woods.

Renjiro (Japanese) virtuous.

Renny (Irish) small but strong. (French) a familiar form of René.

Reno (American) gambler. Geography: a city in Nevada known for gambling.

Renshaw (English) raven woods.

Renton (English) settlement of the roe deer.

Renzo (Latin) a familiar form of Laurence. (Italian) a short form of Lorenzo.

Repucura (Mapuche) jagged rock; rocky road.

Reshad (American) a form of Rashad.

Reshawn (American) a combination of the prefix Re + Shawn.

Reshean (American) a combination of the prefix Re + Sean.

Respicio (Latin) I look behind.

Restituto (Latin) he who returns to God.

Reuben (Hebrew) behold a son.

Reule (French) famous wolf.

Reuquén (Araucanian) tempestuous.

Reuven (Hebrew) a form of Reuben.

Rex (Latin) king.

Rexford (English) king's ford.

Rexton (English) king's town.

Rey (Spanish) a short form of Reynaldo, Reynard, Reynold. (French) a form of Roy.

Reyansh (Hindu) one of Vishnu's avatars.

Reyes (English) a form of Reece.

Reyhan BG (Arabic) favored by God.

Reymond (English) a form of Raymond.

Reymundo (Spanish) a form of Raymond.

Reynaldo (Spanish) a form of Reynold.

Reynard (French) wise; bold, courageous.

Reynold (English) king's advisor. **Réz** BG (Hungarian) copper; redhead.

Rezső

Reza BG (German) a form of Resi (.

Rezin (Hebrew) pleasant, delightful.

Rhett (Welsh) a form of Rhys. Literature: Rhett Butler was the hero of Margaret Mitchell's novel *Gone with the Wind.*

Rhodes (Greek) where roses grow. Geography: an island of southeast Greece.

Rhyan BG (Irish) a form of Ryan.

Rhys (Welsh) enthusiastic; stream.

Rian GB (Irish) little king.

Riberto (German) brilliant because of his power.

Ric (Italian, Spanish) a short form of Rico. (German, English) a form of Rick.

Ricardo, Riccardo (Portuguese, Spanish) forms of Richard.

Ricco, Rico (Italian) short forms of Enrico. (Spanish) familiar forms of Richard.

Rice (English) rich, noble. (Welsh) a form of Reece.

Rich (English) a short form of Richard.

Richard (English) a form of Richart.

Richart (German) rich and powerful ruler.

Richie (English) a familiar form of Richard.

Richman (English) powerful.

Richmond (German) powerful protector.

Rick (German, English) a short form of Cedric, Frederick, Richard.

Rickard **(Swedish) a form of Richard.**

Ricker (English) powerful army.

Rickey, Ricky (English) familiar forms of Richard, Rick.

Ricki GB (English) a familiar form of Richard, Rick.

Rickie BG (English) a familiar form of Richard, Rick.

Rickward (English) mighty guardian.

Rida BG (Arabic) favor.

Riddock (Irish) smooth field.

Rider (English) horseman.

Ridge (English) ridge of a cliff.
Ridgy, Rig, Rydge

Ridgeley (English) meadow near the ridge.

Ridgeway (English) path along the ridge.

Ridley (English) meadow of reeds.

Riel (Spanish) a short form of Gabriel.

Rigby (English) ruler's valley.

Rigel (Arabic) foot. Astronomy: one of the stars in the constellation Orion.

Rigg (English) ridge.

Rigo (Italian) a form of Rigg.

Rigoberto (German) splendid; wealthy.

Rikard (Scandinavian) a form of Richard.

Riker (American) a form of Ryker.

Riki GB (Estonian) a form of Rick.

Rikki GB (Estonian) a form of Rick.

Riley GB (Irish) valiant.

Rimac (Quechua) speaker, eloquent.

Rimachi (Quechua) he who makes us speak.

Rinaldo (Italian) a form of Reynold.

Ring (English) ring.

Ringo (Japanese) apple. (English) a familiar form of Ring.

Rio BG (Spanish) river. Geography: Rio de Janeiro is a city in Brazil.

Río (Spanish) a form of Rio.

Riordan (Irish) bard, royal poet.
Rearden, Reardin, Reardon, Ryordan

Rip (Dutch) ripe; full grown. (English) a short form of Ripley.

Ripley (English) meadow near the river.

Riqui (Spanish) a form of Rickey.

Rishad (American) a form of Rashad.

Rishawn (American) a combination of the prefix Ri + Shawn.

Rishi (Hindi) sage. (English) a form of Richie.

Risley (English) meadow with shrubs.

Risto (Finnish) a short form of Christopher.

Riston (English) settlement near the shrubs. **Ritchard** (English) a form of Richard.

Ritchie (English) a form of Richie.

Rithisak (Cambodian) powerful.

Ritter (German) knight; chivalrous.

River BG (English) river; riverbank.

Riyad (Arabic) gardens.

Riyâd (Arabic) a form of Riyad.

Rizieri (Germanic) army of the leader.

Roald (Norwegian) famous ruler.

Roan (English) a short form of Rowan.

Roano (Spanish) reddish brown skin.

Roar (Norwegian) praised warrior.
Roary

Roarke (Irish) famous ruler.

Rob (English) a short form of Robert.

Robbie BG **(English) a familiar form of Robert.**

Robby (English) a familiar form of Robert.

Robert ⭐

BG (English) famous brilliance. **Roberto** (Italian, Portuguese, Spanish) a form of Robert.

Roberts, Robertson (English) son of Robert.

Robin GB (English) a short form of Robert.

Robinson (English) a form of Roberts.

Robustiano (Latin) strong as the wood of an oak tree.

Roca, Ruca (Aymara) principal; chief.

Rocco (Italian) rock.

Roch (English) a form of Rock.

Rochester (English) rocky fortress.

Rock **(English) a short form of Rockwell.**

Rockford (English) rocky ford.

Rockland (English) rocky land.

Rockledge (English) rocky ledge.

Rockley (English) rocky field.

Rockwell (English) rocky spring. Art: Norman Rockwell was a well-known twentieth-century American illustrator.

Rocky (American) a familiar form of Rocco, Rock.

Rod (English) a short form of Penrod, Roderick, Rodney.

Rodas (Greek, Spanish) a form of Rhodes.

Roddy (English) a familiar form of Roderick.

Rode (Greek) pink.

Roden (English) red valley. Art: Auguste Rodin was an innovative French sculptor.

Roderich (German) a form of Roderick.

Roderick (German) famous ruler.

Rodger (German) a form of Roger.

Rodman (German) famous man, hero.

Rodney (English) island clearing.

Rodolfo (Spanish) a form of Rudolph, Rudolpho.

Rodrick (German) a form of Rodrik.

Rodrigo (Italian, Spanish) a form of Roderick.

Rodriguez (Spanish) son of Rodrigo.

Rodrik (German) famous ruler.

Rodriquez (Spanish) a form of Rodriguez.

Roe (English) roe deer.

Rogan (Irish) redhead.

Rogelio (Spanish) famous warrior. A form of Roger.

Roger (German) famous spearman. **Rogerio** (Portuguese, Spanish) a form of Roger.

Rohan (Hindi) sandalwood.

Rohin (Hindi) upward path.

Rohit (Hindi) big and beautiful fish.

Roi (French) a form of Roy.

Roja (Spanish) red.

Rojelio (Spanish) a form of Rogelio.

Rolán (Spanish) a form of Rolando.

Roland (German) famous throughout the land.

Rolando (Portuguese, Spanish) a form of Roland.

Rolf (German) a form of Ralph. A short form of Rudolph.

Rolland (German) a form of Roland.

Rolle (Swedish) a familiar form of Roland, Rolf.

Rollie (English) a familiar form of Roland.

Rollin (English) a form of Roland.

Rollo (English) a familiar form of Roland.

Rolon (Spanish) famous wolf.

Romain (French) a form of Roman.

Roman (Latin) from Rome, Italy. (Gypsy) gypsy; wanderer.

Román (Latin) a form of Roman.

Romanos (Greek) a form of Roman.

Romany (Gypsy) a form of Roman.

Romario (Italian) a form of Romeo, Romero.

Romea (Latin) pilgrim.

Romel, Romell, Rommel (Latin) short forms of Romulus.

Romelio (Hebrew) God's very beloved one.

Romelo, Romello (Italian) forms of Romel.

Romeo (Italian) pilgrim to Rome; Roman. Literature: the title character of the Shakespearean play *Romeo and Juliet*.

Romero (Latin) a form of Romeo.

Romildo (Germanic) the glorious hero.

Romney (Welsh) winding river.

Romochka (Russian) from Rome.

Romualdo (Germanic) the glorious king.

Rómulo (Greek) he who is full of strength.

Romulus (Latin) citizen of Rome. Mythology: Romulus and his twin brother, Remus, founded Rome.

Romy GB (Italian) a familiar form of Roman.

Ron (Hebrew) a short form of Aaron, Ronald.

Ronald (Scottish) a form of Reginald. (English) a form of Reynold.

Ronaldo (Portuguese) a form of Ronald.

Ronan (Irish) a form of Rónán.

Rónán (Irish) seal.

Rondel (French) short poem.

Rondell (French) a form of Rondel.

Ronel, Ronell, Ronnell (American) forms of Rondel.

Roni GB (Hebrew) my song; my joy. (Scottish) a form of Ronnie.

Ronin (Japanese) History: Ronin were samurai with no lord or master in feudal Japan.

Ronnie BG (Scottish) a familiar form of Ronald.

Ronny BG (Scottish) a familiar form of Ronald.

Ronson (Scottish) son of Ronald.

Ronté (American) a combination of Ron + the suffix Te.

Rony (Hebrew) a form of Roni. (Scottish) a form of Ronnie.

Rooney (Irish) redhead.

Roosevelt (Dutch) rose field. History: Theodore and Franklin D. Roosevelt were the twenty-sixth and thirty-second U.S. presidents, respectively.

Roper (English) rope maker.

Roque (Italian) a form of Rocco.

Rory BG (German) a familiar form of Roderick. (Irish) red king.

Rosalio (Spanish) rose.

Rosario GB (Portuguese) rosary.

Roscoe (Scandinavian) deer forest.

Rosendo (Germanic) the excellent master.

Roshad (American) a form of Rashad.

Roshan BG (American) a form of Roshean.

Roshean (American) a combination of the prefix Ro + Sean.

Rosito (Filipino) rose.

Ross (Latin) rose. (Scottish) peninsula.

(French) red. (English) a short form of Roswald.

Rosswell (English) springtime of roses.

Rostislav (Czech) growing glory.

Roswald (English) field of roses.

Roth (German) redhead.

Rothwell (Scandinavian) red spring.

Rover (English) traveler.

Rowan 🇧🇬 (English) tree with red berries.

Rowdy (American) rowdy.

Rowell (English) roe-deer well.

Rowland (English) rough land. (German) a form of Roland.

Rowley (English) rough meadow.

Rowson (English) son of the redhead.

Roxbury (English) rook's town or fortress.

Roxelio (German) a form of Rogelio.

Roy (French) king. A short form of Royal, Royce.

Royal (French) kingly, royal.

Royce (English) son of Roy.

Royden (English) rye hill.

Ruben, Rubin (Hebrew) forms of Reuben.

Rubén (Hebrew) a form of Ruben.

Rubert (Czech) a form of Robert.

Rucahue (Mapuche) place of construction.

Rucalaf (Mapuche) house of joy.

Ruda (Czech) a form of Rudolph.

Rudd (English) a short form of Rudyard.

Rudecindo (Spanish) a form of Rosendo.

Rudesindo (Teutonic) excellent gentleman.

Rudi (Spanish) a familiar form of Rudolph. (English) a form of Rudy.

Rudiger (German) a form of Rogelio.

Rudo (Shona) love.

Rudolf (German) a form of Rudolph.

Rudolph (German) famous wolf. **Rudolpho** (Italian) a form of Rudolph.

Rudy (English) a familiar form of Rudolph.

Rudyard (English) red enclosure.

Rueben (Hebrew) a form of Reuben.

Ruelle, Rule (French) famous wolf.

Rufay (Quechua) warm.

Ruff (French) redhead.

Rufin (Polish) redhead.

Rufino (Spanish) a form of Rufin, Rufus.

Rufio (Latin) a form of Rufus.

Ruford (English) red ford; ford with reeds.

Rufus (Latin) redhead.

Rugby (English) rook fortress. History: a famous British school after which the sport of Rugby was named.

Ruggerio (Italian) a form of Roger.

Ruhakana (Rukiga) argumentative.

Ruland (German) a form of Roland.

Rumford (English) wide river crossing.

Rumi (Quechua) stone, rock.

Rumimaqui, Rumiñaui (Quechua) he who has strong hands.

Rumisonjo, Rumisuncu (Quechua) hard hearted.

Runacatu, Runacoto (Quechua) short man.

Runako (Shona) handsome.

Rune (German, Swedish) secret.

Runihura (Egyptian) destructor.

Runrot (Tai) prosperous.

Runto, Runtu (Quechua) hailstone.

Rupert (German) a form of Robert.

Ruperto (Italian) a form of Rupert.

Ruprecht (German) a form of Rupert.

Rush (French) redhead. (English) a short form of Russell.

Rushford (English) ford with rushes.

Rusk (Spanish) twisted bread.

Ruskin (French) redhead.

Russ (French) a short form of Russell.

Russel (French) a form of Russell.

Russell (French) redhead; fox colored. **Rustin** (French) a form of Rusty.

Rusty (French) a familiar form of Russell.

Rutger (Scandinavian) a form of Roger.

Rutherford (English) cattle ford.

Rutland (Scandinavian) red land.

Rutledge (English) red ledge.

Rutley (English) red meadow.

Ruy (Spanish) a short form of Roderick.

Ruyan (Spanish) a form of Ryan.

Ryan ☆

⚏ (Irish) little king.

Rycroft (English) rye field.

Ryder ☆ (English) a form of Rider.

Rye (English) a grain used in cereal and whiskey. A short form of Richard, Ryder. (Gypsy) gentleman.

Ryen, Ryon (Irish) forms of Ryan.

Ryerson (English) son of Rider, Ryder.

Ryese (English) a form of Reece.

Ryker (American) a surname used as a first name.

Rylan ⚏ (English) land where rye is grown.

Ryland (English) a form of Rylan.

Ryle (English) rye hill.

Ryley ⚏ (Irish) a form of Riley.

Rylie ⚏ (Irish) a form of Riley.

Ryman (English) rye seller.

Ryne (Irish) a form of Ryan.

Ryo ⚏ (Spanish) a form of Rio.

S

Sa'id (Arabic) happy.

Saa (Egyptian) God's nature.

Saad (Arabic) fortunate, lucky.

Sabas (Hebrew) conversion.

Sabastian (Greek) a form of Sebastian.

Sabastien (French) a form of Sebastian.

Sabatino (Latin) festive day.

Sabelio (Spanish) a form of Sabino.

Saber (French) sword.

Sabin (Basque) a form of Sabine.

Sabino (Basque) a form of Sabin.

Sabiti (Rutooro) born on Sunday.

Sabola (Nguni) pepper.

Saburo (Japanese) third-born son.

Sacchidananda (Indian) total bliss.

Sacha ⚏ (Russian) a form of Sasha.

Sachar (Russian) a form of Zachary.

Sachet, Sachit (Indian) consciousness.

Sachetan (Indian) animated.

Sachin (Indian) another name for the Hindu god Indra.

Sadashiva (Indian) eternally pure.

Saddam (Arabic) powerful ruler.

Sadeepan (Indian) lit up.

Sadiki (Swahili) faithful.

Sadler (English) saddle maker.

Sadoc (Hebrew) sacred.

Sadurní (Catalan) a form of Satordi.

Sadurniño (Spanish) pertaining to the god Saturn.

Safari (Swahili) born while traveling.

Safford (English) willow river crossing.

Sagar (Indian) ocean.

Sage GB (English) wise. Botany: an herb.

Sagun (Indian) possessed of divine qualities.

Sahaj (Indian) natural.

Sahale (Native American) falcon.

Sahas (Indian) bravery.

Sahdev (Indian) one of the Pandava princes, descendents of King Pandu in the Indian epic poem *Mahabharata*.

Sahen (Hindi) above.

Sahib (Indian) lord.

Sahil (Native American) a form of Sahale.

Sahir (Hindi) friend.

Sahúl (Hebrew) requested.

Said (Arabic) a form of Sa'id.

Saîd (Arabic) a form of Said.

Saige GB (English) a form of Sage.

Sainath (Indian) another name for Saibaba, a Hindu guru.

Saipraasad (Indian) blessing.

Saipratap (Indian) blessing of Saibaba.

Sajag (Hindi) watchful.

Sajal (Indian) moist.

Sajan (Indian) beloved.

Saka (Swahili) hunter.

Sakeri (Danish) a form of Zachary.

Saket (Indian) another name for the Hindu god Krishna.

Sakima (Native American) king.

Sakuruta (Pawnee) coming sun.

Sal (Italian) a short form of Salvatore.

Saladin (Arabic) good; faithful.

Salah (Arabic) righteousness. (Hindi) a form of Sala .

Salâh (Arabic) a form of Salah.

Salam (Arabic) lamb.

Salamon (Spanish) a form of Solomon.

Salamón (Spanish) a form of Salamon.

Salarjung (Indian) beautiful.

Salaun (French) a form of Solomon.

Saleem (Arabic) a form of Salím.

Saleh (Arabic) a form of Sálih.

Sâleh (Arabic) a form of Saleh.

Salem GB (Arabic) a form of Salím.

Salene (Swahili) good.

Salih (Egyptian) respectable.

Sálih (Arabic) right, good.

Salil (Indian) water.

Salim (Swahili) peaceful.

Salím (Arabic) peaceful, safe.

Salîm (Arabic) a form of Salim.

Salisbury (English) fort at the willow pool.

Salmalin (Hindi) taloned.

Salman (Czech) a form of Salím, Solomon.

Salmân (Czech) a form of Salman.

Salomé (Hebrew) complete; perfect.

Salomon (French) a form of Solomon.

Salton (English) manor town; willow town.

Salustiano (German) he who enjoys good health.

Salustio (Latin) he who offers salvation.

Salvador (Spanish) savior.

Salvatore (Italian) savior.

Salviano (Spanish) a form of Salvo.

Salvino (Spanish) a short form of Salvador.

Salvio, Salvo (Latin) cured, healthy.

Sam (Hebrew) a short form of Samuel.

Samar (Indian) war.

Samarendra, Samarendu, Samarjit (Indian) other names for the Hindu god Vishnu.

Samarth (Indian) powerful.

Sambo (American) a familiar form of Samuel.

Sameer (Arabic) a form of Samír.

Sami BG (Hebrew) a form of Sammie.

Sâmî (Arabic) tall.

Samín (Quechua) fortunate, lucky.

Samir (Arabic) a form of Samír.

Samír (Arabic) entertaining companion.

Samîr (Arabic) a form of Samír.

Samman (Arabic) grocer.

Sammie BG (Hebrew) a familiar form of Samuel.

Sammy BG (Hebrew) a familiar form of Samuel.

Samo (Czech) a form of Samuel.

Sampson (Hebrew) a form of Samson.

Samson (Hebrew) like the sun. Bible: a judge and powerful warrior betrayed by Delilah.

Samual (Hebrew) a form of Samuel.

Samuel ☆

BG (Hebrew) heard God; asked of God. Bible: a famous Old Testament prophet and judge.
Samuele (Italian) a form of Samuel.

Samuru (Japanese) a form of Samuel.

Samy (Hebrew) a form of Sammie.

Sanat (Hindi) ancient.

Sanborn (English) sandy brook.

Sanchez (Latin) a form of Sancho.

Sancho (Latin) sanctified; sincere. Literature: Sancho Panza was Don Quixote's squire.

Sandeep BG (Punjabi) enlightened.

Sander (English) a short form of Alexander, Lysander.

Sanders (English) son of Sander.

Sándor (Hungarian) a short form of Alexander.

Sandro (Greek, Italian) a short form of Alexander.

Sandy GB (English) a familiar form of Alexander, Sanford.

Sanford **(English) sandy river crossing.**

Sani **(Hindi) the planet Saturn. (Navajo) old.**

Sanjay **(American) a combination of Sanford + Jay.**

Sanjiv **(Hindi) long-lived.**

Sankar (Hindi) another name for the Hindu god Shiva.

Sansón (Spanish) a form of Samson.

Santana GB (Spanish) History: Antonio López de Santa Anna was a Mexican general and political leader.

Santiago (Spanish) a form of James.

Santino (Spanish) a form of Santonio.

Santo (Italian, Spanish) holy.

Santon (English) sandy town.

Santonio (Spanish) Geography: a short form of San Antonio, a city in Texas.

Santos (Spanish) saint.

Santosh (Hindi) satisfied.

Sanya (Russian) defender of men.

Sanyu BG (Luganda) happy.

Sapay (Quechua) unique.

Saqr (Arabic) falcon.

Saquan (American) a combination of the prefix Sa + Quan.

Sarad (Hindi) born in the autumn.

Sargent (French) army officer.

Sargon (Persian) sun prince.

Sarik (Hindi) bird.

Sarito (Spanish) a form of Caesar.

Saritupac (Quechua) glorious prince.

Sariyah (Arabic) clouds at night.

Sarngin (Hindi) archer; protector.

Sarojin (Hindi) like a lotus.

Sasha GB (Russian) a short form of Alexander.

Sasson (Hebrew) joyful.

Satchel (French) small bag.

Satordi (French) Saturn.

Saturio (Latin) protector of the sown fields.

Saturnín (Spanish) gift of Saturn.

Sáturno (Italian) mythological god of planting and harvesting.

Saul (Hebrew) asked for, borrowed. Bible: in the Old Testament, a king of Israel and the father of Jonathan; in the New Testament, Saint Paul's original name was Saul.

Saúl (Hebrew) a form of Saul.

Saulo (Greek) he who is tender and delicate.

Saverio (Italian) a form of Xavier.

Saville (French) willow town.

Savion (American, Spanish) a form of Savon.

Savon (American) a form of Savannah **Saw** (Burmese) early.

Sawyer BG (English) wood worker.

Sax (English) a short form of Saxon.

Saxby (Scandinavian) Saxon farm.

Saxon (English) swordsman. History: the Roman name for the Teutonic raiders who ravaged the Roman British coasts.

Saxton (English) Saxon town.

Sayani (Quechua) I stay on foot.

Sayarumi (Quechua) strong as stone.

Sayer (Welsh) carpenter.

Sayri (Quechua) prince.

Sayyid (Arabic) master.

Scanlon (Irish) little trapper.

Schafer (German) shepherd.

Schmidt (German) blacksmith.

Schneider (German) tailor.

Schön (German) handsome.

Schuman (German) shoemaker.

Schuyler (Dutch) sheltering.

Schyler GB (Dutch) a form of Schuyler.

Scipion (Latin) staff; stick.

Scoey (French) a short form of Scoville.

Scorpio (Latin) dangerous, deadly. Astronomy: a southern constellation near Libra and Sagittarius. Astrology: the eighth sign of the zodiac.

Scot (English) a form of Scott.

Scott (English) from Scotland. A familiar form of Prescott.

Scottie, Scotty (English) familiar forms of Scott.

Scoville (French) Scott's town.

Scribe (Latin) keeper of accounts; writer.

Scully (Irish) town crier.

Seabert (English) shining sea.

Seabrook (English) brook near the sea.

Seamus (Irish) a form of James.

Sean 🆖 (Irish) a form of John.

Seanan (Irish) wise.

Searlas (Irish, French) a form of Charles.

Searle (English) armor.

Seasar (Latin) a form of Caesar.

Seaton (English) town near the sea.

Seb (Egyptian) God of earth.

Sebastian ⭐ (Greek) venerable. (Latin) revered. **Sebastián** (Greek) a form of Sebastian.

Sebastiano (Italian) a form of Sebastian.

Sebastien, Sébastien (French) forms of Sebastian.

Sebastion (Greek) a form of Sebastian.

Secundino (Latin) second.

Secundus (Latin) second-born.
Secondas, Secondus, Secondys

Sedgely (English) sword meadow.

Sedgwick (English) sword grass.

Sedric, Sedrick (Irish) forms of Cedric.

Seeley (English) blessed.

Sef (Egyptian) yesterday. Mythology: one of the two lions that make up the Akeru, guardian of the gates of morning and night.

Sefonías (Hebrew) God protects.

Sefton (English) village of rushes.

Sefu (Swahili) sword.

Segada (Gaelic) admirable.

Seger (English) sea spear; sea warrior.

Segismundo (Germanic) the victorious protector.

Segun (Yoruba) conqueror.

Segundino (Latin) the family's second son.

Segundo (Spanish) second.

Seibert (English) bright sea.

Seif (Arabic) religion's sword.

Seifert (German) a form of Siegfried.

Sein (Basque) innocent.

Sekani (Egyptian) to laugh.

Sekaye (Shona) laughter.
Sekai, Sekay

Sekou (Guinean) learned.

Selby (English) village by the mansion.

Seldon (English) willow tree valley.

Selemías (Hebrew) God rewards.

Selesio (Latin) select.

Selig (German) a form of Seeley.

Selwyn (English) friend from the palace.

Semaj 🆖 (Turkish) a form of Sema .

Semanda (Luganda) cow clan.

Semarias (Hebrew) God guarded him.

Semer (Ethiopian) a form of George.

Semi (Polynesian) character.

Semon (Greek) a form of Simon.

Sempala (Luganda) born in prosperous times.

Sempronio (Latin) name of a Roman family based on male descent.

Sen (Japanese) wood fairy.
Senh

Seneca, Séneca (Latin) an honorable elder.

Sener (Turkish) bringer of joy.

Senior (French) lord.

Sennett (French) elderly.

Senon (Spanish) living.

Senón (Spanish) a form of Senon.

Senwe (African) dry as a grain stalk.

Sepp (German) a form of Joseph.

Septimio, Septimo, Séptimo (Latin) the seventh child.

Septimus (Latin) seventh.

Serafin (Hebrew) a form of Seraphim.

Serafín (Hebrew) a form of Serafin.

Serafino (Portuguese) a form of Seraphim.

Seraphim (Hebrew) fiery, burning. Bible: the highest order of angels, known for their zeal and love.

Serapión (Greek) a form of Serapio.

Sereno (Latin) calm, tranquil.

Serge (Latin) attendant.

Sergei, Sergey (Russian) forms of Serge.

Sergio, Serjio (Italian) forms of Serge.

Serni (Catalan) a form of Saturno.

Serug (Hebrew) interwoven.

Servacio (Latin) he who observes and guards the law.

Servando (Spanish) to serve.

Seth (Hebrew) appointed. Bible: **the third son of Adam.**

Sethos (Egyptian) prince.

Setimba (Luganda) river dweller. Geography: a river in Uganda.

Seumas (Scottish) a form of James.

Severiano (Italian) a form of Séverin.

Séverin (French) severe.

Severino (Spanish) a form of Séverin.

Severn (English) boundary.

Sevilen (Turkish) beloved.

Seward (English) sea guardian.

Sewati (Moquelumnan) curved bear claws.

Sewell (English) sea wall.

Sexton (English) church offical; sexton.

Sextus (Latin) sixth.

Seymour (French) prayer. Religion: name honoring Saint Maur. ,

Shaan (Hebrew, Irish) a form of Sean.

Shabaka (Egyptian) king.

Shabouh (Armenian) king, noble. History: a fourth-century Persian king.

Shad (Punjabi) happy-go-lucky.

Shade BG (English) shade.

Shadi (Arabic) singer.

Shadow BG (English) shadow.

Shadrach (Babylonian) god; godlike. Bible: one of three companions who emerged unharmed from the fiery furnace of Babylon.

Shadrick (Babylonian) a form of Shadrach.

Shadwell (English) shed by a well.

Shady (Arabic) a form of Shadi.

Shae GB (Hebrew) a form of Shai. (Irish) a form of Shea.

Shafiq (Arabic) compassionate.

Shah (Persian) king. History: a title for rulers of Iran.

Shaheed (Arabic) a form of Sa'id.

Shaheem (American) a combination of Shah + Raheem.

Shahid (Arabic) a form of Sa'id.

Shai BG (Irish) a form of Shea. (Hebrew) a short form of Yeshaya.

Shaiming (Chinese) life; sunshine.

Shain, Shaine (Irish) forms of Sean.

Shaka BG (Zulu) founder, first. History: Shaka Zulu was the founder of the Zulu empire.

Shakeel (Arabic) a form of Shaquille.

Shakir (Arabic) thankful.

Shakîr (Arabic) a form of Shakir.

Shakur (Arabic) a form of Shakir.
Shakuur

Shalom (Hebrew) peace.

Shalya (Hindi) throne.

Shaman (Sanskrit) holy man, mystic, medicine man.

Shamar (Hebrew) a form of Shamir.
, Shamare

Shamari BG (Hebrew) a form of Shamir.

Shamir (Hebrew) precious stone.

Shamus (American) slang for detective. (Irish) a form of Seamus.

Shan (Irish) a form of Shane.

Shanahan (Irish) wise, clever.

Shandy (English) rambunctious.

Shane BG (Irish) a form of Sean.
Shaen, Shaene

Shangobunni (Yoruba) gift from Shango.

Shani GB (Hebrew) red. (Swahili) marvelous.

Shanley GB (Irish) small; ancient.

Shannon GB (Irish) small and wise.

Shant (French) a short form of Shantae.

Shantae GB (French) a form of Chante.

Shap (English) a form of Shep.

Shaq (American) a short form of Shaquan, Shaquille.

Shaquan BG (American) a combination of the prefix Sha + Quan.

Shaquell (American) a form of Shaquille.

Shaquile (Arabic) a form of Shaquille.

Shaquill (Arabic) a form of Shaquille.

Shaquille BG (Arabic) handsome.

Shaquon (American) a combination of the prefix Sha + Quon.

Sharad (Pakistani) autumn.

Shareef (Arabic) a form of Sharíf.

Sharif (Arabic) a form of Sharíf.

Sharíf (Arabic) honest; noble.

Sharîf (Arabic) a form of Sharíf.

Sharod (Pakistani) a form of Sharad.
Sharrod

Sharón (Hebrew) a form of Sharron.

Sharron GB (Hebrew) flat area, plain.

Shashenka (Russian) defender of humanity.

Shattuck (English) little shad fish.
Shatuck

Shaun BG (Irish) a form of Sean.

Shavar (Hebrew) comet.

Shavon GB (American) a combination of the prefix Sha + Yvon.

Shaw (English) grove.

Shawn BG (Irish) a form of Sean.

Shawnta GB (American) a combination of Shawn + the suffix Ta.

Shay BG (Irish) a form of Shea.

Shayan (Cheyenne) a form of Cheyenne.

Shaye GB (Irish) a form of Shea.

Shayn (Hebrew) a form of Sean.
Shaynne, Shean

Shayne BG (Hebrew) a form of Sean.

Shea GB (Irish) courteous.

Sheary (Irish) peaceful.
Shearee, Shearey, Sheari, Shearie

Sheba (Hebrew) promise.

Shedrick (Babylonian) a form of Shadrach.

Sheehan (Irish) little; peaceful.

Sheffield (English) crooked field.

Shel (English) a short form of Shelby, Sheldon, Shelton.
Shell

Shelby GB **(English) ledge estate. A form of Selby.**

Sheldon BG **(English) farm on the ledge.**

Shelley GB **(English) a familiar form of Shelby, Sheldon, Shelton. Literature: Percy Bysshe Shelley** was a nineteenth-century British poet.

Shelomó (Hebrew) of peace.

Shelton (English) town on a ledge.

Shem (Hebrew) name; reputation. A form of Samson. (English) a short form of Samuel. Bible: Noah's oldest son.

Shen (Egyptian) sacred amulet. (Chinese) meditation.

Shep (English) a short form of Shepherd.

Shepherd (English) shepherd.

Shepley (English) sheep meadow.

Sherborn (English) clear brook.

Sheridan GB (Irish) wild.

Sherill (English) shire on a hill.

Sherlock (English) light haired. Literature: Sherlock Holmes is a famous British detective character, created by Sir Arthur Conan Doyle.

Sherma (English) one who shears sheep.

Sherman (English) sheep shearer; resident of a shire.

Sherrod (English) clearer of the land.

Sherwin (English) swift runner, one who cuts the wind.

Sherwood (English) bright forest.

Shihab (Arabic) blaze.
Shyhab

Shihâb (Arabic) a form of Shihab.

Shìlín (Chinese) intellectual.

Shilo BG (Hebrew) a form of Shiloh.

Shiloh GB (Hebrew) God's gift.

Shimeón (Hebrew) he heard.

Shimon (Hebrew) a form of Simon.

Shimshon (Hebrew) a form of Samson.

Shing (Chinese) victory.

Shipley (English) sheep meadow.

Shipton (English) sheep village; ship village.

Shiquan (American) a combination of the prefix Shi + Quan.

Shiro (Japanese) fourth-born son.

Shiva (Hindi) life and death. Religion: the most common name for the Hindu god of destruction and reproduction.

Shlomo (Hebrew) a form of Solomon**.**

Shmuel (Hebrew) a form of Samuel.

Shneur (Yiddish) senior.

Shomer (Hebrew) protector.

Shon (German) a form of Schön. (American) a form of Sean.

Shoni (Hebrew) changing.

Shu (Egyptian) air.

Shunnar (Arabic) pheasant.

Si (Hebrew) a short form of Silas, Simon.

Siañu (Quechua) brown like the color of coffee.

Sid (French) a short form of Sidney.

Siddel (English) wide valley.

Siddhartha (Hindi) History: Siddhartha Gautama was the original name of Buddha, the founder of Buddhism.

Sidney GB (French) from Saint-Denis, France.

Sidonio (Spanish) a form of Sidney.

Sidwell (English) wide stream.

Siegfried (German) victorious peace.

Sierra GB (Irish) black. (Spanish) saw-toothed.

Siervo (Spanish) a man who serves God.

Siffre (French) a form of Siegfried.

Siffredo (Italian) a form of Siegfried.

Sig (German) a short form of Siegfried, Sigmund.

Siggy (German) a familiar form of Siegfried, Sigmund.

Sigifredo (German) a form of Siegfried.

Sigismond (French) a form of Sigmund.

Sigismundo (Italian, Spanish) a form of Sigmund.

Sigmund (German) victorious protector. **Sigurd** (German, Scandinavian) victorious guardian.

Sigwald (German) victorious leader.

Silas (Latin) a short form of Silvan.

Silburn (English) blessed.

Silvan (Latin) forest dweller.

Silvano (Italian) a form of Silvan.

Silverio (Spanish) Greek god of trees.

Silvester (Latin) a form of Sylvester.

Silvestre (Spanish) a form of Sylvester.

Silvestro (Italian) a form of Sylvester.

Silvino (Italian) a form of Silvan.

Silvio (Italian) a form of Silvan.

Simão (Portuguese) a form of Samuel.

Simba (Swahili) lion. (Yao) a short form of Lisimba.

Simcha 🇧🇬 (Hebrew) joyful.

Simeon (French) a form of Simon.

Simeón (Spanish) a form of Simón.

Simms (Hebrew) son of Simon.

Simmy (Hebrew) a familiar form of Simcha, Simon.

Simon (Hebrew) he heard. Bible: one of the Twelve Disciples.

Simón (Hebrew) he who has listened to me.

Simon Pierre (French) a combination of Simon + Pierre.

Simplicio (Latin) simple.

Simpson (Hebrew) son of Simon.

Simran 🇬🇧 (Sikh) absorbed in God.

Sina 🇧🇬 (Irish) a form of Seana .

Sinbad (German) prince; sparkling.

Sincere (French) honest; genuine.

Sinche, Sinchi (Quechua) boss, leader; strong; valorous; hard working.

Sinchipuma (Quechua) strong leader and as valuable as a puma.

Sinchiroca (Quechua) strongest prince among the strong ones.

Sinclair 🇬🇧 (French) prayer. Religion: name honoring Saint Clair.

Sinesio (Greek) the intelligent one.

Sinforiano (Spanish) a form of Sinforoso.

Sinforoso (Greek) he who is full of misfortune.

Singh (Hindi) lion.

Sinjin (English) a form of Sinjon.

Sinjon (English) saint, holy man. Religion: name honoring Saint John.

Sione **(Tongan) God is gracious.**

Sipatu (Moquelumnan) pulled out.

Sipho (Zulu) present.

Sir (English) sir, sire.

Siraj (Arabic) lamp, light.

Sirâj (Arabic) a form of Siraj.

Sirio, Siro (Latin) native of Syria.

Sirviente (Latin) God's servant.

Siseal (Irish) a form of Cecil.

Sisebuto (Teutonic) he who fulfills his leadership role whole-heartedly.

Sisi (Fante) born on Sunday.

Sitric (Scandinavian) conqueror.

Siuca (Quechua) youngest son.

Siva (Hindi) a form of Shiva.

Siv

Sivan (Hebrew) ninth month of the Jewish year.

Siwatu (Swahili) born during a time of conflict.

Siwili (Native American) long fox's tail.

Sixto (Greek) the courteous one.

Skah (Lakota) white.

Skai

Skee (Scandinavian) projectile.

Skeeter (English) swift.

Skelly (Irish) storyteller.

Skelton (Dutch) shell town.

Skerry (Scandinavian) stony island.

Skip (Scandinavian) a short form of Skipper.

Skipper (Scandinavian) shipmaster.

Skippie (Scandinavian) a familiar form of Skipper.

Skipton (English) ship town.

Skiriki (Pawnee) coyote.

Skule (Norwegian) hidden.

Sky BG (Dutch) a short form of Skylar.

Skye GB (Dutch) a short form of Skylar.

Skylar GB (Dutch) a form of Schuyler.

Skyler BG (Dutch) a form of Schuyler.

Skylor (Dutch) a form of Schuyler.

Slade (English) a short form of Sladen.

Sladen (English) child of the valley.

Slane (Czech) salty.

Slater (English) roof slater.

Slava (Russian) a short form of Stanislav, Vladislav, Vyacheslav.

Slawek (Polish) a short form of Radoslaw.

Slevin (Irish) mountaineer.

Sloan BG (Irish) warrior.

Smedley (English) flat meadow.

Smith (English) blacksmith.

Snowden (English) snowy hill.

Sobhî (Arabic) sunrise.

Socorro (Spanish) helper.

Socrates (Greek) wise, learned. History: a famous ancient Greek philosopher.

Sócrates (Greek) a form of Socrates.

Socso, Sucsu (Quechua) blackbird.

Sofanor (Greek) the wise man.

Sofian (Arabic) devoted.

Sofiân (Arabic) a form of Sofian.

Sofoclés, Sófocles (Greek) famous for his wisdom.

Sofronio (Greek) prudent; healthy in spirit.

Sohail (Arabic) a form of Suhail.

Sohar (Russian) farmer.

Sohrab (Persian) ancient hero.

Soja (Yoruba) soldier.

Sol (Hebrew) a short form of Saul, Solomon.

Solano (Latin) like the eastern wind.

Solly (Hebrew) a familiar form of Saul, Solomon.

Solomon BG (Hebrew) peaceful. Bible: a king of Israel famous for his wisdom.

Solon (Greek) wise. History: a noted ancient Athenian lawmaker.

Solón (Greek) a form of Solon.

Somac (Quechua) beautiful.

Somer (French) born in summer.

Somerset (English) place of the summer settlers. Literature: William Somerset Maugham was a well-known British writer.

Somerton (English) summer town.

Somerville (English) summer village.

Son (Vietnamese) mountain. (Native American) star. (English) son, boy. A short form of Madison, Orson.

Sonco, Soncoyoc, Sonjoc, Sonjoyoc (Quechua) he who has a good and noble heart.

Songan (Native American) strong.

Sonny (English) a familiar form of Grayson, Madison, Orson, Son.

Sono (Akan) elephant.

Sonu (Hindi) handsome.

Soren (Danish) a form of Sören.

Sören (Danish) thunder; war.

Sorley (Scandinavian) summer traveler; Viking.

Soroush (Persian) happy.

Sorrel GB (French) reddish brown.

Soterios (Greek) savior.

Southwell (English) south well.

Sovann (Cambodian) gold.

Sowande (Yoruba) wise healer sought me out.

Spalding (English) divided field.

Spangler (German) tinsmith.

Spark (English) happy.

Spear (English) spear carrier.

Speedy (English) quick; successful.

Spence (English) a short form of Spencer.

Spencer BG (English) dispenser of provisions.

Spenser BG (English) a form of Spencer. Literature: Edmund Spenser was the British poet who wrote *The Faerie Queene*.

Spike (English) ear of grain; long nail.

Spiridone (Italian) a form of Spiro.

Spiro (Greek) round basket; breath.

Spoor (English) spur maker.

Spreckley (English) twigs.

Springsteen (English) stream by the rocks.

Sproule (English) energetic.

Spurgeon (English) shrub.

Spyros (Greek) a form of Spiro.

Squire (English) knight's assistant; large landholder.

Stacey GB (English) a familiar form of Eustace.

Stacy GB (English) a familiar form of Eustace.

Stafford (English) riverbank landing.

Stamford (English) a form of Stanford.

Stamos (Greek) a form of Stephen.

Stan (Latin, English) a short form of Stanley.

Stanbury (English) stone fortification.

Stancil (English) beam.

Stancio (Spanish) a form of Constantine.

Stancliff (English) stony cliff.

Standish (English) stony parkland. History: Miles Standish was a leader in colonial America.

Stane (Slavic) a short form of Stanislaus.

Stanfield (English) stony field.

Stanford (English) rocky ford.

Stanislaus (Latin) stand of glory.

Stanislav (Slavic) a form of Stanislaus.

Stanislov (Russian) a form of Stanislaus.

Stanley (English) stony meadow.

Stanmore (English) stony lake.

Stannard (English) hard as stone.

Stanton (English) stony farm.

Stanway (English) stony road.

Stanwick (English) stony village.

Stanwood (English) stony woods.

Starbuck (English) challenger of fate. Literature: a character in Herman Melville's novel *Moby-Dick*.

Stark (German) strong, vigorous.

Starling BG (English) bird.

Starr GB (English) star.

Stasik (Russian) a familiar form of Stanislaus.

Stasio (Polish) a form of Stanislaus.

Stavros (Greek) a form of Stephen.

Steadman (English) owner of a farmstead.

Stedman (English) a form of Steadman.

Steel (English) like steel.

Steele (English) a form of Steel.

Steen (German, Danish) stone.

Steenie (Scottish) a form of Stephen.

Steeve (Greek) a short form of Steeven.

Steeven (Greek) a form of Steven.

Stefan (German, Polish, Swedish) a form of Stephen.

Stefano (Italian) a form of Stephen.

Stefanos (Greek) a form of Stephen.

Stefen, Steffen (Norwegian) forms of Stephen.

Steffan (Swedish) a form of Stefan.

Steffon, Stefon (Polish) forms of Stephon.

Stein (German) a form of Steen.

Steinar (Norwegian) rock warrior.

Stepan (Russian) a form of Stephen.

Steph (English) a short form of Stephen.

Stephan (Greek) a form of Stephen.

Stephane, Stéphane (French) forms of Stephen.

Stephaun (Greek) a form of Stephen.

Stephen (Greek) crowned.

Stephenson (English) son of Stephen.

Stephon (Greek) a form of Stephen.

Stephone (Greek) a form of Stephon.

Sterlin (English) a form of Sterling.

Sterling BG (English) valuable; silver penny. A form of Starling.

Stern (German) star.

Sterne (English) austere.

Stetson (Danish) stepson.

Stevan (Greek) a form of Steven.

Steve (Greek) a short form of Stephen, Steven.

Steven (Greek) a form of Stephen.

Stevens (English) son of Steven.

Stevie GB (English) a familiar form of Stephen, Steven.

Stevin, Stevon (Greek) forms of Steven.

Stewart (English) a form of Stuart.

Stian (Norwegian) quick on his feet.

Stig (Swedish) mount.

Stiggur (Gypsy) gate.

Stillman (English) quiet.

Sting (English) spike of grain.

Stirling (English) a form of Sterling.

Stockley (English) tree-stump meadow.

Stockman (English) tree-stump remover.

Stockton (English) tree-stump town.

Stockwell (English) tree-stump well.

Stoddard (English) horse keeper.

Stoffel (German) a short form of Christopher.

Stoker (English) furnace tender.

Stone (English) stone.

Stoney (English) a form of Stone.

Storm BG (English) tempest, storm.

Storr (Norwegian) great.

Stover (English) stove tender.

Stowe (English) hidden; packed away.

Strahan (Irish) minstrel.

Stratford (English) bridge over the river. Literature: Stratford-upon-Avon was Shakespeare's birthplace.

Stratton (Scottish) river valley town.

Strephon (Greek) one who turns.

Strom (Greek) bed, mattress. (German) stream.

Strong (English) powerful.

Stroud (English) thicket.

Struthers (Irish) brook.

Stu (English) a short form of Stewart, Stuart.

Stuart (English) caretaker, steward. History: a Scottish and English royal family.

Studs (English) rounded nail heads; shirt ornaments; male horses used for breeding. History: Louis "Studs" Terkel is a famous American journalist.

Styles (English) stairs put over a wall to help cross it.

Subhi (Arabic) early morning.

Subhî (Arabic) a form of Subhi.

Suck Chin (Korean) unshakable rock.

Sudi (Swahili) lucky.

Sued (Arabic) master, chief.

Suede (Arabic) a form of Sued.

Suelita (Spanish) little lily.

Suffield (English) southern field.

Sufiân (Arabic) consecrated.

Sugden (English) valley of sows.

Suhail (Arabic) gentle.

Suhay (Quechua) he who is like yellow corn: fine and abundant.

Suhuba (Swahili) friend.

Sukhpreet (Sikh) one who values inner peace and joy.

Sukru (Turkish) grateful.

Sulaiman (Arabic) a form of Solomon.

Sullivan BG (Irish) black eyed.

Sully (French) stain, tarnish. (English) south meadow. (Irish) a familiar form of Sullivan.

Sultan (Swahili) ruler.

Sum (Tai) appropriate.

Sumainca (Quechua) beautiful Inca.

Sumarville (French) one who comes from summertime.

Sumeet (English) a form of Summit.

Sumit (English) a form of Summit.

Summit (English) peak, top.

Sumner (English) church officer; summoner.

Suncu, Suncuyuc (Quechua) he who has a good and noble heart.

Sundeep (Punjabi) light; enlightened.

Sunny BG (English) sunny, sunshine.

Sunreep (Hindi) pure.

Suri (Quechua) fast like an ostrich.

Surya BG (Sanskrit) sun.

Susumu (Japanese) move forward.

Sutcliff (English) southern cliff.

Sutherland (Scandinavian) southern land.

Sutton (English) southern town.

Suyai, Suyay (Quechua) hope.

Suycauaman (Quechua) the youngest son of the falcons.

Sven (Scandinavian) youth.

Swaggart (English) one who sways and staggers.

Swain (English) herdsman; knight's attendant.

Swaley (English) winding stream.

Swannee (English) swan.

Sweeney (Irish) small hero.

Swinbourne (English) stream used by swine.

Swindel (English) valley of the swine.

Swinfen (English) swine's mud.

Swinford (English) swine's crossing.

Swinton (English) swine town.

Swithbert (English) strong and bright.

Swithin (German) strong.

Sy (Latin) a short form of Sylas, Symon.

Syed (Arabic) happy.

Sying BG (Chinese) star.

Sylas (Latin) a form of Silas.

Sylvain (French) a form of Silvan, Sylvester.

Sylvan (Latin) a form of Silvan.

Sylvester (Latin) forest dweller.

Symington (English) Simon's town, Simon's estate.
Simington

Symon (Greek) a form of Simon.

Szczepan (Polish) a form of Stephen.

Szygfrid (Hungarian) a form of Siegfried.

Szymon (Polish) a form of Simon.

T

Taaveti (Finnish) a form of David.

Tab (English) a short form of Tabner.

Tabare (Tupi) one who lives apart from the rest.

Tabaré (Tupi) man of the village.

Tabari (Arabic) he remembers.

Tabib (Turkish) physician.

Tabner (German) shining, brilliant; spring. (English) drummer.

Tabo (Spanish) a short form of Gustave.

Tabor (Persian) drummer. (Hungarian) encampment.

Taciano (Spanish) a form of Tacio.

Tacio (Latin) he who is quiet.

Tácito (Spanish) a form of Tacio.

Tad (Welsh) father. (Greek, Latin) a short form of Thaddeus.

Tadan (Native American) plentiful.

Tadarius (American) a combination of the prefix Ta + Darius.

Tadashi (Japanese) faithful servant.

Taddeo (Italian) a form of Thaddeus.

Taddeus (Greek, Latin) a form of Thaddeus.

Tadi (Omaha) wind.

Tadleigh (English) poet from a meadow.

Tadzi (Carrier) loon.

Tadzio (Polish, Spanish) a form of Thaddeus.

Taffy GB (Welsh) a form of David. (English) a familiar form of Taft.

Taft (English) river.

Tage (Danish) day.

Taggart (Irish) son of the priest.

Tâher (Arabic) pure; clean.

Tahir (Indian) holy.

Tahír (Arabic) innocent, pure.

Tai BG (Vietnamese) weather; prosperous; talented.

Taillefer (French) works with iron.

Taima GB (Native American) born during a storm.

Tain (Irish) stream. (Native American) new moon.

Taishawn (American) a combination of Tai + Shawn.

Tait (Scandinavian) a form
of Tate.
Taite, Taitt, Tayt, Tayte

Taiwan (Chinese) island;
island dweller.
Geography: a country off
the coast of China.

Taiwo (Yoruba) first-born
of twins.

Taizeen (Indian)
encouragement.

Taj (Urdu) crown.

Tajdar (Indian) crowned.

Tajo (Spanish) day.

Tajuan (American) a
combination of the prefix
Ta + Juan.

Takeo (Japanese) strong as
bamboo.

Takeshi (Japanese) strong.

Takis (Greek) a familiar
form of Peter.

Takoda (Lakota) friend to
everyone.

Tal (Hebrew) dew; rain.
(Tswana) a form of Tale.

Talâl (Arabic) pleasant;
admirable.

Talat (Indian) prayer.

Talbert (German) bright
valley.

Talbot (French) boot
maker.

Talcott (English) cottage
near the lake.

Tale (Tswana) green.

Tâleb (Arabic) a form of
Talib.

Talen (English) a form of
Talon.

Talib (Arabic) seeker.

Taliesin (Welsh) radiant
brow.

Taliki (Hausa) fellow.

Talleen (Indian) absorbed.

Talli (Delaware) legendary
hero.

Tallis BG (Persian) wise.

Tallon (English, French) a
form of Talon.

Talmadge (English) lake
between two towns.

Talmai (Aramaic) mound;
furrow.

Talman BG (Aramaic)
injured; oppressed.

Talon BG (French, English)
claw, nail.

Talor GB (English) a form
of Tal, Taylor.

Tam BG (Vietnamese)
number eight. (Hebrew)
honest. (English) a short
form of Thomas.

Tamal (Indian) a tree with
very dark bark.

Taman (Slavic) dark, black.

Tamar GB (Hebrew) date;
palm tree.

Tamas (Hungarian) a form
of Thomas.

Tambo (Swahili) vigorous.

Tamir (Arabic) tall as a
palm tree.

Tamkinat (Indian) pomp.

Tammâm (Arabic)
generous.

Tammany (Delaware)
friendly.
Tamany

Tamonash (Indian)
destroyer of ignorance.

Tamson (Scandinavian)
son of Thomas.

Tan (Burmese) million.
(Vietnamese) new.

Tanay, Tanuj (Indian)
son.

Tancredo (Germanic) he
who shrewdly gives
advice.

Tandie (English) team.

Tane (Maori) husband.

Tanek (Greek) immortal.

Taneli (Finnish) God is my
judge.

Taner (English) a form of
Tanner.

Tanguy (French) warrior.

Tani GB (Japanese) valley.

Taniel GB (Estonian) a
form of Daniel.

Tanmay (Sanskrit)
engrossed.

Tanner BG (English)
leather worker; tanner.

Tannin (English) tan
colored; dark.

Tannis GB (Slavic) a form
of Tania, Tanya

Tanny (English) a familiar
form of Tanner.

Tano (Spanish) camp glory.
(Ghanaian) Geography: a
river in Ghana. (Russian)
a short form of
Stanislaus.

Tanton (English) town by the still river.

Tanveer (Indian) enlightened.

Tapan (Sanskrit) sun; summer.

Tapani (Finnish) a form of Stephen.

Tapas (Indian) ascetic.

Tapasendra, Tarakeshwar, Taraknath (Indian) other names for the Hindu god Shiva.

Tapasranjan (Indian) another name for the Hindu god Vishnu.

Täpko (Kiowa) antelope.

Tapomay (Indian) full of moral virtue.

Taquan (American) a combination of the prefix Ta + Quan.

Taquiri (Quechua) he who creates much music and dance.

Tarachand, Taraprashad (Indian) star.

Tarak (Sanskrit) star; protector.

Taral (Indian) honeybee.

Taran BG (Sanskrit) heaven. A form of Tarun.

Taranga (Indian) wave.

Taree GB (Australian) fig tree.

Tarek, Tarik, Tariq (Arabic) forms of Táriq.

Tarell, Tarrell (German) forms of Terrell.

Taren, Tarren (American) forms of Taron.

Târeq (Arabic) name of a star.

Tareton (English) a form of Tarleton.

Tarif (Arabic) uncommon.

Táriq (Arabic) conqueror. History: Tariq bin Ziyad was the Muslim general who conquered Spain.

Tarit (Indian) lightning.

Tarleton (English) Thor's settlement.

Taro (Japanese) first-born male.

Taron (American) a combination of Tad + Ron.

Tarquino (Latin) he who was born in Tarquinia.

Tarrance (Latin) a form of Terrence.

Tarrant (Welsh) thunder.

Tarsicio (Latin) he who belongs to Tarso.

Tarun (Sanskrit) young, youth.

Taruntapan (Indian) morning sun.

Tarver (English) tower; hill; leader.

Taryn GB (American) a form of Taron.

Tas (Gypsy) bird's nest.

Tashawn (American) a combination of the prefix Ta + Shawn.

Tass (Hungarian) ancient mythology name.

Tasunke (Dakota) horse.

Tate BG (Scandinavian, English) cheerful. (Native American) long-winded talker.

Tathagata (Indian) the Buddha.

Tatiano (Latin) he who is quiet.

Tatius (Latin) king, ruler. History: a Sabine king.

Tatum GB (English) cheerful.

Tau (Tswana) lion.

Taua (Quechua) the fourth child.

Tauacapac (Quechua) the fourth lord.

Tauno (Finnish) a form of Donald.

Taurean **(Latin) strong; forceful. Astrology: born under the sign of Taurus.**

Tauro (Spanish) a form of Toro.

Taurus (Latin) Astrology: the second sign of the zodiac.

Tausiq (Indian) reinforcement.

Tavares (Aramaic) a form of Tavor.

Tavaris, Tavarus (Aramaic) forms of Tavor.

Tavarius (Aramaic) a form of Tavor.

Taved (Estonian) a form of David.

Tavey (Latin) a familiar form of Octavio.

Tavi (Aramaic) good.

Tavian (Latin) a form of Octavio.

Tavin, Tavon (American) forms of Tavian.

Tavion (Latin) a form of Tavian.

Tavis (Scottish) a form of Tavish.

Tavish (Scottish) a form of Thomas.

Tavo (Slavic) a short form of Gustave.

Tavor (Aramaic) misfortune.

Tawfiq (Arabic) success.

Tawno (Gypsy) little one.

Tayib (Hindi) good; delicate.

Tayler GB (English) a form of Taylor.

Taylor GB (English) tailor.

Taymullah (Arabic) servant of God.

Tayshawn (American) a combination of Taylor + Shawn.

Tayvon (American) a form of Tavian.

Tayyeb (Arabic) good.

Taz (Arabic) shallow ornamental cup.

Tazio (Italian) a form of Tatius.

Teagan GB (Irish) a form of Teague.

Teague (Irish) bard, poet.

Teale (English) small freshwater duck.

Tearence (Latin) a form of Terrence.

Tearlach (Scottish) a form of Charles.

Tearle (English) stern, severe.

Teasdale (English) river dweller. Geography: a river in England.

Teb (Spanish) a short form of Stephen.

Ted (English) a short form of Edward, Edwin, Theodore.

Teddy (English) a familiar form of Edward, Theodore.

Tedmund (English) protector of the land.

Tedorik (Polish) a form of Theodore.

Tedrick (American) a combination of Ted + Rick.

Teerthankar (Indian) another form of Tirthankar, a type of Jain god.

Teetonka (Lakota) big lodge.

Tefere (Ethiopian) seed.

Tegan GB (Irish) a form of Teague.

Tehuti (Egyptian) god of earth, air, and sea.

Tej (Sanskrit) light; lustrous.

Tejano (Spanish) Texan man.

Tejas (Sanskrit) sharp. (American) a form of Tex.

Tekle (Ethiopian) plant.

Telek (Polish) a form of Telford.

Telem (Hebrew) mound; furrow.

Telémaco (Greek) he who prepares for battle.

Telesforo (Greek) man from the countryside.

Telford (French) iron cutter.

Teller (English) storyteller.

Telly (Greek) a familiar form of Teller, Theodore.

Telmo (English) tiller, cultivator.

Telutci (Moquelumnan) bear making dust as it runs.

Telvin (American) a combination of the prefix Te + Melvin.

Tem (Gypsy) country.

Teman (Hebrew) on the right side; southward.

Temán (Hebrew) a form of Teman.

Tembo (Swahili) elephant.

Temotzin (Nahuatl) one who descends.

Tempest GB (French) storm.

Temple (Latin) sanctuary.

Templeton **(English) town near the temple.**

Tennant (English) tenant, renter.

Tenner (Irish) Religion: a small form of a rosary.

Tennessee (Cherokee) mighty warrior. Geography: a southern U.S. state.

Tennyson (English) a form of Dennison. Literature: Alfred, Lord Tennyson was a nineteenth-century British poet.

Tenyoa (Nahuatl) of a good family name.

Teo (Vietnamese) a form of Tom.

Teobaldo (Italian, Spanish) a form of Theobald.

Teócrito (Greek) God's chosen one.

Teodoro (Italian, Spanish) a form of Theodore.

Teodosio (Greek) a form of Theodore.

Teófano, Teófilo (Greek) loved by God.

Teon (Greek) a form of Teona .

Teotetl (Nahuatl) divine stone.

Teoxihuitl (Nahuatl) turquoise; precious, divine.

Tepiltzin (Nahuatl) privileged son.

Teppo (French) a familiar form of Stephen.

(Finnish) a form of Tapani.

Tequan (American) a combination of the prefix Te + Quan.

Teraj (Hebrew) wild goat.

Teran, Terran, Terren (Latin) short forms of Terrence.

Terance, Terence, Terrance (Latin) forms of Terrence.

Terciero (Spanish) born third.

Tercio, Tertulio (Greek) the third child.

Terel, Terell, Terelle **(German) forms of Terrell.**
Tereall

Teremun (Tiv) father's acceptance.

Terencio (Spanish) a form of Terrence.

Terez (Greek) a form of Teresa .

Teron (Latin) a form of Teran. (American) a form of Tyrone.

Terrell (German) thunder ruler.

Terrelle BG (German) a form of Terrell.

Terrence (Latin) smooth.

Terrick (American) a combination of the prefix Te + Derric.

Terrill (German) a form of Terrell.

Terrin BG (Latin) a short form of Terrence.

Terrion (American) a form of Terron.

Terris (Latin) son of Terry.

Terron (American) a form of Tyrone.

Terry BG (English) a familiar form of Terrence.

Tertius (Latin) third.

Teseo (Greek) the founder.

Teshawn (American) a combination of the prefix Te + Shawn.

Tetley (English) Tate's meadow.

Tetsuya (Japanese) smart.

Teva (Hebrew) nature.

Tevan, Tevon, Tevyn (American) forms of Tevin.

Tevel (Yiddish) a form of David.

Tevin (American) a combination of the prefix Te + Kevin.

Tevis (Scottish) a form of Thomas.

Tewdor (German) a form of Theodore.

Tex (American) from Texas.

Teyo (Spanish) God.

Tezcacoatl (Nahuatl) reflecting serpent; king.

Thâbet (Arabic) a form of Thabit.

Thabit (Arabic) firm, strong.

Thad (Greek, Latin) a short form of Thaddeus.

Thaddeus (Greek) courageous. (Latin) praiser. Bible: one of the Twelve Apostles. ,

Thadeus (Greek, Latin) a form of Thaddeus.

Thady (Irish) praise.

Thai (Vietnamese) many, multiple.

Thalmus (Greek) flowering.

Thaman (Hindi) god; godlike.

Than (Burmese) million.

Thandie BG (Zulu) beloved.

Thane (English) attendant warrior.

Thang (Vietnamese) victorious.

Thanh BG (Vietnamese) finished.

Thaniel (Hebrew) a short form of Nathaniel.

Thanos (Greek) nobleman; bear-man.

Thatcher (English) roof thatcher, repairer of roofs.

Thaw (English) melting ice.

Thayer (French) nation's army.

Thebault (French) a form of Theobald.

Thel (English) upper story.

Thenga (Yao) bring him.

Theo (English) a short form of Theodore.

Theobald (German) people's prince.

Theodore (Greek) gift of God.

Theodoric (German) ruler of the people.

Theophilus (Greek) loved by God.

Theron (Greek) hunter.

Theros (Greek) summer.

Thiago, Tiago (Portuguese) forms of Diego. (Spanish) forms of James, Jacob.

Thian (Vietnamese) smooth.

Thibault (French) a form of Theobald.

Thien (Vietnamese) a form of Thian.

Thierry (French) a form of Theodoric.

Thiery (French) a form of Thierry.

Thom (English) a short form of Thomas.

Thoma (German) a form of Thomas.

Thomas ⭐ (Greek, Aramaic) twin. Bible: one of the Twelve Apostles.

Thommy (Hebrew) a familiar form of Thomas.

Thompson (English) son of Thomas.

Thor (Scandinavian) thunder. Mythology: the Norse god of thunder.

Thorald (Scandinavian) Thor's follower.

Thorbert (Scandinavian) Thor's brightness.

Thorbjorn (Scandinavian) Thor's bear.

Thorgood (English) Thor is good.

Thorleif (Scandinavian) Thor's beloved.

Thorley (English) Thor's meadow.

Thormond (English) Thor's protection.

Thorndike (English) thorny embankment.

Thorne (English) a short form of names beginning with "Thorn."

Thornley (English) thorny meadow.

Thornton (English) thorny town.

Thorpe **(English) village.**

Thorwald (Scandinavian) Thor's forest.

Thuc (Vietnamese) aware.

Thunder (English) thunder.

Thurlow (English) Thor's hill.

Thurman (English) Thor's servant.

Thurmond (English) defended by Thor.

Thurston (Scandinavian) Thor's stone.

Tiago (Spanish) a form of Jacob.

Tiba (Navajo) gray.

Tibault (French) rules of humankind.

Tibbot (Irish) bold.

Tiberio (Italian) from the Tiber River region.

Tibor (Hungarian) holy place.
Tiburcio, Tybor

Tiburón (Spanish) shark.

Tichawanna (Shona) we shall see.

Ticho (Spanish) a short form of Patrick.

Ticiano (Spanish) a form of Tito.

Tico (Greek) adventurous; fortunate.

Tieler (English) a form of Tyler.

Tien (Chinese) heaven.

Tiennan (French) a form of Stephen.

Tiennot (French) a form of Stephen.

Tiernan (Irish) lord.

Tierney 🄶🄱 (Irish) lordly.

Tige (English) a short form of Tiger.

Tiger (American) tiger; powerful and energetic.

Tighe (Irish) a form of Teague. (English) a short form of Tiger.

Tigrio (Latin) tiger.

Tiimu (Moquelumnan) caterpillar coming out of the ground.

Tiktu (Moquelumnan) bird digging up potatoes.

Tilden (English) tilled valley; tiller of the valley.

Tilford (English) prosperous ford.

Till (German) a short form of Theodoric.

Tilo (Teutonic) skillful and praises God.

Tilton (English) prosperous town.

Tim (Greek) a short form of Timothy.

Timin (Arabic) born near the sea.

Timmie, Timmy (Greek) familiar forms of Timothy.

Timmothy (Greek) a form of Timothy.

Timo (Finnish) a form of Timothy.

Timofey (Russian) a form of Timothy.

Timon (Greek) honorable.

Timoteo (Italian, Portuguese, Spanish) a form of Timothy.

Timoteu (Greek) a form of Timothy.

Timothe, Timothee (Greek) forms of Timothy.

Timothy (Greek) honoring God. ,

Timur (Russian) conqueror. (Hebrew) a form of Tamar.

Tin (Vietnamese) thinker.

Tincupuma, Tinquipoma (Quechua) he who creates much music and dance.

Tino (Spanish) venerable, majestic. (Italian) small. A familiar form of Antonio. (Greek) a short form of Augustine.

Tinsley (English) fortified field.

Tiquan (American) a combination of the prefix Ti + Quan.

Tíquico (Greek) very fortunate person.

Tirrell (German) a form of Terrell.

Tirso (Greek) crowned with fig leaves.

Tishawn (American) a combination of the prefix Ti + Shawn.

Tite (French) a form of Titus.

Tito (Italian) a form of Titus.

Titoatauchi, Tituatauchi (Quechua) he who brings luck in trying times.

Titu (Quechua) difficult, complicated.

Titus (Greek) giant. (Latin) hero. A form of Tatius.

History: a Roman emperor.

Tivon (Hebrew) nature lover.

Tiziano (Latin) the giant.

Tj BG (American) a form of TJ.

TJ BG (American) a combination of the initials T. + J.

Tlacaelel (Nahuatl) diligent person.

Tlacelel (Nahuatl) greatest of our heroes.

Tlachinolli (Nahuatl) fire.

Tláloc (Nahuatl) wine of the earth.

Tlanextic (Nahuatl) the light of dawn.

Tlanextli (Nahuatl) radiance, brilliance; majesty, splendor.

Tlatecuhtli (Nahuatl) gentleman of the earth.

Tlazohtlaloni (Nahuatl) one who is loved.

Tlazopilli (Nahuatl) precious noble.

Tlexictli (Nahuatl) fire navel.

Tlilpotonqui (Nahuatl) feathered in black.

Toan (Vietnamese) complete; mathematics.

Tobal (Spanish) a short form of Christopher.

Tobar (Gypsy) road.

Tobi GB (Yoruba) great.

Tobias (Hebrew) God is good.

Tobías (Hebrew) a form of Tobias.

Tobin (Hebrew) a form of Tobias.

Tobit (Hebrew) son of Tobias.

Toby (Hebrew) a familiar form of Tobias.

Tochtli (Nahuatl) rabbit.

Tod (English) a form of Todd.

Todd (English) fox.

Todor (Basque, Russian) a form of Theodore.

Toft (English) small farm.

Togar (Australian) smoke.

Tohías (Spanish) God is good.

Tohon (Native American) cougar.

Tokala (Dakota) fox.

Tokoni BG (Tongan) assistant, helper.

Toland (English) owner of taxed land.

Tolbert (English) bright tax collector.

Tolenka, Tolya (Russian) one who comes from the east.

Toli (Spanish) plowman.

Toller (English) tax collector.

Tolman (English) tax man.

Tolomeo (Greek) powerful in battle.

Toltecatl, Toltecatli (Nahuatl) artist.

Tom (English) a short form of Thomas, Tomas.

Toma (Romanian) a form of Thomas.

Tomas (German) a form of Thomas.

Tomás (Irish, Spanish) a form of Thomas.

Tomasso (Italian) a form of Thomas.

Tomasz (Polish) a form of Thomas.

Tombe (Kakwa) northerners.

Tomé (Hebrew) the identical twin brother.

Tomer (Hebrew) tall.

Tomey, Tomy (Irish) familiar forms of Thomas.

Tomi GB (Japanese) rich. (Hungarian) a form of Thomas.

Tomkin (English) little Tom.

Tomlin (English) little Tom.

Tommie BG (Hebrew) a familiar form of Thomas. Tommee, Tommey, Tommi

Tommy (Hebrew) a familiar form of Thomas.

Tonatiuh (Nahuatl) sunshine.

Tonatiúh (Nahuatl) the highest heaven and greatest honor for the revolutionaries.

Tonauac (Nahuatl) the one who possesses light.

Tonda (Czech) a form of Tony.

Toney, Toni, Tonny
(Greek, Latin, English)
forms of Tony.

Tong (Vietnamese)
fragrant.

Toni GB (Greek, German,
Slavic) a form of Tony.

Tonio (Italian) a short
form of Antonio.
(Portuguese) a form of
Tony.

Tony (Greek) flourishing.
(Latin) praiseworthy.
(English) a short form of
Anthony. A familiar form
of Remington.

Tooantuh (Cherokee)
spring frog.

Toomas (Estonian) a form
of Thomas.

Topa, Tupa (Quechua)
title of honor.

Topher (Greek) a short
form of Christopher,
Kristopher.

Topo (Spanish) gopher.

Topper (English) hill.
Toper

Tor (Norwegian) thunder.
(Tiv) royalty, king.

Torcuato (Latin) adorned
with a collar or garland.

Toren, Torren (Irish)
short forms of Torrence.

Torey BG (English) a
familiar form of Torr,
Torrence.

Tori GB (English) a familiar
form of Torr, Torrence.

Torian (Irish) a form of
Torin.

Toribio (Greek) he who
makes bows.

Torin (Irish) chief. (Latin,
Irish) a form of Torrence.

Torio (Japanese) tail of a
bird.

Torkel (Swedish) Thor's
cauldron.

Tormey (Irish) thunder
spirit.

Tormod (Scottish) north.

Torn (Irish) a short form of
Torrence.

Toro (Spanish) bull.

Torquil (Danish) Thor's
kettle.

Torr (English) tower.

Torrance (Irish) a form of
Torrence.

Torrence (Irish) knolls.
(Latin) a form of
Terrence.

Torrey BG (English) a
familiar form of Torr,
Torrence.

Torrie GB (English) a
familiar form of Torr,
Torrence.

Torrin (Irish, Latin, Irish)
a form of Torin.

Torry (English) a familiar
form of Torr, Torrence.

Torsten (Scandinavian)
thunderstone.

Toru (Japanese) sea.

Toruato (Latin) adorned
with a necklace.

Tory BG (English) a
familiar form of Torr,
Torrence.

Toshi-Shita (Japanese)
junior.

Tosya (Russian) further
than what is expected.

Tototl (Nahuatl) bird.

Toufic (Lebanese) success.

Toussaint (French) all the
saints.

Tovi (Hebrew) good.

Townley (English) town
meadow.

Townsend (English)
town's end.

Tra'von (American) a form
of Travon.

Trabunco (Mapuche)
meeting at the marsh.

Trace (Irish) a form of
Tracy.

Tracey GB (Irish) a form of
Tracy.

Tracy GB (Greek) harvester.
(Latin) courageous.
(Irish) battler.

Trader (English) well-
trodden path; skilled
worker.

Trae (English) a form of
Trey.

Traevon (American) a
form of Trevon.

Traful (Araucanian) union.

Trahern (Welsh) strong as
iron.

Trai (English) a form of
Trey.

Tramaine (Scottish) a form of Tremaine.

Tranamil (Mapuche) low, scattered light

Tranquilino (Roman) tranquil, serene.

Tránsito (Latin) one who goes on to another life.

Traquan (American) a combination of Travis + Quan.

Trashawn BG (American) a combination of Travis + Shawn.

Trasíbulo (Greek) daring counselor.

Traugott (German) God's truth.

Travaris (French) a form of Travers.

Travell (English) traveler.

Traven (American) a form of Trevon.

Traveon (American) a form of Trevon.

Travers (French) crossroads.

Travion (American) a form of Trevon.

Travis (English) a form of Travers.

Travon (American) a form of Trevon.

Travonte (American) a combination of Travon + the suffix Te.

Tray (English) a form of Trey.

Trayton (English) town full of trees.

Trayvion (American) a form of Trayvon.

Trayvon (American) a combination of Tray + Von.

Trayvond (American) a form of Trayvon.

Tre, Tré (American) forms of Trevon. (English) forms of Trey.

Tre Von (American) a form of Trevon.

Trea (English) a form of Trey.

Treat (English) delight.

Treavon (American) a form of Trevon.

Treavor (Irish, Welsh) a form of Trevor.

Trebor (Irish, Welsh) a form of Trevor.

Trecaman (Mapuche) majestic steps of the condor.

Tredway (English) well-worn road.

Tremaine, Tremayne (Scottish) house of stone.

Trent (Latin) torrent, rapid stream. (French) thirty. Geography: a city in northern Italy.

Trenten (Latin) a form of Trenton.

Trenton (Latin) town by the rapid stream. Geography: the capital of New Jersey.

Trequan (American) a combination of Trey + Quan.

Treshaun (American) a form of Treshawn.

Treshawn (American) a combination of Trey + Shawn.

Treston (Welsh) a form of Tristan.

Trev (Irish, Welsh) a short form of Trevor.

Trevar (Irish, Welsh) a form of Trevor.

Trevaughn (American) a combination of Trey + Vaughn.

Trevell (English) a form of Travell.

Trevelyan (English) Elian's homestead.

Treven, Trevin (American) forms of Trevon.

Treveon (American) a form of Trevon.

Trever (Irish, Welsh) a form of Trevor.

Trevion, Trévion (American) forms of Trevon.

Trevis (English) a form of Travis.

Trevon (American) a combination of Trey + Von.

Trévon, Trevonne (American) forms of Trevon.

Trevond (American) a form of Trevon.

Trevonte (American) a combination of Trevon + the suffix Te.

Trevor (Irish) prudent. (Welsh) homestead.

Trey (English) three; third.

Treyton (English) a form of Trayton.

Treyvon (American) a form of Trevon.

Tri (English) a form of Trey.

Trifón (Greek) having a sumptuous, free-spirited life.

Trigg (Scandinavian) trusty.

Trini GB (Latin) a short form of Trinity.

Trinidad (Latin) a form of Trinity.

Trinity GB (Latin) holy trinity.

Trip, Tripp (English) traveler.

Tristan BG (Welsh) bold. Literature: a knight in the Arthurian legends who fell in love with his uncle's wife.

Tristán (Welsh) a form of Tristan.

Tristano (Italian) a form of Tristan.

Tristen BG (Welsh) a form of Tristan.

Tristian BG (Welsh) a form of Tristan.

Tristin BG (Welsh) a form of Tristan.

Triston BG (Welsh) a form of Tristan.

Tristram (Welsh) sorrowful. Literature: the title character in Laurence Sterne's eighteenth-century novel *Tristram Shandy*.

Tristyn BG (Welsh) a form of Tristan.

Trófimo (Greek) fed.

Troilo (Egyptian) he who was born in Troy.

Trot (English) trickling stream.

Trowbridge (English) bridge by the tree.

Troy BG (Irish) foot soldier. (French) curly haired. (English) water.

True (English) faithful, loyal.

Truesdale (English) faithful one's homestead.

Truitt (English) little and honest.

Truman (English) honest. History: Harry S. Truman was the thirty-third U.S. president.

Trumble (English) strong; bold.

Trung (Vietnamese) central; loyalty.

Trustin (English) trustworthy.

Trygve (Norwegian) brave victor.

Trystan BG (Welsh) a form of Tristan.

Trysten, Tryston (Welsh) forms of Tristan.

Tsalani (Nguni) good-bye.

Tse (Ewe) younger of twins.

Tsekani (Egyptian) closed.

Tu BG (Vietnamese) tree.

Tuaco (Ghanaian) eleventh-born.

Tuan (Vietnamese) goes smoothly.

Tuari (Laguna) young eagle.

Tubal (Hebrew) he who tills the soil.

Tubau (Catalan) a form of Teobaldo.

Tucker (English) fuller, tucker of cloth.

Tudor (Welsh) a form of Theodore. History: an English ruling dynasty.

Tufic (Lebanese) success.

Tug (Scandinavian) draw, pull.

Tuketu (Moquelumnan) bear making dust as it runs.

Tukuli (Moquelumnan) caterpillar crawling down a tree.

Tulio (Italian, Spanish) lively.

Tullis (Latin) title, rank.

Tully BG (Irish) at peace with God. (Latin) a familiar form of Tullis.

Tumaini (Mwera) hope.

Tumu (Moquelumnan) deer thinking about eating wild onions.

Tung (Vietnamese) stately, dignified. (Chinese) everyone.

Tungar (Sanskrit) high; lofty.

Tupac (Quechua) the Lord.

Tupacamaru (Quechua) glorious Amaru.

Tupacapac (Quechua) glorious and kind-hearted lord.

Tupacusi (Quechua) happy and majestic.

Tupaquiupanqui, Tupayupanqui (Quechua) memorable and glorious lord.

Tupi (Moquelumnan) pulled up.

Tupper (English) ram raiser.

Turi (Spanish) a short form of Arthur.

Turk (English) from Turkey.

Turlough (Irish) thunder shaped.

Turner (Latin) lathe worker; wood worker.

Turpin (Scandinavian) Finn named after Thor.

Tusya (Russian) surpassing expectations.

Tut (Arabic) strong and courageous. History: a short form of

Tutankhamen, an Egyptian king.

Tutu (Spanish) a familiar form of Justin.

Tuvya (Hebrew) a form of Tobias.

Tuwile (Mwera) death is inevitable.

Tuxford (Scandinavian) shallow river crossing.

Tuyen GB (Vietnamese) angel.

Twain (English) divided in two. Literature: Mark Twain (whose real name was Samuel Langhorne Clemens) was one of the most prominent nineteenth-century American writers.

Twia (Fante) born after twins.

Twitchell (English) narrow passage.

Twyford (English) double river crossing.

Txomin (Basque) like the Lord.

Ty BG (English) a short form of Tyler, Tyrone, Tyrus.

Tybalt (Greek) people's prince.

Tyce (French) a form of Tyson.

Tye (English) a form of Ty.

Tyee (Native American) chief.

Tyger (English) a form of Tiger.

Tyjuan (American) a form of Tajuan.

Tylar BG (English) a form of Tyler.

Tyler ☆
BG (English) tile maker.

Tylor BG (English) a form of Tyler.

Tymon (Polish) a form of Timothy. (Greek) a form of Timon.

Tymothy (English) a form of Timothy.

Tynan (Irish) dark.

Tynek (Czech) a form of Martin.

Tyquan (American) a combination of Ty + Quan.

Tyran, Tyren, Tyrin, Tyron (American) forms of Tyrone.

Tyre (Scottish) a form of Tyree.

Tyrece, Tyrese, Tyrice (American) forms of Tyreese.

Tyree BG (Scottish) island dweller. Geography: Tiree is an island off the west coast of Scotland.

Tyrée (Scottish) a form of Tyree.

Tyreek (American) a form of Tyrick.

Tyreese (American) a form of Terrence.

Tyrek, Tyrik, Tyriq
(American) forms of
Tyrick.

Tyrel, Tyrell, Tyrelle
(American) forms of
Terrell.

Tyrez (American) a form of
Tyreese.

Tyrick (American) a
combination of Ty + Rick.

Tyrone (Greek) sovereign.
(Irish) land of Owen.

Tyrus (English) a form of
Thor.

Tysen (French) a form of
Tyson.

Tyshaun, Tyshon
(American) forms of
Tyshawn.

Tyshawn (American) a
combination of Ty +
Shawn.

Tyson (French) son of Ty.

Tytus (Polish) a form of
Titus.

Tyus (Polish) a form of
Tytus.

Tyvon (American) a
combination of Ty + Von.
(Hebrew) a form of Tivon.

Tywan, Tywon (Chinese)
forms of Taiwan.

Tzadok (Hebrew)
righteous. **Tzion**
(Hebrew) sign from God.
Tzuriel (Hebrew) God is
my rock.

Tzvi (Hebrew) deer.

U

Uaine (Irish) a form of
Owen.

Ualtar (Irish) a form of
Walter.

Ualusi (Tongan) walrus.

Ubadah (Arabic) serves
God.

Ubaid (Arabic) faithful.

Ubalde (French) a form of
Ubaldus.

Ubaldo (Italian) a form of
Ubaldus.

Ubaldus (Teutonic) peace
of mind.

Ubayd (Arabic) faithful.

Ubayda (Arabic) servant of
God.

Ubayy (Arabic) boy.

Uberto (Italian) a form of
Hubert.

Ucello (Italian) bird.

Uche (Ibo) thought.

Uchit (Indian) correct.

Uchu (Quechua) hot like
pepper.

Ucumari (Quechua) he
who has the strength of a
bear.

Udant (Hindi) correct
message.

Udar (Indian) generous.

Udarsh (Hindi) brimming.

Uday (Sanskrit) to rise.

Udayachal (Indian)
eastern horizon.

Udayan (Indian) rising;
king of the city of Avanti.

Udbal (Hindi) mighty.

Udbhav (Indian) creation;
to arise from.

Uddhar (Indian)
liberation.

Uddhav (Indian) friend of
the Hindu god Krishna.

Uddip (Indian) giving light.

Uddiyan (Indian) flying
speed.

Udell (English) yew-tree
valley.

Udeep (Indian) flood.

Udit (Sanskrit) grown;
shining.

Udo (Japanese) ginseng
plant. (German) a short
form of Udolf.

Udolf (English) prosperous
wolf.

Udu (Hindi) water.

Udyam (Indian) effort.

Udyan (Indian) garden.

Ueli (Swiss) noble ruler.

Ueman (Nahuatl)
venerable time.

Uetzcayotl (Nahuatl) the
essence of light.

Ufa (Egyptian) flower.

Uffo (German) wild bear.

Ugo (Italian) a form of
Hugh, Hugo.

Ugutz (Basque) a form of
John.

Uhila (Tongan) lightning.

Uilliam (Irish) a form of
William.

Uinseann (Irish) a form of
Vincent.

Uistean (Irish) intelligent.

Uja (Sanskrit) growing.

Ujagar, Ujala, Ujjala, Ujwal (Indian) bright.

Ujas (Indian) first light.

Ujendra (Indian) conqueror.

Ujesh (Indian) one who bestows light.

Ujjay (Indian) victorious.

Ujjwal (Indian) splendorous.

Uku (Hawaiian) flea, insect; skilled ukulele player.

Ulan (African) first-born twin.

Ulbrecht (German) a form of Albert.

Uldric (Lettish) a form of Aldrich.

Uleki (Hawaiian) wrathful.

Ulf (German) wolf.

Ulfer (German) warrior fierce as a wolf.

Ulfred (German) peaceful wolf.

Ulfrido (Teutonic) he imposes peace through force.

Ulger (German) warring wolf.

Ulhas (Indian) happiness.

Ulices (Latin) a form of Ulysses.

Ulick (Scandinavian) bright, rewarding mind.

Ulises, Ulisses (Latin) forms of Ulysses.

Ullanta, Ullantay (Aymara) the warrior who sees everything from his watchtower.

Ullas (Indian) light.

Ullivieri (Italian) olive tree.

Ullock (German) sporting wolf.

Ulmer (English) famous wolf.

Umio (Japanese) sea hero.

Ulmo (German) from Ulm, Germany.

Ulpiano, Ulpio (Latin) sly as a fox.

Ulric (German) a form of Ulrich.

Ulrich (German) wolf ruler; ruler of all.

Ultan (German) noble stone.

Ultman (Hindi) god; godlike.

Ulyses (Latin) a form of Ulysses.

Ulysses (Latin) wrathful. A form of Odysseus.

Umanant, Umakant, Umanand, Umashankar, Umesh (Indian) other names for the Hindu god Shiva.

Umang (Sanskrit) enthusiastic.

Umaprasad (Indian) blessing of the Hindu goddess Parvati.

Umar (Arabic) a form of Omar.

Umara (Arabic) a form of Umar.

Umberto (Italian) a form of Humbert.

Umed (Indian) hope.

Umi (Yao) life.

Umit (Turkish) hope.

Umrao (Indian) noble; king.

Unai (Basque) shepherd.

Unay (Quechua) remote, underlying.

Uner (Turkish) famous.

Unika GB (Lomwe) brighten.

Unique GB (Latin) only, unique.

Unity GB (English) unity.

Unmesh (Indian) revelation.

Unnabh (Hindi) highest.

Unnat, Urjita (Indian) energized.

Uno (Latin) one; first-born.

Unwin (English) nonfriend.
Unwinn, Unwyn

Upagupta (Indian) Buddhist monk.

Upamanyu (Indian) devoted pupil.

Upanshu (Indian) chanting of hymns or mantras in low tone.

Upendra (Indian) another name for the Hindu god Vishnu.

Uppas (Indian) gem.

Upshaw (English) upper wooded area.

Upton (English) upper town.

Upwood (English) upper forest.

Uqbah (Indian) the end of everything.

Urav (Indian) excitement.

Ur, Uratum (Egyptian) great.

Urania (Greek) blind.

Urban (Latin) city dweller; courteous.

Urbane (English) a form of Urban.

Urbano (Italian) a form of Urban.

Urcucolla (Quechua) hill.

Uri 🄱🄶 (Hebrew) a short form of Uriah.

Uriá (Hebrew) a form of Uriah.

Uriah (Hebrew) my light. Bible: a soldier and the husband of Bathsheba.

Urian (Greek) heaven.

Urías (Greek) light of the Lord.

Uriel (Hebrew) God is my light.

Urso (Latin) a form of Urson.

Urson (French) a form of Orson.

Urtzi (Basque) sky.

Urvang (Indian) mountain.

Urvil (Hindi) sea.

Usaamah (Indian) description of a lion.

Usaku (Japanese) moonlit.

Usama (Arabic) a form of Usamah.

Usamah (Arabic) like a lion.

Usco, Uscouiyca, Uscu, Uscuiyca (Quechua) wild cat.

Useni (Yao) tell me.

Ushakanta (Indian) sun.

Ushapati (Indian) husband of dawn.

Usher (English) doorkeeper.

Ushi (Chinese) ox.

Usi (Yao) smoke.

Usman (Arabic) a form of Uthman.

Ustin (Russian) a form of Justin.

Usuy (Quechua) he who brings abundances.

Utanka (Indian) a disciple of the sage Veda.

Utatci (Moquelumnan) bear scratching itself.

Utba (Arabic) boy.

Uthman (Arabic) companion of the Prophet.

Utkarsh (Hindi) high quality.

Utkarsha (Indian) advancement.

Utpal (Indian) burst open.

Utsav (Indian) festival.

Uttam (Sanskrit) best.

Uttiya (Indian) a name in Buddhist literature.

Uturuncu (Quechua) jaguar.

Uturuncu Achachi (Quechua) he who has brave ancestors.

Uwe (German) a familiar form of Ulrich.

Uxío (Greek) born into nobility.

Uzair (Arabic) helpful.
Uzaire, Uzayr, Uzayre

Uzi (Hebrew) my strength.

Uziel (Hebrew) God is my strength; mighty force.

Uzoma (Nigerian) born during a journey.

Uzumati (Moquelumnan) grizzly bear.

V

Vachan (Indian) speech.

Vachel (French) small cow.

Vaclav (Czech) wreath of glory.

Vadin (Hindi) speaker.

Vaibhav (Indian) riches.

Vaijnath (Indian) another name for the Hindu god Shiva.

Vail 🄱🄶 (English) valley.

Vaina (Finnish) river's mouth.

Vajra (Indian) great-grandson of the Hindu god Krishna; diamond.

Vajradhar, Vajrapani (Indian) other names of the Hindu god Indra.

Val BG **(Latin) a short form of Valentin.**

Valarico (Germanic) leader of the battle.

Valborg (Swedish) mighty mountain.

Valdemar (Swedish) famous ruler.

Valdo (Teutonic) he who governs.

Valdus (German) powerful.

Valente (Italian) a form of Valentin.

Valentin (Latin) strong; healthy.

Valentín (Latin) a form of Valentin.

Valentino (Italian) a form of Valentin.

Valere (French) a form of Valerian.

Valerian (Latin) strong; healthy.

Valerii (Russian) a form of Valerian.

Valero (Latin) valiant.

Valfredo (Germanic) the peaceful king.

Valfrid (Swedish) strong peace.

Valgard (Scandinavian) foreign spear.

Vali (Tongan) paint.

Valiant (French) valiant.

Valin (Hindi) a form of Balin.

Vallabh (Indian) beloved.

Vallis (French) from Wales.

Valmik, Valmiki (Indian) author of the Indian epic poem *Ramayana*.

Valter (Lithuanian, Swedish) a form of Walter.

Vaman (Indian) fifth incarnation of the Hindu god Vishnu.

Vamana (Sanskrit) praiseworthy.
Vamanah

Vamsi (Indian) name of a raga, an ancient form of Hindu devotional music.

Van BG (Dutch) a short form of Vandyke.
Vane,

Vanajit (Indian) lord of the forest.

Vance (English) thresher.

Vanda GB (Lithuanian) a form of Walter.

Vandan (Hindi) saved.

Vander (Dutch) belongs.

Vandyke (Dutch) dyke.

Vann (Dutch) a short form of Vandyke.

Vanya BG (Russian) a familiar form of Ivan.

Vanyusha (Russian) gift from God.

Varad (Hungarian) from the fortress.

Vardhaman (Indian) another name for Mahavir, the twenty-fourth and last Tirthankar, a type of Jain god.

Vardon (French) green knoll.

Varen (Hindi) better.

Varian (Latin) variable.

Varick (German) protecting ruler.

Varij (Indian) lotus.

Varil (Hindi) water.
Varal, Varel, Varol, Varyl

Varindra (Indian) another name for the Hindu god Varun, lord of the waters.

Vartan (Armenian) rose producer; rose giver.

Varun (Hindi) rain god.

Vasant (Sanskrit) spring.

Vashawn (American) a combination of the prefix Va + Shawn.

Vashon (American) a form of Vashawn.

Vasilios (Italian) a form of Vasilis.

Vasilis (Greek) a form of Basil.

Vasily (Russian) a form of Vasilis.

Vasin (Hindi) ruler, lord.

Vasishtha, Vasistha (Indian) an ancient Indian sage.

Vasu (Sanskrit) wealth.

Vasudev (Indian) father of the Hindu god Krishna.

Vasudha (Indian) earth.

Vasyl (German, Slavic) a form of William.

Vatsal (Indian) affectionate.

Vaughan (Welsh) a form of Vaughn.

Vaughn (Welsh) small.

Veasna (Cambodian) lucky.

Ved (Sanskrit) sacred knowledge.

Vedanga (Indian) meaning of Vedas, Hindu scriptures.

Vedavrata (Indian) vow of the Vedas, Hindu scriptures.

Vedie (Latin) sight.

Vedmohan (Indian) another name for the Hindu god Krishna.

Vedprakash (Indian) light of the Vedas, Hindu scriptures.

Veer (Sanskrit) brave.

Veera (Indian) brave.

Vegard (Norwegian) sanctuary; protection.

Veiko (Finnish) brother.

Veit (Swedish) wide.

Velvel (Yiddish) wolf.

Venancio (Latin) a fan of hunting.

Vencel (Hungarian) a short form of Wenceslaus.

Venceslao (Slavic) crowned with glory.

Venedictos (Greek) a form of Benedict.

Veni (Indian) another name for the Hindu god Krishna.

Veniamin (Bulgarian) a form of Benjamin.

Venkat (Hindi) god; godlike. Religion: another name for the Hindu god Vishnu.

Ventura (Latin) he who will be happy.

Venturo (Spanish) good fortune.

Venya (Russian) a familiar form of Benedict.

Verdun (French) fort on a hill. Geography: a city in France and in Quebec, Canada.

Vere (Latin, French) true.

Vered (Hebrew) rose.

Vergil (Latin) a form of Virgil. Literature: a Roman poet best known for his epic poem *Aenid*.

Verlin (Latin) blooming.

Vermundo (Spanish) protective bear.

Vern (Latin) a short form of Vernon.

Vernados (German) courage of the bear.

Vernell **(Latin) a form of Vernon.**

Verner (German) defending army.

Verney (French) alder grove.

Vernon (Latin) springlike; youthful.

Vero (Latin) truthful, credible.

Verrill (German) masculine. (French) loyal.

Vespasiano (Latin) the name of a Roman emperor.

Veston (English) church town.

Veto (Spanish) intelligent.

Vian (English) a short form of Vivian .

Vibert (American) a combination of Vic + Bert.

Vic (Latin) a short form of Victor.

Vicar (Latin) priest, cleric.

Vicente (Spanish) a form of Vincent.
Vicent, Visente

Vicenzo (Italian) a form of Vincent.

Victoir (French) a form of Victor.

Victor (Latin) victor, conqueror.

Víctor (Spanish) a form of Victor.

Victoriano (Spanish) a form of Victor.

Victorio (Spanish) a form of Victor.

Victormanuel (Spanish) a combination of Victor + Manuel.

Victoro (Latin) a form of Victor.

Vidal ⓑⓖ (Spanish) a form of Vitas.

Vidar (Norwegian) tree warrior.

Videl (Spanish) a form of Vidal.

Vidor (Hungarian) cheerful.

Vidur (Hindi) wise.

Vidya (Sanskrit) wise.

Viet (Vietnamese) Vietnamese.

Vigberto (Germanic) one who shines in battle.

Vihaan (Sanskrit) first ray of light; dawn; morning.

Viho (Cheyenne) chief.

Vijai (Hindi) a form of Vijay.

Vijay (Hindi) victorious.

Vikas (Hindi) growing.

Viking (Scandinavian) Viking; Scandinavian.

Vikram (Hindi) valorous.

Vikrant (Hindi) powerful.

Viktor (German, Hungarian, Russian) a form of Victor.

Vilfredo (Germanic) the peaceful king.

Vilhelm (German) a form of William.

Vili (Hungarian) a short form of William.

Viliam (Czech) a form of William.

Viljo (Finnish) a form of William.

Ville (Swedish) a short form of William.

Vimal (Hindi) pure.

Vin (Latin) a short form of Vincent.

Vinay (Hindi) polite.

Vince (English) a short form of Vincent.

Vincens (German) a form of Vincent.

Vincent ⓑⓖ (Latin) victor, conqueror. .

Vincente (Spanish) a form of Vincent.

Vincenzo (Italian) a form of Vincent.

Vinci (Hungarian, Italian) a familiar form of Vincent.

Vinny (English) a familiar form of Calvin, Melvin, Vincent.

Vinod (Hindi) happy, joyful.

Vinson (English) son of Vincent.

Vipul (Hindi) plentiful.

Viraj (Hindi) resplendent.

Virat (Hindi) very big.

Virgil (Latin) rod bearer, staff bearer.

Virgilio (Spanish) a form of Virgil.

Virginio (Latin) he is pure and simple.

Virote (Tai) strong, powerful.

Virxilio (Latin) a form of Virgil.

Vishal (Hindi) huge; great.

Vishnu (Hindi) protector.

Vitaliano, Vitalicio (Latin) young and strong.

Vitalis (Latin) life; alive.

Vitas (Latin) alive, vital.

Vito (Latin) a short form of Vittorio.

Vítor (Latin) a form of Victor.

Vitoriano (Latin) the victor.

Vittorio (Italian) a form of Victor.

Vitya (Russian) a form of Victor.

Vivaan (Hindi) full of life.

Vivek (Hindi) wisdom.

Viviano (Spanish) small man.

Vlad (Russian) a short form of Vladimir, Vladislav. Vladd, Vladik, Vladko

Vladimir (Russian) famous prince.
  Vladimiro (Spanish) a form of Vladimir.

Vladislav (Slavic) glorious ruler. **Vlas** (Russian) a short form of Vladislav.

Vogel (German) bird.

Volker (German) people's guard.

Volley (Latin) flying.

Volney (German) national spirit.

Von (German) a short form of many German names. (Welsh) a form of Vaughn.

Vova (Russian) a form of Walter.

Vuai (Swahili) savior.

Vulpiano (Latin) sly as a fox.

Vyacheslav (Russian) a form of Vladislav. .

W

Wa`El (Arabic) one who goes toward salvation.

Waban (Ojibwa) white.

Wade (English) ford; river crossing.

Wâdî (Arabic) calm, peaceful.

Wadih (Lebanese) alone.

Wadley (English) ford meadow.

Wadsworth (English) village near the ford.

Wael (English) a form of Wales.

Wafic (Lebanese) arbitrator.

Wafiq (Arabic) successful.

Wagner (German) wagoner, wagon maker. Music: Richard Wagner was a famous nineteenth-century German composer.

Wahab (Indian) large-hearted.

Wâhed (Arabic) a form of Wahid.

Wahid (Arabic) single; exclusively unequaled.

Wahkan (Lakota) sacred.

Wahkoowah (Lakota) charging.

Wain (English) a short form of Wainwright. A form of Wayne.

Wainwright (English) wagon maker.

Waite (English) watchman.

Wajidali (Indian) obsessed.

Wake (English) awake, alert.

Wakefield (English) wet field.

Wakely (English) wet meadow.

Wakeman (English) watchman.

Wakîl (Arabic) lawyer.

Wakiza (Native American) determined warrior**.**

Walberto (Germanic) one who remains in power.

Walby (English) house near a wall.

Walcott (English) cottage by the wall.

Waldemar (German) powerful; famous.

Walden (English) wooded valley. Literature: Henry David Thoreau made Walden Pond famous with his book *Walden*.

Waldino (Teutonic) having an open and bold spirit.

Waldo (German) a familiar form of Oswald, Waldemar, Walden.

Waldron (English) ruler.

Waleed (Arabic) newborn.

Walerian (Polish) strong; brave.

Wales (English) from Wales.

Walford (English) Welshman's ford.

Walfred (German) peaceful ruler.

Wali (Arabic) all-governing.

Walid (Arabic) a form of Waleed.

Walîd (Arabic) a form of Walid.

Walker 🇧🇬 (English) cloth walker; cloth cleaner.

Wallace (English) from Wales.

Wallach (German) a form of Wallace.

Waller (German) powerful. (English) wall maker.

Wallis 🇬🇧 (English) a form of Wallace.

Wally (English) a familiar form of Walter.

Walmond (German) mighty ruler.

Walsh (English) a form of Wallace.

Walt (English) a short form of Walter, Walton.

Walter (German) army ruler, general. (English) woodsman.

Walther (German) a form of Walter.

Waltier (French) a form of Walter.

Walton (English) walled town.

Waltr (Czech) a form of Walter.

Walworth (English) fenced-in farm.

Walwyn (English) Welsh friend.

Wamblee (Lakota) eagle.

Wanbi (Australian) wild dingo.

Wanda (Germanic) boss of the hoodlums.

Wang (Chinese) hope; wish.

Wanikiya (Lakota) savior.

Wanya (Russian) a form of Vanya.

Wapi (Native American) lucky.

Warburton (English) fortified town.

Ward (English) watchman, guardian.
Warde

Wardell (English) watchman's hill.

Warden (English) valley guardian.

Wardley (English) watchman's meadow.

Ware (English) wary, cautious. (German) a form of Warren.

Warfield (English) field near the weir or fish trap.

Warford (English) ford near the weir or fish trap.

Warick (English) town hero.

Warley (English) meadow near the weir or fish trap.

Warmond (English) true guardian.

Warner (German) armed defender. (French) park keeper.

Warren (German) general; warden; rabbit hutch.

Warton (English) town near the weir or fish trap.

Warwick (English) buildings near the weir or fish trap.

Waseem (Arabic) a form of Wasim.

Washburn (English) overflowing river.

Washington (English) town near water. History: George Washington was the first U.S. president.

Wasili (Russian) a form of Basil.

Wasim (Arabic) graceful; good-looking.
Wassim, Wasym

Wâsim (Arabic) a form of Wasim.

Watende (Nyakyusa) there will be revenge.
Watend

Waterio (Spanish) a form of Walter.

Watford (English) wattle ford; dam made of twigs and sticks.
Wattford

Watkins (English) son of Walter.

Watson (English) son of Walter.

Waverly GB (English) quaking aspen-tree meadow.

Wayde (English) a form of Wade.

Wayland (English) a form of Waylon.

Waylon (English) land by the road.

Wayman (English) road man; traveler.

Wayne (English) wagon maker. A short form of Wainwright.

Wazir (Arabic) minister.
Wazyr

Wazîr (Arabic) a form of Wazir.

Webb (English) weaver.

Weber (German) weaver.

Webley (English) weaver's meadow.

Webster (English) weaver.
Webstar

Wcddel (English) valley near the ford.
Weddell, Wedel, Wedell

Wei-Quo (Chinese) ruler of the country.

Weiss (German) white.

Welborne (English) spring-fed stream.

Welby (German) farm near the well.

Weldon (English) hill near the well.

Welfel (Yiddish) a form of William.
Welvel

Welford (English) ford near the well.
Wellford

Wellington (English) rich man's town. History: the Duke of Wellington was the British general who defeated Napoleon at Waterloo.

Wells (English) springs.

Welsh (English) a form of Wallace, Walsh.

Welton (English) town near the well.

Wemilat (Native American) all give to him.

Wemilo (Native American) all speak to him.

Wen (Gypsy) born in winter.

Wenceslaus (Slavic) wreath of honor.

Wendel (German, English) a form of Wendell.

Wendell (German) wanderer. (English) good dale, good valley.

Wene (Hawaiian) a form of Wayne.

Wenford (English) white ford.

Wenlock (Welsh) monastery lake.
Wenloc, Wenloch, Wenlok

Wensley (English) clearing in a meadow.

Wentworth (English) pale man's settlement.

Wenutu (Native American) clear sky.

Wenzel (Slavic) knowing. A form of Wenceslaus.

Werner (English) a form of Warner.

Wes (English) a short form of Wesley.

Wesh (Gypsy) woods.

Wesley BG (English) western meadow.

Wesly (English) a form of Wesley.

West (English) west. A short form of Weston.

Westbrook (English) western brook.

Westby (English) western farmstead.

Westcott (English) western cottage.

Westin (English) a form of Weston.

Westley (English) a form of Wesley.

Weston (English) western town.

Wetherby (English) wether-sheep farm.

Wetherell (English) wether-sheep corner.

Wetherly (English) wether-sheep meadow.

Weylin (English) a form of Waylon.

Whalley (English) woods near a hill.

Wharton (English) town on the bank of a lake.

Wheatley (English) wheat field.

Wheaton (English) wheat town.

Wheeler (English) wheel maker; wagon driver.

Whistler (English) whistler, piper.

Whit (English) a short form of Whitman, Whitney.

Whitby (English) white house.

Whitcomb (English) white valley.

Whitelaw (English) small hill.

Whitey (English) white skinned; white haired.
Whitee, Whiti, Whitie, Whity

Whitfield (English) white field.

Whitford (English) white ford.

Whitley GB (English) white meadow.

Whitlock (English) white lock of hair.

Whitman (English) white-haired man.
Whit, Whitmen, Whytman, Whytmen

Whitmore (English) white moor.

Whitney GB (English) white island; white water.

Whittaker (English) white field.

Wicasa (Dakota) man.

Wicent (Polish) a form of Vincent.

Wichado (Native American) willing.

Wickham (English) village enclosure.

Wickley (English) village meadow.

Wid (English) wide.

Wies (German) renowned warrior.

Wikoli (Hawaiian) a form of Victor.

Wiktor (Polish) a form of Victor.

Wil, Will (English) short forms of Wilfred, William.

Wilanu (Moquelumnan) pouring water on flour.

Wilber (English) a form of Wilbur.

Wilbert (German) brilliant; resolute.

Wilbur (English) wall fortification; bright willows.

Wilder (English) wilderness, wild.

Wildon (English) wooded hill.

Wile (Hawaiian) a form of Willie.

Wiley (English) willow meadow; Will's meadow.

Wilford (English) willow-tree ford.

Wilfred (German) determined peacemaker.

Wilfredo, Wilfrido (Spanish) forms of Wilfred.

Wilhelm (German) determined guardian.

Wiliama (Hawaiian) a form of William.

Wilkie (English) a familiar form of Wilkins.

Wilkins (English) William's kin.

Wilkinson (English) son of little William.

Willard (German) determined and brave.

Willem (German) a form of Wilhelm, William.

William ☆

BG (English) a form of Wilhelm.

Williams (German) son of William.

Willie BG (German) a familiar form of William.

Willis (German) son of Willie.

Willoughby (English) willow farm.

Wills (English) son of Will.

Willy (German) a familiar form of William.

Wilmer (German) determined and famous.

Wilmot (Teutonic) resolute spirit.

Wilny (Native American) eagle singing while flying.

Wilson (English) son of Will.

Wilstan (German) wolf stone.

Wilt (English) a short form of Wilton.

Wilton (English) farm by the spring.

Wilu (Moquelumnan) chicken hawk squawking.

Win BG (Cambodian) bright. (English) a short form of Winston and names ending in "win."

Wincent (Polish) a form of Vincent.

Winchell (English) bend in the road; bend in the land.

Windell (English) windy valley.

Windsor (English) riverbank with a winch. History: the surname of the British royal family.

Winfield (English) friendly field.

Winfred (English) a form of Winfield. (German) a form of Winfried.

Winfried (German) friend of peace.

Wing GB (Chinese) glory.

Wingate (English) winding gate.

Wingi (Native American) willing.

Winslow (English) friend's hill.

Winston (English) friendly town; victory town.

Winter GB (English) born in winter.

Winthrop (English) victory at the crossroads.

Winton (English) a form of Winston.

Winward (English) friend's guardian; friend's forest.

Wit (Polish) life. (English) a form of Whit. (Flemish) a **short form of DeWitt.**

Witek (Polish) a form of Victor.

Witha (Arabic) handsome.

Witter (English) wise warrior.

Witton (English) wise man's estate.

Wladislav (Polish) a form of Vladislav.

Wolcott (English) cottage in the woods.

Wolf (German, English) a short form of Wolfe, Wolfgang.

Wolfe (English) wolf.

Wolfgang (German) wolf quarrel. Music: Wolfgang Amadeus Mozart was a famous eighteenth-century Austrian composer.

Wood (English) a short form of Elwood, Garwood, Woodrow.

Woodfield (English) forest meadow.
Woodfyeld

Woodford **(English) ford through the forest.**

Woodley **(English) wooded meadow.**

Woodrow (English) passage in the woods. History: Thomas Woodrow Wilson was the twenty-eighth U.S. president.

Woodruff (English) forest ranger.

Woodson (English) son of Wood.

Woodville (English) town at the edge of the woods.

Woodward (English) forest warden.

Woody (American) a familiar form of Elwood, Garwood, Wood, Woodrow.

Woolsey (English) victorious wolf.

Worcester (English) forest army camp.

Wordsworth (English) wolf-guardian's farm. Literature: William Wordsworth was a famous British poet.

Worie (Ibo) born on market day.

Worrell (English) lives at the manor of the loyal one.

Worth (English) a short form of Wordsworth.

Worton (English) farm town.

Wouter (German) powerful warrior.

Wrangle (American) a form of Rangle.

Wray (Scandinavian) corner property. (English) crooked.

Wren BG (Welsh) chief, ruler. (English) wren.

Wright (English) a short form of Wainwright.

Wrisley (English) a form of Risley.

Wriston (English) a form of Riston.

Wuliton (Native American) will do well.

Wunand (Native American) God is good.

Wuyi (Moquelumnan) turkey vulture flying.

Wyatt ☀ (French) little warrior.

Wybert (English) battle bright.

Wyborn (Scandinavian) war bear.

Wyck (Scandinavian) village.

Wycliff (English) white cliff; village near the cliff.

Wylie (English) charming.

Wyman (English) fighter, warrior.

Wymer (English) famous in battle.

Wyn (Welsh) light skinned; white. (English) friend. A short form of Selwyn.

Wyndham (Scottish) village near the winding road.

Wynono (Native American) first-born son.

Wynton (English) a form of Winston.

Wythe (English) willow tree.

X

Xabat (Basque) savior.

Xacinto (Greek) the hyacinth flower.

Xacob (Galician) a form of Jacob.

Xacobo, Xaime (Hebrew) second son.

Xaiver (Basque) a form of Xavier.

Xalbador, Xalvador (Spanish) savior.

Xan (Greek) a short form of Alexander.

Xander (Greek) a short form of Alexander.

Xanthippus (Greek) light-colored horse.

Xanthus (Latin) golden haired.

Xarles (Basque) a form of Charles.

Xaver (Spanish) a form of Xavier.

Xavier
BG (Arabic) bright. (Basque) owner of the new house.

Xenaro (Latin) porter.

Xeneroso (Latin) generous.

Xenophon (Greek) strange voice.

Xenos (Greek) stranger; guest.

Xenxo (Greek) protector of the family.

Xerardo (German) a form of Gerardo.

Xerman (Galician) a form of German.

Xerome, Xerónimo, Xes (Greek) saintly name.

Xerxes (Persian) ruler. History: a king of Persia.
Xeres, Xerus, Zerk, Zerzes

Xesús (Hebrew) savior.

Xeven (Slavic) lively.
Xyven

Xian (Galician) a form of Julian.

Xián, Xiao, Xillao, Xulio (Latin) from the Lulia family.

Xicohtencatl (Nahuatl) angry bumblebee.

Xicoténcatl (Nahuatl) from the place of the reefs.

Xihuitl (Nahuatl) year; comet.

Xil (Greek) young goat.

Xilberte, Xilberto (German) forms of Gilbert.

Xildas (German) taxes.

Ximén (Spanish) obedient.

Ximenes (Spanish) a form of Simon.

Xipil (Nahuatl) noble of the fire.

Xipilli (Nahuatl) jeweled prince.

Xiuhcoatl (Nahuatl) fire serpent; weapon of destruction.

Xiutecuhtli (Nahuatl) gentleman of the fire.

Xoan (Hebrew) God is good.

Xoaquín (Hebrew) a form of Joaquín.

Xob (Hebrew) persecuted, afflicted.

Xochiel, Xochitl, Xochtiel (Nahuatl) flower.

Xochipepe (Nahuatl) flower gatherer.

Xólotl (Nahuatl) precious twin.

Xorxe, Xurxo (Greek) tiller of the soil.

Xose (Galician) a form of Jose.

Xosé (Hebrew) seated on the right-hand side of God.

Xudas (Hebrew) a form of Judas.

Xusto (Latin) fair, just.

Xylon (Greek) forest.

Xzavier (Basque) a form of Xavier.

Y

Yaaseen (Indian) another name for Muhammad, the founder of Islam.

Yabarak (Australian) sea.

Yacu (Quechua) water.

Yad (Lebanese) jade.

Yadav, Yadavendra, Yadunandan, Yadunath, Yaduraj, Yaduvir, Yajnarup (Indian) other names for the Hindu god Krishna.

Yadid (Hebrew) friend; beloved.

Yadon (Hebrew) he will judge.

Yael 🇬🇧 (Hebrew) a form of Jael.

Yafeu (Ibo) bold.

Yagil (Hebrew) he will rejoice.

Yagna (Indian) ceremonial rites to God.

Yago (Spanish) a form of James.

Yaguatí (Guarani) leopard.

Yahto (Lakota) blue.

Yahya (Arabic) living.

Yahyaa (Indian) prophet.

Yahye (Arabic) a form of Yahya.

Yair (Hebrew) he will enlighten.

Yaj (Indian) a sage.

Yajat, Yamajit (Indian) other names for the Hindu god Shiva.

Yajnadhar, Yajnesh, Yamahil (Indian) other names for the Hindu god Vishnu.

Yakecen (Dene) sky song.

Yakez (Carrier) heaven.

Yakir (Hebrew) honored.

Yakov (Russian) a form of Jacob.

Yale (German) productive. (English) old.

Yaman (Indian) another name for Yama, the Hindu god of death.

Yamil (Arabic) a form of Yamila .

Yamir (Indian) moon.

Yamqui (Aymara) title of nobility.

Yan, Yann (Russian) forms of John.

Yana 🇧🇬 (Native American) bear.

Yanamayu (Quechua) black river.

Yancey (Native American) a form of Yancy.

Yancy (Native American) Englishman, Yankee.

Yang (Chinese) people of goat tongue.

Yanick, Yanik, Yannick (Russian) familiar forms of Yan.

Yanka (Russian) a familiar form of John.

Yanni (Greek) a form of John.

Yanton (Hebrew) a form of Johnathon, Jonathen.

Yanuario (Latin) voyage.

Yao (Ewe) born on Thursday.

Yaotl (Nahuatl) war; warrior.

Yaphet (Hebrew) a form of Japheth.
Yapheth, Yefat, Yephat

Yarb (Gypsy) herb.

Yardan (Arabic) king.

Yarden (Hebrew) a form of Jordan.

Yardley (English) enclosed meadow.

Yarom (Hebrew) he will raise up.

Yaron (Hebrew) he will sing; he will cry out.

Yasaar (Indian) ease; wealth.

Yasâr, Yassêr (Arabic) forms of Yasir.

Yasashiku (Japanese) gentle; polite.

Yash (Hindi) victorious; glory.

Yasha (Russian) a form of Jacob, James.

Yashas (Indian) fame.

Yashodev (Indian) lord of fame.

Yashodhan (Indian) rich in fame.

Yashodhara (Indian) one who has achieved fame.

Yashpal (Indian) protector of fame.

Yashwant (Hindi) glorious.

Yasin (Arabic) prophet.

Yasir (Afghan) humble; takes it easy. (Arabic) wealthy.

Yasuo (Japanese) restful.

Yates (English) gates.

Yatin (Hindi) ascetic.

Yatindra (Indian) another name for the Hindu god Indra.

Yatish (Indian) lord of devotees.

Yauar (Quechua) blood.

Yauarguacac (Quechua) he sheds tears of blood.

Yauarpuma (Quechua) puma blood.

Yauri (Quechua) lance, needle.

Yavin (Hebrew) he will understand.

Yawo (Akan) born on Thursday.

Yayauhqui (Nahuatl) black smoking mirror.

Yazid (Arabic) his power will increase.

Yâzid (Arabic) a form of Yazid.

Yechiel (Hebrew) God lives.

Yedidya (Hebrew) a form of Jedidiah.

Yegor (Russian) a form of George.

Yehoshua (Hebrew) a form of Joshua.

Yehoyakem (Hebrew) a form of Joachim.

Yehuda, Yehudah (Hebrew) forms of Yehudi.

Yehudi (Hebrew) a form of Judah.

Yelutci (Moquelumnan) bear walking silently.

Yeoman (English) attendant; retainer.

Yeremey (Russian) a form of Jeremiah.

Yervant (Armenian) king, ruler. History: an Armenian king.

Yeshaya (Hebrew) gift. .

Yeshurun (Hebrew) right way.

Yeska (Russian) a form of Joseph.

Yestin (Welsh) just.

Yeudiel (Hebrew) I give thanks to God.

Yevgeny (Russian) a form of Yevgenyi.

Yevgenyi (Russian) a form of Eugene.

Yigal (Hebrew) he will redeem.
Yagel, Yigael

Yihad (Lebanese) struggle.

Yirmaya (Hebrew) a form of Jeremiah.

Yishai (Hebrew) a form Yisrael (Hebrew) a form of Israel.

Yisroel (Hebrew) a form of Yisrael.

Yitro (Hebrew) a form of Jethro.

Yitzchak (Hebrew) a form of Isaac.

Yngve (Swedish) ancestor; lord, master.

Yo (Cambodian) honest.

Yoakim (Slavic) a form of Jacob.

Yoan, Yoann (German) forms of Johann.

Yoav (Hebrew) a form of Joab.

Yobanis (Spanish) percussionist.

Yochanan (Hebrew) a form of John.

Yoel (Hebrew) a form of Joel.

Yogesh (Hindi) ascetic. Religion: another name for the Hindu god Shiva.

Yogi (Sanskrit) union; person who practices yoga.

Yohan, Yohann (German) forms of Johann.

Yohance (Hausa) a form of John.

Yolotli (Nahuatl) heart.

Yoltic (Nahuatl) he who is alive.

Yolyamanitzin (Nahuatl) just; tender and considerate person.

Yonah (Hebrew) a form of Jonah.

Yonatan (Hebrew) a form of Jonathan.

Yonathan (Hebrew) a form of Yonatan.

Yong (Chinese) courageous.

Yong-Sun (Korean) dragon in the first position; courageous.

Yoni (Greek) a form of Yanni.

Yonis (Hebrew) a form of Yonus.

Yonus (Hebrew) dove.

Yoofi (Akan) born on Friday.

Yooku (Fante) born on Wednesday.

Yoram (Hebrew) God is high.

Yorgos (Greek) a form of George.

Yorick (English) farmer. (Scandinavian) a form of George.

York (English) boar estate; yew-tree estate.

Yorkoo (Fante) born on Thursday.

Yosef (Hebrew) a form of Joseph.

Yóshi (Japanese) adopted son.

Yoshiyahu (Hebrew) a form of Josiah.

Yoskolo (Moquelumnan) breaking off pine cones.

Yosu (Hebrew) a form of Jesus.

Yotimo (Moquelumnan) yellow jacket carrying food to its hive.

Yottoko (Native American) mud at the water's edge.

Younes (Lebanese) prophet.

Young (English) young.

Young-Jae (Korean) pile of prosperity.

Young-Soo (Korean) keeping the prosperity.

Youri (Russian) a form of Yuri.

Youseef, Yousef (Yiddish) forms of Joseph.

Youssel (Yiddish) a familiar form of Joseph.

Yov (Russian) a short form of Yoakim.

Yovani (Slavic) a form of Jovan.

Yoyi (Hebrew) a form of George.

Yrjo (Finnish) a form of George.

Ysidro (Greek) a short form of Isidore.

Yu 🆑 (Chinese) universe.

Yuçef (Arabic) a form of José.

Yudan (Hebrew) judgment.**Yudell** (English) a form of Udell.

Yuhannà (Arabic) a form of Juan.

Yuki 🆑 (Japanese) snow.

Yul (Mongolian) beyond the horizon.

Yule (English) born at Christmas.

Yuli (Basque) youthful.

Yuma (Native American) son of a chief.

Yunes (Lebanese) prophet.

Yunus (Turkish) a form of Jonah.

Yupanqui (Quechua) he who honors his ancestors.

Yurac (Quechua) white.

Yurcel (Turkish) sublime.

Yuri 🆑 (Russian, Ukrainian) a form of George. (Hebrew) a familiar form of Uriah.

Yurochka (Russian) farmer.

Yusef, Yusuf (Arabic, Swahili) forms of Joseph.

Yusif (Russian) a form of Joseph.

Yustyn (Russian) a form of Justin.

Yutu (Moquelumnan) coyote out hunting.

Yuuki (Japanese) a form of Yuki.

Yuval (Hebrew) rejoicing.

Yves (French) a form of Ivar, Ives.

Yvet (French) archer.

Yvon (French) a form of Ivar, Yves.

Ywain (Irish) a form of Owen.

Z

Zabdi (Hebrew) a short form of Zabdiel.

Zabdiel (Hebrew) present, gift.

Zabulón (Hebrew) purple house.

Zac (Hebrew) a short form of Zachariah, Zachary.

Zacarias (Portuguese, Spanish) a form of Zachariah.

Zacarías (Spanish) a form of Zacarias.

Zacary, Zaccary (Hebrew) forms of Zachary.

Zacchaeus (Hebrew) a form of Zaccheus.

Zaccheus (Hebrew) innocent, pure.

Zach (Hebrew) a short form of Zachariah, Zachary.

Zacharey, Zachari (Hebrew) forms of Zachary.

Zacharia (Hebrew) a form of Zachariah.

Zachariah (Hebrew) God remembered.

Zacharias (German) a form of Zachariah.

Zacharie BG (Hebrew) a form of Zachary.

Zachary ✿

BG (Hebrew) a familiar form of Zachariah. History: Zachary Taylor was the twelfth U.S. president.

Zacheriah (Hebrew) a form of Zachariah.

Zachery (Hebrew) a form of Zachary.

Zachory (Hebrew) a form of Zachary.

Zachrey, Zachry (Hebrew) forms of Zachary.

Zack (Hebrew) a short form of Zachariah, Zachary.

Zackariah (Hebrew) a form of Zachariah.

Zackary (Hebrew) a form of Zachary.

Zackery (Hebrew) a form of Zachary.

Zackory (Hebrew) a form of Zachary.

Zadok (Hebrew) a short form of Tzadok.

Zadornin (Basque) Saturn.

Zafir (Arabic) victorious.

Zah (Lebanese) bright, luminous.

Zahid (Arabic) self-denying, ascetic.

Zâhid (Arabic) a form of Zahid.

Zahir (Arabic) shining, bright.

Zahîr (Arabic) a form of Zahir.

Zahur (Swahili) flower.

Zaid (Arabic) increase, growth.

Zaide (Hebrew) older.

Zaim (Arabic) brigadier general.

Zain (English) a form of Zane.

Zaire BG (Arabic) a form of Zahir. Geography: a country of central Africa.

Zak (Hebrew) a short form of Zachariah, Zachary.

Zakari, Zakary, Zakkary (Hebrew) forms of Zachary.

Zakaria, Zakariya (Hebrew) forms of Zachariah.

Zakariyya (Arabic) prophet. Religion: an Islamic prophet.

Zakery (Hebrew) a form of Zachary.

Zaki (Arabic) bright; pure. (Hausa) lion.

Zakia GB (Swahili) intelligent.

Zako (Hungarian) a form of Zachariah.

Zale (Greek) sea strength.

Zalmai (Afghan) young.

Zalman (Yiddish) a form of Solomon.

Zalmir (Hebrew) songbird.

Zamiel (German) a form of Samuel.

Zamir (Hebrew) song; bird.

Zan (Italian) clown.

Zander (Greck) a short form of Alexander.

Zane (English) a form of John.

Zanis (Latvian) a form of Janis.

Zanthippus (Greek) a form of Xanthippus.

Zanthus (Latin) a form of Xanthus.

Zanvil (Hebrew) a form of Samuel.

Zaquan (American) a combination of the prefix Za + Quan.

Zaqueo (Hebrew) pure, innocent.

Zareb (African) protector.

Zared (Hebrew) ambush.

Zarek (Polish) may God protect the king.

Zavier (Arabic) a form of Xavier.

Zayden (American) a name that begins with "Z" and rhymes with Jayden and Hayden.

Zayed (Arabic) growth.

Zayit BG (Hebrew) olive.

Zayne (English) a form of Zane.

Zdenek (Czech) follower of Saint Denis.

Zeb (Hebrew) a short form of Zebediah, Zebulon.

Zebadiá (Hebrew) a form of Zebadiah.

Zebadiah (Hebrew) a form of Zebediah.

Zebedee (Hebrew) a familiar form of Zebediah.

Zebediah (Hebrew) God's gift.

Zebedías (Hebrew) given by Yahweh.

Zebulon (Hebrew) exalted, honored; lofty house.

Zebulún (Hebrew) a form of Zebulon.

Zecharia BG (Hebrew) a form of Zachariah.

Zechariah (Hebrew) a form of Zachariah.

Zed (Hebrew) a short form of Zedekiah.

Zedekiah (Hebrew) God is mighty and just.

Zedequías (Hebrew) a form of Zedekiah.

Zedidiah (Hebrew) a form of Zebediah.

Zeeman (Dutch) seaman.

Zeév (Hebrew) wolf.

Zeheb (Turkish) gold.

Zeke (Hebrew) a short form of Ezekiel, Zachariah, Zachary, Zechariah.

Zeki (Turkish) clever, intelligent.

Zelgai (Afghan) heart.

Zelig (Yiddish) a form of Selig.

Zelimir (Slavic) wishes for peace.

Zemar (Afghan) lion.

Zen (Japanese) religious. Religion: a form of Buddhism.

Zenda GB (Czech) a form of Eugene.

Zeno (Greek) cart; harness. History: a Greek philosopher.

Zenobio (Greek) life of Zeus.

Zenón (Greek) he who lives.

Zenzo (Italian) a form of Lorenzo.

Zephaniah (Hebrew) treasured by God.

Zephyr BG (Greek) west wind.

Zerach (Hebrew) light.

Zero (Arabic) empty, void.

Zeroun (Armenian) wise and respected.

Zeshan (American) a form of Zeshawn.

Zeshawn (American) a combination of the prefix Ze + Shawn.

Zesiro (Luganda) older of twins.

Zethan (Hebrew) shining.

Zeus (Greek) living. Mythology: chief god of the Greek pantheon.

Zeusef (Portuguese) a form of Joseph.

Zev (Hebrew) a short form of Zebulon.

Zevi (Hebrew) a form of Tzvi.

Zhek (Russian) a short form of Evgeny.

Zhìxin (Chinese) ambitious.

Zhora (Russian) a form of George.

Zhuàng (Chinese) strong.

Zia GB (Hebrew) trembling; moving. (Arabic) light.

Zigfrid (Latvian, Russian) a form of Siegfried.

Ziggy (American) a familiar form of Siegfried, Sigmund.

Zigor (Basque) punishment.

Zikomo (Nguni) thank-you.

Zilaba (Luganda) born while sick.

Zimon (Hebrew) a form of Simon.

Zimra BG (Hebrew) song of praise.

Zimraan (Arabic) praise.

Zimri (Hebrew) valuable.

Zimrí (Hebrew) a form of Zimri.

Zinan (Japanese) second son.

Zindel (Yiddish) a form of Alexander.

Zion BG (Hebrew) sign, omen; excellent. Bible: the name used to refer to Israel and to the Jewish people.

Zipactonal (Nahuatl) harmonic light.

Ziskind (Yiddish) sweet child.

Ziv (Hebrew) shining brightly. (Slavic) a short form of Ziven.

Ziven (Slavic) vigorous, lively.

Ziyad (Arabic) increase.

Ziyâd (Arabic) a form of Ziyad.

Zlatan (Czech) gold.

Zoel (Hebrew) son of Babel.

Zohar BG (Hebrew) bright light.

Zola GB (German) prince. (Italian) ball of earth. Literature: Émile Zola was a nineteenth-century French writer and critic.

Zolin (Nahuatl) quail.

Zollie, Zolly (Hebrew) forms of Solly.

Zoltán (Hungarian) life.

Zonar (Latin) sound.

Zorba (Greek) live each day.

Zorion (Basque) a form of Orion.

Zorya (Slavic) star; dawn.

Zosime (French) a form of Zosimus.

Zósimo (Greek) he who fights.

Zosimus (Greek) full of life.

Zótico (Greek) of a long life.

Zotikos (Greek) saintly, holy. Religion: a saint in the Eastern Orthodox Church.

Zotom (Kiowa) a biter.

Zsigmond (Hungarian) a form of Sigmund.

Zuberi (Swahili) strong.

Zubin (Hebrew) a short form of Zebulon.

Zuhayr (Arabic) brilliant, shining.

Zuka (Shona) sixpence.

Zuriel (Hebrew) God is my rock.

Zygmunt (Polish) a form of Sigmund.

Chapter 2
Inspiring Baby Names from Hindu

Baby Boy Names
It seems that Hindus come up with the most interesting names. Their respective Sanskrit meaning adds more depth to the names. Each name represents virtue and value. If you want a spiritual start for your bundle of joy, consider the following baby boy names based in Hinduism.

ABHAS [AH-bahs]
This is a Sanskrit name which means "awareness or realization." Abhas is inspirational and creative. He strives to achieve harmony within himself. He is a loving and caring person who does not hesitate to help others. Outgoing and friendly, Abhas makes friends easily.

AADIR [AH-deer]
Indian by origin, this Hindi name means "beginning or origin." It signifies a source. Aadir is a source of unity and harmony. He is a peacemaker. Reliable, responsible and consistent, he is someone who makes other people feel secure. He treats his loved ones with respect and devotion. Aadir has set clear goals and takes actions guided by his vision of the future.

AADRIK [AHD-reek]
Telugu by origin, Aadrik is the "rising sun between the mountains." He is indeed a symbol of hope and harmony. He is excellent in bridging gaps. Compassionate and protective of others, Aadrik's devotion is unquestionable. He is someone who is dedicated to his work and is likely to accomplish something significant.

AAGAR [AH-guhr]
In Sanskrit, the name refers to someone who is musically inclined. Aagar does not fall short in creativity and inspiration. He is filled with confidence, blessed with wisdom and spirituality. He is someone who takes initiative for others to follow. Outgoing and sociable, he builds friendship easily.

AANAND [AH-nand]
In Sanskrit, this Hindu name is a symbol of good fortune. It signifies delight, happiness and bliss. A gift to the community, Aanand is socially active and born leader. He is guided by his passion. Adventurous in spirit, he is an explorer. While he enjoys his freedom, he does not forget his responsibilities. He works hard to be able to succeed in his life.

ABHAI [AHB-bhay]
Abhai means "fearless." He has a deep sense of purpose. This motivates him to work hard. He tackles life with great enthusiasm. His positivity is an inspiration to others. Dynamic, devoted and capable, Abhai is able to bring forth the best in people.

ABHAIVEER [AH-bay-veer]
Sikh by origin, this name refers to someone "who is bold and brave." Born with an adventurous spirit, Abhaiveer does not let anything hold him back. He likes to explore and experience new things. He is passionate and socially active. With a knack for creativity, he inspires others. He is hardworking and will stop at nothing until he succeeds.

ABHATA [AH-buh-tah]
In Sanskrit, Abhata is synonymous to shining and glorious, blazing and splendid. He is admirable in his creative thinking. He shines socially as a natural entertainer. He is a stand out with his social, outgoing and friendly personality. His love and care for his loved ones are unwarranted.

AINESH [AY-nesh]
Of Indian origin, Ainesh means "sun's glory." His passions are as bright as the sun. His adventurous spirit is blinding. His insights and ideas are always grand. His art and creativity are unyielding. And he does splendid things with his generous heart.

AIVANNAN [AY-vahn-nuhn]
Aivannan is one of Lord Shiva's name in Tamil. Aivannan is moved with a purpose in mind. His creative approach to things allows him to come up with innovative ideas. He is dynamic and efficient at work. An inspirational character, he has the ability to motivate people.

BHUDHARA [BOOHD-hah-ruh]

Its Indian roots suggest a link to Lord Krishna. The name itself means "supporter of the earth." Reliable support to others, Bhudhara has a sense of duty. Other people find him trustworthy because of his reliability and consistency. He lives a life of kindness and generosity. He finds happiness in being able to help others. His versatility and remarkable enthusiasm allow him to overcome challenges that may come his way.

BIJENDER [bee-JEHN-der]
This Hindu name is synonymous to courage. With a brave spirit, Bijender takes the initiative and leads. He is capable of handling responsibilities. He fulfills his duties with precision. He recognizes opportunities when they come his way. He is independent and he calls the shots in his life.

CATAKA [KAH-tuh-kah]
From India, this name refers to someone "which is a poet." Cataka's wisdom and spirituality along with his ability for keen observation allow him to have a deep understanding of people and situations. Although he may be introverted, he is intelligent and confident about his skills. He possesses inspired creativity. When given a chance, Cataka can prove himself to be a worthy leader.

DEEPIKA [deeh-PEEH-kuh]
Of Indian origin, this Hindu name means "sun's light" or "lord of heat." Deepika's warmth can be felt through his deep love and caring for his loved ones. He is devoted, generous and selfsacrificing. He has a way of making people feel at ease. He holds a strong sense of duty.

DEESHAN [DEEH-shahn| DEY-shan]
This Hindu name refers to "someone who shows direction." Born with leadership skills, Deeshan is likely to take the initiative and be in control. He is also a born diplomat with his ability to bridge gaps. He is idealistic, compassionate and devoted. Naturally charming, he attracts draws people in.

RAAJEEV [rah-JEEV]
Of Indian origin, Raajeev refers to "Blue Lotus." It signifies someone who is an achiever or "one who rules all." A passionate leader, he is active in social matters and he tries to involve others. He is an inspirational character whose creativity is well admired. He strives for success and recognition.

RAAVI [rah-VEE]
Raavi refers to the sun. It signifies brightness and radiance. He shines through his ability to make people trust and feel secure around him. He has a clear vision of his future and makes decisions in the present accordingly. Responsible and consistent with deep patriotism, Raavi is likely to fill an important position in society. Raavi's genuine concern and sympathy for others make him a natural peacemaker. He is loving and makes sure to look after his loved ones. Charity gives him a sense of inner harmony.

SAADAR [sah-DUHR]
In Sanskrit, Saadar is synonymous to respect. A passionate person with a zest for life, Saadar is respected for his work ethic. He is admired for his highly creative ideas and insights. He is well-liked for his outgoing personality

SANTOSO [sahn-TOW-sow]
In Sanskrit, this Hindu name means "peaceful." Santoso has a warm presence about him. His personality signifies grace and charm. His idealism, kind heart and compassion, deep understanding, sincerity and honesty makes him well-loved as a leader.

TANSHU [tahn-SHOO] This Indian name means "wholly natural." Intelligent, introverted and independent, Tanshu seems like a mystery. He embodies wisdom and spirituality. He has a gift of seeing through people and acts with honesty and sincerity. He is responsible and practical which makes him an excellent team player.

VACHASYA [vah-KASH-yuh] In Sanskrit, the name refers to someone who is "well-spoken of." Vachasya's passion, creativity, leadership, adventurous and inspirational spirit are well celebrated. He is someone who works relentlessly to accomplish something important.

YATHART [YAH-thart] This Sanskrit name means "truth or complete." A natural peacemaker, Yathart's ability to bring people together is remarkable. He is idealistic and compassionate. He has the marks of a leader. His presence is always welcome. He embodies grace and charm which draws people in. He possesses clarity of mind and contributes innovative ideas.

Baby Girl Names

Hindu inspired baby girl names are like flowers that exude a pleasant smell. More than the lovely sound they create though is a gentle feeling it leaves you as you find out what they mean. They are uniquely beautiful and anyone, including your little pretty darling, will be honored to bear any of these meaningful names.

AABHA [AHB-bah]
From Sanskrit, this Hindu name means "light, brilliance or glow." It also signifies "gloriousness" and "splendor." Aabha exudes her radiance with her outgoing and friendly personality. Her creativity is inspired. Dynamic and capable, she approaches things in a unique way. She upholds a purpose and she uses this as motivation. A responsible individual, Aabha is a capable leader.

AABHARANA [AHB-ha-rah-nah]
This Hindi name refers to valuables like ornaments and jewels. In a deeper sense, it signifies honor, happiness and prosperity. Aabharana is filled with understanding and compassion. She has clarity in her thoughts and is able to come up with great ideas and insights. She brings honor to her name by living a life of generosity. To her family, she is protective and faithful. Versatile and adaptable, she takes on life with enthusiasm and a positive attitude.

AADARSHINI [ah-DAHR-shee-nee]
Tamil by origin, Aadarshini means "idealistic." Her idealism is inspirational. She exudes grace and charm. Her friendly and outgoing personality along with her optimistic attitude draws people in. Aadashini is kindhearted and compassionate. She possesses great qualities of a leader.

AADHILA [AHD-hee-lah]
This name means "honesty." Aadhila is a girl who won't lie. She brings beauty to the world with her inspired creativity and artistry. She can be described as charitable and a promoter of peace. Her easygoing personality is loved by all. She is a kind heart. With compassion and understanding, she gives with a generous heart. To her loved ones, she is caring and protective.

AADHIRAI [AHD-hee-ray]
Tamil by origin, Aadhirai refers to "a special star." She glows like a star with her attractiveness and creativity. Her passion and inspiration shine through. She is bright with genuine love and concern for others. She strives for peace and harmony.

AADRITA [AHD-ree-tah]
Indian by origin, Aadrita is synonymous to adorable and charming. The name also signifies one with lots of love to give. Aadrita is indeed a charmer with her romantic, outgoing and friendly persona. She is highly creative and artistic. With a huge heart, she lives her life with kindness, compassion and generosity.

AAGARNA [ah-GAHR-nah]
This Hindu name is synonymous to music or "one who has the gift of music." With an attractive personality, Aagarna draws people in. Her creativity is admirable. She strives for perfection. She is practical and responsible. She has excellent organization skills. She deals with people and life guided by sincerity and honesty.

AALAYA [AH-lah-yah]
In Sanskrit, Aalaya means "home or refuge." She is attracted to the excitement that adventures bring. She enjoys the freedom and lives her life to the fullest. A leader in her own right, Aalaya is responsible, reliable, dynamic, practical and inspiring. She follows a purpose and she acts with immense motivation.

AAMAYA [AH-mah-yah]
Bengali by origin, this name refers to "the pleasant night rain that brings new hope." Aamaya is the calmness after a storm. Loving and caring, she is most genuine. She is remarkable in her skills of the organization. She is practical in dealing with matters. She is always reliable. Her honesty and sincerity are inspiring.

AAMUKTA MALYA [ah-MOOKH-tuh MAHL-yah]
This Hindu name is taken from a poem which is authored by an Indian king named, Sri Krishna Deva Raya. Aamukta Malya has a sense of responsibility. She is consistent and reliable

in her words and actions. She likes to lead and supervise. Her confidence may be intimidating but she means well. With great optimism and natural enthusiasm, she inspires others to be the best they can be.

AARINI [AH-ree-nee]
Bengali by origin, Aarini means "someone who is adventurous." Attractive and athletic, she is passionate about like. True to her adventurous spirit, she enjoys exploring and traveling. Rather than resisting, she is one who embraces change. She acts with devotion and genuine concern for others. She finds fulfillment in being able to contribute to the improvement of others.

AARAVI [ah-RAH-vee]
Another Bengali name, Aaravi means "harmony" or a "state of tranquility." She finds inner peace and harmony by teaching others. A consistent and responsible person, Aaravi easily earns the trust of others. She is blessed with creativity. Outgoing and friendly, Aaravi is agreeable and inspirational. She thinks ahead of her time. Her decisions are guided by her vision of her future.

AARADHAYA [ah-RAHD-hah-yah]
This Hindu name means "esteem" and "respect." It also signifies "sentiment of affection." Loving and caring, Aaradhaya puts her loved ones' needs before hers. Being able to care for others gives her a sense of fulfillment. Armed with a sense of purpose, she is versatile, smart and efficient. She is capable of being a leader. She is a great motivator. She lives a life of example and serves as an inspiration to others. She takes on life with enthusiasm.

ABHISARIKAA [ah-BEE-sah-ree-kah]
In Sanskrit, the name means "beloved one." Among Abhisarikaa's lovable qualities are her diligence, consistency, reliability, practicality and sincerity. She is practical and always thinks about her future. She strives to accomplish her goals. She pushes herself to achieve success and recognition.

ABHITA [ah-BEEh-tah]
This Sanskrit name means "courageous or brave." It refers to someone who is fearless. Indeed, Abhita enjoys her freedom and is not afraid to take risks. She treats life as a series of adventures. She is someone who embraces change and lives her life to the fullest no matter what.

ADISHAKTI [ah-deeh-SHAHK-teeh]
In Sanskrit, Adishakti refers to the "goddess of supreme power." Adishakti embodies this meaning. She exudes confidence, strength and power. She strives hard to accomplish higher goals. She continues to challenge herself. Adishakti has the strength of character to become a notable leader. She takes initiative and takes control. She is her own person. Her devotion and sympathetic side further add to her admirable qualities.

ANTARA [AHN-tah-rah]
In Sanskrit, Antara refers to the "heart and soul." It signifies that is within. Blessed with wisdom and spirituality, Antara is capable of leading. She is creative and intelligent. She may be introverted but this is what allows her to reflect upon herself and others. She works and acts independently. Although she may seem mysterious, Antara is social, outgoing and friendly.

CHANKRISNA [chahn-KREESH-nah]
This Hindu name refers to a "sweet-smelling tree." Creative, romantic and artistic, Chankrisna possesses many great qualities she can be proud of. With her sympathetic persona, she is a natural peacemaker. To her loved ones, she is devoted, faithful and protective. She is easy-going and understanding. Chankrisna is a hardworking individual who has clear goals for herself. She acts compassionately towards others.

DHARMI [DAHR-meeh]
In Sanskrit, Dharmi refers to one "who is religious." She embodies wisdom and spirituality. She has a deep understanding of people. Intelligent but introverted, she exudes an air of mystery. She is independent and a natural-born leader. She is in full control of her fate.

EKISHA [ey-KEEH-shah]
Indian by origin, this is the name of a Hindu goddess. Ekisha reflects a warm and serene persona. She is genuine in her relationships. Her unpretentious and friendly character draw

people in. Patient and understanding, she strives to achieve success. Her family takes her top priority. She is generous to the point of self-sacrificing. She is inclined towards the arts.

HASRI [HAHS-ree]

In Sanskrit, Hasri refers to someone who is "always joyful or happy." She brings joy to those around her with her grace and charm. She acts with compassion. She has a kind heart. Born with leadership skills, Hasri is intelligent and skillful. She is independent. She likes to be in control.

INIYA [ee-NEE-yah]

This Hindu name means "sweet." Iniya is an attractive person. She takes her responsibilities seriously. In control and independent, she possesses the marks of a capable leader.

KANNITHA [kahn-NEET-huh]

This Hindu name traces its origin from Cambodia and Sanskrit. It means "angels." Angelic in appearance and personality, Kannitha is genuinely loving and caring. She brings peace and harmony by helping others. She is trustworthy. A natural peacemaker, she strives to bridge gaps that separate people. She is devoted and sympathetic. With her many great qualities, she is likely to play an important role in her community.

MONISHA [mow-NEE-shah]

Indian by origin, Monisha refers to someone who is "brilliant, wise and well-learned." She is destined to share her wisdom by teaching others. Her idealism is inspiring and she is bound to lead. Monisha's charm and grace attract people. Her kind and compassionate heart is well admired.

PADMINI [PAHD-mee-nee]

This Hindu name refers to a "multitude of lotuses" or "someone who resides in a lotus." It is also among the various names of the goddess Lakshmi. Padmini is real and unpretentious. She exudes a warm and friendly nature. She is patient and understanding but also independent. She dreams of taking the lead. Padmini has a positive outlook on life. She has incredible enthusiasm. With this, she is capable of helping people become the best versions of themselves.

SAARYA [SARH-yuh]

This Hindu name refers to someone who lives in piety. Pious in her ways, Saarya exudes a strong and powerful character at the same time. She is confident about herself and her abilities. She challenges herself to achieve higher goals. Creative and inspirational, Saarya's unique gifts allow her to make a significant 118 impact on other people's lives.

SRAVANTI [SHRA-vahn-tee]

Indian by origin, this Hindu name refers to someone "who flows like a river." Fluid and attractive, Sravanti allows creativity to flow through her veins. She feels the excitement in a rush of adventures. She tends to live her life to the fullest.

YASHICA [yah-SHEE-kuh]

In Sanskrit, Yahica refers to someone who is "intelligent, brave and successful." Smart, independent and bold, Yashica is capable many great things. Her deep sense of purpose is inspiring. She has remarkable enthusiasm. She always looks at the glass half full.

Chapter 3
Traditional names that never fade

Traditional names are names that are dedicated, strong and have a long history and tradition behind them. Many times, they are passed down through the generations from father to son or daughter and have sustained their popularity despite the passage of years. They tend to maintain their appeal from generation to generation and they will remain commonly used by young parents in any given year. Many traditional names are biblical in origin, and many of these names have been used by royalty and others in high office or in history books. Make your choice and don't worry about his name going out of style.

Adam	Eric	Richard
Abigail	Hope	Valerie
Andrew	Graham	Samuel
Andrea	Ivy	Samantha
Garret	Isaac	
Anna	Jean	
Thomas	John	
Bethany	Lydia	
William	Lucas	
Caroline	Maria	
Charles	Mark	
Delia	Nicole	
Darren	Matthew	
Eliza	Phoebe	
David	Michael	
Felicia	Rebecca	
Edward	Philip	
Gabrielle	Sarah	

Chapter 4

FAQs

Here are some of the most asked questions from parents who are in the process of choosing a name for their baby.

1. My partner and I disagree with names, what do we do?

This scenario is extremely common. You and your partner are different people with different opinions. Baby-names are like flavors of ice cream. Everyone is different. The best situation is if you both compromise and find a middle ground. In order to do this, sit your partner down and you should both write a list of three names which you like. When you've done this, hand your list to your partner and take theirs. You both have to cross out two names. The name that remains on both lists will be your final two names. From there, you both have to have a conversation about the name choice. Come to a mutual decision. If you still can't come to an understanding because one of you is not okay with the names they chose, then sit down with this book and go through names again. There is bound to be at least one name you can both agree on.

2. Is it okay to choose a masculine name for my daughter/ a feminine name for my son?

Absolutely! You're the parent and you decide. I've met many Leslies who are men and many Joes who are women. Of course you have to consider the social impact doing this will have on your baby. While there is nothing wrong with naming your son 'Emily', be aware of the impact that will have on your son's life. While it sounds harsh, many kids who are named unisex and opposite sex names are more likely to be taunted or bullied at school.

3. Can I make up a name for my baby?

Yes. Again, you have to be very careful with how you go about this. Making up a name based on another name is 100% fine but naming a child a word which out of context would be misinterpreted is not a good idea. Here are some examples of what is appropriate and what is not. The following are real names which people have named their babies. You have to make the responsible decision if you have a name in mind which isn't usual.

4. Can I use an alternate spelling for my baby's name?

Of course. In fact, this is encouraged in a lot of cases because alternate spellings can make for some of the most original and beautiful names in the world. For example: -
-Adrienn instead of Adrien
- Melisha instead of Melissa
- Franceen instead of Francine
- Lili instead of Lily
Once more, responsibility is key. Not going overboard is a principal aspect of using alternate spellings for baby names.

5. Can I call my baby a name from a different culture to my own?

Can you? Yes.

Should you? It depends.

There are times when doing this could be misconstrued as offensive if you aren't 100% sure of the meaning of a name in another language. In 2012, a man famously made it onto the local newspapers in the South of England because he named his daughter a Chinese name without properly researching the etymology and meaning of the name. It turns out he called her 'Loud Peanut' which is funny but unfortunate.

If you admire a certain culture or language and do the right research behind an ethnic/cultural name, then it would be a lovely tribute to name your child in that language.

Carnivores:Tiger
Panther
Cougar
Python
Cobra
Suggestive of impropriety?:Rome
o

Shady
Dream
Fantasy
Hustler
Floozy
Free
Lingerie
Cayenne

Abandon
Inappropriate expectations:Beauty
Barbie
Champ
Hercules

Unfortunate Surnames for which a variant might be considered:

Note: In every case but one (Shyster), suggestions are based first upon the intended meaning of the name. In that one exception, suggestions are loosely related or are "sounds-similar" words that do not appear to have such negative meanings. Possible adjustments to other "problem" names might be approached in the same way.

Hooker (Hook maker) - Hooke, Hookmaker, Hookmacher?
Dick (Short for Richard) - Richards, Richard?
Seaman (Sea Man) - Seaworth, Seaworthy, Seafarer, Seaside?
Gay (Glad) - Glad, Gladd, Glade?
Gayward (Glad-like) - Gladward, Gladdward?
Butts (Bulls-eye, Target) - Archer, Arrow, Aim, Aims, Aimes?
Fuchs (Fox), Fucks, Fucksman, Focker - Fox, Fox, Foxman, Foxman, Foxer?
Virgin - Virgo, Virge, Virtue?
Manlove - Loveman, Loveman, Mann, Love?

Dicker (Dyke worker/builder) - Dyker, Diggar, Digman, Dykeman?
Frick (Smith) - Fevre, Feaver, Smith?
Heine (Home rule) - Henrich, Hendrich, Henrick, Hendry, Henric?
Roach (Rock) - Rock, Stone, Rockman, Stoneman
Pot (Pit) - Phillips, Pitt, Pittman
Schmuck (Jeweller or Neat and tidy) - Jew
Schmuck (Jeweller or Neat and tidy) - Jeweller, Bright, Order?
Shyster (Ohboy... let's just make up something!) - Lawman, Lawman, Schist, Christ?

Messer (Hayward, one responsible for gathering/keeping hay) - Hayer, Hayman, Hay?
Raper (Rope maker) - Roper, Ropere, Ropemaker, Rope?
Gasser (Road or Alley resident) - Alley, Streeter, Street, Lane?
Loser - (Lazarus/Eleazer/Elieser) - Lazar, Eleazer, Elieser, Eli?
Klutz (Clumsy) - Tripp (Existing name that means the same thing, but sounds better.)?
Fly (Flageum / Flavius) - Flyer, Flyman, Flymann?
Slaughter (various) - Sloh, Slough, Sloetree?
Boner (de bonne aire) - Bonnaire, Bonaire, Bonne?

Chapter 5
Famous Names

Popular Names from Politicians and Influential People Some people like to name their children after presidents and influential people.

So if you are passionate about politics, this list may help narrow down your choices. Nothing grand here. Remember, plain works. Feel free to use a variation of the names as well, these are just here to give you a few more ideas!

Names of Presidents for Boys

George Washington	Andrew Johnson	James Polk
James Monroe	Ulysses Grant	William McKinley
William Henry	John Quincy Adams	William Taft
James Garfield	Thomas Jefferson	Benjamin Harrison
Franklin Pierce	Martin Van Buren	Warren Harding
John Adams	John Tyler	Ronald Reagan
James Madison	Zachary Taylor	Bill Clinton
Theodore Roosevelt	Millard Fillmore	George Bush
Calvin Coolidge	Rutherford Hayes	Barack Obama
James Buchanan	Chester Arthur	

Other Notable Politicians

Moon Landrieu – Secretary of Housing and Urban Development

Oveta Culp Hobby – Secretary of Health, Education and Welfare

Alben Barkley – Vice President under Harry Truman

Schuyler Colfax – Vice President under Ulysses Grant

Danforth Quayle – Vice President under George Bush

Famous Names of Writers and Artists

If you adore Shakespeare, Agatha Christie, and Maya Angelou among others, you might consider naming your child after one of the people listed below.

Boy's Names

Gabriel Garcia	Walt Whitman	Geoffrey Chaucer
Herman Melville	Gustave Klimt	Salvador Dali
Nathaniel Hawthorne	David Hockney	

Girl's Names

Alice Walker	Georgia O' Keeffe	Gloria Steinem
Agatha Christie	Jane Austen	
Frida Kahlo	Nora Ephron	

Famous Rock and Roll Names

Boy's Names

Elton John	John Lennon	David Lee Roth
Freddie Mercury	Paul McCartney	Kurt Cobain
Jimmy Buffett	Robert Palmer	Bruce Springsteen

Girl's Names

Alanis Morrissett	Popular Celebrity	Christopher Reeves
Annie Lennox	Names	Dennis Quaid
Janis Joplin	Boy's Names	Eddie Murphy
Tina Turner	Andy Garcia	Clint Eastwood
Melissa Etheridge	Antonio Banderas	Harry Hamlin
Alison Moyet	Brad Pitt	Dean Cain

Harvey Keitel
James Dean
Jimmy Stewart
Lenny Bruce

Girl's Names

Alicia Silverstone
Angela Bassett
Bette Davis Demi Moore
Glenn Close
Goldie Hawn
Meryl Streep
Michelle Pfeiffer

Macaulay Culkin
Ralph Macchio
Mel Gibson
Matt Dillon

Sharon Stone
Angelina Jolie
Julia Roberts
Emma Thompson
Gilda Radner
Halle Berry
Jennifer Lawrence

Sammy Davis
Steven Seagal
Wesley Snipes
William Baldwin

Sandra Bullock
Sharon Stone
Selina Gomez
Vanessa Hudgens
Winona Ryder

What Famous Celebrities are Naming their Babies

Americans adore celebrities and this fact can't help but be mirrored in the names given to kids. Not only do parents name their kids after their Hollywood idols, but they also go out of their way naming them after the kids that the stars are having.

For Girls

Claudia Rose – daughter of Michelle
Pfeiffer Zoe – daughter of Amanda
Bearse Sasha – daughter of Steven Spielberg

Annie – daughter of Jamie Lee Curtis
Molly – daughter of Terri Garr
Tara – daughter of Oliver Stone

Danielle – daughter of Jerry Lewis
Renee – daughter of Rod Stewart
Matalin Mary – daughter of Mary Matalin

For Boys

Nicolas – son of Jean-Claude Van Damme
Jett – son of Jon Travolta
Cody – son of Robin Williams

Jack Henry - son of Meg Ryan
Alexander James - son of Andy Mill

Christian Aurelia - son of Arnold Schwarzenegger
Michael Garrett – son of Melissa Gilbert

Famous Country Music Names

Country music is a big hit. This is precisely the reason why many parents would love to have their babies named after their favorite country music singer.

Boy's names

Chet Atkins
Garth Brooks

George Jones
Kenny Rogers

Waylon Jennings
Lee Clayton

Girl's Names

Crystal Gayle
Loretta Lynn
Taylor Swift

Shania Twain
Wynonna Judd
Dolly Parton

Naomi Judd
Reba McEntire
Patty Lovelace

Chapter 6
Biblical Namesand Meanings

In this chapter, I have a list of names from the bible along with a brief description of that person's role in the book and a description of the origins of the name. As you will see, the majority, but not all, of these names have origins in the Hebrew language.

Key – Name – boy's name

Name – girl's name

Name – gender-neutral name

A

Aaron – (role in the bible) the brother of Moses – (meaning) it's Hebrew origins mean a teacher, or a high mountain, metaphorically a mountain of strength or wisdom.

Abda – a servant of Solomon – it originates from the Arabic for extraordinary, or beautiful.

Abdeel – the father of Shelemiah – a Hebrew word meaning a cloud from God, or a servant to God

Abigail – sister of David – from the Hebrew meaning the joy of the father.

Abraham – father to Isaac – a Hebrew name which means father to the multitude.

Adah – a wife of Lamech – a Hebrew name meaning adornment.

Adam – first man, in the Garden of Eden – this is the Hebrew word for man.

Adina – a mighty member of the army of David – it means slender one, and is from Hebrew.

Ahab – a king of Israel – uncle, or father's brother, from Hebrew.

Aisha – a senior member of the household of Solomon – the brother of a prince, from Hebrew.

Ajah – Son of Ezer – an old English name, which means a goat, sometimes a hawk.

Amos – an ancestor of Jesus – the name is from Hebrew and means borne by God.

Amzi – an Israelite exile – strong or one's own strength. Although the name is biblical, and is therefore probably of Hebrew origin, it is uncertain from where the name originated.

Anah – a daughter of Zibeon and a son of Seir – a discoverer or explorer; one who finds the answer. The name is from Hebrew.

Anaiah – a supporter of Ezra – an answer to God – the Hebrew name was originally a boy's name but of late it has become more popular for girls.

Andrew – an Apostle of Jesus Christ – a word derived from Greek, and which means manly.

Anna – a prophet – originally from Latin, it means given grace or favor

Arah – son of Ulla – a traveler or wayfarer, the name is of indeterminate origin, and can be applied for boys or girls.

Asher – a son of Jacob – from Hebrew origins, it means happiness.

Azzan – the father of a prince – from Hebrew, it means strong.

B

Barkos – the father to the Nethinim – most probably this means a painter, but its entomology is uncertain.

Barnabus – a minor apostle – an Aramaic word, which means consolation.

Bartholomew – an Apostle of Jesus Christ – another name with Aramaic origins, it means a son.

Basemath – wife of Esau – sweet-smelling or sweet of smile, it is a Hebrew word.

Ben Dekar – one of Solomon's main administrators – a son (of Pick), this is a name with Hebrew origins.

Benjamin - a son of Jacob – a Hebrew word, and as a name often given to the youngest son. It means right-hand son.

C

Caleb – son of Hezron – a Hebrew name which means one who is bold.

Candace (Candice) – an Ethiopian Queen who found God – this is from Latin, and means purity or whiteness.

Carshena (Karshena) – A high ranking official in the court of King Ahasuerus – wolf-like or wolfish for a boy, lamb-like for a girl. The derivation of the name is unknown.

Chalcol – a man almost as wise as Solomon – steady or reliable. This is from the Hebrew language.

Claudia – an associate of the Apostle Paul – the name is from the Latin for lame.

D

Dalphon – a son of Haman – from the Hebrew to weep

Dan - a son of Jacob – a Hebrew name which means God is my judge.

Daniel – savior of Susanna, who had been falsely accused of adultery – the full form of Dan (above)

Deborah – a nursemaid – it is the Hebrew for a bee.

Delilah – the love of Samson – this is also a Hebrew name, and it means lovelorn, and also seductive.

Dodo – a hero from Bethlehem – beloved, or father's brother this is from Hebrew.

E

Elasah – a descendent of Saul – a Hebrew word meaning made by God

Eli – a priest – a name descended from Greek, and meaning a defender of man.

Elijah – a prophet – a Hebrew name which means Jehovah is God, or God the lord.

Eliphalet or Eliphelet – one of the sons of David (note, there are several spelling variations for this name) – it comes from the Hebrew for God delivers.

Elisheba – The sister in law of Moses, and wife of Aaron – God is my oath is the meaning of this name, which is a Hebrew term.

Elnathan (much more commonly known as Nathan) – the father of Nehushta – a Hebrew term which means given by God

Elon – a judge of Israel – it refers to an oak tree in Hebrew.

Enoch – the first son of Cain – it is a Hebrew name which means dedicated.

Eri – a son of Gad – watchful or careful; a Hebrew name.

Eve – the first woman, in the Garden of Eden – it is a Latin word which means life.

G

Gad - a son of Jacob – possibly a Hebrew word for the Juniper tree, or a Scandinavian term meaning to cut, or invade.

Gamul (more usually chosen in the form of Samuel) – an important priest – a rewarded one, one whom God has heard. It is a Hebrew name.

Gideon – the son of Joash – a Hebrew name that means a hewer, or one who cuts down.

H

Hakkatan – the father of Johanan, and leader of a line of descendants from Ezra – the small one, or simply small, it is from the Hebrew for being small.

Hannah – a person of Jerusalem, and a prophet – it is from the Hebrew, and means favor or grace.

I

Ira – the priest of David – it comes from the Latin for wrath.

Isaac – son of Abraham - it is from the Hebrew for laughter.

Issachar - a son of Jacob – a Hebrew word which comes to mean 'his reward will come'.

J

James – a brother of Jesus – a Latin term, with links to Greek and Hebrew, which means one who supplants another.

Jamin (also, Benjamin) – one of the sons of Simeon – right-hand man, a Hebrew form.

Jareb – a king of Assyria – a Hebrew word for a great king, although it might specifically relate to an epithet for an Assyrian king.

Jemima – a daughter of Job – a Hebrew word meaning a dove

Joanna – helped to prepare the body of Jesus for burial – from the Greek meaning God is gracious.

Jochebed – the mother of Moses – a Hebrew

term meaning God's glory.

Joel – the eldest son of Samuel, a prophet – a Hebrew name which means one who commands.

John – an Apostle of Jesus Christ – another Hebrew name which means that God has been gracious.

Jonathan – a survivor of the destruction of Jerusalem – being another version of John, its origins are also Hebrew, and the meaning is similar to John, in this case, God-given

Joseph – the father of Jesus, and a son of Jacob – a Hebrew name is meaning increased by God.

Joshua – the owner of the field where the Ark finally came to rest – From the Hebrew, meaning God saves, there are links through the Latin Iesus, which means Jesus in English.

Judith – wife of Esau – a Hebrew name meaning a woman of Judea.

Judah - a son of Jacob – meaning one who is praised, the name is derived from Hebrew.

Jude – a brother of Jesus – a different version of Judah, this is from Greek, but has the same meaning as Judah.

Julia – a Christian woman of Rome – the female equivalent to Julius, the name is from Latin and means young.

Junia - a person respected by St Paul – another version of Julia and Julius, it can be for both boys and girls, and comes from the Latin meaning young.

K

Keren – one of Job's daughters – a Hebrew name which means glorious dignity.

Keziah (sometimes Kezia or Cassia) – the second daughter of the Job – a Hebrew name meaning smelling of sweet-scented spice.

L

Lael – the father of Eliasaph – a Hebrew, gender-neutral name meaning belonging to God

Lazarus – a believer in Jesus Christ – a Hebrew name meaning helped by God.

Leah – the first wife of Jacob – a Hebrew name is meaning weary.

Levi - a son of Jacob – a Hebrew name which means an ally, or friend.

Linus - one of the associates of Paul, the Apostle – a Greek name, which translates to fair or flaxen-haired.

Lois (more often Louise) – St Timothy's grandmother - A name of Greek origins, it means superior.

Luke – a believer in Jesus Christ – from the Latin meaning light.

Lydia – an early convert to Christianity – a Greek name, meaning a beautiful or noble one.

M

Mahalath – a wife of Esau – a Hebrew name meaning a tender one.

Malchiel – the grandson of Asher – a Hebrew name meaning my God is my King

Mark – a believer in Jesus Christ – a Latin name meaning a hammer, or a warrior.

Martha – a believer in Jesus Christ – an Aramaic name, which means the mistress of the house.

Mary – mother of Jesus Christ – a Latin name which means star of the sea.

Matthew – an Apostle of Jesus Christ – a Hebrew name meaning a gift from God.

Matthias – a minor apostle – also meaning a gift from God, it is similar to Matthew, but also has Greek origins.

Mehetable or Mehitable – the wife of Hadad – made good by God, most probably from Hebrew.

Melea – the father of Eliakim – in the genealogy of God; probably from Greek.

Merab – in the bible, a daughter of Saul, this name is also used for boys – it is from Hebrew, and means abundant.

Michael – a member of the House of Asher – a Hebrew name which means like God.

Miriam – the sister of Moses – a Hebrew version of Mary, likewise meaning a star of the sea.

N

Naomi – Ruth's mother in law – a Hebrew name is meaning pleasant.

Naphtali - a son of Jacob – a Hebrew variant is meaning a wrestler.

Noah – the man who built the ark, also the daughter of Zelophehad

– a Hebrew name meaning consolation. In a biblical context, it could also mean long-lived.

O

Obadiah – one of David's descendants – a Hebrew name meaning servant of the Lord.

Obil – as Ishmaelite – a keeper of animals, especially camels. A shepherd when used for boys, or one who weeps for the weepers, more often for girls. It is a Hebrew name.

Onesimus – a believer in Jesus Christ – a Latin name for one who will be profitable.

Orpah – the sister in law of Ruth – a Moabite name is meaning a fawn.

P

Paul – a minor apostle – from the Latin meaning small.

Peter – an apostle of Jesus – from the Latin meaning a rock

Philemon (Philomena) – a believer in Jesus Christ – a Greek name, meaning one who kisses.

Phoebe – a deaconess – from the Greek for a shining one.

Priscilla – a believer in Jesus Christ – from the Latin for venerable.

R

Rachel – Jacob's second wife – a Hebrew name is meaning lamb.

Rapha (a form of Raphael) – a parent of Jessi – from the Hebrew meaning the healing powers of God.

Repeal (another form of Raphael) – a son of

.

Shemaiah – the same meaning as Rapha.

Reuben - a son of Jacob – this is from Hebrew for who sees the son?

Ruth – the wife of Boaz – a Hebrew name, meaning friend.

S

Salome – daughter of Herodias – a Hebrew name, meaning peace

Saph – an enemy of David – a Hebrew name meaning giant, or from a family of giants

Sarah – the wife of Abraham, and Isaac's mother – from the Hebrew meaning princess.

Silas – a believer in Jesus Christ – a word from the Greek, which means woods or forest.

Simeon - a son of Jacob – it is a Hebrew term, meaning a listener.

Simon – an Apostle of Jesus Christ – A Greek name with a slightly different meaning to Simeon above, Simon means heard by God.

Stephen – the first martyr – a Greek name which means a crown or wreath.

Susanna – a victim of false accusations, saved by Daniel – a Hebrew name meaning lily.

T

Tabitha – a doer of good and aid to the poor – a person who is graceful. It is from Greek origins, although has links to Hebrew and Aramaic, where it means a gazelle.

Tamar (more often, Tamara) – a daughter of David – the name is

from the Hebrew, and means a date palm.

Tapath (a variant of Tabitha) – a daughter of Solomon – see Tabitha above.

Timothy – a believer in Jesus Christ – from the Greek, and means to honor God.

Titus – a believer in Jesus Christ – in this context, from the Latin for saved. It also has Green connotations, where it means a giant.

U

Uri (from Uriah) – a member of the Judah tribe – my flame, or my light from Hebrew.

Uriah – a prophet – see Uriah above.

V

Vanish (Vania for girls) – one of the sons of Bani – In this context it is from the Hebrew meaning nourishment of the Lord, or gift to God. It has a Latin background also, where the meaning is slightly different, being a bringer of good news.

Z

Zabud - a priest and friend of King Solomon – endowed, most probably from Hebrew origins.

Zebediah (also Zebedee) – a son of Ishmael - given by good, from the Hebrew.

Zebulun - a son of Jacob – from the Ugaritic (Ugarit is a coastal part of Syria) for a prince.

Zephon – a son of Gad – a Hebrew name which means an angel, or one who expects good

Chapter 7
Names Based on Locations

A name stemming from a location can have personal meaning, such as where the parents' wedding took place, or even where their baby was born. Or, it can simply be chosen because of the beautiful phonetic sounds these names have.

Girls

Adelaide - City in Australia - German

Africa - Continent - Latin

Albany- white, fair" - the capital of New York - Latin

Alberta - Province in Canada - Anglo-Saxon

Alexandria - City in Virginia, USA - Greek

America - Country in North America - Latin

Andorra - European Principality in Eastern Pyrenees mountains – English

Arabia - "Desert, Evening, Ravens," - Saudi Arabia in Asia – Biblical

Arizona - "little springs" - state in USA - Native American

Asia- Means "east," Continent - Greek

Aspen - City in Colorado, USA - English

Atlanta - City in Georgia, USA - Greek/Latin

Austin - means "Majestic dignity," - a city in Texas, USA - Latin

Avalon - "island of apples" - City in California, USA - Celtic

Bailey - Means "able," - a city in Colorado, USA - German

Berlin - "river rake" or "bear" - City in Germany, German

Bethany - "house of figs" - Village outside of Jerusalem in Bible - Biblical/Hebrew

Bolivia - Country in South America; Spanish

Boston - City in Massachusetts, USA; English

Albany- white, fair" - the Brazil - Country in South America, Portuguese

Brittany - Region in France; English/Celtic

Brooklyn - "stream" - City in NY, USA - English

Cairo - "the victorious" - City in Egypt - Arabic

Calais - City in France 3 hrs from Paris - French

Canada - "villiage" - Country in North America - Iroquois

Carolina - "Strong" - States North and South Carolina, USA - Latin

Catalina - "Pure" - Santa Catalina Island (California), Spanish

Charlotte - "free man" - City in North Carolina, USA - French

Chelsea - "seaport" - District of London, England; English

Cheyenne - City and capital of Wyoming; Native American

China - "Qin's kingdom" - a country in Asia; English

Dakota - "friend" - states North and South Dakota, USA - Native American; Sioux

Devon - "defender" - County in England - Gaelic

Dijon - City in France - French

Dixie - "tenth" - an old, generic term for the southern states of USA- Latin

Eden - "paradise" - Biblical location (ie: garden of paradise) - Hebrew

Egypt - Country in N. Africa - (origin debated: Ancient Egyptian, Greek, and/or Arabic)

Everest - tallest mountain in the world - Nepal and China - English

Fatima – City in Portugal - Portuguese

Florence - "blooming" - a city in Tuscany, Italy – Latin

Florida - "flourishing" - State in USA - Latin

France - "French" - Country in Europe - English

Gaza - the largest city in Palestine - Arabic

Geneva- "estuary" or "race of women" or "juniper"- a city in Switzerland - Latin/French

Genoa - city in Italy - Latin

Georgia - "earth-worker" - State in USA – English

Havana - "beauty" - the capital city of Cuba - Spanish

Haven - "safe place" - city New Haven, Michigan, USA - English

Heaven - "paradise" - Biblical location of Paradise – English

Helena - "bright, shining light" - city in Montana - Greek

Holland - location in The Netherlands – Dutch

India - Country in South Asia - Latin

Indiana - State in USA - English

Ireland - 3rd largest island in Europe - English

Java - island in Indonesia - English

Jordan - "descending" - kingdom in Asia – Hebrew

Juneau - Capital of Alaska, USA - French

Juno - Town in Texas, USA – English

Kenya - "yes to God" - a country in Africa - Hebrew

Kimberley - "royal fortress, meadow" - a town in Tasmania, Australia – English

Kimberly - "royal fortress, meadow" - a ghost town in Nevada, USA – English

Lisbon - the capital of Portugal - Portuguese

London - Capital of the UK - English

Lorraine - a city in France - French

Lourdes - city in France - Spanish

Lydia - Kingdom in Asia - Greek

Madison - "Madison Square Garden" in Wisconsin, USA - English

Maison- "house" - Maisons-Laffitte - Commune in north-central France - French

Malta - "honey-sweet" - Mediterranean island - Greek

Marina - "man/woman of the sea" - city in California, USA - Latin

Marsala - city in Sicily - Italian

Mecca - City in Saudi Arabia – Arabic

Mercia - Kingdom in Britain - English

Miami - city in Florida - English

Milan - a city in Italy – Italian

Montana - "mountain" - state in USA - Latin

Myrtle - city in Minnesota, USA - Greek

Nevada - "snow-capped" - State in USA - Spanish

Oasis - area of vegetation in the desert - Greek

Odessa - a city in Ukraine – Russian

Panama - "many butterflies" or "an abundance of fish" - region/ republic in Central America - Spanish

Paris - the capital of France - Greek

Persia - Empire (Officially Islamic Republic of Iran) in Asia - Latin

Regina - "queen" - the capital of Saskatchewan, Canada - Latin

Rome - "strength, power" - Capital of Italy – Latin

Russia - the largest country in the world in Eurasia - Greek

Sahara - "dawn, desert" - desert in N. Africa - Arabic

Samaria - "watch mountain, watchtower" - ancient city/capital of Northern Kingdom of Isreal- Latin/Hebrew

Savannah - "treeless plain" - a city in Georgia, USA - Spanish

Seville - "prophetess, oracle" - city in Spain - Spanish

Shannon - "wise river" - river in Ireland - Irish

Sharon - "plain (geographic)" - plain in Palestine - Hebrew

Shasta - "teacher" - volcanic peak in California - English/Sanskrit

Sicily -Island in Mediterranean - Italian

Sierra - "mountain range" - the Sierra Madre in the Philippines on Luzon Island - Spanish Sonoma - "valley of the moon" –

Sonoma Valley County in California - English/Native American

Svea - ancient name for Sweden - Swedish

Sydney - a city in Australia - French

Tulsa - "strength, power" - Capital of Italy - Latin

Valencia - "brave" - a city in Italy - Italian/Latin

Venice - City in Italy - Italian

Venezia - "from the city of Venice" - relation to Venice, Italy - Italian

Verona - City in Italy - Latin

Victoria - "triumphant" - the capital of British Columbia, Canada - Latin

Vienna - "chosen one" - the capital of Austria - German

Virginia - "virgin" - State in USA - Latin

Return to Table of Contents

Boys

Africa - continent - Latin

Albany - "white, fair" - the capital of New York - Latin

Arlington - city in Virginia, USA - English

Arizona - "little springs" - state in USA - Native American

Aspen - city in Colorado - English

Austin - "great, magnificent" - city in Texas, USA - Latin

Bailey - "able" - a city in Colorado - German

Berlin - "river rake" or "bear" -the capital of Germany - German

Brazil - Country in S. America - Portuguese

Bremen - state and city in Germany - German

Brighton - "bright settlement" - a city in England - English

Boston - the capital of Massachusetts, USA - English

Bristol - "bridge location" - a city in England - English

Brooklyn - "stream" - City in NY, USA - English

Bronx - county of New York City, USA - English

Camden - "from the valley" - historic town in New South Whales - Celtic

Carson - City in California, USA - Celtic

Caspian - "The Caspian Sea" between Europe and Asia - English

Chad - "battle, warrior" - a country in Africa - Welch

Chandler - "candle maker" - Island in Antarctica - French

Cody - "helpful" - city in Florida, USA - English

Columbus - the capital of Ohio, USA - English

Cuba - Republic and island in the Caribbean Sea - Spanish

Dakota - "friend" - states North and South Dakota, USA - Native American; Sioux

Dale - "valley" - community in Ontario, Canada - Old English

Dallas - "valley of water" - city in Texas, USA - Irish

Dayton - "dairy town" - city in Ohio, USA - English

Denver - "valley" - a city in Colorado, USA - English

Devon - "defender" - county in England - Irish

Diego - "teacher" - city San Diego, California, USA - Spanish

Dijon - City in France - French

Eugene - "well-born" - county in Oregon, USA - Greek

Everest - largest mountain in the world, Mt. Everest - China and Nepal - English

Forrest - a river in Kimberley, Australia - Latin

France - "French" - a country in Europe - Latin

Francisco - "San Francisco" city in California, USA - Spanish

Gary - "spear-carrier"- a city in Indiana - English

Glen - "secluded valley" - "Great Glen" large, famous valley in Scotland - Irish/Scottish

Guadalupe - "wolf river" - city in Mexico - Spanish

Hamilton - "beautiful mountain" - City in Ontario, Canada - English

Holland - region in The Netherlands - Dutch

Houston - "hill town" - city in Texas, USA - English

Hudson - "The Hudson River" in NY, USA - English

Indiana - State in USA - English

Indio - "indigenous people" - City in California, USA - Spanish

Ireland - 3rd largest island in Europe - English

Israel - "may God prevail" - Republic in the Middle East - Hebrew

Jackson - the capital of Mississippi, USA - Hebrew

Jerico - "city of the moon" - City in Columbia, South America - Spanish

Jersey - "grassy island" - location in the UK on the coast of Normandy, France - English

Jordan - "descend, flow down" - a kingdom in Western Asia - Hebrew

Kent - "coast" - county in England - Welsh/English

Kingston - "King's field" - the capital of Jamaica - English

Kyle - "channel, strait, handsome" - town in Saskatchewan, Canada - Gaelic

Laredo - city in Texas, USA - Spanish

Lincoln - "lithe" - city in Buenos Aires, Argentina - Latin

London - the capital of the UK - English

Madison - "Madison Square Garden" in Wisconsin, USA - English

Maison - "house" - Maisons-Laffitte - Commune in north-central France - French

Marshall - "horse keeper" - a city in Alaska, USA - French

Melbourne - "mill stream" - the capital of Victoria, Australia - English

Memphis - "enduring, beautiful" - city in Tennessee, USA - Latin/Greek/Egyptian

Mitchell - "big" - Mitchell Island in British Columbia, Canada - Middle English

Montreal - city in Quebec, Canada - French

Orlando - "famous island, famed land" city in Florida, USA - German/Spanish

Oslo - the capital of Norway – Norwegian

Paris - Capital of France - Greek

Peyton - "royal" - location in El Paso County, Colorado, USA - Scottish

Phoenix - "mythical, beautiful bird of rebirth" - city in Arizona, USA - Latin/Greek

Raleigh - "roe deer clearing" - the capital of North Carolina, USA - Old English

Reno - city in Nevada - English

Richmond - "wise protector" - the capital of Virginia, USA - German

Rio - "river" - city Rio de Janeiro in Brazil - Spanish

Rome - "strength, power" - Capital of Italy - Latin

Salem - "peace" - (in Bible) Ancient Jerusalem - Hebrew

Santiago - the capital of Chile - Spanish

Sydney - a city in Australia - French

Texas - "friends, allies" - the state is USA - Spanish

Trenton - "river" - a town in Nova Scotia, Canada - English

Troy - "curly-haired" - ancient city in ruins in Asia Minor - English

Vegas - "meadows" - city Las Vegas in Nevada, USA - Spanish

Washington - "active" - Washington D.C. - the capital of USA - English

York - a city in NE England – English

Zaire - "river that swallows all rivers" - former name of the Democratic Republic of the Congo, Africa – African

Zion - "promised land, eutopia" - hill in Jerusalem - Hebrew

Zurich - a city in Switzerland – German

Name:_____ _____

Factors	Positive	Neutral	Negative
1. Spelling	❏ easy	❏ medium	❏ hard
2. Pronunciation	❏ easy	❏ medium	❏ hard
3. Sound	❏ pleasing	❏ okay	❏ unpleasing
4. Last Name	❏ fits well	❏ fits okay	❏ doesn't fit
5. Gender ID	❏ clear	❏ neutral	❏ unclear
6. Nicknames	❏ appealing	❏ okay	❏ unappealing
7. Popularity	❏ not too popular	❏ popular	❏ too popular
8. Uniqueness	❏ not too unique	❏ unique	❏ too unique
9. Impression	❏ positive	❏ okay	❏ negative
10. Namesakes	❏ positive	❏ okay	❏ negative
11. Initials	❏ pleasing	❏ okay	❏ unpleasing
12. Meaning	❏ positive	❏ okay	❏ negative

Mom's Top Five Names

1._____ Mom's Score: ____ Dad's Score: ____
2._____ Mom's Score: ____ Dad's Score: ____
3._____ Mom's Score: ____ Dad's Score: ____
4._____ Mom's Score: ____ Dad's Score: ____
5._____ Mom's Score: ____ Dad's Score: ____

Dad's Top Five Names
1._____ Dad's Score: ____ Mom's Score: ____
2._____ Dad's Score: ____ Mom's Score: ____
3._____ Dad's Score: ____ Mom's Score: ____
4._____ Dad's Score: ____ Mom's Score: ____
5._____ Dad's Score: ____ Mom's Score: ____

The name we chose is: _____.

Conclusion

Y ou're here, you've made it to the end of the book. We sincerely hope that you've benefitted from it. Perhaps you've found your perfect name , or you haven 't quite decided yet. Hopefully , you at least have some prospects that you can think about. Our recommendation is to write them down and to think about them for a couple of weeks . Say or shout the names out loud and you will begin to get a feel for the names. Thank you very much for reading this book, we wish you all the best! Now that you have come to the end of this book, we would first like to express our gratitude for choosing this particular source and taking the time to read through it. We hope you found it useful and you can now use it as a guide anytime you want. You may also want to recommend it to any family or friends that you think might find it useful as well.

Printed in Great Britain
by Amazon